P9-EEB-583

LATIN AMERICAN LITERARY AUTHORS:

An Annotated Guide to Bibliographies

by

DAVID ZUBATSKY

The Scarecrow Press, Inc.
Metuchen, N.J., & London
1986

Portions of this bibliography first appeared as "An Annotated Bibliography of Latin American Author Bibliographies," Chasqui (Monterrey), 6 (Nov. 1976), 43-70; 6 (Feb. 1977), 41-72; 6 (May 1977), 45-68; 7 (Nov. 1977), 35-54; 7 (May 1978), 34-78; 8 (Feb. 1979), 47-94. Reprinted by permission of Chasqui (Monterrey).

Library of Congress Cataloging-in-Publication Data

Zubatsky, David S., 1939-
Latin American literary authors.

1. Bibliography--Bibliography--Latin American literature. 2. Bibliography--Bibliography--Authors, Latin American. 3. Latin American literature--Bibliography. 4. Authors, Latin American--Bibliography. I. Title.
Z1609.L7Z82 1986 [PQ7081] 016.01686'08'098 86-10086
ISBN 0-8108-1900-7

Manufactured in the United States of America

CONTENTS

PREFACE

The purpose of this compilation is to present, through an author arrangement, an annotated bibliography of personal bibliographies of Brazilian and Spanish American writers of novels, drama, poetry, and short stories, as well as essayists, journalists, linguists, and literary critics. Personal bibliographies are defined as bibliographies of a writer's works and/or those works written about the writer and the writer's works. The works of Spanish writers in exile in Latin America have been excluded; however, such early Spanish chroniclers as Bartolomé de las Casas, Hernán Cortés, Bernal Díaz del Castillo, and Alonso de Ercilla y Zúñiga have been included because of their importance in colonial Latin American literature.

This guide includes citations that appear in periodicals, books, dissertations, and festschrift volumes. Because of the limited distribution in the United States of the works by and about the authors covered in this volume, many of which have been published in short-lived little magazines, pamphlets, festschrift volumes, or anthologies, the compiler has been inclusive rather than exclusive in the choice of bibliographies to be included. In most instances, the annotations will indicate the difference to the user by noting the bibliography's contents, coverage, number of entries, and any other pertinent information.

As noted earlier, the arrangement of the bibliography is alphabetical by author. Whenever an author is better known by a pseudonym, he or she is so listed with appropriate cross-references provided. A listing of the general bibliographies and biobibliographies which should be consulted further by researchers appears after the author section.

I wish to thank the staff of the Interlibrary Loan Section of the University of Illinois Libraries for providing most valuable assistance in my searches. I am also most indebted to Dr. Hensley C. Woodbridge, professor of Spanish at Southern Illinois University, Carbondale, for his advice and resource assistance in the preparation of this guide.

ABBREVIATIONS FOR BIBLIOGRAPHIES INDEXED

Anderson	Robert Roland Anderson, Spanish American Modernism: A Selected Bibliography (Tucson, Ariz.: The University of Arizona Press, 1970), 167 p.
Becco and Foster	Horacio Jorge Becco and David W. Foster, La nueva narrativa hispanoamericana: bibliografía (Buenos Aires: Caso Pardo, S.A., 1976), 226p.
Cardozo, Poesía	Lubio Cardozo, La poesía en Mérida de Venezuela (Maracaibo: Universidad del Zulia, Facultad de Humanidades y Educación, 1971), 215p.
Corvalán	Graciela N.V. Corvalán, Latin American Women Writers in English Translation: A Bibliography (Los Angeles: California State University, Latin American Studies Center, 1980), 190p.
Escudero	Alfonso M. Escudero, "Fuentes de consulta sobre los poetas románticos chilenos," AISTHESIS, Núm. 5 (1970), pp. 295-307.
Flores, BEH	Angel Flores, Bibliografía de escritores hispanoamericanos; A Bibliography of Spanish-American Writers, 1609-1974 (New York: Gordian Press, 1975), 319p.
Flores, NH	Angel Flores, Narrativa hispanoamericana, 1816-1981: Historia y

antología (México: Siglo XXI, 1981-1984), 5vs.

Foster, Arg. Lit.	David W. Foster, Argentine Literature: A Research Guide, 2nd Edition, Revised and Expanded (New York: Garland, 1982), 778p.
Foster, Chilean Lit.	David W. Foster, Chilean Literature: A Working Bibliography of Secondary Sources (Boston: G.K. Hall, 1978), 236p.
Foster, Cuban Lit.	David W. Foster, Cuban Literature: A Research Guide (New York: Garland, 1985), 522p.
Foster, Mex. Lit.	David W. Foster, Mexican Literature: A Bibliography of Secondary Sources (Metuchen, N.J.: Scarecrow Press, 1981), 386p.
Foster, Peruvian Lit.	David W. Foster, Peruvian Literature: A Bibliography of Secondary Sources (Westport, Conn.: Greenwood Press, 1981), 324p.
Foster, P.R. Lit.	David W. Foster, Puerto Rican Literature: A Bibliography of Secondary Sources (Westport, Conn.: Greenwood Press, 1982), 232p.
Foster, 20th Century	David W. Foster, The 20th Century Spanish Novel: A Bibliographic Guide (Metuchen, N.J.: Scarecrow Press, 1975), 227p.
Jackson, Afro-Spanish	Richard L. Jackson, The Afro-Spanish American Author: An Annotated Bibliography of Criticism (New York: Garland, 1980), 129p.
Moraes	Jomar Moraes, Bibliografia crítica da literatura maranhense (São Luís:

	Departamento de Cultura do Maranhão, 1972), 122p.
Porras Collantes	Ernesto Porras Collantes, Bibliografía de la novela en Colombia, con notas de contenido y crítica de las obras y guías de comentarios sobre los autores (Bogotá: Instituto Caro y Cuervo, 1976), 888p.
Porter	Dorothy B. Porter, Afro-Braziliana: A Working Bibliography (Boston: G.K. Hall, 1978), 294p.

THE GUIDE

ABELLA CAPRILE, MARGARITA (Argentina, 1901-1960)
Becco, Horacio Jorge. "Bibliografía de Margarita Abella Caprile" in Margarita Abella Caprile's Obras Completas (Buenos Aires: Emecé Editores, 1964), pp. 397-404. Contents: I. Poesía (by year, 1917-1962). II. Prosa (1936-1958). III. Crítica.

ABREU, JOAO CAPISTRANO DE (Brazil, 1853-1927)
Paiva, Tancredo de Barros. "Bibliografia capistraneana," ANAIS DO MUSEU PAULISTA, 4 (1931), 481-512.
Vianna, Hélio. CAPISTRANO DE ABREU: ENSAIO BIO-BIBLIOGRAFICO. Rio de Janeiro: Ministério da Educação e Cultura, 1955. 126p.

ABREU GOMEZ, ERMILO (Mexico, 1894-1971)
Silva de Rodríguez, Cecilia. VIDA Y OBRAS DE ERMILO ABREU GOMEZ. México, D.F.: Publicaciones del Boletín Bibliográfico de la Secretaría de Hacienda y Crédito Público, 1971. 182p. "Bibliografía," pp. 172-178. Contents: I. Libros. II. Revistas (articles). III. Fuentes inéditas.
Valle, Rafael Heliodoro. "Ermilo Abreu Gómez: notas bibliográficas," HISPANIA, 33, No. 3 (August 1950), 230-232. Contents: I. Obras. A. En revistas. B. Prólogos. C. En antologías. D. Traducciones. II. Referencias. This work does not pretend to be complete. The compiler only included the most important works: "Queda sin registro su copiosa colaboración en las revistas: CONTEMPORANEAS, LETRAS DE MEXICO y EL HIJO PRODIGO."

ACEVEDO, EDUARDO (Uruguay, 1815-1863)
Montevideo. Biblioteca Nacional. EXPOSICION EDUARDO ACEVEDO CENTENARIO. CENTENARIO DE SU MUERTE (1815-1863). Montevideo: Biblioteca Nacional, 1963. 81p. Contents: I. Iconografía, pp. 41-43. entries 1-18. II. Manuscritos, pp. 44-48, entries 19-33. III. Biblioteca del Doctor Eduardo Acevedo, pp. 71-75, entries 35-72. V. Obras y referencias periodísticas sobre el doctor Eduardo Acevedo, pp. 76-81, entries 73-124.

ACEVEDO DIAZ, EDUARDO (Uruguay, 1851-1921)
EXPOSICION BIBLIOGRAFICO Y DOCUMENTAL EDUARDO ACEVEDO DIAZ, 1851-1921. Montevideo: Biblioteca Nacional, 1981. 86p. 582 items. Contents: I. Imagen familiar e íntima. A. Correspondencia. B. Iconografía. II. Imagen del político; del

periodista; del diplomático. A. Originales. B. Correspondencia. 1. De Eduardo Acevedo Díaz. 2. A Eduardo Acevedo Díaz. B. Libros. C. Revistas. D. Diarios. E. Iconografía. III. Imagen del escritor. A. Originales. B. Correspondencia. A. De Eduardo Acevedo Díaz. B. A Eduardo Acevedo Díaz. C. Libros. D. Revistas. E. Iconografía. IV. Biocrítica. A. Libros y folletos. B. Revistas. V. Testimonios varios. VI. Objetos personales.

Flores, BEH, pp. 71-72. Contents: I. Ediciones. II. Referencias. III. Bibliografía selecta (criticism).

Rela, Walter. EDUARDO ACEVEDO DIAZ: GUIA BIBLIOGRAFICA. Montevideo: Ulises, 1967. 83p. 397 entries under the following categories: I. Cuadro biográfico-cronológico. II. Obras del autor. A. Novela y cuento. B. Trabajos varios. III. Colaboraciones en diarios, periódicos y revistas. A. Artículos literarios. B. Artículos públicos (selección). C. Páginas de Eduardo Acevedo Díaz (publicadas o reproducidas después su muerte). D. Recopilaciones de textos del autor. E. Textos del autor en diversas antologías. F. Traducciones de textos del autor. IV. Obras sobre el autor. A. Biografía. B. Historias literarias. C. Ensayo y crítica. D. Artículos en diarios, periódicos y revistas. 1. Firmados. 2. Sin firma. V. Varios. A. Bibliografía individual. B. Historias nacionales. C. De referencia general. D. Diccionarios. E. Folletos. VI. Indice onomástico.

ACOSTA, AGUSTIN (Cuba, 1886-1979)

Foster, Cuban Lit., pp. 83-84. Contents: I. Dissertation. II. Critical Essays.

ACOSTA, CECILIO (Venezuela, 1818-1881)

Sambrano Urdaneta, Oscar. CECILIO ACOSTA, VIDA Y OBRA. Caracas: Ministerio de Educación, Departamento de Publicaciones, 1969. 171p. (Colección Vigilia, 20). "Apéndice bibliográfico," pp. 105-113. Contents: I. Compilaciones y antologías. II. Obras de Cecilio Acosta. III. Estudios sobre Cecilio Acosta.

ACOSTA DE SAMPER, SOLEDAD (Colombia, 1833-1913)

Otero Muñoz, Gustavo. "Soledad Acosta de Samper: Bibliografía," BOLETIN DE HISTORIA Y ANTIGÜEDADES (Bogotá), 24 (1937), 27-283. Contents: I. Ciencias y religión. II. Crítica y estudios literarios. III. Estudios sociales. IV. Historia. V. Narraciones breves. VI. Novelas. VII. Periódicos. VIII. Teatro. IX. Traducciones. X. Viajes.

Porras Collantes, pp. 6-27. Includes works of and critical studies about the author.

ACUNA, MANUEL (Mexico, 1849-1873)

Flores, BEH, p. 1. Contents: I. Edición principal. II. Otras ediciones. III. Referencias. IV. Bibliografía selecta (criticism).

ADAN, MARTIN (pseudonym of RAFAEL DE LA FUENTES BENAVIDES) (Peru, 1908-1985)

Foster, Peruvian Lit., pp. 51-55. Contents: I. Bibliographies. II. Critical Monographs and Dissertations. III. Critical Essays.

Weller, Hubert P. BIBLIOGRAFIA ANALITICA Y ANOTADA DE Y SOBRE MARTIN ADAN (RAFAEL DE LA FUENTE BENAVIDES, 1927-1974). Lima: Instituto Nacional de Cultura, 1975. 141p. Contents: I. La obra de Martín Adán (1927-1974). A. Clasificación. 1. Verso. 2. Prosa poética (1927-1942). 3. Prosa expositiva (1928-1968). 4. Estudios bibliográficos (1939-1942) II. Análisis bibliográfico. III. Bibliografía de Martín Adán (169 works analyzed alphabetically). IV. Bibliografía anotada sobre Martín Adán (290 items annotated). V. Referencias anecdóticas y biobibliográficas de menor importancia (83 items).

AGUAYO, ALFREDO MIGUEL (Cuba, 1866-1948)

Aguayo, Jorge. BIBLIOGRAFIA DE ALFREDO M. AGUAYO. La Habana: Cultural, S.A., 1950. 119p. The entries are divided into bibliografía activa (422 items; by subject) and bibliografía pasiva (works about the author and his work) sections.

AGUEROS, VICTORIANO (Mexico, 1854-1911)

Agüeros, Victoriano. OBRAS LITERARIAS. TOMO 1: ARTICULOS SUELTOS. México, D.F.: Imprenta de V. Agüeros, edit., 1897. 483p. (Biblioteca de Autores Mexicanos, 8). "Noticia del autor y de sus escritos," pp. v-xxix. Contents: I. Biografía. II. Juicios.

AGUILAR Y CORDOBA, DIEGO DE (Peru, 1550?-1613)

Rivera Calderón, Carmen. "DIEGO DE AGUILAR Y DE CORDOBA (S. XVI): BIOBIBLIOGRAFIA." Tesis. Lima: Biblioteca Nacional, Escuela de Bibliotecarios, Lima, 1959.

AGUILERA-MALTA, DEMETRIO (Ecuador, 1909-1981)

Fama, Antonio. REALISMO MAGICO DE LA NARRATIVA DE AGUILERA-MALTA. Madrid: Playor, 1977. 169p. Contents: I. "Obras en prosa de Demetrio Aguilera-Malta (en orden cronológico)," pp. 151-152. II. "Obras dramáticas de Demetrio Aguilera-Malta," pp. 152-157. III. "Obras de consulta general," pp. 157-169 (includes critical works about the author and his work).

Luzuriaga, Gerardo. DEL REALISMO AL EXPRESIONISMO: EL TEATRO DE AGUILERA-MALTA. Madrid: Playor, 1973. 204p. Contents: I. "Estudios y referencias sobre Demetrio Aguilera-Malta," pp. 194-195. II. "Obras no dramáticas de Demetrio Aguilera-Malta," pp. 195-196. III. "Obras dramáticas de Demetrio Aguilera-Malta," pp. 196-197.

Rabassa, Clementine Christos. DEMETRIO AGUILERA-MALTA AND SOCIAL JUSTICE: THE TERTIARY PHASE OF EPIC TRADITION IN LATIN AMERICAN LITERATURE. Rutherford, N.J.: Fairleigh Dickinson University Press, 1980. 301p. "Selected

Bibliography," pp. 265-277. Contents: I. Works and Editions. A. Short Stories. B. Novels. C. Theater. D. Essays (by year, 1930-1971). E. Miscellaneous. F. Unpublished Works. II. Criticism and Studies of the Works of Demetrio Aguilera-Malta.

AGUIRRE, JUAN BAUTISTA (Ecuador, 1725-1786
Flores, BEH, pp. 185-186. Contents: I. Ediciones. II. Bibliografía selecta (criticism).

AGUIRRE, NATANIEL (Bolivia, 1843-1888)
Flores, BEH, p. 57. Contents: I. Edición principal. II. Otras ediciones. III. Bibliografía selecta (criticism).
Flores, NH, v. 1, pp. 237-238. Contents: I. Ediciones principales. II. Referencias. III. Bibliografía selecta (criticism).

AGUSTIN, JOSE (Mexico, 1944-)
Foster, Mex. Lit., pp. 83-84. Contents: I. Critical Monographs and Dissertations. II. Critical Essays.
Foster, 20th Century, p. 22. Contents: I. Critical Books. II. Critical Essays.
Minovés-Myers, Concepción M. "TECNICAS NARRATIVAS DE JOSE AGUSTIN." Ph.D., University of Illinois, 1981. 182p. "Bibliografía," pp. 167-170. Contents: I. Publicaciones de José Agustín. A. Obras de creación. B. Estudios. II. Estudios sobre José Agustín y la Onda

AGUSTINI, DELMIRA (Uruguay, 1886-1914)
Corvalán, pp. 29-30. Contents: I. Poetry. II. Critical Works On.
Flores, BEH, pp. 186-187. Contents: I. Ediciones. II. Bibliografía selecta (criticism).
Stephens, Doris T. DELMIRA AGUSTINI AND THE QUEST FOR TRANSCENDENCE. Montevideo: Ediciones Géminis, 1975. 220 p. "Bibliography," pp. 207-220. Contents: I. Works (listed chronologically). II. Poetry. III. Correspondence. IV. Anthologies. V. Books. VI. Periodicals. VII. Unpublished Dissertations.

AIRES, FELIX (Brazil, 1904-)
Moraes, pp. 99-101. Major works by and about the author.

AIRES, MATIAS (Brazil, 1705-1763)
"Bio-bibliografia: Cadeira No. 3, Patronato Matias Aires Ramos da Silva Eça," REVISTA DA ACADEMIA PAULISTA DE LETRAS, 1 (12 agosto de 1938), 148-152.

ALAYZA Y PAZ, SOLDAN, LUIS (Peru, 1883-)
Moreyra Paz Soldán, Carlos. LA OBRA DE LOS PAZ SOLDAN. Lima, 1974. 232 p. "Bibliografía," pp. 117-127. Contents:

I. Libros y folletos. II. Prólogos. III. Discursos y conferencias. IV. Artículos periodísticos.

ALECIO, ADRIANO DE (Peru, ?-1650)
Ordoñez López, María Angélica. "BIO-BIBLIOGRAFIA DE ADRIANO DE ALECIO." Tesis. Lima: Biblioteca Nacional, Escuela de Bibliotecarios, 1965.

ALEGRIA, ALONSO (Peru, 1941-)
Foster, Peruvian Lit., p. 56. Critical Essays.

ALEGRIA, CIRO (Peru, 1909-1967)
"Bibliografía de Ciro Alegría Bazán," ANUARIO BIBLIOGRAFICO PERUANO, 1967/69 (i.e. 1975), 538-575. Partially annotated contents. Contents: I. Libros y folletos (By year, 1935-1973). II. Otras publicaciones (Anthologies mainly). III. Artículos y ensayos. IV. Poesías. V. Traducciones. VI. Notas bibliográficas (revistas). VII. Reportajes. VIII. Referencias (Criticism, biographical sketches).
Flores, BEH, pp. 72-73. Contents: I. Ediciones. II. Referencias. III. Bibliografía selecta (criticism).
Foster, Peruvian Lit., pp. 57-65. Contents: I. Bibliographies. II. Critical Monographs and Dissertations. III. Critical Essays.
Foster, 20th Century, pp. 22-24. Contents: I. Bibliographies. II. Critical Books. III. Critical Essays.
Rodríguez-Florido, Jorge J. "Bibliografía de y sobre Ciro Alegría," CHASQUI, 4, Núm. 3 (mayo de 1975), 23-54. 336 entries. Contents: I. Obras de Alegría. A. Novelas. B. Cuentos, leyendas y relatos. C. Colecciones de cuentos y novelas. D. Colecciones de artículos periodísticos y libros de ensayos. E. Fragmentos de novelas, cuentos y adaptaciones. F. Traducciones de sus obras. G. Ensayos, reseñas y artículos periodísticos. H. Poesías y poemas en prosa. I. Piezas teatrales. J. Entrevistas e intervenciones orales. K. Prólogos. II. Crítica sobre la obra de Alegría. A. Libros, tesis y colecciones de ensayos. B. Estudios, notas y reseñas.
Vilariño de Olivieri, Matilde. LA NOVELISTICA DE CIRO ALEGRIA. EDICION REVISADA Y AUMENTADA. Río Piedras: Editorial Universitaria, Universidad de Puerto Rico, 1980. 231 p. "Bibliografía," pp. 225-231. Contents: I. Obras de Ciro Alegría. A. Cuentos y relatos. B. Novelas. C. Poesías. D. Teatro. E. Notas bibliográficas. F. Traducciones. II. Estudios y apuntes sobre Ciro Alegría.

ALEGRIA, FERNANDO (Chile, 1918-)
Foster, Chilean Lit., pp. 47-50. Contents: I. Critical Books and Theses. II. Critical Essays.
Foster, 20th Century, pp. 25-27. Contents: I. Critical Books. II. Critical Essays.
Reeves, Rosa E. "Bibliografía de Fernando Alegría," TEXTO CRITICO, Núm. 22/23 (julio/diciembre de 1981), 31-58. Con-

tents: I. Bibliografía primaria. A. Libros. B. Artículos y otras publicaciones. II. Bibliografía secundaria. A. Libros y artículos. B. Traducciones de su obra.

ALEGRIA, JOSE A. (Puerto Rico, 1886/87-1965).
Foster, P.R. Lit., p. 65. Critical Essays.

ALENCAR, JOSE MARTINIANO DE (Brazil, 1829-1877)
Alencar, José de. ALENCAR, OS BASTIDORES E A POSTERIDADE. INTRODUÇAO, BIBLIOGRAFIA PASSIVA, TEXTOS EDITOS E INEDITOS, NOTAS A CARGO DE FABIO FREIXEIRO. Rio de Janeiro: Museu Histórico Nacional, 1977. 237 p. (Coleção Estudos e Documentos, v. 4, t. 1). "Bibliografia sôbre Alencar," pp. 81-105.
______. "IRACEMA." EDIÇAO CRITICA DE M. CAVALCANTI PROENÇA. 2a edição. Rio de Janeiro: Livros Técnicos e Científicos; São Paulo: Editôra da Universidade de São Paulo, 1979. 315 p. (Biblioteca Universitária de Literatura Brasileira; Série C; 3). "Pequena bibliografia de Iracema," pp. 273-294. The bibliography is a descriptive one listing all editions, including translations, from 1865 to 1965.
______. OBRA COMPLETA. Rio de Janeiro: Editôra José Aguilar, Ltda., 1958-1960. 4 vs. "Bibliografia," v. 4, pp. 1321-1328. Contents: I. Fontes. II. Obras do autor. A. Ficção. B. Teatro. C. Poesia. D. Ensaios literários, críticos e filológicos. E. Escritos e discursos políticos e jurídicos. F. Inéditos. G. Antologias. III. Estudos sôbre o autor.
Castelo, José Aderaldo. "Bibliografia e plano das obras completas de José de Alencar," BOLETIM BIBLIOGRAFICO (Biblioteca Pública Municipal de São Paulo), 13(1949), 37-57. Contents: I. Ficção-Romance. II. Teatro. III. Poesia. IV. Crítica-Biografias-Estudos gramaticais-Correspondência. V. Jornalismo-Crônicas-Escritos políticos. VI. Discursos políticos. VII. Escritos jurídicos. VIII. Antologias.
Mota, Artur. JOSE DE ALENCAR (O ESCRIPTOR E O POETIRO). SUA VIDA E SUA OBRA. Rio de Janeiro: F. Briguiet, 1921. 307 p. Contents: I. "As fontes para o estudo de sua individualidade," pp. 295-297. II. "Bibliographia. Collaboração em jornaes e revistas," pp. 299-300. III. "Obras publicadas em volumes ou folhetos," pp. 300-304. IV. "Obras inéditas ou de publicação posthuma em revistas," pp. 304-307.
______. "Perfis acadêmicos; Cadeira No. 23: José de Alencar," REVISTA DA ACADEMIA BRASILEIRA DE LETRAS, Núm. 146 (fevereiro de 1934), 131-182. Contents: "Bibliografia," pp. 131-143. I. Obras (arranged by year, 1846-1877). II. Obras publicadas em livros e folhetos (1856-1893). III. Obras inéditas. IV. Fontes o estudo crítico.
Orico, Osvaldo. A VIDA DE JOSE DE ALENCAR. São Paulo: Companhia Editôra Nacional, 1929. 214 p. "Bibliografia de José de Alencar, por Mário de Alencar," pp. 209-214.

Rio de Janeiro. Biblioteca Nacional. JOSE DE ALENCAR, CATALOGO DA EXPOSIÇAO COMEMORATIVA DO CENTENARIO DE MORTE, 1877-1977. ORGANIZADO PELA SEÇAO DE PROMOÇOES CULTURAIS. Rio de Janeiro: Biblioteca Nacional, 1977. 91p. 523 entries. Contents: I. Manuscritos. A. Cartas. B. Poesia. II. Obras. III. Teatro. IV. Músicas (inspiradas em obras de Alencar). V. Ilustrações.

ALENCAR, MARIO DE (Brazil, 1872-1925)

Mota, Artur. "Perfis acadêmicos: Mário de Alencar," REVISTA DA ACADEMIA BRASILEIRA DE LETRAS, Núm. 120 (1931), 402-415. Contents: I. "Bibliografia," pp. 402-403 (arranged by year, 1888-1922). II. "Fontes para o estudo crítico," pp. 403-404.

ALFONSO, PACO (Cuba, 1906-)

Foster, Cuban Lit., p. 85. Critical Essays.

ALIX, JUAN ANTONIO (Dominican Republic, 1833-1918)

Alfau Durán, Vetilio. "Contribución a la bibliografía del gran poeta popular dominicano Juan Antonio Alix," ANALES DE LA UNIVERSIDAD DE SANTO DOMINGO, 9, Núm. 69/70 (enero/junio de 1954), 27-63. I. Acerca de Alix. II. Volúmenes (published). III. Décimas (by date 1873-1911). IV. Sin fecha. V. Sin fechas anteriores a 1893.

"ALMAFUERTE" (Pseudonym of PEDRO B. PALACIOS) (Argentina, 1854-1917)

Foster, Arg. Lit., pp. 610-614. Contents: I. Critical Monographs. II. Critical Essays.

ALMEIDA, MANUEL ANTONIO DE (Brazil, 1831-1861)

Rebêlo, Marques. BIBLIOGRAFIA DE MANUEL ANTONIO DE ALMEIDA. Rio de Janeiro: Ministério da Educação e Saúde, Instituto Nacional do Livro, 1951. 188p. (Coleção B1; Bibliografia 7). An exhaustive bibliography of 258 items of both his work and of works about him. Partially annotated entries.

_______. VIDA E OBRA DE MANUEL ANTONIO DE ALMEIDA. 2a. edição revista. São Paulo: Livraria Martins Editôra, 1963. 147p. "Breve bibliografia," pp. 131-147. Contents: I. Memórias de um Sargento de Milícias. A. Edições em vida do autor (arranged by year, 1852-1855). B. Edições póstumas (arranged by year, 1862-1962). C. Traduções. D. Peças de teatro extraídas do romance. II. Outras obras. III. Estudos principais (criticism).

ALONE (Pseudonym of HERNAN DIAZ ARRIETA) (Chile, 1891-1984).

"Cartillas biobibliográficas de autores chilenos: Hernán Díaz Arrieta (seud. Alone), Santiago, 1891, crítico literario, ensayista y novelista," BOLETIN DEL INSTITUTO DE LITERATURA CHILENA (Universidad de Chile, Santiago), Año V,

Núm. 12 (julio de 1966), 6-18. Contents: I. Obras. A. Traducciones. B. Prólogos. C. Novelas. D. Ensayos. E. Antologías. II. Referencias. III. Vida. IV. Otros datos.

Leyton Soto, Mario. ALONE: 65 AÑOS DE CRITICA LITERARIA. BIBLIOGRAFIA. Santiago de Chile: Ministerio de Educación, Centro de Perfeccionamiento, Experimentación e Investigaciones Pedagógicas, 1973. 5 vs. Contents: I. Comentarios sobre Alone publicados entre 1909-1972. II. Comentarios sobre libros y autores redactados por Alone. III. Artículos de Alone sobre temas varios.

ALONSO, DORA (Cuba, 1910-)

Foster, Cuban Lit., p. 86. Critical Essays.

ALONSO, MANUEL ANTONIO (Puerto Rico, 1822-1889)

Foster, P.R. Lit., pp. 66-67. Contents: I. Critical Monographs and Dissertation. II. Critical Essays.

ALTAMIRANO, IGNACIO MANUEL (Mexico, 1834-1893)

Flores, BEH, pp. 2-3. Contents: I. Edición principal. II. Otras ediciones (novela y cuento). III. Referencias. IV. Bibliografía selecta (criticism).

Foster, Mex. Lit., pp. 84-90. Contents: I. Bibliographies. II. Critical Monographs and Dissertations. III. Critical Essays.

Valle, Rafael Heliodoro. BIBLIOGRAFIA DE IGNACIO MANUEL ALTAMIRANO. México, D.F.: D.A.P.P., 1939. 155p. (Bibliografías mexicanas, 8). Contents: I. Discursos. II. Hemerobibliografía. III. Inéditos. IV. Periódicos (he edited or collaborated in). V. Prólogos. VI. Prosa. VII. Traducciones. VIII. Verso. IX. Cronología. X. Iconografía. XI. Seudónimos. XII. Sobre Altamirano. XIII. Nombres en esta bibliografía. Partially annotated entries.

Warner, Ralph E. BIBLIOGRAFIA DE IGNACIO MANUEL ALTAMIRANO. México, D.F., 1955. 220p. 458 items, partially annotated. Contents: I. Obras. A. Colecciones de géneros varios. B. Poesía. C. Novela y novela corta. D. Paisajes y leyendas. E. Crítica literaria, bibliografía, biografía, crónicas y revistas. F. Prólogos. Cartas-Prólogos, introducciones, etcétera. G. Discursos. H. Cartas. I. Artículos varios. J. Traducciones y adaptaciones. II. Sobre la vida y obras de Altamirano. III. Indice de personas.

_______. "Bibliografía de las obras de Ignacio Manuel Altamirano," REVISTA IBEROAMERICANA, 3 (1941), 465-512. 329 partially annotated titles. Contents: I. Poesía. II. Novela y novela corta. III. Paisajes y leyendas. IV. Crítica literaria. V. Bibliografía, biografía, prólogos. VI. Discursos. VII. Artículos varios. VIII. Traducciones y adaptaciones. IX. Indice de personas y corporaciones.

ALVARENGA, MANUEL IGNACIO DA SILVA (Brazil, 1749-1814)

Porter, pp. 265-267. Contents: I. Writings. II. References, Critical and Biographical.

ALVAREZ, AGUSTIN (Argentina, 1857-1914)
Roig, Arturo Andrés. "Ensayo bibliográfico sobre un positivista argentino; Agustín Alvarez," REVISTA DE BIBLIOGRAFIA INTERAMERICANA, 12 (1962), 279-298. Contents: I. Escritos de Agustín Alvarez. A. Libros y folletos. B. Colaboraciones en revistas y otras publicaciones. II. Escritos sobre Agustín Alvarez. 168 titles, partially annotated.

ALVAREZ, JOSE SIXTO see "FRAY MOCHO"

ALVAREZ BARAGANO, JOSE (Cuba, 1932-1962)
Foster, Cuban Lit., p. 87. Critical Essays.

ALVAREZ MARRERO, FRANCISCO (Puerto Rico, 1847-1881)
Foster, P.R. Lit., pp. 67-68. Critical Essays.

ALVES, ANTONIO DE CASTRO (Brazil, 1847-1871)
Horch, Hans Jürgen W. ANTONIO DE CASTRO ALVES (1847-1871). SEINE SKLAVENDICHTUNG UND IHRE BEZIECHUNGEN ZUR ABOLITION IN BRASILIEN. Hamburg: Cram, de Gruyter & Co., 1958. 384 p. (Hamburger Romanistische Studien, B 26). "Bibliographie," 239-379. Contents: Bibliographie der Ausgaben des Dichters (136 entries, partially annotated). II. Bibliographie der Veröffentlichung von Gedichten im periodischen Schrifttum unter besonderer Berücksichtigung der Feststellung einer Erstveröffentlichung sowie Angaben für übertragungen in fremde Sprachen. (120 entries by work). III. Bibliographie über Castro Alves (1227 entries). IV. Zusammenstellung bibliographischer Angaben, die für eine Einbeziehung unter III nicht ausreichende Anhaltspunkte ergaben (61 entries). V. Übersicht der sonstigen in der Darstellung benutzten Schrifttums (71 entries). VI. Titelregister der Gedichte. VII. Namenregister.
______. BIBLIOGRAFIA DE CASTRO ALVES. Rio de Janeiro: Ministério da Educação e Cultura, Instituto Nacional de Livro, 1960. 259p. (Coleção B1, Bibliografia, 12). A descriptive bibliography of 563 entries. Contents: I. Manuscritos e facsímiles. II. Obra poética (em periódicos, em obras diversas). III. Traduções. IV. Poesias musicadas. V. Poesia perdidas. VI. Trabalhos em prosa. VII. Correspondência (ativa, passiva). VIII. Edições. IX. Indice das poesias e obras do poeta. X. Indice onomástico. XI. Indice das publicações periódicas.
Porter, pp. 203-207. Contents: I. Writings. II. References, Critical and Biographical.
Rio de Janeiro. Biblioteca Nacional. CASTRO ALVES: CATALOGO DA EXPOSIÇAO (COMEMORATIVA DO CENTENARIO DA MORTE DE ANTONIO DE CASTRO ALVES, 1871-1971). Rio de Janeiro: Biblioteca Nacional, Divisão de Publicações e Divulgação, 1971. 68p. Contents: I. Obras de Castro Alves. A. Manuscritos autógrafos. B. Correspondência. 1. Manuscrita (autógrafos). 2. Impressa. C. Desenhos, pintura,

caricaturas. D. Obras Completas. E. Poesias completas. F. Obras reunidas. G. Obras e poemas isolados. 1. Obras. 2. Poemas. H. Poemas musicados (partituras). I. Avulsos (poesia e prosa). J. Antologias. K. Traduções. L. Jornais. II. Influências literárias. III. Documentário. IV. Bibliografia. V. Retratos de Castro Alves. VI. Outros retratos. VII. Ilustrações.

ALVES, JOAO LUIZ (Brazil, 1870-1925)

Mota, Artur. "Perfis acadêmicos, Cadeira No. 11: João Luiz Alves," REVISTA DA ACADEMIA BRASILEIRA DE LETRAS, Núm. 83 (novembro de 1928), 313-320. Contents: I. "Bibliografia," pp. 313-314 (1902-1927). II. "Fontes para o estudo crítico," p. 315.

AMADO, JORGE (Brazil, 1912-)

Almeida, Alfredo Wagner Berno de. JORGE AMADO; POLITICA E LITERATURA: UM ESTUDO SOBRE A TRAJETORIA INTELECTUAL DE JORGE AMADO. Rio de Janeiro: Editôra Campus, 1979. 313p. "Bibliografia," pp. 282-313. Contents: I. A produção intelectual do autor (includes books, newspaper and journal articles, speeches, and prefaces). II. Entrevistas, depoimentos, inquéritos e declarações. III. A produção intelectual sôbre Jorge Amado e sua obra (very comprehensive in all genres). 595 entries.

"Bibliografia," in JORGE AMADO'S POVO E TERRA: 40 ANOS DE LITERATURA. (São Paulo: Livraria Martins Editôra, 1972), pp. 245-247. Contents: I. Títulos. II. Prêmios. III. Livros publicados. IV. Aptações. A. Para o cinema. B. Para o teatro. C. Para o rádio. D. Para a televisão.

Porter, pp. 174-178. Contents: Writings. II. References, Critical and Biographical.

Tavares, Paulo. O BAIANO JORGE AMADO E SUA OBRA. Rio de Janeiro: Editôra Record, 1980. 196p. "Bibliografias," pp. 53-139. Contents: I. Bibliografia de Jorge Amado. A. Obras publicadas (sequência cronológica). 1. Os romances (by work, and includes synopses, publishing history, and any translations). 2. Os contos (same information provided as in no. 1). 3. As biografias (same information provided as in no. 1). 4. Poesia. 5. Teatro. 6. Viagem. 7. Guias. 8. Literatura infantil-juvenil. B. Co-autorais. C. Adaptaçoes. 1. Para o teatro. 2. Para o cinema. 3. Para o rádio. 4. Para a televisão. 5. Para fotonovela. 6. Para histórias em quadrinhos. 7. Músicas. II. Bibliografia sôbre Jorge Amado. A. Em trabalhos especializados (by year, 1961-1979). B. Em algumas obras de crítica e de referência (by year, 1938-1978). C. Tesis e ensaios (não editados; by year, 1954-1976).

Vsesoiuznaia Gosudarstvennaia Biblioteka Inostrannoi Literatury. ZHORZHI AMADU. Moskva: Izdatel'stvo "Kniga," 1965. 47p. Includes bibliographies of Jorge Amado's works and of works concerning him in Portuguese and Russian. 80 listings.

AMALIA, NARCISA (Brazil, 1852-1924)
Reis, Antônio Simões dos. NARCISA AMALIA. Rio de Janeiro: Organizações Simões, 1949. 192p. (His Bibliografia brasileira, 2). "Bibliografia de Narcisa Amália," pp. 179-184 (works arranged by year, 1867-1902). "Bibliografia sôbre Narcisa Amália," pp. 184-188.

AMEZAGA, CARLOS GERMAN (Peru, 1862-1906)
Prado Prado, Rosario. "CARLOS GERMAN AMEZAGA." Tesis. Lima: Biblioteca Nacional, Escuela de Bibliotecarios, 1957.

AMORIM, ENRIQUE (Uruguay, 1900-1960)
Flores, BEH, pp. 187-188. Contents: I. Ediciones. II. Referencias. III. Bibliografía selecta (criticism).
Foster, 20th Century, pp. 27-28. Contents: I. Bibliographies. II. Critical Books. III. Critical Essays.
Mose, K. E. A. ENRIQUE AMORIM: THE PASSION OF A URUGUAYAN. Madrid: Editorial Playor, S.A., 1973. 255p. "Selected, Classified Bibliography," pp. 234-254. Contents: I. Books by Amorim, 1920-1970 (by year). II. Stories of Amorim in Anthologies. III. Amorim's Work in Translation. IV. Work Unpublished in Volumes or Not Published at All. V. Articles by Amorim (by year, 1917-1960). VI. Reportage on Amorim (Criticism by year, 1924-1968). VII. Letters from Amorim; Letters Written or Forwarded to Amorim. VIII. Reviews of Amorim's Work (By Work). IX. Other Criticism. X. General.

AMUNATEGUI, MIGUEL LUIS (Chile, 1828-1888)
Rosales, Justo Abel. BIBLIOGRAFIA DEL LITERATO DON MIGUEL LUIS AMUNATEGUI. Santiago de Chile: Imprenta de la Libertad Electoral, 1888. 30p. In an alphabetical arrangement, the author lists 37 books and pamphlets, 9 articles from literary reviews and 7 publications which appeared in newspapers.

AMUNATEGUI REYES, MIGUEL LUIS (Chile, 1862-1949)
Silva Castro, Raúl. MIGUEL LUIS AMUNATEGUI REYES (1862-1949). Santiago de Chile: Editorial Jurídica de Chile, 1951. 315p. (Colección de Estudios Jurídicos y Sociales, v. 20). "Bibliografía," pp. 241-262. 47 annotated entries arranged chronologically, 1878-1943. Newspaper articles and other notices are not included.

AMUNATEGUI SOLAR, DOMINGO (Chile, 1860-1946)
Feliú Cruz, Guillermo. "Ensayo de una bibliografía de Domingo Amunátegui Solar (1876-1946)," ANALES DE LA UNIVERSIDAD DE CHILE, Año 119, Núm. 121/122 (1º y 2º trimestres de 1961), 350-431. Also published as an offprint: Santiago de Chile: Editorial Nascimento, 1961. 336-431p. 587 entries, partially annotated, are arranged by year, 1876-1946.

ANCHIETA, JOSE DE (Brazil, 1534-1597)

Anchieta, José de. POEMA DA BEM-AVENTURADA VIRGEM MARIA, MÃE DE DEUS. São Paulo: Instituto Nacional do Livro, 1980. 2vs. (Obras completas, v. 4). "Bibliografia principal," v. 1, pp. 9-12. Includes works by and about the author.

Mota, Artur. "Bio-bibliografia: José de Anchieta," REVISTA DA ACADEMIA PAULISTA DE LETRAS, 1 (11 dezembro de 1938), 129-133.

Rela, Walter. "Teatro brasileño: de las piezas del P. Anchieta a la comedia costumbrista," REVISTA IBEROAMERICANA DE LITERATURA (Montevideo), 4, Núm. 4 (1962), 29-62. Includes a useful bibliography of items available in Rio de Janeiro and São Paulo libraries.

ANDERSON IMBERT, ENRIQUE (Argentina, 1910-)

Becco, Jorge Horacio. CUENTISTAS ARGENTINOS. Buenos Aires: Ediciones Culturales Argentinas, Ministerio de Educación y Justicia, Dirección General de Cultura, 1961. 381p. "Bibliografía de Enrique Anderson Imbert," pp. 355-357.

Foster, Arg. Lit., pp. 150-154. Contents: I. Critical Monograph and Dissertations. II. Critical Essays.

ANDRADE, CARLOS DRUMMOND DE (Brazil, 1902-)

Andrade, Carlos Drummond de. OBRA COMPLETA. Rio de Janeiro: Companhia Aguilar Editôra, 1964. 959p. "Bibliografia," pp. 925-937. Contents: I. Obras do autor. A. Edições brasileiras. B. Em língua castelhana. C. Traduções de outros autores. D. Entre vistas. II. Estudos, artigos e reportagens sôbre o autor. III. Composições musicais sôbre o autor.

_______. 70 HISTORINHAS: ANTOLOGIA. Rio de Janeiro: Livraria José Olympio, 1978. 158p. "Bibliografia de e sôbre Carlos Drummond de Andrade," pp. ix-xi. Contents: I. Do autor. A. Prosa. B. Poesia. C. Antologias. D. Conjunto de obra. II. Sôbre o autor. A. Livros. B. Alguns estudos em livro.

Netto, José Paulo. "Drummond: breve presentación bibliográfica," REVISTA DE CRITICA LITERARIA LATINOAMERICANA, 2, Núm. 4 (1976), 145-149. Contents: I. Obra poética de Drummond. A. Libros. B. Antologías. C. Obra completa. II. Textos de referencia general de la historia de la literatura brasileña. III. Textos de referencia del movimiento modernista. IV. Textos analíticos referidos a la obra de Drummond. V. Textos que presentan análisis de la obra de Drummond.

Py, Fernando. BIBLIOGRAFIA COMENTADA DE CARLOS DRUMMOND DE ANDRADE (1918-1930). Rio de Janeiro: Livraria J. Olympio Editôra con convênio como o Instituto Nacional do Livro, 1980. 176p. Contents: I. Indice cronológico (works are listed by year, 1918-1930). II. Pseudônimos e afins. III. Edição. IV. Indice geral de títulos. V. Indice onomástico geral.

Rio de Janeiro. Biblioteca Nacional. CARLOS DRUMMOND DE ANDRADE: EXPOSIÇAO COMEMORATIVA DOS 80 ANOS. Catálogo organizado pelo Seção de Promoções Culturais. Apresentação de Célia Ribeiro Zaher. Rio de Janeiro, 1983. 53p.

Santiago, Silviano. CARLOS DRUMMOND DE ANDRADE. Petrópolis: Editôra "Vozes," 1976. 131p. "Bibliografia," pp. 127-131. Contents: I. Obras de Carlos Drummond de Andrade. A. Poesia (1930-1973). B. Prosa (1944-1972). C. Conjunto de obra. D. Traduções. E. Versões no estrangeiro. II. Estudos sôbre Carlos Drummond de Andrade (bibliografia resumida). A. Livros. B. Artigos.

ANDRADE, MARIO DE (Brazil, 1893-1945)

Lopes, Telê Pôrto Ancora. "Cronologia geral da obra de Mário de Andrade publicada em volume," REVISTA DO INSTITUTO DE ESTUDIOS BRASILEIROS (São Paulo), 7 (1969), 139-172. Contents: I. Cronologia da edição. A. Arte literária. 1. Conto. 2. Crônica. 3. Poesia. 4. Romance. B. Estudos. 1. Folclore e música. 2. Arte literária. II. Cronologia da composição (1914-1944; arranged by type of work). Also published in the BOLETIM BIBLIOGRAFICO (BIBLIOTECA MUNICIPAL "MARIO DE ANDRADE," SAO PAULO), Número especial (fevreiro de 1970), 117-149.

Porter, pp. 178-182. Contents: I. Writings. II. References, Critical and Biographical.

Reis, Antônio Simões dos. MARIO DE ANDRADE: BIBLIOGRAFIA SOBRE A SUA OBRA. Rio de Janeiro: Instituto Nacional do Livro, 1960. 47p. (Suplemento da Revista do Livro, 3).

Rio de Janeiro. Biblioteca Nacional. EXPOSIÇAO MARIO DE ANDRADE. EXPOSIÇAO COMEMORATIVA DO 25o ANIVERSARIO DA MORTE DO ESCRITOR MARIO DE ANDRADE (1945-1970), ORGANIZADA PELA SEÇAO DE EXP. E INAUGURADA-EM 26 DE MAIO DE 1970. 589 entries. Contents: I. Obras de Mário de Andrade. A. Obras reunidas. B. Poesias. C. Contos. D. Romances. E. Opera cômica. F. Estudos, ensaios crônicos e outros trabalhos sôbre música e folclore. G. Sôbre literatura, arte e outros assuntos. H. Cartas. I. Desenhos. J. Músicas. K. Textos musicados. II. Antologias. III. Documentário. IV. Poemas dedicados a Mário de Andrade. V. Bibliografia (biographies, critical studies, etc.). VI. Caricaturas. VII. Fotografias.

ANDRADE, MARTIM FRANCISCO RIBEIRO DE (Brazil, 1775-1844)

Mota, Artur. "Bio-bibliografia: Martim Francisco Ribeiro de Andrade," REVISTA DA ACADEMIA PAULISTA DE LETRAS, Núm. 14 (1941), 112-114. "Bibliografia," pp. 112-113 (1799-1890).

ANDRADE, OLEGARIO VICTOR (Argentina, 1839-1882)

Foster, Arg. Lit., pp. 155-157. Contents: I. Critical Monographs. II. Critical Essays.

ANDRADE, PEDRO (Venezuela, 1895-)
Cordozo, Poesía, pp. 169-170. Includes poetical works by and critical studies about the author.

ANDREU IGLESIAS, CESAR (Puerto Rico, 1915-)
Foster, P.R. Lit., p. 68. Contents: I. Critical Monographs. II. Critical Essays.

ANGELIS, PEDRO DE (Argentina, 1784-1859)
Arana, Enrique. BIO-BIBLIOGRAFIA DE DON PEDRO DE ANGELIS, 1784-1859: LABOR HISTORICA, PERIODISTICA Y LITERARIA. Buenos Aires: Imprenta C. H. Ricardo Gutiérrez, 1933. 75p. Reprinted from BOLETIN DE LA BIBLIOTECA DE LA FACULTAD DE DERECHO Y CIENCIAS SOCIALES (BUENOS AIRES), Año 1, Núm. 5 (junio de 1933).

ANJOS, AUGUSTO DOS (Brazil, 1884-1913)
Porter, pp. 182-183. Contents: I. Writings. II. References, Critical and Biographical.

APARICIO, RAUL (Cuba, 1913-1970)
Foster, Cuban Lit., p. 88. Critical Essays.

ARANHA, JOSE PEREIRA DA GRAÇA (Brazil, 1868-1931)
Aranha, Graça. OBRA COMPLETA. ORGANIZADA SOB A DIREÇAO DE AFRANIO COUTINHO. Rio de Janeiro: Instituto Nacional do Livro, 1968. 912p. "Bibliografia," pp. 36-42. Contents: I. Obras do autor. A. Livros. B. Traduções. II. Estudos, artigos e reportagens sôbre o autor.
Moraes, pp. 70-77. Major works by and about the author.
Rio de Janeiro. Biblioteca Nacional. CATALOGO DA EXPOSIÇAO COMEMORATIVA DO CENTENARIO DE NASCIMENTO DE GRAÇA ARANHA. Rio de Janeiro: Biblioteca Nacional, Divisão de Publicações e Divulgação, Seção de Exposições, 1968. 47p. Contents: I. Obras de Graça Aranha. A. Livros (by year, 1902-1938). B. Trabalhos esparsos (by title). C. Prefácios. D. Correspondência ativa. E. Correspondência passiva. F. Correspondência de terceiros. G. Antologias. H. Números de revistas dedicados a Graça Aranha. II. Bibliografia (critical studies about Graça Aranha and his work). III. Documentos. IV. Objetos que pertenceram a Graça Aranha. V. Outros retratos. VI. Ilustrações. 305 items.

ARARIPE JUNIOR, TRISTAO DE ALENCAR (Brazil, 1848-1911)
Araripe Júnior. ARARIPE JUNIOR: TEORIA, CRITICA E HISTORIA LITERARIA. SELEÇAO E APRESENTAÇAO DE ALFREDO BUSI. Rio de Janeiro: Livros Técnicos e Científicos; São Paulo: Editôra da Universidade de São Paulo, 1978. 436p. "Bibliografia," pp. 421-426. Contents: I. Obras de Araripe Jr. A. Ficção. B. Crítica. 1. Em livro. 2. Em artigos de jornais e de revistas. 3. Prefácios. II. Sôbre Araripe Jr.

Mota, Artur. "Perfis acadêmicos, Cadeira No. 16: Araripe Júnior," REVISTA DA ACADEMIA BRASILEIRA DE LETRAS, Núm. 92 (agôsto de 1929), 473-490. Contents: I. "Bibliografia," pp. 472-476 (1868-1911). II. "Fontes para o estudo crítico," pp. 476-477.

ARAUJO, RAIMUNDO CORREA DE (Brazil, 1885-1951)
Moraes, pp. 92-94. Major works by and about the author.

ARAYA, GUILLERMO (Chile, 1931-1983)
Epple, Juan Armando. "Cronología biográfica y académica y bibliografía de Guillermo Araya," LITERATURA CHILENA: CREACION Y CRITICA, Núm. 24 (abril/junio de 1983), 14-16. Contents: I. Artículos y reseñas (arranged by year, 1955-1983). II. Ediciones (arranged by year, 1969-1981). III. Libros (arranged by year, 1968-1983). IV. Narrativa (arranged by year, 1980-1983).

ARCE DE VAZQUEZ, MARGOT (Puerto Rico, 1904-)
Arrigoitia, Luis de. "Margot Arce de Vázquez y la crítica literaria en Puerto Rico," REVISTA DE ESTUDIOS HISPANICOS (Río Piedras, Puerto Rico), Año II, Núm. 1/4 (enero/diciembre de 1972), 283-292. Contents: I. Ediciones. II. Traducciones. III. Artículos sueltos. IV. Reseñas. V. Prólogos. VI. Estudios.
Foster, P.R. Lit., pp. 69-70. Contents: I. Bibliography. II. Critical Essays.

ARELLANO, JORGE EDUARDO (Nicaragua, 1946-)
"Bibliografía analítica de Jorge Eduardo Arellano," LA PRENSA LITERARIA (Managua), 24 de julio de 1976, 6-7. 50 items. Contents: I. Libros. II. Plaquets y folletos. III. Separatas. IV. Ediciones. V. Trabajos en revistas especializadas. VI. Hemerografía dispersa. Includes reviews where applicable.
"Bibliografía de Jorge Eduardo Arellano, 1962-1976," BOLETIN NICARAGUENSE DE BIBLIOGRAFIA Y DOCUMENTACION, Núm. 11 (mayo/junio de 1976), 15-33. 520 items. Contents: I. Libros. II. Plaquets y folletos. III. Separatas. IV. Ediciones. V. Trabajos en revistas especializadas. VI. Hemerografía dispersa.

ARENAS, REINALDO (Cuba, 1943-)
Foster, Cuban Lit., pp. 89-91. Contents: I. Critical Monographs and Dissertations. II. Critical Essays.

AREVALO MARTINEZ, RAFAEL (Guatemala, 1884-1975)
Biblioteca Nacional de Guatemala. ALGUNOS JUICIOS DE ESCRITORES GUATEMALTECOS Y EXTRANJEROS SOBRE LA PERSONALIDAD LITERARIA DE RAFAEL AREVALO MARTINEZ Y LISTA BIBLIOGRAFICA DE SU PRODUCCION INTELECTUAL ORDENADA ALFABETICAMENTE POR TITULOS (1909-1959).

Guatemala: Editorial del Ministerio de Educación Pública, 1959. 84p. "Lista bibliográfica...," pp. 59-84. By title.

Dardón Córdova, Gonzalo. "Bibliografía de Rafael Arévalo Martínez," in RAFAEL AREVALO MARTINEZ: HOMENAJE (Guatemala: Instituto Guatemalteco-Americano, 1959), pp. 45-50. Contents: I. Obras escogidas. II. Biografías, ensayos, novelas, artículos (contained in the BOLETIN DE LA BIBLIOTECA NACIONAL, GUATEMALA, 1932-, BOLETIN DE MUSEOS Y BIBLIOTECAS, Guatemala, 1941-1945). III. Trabajos sobre el autor y sus obras.

Estrada L., Hugo. LA POESIA DE RAFAEL AREVALO MARTINEZ. Guatemala, C.A.: Universidad de San Carlos de Guatemala, 1971. 176p. "Principales obras de Arévalo Martínez," pp. 171-176. Contents: I. En verso. II. En prosa. III. Teatro. IV. Bibliografía general (includes a few studies on Arévalo Martínez and his work).

Flores, BEH, pp. 188-190. Contents: I. Ediciones. II. Bibliografiia selecta (criticism).

Salgado, María A. RAFAEL AREVALO MARTINEZ. Boston: G. K. Hall, 1979. 140p. "Selected Bibliography," pp. 135-137. Contents: I. Primary Sources. A. Principal Works. B. Anthologies and Collections. II. Secondary Sources. (briefly annotated).

ARGUEDAS, ALCIDES (Bolivia, 1879-1946)

Albarracín Millán, Juan. ALCIDES ARGUEDAS: LA CONCIENCIA CRITICA DE UNA EPOCA. La Paz: Empresa Editorial Universo, 1979. 340p. "Tabla biobibliográfica," pp. 319-322 (arranged by year, 1879-1920).

Flores, BEH, pp. 190-191. Contents: I. Edición principal. II. Otras ediciones. III. Bibliografía selecta (criticism).

ARGUEDAS, JOSE MARIA (Peru, 1911-1969)

Anderson, pp. 20-23. Critical essays.

"Bio-bibliografía de José María Arguedas Altamirano," ANUARIO BIBLIOGRAFICO PERUANO, 1967/69 (i.e. 1975), 596-633. Contents: I. Libros y folletos (1935-1973). II. Otras publicaciones. III. Artículos y ensayos. IV. Poesías. V. Traducciones. VI. Cartas. VII. Reportajes. VIII. Notas bibliográficas (revistas). IX. Referencias (Criticism, biographical sketches, etc.).

Flores, BEH, pp. 73-75, 180. Contents: I. Ediciones. II. Referencias. III. Bibliografía selecta (criticism).

Foster, Peruvian Lit., pp. 68-81. Contents: I. Bibliographies. II. Critical Monographs and Dissertations. III. Critical Essays.

Foster, 20th Century, pp. 28-31. Contents: I. Bibliographies. II. Critical Books. III. Critical Essays.

Merino de Zela, E. Mildred. "Vida y obra de José María Arguedas," REVISTA PERUANA DE CULTURA, Núm. 13/14 (diciembre de 1970), 146-178. 299 entries arranged in the following manner: I. Historia y arqueología, museos. II. Religión y magia, mitos. III. Arte, arte popular, artesanía. IV. Folklore. V. Lingüística y educación. VI. Literatura. VII. Etnología, sociología. VIII. Política. IX. Varia.

Muñoz, Silverio. JOSE MARIA ARGUEDAS Y EL MITO DE LA SALVACION POR LA CULTURA. Minneapolis: Instituto Para el Estudio de Ideologías y Literatura, 1980. 152p. "Bibliografía," pp. 147-152. Includes a listing of the author's major works and critical studies about the author and his work.

Rowe, William. "Bibliografía sobre José María Arguedas," REVISTA PERUANA DE CULTURA, Núm. 13/14 (diciembre de 1970), 179-197. 103 entries; some annotations.

_______. MITO E IDEOLOGIA EN LA OBRA DE JOSE MARIA ARGUEDAS. Lima: Instituto Nacional de Cultura, 1979. 220p. Contents: I. "Bibliografía de José María Arguedas," pp. 216-217. II. "Estudios sobre Arguedas," pp. 217-219.

Urrello, Antonio. JOSE MARIA ARGUEDAS; EL NUEVO ROSTRO DEL INDIO: UNA ESTRUCTURA MITICO-POETICA. Lima: Librería-Editorial Juan Mejía Baca, 1974. 205p. Contents: I. "Obra narrativa," pp. 195-196. II. "Otros libros y poemas," pp. 196-197. III. "Artículos," pp. 197-200. IV. "Artículos y libros sobre José María Arguedas," pp. 200-205.

ARGUELLO, SANTIAGO (Nicaragua, 1872-1940)

Arellano, Jorge Eduardo. "Otra contribución de la bibliografía de Santiago Argüello," BOLETIN NICARAGUENSE DE BIBLIOGRAFIA Y DOCUMENTACION, Núm. 46 (marzo/abril de 1982), 108-110. Contents: I. Artículos y poemas en revistas, periódicos y antologías. II. Crítica referente a Argüello.

Cerutti, Franco. "Contribución a la bibliografía de Santiago Argüello," BOLETIN NICARAGUENSE DE BIBLIOGRAFIA Y DOCUMENTATION, Núm. 4 (marzo/abril de 1975), 30-33. Additions to the Moore bibliography. Contents: I. Libros y folletos de Santiago Argüello (61 items). II. Crítica referente a Argüello (23 items). III. Obras inéditas. Reprinted: BOLETIN NICARAGUENSE DE BIBLIOGRAFIA Y DOCUMENTACION, Núm. 46 (marzo/abril de 1982), 95-103.

Moore, E. R., J. T. Reid, and R. E. Warner. "Bibliografía de Santiago Argüello," REVISTA IBEROAMERICANA, 5 (1942), 427-437. Contents: I. Libros y folletos. II. Artículos y poemas en revistas, periódicos y antologías. III. Crítica referente a Argüello. Reprinted in BOLETIN NICARAGUENSE DE BIBLIOGRAFIA Y DOCUMENTACION, Núm. 3 (enero/febrero de 1975), 12-22; Ibid., Núm. 46 (enero/abril de 1982), 104-107.

ARGUELLO MORA, MANUEL (Costa Rica, 1834-1902)

Argüello Mora, Manuel. OBRAS LITERARIAS E HISTORICAS. San José, C.R.: Editorial Costa Rica, 1963. 495p. Contents: I. "Bibliografía de don Manuel Argüello Mora," pp. 489-491. II. "Bibliografía sobre Argüello Mora," p. 491.

ARIAS LARETTA, FELIPE (Peru, 1910-1954)
"Felipe Arias Laretta," ANUARIO BIBLIOGRAFICO PERUANO, 1953/1954, 301-303. Contents: I. Biografía. II. Libros y folletos. III. Otras publicaciones. IV. Poesías. V. Notas bibliográficas. VI. Referencias (Criticism, biographical sketches, etc.).

ARIDJIS, HOMERO (Mexico, 1940-)
Foster, Mex. Lit., pp. 90-91. Critical Essays.

ARINOS, AFONSO (Brazil, 1868-1916)
Gravatá, Hélio. "Bibliografia de/sôbre Afonso Arinos," REVISTA DO LIVRO, Núm. 33 (1968), 143-155. Contents: I. Trabalhos de Afonso Arinos. A. Livros e folhetos. B. Artigos em periódicos. C. Antologias. D. Discursos. E. Conferências. II. Trabalhos sôbre Afonso Arinos. A. Bibliografias. B. Livros, parte de obras. C. Verbêtes. D. Artigos em periódicos. III. Indices (by part and anônimos). 111 titles.

ARLT, ROBERTO (Argentina, 1900-1942)
Arlt, Roberto. LAS AGUAFUERTES PORTENAS DE ROBERTO ARLT PUBLICADAS EN "EL MUNDO," 1928-1933. Buenos Aires: Ediciones Culturales Argentinas, Ministerio de Cultura y Educación, 1981. 296p. "Bibliografía," pp. 272-296. The aguafuertes are arranged chronologically.
Becco, Horacio Jorge, and Oscar Masotta. ROBERTO ARLT. Buenos Aires: Universidad de Buenos Aires, Facultad de Filosofía y Letras, Instituto de Literatura Argentina "Ricardo Rojas," 1959. 10p. (Guías bibliográficas, 2). Contents: I. Ediciones. II. Teatro. III. Teatro estrenada. IV. Estudios.
Flores, BEH, pp. 191-193. Contents: I. Ediciones principales. II. Otras ediciones. III. Referencias. IV. Bibliografía selecta (criticism).
Flores, NH, v. 4, pp. 92-96. Contents: I. Ediciones principales de su narrativa. II. Referencias. III. Antología crítica y homenajes en revistas. IV. Bibliografía selecta (criticism).
Foster, Arg. Lit., pp. 158-166. Contents: I. Bibliographies. II. Critical Monographs and Dissertations. III. Critical Essays.
Foster, 20th Century, pp. 31-34. Contents: I. Bibliographies. II. Critical Books. III. Critical Essays.
Guerro, Diana. ROBERTO ARLT: EL HABITANTE SOLITARIO. Buenos Aires: Gránica, 1972. 223p. "Bibliografía," pp. 191-223. Contents: I. Trabajos de Roberto Arlt. A. Novelas. Cuentos. Obras completas (arranged by year, 1926-1969). B. En prensa. C. Teatro (by year, 1930-1968). D. Cine. Televisión. E. Cuentos, epístolas, ensayos, etc. publicados en periódicos y revistas (by year, 1920-1971). F. Material existente cuyos datos no se han podido precisar. G. Antologías de Roberto Arlt. H. Antologías que incluyen trabajos de Arlt. II. Estudios críticos. Ensayos. Reseñas.

Juicios ocasionales. Homenajes, etc. (alphabetically arranged by author).

ARMAS, AUGUSTO (Cuba, 1869-1893)
Foster, Cuban Lit., p. 92. Critical Essays.

ARMAS Y CARDENAS, JOSE DE ("JUSTO DE LARA") (Cuba, 1866-1919)
Coronado y Alvaro, Francisco de Paula. "Justo de Lara," REVISTA DE LA UNIVERSIDAD DE LA HABANA, 30 (enero/junio de 1920), 193-204. Works are arranged chronologically (1884-1916) under the following categories: I. Su seudónimo. II. Sus libros. III. Escritos inéditos. Entries are annotated.
Foster, Cuban Lit., pp. 93-94. Contents: I. Bibliography. II. Critical Monographs. III. Critical Essays.
Soler Mirabent, Antonia. "Bibliografía de José de Armas y de Cárdenas (1909-1915)," BOLETIN DEL INSTITUTO DE LITERATURA Y LINGUISTICA (La Habana), 1 (enero/marzo de 1967), 63-76. The bibliography's 322 entries are arranged chronologically.
Valverde y Maruri, Antonio L. ELOGIO DEL LIC. JOSE DE ARMAS Y CARDENAS ("JUSTO DE LARA"). La Habana: Imprenta "El Siglo," 1923. 225p. "Bibliografía": pp. 148-176. 352 items are listed by year, 1882-1919. This work is up-dated by Antonio Salera's "Bibliografía de José de Armas y Cárdenas (1909-1915)," L/L (Boletín del Instituto de Literatura y Lingüística, Academia de Ciencias de Cuba), Año 1, Núm. 1 (enero/marzo de 1967), 63-76. 322 entries are listed by year.

ARONA, JUAN DE (Pseudonym of PEDRO PAZ SOLDAN Y UNANUE) (Peru, 1839-1895)
Moreyra Paz Soldán, Carlos. LA OBRA DE LOS PAZ SOLDAN. Lima, 1974. 232p. "Bibliografía," pp. 69-76. Contents: I. Libros y folletos. II. Comedias. III. Cartas. IV. Periódicos. V. Artículos periodísticos. VI. Poesía (en periódicos). VII. Manuscritos.

AROZARENA, MARCELINO (Cuba, 1912-)
Jackson, Afro-Spanish, p. 51. Contents: I. Works. II. Criticism.

ARRAIZ, ANTONIO (Venezuela, 1903-1963)
Araujo, Orlando and Oscar Sambrano Urdaneta. ANTONIO ARRAIZ. Caracas: Ediciones de la Biblioteca, Universidad Central de Venezuela, 1975. 146p. (Colección Los creadores, 8). "Biobibliografía," pp. 136-146. Contents: I. Obras publicadas en volumen. A. Poesía. B. Novela. C. Cuento. D. Ensayo. E. Obra didáctica. II. Bibliografía indirecta (criticism, etc.).
Arráiz, Antonio. SUMA POETICA. Caracas: Instituto Nacional de Cultura y Bellas Artes, 1966. 313p. "Probable cronología de la poesía de Antonio Arráiz," pp. 300-303.

Caracas. Universidad Católica "Andrés Bello." Seminario de Literatura Venezolana. CONTRIBUCION A LA BIBLIOGRAFIA DE ANTONIO ARRAIZ, 1903-1963. Caracas: Gobernación del Distrito Federal, 1969. 199p. (Colección bibliografías, 3). 1,042 entries. Contents: I. Fuentes bibliográficas. II. Bibliografía directa. A. Obras mayores. 1. Novela. 2. Cuento. 3. Poesía. 4. Ensayo. 5. Obras didácticos. 6. Prólogos. B. Obra dispersa (journal and newspaper articles mainly). III. Bibliografía indirecta (libros, folletos, capítulos, artículos y referencias sobre el autor y su obra).

Flores, BEH, pp. 193-194. Contents: I. Ediciones. II. Bibliografía selecta (criticism).

ARREOLA, JUAN JOSE (Mexico, 1918-)

Flores, BEH, pp. 75-77. Contents: I. Ediciones. II. Bibliografía selecta (criticism).

Foster, Mex. Lit., pp. 91-95. Contents: I. Bibliographies. II. Critical Monographs and Dissertations. III. Critical Essays.

Ramírez, Arthur and Fern L. Ramírez. "Hacia una bibliografía de y sobre Juan José Arreola," REVISTA IBEROAMERICANA, 45, Núm. 108-109 (julio/diciembre de 1979), 651-667. 284 entries. Contents: I. Obras de Juan José Arreola. A. Obras primarias en sus ediciones principales. B. Antologías y compilaciones. C. Cuentos. D. Ensayos. E. Traducciones. F. Discos. II. Estudios bibliográficos. III. Entrevistas y material biográfico. IV. Referencias en general a la obra de Arreola. V. Crítica sobre Confabulario y otras narraciones breves. VI. Crítica sobre La hora de todos, el teatro de Arreola. VII. Crítica sobre La feria, la novela de Arreola. VIII. Addendum.

Washburn, Yulan M. JUAN JOSE ARREOLA. Boston: Twayne Publishers, 1983. 143p. "Selected Bibliography," pp. 136-140. Contents: I. Primary Sources. II. Secondary Sources (partially annotated).

ARRIETA, RAFAEL ALBERTO (Argentina, 1889-1968)

Becco, Horacio Jorge. "Bibliografía de don Rafael Alberto Arrieta, 1889-1968," BOLETIN DE LA ACADEMIA ARGENTINA DE LETRAS, 33, Núm. 127/128 (enero/junio de 1968), 15-21. Contents: I. Poesía. II. Prosa. III. Folletos. IV. Prólogos y selecciones. V. Traducciones. VI. Antologías.

Giusti, Roberto F. RAFAEL ALBERTO ARRIETA. Buenos Aires: Ediciones Culturales Argentinas, 1962. 167p. Contents: I. "Bibliografía del autor," pp. 159-160. II. "Bibliografía firmada sobre el autor," pp. 161-165.

López, Susana Beatriz. CONTRIBUCION A LA BIBLIOGRAFIA DE RAFAEL ALBERTO ARRIETA. Buenos Aires: Fondo Nacional de las Artes, 1970. 71p. (Bibliografía Argentina de Artes y Letras, Compilaciones Especiales, Nos. 37/38). Contents: I. Obras del autor. A. Poesía. B. Ensayos. C. Prosa varia. II. Colaboraciones en publicaciones periódicas. A. Poesía. B. Ensayos y notas. III. Discursos y conferencias.

IV. Entrevistas, encuestas, reportajes. V. Ediciones, prólogos. VI. Antologías de textos del autor. VII. Antologías diversas. VIII. Traducción de obras de otras autores. A. Francés. B. Inglés. IX. Traducciones de obras del autor. A. Francés. Inglés. C. Italiano. D. Portugués. X. Crítica y biografía (trabajos firmados). XI. Bibliografía. XII. Homenajes (trabajos firmados, artículos sin firmar). XIII. Cuadro biográfico cronológico. XIV. Indices (de títulos, onomástico). XV. Ilustraciones.

ARRIVI, FRANCISCO (Puerto Rico, 1915-)
Foster, P.R. Lit., pp. 70-71. Critical Essays.

ARRUFAT, ANTON (Cuba, 1935-)
Foster, Cuban Lit., pp. 95-96. Contents: I. Dissertation. II. Critical Essays.

ARTEAGA ALEMPARTE, DOMINGO (Chile, 1834-1882)
Escudero, p. 302. Criticism.

ARTEL, JORGE (Columbia, 1909-)
Jackson, Afro-Spanish, pp. 51-52. Contents: I. Works. II. Criticism.

ASCASUBI, HILARIO (Argentina, 1807-1875)
Foster, Arg. Lit., pp. 167-170. Contents: I. Bibliography. II. Critical Monographs and Dissertations. III. Critical Essays.
Rodríguez Molas, Ricardo. "Contribución a la bibliografía de Hilario Ascasubi, 1807-1875," BIBLIOGRAFIA ARGENTINA DE ARTES Y LETRAS, Núm. 12 (octubre/diciembre de 1961), 2ª sección, 51-84. Contents: I. Obras del autor. A. Libros. B. Colaboraciones en publicaciones periódicas. C. Textos del autor en diversas antologías. D. Correspondencia en periódicos y recopilaciones documentales. II. Seudónimos usados por Ascasubi. III. Crítica y biografía. IV. Cuadro biográfico-cronológico. V. Indice (de títulos, onomástico). VI. Ilustraciones.
Sosa de Newton, Lily. GENIO Y FIGURA DE HILARIO ASCASUBI. Buenos Aires: Editorial Universitaria de Buenos Aires, 1981. 346p. "Bibliografía," pp. 313-343. Contents: I. Obras de Hilario Ascasubi. A. Libros, folletos. B. Periódicos propios. C. Publicaciones en otros periódicos. D. Correspondencia. E. Antologías. II. Sobre Hilario Ascasubi. A. Crítica. B. Biografía. C. Información periodística.

ASTOL, EUGENIO (Puerto Rico, 1868-1948)
Foster, P.R. Lit., pp. 71-72. Critical Essays.

ASTURIAS, MIGUEL ANGEL (Guatemala, 1899-1974)
Andrea, Pedro F. de. "Miguel Angel Asturias: anticipo bibliográfico," REVISTA IBEROAMERICANA, 35, Núm. 67 (enero/

abril de 1969), 133-269. 1,460 items. Contents: I. Obras de Miguel Angel Asturias. A. Ensayos, poesías, novelas, cuentos, leyendas. B. Teatro. C. Algunas antologías. D. Obras de conjunto. E. Miscelánea. F. Hemerografía de Asturias en español. II. Traducciones. A. Traducciones de obras asturianas. B. Asturias traductor. C. Hemerografía de Asturias en traducciones. D. Traducciones de Asturias incluídas en antologías. III. Referencias sobre Asturias. A. Libros, folletos y separatas. B. Tesis. C. Algunos homenajes. D. Algunas conferencias. E. Referencias: hemerografía sobre Asturias. G. Estudios, artículos, reseñas. Bibliography also published as a book: México, D.F.: Ediciones De Andrea, 1969. 135p.

_______. "Miguel Angel Asturias en México: ensayo bibliográfico," BOLETIN DE LA COMUNIDAD LATINOAMERICANA DE ESCRITORES (México), 2 (1968), 10-26. This work of 217 entries is divided into four sections: I. Obras impresas en México. II. Traducciones publicadas en México. III. Hemerografía mexicana de Asturias. IV. Referencias sobre Asturias en la prensa nacional y en libros impresos en México.

Barkan, Pierre. "Bibliographie," pp. 355-370 in MIGUEL ANGEL ASTURIAS. Cette édition de Monsieur le Président de Miguel Angel Asturias lauréat 1967 (Guatemala) réalisée par les presses du compagnonnage est une sélection des Editions Rombaldi réservée a la Guilde des Bibliophiles, 1970. 371p. Chronologically arranged, 1912-1969. Each Spanish language title is followed by translations whenever they were published.

_______. "Le don Miguel Angel Asturias à la Bibliothèque Nationale de Paris," Europe, No. 553/554 (1975), 201-208. Contents: I. Manuscripts des oeuvres. II. Oeuvres imprimées.

Bellini, Giuseppe. "Bibliografía," in Miguel Angel Asturias' TRES OBRAS; INTRODUCCION, NOTAS CRITICAS Y CRONOLOGIA DE GUISEPPE BELLINI (Caracas: Biblioteca Ayacucho, 1977), pp. 563-568. Contents: I. Obras de Miguel Angel Asturias. A. Poesía. B. Novelas y cuentos. C. Teatro. D. Guiones. E. Tesis y ensayos. F. Varia. G. Obras completas y antologías. II. Ediciones críticas (critical studies on Asturias).

Cheymol, Marc. "M. A. Asturias: bibliographie critique essentielle, 1967-1977," CAHIERS DU SEMINAIRE ASTURIAS (Nanterre), 3 (10 mai 1977), 71-77. Very few non-French citations in this bibliography. Contents: I. Pour situer Asturias dans son contexte latino-américain. II. Volumes entièrement consacrés à Asturias. III. Articles de présentation générale. IV. Articles spécialisés: études de critique littéraire sur un problème précis. V. Thèses: travaux universitaires en cours.

_______. "Miguel Angel Asturias: Bibliographie critique essentielle, 1967-1977 (France)," CAHIERS DU SEMINAIRE ASTURIAS (Nanterre), 4 (décémbre 1977), 1-14. Same type of entries as above.

Couffon, Claude. MIGUEL ANGEL ASTURIAS. Paris: Editions Seghers, 1970. 187p. (Poètes d'aujourd'hui, 196). "Bibliographie," pp. 183-187. Contents: I. Oeuvres de Miguel Angel Asturias. A. Poésie. B. Romans, contes, légendes. C. Théâtre. D. Thèse et essais. E. Oeuvres, choisies ou complètes. F. Prologues et anthologies. II. Traductions de Miguel Angel Asturias. III. Traductions françaises. IV. Quelques textes non recueillis en volumes.

Flores, BEH, pp. 77-79. Contents: I. Ediciones principales. II. Otras ediciones. III. Referencias. IV. Bibliografía selecta (criticism).

Foster, 20th Century, pp. 34-43. Contents: I. Bibliographies. II. Critical Books. III. Critical Essays.

Martin, Gerald. "Miguel Angel Asturias in Great Britain and North America: A Brief Bibliographical Survey (1967-1977)," CAHIERS DU SEMINAIRE ASTURIAS (Nanterre), 4 (décémbre 1977), 58-61. Contents: I. Translations. II. Books. III. Dissertations. IV. Articles.

Moore, Richard E. ASTURIAS: A CHECKLIST OF WORKS AND CRITICISM. New York: The American Institute for Marxist Studies, 1979. 121p. (Bibliographical Series, 13). Contents: I. Asturias: His Major Works and Criticisms. II. Asturias: His Minor Works and Criticisms. III. Translations by Asturias. IV. Prologues. V. Book of Criticisms. VI. General Items on Asturias (articles, etc.). VII. Index by Author.

_______. "Miguel Angel Asturias: A Biobibliography," BULLETIN OF BIBLIOGRAPHY, 27 (1970), 85-90, 107-111. Contents: I. Biography. II. Publications (includes reviews and translations). III. General works about Asturias (partially annotated).

Segala, Amos. "Les fonds Asturias à la Bibliothèque Nationale: description et recherches," CAHIERS DU SEMINAIRE ASTURIAS (Nanterre), 5 (1980).

Serafin, Silvana. MIGUEL ANGEL ASTURIAS: BIBLIOGRAFIA ITALIANA Y ANTOLOGIA CRITICA. Cisalpino: Goliardica, 1979. 87p. "Bibliografía," pp. 1-14. Contents: I. Bibliografía. II. Estudios biobibliográficos. III. Estudios de conjunto. IV. Estudios sobre el realismo mágico. V. Estudios sobre novelas singular. VI. Estudios sobre poesía. VII. Estudios sobre teatro. VIII. Relaciones literarias. IX. Homenajes italianos. X. Traducciones. XI. Inéditos publicados en Italia por primera vez.

AUGIER, ANGEL I. (Cuba, 1910-)

Perdomo Correa, Omar. BIBLIOGRAFIA MARTIANA DE ANGEL AUGIER. La Habana: Casa Natal de José Martí, 1980. 46p.

_______, and José Antonio Portuondo. "Angel Augier: biobibliografía," LA GACETA DE CUBA, Núm. 141 (diciembre de 1975), 26-30. A selected bibliography arranged under the following topics: I. Prólogo. II. Cronología (1910-1975). III. Bibliografía activa. A. Libros y folletos. B. Compilaciones, introducciones y notas. IV. Bibliografía pasiva. A. Libros y folletos. B. Publicaciones periódicas.

AYERRA SANTA MARIA, FRANCISCO DE (Puerto Rico, 1630-1708)
Rosa-Nieves, Cesáreo. FRANCISCO DE AYERRA SANTA MARIA: POETA PUERTORRIQUENO, 1630-1708. San Juan: Editorial Universitaria, Universidad de Puerto Rico, 1948. 31p. "Bibliografía mínima," pp. 28-30. Contents: I. Obras poéticas de Francisco de Ayerra Santa María. II. Obras de consulta sobre Ayerra Santa María.

AYLLON, JUAN (Peru, 1604?- ?)
Indacochea, Luisa. "BIO-BIBLIOGRAFIA DE FRAY JUAN DE AYLLON." Tesis. Lima: Biblioteca Nacional, Escuela de Bibliotecarios, 1959.

AZEVEDO, ALUISIO (Brazil, 1857-1913)
Andrade, Antônio. "A Gênese d'O Mulato de Aluísio Azevedo." Ph.D., Indiana University, 1975. 640p. "Bibliografia," pp. 188-203.
Brayner, Sonia. A METAFORA DO CORPO NO ROMANCE NATURALISTA: ESTUDO SOBRE "O CORTIÇO." Rio de Janeiro: Livraria São José, 1973. 129p. "Obras de Aluísio Azevedo," pp. 126-129.
Epple, Juan Armando. Bibliografía de Aluísio Azevedo," REVISTA DE CRITICA LITERARIA LATINOAMERICANA, Núm. 11 (1980), 129-136. Contents: I. Obras de ficción. A. Novelas. B. Cuentos. C. Teatro publicado. II. Otras publicaciones. III. Bibliografía sobre Aluísio Azevedo.
Menezes, Raimundo de. ALUISIO AZEVEDO: UMA VIDA DE ROMANCE. São Paulo: Livraria Martins, 1958. 343p. Contents: I. Obras de Aluísio Azevedo," pp. 333-335. A. Romances (by year, 1879-1890). B. Contos. C. Teatro (by year, 1882-1905). D. Diversos. E. Jornais e revistas. F. Traduções. G. Pseudônimos. II. "Bibliografia," pp. 337-339 (includes a selected number of studies on Azevedo).
Moraes, pp. 54-58. Major works by and about the author.
Pires, Homero. ALVARES DE AZEVEDO. ENSAIO BIO-BIBLIOGRAFICO. Rio de Janeiro: Officina Industrial Graphica, 1931. 96p. (Publicações da Academia Brasileira, III, Bibliografia 3). Contents: I. Nota biográfica. II. Bibliografia. A. Manuscritos. B. Obras impresas (by year, 1849-1919; descriptive bibliography approach). III. Iconografia. IV. Escritos e opiniões sôbre Alvarez de Azevedo. V. Depoimentos.
Sales, Herberto. PARA CONHECER MELHOR ALUISIO AZEVEDO. Rio de Janeiro: Bloch Editôres, 1973. 136p. "Bibliografia," pp. 19-21. Contents: I. Romances. II. Contos. III. Teatro (publicado). IV. Crônicos e epistolário. V. Algumas traduções.

AZEVEDO, ARTUR (Brazil, 1855-1908)

Moraes, pp. 52-54. Major works by and about the author.

Santos, Miguel dos. "Pseudônimos de Artur Azevedo," BOLETIM DA SOCIEDADE BRASILEIRA DE AUTORES TEATRAIS, Núm. 275 (novembro/dezembro de 1953), 14.

Seidl, Roberto. ARTUR AZEVEDO: ENSAIO BIO-BIBLIOGRAFICO. Rio de Janeiro: Empresa Editôra ABC Limitada, 1937. 175p. (Publicações da Academia Brasileira. Clássicos brasileiros 3: Bibliografia 8). Contents: I. Nota biográfica. II. Ensaio de bibliografia (A descriptive bibliography by year, 1871-1932). III. Escritos de Artur Azevedo impressos em compêndios de literatura, florilégios, seletas e antologias (1884-1935). IV. Prefácios. V. Inéditos. VI. Manuscritos. VII. Principais opiniões sôbre o escritor. VIII. Depoimentos sôbre e escritor.

AZEVEDO, MANUEL ANTONIO ALVARES DE (Brazil, 1831-1852)

Lacerda, Virgínia Côrtes de. "Bibliografia de Alvares de Azevedo," LEITORES E LIVROS, 3, Núm. 10 (outubre/dezembro de 1952), 78-82. The entries are accompanied by critical comments.

Mota, Artur. "Alvares de Azevedo," REVISTA NOVA, 1, Núm. 3 (setembro de 1931), 397-415. Bibliographical study.

AZUELA, MARIANO (Mexico, 1873-1952)

Flores, BEH, pp. 79-81. Contents: I. Edición principal. II. Otras ediciones. III. Referencias. IV. Bibliografía selecta (criticism).

Foster, Mex. Lit., pp. 95-107. Contents: I. Bibliographies. II. Critical Monographs and Dissertations. III. Critical Essays.

Foster, 20th Century, pp. 43-47. Contents: I. Bibliographies. II. Critical Books. III. Critical Essays.

González, Manuel Pedro. "Bibliografía del novelista Mariano Azuela," REVISTA BIMESTRE CUBANA, 48, Núm. 1 (julio/agosto de 1941), 50-72. Contents: I. Bibliografía original. A. Primeras notas (1896-1910). B. Labor varia. Impresiones y artículos (1912-1938). C. Cuentos (1903-1939). D. Novelas. 1. Los de abajo. 2. Traducciones de Los de abajo. E. Teatro. II. Bibliografía crítica.

- B -

BACHILLER Y MORALES, ANTONIO (Cuba, 1812-1889)

Peraza Sarausa, Fermín. ANTONIO BACHILLER Y MORALES. La Habana: Municipio de La Habana, Departamento de Cultura, 1942. 7p. (Publicaciones de la Biblioteca Municipal de La Habana, Serie C: Guías Bibliográficas, 5). Contents: I. Bosquejo biográfico. II. Relación de libros y folletos para el estudio de la vida y de la obra de Antonio Bachiller y Morales existentes en nuestras principales bibliotecas.

BALBOA TROYA Y QUESADA, SILVESTRE DE (Cuba, 1563-1624)
Foster, Cuban Lit., pp. 97-98. Contents: I. Critical Monographs. II. Critical Essays.

BALBUENA, BERNARDO DE (Mexico and Puerto Rico, 1568-1627)
Flores, BEH, pp. 3-4. Contents: I. Ediciones. II. Referencias. III. Bibliografía selecta (criticism).
Foster, P.R. Lit., pp. 72-75. Contents: I. Critical Monographs. II. Critical Essays.
Rojas Garcidueñas, José. BERNARDO DE BALBUENA: LA VIDA Y LA OBRA. México, D.F.: UNAM, Instituto de Investigaciones Estéticas, 1958. 213p. "Obras de Bernardo de Balbuena" (selected; arranged by year 1608-1954). "Bibliografía," pp. 211-213 (includes works about Bernardo de Balbuena).

BALLAGAS, EMILIO (Cuba, 1908-1954)
Flores, BEH, pp. 81-82. Contents: I. Ediciones principales. II. Otras ediciones. III. Bibliografía selecta (criticism).
Foster, Cuban Lit., pp. 99-101. Contents: I. Critical Monographs and Dissertations. II. Critical Essays.
Rice, Argyill Pryor. EMILIO BALLAGAS: POETA O POESIA. México, D.F., Ediciones De Andrea, 1966. 237p. (Colección Studium, 56). "Bibliografía," pp. 231-234. Contents: I. Bibliografía activa. A. Poesía. B. Prosa. II. Bibliografía pasiva. A. Obras específicas sobre Ballagas. B. Obras generales.

BALSEIRO, JOSE A. (Puerto Rico, 1900-)
Foster, P.R. Lit., pp. 76-77. Critical Essays.

BANCHS, ENRIQUE (Argentina, 1888-1968)
Becco, Horacio Jorge. "Bibliografía de don Enrique Banchs," BOLETIN DE LA ACADEMIA ARGENTINA DE LETRAS, 33, Núm. 127/128 (enero/junio de 1968), 27-29. Contents: I. Obra poética. II. Prosa. III. Antologías. IV. Bibliografías.
_______. "Bibliografía de Enrique Banchs," in Leónidas de Vedia's ENRIQUE BANCHS (Buenos Aires: Edición de Cultura Argentina, Ministerio de Educación y Justicia, Dirección General de Cultura, 1964), pp. 189-199. 172 entries. Contents: I. Obra poética. II. Prosa. III. Antologías. IV. Antologías con textos de Banchs. V. Traducciones. VI. Estudios sobre su obra. VII. Bibliografía.
Flores, BEH, pp. 194-195. Contents: I. Edición principal. II. Otras ediciones. III. Referencias. IV. Bibliografía selecta.
Foster, Arg. Lit., pp. 171-175. Contents: I. Bibliographies. II. Critical Monographs and Dissertation. III. Critical Essays.

BANDEIRA, MANUEL (Brazil, 1886-1968)
Bandeira, Manuel. MANUEL BANDEIRA. SELEÇAO DE TEXTOS: SONIA BRAYNER. Rio de Janeiro: Civilização Brasileira,

1980. Contents: I. "Cronologia de Manuel Bandeira escrita por o mesmo," pp. 11-21. II. Bibliografia ativa," pp. 22-26. A. Poesia. B. Prosa. C. Antologias e edições. D. Teatro traduzido. E. Poemas musicados. III. "Bibliografia passiva," pp. 27-29. This bibliography up-dates bibliography in the 1967 edition of Bandeira's Poesia completa e prosa.

_______. POESIA COMPLETA E PROSA. Rio de Janeiro: Companhia José Aguilar Editora, 1967. 814p. "Bibliografia," pp. 781-792. Contents: I. Obras. II. Edições e antologias. III. Traduções. IV. Músicas. V. Estudos, reportagens, homenagens.

Flores, BEH, pp. 195-197. Contents: I. Ediciones principales. II. Otras ediciones. III. Referencias. IV. Bibliografía selecta (criticism).

BARBA-JACOB, PORFIRIO (Pseudonym of MIGUEL ANGEL OSORIO) (Colombia, 1883-1942)

Barba-Jacob, Porfirio. OBRAS COMPLETAS. Medellín: Editorial Montoya, 1962. 553p. "Bibliografía," pp. 475-546. Contents: I. Libros y opúsculos (By year, 1907-1960). II. Libros y opúsculos sin fecha. III. Artículos de prensa (1907-1959). IV. Artículos de prensa sin fecha. V. Poesías sin fecha. VI. Obras inéditas. VII. Periódicos que fundó. VIII. Bibliografía sobre Barba-Jacob (by author).

Valle, Rafael Heliodoro. BIBLIOGRAFIA DE PORFIRIO BARBA-JACOB. ORDENADA POR EMILIA ROMERO DE VALLE. Bogotá: Instituto Caro y Cuervo, 1961. 107p. Originally published in THESAURUS (Boletín del Instituto Caro y Cuervo), 15 (1960), 71-173. Contents: I. Libros y opúsculos (1907-1960). II. Libros y opúsculos sin fecha. III. Artículos de prensa (1907-1959). IV. Artículos sin fecha. V. Poesías sin fecha. VI. Obras inéditas. VII. Periódicos que fundó (1909-1936). VIII. Bibliografía sobre Barba-Jacob. Partially annotated.

BARBIERI, VICENTE (Argentina, 1903-1956)

Becco, Horacio Jorge. "Bibliografía," in Vicente Barbieri's OBRA POETICA: ANOTACION PRELIMINAR DE CARLOS MASTRONARDI (Buenos Aires: Emecé, 1961), pp. 403-427. 603 entries. Contents: I. Poesía. II. Prosa. III. Teatro. IV. Otros trabajos y prólogos. V. Discografía. VI. Poemas, prosas y ensayos. VII. Antologías. VIII. Crítica. IX. Poemas dedicados. X. Iconografía. XI. Homenajes.

Flores, BEH, pp. 197-198. Contents: I.Edición principal. II. Otras ediciones. III. Referencias. IV. Bibliografía selecta (criticism).

Foster, Arg. Lit., pp. 176-178. Contents: I. Bibliographies. II. Critical Monographs. III. Critical Essays.

Garat, Aurelia, and Lorenzo, Ana María. "Contribución a la bibliografía de Vicente Barbieri," in Vicente Barbieri's PROSA

DISPERSAS DE VICENTE BARBIERI. (La Plata: Universidad Nacional de La Plata, Facultad de Humanidades y Ciencias, 1970), pp. 215-299. 809 entries. Contents: I. Del autor. A. Obras. 1. Poesía. 2. Prosa. 3. Teatro. B. Colaboraciones en publicaciones periódicas. Nómina de publicaciones periódicas en las que colaboró Vicente Barbieri. 1. Poesía. Seudónimos usados por Vicente Barbieri. 2. Cuentos y relatos. 3. Prosa varia. 4. Teatro. C. Discursos. Conferencias. Entrevistas. D. Prólogos a obras de otros autores. E. Antología de textos del autor. F. Colaboraciones en libros. G. Textos del autor en diversas antologías. H. Traducciones de obras del autor. I. Traducciones de textos de otros autores. J. Textos inéditos. K. Discografía. L. Colección literaria dirigida por el autor. M. Material existente cuya fecha no podido determinarse. II. Crítica y biografía. A. Trabajos firmados. B. Artículos sin firmar. C. Bibliografías. D. Homenajes. E. Poemas dedicados. F. Iconografía. G. Notas periodísticas. H. Crónicas de estreno. I. Notas necrológicas. J. Homenajes póstumas. K. Indices.

BARBOSA, DOMINGOS (Brazil, 1880-1946)
Moraes, pp. 86-87. Major works by and about the author.

BARBOSA, DOMINGOS CALDAS (Brazil, 1740-1800)
Porter, p. 195. Contents: I. Writings. II. References, Critical and Biographical.

BARBOSA, RUI (Brazil, 1849-1923)
Néry, Fernando. RUI BARBOSA (ENSAIO BIO-BIBLIOGRAFICO). Rio de Janeiro: Editôra Guanabara, 1932. 282p. Contents: I. "Principais livros e trabalhos acerca de Rui Barbosa," p. 189. II. "Bibliografia," pp. 191-282.
Pereira, Antônio Batista. RUI BARBOSA: CATALOGO DAS OBRAS. Rio de Janeiro: n.p., 1926. 226p.

BARNET, MIGUEL (Cuba, 1940-)
Foster, Cuban Lit., pp. 102-103. Critical Essays.

BARNOLA, PEDRO PABLO (Venezuela, 1908-)
Becco, Horacio Jorge. R.P. PEDRO PABLO BARNOLA, S.J..: BIBLIOGRAFIA (1935-1983). San Cristóbal, Venezuela: Universidad Católica del Tachira, 1985. 16p. (Separata de la revista, PARAMILLO, Núm. 2/3). Contents: I. Libros y folletos. Ordenamiento cronológico. II. Prólogos, estudios y participaciones en otras obras.

BARRA, EDUARDO DE LA (Chile, 1839-1900)
Escudero, pp. 303-304. Criticism.

BARRETO, AFONSO HENRIQUE DE LIMA (Brazil, 1881-1922)
Barbosa, Francisco de Assis. A VIDA DE LIMA BARRETO

(1881-1922). Terceira edição definitiva. Rio de Janeiro: Editôra Civilização Brasileira, 1964. 387p. Pages 346-369 contain an inventory of Lima Barreto's library.

Barreto, Lima. DOS NOVELAS: "RECUERDOS DEL ESCRIBIENTE ISIAS CAMINHA/EL TRISTE FIN DE POLICARIO QUARESMA. PROLOGO Y CRONOLOGIA DE FRANCISCO DE ASSIS BARBOSA. Caracas: Biblioteca Ayacucho, 1978. 390p. "Bibliografía," pp. 385-390. Contents: I. Obras de Lima Barreto. II. Escritos sobre Lima Barreto.

Nunes, Maria Luisa. LIMA BARRETO: BIBLIOGRAPHY AND TRANSLATIONS. Boston: G. K. Hall, 1979. 227p. Contents: I. "Bibliography of the Works of Lima Barreto," pp. 11-15 (by year, 1909-1953). Annotated entries. II. "Selected Bibliography of Works about Lima Barretto," pp. 17-27. Annotated entries.

Porter, pp. 230-232. Contents: I. Writings. II. References, Critical and Biographical.

Prado, Antônio Arnoni. LIMA BARRETO: O CRITICO E A CRISE. Rio de Janeiro: Livraria Editôra Cátedra, 1976. 123p. "Bibliografia," pp. 117-119. Contents: I. Sôbre o autor. II. Do autor.

Rio de Janeiro. Biblioteca Nacional. LIMA BARRETO: 1881-1922. CATALOGO DA EXPOSIÇAO COMEMORATIVA DO CENTENARIO DE NASCIMENTO. Organizado pela Seção de Promoções Culturais. Apresentação de Plínio Doyle. Rio de Janeiro, 1981. 70p.

BARRETO, PAULO see RIO, JOAO DO

BARRETT, RAFAEL (Argentina, Paraguay, or Uruguay, 1876-1910)

"Bibliografía de Rafael Barrett en La razón," REVISTA DE LA BIBLIOTECA NACIONAL (MONTEVIDEO), 16 (diciembre de 1976), 51-59.

BARRIOS, EDUARDO (Chile, 1884-1963)

"Cartillas biobibliográficas de autores chilenos: Eduardo Barrios Hudtwalcker, Valparaíso, 1884. Novelista, cuentista y dramaturgo," BOLETIN DEL INSTITUTO DE LITERATURA CHILENA (Universidad de Chile, Santiago), Año 2, Núm. 3 (octubre de 1962), 14-24. Contents: I. Obras. II. Referencias (Criticism, biographical sketches, etc.). III. Tabla biográfica.

Flores, BEH, pp. 198-200. Contents: I. Edición principal. II. Otras ediciones. III. Referencias. IV. Bibliografía selecta (criticism).

Foster, Chilean Lit., pp. 50-56. Contents: I. Bibliographies. II. Critical Books and Theses. III. Critical Essays.

Foster, 20th Century, pp. 47-51. Contents: I. Bibliographies. II. Critical Books. III. Critical Essays.

Martínez López, Benjamín. EDUARDO BARRIOS: VIDA Y OBRA. Río Piedras, Puerto Rico: Editorial Universitaria, Universidad de Puerto Rico, 1977. 163p. "Bibliografía," pp. 159-162.

Contents: I. Obras de Eduardo Barrios. A. Novelas. B. Cuentos. C. Teatro. D. Artículos. II. Estudios críticos sobre Eduardo Barrios.

BARRIOS, PILAR (Uruguay, 1889-)
Jackson, Afro-Spanish, pp. 52-53. Contents: I. Works. II. Criticism.

BARROS, LEANDRO GOMES DE (Brazil, 1865-1918)
Batista, Sebastião Nunes. BIBLIOGRAFIA PREVIA DE LEANDRO GOMES DE BARROS. Rio de Janeiro: Divisão de Publicações e Divulgação, Biblioteca Nacional, 1971. 97p. Contents: I. Resumo biográfico. II. Critério de registro dos poemas. III. Bibliografia prévia (by title). IV. Folhetos de autoria também atribuída a Leandro Gomes de Barros (by title). V. Adulterações de acróstico. VI. Folhetos de outros poetas populares baseados em poemas de Leandro Gomes de Barros.

BATRES MONTUFAR, JOSE (Guatemala, 1809-1844)
Flores, BEH, pp. 4-5. Contents: I. Ediciones. II. Bibliografía selecta (criticism).

BAUZA, OBDULIO (Puerto Rico, 1907-)
Foster, P.R. Lit., p. 77. Critical Essays.

BAZAN VELAZQUEZ, ARMANDO (Peru, 1902-1962)
Márquez P., María Antonieta. "Armando Bazán Velázquez," ANUARIO BIBLIOGRAFICO PERUANO, 1961/1963, 460-468. Contents: I. Cronobiografía. II. Libros y folletos. III. Otras publicaciones. IV. Artículos y ensayos, cuentos, poesías. V. Notas bibliográficas. VI. Reportajes. VII. Referencias, necrológicas.

BECERRA, JOSE CARLOS (Mexico, 1936-1970)
Becerra, José Carlos. EL OTONO RECORRE LAS ISLAS: OBRA POETICA 1961/1970. PROLOGO DE OCTAVIO PAZ. EDICION PREPARADA POR JOSE EMILIO PACHECO Y GABRIEL ZARD. México, D.F.: Biblioteca Era, 1973. 311p. "Bibliografía," pp. 32-34. Contents: I. Libros de José Carlos Becerra (by year, 1965-1970). II. Poemas en antologías y publicaciones periódicas (by year, 1962-1973).

BEINGOLLA, MANUEL (Peru, 1881-1953)
"Manuel Beingolla," ANUARIO BIBLIOGRAFICO PERUANO, 1953/1954, 324-332. Contents: I. Biografía. II. Libros y folletos. III. Otras publicaciones. IV. Traducciones. VII. Referencias (Criticism, biographical sketches, etc.).

BELAVEL, EMILIO S. (Puerto Rico, 1903-1972)
Foster, P.R. Lit., pp. 78-79. Contents: I. Bibliography. II. Critical Monographs. III. Critical Essays.

Lugo de Marichal, Flavia. "Bibliografía," SIN NOMBRE, 4 (abril/junio de 1974), 105-110. Contents: I. Obras de Emilio S. Belavel A. Libros de cuentos. B. Cuentos en el Puerto Rico Ilustrado. C. Teatro. D. Ensayos, artículos y crítica literaria. II. Estudios sobre Emilio S. Belavel.

BELLI, CARLOS GERMAN (Peru, 1927-)

Flores, BEH, pp. 200-201. Contents: I. Ediciones. II. Bibliografía selecta (criticism).

Foster, Peruvian Lit., pp. 82-83. Critical Essays.

BELLO, ANDRES (Chile and Venezuela, 1781-1865)

Becco, Horacio Jorge. EDICIONES CHILENAS DE ANDRES BELLO (1830-1893). Caracas: La Casa de Bello, 1980. 87p. 190 entries. Contents: I. Obras de referencia. II. Obras de Bello. III. Mensajes presidenciales redactados por Andrés Bello. IV. Memorias de relaciones exteriores redactadas por Andrés Bello. V. Obras completas. VI. Andrés Bello, editor. VII. Diarios y revistas donde colaboró Andrés Bello. VIII. Ordenamiento cronológico de las ediciones chilenas. IX. Indice onomástico. X. Indice de títulos. XI. Indice general.

Bello, Andrés. OBRA LITERARIA. SELECCION Y PROLOGO DE PEDRO GRASES. CRONOLOGIA DE OSCAR SAMBRANO URDANETA. Caracas: Biblioteca Ayacucho, 1979. 735p. "Fuentes bibliográficas y ediciones de Obras Completas de Andres Bello," pp. xlviii-lvi. Contents: I. Fuentes bibliográficas de Andrés Bello. II. Ediciones de Obras Completas de Andrés Bello.

Caro, Miguel Antonio. "Apuntes bibliográficos relativos a D. Andrés Bello," in A LA MEMORIA DE ANDRES BELLO EN SU CENTENARIO. HOMENAJE DEL "REPERTORIO COLOMBIANO" (Bogotá: Librería Americana, 1881), pp. 90-125 and reprinted in BELLO EN COLOMBIA. ESTUDIO Y SELECCION DE RAFAEL TORRES QUINTERO (Bogotá: Instituto Caro y Cuervo, 1952), pp. 61-113. Contents: I. Composiciones en verso. II. Opúsculos. III. Obras mayores. IV. Publicaciones relativas a Bello.

"Catálogo de la exposición bibliográfica e iconográfica de Andrés Bello," in PRIMER LIBRO DE LA SEMANA DE BELLO EN CARACAS (Caracas: Ediciones del Ministerio de Educación, 1952), pp. 323-352. Contents: I. Manuscritos y Fotocopias. II. Obras impresas de Bello. III. Bibliografía sobre A.B. IV. La época de Bello. V. Recortes de prensa. VI. Iconografía.

Cifuentes, Manuel. "Catálogo de la exposición bibliográfica, iconográfica y de objetos personales de Andrés Bello efectuada en la Biblioteca Nacional con motivo del centenario de su fallecimiento 1865-15 de octubre-1964," MAPOCHO, Tomo IV, Vol. 12, Núm. 3 (1965), 355-377. Contents: I. Recuerdos de Andrés Bello. II. Obras completas, antologías y selecciones. III. Diarios y revistas en que escribió Bello. IV. Rest of exhibit arranged books, etc., by topic.

Flores, BEH, pp. 5-7. Contents: I. Ediciones principales. II. Antologías. III. Referencias. IV. Bibliografía selecta (criticism).

Grases, Pedro. "Bibliografía sumaria de Andrés Bello," MAPOCHO, Tomo IV, Vol. 12, Núm. 3 (1965), 332-344. Contents: I. Bibliografía de Andrés Bello. II. Las obras completas de Andrés Bello. III. Ediciones de obras completas y antologías. IV. Referencias bibliográficas. V. Referencias por temas. A. Obras biográficas y misceláneas. B. Poesía. C. Filosofía, educación, administración pública y legislación. D. Temas jurídicos, derecho internacional. E. Historia, periodismo, ciencias, ideario. Partially annotated.

_______. "Bibliografía de Andrés Bello," REVISTA NACIONAL DE CULTURA UNIVERSITARIA (Caracas), Núm. 4 (noviembre/diciembre de 1947), 211-230. "Reúno en lista parcial de libros, folletos y artículos, una serie de publicaciones acerca de la vida y la obra del gran humanista caraqueño." Contents: I. Fuentes bibliográficas. II. Estudios generales (biografías y apreciaciones de conjunto). III. Estudios monografías (aspectos de la vida y la obra de Bello; includes journal articles). 163 entries. The above article is also reprinted in DOCE ESTUDIOS SOBRE ANDRES BELLO (Buenos Aires: Nova, 1950), pp. 157-178.

_______. CONTRIBUCION AL ESTUDIO DE LA BIBLIOGRAFIA CARAQUEÑA DE DON ANDRES BELLO. Edición ordenada por el Comité de la Quinta Exposición del Libro Venezolano (29 noviembre-6 diciembre de 1943). Caracas: Tipografía Americana, 1944. 53p. "He aquí una pequeña relación bibliográfica, forzosamente incompleta, de ediciones de obras y escritos de Andrés Bello, realizadas en Caracas, o desde Caracas, la ciudad natal del gran humanista." 50 items annotated, 1837-1943. Bibliography also appears in BOLETIN DE LA ACADEMIA VENEZOLANA, Núm. 40 (1943), 245-266, and in ANDRES BELLO: EL PRIMER HUMANISTA DE AMERICA (Buenos Aires: Tridente, 1946), pp. 107-152.

_______. LIBROS DE BELLO EDITADOS EN CARACAS EN EL SIGLO XIX. Caracas: La Casa de Bello, 1978. 61p. A descriptive bibliography of Bello's works, arranged by year, 1810-1881.

_______. MEDIO SIGLO DE BELLISMO EN CHILE, 1846-1900. Caracas: La Casa de Bello, 1980. 50p. Contents: I. Fuentes generales. II. Crítica: libros y folletos. III. Crítica: hemerografía. IV. Addenda. V. Indice onomástico. VI. Indice cronológico.

Millares Carlo, Agustín. BIBLIOGRAFIA DE ANDRES BELLO. Madrid: Fundación Universitaria Española, 1978. 237p. Contents: I. Bibliografía "A." A. Obras completas. B. Compilaciones parciales. C. Antologías. D. Colecciones poéticas. E. Traducciones. II. Registro alfabético de títulos de la producción de Andrés Bello. III. Bibliografía "B." A. Fuentes bibliográficas. B. Bibliografía sobre Andrés Bello. IV.

Adiciones y correciones. V. Indice onomástico. The 1,067 items in this volume are almost exclusively published in the Hispanic world. The occasional annotations are not evaluative in nature.

_______. "Don Andrés Bello. Ensayo bibliográfico, adiciones y correciones," BOLETIN DE LA BIBLIOTECA GENERAL, Universidad del Zulia (Maracaibo), Años IX-X, Núms. 15/16 (julio 1969/julio de 1970), 239-277. Contents: I. Bibliografía "A." A. Indexes volumes 21 and 22 of OBRAS COMPLETAS (by title). II. Bibliografía "B." A. Fuentes bibliográficas. B. Bibliografía sobre Andrés Bello.

_______. "Don Andrés Bello (1781-1865): ensayo bibliográfico," REVISTA DE HISTORIA DE AMERICA, Núm. 67/68 (enero/diciembre de 1969), 211-331. Annotated entries. 757 total entries. Contents: I. Bibliografía de los escritos de don Andrés Bello. A. Obras completas. B. Compilaciones parciales. C. Antologías. D. Colecciones poéticas. E. Traducciones. F. Registro alfabético de títulos de la producción de Andrés Bello. II. Bibliografía. A. Fuentes bibliográficas. B. Bibliografía sobre Andrés Bello. III. Addenda. Reprinted: México, D.F.: Instituto Panamericano de Geografía e Historia, 1970. 130p. (Publicación 310; Bibliografías, 4).

Venezuela. Biblioteca Nacional. Hemeroteca. DON ANDRES BELLO: BIBLIOGRAFIA DE TRABAJOS SOBRE SU VIDA Y OBRA. Caracas: Biblioteca Nacional, 1956, 119p. (Its Catálogo analítico, entrega 1). This bibliography only includes those works in the Biblioteca Nacional's catalog. Contents: I. Autores. II. Crónicas, ensayos y discursos. III. Reseñas gacetillas.

BELMONTE BERMUDEZ, LUIS DE (Peru, 1582-1630)

Fuente Benavides, Rafael de la. "Luis de Belmonte Bermúdez, contribución a una bibliografía del primer siglo de la literatura peruana," BOLETIN BIBLIOGRAFICO (Biblioteca de la Universidad de San Marcos, Lima), Año 13, Vol. 10, Núm. 4 (diciembre de 1940), 347-362. A descriptive bibliography arranged by work.

BENCOMO BARRIOS, CARMEN DELIA (Venezuela, 1923-)

Cardozo, Poesía, pp. 170-172. Includes poetical works of and critical works about the author.

BENEDETTI, MARIO (Uruguay, 1920-)

Flores, BEH, pp. 201-202. Contents: I. Ediciones. II. Bibliografía selecta (criticism).

MARIO BENEDETTI. VARIACIONES CRITICAS. EDICION A CARGO DE RUFFINELLI. Montevideo: Libros de Astillero, 1973. 221p. "Bibliografía," pp. 193-219. Contents: I. Obras de Mario Benedetti (only books). II. Sobre Mario Benedetti. III. Anexos. A. Prólogos de Mario Benedetti. B. Discos, partituras, etc. C. Obras y trabajos de Mario Benedetti traducidos a otras lenguas.

Pérez Buberfall, Freda. "Bibliografía de y sobre Mario Benedetti," REVISTA IBEROAMERICANA, Núm. 114/115 (enero/junio de 1981), 359-411. Contents: I. Obras de Mario Benedetti (por orden cronológico de la publicación). A. Poesía. B. Prosa. 1. Novelas. 2. Cuentos. 3. Ensayos. C. Teatro. D. Antologías y prólogos. E. Miscelánea. F. Traducciones de obras de Mario Benedetti. II. Sobre Mario Benedetti.

RECOPILACION DE TEXTOS SOBRE MARIO BENEDETTI. COMPILACION Y PROLOGO DE AMBROSIO FORNET. La Habana: Casa de las Américas, 1976. 299p. Contents: I. "Obras de Mario Benedetti," pp. 275-276 (by year, 1945-1974). II. "Sobre Mario Benedetti," pp. 277-295.

BENITEZ ROJO, ANTONIO (Cuba, 1931-)

Foster, Cuban Lit., pp. 104-105. Critical Essays.

BENITEZ Y DE ARCE DE GAUTIER, ALEJANDRINA (Puerto Rico, 1819-1879)

Foster, P.R. Lit., pp. 79-80. Contents: I. Critical Monographs. II. Critical Essays.

BERNAOLA, PEDRO (Puerto Rico, 1916/19-1972)

Foster, P.R. Lit., p. 80. Critical Essays.

BERNARDEZ, FRANCISCO LUIS (Argentina, 1900-)

Becco, Horacio Jorge. "Bibliografía de Francisco Luis Bernárdez," in Rogelio Barufaldi's FRANCISCO LUIS BERNARDEZ (Buenos Aires: Ediciones Culturas Argentinas, Ministerio de Educación y Justicia, Dirección General de Cultura, 1963), pp. 163-171. 115 entries. Contents: I. Poesía (By year, 1922-1958). II. Prosa. III. Recopilaciones. IV. Discografía. V. Antologías. VI. Estudios críticos. VII. Bibliografía.

Flores, BEH, pp. 202-204. Contents: I. Ediciones. II. Referencias. III. Bibliografía selecta (criticism).

Foster, Arg. Lit., pp. 181-184. Contents: I. Bibliographies. II. Critical Monographs. III. Critical Essays.

Lacunza, Angélica Beatriz. BIBLIOGRAFIA DE FRANCISCO LUIS BERNARDEZ. Buenos Aires: Universidad de Buenos Aires, Facultad de Filosofía y Letras, Instituto de Literatura "Ricardo Rojas," 1962. 26p. (Guías bibliográficas, 7). Contents: I. Obras del autor (by year, 1922-1961). II. Crítica.

_______. "Bibliografía de Francisco Luis Bernárdez," in her LA OBRA POETICA DE FRANCISCO LUIS BERNARDEZ. (Buenos Aires: Editorial Huemul, 1964), pp. 199-228. Bibliography of Bernárdez's writings which appeared in Argentina from 1922-1961. Works are arranged by year.

BEROES, PEDRO (Venezuela, 1912-)

Vannani de Gerulevicz, Marisa. PEDRO BEROES. Caracas: Escuela de Biblioteconomía y Archivos, Universidad Central de Venezuela, 1967. 77p. (Serie bibliografica, 4). Contents: I.

Actualidades y crónicas. A. EL MUNDO. B. EL NACIONAL. C. ULTIMA NOTICIAS. II. Crítica artística. III. Historia. IV. Literatura y crítica literaria. V. Política. The citings are by newspaper, then by year, and date of issue.

BETANCES, RAMON EMETERIO (Puerto Rico, 1827-1898)
Foster, P.R. Lit., pp. 81-82. Contents: I. Critical Monographs. II. Critical Essays.

BETANCOURT, JOSE RAMON DE (Cuba, 1823-1890)
Foster, Cuban Lit., p. 106. Critical Essays.

BETANCOURT, LUIS VICTORIANO (Cuba, 1843-1885)
Foster, Cuban Lit., p. 107. Contents: I. Critical Monographs. II. Critical Essays.

BEVILACQUA, CLOVIS (Brazil, 1859-1944)
Rio de Janeiro. Biblioteca Nacional. COMEMORAÇAO DO CENTENARIO DE NASCIMENTO DE CLOVIS BEVILACQUA. Rio de Janeiro, 1959. 27p. Bibliography.

BILAC, OLAVO (Brazil, 1865-1918)
Carvalho, Afonso de. BILAC: O HOMEM, O POETA, O PATRIOTA. Rio de Janeiro: José Olympio, 1942. 334p. "Bibliografia," pp. 323-327. Includes critical studies on Bilac and his work.
Mota, Artur. "Perfis Acadêmicos, Cadeira No. 15: Olavo Bilac," REVISTA DA ACADEMIA BRASILEIRA DE LETRAS, Núm. 90 (junho de 1929), 198-214. Contents: I. "Bibliografia," pp. 198-201 (1888-1924). II. "Fontes para o estudo crítico," pp. 201-203.
Porter, pp. 190-192. Contents: I. Writings. II. References, Critical and Biographical.

BIOY CASARES, ADOLFO (Argentina, 1914-1984)
Becco, Horacio Jorge. "Bibliografía de Jorge Luis Borges y Adolfo Bioy Casares," in Jorge Luis Borges and Adolfo Bioy Casares' Dos fantasías memorables (Buenos Aires: Edicom, 1971), pp. 65-77. Includes a list of the various collaborations by the two authors and a list of the studies that have been published on their collaborations.
Borello, Rodolfo A. "Bibliografía sobre Adolfo Bioy Casares," REVISTA IBEROAMERICANA, 41, Núm. 91 (abril/junio de 1975), 367-368. Up-dates Section V: "Crítica sobre Adolfo Bioy Casares" of Raquel Puig Zaldívar's work.
Flores, BEH, pp. 204-205. Contents: I. Ediciones. II. Bibliografía selecta (criticism).
Foster, Arg. Lit., pp. 185-191. Contents: I. Bibliographies. II. Critical Monographs and Dissertations. III. Critical Essays.
Levine, Suzanne Jill. GUIA DE ADOLFO BIOY CASARES. Madrid:

Fundamentos, 1982. 272p. (Colección Espiral, 61). "Bibliografía," pp. 241-254. Contents: I. Fuentes principales. A. Obras de Adolfo Bioy Casares. B. Obras en colaboración. 1. Obras originales. 2. Ediciones. 3. Traducción con Jorge Luis Borges. II. Fuentes secundarias.

Puig Zaldívar, Raquel. "Bibliografía de y sobre Adolfo Bioy Casares," REVISTA IBEROAMERICANA, 40, Núm. 86 (enero/marzo de 1974), 173-178. Contents: I. Obras del autor. II. Libros co-autores. III. Miscelánea. IV. Traducciones. V. Crítica sobre Adolfo Bioy Casares.

Villordo, Oscar Hermes. GENIO Y FIGURA DE ADOLFO BIOY CASARES. Buenos Aires: EUDEBA, 1983. 207p. "Bibliografía," pp. 199-206. Contents: I. Libros anteriores a La invención de Morel. II. A partir de La invención de Morel. III. Obras firmadas con seudónimo. IV. Obras en colaboración. A. Con Jorge Luis Borges. B. Con Jorge Luis Borges y Silvina Ocampo. V. Obras en colaboración firmadas con seudónimo. A. Con Jorge Luis Borges. VI. Obras traducidas (by work). VII. Obras sobre Adolfo Bioy Casares. A. Hasta 1960. B. De 1960 en adelante.

BLANCO, ANDRES ELOY (Venezuela, 1897-1955)

Flores, BEH, pp. 82-83. Contents: I. Ediciones principales. II. Otras ediciones. III. Bibliografía selecta (criticism).

BLANCO, ANTONIO NICOLAS (Puerto Rico, 1887-1945)

Foster, P.R. Lit., p. 83. Contents: I. Dissertation. II. Critical Essays.

BLANCO, EDUARDO (Venezuela, 1838-1912)

Caracas. Universidad Católica "Andrés Bello." Seminario de Literatura Venezolano. CONTRIBUCION A LA BIBLIOGRAFIA DE EDUARDO BLANCO, 1838-1912. Caracas: Gobernación del Distrito Federal, 1971. 82p. (Colección bibliografías, 9). 176 references. Contents: I. Referencias bibliográficas. II. Obras mayores. A. Novela. B. Cuento. C. Historia. D. Drama. III. Miscelánea. IV. Obra dispersa (mainly journal and newspaper articles). V. Biografía y crítica (libros, folletos, capítulos, artículos y referencias sobre el autor y su obra).

BLANCO, TOMAS (Puerto Rico, 1896/1900-1975)

Blanco, Tomás. LOS VATES. SEGUNDA EDICION. Río Piedras, 1981. 96p. (Obras completas, 2). Contents: I. "Bibliografía de Tomás Blanco," pp. 91-93. A. Obras publicadas (libros). B. Artículos publicados (selección). II. "Cronología de Tomás Blanco," pp. 95-96.

Foster, P.R. Lit., pp. 83-84. Contents: I. Dissertation. II. Critical Essays.

BLANCO FERNANDEZ, LUIS AMADO (Cuba, 1903-1975)

"Luis Amado Blanco Fernández (1903-1975): Bío-bibliografía," BIBLIOGRAFIA CUBANA, 1975, 201-203. Contents: I. Biografía. II. Bibliografía activa.

BLANCO FOMBONA, RUFINO (Venezuela, 1874-1944)

Gabaldón Márquez, Edgar. "Estudio bibliográfico sobre Rufino Blanco-Fombona," in Rufino Blanco-Fombona's OBRAS SELECTAS: ESTUDIO PRELIMINAR POR EDGAR GABALDON MARQUEZ (Caracas, Madrid: Edición Edime, 1958), pp. xvii-xlvii. The 504 entries are partially annotated. Contents: I. Poesía. II. Cuentos. III. Novela. IV. Crítica literaria: estudios. V. Crítica literaria: artículos en periódicos y revistas. VI. Crítica literaria: prólogos. VII. Historia: obra propia. VIII. Historia: Prólogos de editor. IX. Historia: obras editadas y anotadas. X. Periodismo político y literario. XI. Autobiografía. XII. Traducciones de obra ajena. XIII. Traducciones de sus obras. XIV. Estudios sobre Rufino Blanco-Fombona. XV. Obras publicadas por R.B.F.

Lovera de Sola, Roberto. "Contribución a la bibliografía de Rufino Blanco-Fombona," IMAGEN (Caracas), Núm. 101/102 (enero/febrero de 1975), 200-205. Partially annotated entries. Contents: I. Ediciones en conjunto: obras selectas. II. Poesía. III. Crítica/literaria. IV. Historia. V. Autobiografías. VI. Política. VII. Epistolario. VIII. Textos en antologías. A. Poemas. B. Cuentos. IX. Compilaciones. X. Traducciones. XI. Prólogos. XII. Labor editorial. XIII. Fuentes de este trabajo.

Rivas, Rafael Angel. FUENTES DOCUMENTALES PARA EL ESTUDIO DE RUFINO BLANCO FOMBONA. Caracas: Centro de Estudios Latinoamericanos "Rómulo Gallegos"; Consejo Nacional de la Cultura, 1979. 244p. Contents: I. Préfacio. II. Introducción. III. Cronología. IV. Bibliografía directa. A. Libros, folletos y ensayos en libros. B. Compilaciones. C. Prólogos. D. Notas. E. Traducciones. F. Ensayos, cuentos y poemas en antologías. G. Cartas. H. Hemerografía. V. Bibliografía indirecta. A. Fuentes generales. B. Bibliografías. C. Enciclopedias, historias. D. Monografías y ensayos en libros. E. Hemerografía. VI. Indice analítico. Work contains 1,722 entries.

"Rufino Blanco Fombona, 1874-1944," in ESCRITORES VENEZOLANOS FALLECIDOS ENTRE 1942 y 1947 (Caracas: Biblioteca Nacional, 1948), pp. 16-23. Contents: I. Bibliografía. A. Obras. B. Prologuista. C. Editor y compilador. D. Traductor. II. Fuentes (criticism, etc.).

Stegmann, Wilhelm. RUFINO BLANCO-FOMBONA UND SEIN EPISCHES WERK MIT EINER GESAMTBIBLIOGRAPHIE ZU BLANCO-FOMBONA. Hamburg: Kommissionverlag: Cram, de Gruyter & Co., 1959. 159p. (Hamburger Romanistische Studien, 27). "Bibliographie," pp. 143-159. Contents: I. Werke. A. Vers-und Prosadichtung. B. Literaturkritik, Geschichte, Sociologie und Polemik. C. Reise Literatur und Tagebücher. D. Beiträge zu Zeitsschriften und Zeitungen.

E. Kommentare, Vorreden, Editionen, kleinere Buchbeiträge. F. Anthologien, in denen Blanco-Fombona vertreten ist. G. Übersetzungen von Werken Blanco-Fombonas. II. Spezialliteratur über Blanco-Fombona. A. Monographien und Studien. B. Zeitschriftenaufsätze. C. Buchbesprechungen. D. Literaturgeschichten. E. Hilfsmittel zur Blanco-Fombona-Bibliographie.

BLEST GANA, ALBERTO (Chile, 1830-1920)

Blest Gana, Alberto. MARTIN RIVAS (NOVELA DE COSTUMBRES POLITICO-SOCIALES). PROLOGO, NOTAS Y CRONOLOGIA DE JAIME CONCHA. Caracas: Biblioteca Ayacucho, 1977. 459p. "Bibliografía de Alberto Blest Gana (1830-1920)," pp. 455-459. Contents: I. Obra publicada. Novelas. II. Otras publicaciones. III. Ediciones de Martín Rivas. IV. Crítica.

Flores, BEH, pp. 8-9. Contents: Ediciones. II. Referencias. III. Bibliografía selecta (criticism).

Foster, Chilean Lit., pp. 57-62. Contents: I. Bibliographies. II. Critical Books. III. Critical Essays.

Román-Lagunas, Jorge. "Bibliografía anotada de y sobre Alberto Blest Gana," REVISTA IBEROAMERICANA, Núm. 112/113 (julio/diciembre de 1980), 605-647. 484 partially annotated entries. Contents: I. Obras de Alberto Blest Gana. A. Novelas. B. Teatro. C. Artículos de costumbres. D. Trabajos sobre literatura. E. Viajes. F. Traducciones (de sus novelas). G. Compilaciones. II. Sobre Alberto Blest Gana. A. Bibliografías. B. Libros, tesis, memorias de grado. C. Ensayos críticos. D. Prólogos. E. Historias de la literatura, panoramas, diccionarios, etc. F. Reseñas, notas, referencias. III. Indice onomástico.

Silva Castro, Raúl. ALBERTO BLEST GANA (1830-1920). ESTUDIO BIOGRAFICO Y CRITICO. Santiago de Chile: Imprenta Universitaria, 1941. 652p. "Bibliografía," pp. 593-632. Contents: I. Obras literarias (by year, 1858-1936). II. Documentos oficiales. III. Colaboración en periódicos (1853-1864). IV. Varios. V. Principales obras consultadas.

BLEST GANA, GUILLERMO (Chile, 1829-1905)

Escudero, p. 301. Criticism.

BOBADILLA, EMILIO ("FRAY CANDIL") (Cuba, 1862-1921)

Barinaga y Ponce de León, Graziela. ESTUDIO CRITICO BIOGRAFICO DE EMILIO BOBADILLA. La Habana: Carasa y Cía. Impresores, 1926. 323p. "Bibliografía sobre Emilio Bobadilla," pp. 319-322.

Foster, Cuban Lit., pp. 108-109. Contents: I. Critical Monographs and Dissertations. II. Critical Essays.

BOMBAL, MARIA LUISA (Chile, 1910-1980)

Bombal, María Luisa. LA HISTORIA DE MARIA GRISELDA. Quillota, Chile: Editorial "El Observador," 1976. 91p.

"Cronología de María Luisa Bombal," pp. 81-85. "Obras inéditas," p. 85. "Bibliografía (criticism)," pp. 87-89.

Cortés, Darío A. "Bibliografía de y sobre María Luisa Bombal," HISPANIC JOURNAL, 1 (Spring 1980), 125-142. 316 entries. Contents: I. Bibliografía de Bombal. A. Novelas. B. Traducciones de sus novelas. C. Cuentos, publicación inicial. D. Sus cuentos recogidos en antologías. E. Artículos. F. Obras inéditas. II. Bibliografía sobre Bombal. A. Libros y monografías. B. Artículos. C. Notas y reseñas. D. Referencias breves en algunas historias literarias, manuales y artículos de crítica. E. Tesis y entrevistas.

Corvalán, pp. 35-36. Contents: I. Works. II. Critical Works On.

Foster, Chilean Lit., pp. 62-64. Contents: I. Critical Books and Theses. II. Critical Essays.

Gligo, Agata. MARIA LUISA (SOBRE LA VIDA DE MARIA LUISA BOMBAL). Santiago de Chile: Editorial Andrés Bello, 1984. 180p. "Algunos ensayos, estudios y juicios críticos sobre la obra de María Luisa Bombal," pp. 177-180.

BONET, CARMELO M. (Argentina, 1886-1977)

"Bibliografía de Don Carmelo M. Bonet (1886-1977)," BOLETIN DE LA ACADEMIA ARGENTINA DE LETRAS, Núm. 165/166 (julio/diciembre de 1977), 363-366. Contents: I. Libros. II. Folletos.

BONIFAZ NUNO, RUBEN (Mexico, 1923-)

Foster, Mex. Lit., pp. 106-107. Contents: I. Dissertation. II. Critical Essays.

BOPP, RAUL (Brazil, 1898-)

Bopp, Raúl. SELETA EM PROSA E VERSO DE RAUL BOPP. ORGANIZAÇAO, ESTUDO E NOTAS DO PROF. A. GUIMARAES. Rio de Janeiro: Livraria José Olympio, 1975. 169p. "Bibliografia," pp. 162-163. Contents: I. Obras do autor. II. Em colaboração. III. Bibliografia sôbre o autor.

BORGES, JORGE LUIS (Argentina, 1899-)

Alazraki, Jaime. PROSA NARRATIVA DE JORGE LUIS BORGES. 3ed. aumentada. Madrid: Gredos, 1983. 489p. "Bibliografía," pp. 457-467. Contents: Bibliografía. II. Ediciones (cuentos). III. Colecciones. IV. Crítica: estudios y artículos. Emphasis on works published since 1960.

Becco, Horacio Jorge. "Bibliografía de Jorge Luis Borges y Adolfo Bioy Casares," in Jorge Luis Borges and Adolfo Bioy Casares' Dos fantasías memorables (Buenos Aires: Edicom, 1971), pp. 65-77. Includes a list of the various collaborations by the two authors and a list of the studies that have been published on their collaborations.

______. JORGE LUIS BORGES: BIBLIOGRAFIA TOTAL, 1923-1973. Buenos Aires: Casa Pardo, S.A., 1973. 245p. This work is far from a total or complete bibliography as the title would indicate. A large amount of material published outside Argentina has not been included due to its "inaccessibility," and "hemos suprimido aquí las colaboraciones en publicaciones periódicas, en antologías o dentro de trabajos críticos, que dejamos para un segundo tomo...." Many newspaper citings are incomplete bibliographically. Contents: I. Introducción. II. Cronología bibliográfica. III. Tabla cronológica de primeras ediciones. IV. Obras del autor. A. Obras completas. B. Poesías. C. Cuento. D. Ensayo. E. Antologías. V. Obras en colaboración. A. Literarias. B. Antologías. VI. Ediciones privadas. VII. Prólogos y ediciones. VIII. Traducciones de su obra. IX. Discografía. A. Discos. B. Partitura. X. Crítica y biografía. XI. Diálogos y reportajes. XII. Bibliografías. A. Generales. B. Sobre el autor. XIII. Iconografía. XIV. Indices. A. Indice de ilustraciones. B. Indice de títulos. C. Indice Onomástico.

Berveiller, Michel. LE COSMOPOLITISME DE JORGE LUIS BORGES. Paris: Didier, 1973. 507p. (Publications de la Sorbonne, Littératures, 4). "Bibliographie," pp. 461-484. Contents: I. Textes et propos de J. L. Borges. A. Livres. B. Livres écrits en collaboration (by collaborator). C. Anthologies, éditions et préfaces. D. Traductions. E. Textes publiés dans des périodiques. F. Entretiens avec J. L. Borges. G. Oeuvres traduites (by language). II. Etudes sur J. L. Borges. A. Livres. B. Oeuvrages contenant des appreciations sur J. L. Borges. C. Articles sur J. L. Borges. D. Filmographie. E. Discographie.

Fiore, Robert L. "Toward a Bibliography on Jorge Luis Borges," in Lowell Dunham and Ivar Ivask's THE CARDINAL POINTS OF BORGES (Norman: University of Oklahoma Press, 1971), pp. 83-105. "The bibliographies of Ana María Barrenchea, Nodier Lucio, and Lydia Revello and the one included in L'HERNE have proved to be useful. The present study is an attempt to verify, to correct, and to add to the bibliographical data previously published. Included in an addendum are entries which have not been verified because of lack of information." Includes U.S. dissertations.

________. "Critical Studies on Jorge Luis Borges," MODERN FICTION STUDIES, 19 (1973), 475-480. Updates his work in THE CARDINAL POINTS OF BORGES.

Flores, BEH, pp. 84-89, 180. Contents: I. Ediciones principales. II. Otras ediciones. III. Referencias. IV. Bibliografía selecta (criticism).

Foster, Arg. Lit., pp. 192-267. Contents: I. Bibliographies. II. Critical Monographs and Dissertations. III. Critical Essays.

Foster, David William. JORGE LUIS BORGES: AN ANNOTATED PRIMARY AND SECONDARY BIBLIOGRAPHY. INTRODUCTION BY MARTIN S. STABB. New York: Garland, 1984. 327p. Contents: I. Works by Borges. II. General Studies: Monographs. III. General Studies: Articles. IV. General Studies on the Poetry. V. General Studies on the Fiction. VI. General Studies on the Essays. VII. Criticism on Specific Texts. VIII. Special Topics. A. General Themes. B. Philosophical Themes and Issues. C. Sociocultural and Political Commitment in Borges. D. Argentina and Buenos Aires in Borges. E. The Kabbalah and Other Jewish Motifs in Borges. F. Literary Theory in Borges's Writings. G. Stylistic Considerations of Borges's Writings. IX. Borges and Other Writers and Literatures. X. Commentaries on Borges by Other Writers. XI. Negative Criticism on Borges's Writings. XII. Interviews. XIII. Chronology, Biography, Memorabilia. XIV. Bibliographies. XV. Collections of Articles. XVI. Review Surveys. XVII. Index of Original Titles of Borges's Works. XVIII. Index of Criticism, Translators, Illustrators, and Coauthors.

Lucio, Nodier, and Revello, Lydia. "Contribución a la bibliografía de Jorge Luis Borges," BIBLIOGRAFIA ARGENTINA DE ARTES Y LETRAS, Núm. 10/11 (abril/setiembre de 1961), 46-111. Despite the absence of many foreign items among the total 873 entries, this bibliography is excellent in method and presentation. Contents: I. Obras del autor. A. Libros-poesía. B. Cuento. C. Ensayo. D. Prosa. II. Obras en colaboración. III. Colaboraciones en publicaciones periódicas. IV. Prólogos y ediciones. V. Traducciones de obras de otros autores (francés, inglés). VI. Traducción de obras del autor (alemán, español, francés, inglés, italiano). VII. Antologías de textos de Borges. VIII. Textos del autor en diversas antologías. IX. Crítica y biografía. X. Cronología bio-bibliografía. XI. Indices. A. De títulos. B. De Onomástico.

_______. "Contribution a la bibliographie de Borges," in JORGE LUIS BORGES (Paris: L'HERNE, 1964), pp. 485-516. Contents: I. Oeuvres. A. Livres. B. Poésies. C. Contes. D. Essais. E. Poésie et prose. II. Oeuvre en collaboration. III. Collaboration aux journaux et revues. IV. Préfaces. V. Traductions par Borges. VI. Traductions des oeuvres de Borges. VII. Critique.

Lyon, T. E. "Jorge Luis Borges: Selected Bibliography of First Editions and English Translations," in Dunham and Ivask's THE CARDINAL POINTS OF BORGES, pp. 107-109. "The present bibliography embodies only first editions and important innovative reeditions essential for a comprehension of Borges' literary trajectory. In recent years Borges has published considerable creative work in collaboration with several Argentine writers and this prose is included as part of the bibliography." Contents: I. Poetry. II. Fiction. III. Essay. IV. Works done in Collaboration. V. English Translations.

Molloy, Sylvia. LA DIFFUSION DE LA LITTERATURE HISPANO-AMERICAINE EN FRANCE AU XXe SIECLE. Paris: Presses Universitaires de France, 1972. 355p. (Publications de la Faculté des Lettres et Sciences Humaines de Paris-Sorbonne, Série Recherches, tome 68). This volume contains two chapters on Borges: "Jorge Luis Borges," pp. 194-237 and "La traduction de l'oeuvre de Borges en France," pp. 238-248; as well as a listing of over one hundred items in French on Borges (pp. 318-322), many of which are not reported by Becco.

BORRERO, JUANA (Cuba, 1877-1896)
Borrero, Juana. POESIAS. La Habana: Instituto de Literatura y Lingüística, 1966. 220p. "Bibliografía de Juana Borrero," pp. 183-187. Contents: I. Bibliografía activa (arranged chronologically, 1891-1896). II. Bibliografía pasiva.
Foster, Cuban Lit., pp. 110-111. Contents: I. Critical Monographs. II. Critical Essays.

BOSCH, JUAN (Dominican Republic, 1909-)
Fernández Olmos, Margarita. LA CUENTISTICA DE JUAN BOSCH: UN ANALISIS CRITICO-CULTURAL. Santo Domingo: Editora Alfa & Omega, 1982. "Bibliografía," pp. 175-182. The bibliography includes both works by Bosch and critical studies on Bosch and his work.

BOTI, REGINO E. (Cuba, 1878-1958)
Foster, Cuban Lit., pp. 112-113. Contents: I. Critical Monographs and Dissertations. II. Critical Essays.
Suarée, Octavia de la. LA OBRA LITERARIA DE REGINO E. BOTI. New York: Senda Nueva de Ediciones, 1977. 211p. "Bibliografía general," pp. 183-201. Contents: I. Obras de Regino E. Boti. A. Poesía. B. Prosa. II. Obras en que se incluyen menciones y observaciones sobre el autor. A. Libros. B. Artículos y conferencias.

BRAGA, GENTIL (Brazil, 1835-1876)
Moraes, pp. 37-39. Major works by and about the author.

BRANNON BEERS, CARMEN see LARS, CLAUDIA

BRAU, SALVADOR (Puerto Rico, 1842-1912)
Foster, P.R. Lit., p. 85-86. Contents: I. Critical Monographs and Dissertation. II. Critical Essays.

BRICENO-IRAGORRY, MARIO (Venezuela, 1897-1958)
Mancera Galletti, Angel. DE LA OSCURIDAD A LA LUZ: ESTUDIO CRITICO BIOGRAFICO DE MARIO BRICENO-IRAGORRY. Caracas: Tipografía Vargas, 1960. (Ediciones Casa del Escritor, 1). "Ficha biobibliográfica de Mario Briceño-Iragorry," pp. 189-196. Contents: I. Ficha bio-bibliográfica. II. Libros. III. Conferencias. IV. Discursos y monografías. V. Prólogos.

BRINDAS DE SALAS, VIRGINIA (Uruguay)
Jackson, Afro-Spanish, pp. 53-54. Contents: I. Works. II. Criticism.

BRITO, FRANCISCO DE PAULA (Brazil, 1809-1861)
Porter, p. 192. Contents: I. Writings. II. References, Critical and Biographical.

BRULL, MARIANO (Cuba, 1891-1956)
Foster, Cuban Lit., pp. 114-115. Contents: I. Dissertation. II. Critical Essays.
Larraga, Ricardo. "MARIANO BRULL Y LA POESIA PURA EN CUBA: BIBLIOGRAFIA Y EVOLUCION." Ph.D., New York University, 1981. 267p.

BRUNET, MARTA (Chile, 1901-1967)
Brunet, Marta. ANTOLOGIA DE CUENTOS. SELECCION, PROLOGO, NOTAS Y BIBLIOGRAFIA DE NICOMEDES GUZMAN. 3. ed. Santiago: Editorial Zig-Zag, 1970. 238p. Contents: I. "Obras," pp. 234-235. II. "Referencias," pp. 236-238.
_______. OBRAS COMPLETAS. PROLOGO DE ALONE. Santiago de Chile: Zig-Zag, 1963. 871p. Contents: I. "Obras," pp. 867-868. II. "Referencias," pp. 869-871.
Durán Cerda, Julio. "Cartillas biobibliográficas de autores chilenos: Marta Brunet Caraves, Chillán, 1901. Novelista y cuentista," BOLETIN DEL INSTITUTO DE LITERATURA CHILENA (Universidad de Chile, Santiago), Año I, Núm. 1 (septiembre de 1961), 24-26.
Flores, BEH, pp. 205-206. Contents: I. Edición principal. II. Otras ediciones. III. Referencias. IV. Bibliografía selecta (criticism).
Foster, Chilean Lit., pp. 64-67. Contents: I. Bibliographies. II. Critical Books and Theses. III. Critical Essays.

BRYCE ECHENIQUE, ALFREDO (Peru, 1939-)
Foster, Peruvian Lit., pp. 84-85. Contents: I. Critical Monographs and Dissertations. II. Critical Essays.

BULLRICH, SILVINA (Argentina, 1915-)
Bullrich, Silvina. PAGINAS DE SILVINA BULLRICH, SELECCIONADAS POR LA AUTORA. ESTUDIO PRELIMINAR DE NICOLAS COCARO. Buenos Aires: Editorial Celtia, 1983. 189p. "Bibliografía sobre Silvina Bullrich," pp. 181-183. Contents: I. Estudios generales. II. Notas bibliográficas (book reviews).
Corvalán, p. 37. Contents: I. Works. II. Critical Works.
Foster, Arg. Lit., pp. 268-270. Contents: I. Critical Monograph and Dissertations. II. Critical Essays.

BURGOS, JULIA DE (Puerto Rico 1914/17-1953)
Corvalán, p. 38. Contents: I. Works. II. Critical Works On.
Foster, P.R. Lit., pp. 87-89. Contents: I. Critical Monographs and Dissertations. II. Critical Essays.
Jiménez de Báez, Yvette. JULIA DE BURGOS: VIDA Y POESIA. San Juan: Ediciones Borinquen, Editorial Coquí, 1966. 210p.

"Bibliografía," pp. 203-206. Contents: I. Obras de Julia de Burgos. A. Publicaciones. 1. Poesías. 2. Prosa. B. Inéditas. 1. Poesía. 2. Prosa. II. Estudios críticos sobre Julia de Burgos y artículos de periódicos.

BURNETT, JOSE CARLOS LAGO (Brazil, 1929-)
Moraes, pp. 115-117. Major works by and about the author.

BUZZI, DAVID (Cuba, 1933-)
Foster, Cuban Lit., p. 116. Critical Essays.

BYRNE, BONIFACIO (Cuba, 1861-1936)
Foster, Cuban Lit., pp. 117-118. Contents: I. Bibliography. II. Critical Monograph. III. Critical Essays.
Moliner, Israel M. INDICE BIO-BIBLIOGRAFICO DE BONIFACIO BYRNE. Matanzas: Atenas de Cuba, 1943. 11p. Contents: I. "Bibliografía de Bonifacio Byrne," pp. 8-9. II. "De Bonifacio Byrne han escrito," pp. 9-11 (criticism).

- C -

CABALLERO CALDERON, EDUARDO (Colombia, 1910-)
Flores, BEH, pp. 206-207. Contents: I. Edición principal. II. Otras Ediciones. III. Bibliografía selecta (criticism).
Foster, 20th Century, pp. 51-52. Contents: Critical Essays.
Porras Collantes, pp. 95-109. Includes works of and critical studies about the author.

CABALLERO Y RODRIGUEZ, JOSE AGUSTIN (Cuba, 1762-1835)
Foster, Cuban Lit., pp. 119-121. Contents: I. Bibliographies. II. Critical Monographs. III. Critical Essays.
González del Valle y Ramírez, Francisco. "Bibliografía: José Agustín Caballero y Rodríguez," REVISTA BIMESTRE CUBANA, 35 (1935), 177-183. Contents: I. Obras (24 items arranged chronologically). II. Traducciones. III. Bibliografía sobre José Agustín Caballero y Rodríguez (15 items).

CABELLO DE CARBONERA, MERCEDES (Peru, 1849-1909)
Flores, NH, v. 2, p. 26. Contents: I. Obras de ficción. II. Bibliografía selecta (criticism).

CABRERA, LYDIA (Cuba, 1899/1900-)
Foster, Cuban Lit., pp. 122-124. Contents: I. Critical Monographs. II. Critical Essays.
Perera, Hilda. IDAPO: EL SINCRETISMO EN LOS CUENTOS NEGROS DE LYDIA CABRERA. Miami: Ediciones Universal, 1971. 118p. (Colección Polymita, 3). "Bibliografía," pp. 113-118. Contents: I. Obras de Lydia Cabrera. II. Artículos sobre Lydia Cabrera y su producción literaria. III. Obras sobre temas negros.

Valdés-Cruz, Rosa. LO ANCESTRAL AFRICANO EN LA NARRATIVA DE LYDIA CABRERA. Barcelona: Editorial Vosgos, 1974. 113p. "Bibliografía," pp. 108-113. Contents: I. Obras de Lydia Cabrera. II. Obras específicas sobre Lydia Cabrera.

CABRERA INFANTE, GUILLERMO (Cuba, 1929-)

Alvarez-Borland, Isabel. DISCONTINUIDAD Y RUPTURA EN GUILLERMO CABRERA INFANTE. Gaithersburg, Md.: Ediciones Hispamérica, 1982. 146p. "Bibliografía," pp. 139-146. Contents: I. Bibliografía de Cabrera Infante. II. Bibliografía consultada (includes works about the author).

Flores, BEH, pp. 207-208. Contents: I. Ediciones. II. Bibliografía selecta (criticism).

Foster, Cuban Lit., pp. 125-133. Contents: I. Bibliography. II. Critical Monographs and Dissertations. III. Critical Essays.

Foster, 20th Century, pp. 52-54. Contents: I. Bibliographies. II. Critical Books. III. Critical Essays.

CADILLA DE MARTINEZ, MARIA (Puerto Rico, 1884/86-1951)

Foster, P.R. Lit., pp. 89-90. Critical Essays.

CAMARA, JOAQUIM MATTOSO, JR. (Brazil, 1904-1970)

Azevedo Filho, Leodegário A. de. "Bibliografia de J. Mattoso Câmara, Jr.," in II CONGRESSO BRASILEIRO DE LINGUA E LITERATURA (De 6 A 17 DE JULHO DE 1970): HOMENAGEM A J. MATTOSO CAMARA, JR. (Rio de Janeiro: Edições Gernasa e Artes Gráficas Ltda., 1971), pp. 20-31. Arranged chronologically.

"Bibliografia de Joaquim Mattoso Câmara, Jr.," VOZES (Petrópolis), 67 (5), 1973, 81-85. By year, 1934-1972. Includes books, reviews, articles, essays, and translations. Reprinted from DISPERSOS DE J. MATTOSO CAMARA, JR. SELEÇAO E INTROD. POR CARLOS EDUARDO FALCAO UCHOA. Rio de Janeiro: Fundação Getúlio Vargas, Instituto de Documentação, Serviço de Publicações, 1972. 273p. (Coleção Estante de Língua Portuguêsa. Série Dispersos, 1). "Bibliografia," pp. xxiii-xlii.

Naro, Anthony J., and John Reighard. "Analytical Bibliography of the Writings of Joaquim Mattoso Câmara, Jr.," in J. Mattoso Câmara, Jr. THE PORTUGUESE LANGUAGE. Translated by Anthony J. Naro (Chicago: The University of Chicago Press, 1972), pp. 235-260. The bibliography excludes "nearly all works intended for the secondary level, brief commentaries and letters, shorter non-critical notices of publications, and reviews that did not seem to us to attain a certain minimum of substantive content. Some of the items of this sort are, however, mentioned in the translator's preface." Contents: I. Grammatical Studies in Portuguese. II. Stylistic Studies in Portuguese. III. Linguistic Studies in Indigenous Languages of Brazil. IV. Reference and Bibliography. V. Commentary and Discussion. VI. Reviews. VII. Texts. VIII. Translations. IX. Index of Reviewers.

CAMARILLO ROA DE PEREYRA, MARIA ENRIQUETA see ENRIQUETA, MARIA)

CAMBACERES, EUGENIO (Argentina, 1843-1890)
Borello, Rodolfo A. "Contribución a la bibliografía de Eugenio Cambaceres (Buenos Aires, 1843-1899)," OTTAWA HISPANICA, 1 (1979), 85-97. Contents: I. Obras de Cambaceres (chronologically arranged). II. Estudios sobre Cambaceres y su vida.
Flores, BEH, pp. 58-59. Contents: I. Edición principal. II. Otras ediciones. III. Bibliografía selecta (criticism).
Flores, NH, v. 2, pp. 18-19. Contents: I. Edición principal. II. Referencias. III. Bibliografía selecta (criticism).
Foster, Arg. Lit., pp. 271-274. Contents: I. Critical Monographs and Dissertations. II. Critical Essays.

CAMBOURS OCAMPO, ARTURO (Argentina, 1908-)
Lafleur, Héctor René. ARTURO CAMBOURS OCAMPO. Buenos Aires: Ediciones Culturales Argentinas, Ministerio de Cultura y Educación, 1972. 158p. "Bibliografía," pp. 139-158. Contents: I. Libros. II. Folletos. III. Traducciones de la obra de A.C.O. IV. Labor editora. V. Dirección de revistas, periódicos y cuadernos. VI. Artículos, ensayos y comentarios sobre la obra de A.C.O. (By work). VII. Historias de la literatura, diccionarios, antologías, libros y artículos donde se cita la obra de A.C.O. VIII. Reportajes y declaraciones de A.C.O. (Por orden cronológico). IX. Cargos docentes. Designaciones oficiales y conferencias de A.C.O. The Bibliography excludes A.C.O.'s articles in reviews and newspapers.

CAMINO CALDERON, CARLOS (Peru, 1884-1956)
Gerbi, Juana. "Carlos Camino Calderón," ANUARIO BIBLIOGRAFICO PERUANO, 1955/1957, 450-457. Contents: I. Biografía. II. Libros y folletos. III. Artículos y ensayos. IV. Cuentos y leyendas. V. Poesías. VI. Notas bibliográficas. VII. Referencias (Criticism, etc.). VIII. Notas necrológicas.

CAMPO, ANGEL DEL (Mexico, 1868-1908)
Hale, Dennis Lee. "POSITIVISM AND THE SOCIAL ASPECTS OF THE WRITINGS OF ANGEL DEL CAMPO." Ph.D., Florida State University, 1977. 429p. "A lengthy bibliography, containing an extensive listing of Campos's writings, concludes this study."

CAMPO, ESTANISLAO DEL (Argentina, 1834-1880)
Flores, BEH, pp. 59-60. Contents: I. Ediciones. II. Referencias. III. Bibliografía selecta (criticism).
Foster, Arg. Lit., pp. 275-279. Contents: I. Critical Monographs. II. Critical Essays.

CAMPOS, HUMBERTO (Brazil, 1886-1934)
Moraes, pp. 94-96. Works by and about the author.

Porter, pp. 197-200. Contents: I. Writings. II. References, Critical and Biographical.

CANAL FEIJOO, BERNARDO (Argentina, 1897-)
Corvalán, Octavio. LA OBRA POETICA DE BERNARDO CANAL FEIJOO. San Miguel de Tucumán: Universidad Nacional de Tucumán, Facultad de Filosofía y Letras, 1976. 127p. (Cuadernos de Humanitas, 50). "Obras de Bernardo Canal Feijóo," pp. 59-60.

CANALES, NEMESIO R. (Puerto Rico, 1878-1923)
Foster, P.R. Lit., pp. 90-92. Contents: I. Critical Monographs and Dissertation. II. Critical Essays.

CANE, MIGUEL (Argentina, 1851-1905)
Foster, Arg. Lit., pp. 280-282. Contents: I. Critical Monographs. II. Critical Essays.

CANTON, WILBERTO L. (Mexico, 1923-1979)
Shirley, Carl R. "A Curriculum Operum of Mexico's Wilberto Cantón," LATIN AMERICAN THEATRE REVIEW, 13, No. 2 (1980), 47-56. 63 items, mostly annotated, are arranged by year, 1942-1980.

CAPDEVILA, ARTURO (Argentina, 1889-1967)
Becco, Horacio Jorge. "Bibliografía de don Arturo Capdevila, 1889-1967," BOLETIN DE LA ACADEMIA ARGENTINA DE LETRAS, 32, Núm. 125/126 (julio/diciembre de 1967), 329-338. Contents: I. Poesía. II. Teatro. III. Novela y cuentos. IV. Historia y evocación. V. Ensayos. VI. Derecho. VII. Prólogos y recopilaciones. VIII. Obra escogida. IX. Labor científica.
Foster, Arg. Lit., pp. 283-287. Contents: I. Bibliographies. II. Critical Monograph. III. Critical Essays.

CARBALLIDO, EMILIO (Mexico, 1925-)
Foster, Mex. Lit., pp. 107-110. Contents: I. Bibliographies. II. Critical Monographs and Dissertations. III. Critical Essays.
Peden, Margaret Sayers. EMILIO CARBALLIDO. Boston: Twayne Publishers, 1980. 192p. "Selected Bibliography," pp. 183-189. Contents: I. Primary Sources. A. Bibliography. B. Drama. C. Prose. D. Translations. II. Secondary Sources.
_______. "Emilio Carballido; curriculum operum," LATIN AMERICAN THEATER RESEARCH REVIEW, 1, No. 1 (Fall 1967), 38-42. 85 titles, arranged by year, 1948-1967.
_______. "Emilio Carballido: Curriculum Operum," TEXTO CRITICO, Núm. 3 (enero/abril de 1976), 94-112.

CARDENAL, ERNESTO (Nicaragua, 1925-)

Borgeson, Paul W. "Bibliografía de y sobre Ernesto Cardenal," REVISTA IBEROAMERICANA, Núm. 108/109 (julio/diciembre de 1979), 641-650. Contents: I. Publicaciones de Ernesto Cardenal. A. Obras principales (by work). B. Antologías (en orden de su publicación). C. Antologías en traducción. D. Obras en traducción. E. Artículos y antologías por Ernesto Cardenal. F. Traducciones por Ernesto Cardenal. G. Miscelánea. II. Estudios sobre Ernesto Cardenal.

Flores, BEH, p. 208. Contents: I. Ediciones. II. Bibliografía selecta (criticism).

Smith, Janet Lynne. AN ANNOTATED BIBLIOGRAPHY OF AND ABOUT ERNESTO CARDENAL. Tempe, Arizona: Arizona State University, Center for Latin American Studies, 1979. 61p. (Special Studies, 21). Contents: I. Criticism. II. Obra. III. Poesía suelta. IV. Writings. V. Introductions, Compilations and Works Edited by Ernesto Cardenal. VI. Translations into English. VII. Translations by Ernesto Cardenal and Others. A. General Collections. B. Works by Individuals. This bibliography is not as comprehensive as the author states in her introductory remarks, e.g., critical studies are only included if they are written in English, Spanish, and German and she does not include foreign language translations of Cardenal's works other than English.

CARDOSO, ONELIO JORGE (Cuba, 1914-)

Foster, Cuban Lit., pp. 134-136. Contents: I. Bibliography. II. Critical Essays.

CARDOZA Y ARAGON, LUIS (Guatemala, 1904-)

Cardoza y Aragón, Luis. POESIAS COMPLETAS Y ALGUNAS PROSAS. México, D.F.: Tezontle, 1977. 669p. "Bibliografía mínima de Luis Cardoza y Aragón," pp. 661-662.

CARO, JOSE EUSEBIO (Colombia, 1817-1853)

Aljure-Chalelea, Simón. JOSE EUSEBIO CARO: BIBLIOGRAFIA. Charlottesville, Va.: Bibliographical Society of the University of Virginia, 1967. 82p. Contents: I. Poesías (By title). II. Prosa (By title). III. Versiones. IV. Epistolario. V. Bibliografía sobre José Eusebio Caro.

Martín, José Luis. LA POESIA DE JOSE EUSEBIO CARO: CONTRIBUCION ESTILISTICA AL ESTUDIO DEL ROMANTICISMO HISPANOAMERICANO. Bogotá: Instituto Caro y Cuervo. (Publicaciones del Instituto Caro y Cuervo, 22), 1966. 510p. "Bibliografía especial," pp. 459-474. Contents: I. Obras de José Eusebio Caro. A. Ediciones basicas de sus poemas. B. Obras en prosa (publicaciones e inéditas) y otros poemas sueltos. C. Periódicos donde Caro colaboró asiduamente. D. Versiones célebres de sus poemas. II. Antologías y colecciones con algunos poemas de José Eusebio Caro. III. Estudios sobre José Eusebio Caro. A. Estudios especializados. B. Estudios generales. "Bibliografía general," pp. 474-497. I. Romanticismo en Colombia. II. Romanticismo en Hispanoamérica. III. Romanticismo general. IV. Obras consultadas sobre estilística y disciplinas afines. V. Otras obras consultadas. "Repertorios bibliográficos consultados," pp. 497-500. I. Bibliografías sobre José Eusebio Caro. II. Otras fuentes bibliográficas consultadas.

CARO, MIGUEL ANTONIO (Colombia, 1843-1909)

Caro, Víctor E. "Bibliografía de don Miguel Antonio Caro," pp. 1-130 in BIBLIOGRAFIAS DE DON MIGUEL ANTONIO CARO, POR VICTOR E. CARO Y DE DON RUFINO JOSE CUERVO, POR AUGUSTO TOLEDO. Bogotá: Editorial ABC, 1945. 183p. Contents: I. Poesías, libros y folletos. A. Poesías originales y traducciones poéticas. B. Antologías y colecciones. II. Prosa: libros y folletos. A. Literatura, filología, gramática. B. Prólogos, estudios, biográficos y críticos. C. Filosofía. D. Jurisprudencia. E. Ciencias económicas. F. Mensajes al Congreso. G. Varios. H. Obras completas y publicaciones póstumas. I. Obras en prensa. III. Periodismo.

Vismara, Marisa. LA POESIA LATINA DI MIGUEL ANTONIO CARO. PRESENTAZIONE DI BENEDETTO RIPOSATI. Milano: Vita e Pensiero, 1980. 228p. (Scienze filologiche e letteratura, 17). "Bibliografia," pp. 225-228. Contents: I. Edizioni delle opere poetiche di Miguel Antonio Caro. A. Studi particolari. B. Studi generali.

CARPENTIER, ALEJO (Cuba, 1904-1980)

Flores, BEH, pp. 89-92, 180. Contents: I. Ediciones. II. Referencias. III. Bibliografía selecta (criticism).

Foster, Cuban Lit., pp. 137-174. Contents: I. Bibliographies. II. Critical Monographs and Dissertations. III. Critical Essays.

Foster, 20th Century, pp. 55-63. Contents: I. Bibliographies. II. Critical Books. III. Critical Essays.

García-Caranza, Araceli. "Bibliografía de una exposición," REVISTA DE LA BIBLIOTECA NACIONAL "JOSE MARTI" (La Habana), 3ª época, 17, Núm. 1 (enero/abril de 1975), 45-87. Exposition of his works sponsored by the Biblioteca Nacional "José Martí" entitled "Un camino de medio siglo," Dec. 25, 1975. Contents: I. Carpentier novelista (muestra de sus novelas y relatos en español y otros idiomas). Spanish, 1933-1974. List includes all published editions in Spanish and 17 other languages. II. Carpentier dona sus manuscritos a la Biblioteca Nacional (parte de muestra). III. Carpentier periodista (excerpts from works, 1922-1973). IV. Algo de su bibliografía pasiva, no antología, de los últimos años, 1959-1974.

González Echevarría, Roberto. ALEJO CARPENTIER: THE PILGRIM AT HOME. Ithaca, N.Y.: Cornell University Press, 1977. 307p. "Selected Bibliography," pp. 275-299. Contents: I. Books. II. Poems. III. Scenarios and Ballets. IV. Short Stories. V. Articles, Essays, and Notes. VI. Chapters of Novels. VII. Works Cited (critical). VIII. Dissertations. IX. Articles and Pamphlets (critical).

_______, and Klaus Müller-Bergh. ALEJO CARPENTIER: BIBLIOGRAPHICAL GUIDE. ALEJO CARPENTIER: GUIA BIBLIOGRAFICA. Westport, Conn.: Greenwood Press, 1983. 271p. 3,191 entries. Contents: I. Primary Bibliography/bibliografía activa. A. Books and Pamphlets/libros y panfletos. B. Journals/publicaciones periódicas (by journal). C. In Miscellaneous Publications/en publicaciones misceláneas (1923-1980). II. Secondary Bibliography/bibliografía pasiva. A. Books and pamphlets/libros y panfletos. B. Dissertations/tesis de grado. C. Interviews/entrevistas (1945-1980). D. Articles and Notes in Books, Magazines and Other Journals/artículos y notas en libros, revistas y otras publicaciones periódicas. E. Special Issues of Journals/números especiales. III. Records/discos. IV. Late Entries/fichas rezagadas. A. Primary/activa. B. Secondary/pasiva. C. Post-1980. V. Index of Names/índice onomástico. A. Primary/activa. B. Secondary/pasiva.

La Habana. Biblioteca Nacional "José Martí." 45 AÑOS DE TRABAJO INTELECTUAL. La Habana, 1966. 1v. (unpaged). A bibliography-catalogue of an exhibit of the works of Carpentier prepared by Graziella Pogolotti. Editions in Spanish and translations of his books as well as articles in Cuban and foreign periodicals. Although the bibliography is admittedly incomplete, it is still very useful.

CARRASQUILLA, TOMAS (Colombia, 1854-1940)

Flores, BEH, pp. 92-94. Contents: I. Ediciones principales. II. Otras ediciones. III. Referencias. IV. Bibliografía selecta (criticism).

Levy, Kurt. TOMAS CARRASQUILLA. Boston: Twayne, 1980. 150p. "Selected Bibliography," pp. 140-145. Contents: I. Primary Sources. A. Editions of Complete Work. B. Editions of Collections (listed in chronological order). C. Editions of Individual Works (listed in chronological order). II. Secondary Works. A. Critical Material. B. Background Works.

_______. VIDA Y OBRAS DE TOMAS CARRASQUILLA: GENITOR DEL REGIONALISMO EN LA LITERATURA HISPANO-AMERICANA. VERSION ESPAÑOLA, DIRECTAMENTE DEL INGLES, POR CARLOS LOPEZ NARVAEZ. Medellín: Editorial Bedout, 1958. 397p. "Bibliografía," pp. 289-308. Contents: I. Obras de Tomás Carrasquilla. A. Novelas y novelas cortas. B. Cuentos. C. Cuadros de costumbres. D. Crónicas. E. Ensayos. F. Miscelánea. II. Artículos sobre Carrasquilla. III. Tesis sobre Carrasquilla para grados de MAGISTER ARTIUM. IV. Obras que contienen comentarios sobre, o referencias a, Tomás Carrasquilla. V. Otras obras consultadas para este estudio.

Mango, Nancy. "Tomás Carrasquilla, una bibliografía," REVISTA INTERAMERICANA DE BIBLIOGRAFIA, 9, Núm. 3 (julio/diciembre de 1959), 249-254. A very selective bibliography of 63 references, of which most are located in the collections of the Organization of American States' Columbus Memorial Library. Contents: I. Escritos de Carrasquilla. II. Estudios sobre Carrasquilla.

Porras Collantes, pp. 126-158. Includes works of and critical studies about the author.

CARRERA ANDRADE, JORGE (Ecuador, 1903-)

Flores, BEH, pp. 209-210. Contents: I. Ediciones. II. Referencias. III. Bibliografía selecta (criticism).

Harth, Dorothy E. JORGE CARRERA ANDRADE: A BIBLIOGRAPHY, 1922-1970. Syracuse, N.Y.: Centro de Estudios Hispánicos, Syracuse University, 197? 24p. (Bibliotheca Hispana-Novissima, 2).

Ojeda, Enrique. JORGE CARRERA ANDRADE: INTRODUCCION AL ESTUDIO DE SU VIDA Y DE SU OBRA. New York: Eliseo Torres & Sons, 1972. 431p. "Bibliografía," pp. 385-430. Contents: I. Colección y archivo personal de Jorge Carrera Andrade (in the Special Collections Department of the State University of New York/Stony Brook). II. Obras de Jorge Carrera Andrade. A. Libros de poesía. B. Libros de prosa. C. Poesías sueltas. 1. No recogidas en libros. D. Libros traducidos a otros idiomas. E. Poesía traducida por Carrera Andrade al español. F. Prosa traducida por Carrera Andrade al español. G. Antologías que contienen poemas de Carrera Andrade. H. Artículos publicados en revistas. I. Discursos. J. Obras inéditas. III. Estudios y referencias críticas sobre la obra de Jorge Carrera Andrade. A. Libros, opúsculos y estudios especiales. B. Artículos.

CARRIEGO, EVARISTO (Argentina, 1883-1912)

Eggers-Lan de Telecki, Beatriz. CARRIEGO Y SU POESIA DE BARRIO DEL 900. México: Costa-Amic, 1977. 141p. "Bibliografía," pp. 133-136. Contents: I. Bibliografía de Evaristo Carriego. II. Bibliografía sobre Evaristo Carriego.

Flores, BEH, pp. 94-95. Contents: I. Ediciones. II. Bibliografía selecta (criticism).

Foster, Arg. Lit., pp. 288-291. Contents: I. Critical Monographs and Dissertation. II. Critical Essays.

Teleki, Beatriz Eggers. "LA POESIA ARGENTINA DE EVARISTO CARRIEGO (1883-1912)." Ph.D., University of California/Berkeley, 1977. Includes an extensive bibliography and illustrations.

CARRIO DE LA VANDERA, ALONSO see "CONCOLORCORVO"

CARRION, MIGUEL DE (Cuba, 1875-1929)

Anderson, pp. 16-19. Contents: Critical Essays.

"En el centenario de Miguel Carrión: bibliografía de su obra narrativa," L/L (Anuario del Instituto de Literatura y Lingüística de la Academia de Ciencias de Cuba, La Habana), Núm. 6 (1975), 190-196. Contents: I. Bibliografía activa. II. Bibliografía pasiva. III. Indice temático de su bibliografía pasiva.

Foster, Cuban Lit., pp. 175-176. Contents: Bibliography. II. Critical Monographs. III. Critical Essays.

González, Mirza L. NOVELA Y EL CUENTO PSICOLOGICOS DE

MIGUEL DE CARRION: ESTUDIO PSICOSOCIAL CUBANO. Miami: Universal, 1979. 180p. "Bibliografía," pp. 158-163. Contents: I. Novelas y cuentos publicados de Carrión. II. Cuentos inéditos de Carrión. III. Referencias críticas sobre Carrión.

Jackson, Afro-Spanish, pp. 57-84. Contents: I. Works. II. Criticism. A. Bibliography. B. Books. C. Articles, Shorter Studies, and Dissertations. Annotated entries.

CASACCIA, GABRIEL (Paraguay, 1907-)

Feito, Francisco E. EL PARAGUAY EN LA OBRA DE GABRIEL CASACCIA. Buenos Aires: Fernando García Cambeiro, 1977. 185p. "Bibliografía," pp. 178-182. Contents: I. Obras del autor (arranged by year, 1930-1975). A. Libros. B. Obra suelta. C. Traducciones. II. Miscelánea. A. Prosa. B. Entrevistas. C. Correspondencia. D. Opiniones crítico-literarias. III. Libros, artículos, reseñas y notas sobre el autor y su obra.

Flores, BEH, pp. 210-211. Contents: I. Ediciones. II. Bibliografía selecta (criticism).

CASAL, JULIAN DEL (Cuba, 1863-1893)

Casal, Julián del. THE POETRY OF JULIAN DEL CASAL: A CRITICAL EDITION, EDITED BY ROBERT JAY GLICKMAN. Gainesville: The University Presses of Florida, 1976-1978. 2 vs. "Bibliography," v. 2, pp. 443-451. A selected bibliography of works by and about Casal.

_______. PROSA. La Habana: Consejo Nacional de Cultura, 1963-1964. 3 vs. "Bibliografía," v. 3, pp. 193-240. Contents: I. Activa (Casal's works listed chronologically, 1881-1945; 367 entries). II. Bibliografía pasiva de Julián del Casal (titles about Casal and his works).

Figueroa, Esperanza. "Bibliografía cronológica de la obra de Julián del Casal," REVISTA IBEROAMERICANA, 35, Núm. 68 (mayo/agosto de 1969), 385-399. Entries are by year, 1881-1893. Within the year, items are listed under the following subject categories: poesías, prosa, crónicas, crítica, traducciones, poemas en prosa, cuentos, and ediciones.

Flores, BEH, pp. 9-10. Contents: I. Ediciones. II. Referencias. III. Bibliografía selecta (criticism).

Foster, Cuban Lit., pp. 177-187. Contents: I. Bibliographies. II. Critical Monographs and Dissertations. III. Critical Essays.

Prulletti, Rita Geada de. "Bibliografía de y sobre Julián del Casal (1863-1893)," REVISTA IBEROAMERICANA, 33, Núm. 63 (enero/junio de 1967), 133-139. Contents: I. Obras del autor. II. Obras sobre el autor. III. Bibliografía general.

CASAS, BARTOLOME DE LAS (1474-1566)

Cantú, Francesca. "Italia: Documentos lascasianos," HISTORIOGRAFIA Y BIBLIOGRAFIA, Núm. 19/20 (1975/76), 127-155.

Becerra de León, Berta. BIBLIOGRAFIA DEL PADRE BARTOLOME DE LAS CASAS. La Habana: Sociedad Económica de Amigos del País, 1949. 67p. (Ediciones de su Biblioteca Pública, 4). 256 titles are registered, limited mainly to those titles in Cuban collections. Contents: I. Obras bibliográficas. II. Obras del Padre Las Casas (se ordenan por la fecha aproximada de su composición). III. Obras inéditas. IV. Impugnadores. V. Obras sobre las Casas. VI. Referencias.

Hanke, Lewis and Manuel Giménez Fernández. BARTOLOME DE LAS CASAS 1474-1566; BIBLIOGRAFIA CRITICA Y CUERPO DE MATERIALES PARA EL ESTUDIO DE SU VIDA, ESCRITOS, ACTUACION Y POLEMICAS QUE SUSCITARON DURANTE CUATRO SIGLOS. Santiago de Chile: Fondo Histórico y Bibliográfico "José Toribio Medina," 1954. 394p. 849 entries which are partially annotated. Bibliography covers 1492-1953. Library sources are given.

Julián, Amadeo. "Bibliografía de Fray Bartolomé de las Casas," REVISTA DOMINICANA DE ANTROPOLOGIA E HISTORIA, Núm. 7/8 (enero/diciembre de 1974), 29-99. Las Casas' writings are arranged by year: 1515-1566.

Mejía Sánchez, Ernesto. LAS CASAS EN MEXICO; EXPOSICION BIBLIOGRAFICA CONMEMORATIVA DEL CUARTO CENTENARIO DE SU MUERTE (1566-1966), México, D.F.: Instituto Bibliográfico Mexicano, 1967. 170p. (Anejos al BOLETIN DE LA BIBLIOTECA NACIONAL, 2). Bibliography annotates locations of sources of items exhibited (libraries, archives, etc.). Contents: I. Manuscritos. II. Tratados. III. Traducciones. IV. LA BREVISIMA DESTRUCCION. V. DIALOGO. VI. OBRAS. VII. HISTORIA DE LAS INDIAS. VIII. LA APOLGETICA HISTORIA. IX. BIOGRAFIAS Y ESTUDIOS.

Wagner, Henry Raupp. THE LIFE AND WRITINGS OF BARTOLOME DE LAS CASAS, WITH THE COLLABORATION OF HELEN RAND PARISH. Albuquerque: University of New Mexico Press, 1967. 310p. "Narrative and Critical Catalogue of Casas' Writing: pp. 253-298."

CASTELLANOS, JESUS (Cuba, 1879-1912)

Foster, Cuban Lit., pp. 188-189. Contents: I. Critical Monographs and Dissertations. II. Critical Essays.

CASTELLANOS, ROSARIO (Mexico, 1925-1974)

Ahern, Maureen. "A Critical Bibliography of and about the Works of Rosario Catellanos," in HOMENAJE A ROSARIO CASTELLANOS (Valencia, Spain: Albatros/Hispanófila, 1980), pp. 121-174. Briefly annotated entries. Contents: I. Bibliography of the Works of Rosario Castellanos. A. Poetry. 1. Published Collections. 2. Uncollected Poems. B. Prose Fiction. Novel and Short Story. C. Theatre. D. Essays and Other Texts. 1. Published Collections. 2. Uncollected Essays and Reviews. E. Translations by Rosario Castellanos. F. Bibliography of the Works of Rosario Castellanos in Translation. 1. Poems and

Prose. a. Poems in Translation. b. Prose in Translation. II. Critical Bibliography of Selected Castellanos Criticism.

Corvalán, pp. 42-44. Contents: I. Works. II. Critical Works On.

Fiscal, María Rosa. LA IMAGEN DE LA MUJER IN LA NARRATIVA DE ROSARIO CASTELLANOS. México, D.F.: UNAM, 1980. 123p. Contents: I. "Bibliografía de Rosario Castellanos," pp. 109-110. II. "Hemerobibliografía sobre Rosario Castellanos," pp. 113-115.

Foster, Mex. Lit., pp. 110-115. Contents: I. Bibliographies. II. Critical Monographs. III. Critical Essays.

Foster, 20th Century, pp. 63-64. Contents: Critical Essays.

CASTILLO Y GUEVARA, VENERABLE MADRE MARIA FRANCISCA JOSEF A DE (Columbia, 1671-1742)

"Ficha biográfica y bibliográfica de la Madre de Castillo," BOLETIN DE LA ACADEMIA COLOMBIANA, Núm. 91 (febrero/marzo de 1972), 5-8. Includes pertinent recent studies of Madre de Castillo's life and works.

Morales Borrero, María Teresa. LA MADRE CASTILLO: SU ESPIRITUALIDAD Y SU ESTILO. Bogotá: Instituto Caro y Cuervo, 1968. 493p. (Its Publicaciones, 25). "Bibliografía," pp. 449-464. Contents: I. Escritos de la Madre Castillo (arranged by year, 1817-1968). II. Escritos sobre la Madre Castillo.

CASTRO, FRANCISCO DE (Brazil, 1857-1901)

Mota, Artur. "Perfis acadêmicos, Cadeira No. 13: Francisco de Castro," REVISTA DA ACADEMIA BRASILEIRA DE LETRAS," Núm. 86 (fevereiro de 1929), pp. 150-157. Contents: I. "Bibliografia," pp. 150-151 (1878-1905). "Fontes para o estudo crítico," pp. 151-152.

CASTRO, OSCAR (Chile, 1910-1947)

Foster, Chilean Lit., pp. 68-69. Contents: I. Critical Books and Theses. II. Critical Essays.

CESPEDES, AUGUSTO (Bolivia, 1904-)

Flores, BEH, p. 211. Contents: I. Ediciones. II. Bibliografía selecta (criticism).

CESPEDES Y CASTILLO, CARLOS MANUEL DE (Cuba, 1819-1874)

"Bibliografía sobre Carlos Manuel de Céspedes en la Biblioteca de la Universidad Central," ISLAS (SANTA CLARA), 11 (octubre/diciembre de 1965), 311-322. 109 entries. Contents: I. Libros y folletos. II. Revistas y periódicos. III. Documentos. IV. Cartas. V. Manuscritos.

CESTERO, FERDINAND R. (Puerto Rico, 1864-1945)

Foster, P.R. Lit., p. 92. Critical Essays.

CID-PEREZ, JOSE (Cuba, 1906-)
Foster, Cuban Lit., p. 193. Contents: I. Critical Monographs and Dissertations. II. Critical Essays.
"José Cid-Pérez: Bibliografía y curriculum vitae," in FESTSCHRIFT JOSE CID-PEREZ (New York: Senda Nueva de Ediciones, 1981), 11-15. Contents: I. Publicaciones. II. Sin publicar. III. Obras de teatro puestas en escena. IV. Obras sin estrenar. V. Labor periodística. VI. Premios, honores y condecoraciones. VII. Conferencias y cursos.

CISNEROS, ANTONIO (Peru, 1942-)
Foster, Peruvian Lit., p. 96. Contents: I. Critical Monographs and Dissertations. II. Critical Essays.

CISNEROS, LUIS BENJAMIN (Peru, 1837-1904)
Montes de Oca, Mireya. "BIOBIBLIOGRAFIA DE LUIS BENJAMIN CISNEROS (1837-1904)." Tesis. Lima: Biblioteca Nacional, Escuela de Bibliotecarios, 1956.

COEHLO NETTO, HENRIQUE (Brazil, 1864-1934)
Coelho Netto, Paulo. BIBLIOGRAFIA DE COELHO NETTO. COM A COLABORAÇAO DE NEUZA NASCIMENTO KUHN. Rio de Janeiro: Instituto Nacional do Livro, 1972. 326p. (Coleção documentos, 4). 2,966 partially annotated titles. Contents: I. Pseudônimos. II. Cronologia. III. Bibliografia. A. Obra seleta. B. Obras escolhidas. C. Contribuição em obras de outros autores. D. Literatura brasileira. E. Obras individuais do autor. 1. Teatro. 2. Romance. 3. Novela. 4. Conto. 5. Discursos conferências e mensagens. 6. Crônicas e memórias. F. Traduções. G. Trabalhos esparsos (em capítulos de livros revistas e jornais). H. Trabalhos esparsos (em manuscrito). IV. Fontes de informação. A. Estudos bio-bibliográficos (em livros, capítulos de livros separatas, revistas ou jornais). B. Documentos iconográficos. V. Notas finais do autor. A. Obras inéditas. B. Teatro. C. Teatro infantil. D. Traduções. VI. Indices. A. Pseudônimos. B. Analítico.
Moraes, pp. 66-70. Major works by and about the author.

COFINO LOPEZ, MANUEL (Cuba, 1936-)
Foster, Cuban Lit., pp. 194-195. Critical Essays.

COLL, PEDRO EMILIO (Venezuela, 1872-1947)
Briceño-Iragorry, Mario. "Apuntes para un retrato de Pedro Emilio Coll," CULTURA UNIVERSITARIA (Caracas), Núm. 1 (mayo/junio de 1947), 9-43. Evaluation of the writer, followed by a chronology and a bibliography. Published also in the BOLETIN DE LA ACADEMIA VENEZOLANA, 14, Núm. 58 (julio/septiembre de 1947), 257-296.
Paz Castillo, Fernando. "Seudónimos de Pedro Emilio Coll," in his DE LA EPOCA MODERNISTA (Caracas: Instituto Nacional de Cultura y Bellas Artes, 1968), pp. 283-298.

"Pedro Emilio Coll, 1872-1947," in ESCRITORES VENEZOLANOS FALLECIDOS ENTRE 1942 y 1947 (Caracas: Biblioteca Nacional, 1948), pp. 28-31. Contents: I. Bibliografía. A. Obras. B. Prologuista. C. Editor. D. Traductor. II. Fuentes (criticism, etc.).

COLL Y TOSTE, CAYETANO (Puerto Rico, 1850-1930)
Arana-Soto, S. LAS POESIAS DEL DOCTOR CAYETANO COLL Y TOSTE. San Juan: Tipografía Miguza, 1970. 151p. "Bibliografía de Coll y Toste," pp. 39-43. Contents: I. Libros y folletos. II. Artículos.
Foster, P.R. Lit., pp. 93-94. Contents: I. Critical Monographs. II. Critical Essays.

COLL Y VIDAL, ANTONIO (Puerto Rico, 1898-)
Foster, P.R. Lit., pp. 94-95. Critical Essays.

COLOANE CARDENAS, FRANCISCO (Chile, 1910-)
"Cartillas biobibliográficas de autores chilenos: Francisco Vicente Coloane Cárdenas. Quemchi, Isla Grande de Chile, 1910. Cuentista, novelista y autor teatral," BOLETIN DEL INSTITUTO DE LITERATURA CHILENA (Universidad de Chile, Santiago), Año 4, Núm. 9 (enero de 1965), 13-22. Contents: I. Obra. II. Referencias. III. Vida.

CONCHA RIFFO, GILBERTO see VALLE, JUVENCIO

"CONCOLORCORVO" (Pseudonym of ALONSO CARRIO DE LA VANDERA) (Peru, ca. 1715-1778?)
Foster, Peruvian Lit., pp. 97-100. Contents: I. Critical Monographs and Dissertations. II. Critical Essays.

CONDE Y OQUENDO, FRANCISCO (Cuba, 1733-1799)
Toussaint, Manuel. "La obra de un ilustre cubano en México: El Dr. D. Francisco J. Conde y Oquendo," UNIVERSIDAD DE LA HABANA, 4, Núm. 22 (1939), 125-135. Critical bibliography.

CONTI, HAROLDO (Argentina, 1925-)
Foster, Arg. Lit., pp. 292-293. Contents: I. Critical Monographs. II. Critical Essays.

CONTRERAS, FRANCISCO (Chile, 1877-1933)
"Cartillas biobibliográficas de autores chilenos: Francisco M. A. Contreras Valenzuela. Quirihué, 1877-1933, París. Poeta, crítico literario, novelista y cuentista," BOLETIN DEL INSTITUTO DE LITERATURA CHILENA (Universidad de Chile, Santiago), Año 3, Núm. 6 (diciembre de 1963), 4-12. Contents: I. Obra: en antologías poéticas. II. Referencias. III. Tabla biográfica. IV. Otros datos.

CORCHADO Y JUARBE, MANUEL (Puerto Rico, 1840-1884)
Foster, P.R. Lit., pp. 95-96. Contents: I. Critical Monographs. II. Critical Essays.

CORONADO, MARTIN (Argentina, 1850-1919)
Foster, Arg. Lit., pp. 294-295. Contents: Critical Monographs. II. Critical Essays.

CORONEL URTECHO, JOSE (Nicaragua, 1906-)
Arellano, Jorge Eduardo. "Bibliografía básica de José Coronel Urtecho," BOLETIN NICARAGUENSE DE BIBLIOGRAFIA Y DOCUMENTACION, Núm. 16 (marzo/abril de 1977), 60-65. 160 entries. Contents: I. Libros, folletos y separatos. II. Hemerografía inicial (1920-1934). III. Algunos textos en publicaciones periódicas (1935-1974). IV. Algunas traducciones. Same bibliography also in ENCUENTRO (LEON), Núm. 9 (abril/setiembre de 1976), 129-132.

CORPANCHO, MANUEL NICOLAS (Peru, 1830-1863)
Romero, Emilia. "Bibliografía literaria de Corpancho en México," BOLETIN BIBLIOGRAFICO (Biblioteca de la Universidad de San Marcos, Lima), Año 21, Vol. 18, No. 1/2 (junio de 1948), 39-43. "En las siguientes líneas podrá apreciarse la labor literaria que Manuel Nicolás Corpancho pudo realizar durante su estada en México en 1862-63." Works are listed by year (within year by day and month). Critical commentaries and other annotations.

CORREA, FREDERICO JOSE (Brazil, 1817-1881)
Moraes, pp. 17-18. Major works by and about the author.

CORREA, GUSTAVO (Colombia, 1914-)
"Publicaciones de Gustavo Correa," NOTICIAS CULTURALES (Instituto Caro y Cuervo, Bogotá), Núm. 77 (1967), 3-5. Contents: I. Libros y monografías (By year, 1955-1962). II. Artículos (By year, 1948-1966). III. Reseñas (By year, 1952-1964).

CORREA, LUIS (Venezuela, 1884-1940)
Grases, Pedro. "Contribución a la bibliografía de Luis Correa," in Luis Correa's TERRA PATRUM (Caracas: Monte Avila, 1972), v. 1, pp. xxvii-l. 111 entries.
_______. "Contribución a la bibliografía de don Luis Correa," REVISTA NACIONAL DE CULTURA (Caracas), Año 2, Núm. 18 (mayo de 1940), 108-114. 61 entries, but the compiler makes no claim to completeness.
_______. DON LUIS CORREA: SUMA DE GENEROSIDAD EN LAS LETRAS VENEZOLANAS. Caracas, 1941. 73p. "Contribución a la bibliografía de don Luis Correa," pp. 43-66. 94 items listed chronologically, 1905-1940.

CORREA, VIRIATO (Brazil, 1884-1967)
Moraes, pp. 88-90. Major works by and about the author.
Porter, pp. 208-209. Contents: I. Writings. II. References, Critical and Biographical.

CORREIA, RAIMUNDO (Brazil, 1859-1911)
Correia, Raimundo. OBRAS COMPLETAS. São Paulo: Companhia Editôra Nacional, 1948. 2 vs. "Bibliografia de Raimundo Correia," v. 1, pp. 20-33. Contents: I. Poesia. II. Prosa. III. Publicações em antologias, seletas, etc. (all entries in parts I, II, and III are arranged by year). IV. Fontes de estudo sôbre Raimundo Correia.
_______. POESIA COMPLETA E PROSA. Rio de Janeiro: Editôra José Aguilar Ltda., 1961. 694p. "Bibliografia esencial," pp. 667-674. Contents: I. Obras do autor. II. Estudos sôbre o autor.
Moraes, pp. 58-63. Major works by and about the author.
Val, Waldir Ribeiro do. VIDA E OBRA DE RAIMUNDO CORREIA. Rio de Janeiro: Livraria Editôra Cátedra; Brasília: Instituto Nacional do Livro, 1980. 293p. Contents: I. "Bibliografia de Raimundo Correia," pp. 275-276 (By year, 1879-1961). II. "Colaboração em periódicos," pp. 276-277 (By year, 1879-1911; incomplete).

CORRETJER, JUAN ANTONIO (Puerto Rico, 1908-)
Foster, P.R. Lit., pp. 96-97. Critical Essays.

CORTAZAR, JULIO (Argentina, 1914-1984)
Alazraki, Jaime. "Cortázar en la epoca de 1940: 42 títulos desconocidos," REVISTA IBEROAMERICANA, Núm. 110/111 (enero/junio de 1980), 647-667. Lists book reviews by Cortázar that appeared in Gabalgata, 1947-1948.
Flores, BEH, pp. 95-99, 181-182. Contents: I. Ediciones. II. Referencias. III. Bibliografía selecta (criticism).
Foster, Arg. Lit., pp. 296-341. Contents: I. Bibliographies. II. Critical Monographs and Dissertations. III. Critical Essays.
Foster, 20th Century, pp. 64-75. Contents: I. Bibliographies. II. Critical Books. III. Critical Essays.
Paley de Francescato, Martha. "Bibliografía de y sobre Julio Cortázar," REVISTA IBEROAMERICANA, 39, Núm. 84/85 (julio/diciembre de 1973), 697-726. Contents: I. Libros de Cortázar. II. Reseñas, artículos, notas, ensayos, cartas, poemas y relatos no coleccionadas de Cortázar. III. Traducciones de obras de Cortázar. IV. Libros sobre Cortázar (annotated). V. Libros de conjunto sobre Cortázar. VI. Tesis doctorales. VII. Artículos, notas y reseñas de las obras sobre Cortázar.
_______. "Bibliography," in THE FINAL ISLAND: THE FICTION OF JULIO CORTAZAR (Norman, Okla.: University of Oklahoma Press, 1978), pp. 171-199. Contents: I. Works by Julio Cortázar. A. Books. B. Translations of the Works of Julio Cortázar (by language; books only). C. Reviews, Articles, Stories, Essays, Poems by Julio Cortázar. D. Cortázar as

Translator. II. Interviews with Julio Cortázar. III. Bibliography of Works about Julio Cortázar. A. Bibliographies. B. Books. C. Doctoral Theses. D. Articles and Reviews.

_______. "Selected Bibliography (1938-1976)," BOOKS ABROAD, 50 (1976), 513-516. Contents: I. Books by Cortázar. II. Books on Cortázar. III. English Translations of Cortázar's Works. IV. Articles in English.

Rey Zabal, María Víctor. "Bibliografía de y sobre Cortázar," CUADERNOS HISPANOAMERICANOS, Núm. 364/366 (octubre/diciembre de 1976), 649-667. Contents: I. Libros de Julio Cortázar. II. Otras publicaciones. III. Estudios sobre la obra de Julio Cortázar. IV. Obras de conjunto. V. Otras publicaciones sobre la obra de Julio Cortázar.

CORTES, ALFONSO (Nicaragua, 1893-)

Varela-Ibarra, José. LA POESIA DE ALFONSO CORTES. León, Nicaragua: Universidad Nacional Autónoma de Nicaragua, 1976. 172p. (Ensayos, 5). "Bibliografía," pp. 170-172. Contents: I. Obras de Alfonso Cortés. II. Sobre Alfonso Cortés.

CORTES, HERNAN (Mexico, 1485-1547)

Medina, José Toribio. ENSAYO BIO-BIBLIOGRAFICO SOBRE HERNAN CORTES: OBRA POSTUMA. INTRODUCCION DE GUILLERMO FELIU CRUZ. Santiago de Chile: Fondo Histórico y Bibliográfico José Toribio Medina, 1952. 243p. 253 entries are listed under the following categories: I. Las cartas de relación de Hernán Cortés: su historia, su bibliografía. II. Ensayo bibliográfico sobre otros documentos cortesianos, 1522-1930. III. Bibliógrafos de Cortés. IV. Indice de nombres de personas.

Valle, Rafael Heliodoro. BIBLIOGRAFIA DE HERNAN CORTES. México, D.F.: Editorial Jus, 1953. 269p. (Publicación de la Sociedad de Estudios Cortesianos, 7). 611 entries are listed under the following categories: I. Hernán Cortés en su ámbito. II. Las cartas de Cortés. III. Cronología de las cartas de relación. IV. Cartas de relación (1519-1946). V. Otras cartas y papeles de Cortés, 1520-1767. VI. Escritos cortesianos sin fecha. VII. Documentos sobre Cortés (1518-1570). VIII. Documentos, sin fecha.

COSTA, CLAUDIO MANUEL DA (Brazil, 1729-1789)

Costa, Cláudio Manuel da. POEMAS DE CLAUDIO MANUEL DA COSTA. INTRODUÇAO, SELEÇAO E NOTAS DE PERICLES EUGENIO DA SILVA RAMOS. São Paulo: Editôra Cultrix, 1966. 191p. "Bibliografia sôbre o autor," pp. 31-32.

Lousada, Wilson. PARA CONHECER MELHOR CLAUDIO MANUEL DA COSTA. Rio de Janeiro: Bloch Editores, 1974. 121p. Contents: I. "Bibliografia," pp. 19-21 (his works). II. "Fontes para estudo," pp. 21-23 (criticism).

COSTA FILHO, ODYLO (Brazil, 1914-)

Moraes, pp. 101-102. Major works by and about the author.

COUTO, RUI RIBEIRO (Brazil, 1898-1963)
Monteiro, Adolfo Casais. A POESIA DE RIBEIRO COUTO. Rio de Janeiro: Edições Presença, 1935. 46p. "Obra de Ribeiro Couto," pp. 45-46. Contents: I. Poesia. II. Contos, novelas. III. Crônica e viagens. IV. Ensaios, crítica.

CREMA, EDOARDO (Venezuela, 1902-)
León, Carlos Augusto. "Catálogo bibliográfico," in EDOARDO CREMA Y SU OBRA (Caracas: Universidad Central de Venezuela, Dirección de Cultura, 1967), pp. 223-249. Contents: I. Literaturas venezolana e hispanoamericana. II. Bellas artes, teatro y cine. III. Heterogéneas. IV. Presencia de Grecia y Roma. V. Presencia de Italia.

CRESPO, ANTONIO CALIDO CONÇALVES (Brazil, 1846-1883)
Porter, pp. 221-222. Contents: I. Writings. II. References, Critical and Biographical.

CRUCHAGA SANTA MARIA, ANGEL C. (Chile, 1893-1964)
"Cartillas biobibliográficas de autores chilenos: Angel C. Cruchaga Santa María. Santiago, 1893-1964, Santiago. Poeta y cuentista," BOLETIN DEL INSTITUTO DE LITERATURA CHILENA (Universidad de Chile, Santiago), Año 3, Núm. 7/8 (agosto de 1964), 17-26. Contents: I. Obra: en antologías poéticas. II. Referencias. III. Vida. IV. Otros datos.
Foster, Chilean Lit., pp. 69-70. Contents: I. Bibliographies. II. Critical Books and Theses. III. Critical Essays.

CRUZ, MANUEL DE LA (Cuba, 1861-1896)
Foster, Cuban Lit., pp. 196-197. Contents: I. Critical Monographs. II. Critical Essays.

CUADRA, JOSE DE LA (Ecuador, 1903-1941)
Flores, BEH, pp. 99-100. Contents: I. Edición principal. II. Otras ediciones. III. Bibliografía selecta (criticism).

CRUZ, SOR JUANA INES DE LA (Mexico, 1648?-1695)
Abreu Gómez, Ermilo. SOR JUANA INES DE LA CRUZ: BIBLIOGRAFIA Y BIBLIOTECA. México, D.F.: Imprenta de la Secretaría de Relaciones Exteriores, 1934. 455p. Contents: I. Ediciones completas. II. Ediciones comprobadas. III. Ediciones supuestas. IV. Indice de autoridades. V. Indice de apologistas. VI. Bibliografía de las ediciones. VII. Coplas de música-decasílabos (romance), décimas. VIII. Endecasílabos-endechas, glosas. IX. Letras profanas. X. Letras sagradas. XI. Liras-octavas-quintillas. XII. Quintillas-redondillas. XIII. Redondillas-romances. XIV. Silvas. XV. Sonetos. XVI. Villancicos. XVII. Prosa. XVIII. Teatro. XIX. Sainetes y saraos. XX. Apéndices. XXI. Cronología, Biblioteca de Sor Juana Inés de la Cruz. XXII. Bibliografía. XXIII. Indice de obras citadas y consultadas. "Fotograbados de las portadas de las principales ediciones de Sor Juana," pp. 423-451.

Benassy-Berling, Marie-Cécile. HUMANISME ET RELIGION CHEZ SOR JUANA INES DE LA CRUZ: LA FEMME ET LA CULTURE AU XVIIe SIECLE. Paris: Editions Hispaniques, 1982. 510p. "Bibliographie," pp. 471-482. Contents: I. Textes anciens. A. Textes. B. Textes manuscrits. C. Textes imprimés. II. Travaux sur sor Juana.

Corvalán, pp. 46-50. Contents: I. Works. II. Critical Works On.

Flores, BEH, pp. 10-13. Contents: I. Edición principal. II. Otras ediciones. III. Referencias. IV. Bibliografía selecta (criticism).

Foster, Mex. Lit., pp. 199-218. Contents: I. Bibliographies. II. Critical Monographs and Dissertations. III. Critical Essays.

Henríquez Ureña, Pedro. "Bibliografía de Sor Juan Inés de la Cruz," REVUE HISPANIQUE, 40, Núm. 97 (1917), 161-214. An annotated bibliography of the editions of the works of Sor Juana. This article was reprinted with notes by Ermilo Abreu Gómez in EL LIBRO Y EL PUEBLO (México), 12 (1934), 72-78, 137-143, 175-179.

Iguíniz, Juan B. "Catálogo de las obras de y sobre Sor Juana Inés de la Cruz existentes en la Biblioteca Nacional," BOLETIN DE LA BIBLIOTECA NACIONAL (México), 2ª época, 2, Núm. 4 (octubre/diciembre de 1951), 9-18. Contents: I. Obras de Sor Juana. II. Poesía. III. Teatro. IV. Obras sobre Sor Juana. A. Bibliografía. B. Biografía. C. Crítica e interpretación. D. Genealogía. E. Poesías.

Salceda, Alberto. "Cronología del teatro de Sor Juana," ABSIDE (México), 17, Núm. 3 (julio/septiembre de 1953), 333-358.

Schons, Dorothy. BIBLIOGRAFIA DE SOR JUANA INES DE LA CRUZ. TRADUCCION DEL INGLES POR J. MAURICIO CARRANZA. México, 1927. (Bibliografías mexicanas, 7). 67p.

_______. SOME BIBLIOGRAPHICAL NOTES ON SOR JUANA INES DE LA CRUZ. Austin, Tex.: The University of Texas, 1925. 30p. (University of Texas Bulletin, No. 2526). Both of the above list editions (mainly from the University of Texas Library) and articles and studies on Sor Juana and her work.

SOR JUANA INES DE LA CRUZ ANTE LA HISTORIA (BIOGRAFIAS ANTIGUAS. "LA FAMA" DE 1700. NOTICIAS DE 1667 a 1892). RECOPILACION DE FRANCISCO DE LA MAZA. REVISION DE ELIAS TRABUESE. México, D.F.: Universidad Nacional Autónoma de México, 1980. 612p. "Bibliografía," pp. 570-608. Critical works about Sor Juana and her work.

CUADRA, MANOLO (Nicaragua, 1907-1957)

Calatayud Bernabeu, José. MANOLO CUADRA: EL YO E LAS CIRCUNSTANCIAS. Managua, Nicaragua: Editorial "Hospicio," 1968. 175p. Contents: I. "Obras de Manolo Cuadra," p. 171. II. "Antologías y selecciones de las obras de Manolo Cuadra," p. 172. III. "Obras sobre Manolo Cuadra," pp. 172-174.

CUADRA, PABLO ANTONIO (Nicaragua, 1912-)

Cuadra, Pablo Antonio. EL JAGUAR Y LA LUNA. Buenos Aires: Ediciones Carlos Lohlé, 1971. 90p. "Bibliografía," pp. 85-87. Contents: I. Obras de Pablo Antonio Cuadra. A. Poesía. B. Teatro. C. Ensayos literarios. D. Narrativa. E. Otras. II. Algunas traducciones de sus obras.

Flores, BEH, pp. 211-212. Contents: I. Ediciones. II. Bibliografía selecta (criticism).

Guardia de Alfaro, Gloria. ESTUDIO SOBRE EL PENSAMIENTO POETICO DE PABLO ANTONIO CUADRA. Madrid: Gredos, 1971. 259p. "Bibliografía," pp. 249-256. Contents: I. Obra de Pablo Antonio Cuadra. A. Poesía. B. Ensayo. C. Narrativa. D. Teatro. II. Estudios particulares sobre la obra del poesía. III. Estudios generales sobre la obra del poeta. IV. Bibliografía general.

CUENCA, AGUSTIN F. (Mexico, 1850-1884)

Kuehne, Alyce G. de. "Hemerografía de Agustín F. Cuenca," BOLETIN DE LA BIBLIOTECA NACIONAL (México), 2ª época, 17, Núm. 3/4 (julio/diciembre de 1966), 53-72. A chronological, partially annotated listing of 80 items, extending from 1870-1884, of contributions to several Mexican periodicals by Agustín F. Cuenca, precursor of modernism. Bibliography includes both literary and political writings.

CUERVO, RUFINO JOSE (Colombia, 1844-1911)

Torres Quintero, Rafael. BIBLIOGRAFIA DE RUFINO JOSE CUERVO. Bogotá: Lit. Colombia, 1951. 194p. (Publicaciones del Instituto Caro y Cuervo; Series Minor, 2). Sixty-two entries divided into the following categories: I. Bibliografía de Cuervo: índice cronológico. II. Bibliografía sobre Cuervo.

_______. "Bibliografía de Rufino José Cuervo," in Rufino José Cuervo's OBRAS (Bogotá: Publicaciones del Instituto Caro y Cuervo, 1954), v. 2, pp. 1741-1817. (Clásicos colombianos, 2). Updates and revises his 1951 edition. Contents: I. Bibliografía de Cuervo; índice cronológico. II. Bibliografía sobre Cuervo. This work was reprinted in Fernando Antonio Martínez and Rafael Torres Quintero's RUFINO JOSE CUERVO (Bogotá: Librería Voluntad, 1954), pp. 145-221. (Instituto Caro y Cuervo. Filólogos colombianos, 1).

CUNHA, EUCLIDES DA (Brazil, 1866-1909)

Cunha, Euclides da. OBRA COMPLETA. ORGANIZADA SOB A DIREÇAO DE AFRANIO COUTINHO. Rio de Janeiro: Companhia José Aguilar, 1966. 2 vs. "Bibliografia," v. 1, pp. 57-80. Contents: I. Do autor. A. Livros publicados em vida do autor. B. Livros publicados após a morte do autor. C. Reimpressões. D. Traduções. E. Adaptações. F. Obras completas. II. Sôbre o autor.

Reis, Irene Monteiro. BIBLIOGRAFIA DE EUCLIDES DA CUNHA. Rio de Janeiro: Instituto do Livro, 1971. 422p. (Coleção documentos, 2). Contents: I. Cronologia de Euclides. II.

Obras de Euclides da Cunha. A. Obras completas. B. Antologias. C. Livros e folhetos. D. Trabalhos esparsos. E. Prefácios. F. Desenhos. G. Cartografia. H. Correspondência impresa. 1. C. ativa. 2. C. passiva. 3. C. de terceiros. I. Manuscritos. III. Iconografia. IV. Obras sôbre Euclides da Cunha: em livros, folhetos, capítulos de livros, separatas, artigos de revistas e jornais. V. Indice (author-title-subject). 3,010 items.

Rio de Janeiro. Biblioteca Nacional. EXPOSIÇAO COMEMORATIVA DO CENTENARIO DE NASCIMENTO DE EUCLIDES DA CUNHA, 1866-1966. Rio de Janeiro: Divisão de Publicações e Divulgação, 1966. 72p. Bibliography.

Venâncio, Francisco. A GLORIA DE EUCLIDES DA CUNHA. São Paulo: Companhia Editôra Nacional, 1940. 323p. (Biblioteca Pedagógica Brasileira, Série 5.a., Brasiliana, 193). Contents: I. "Bibliografia do autor," pp. 256-264. A. Livros. B. Trabalhos esparsos. II. "Iconografia," pp. 265-267. III. "Bibliografia sôbre o autor," pp. 267-295 (263 entries are arranged chronologically, 1902-1939).

CUZZANI, AGUSTIN (Argentina, 1924-)

Foster, Arg. Lit., pp. 342-343. Contents: I. Dissertations. II. Critical Essays.

- Ch -

CHACON Y CALVO, JOSE MARIA (Cuba, 1893-1969)

Foster, Cuban Lit., pp. 190-191. Contents: I. Bibliography. II. Critical Monographs. III. Critical Essays.

Gutiérrez-Vega, Zenaida. ESTUDIO BIBLIOGRAFICO DE JOSE MARIA CHACON (1913-1969). Madrid: Fundación Universitaria Española, 1982. 163p. (Biblioteca Histórica Hispanoamericana, 5). Contents: I. Bibliografía activa. A. Libros. B. Prólogos, notas preliminares. C. Notas bibliográficas. D. Discursos. E. Conferencias. F. Notas cronológicas. G. Artículos históricos. H. Artículos varios. All the above sections are arranged chronologically. II. Bibliografía pasiva. A. Libros. B. Artículos. C. Entrevistas. D. Notas bibliográficas. E. Críticas en libros. III. Indice onomástico.

CHAPLE, SERGIO (Cuba, 1938-)

Foster, Cuban Lit., p. 192. Critical Essays.

CHASE, ALFONSO (Costa Rica, 1945-)

Chase, Alfonso. OBRA EN MARCHA: POESIA, 1965-1980. San José, C.R.: Editorial Costa Rica, 1982. 285p. "Bibliografía," pp. 275-285. Contents: I. Poesía. II. Narrativa. III. Ensayos e investigaciones. IV. Traducciones. V. Estudios generales sobre su poesía. VI. Poesías reproducidas en antologías. VII. Bibliografía en diarios: Costa Rica (criticism). VIII. Bibliografía en diarios: extranjeros sobre su poesía.

CHIAPPORI, ATILIO (Argentina, 1880-1947)
"Bibliografía de don Atilio Chiappori," BOLETIN DE LA ACADEMIA ARGENTINA DE LETRAS, 16, Núm. 59 (abril/junio de 1947), 213-214. Eleven titles, arranged by year, 1907-1944.

CHIRVECHES, ARMANDO (Bolivia, 1881-1926)
Albarracín Millán, Juan. ARMANDO CHIRVECHES. La Paz: Talleres Gráficos "San Antonio," 1979. 295p. Contents: I. "Resumen biobibliográfico," pp. 261-263. II. "Citas bibliográficas," pp. 265-275.

CHOCANO, JOSE SANTOS (Peru, 1875-1934)
Anderson, pp. 20-23. Critical Essays.
Chocano, José Santos. POESIA. PROLOGO SELECCION Y NOTAS DE LUIS ALBERTO SANCHEZ. Lima: Universidad Nacional Mayor de San Marcos, 1959. 159p. (Biblioteca de Cultura General, Serie Literatura, 2). "Bibliografía," pp. 150-158. Contents: I. Del autor (books, pamphlets, arranged by year, 1895-1958). II. Sobre el autor (books only). "Resumen cronológico, 1875-1934," pp. 22-31.
Flores, BEH, pp. 212-214. Contents: I. Edición principal. II. Otras ediciones. III. Referencias. IV. Bibliografía selecta (criticism).
Foster, Peruvian Lit., pp. 86-95. Contents: I. Bibliographies. II. Critical Monographs and Dissertations. III. Critical Essays.
Mortheiru Salgado, Pedro, "Sobre José Santos Chocano (Bibliografía)," ATENEA (Santiago de Chile), Año 14, Tomo 40, Núm. 149 (noviembre de 1937), 438-447. Works about Chocano and his work listed alphabetically.
Rosenbaum, Sidonia C. "Bibliografía de Santos Chocano," REVISTA HISPANICA MODERNA, 1, Núm. 3 (abril de 1935), 191-193. Contents: I. Ediciones. A. Poesía. B. Traducciones. C. Prosa. II. Estudios. A. Generales. B. Biografías. C. Críticos.

CHUECOS PICON, RAUL (Venezuela, 1891-1937)
Cardozo, Poesía, pp. 172-176. Includes poetical works of and critical studies about the author.

CHUMACERO, ALI (Mexico, 1918-)
Foster, Mex. Lit., p. 115. Critical Essays.

CHURATA, GAMALIEL (Pseudonym of ARTURO PERALTA) (Peru, 1897-1969)
"Biobibliografía de Gamaliel Churata (seudónimo de Arturo Peralta)," ANUARIO BIBLIOGRAFICO PERUANO, 1967/1969 (i.e. 1975), 677-683. Contents: I. Libros y folletos. II. Otras publicaciones. III. Artículos y ensayos. IV. Cuentos, poesías. V. Reportajes. VI. Referencias (criticism, etc.). VII. Necrológicas y homenajes póstumas.

- D -

DARIO, RUBEN (Nicaragua, 1867-1916)

Anderson, pp. 24-61. Critical essays.

Becco, Horacio Jorge. "Rubén Darío visto por argentinos," CUADERNOS DEL IDIOMA, Año 2, Núm. 9 (1968), 157-162. Bibliography is arranged by author.

Caillet-Bois, Julio. "Rubén Darío: apuntes para una bibliografía de sus obras malogradas," SUR, Año 16, Núm. 162 (Abril de 1948), 101-109. Bibliography lists projected works never completed, such as LIBRO DEL TROPICO, and projects never launched, such as a children's magazine to be entitled LA NUEVA INFANCIA.

Cozad, Mary Lee. "Los prólogos de Rubén Darío: estudio bibliográfico," THESAURUS (BOGOTA), 29 (1974), 457-488. Pages 471-485 contains a list of Darío's prólogos by year, 1884-1916. 45 entries.

Darío, Rubén. OBRAS DESCONOCIDAS ... ESCRITAS EN CHILE Y NO RECOPILADAS EN NINGUNO DE SUS LIBROS. EDICION RECOGIDA POR RAUL SILVA CASTRO. Santiago de Chile: Prensas de la Universidad, 1934. 316p. "Bibliografía," pp. lxxxii-cxxxii.

________. POESIAS COMPLETAS. Edición, introducción y notas de Alfonso Méndez Plancarte, aumentada con nuevas poesías y otras adiciones de Antonio Oliver Belmas. Décima edición. Madrid: Aguilar, 1967. 1,309p. "Notas bibliográficas y textuales, variantes-fuentes-cronología," pp. 1147-1232. By work. "Nuevas notas bibliográficas y textuales," pp. 1234-1267. By work. "Indice alfabético de títulos de poesías y de primeros versos," pp. 1269-1287.

Del Greco, Arnold Armand. REPERTORIO BIBLIOGRAFICO DEL MUNDO DE RUBEN DARIO. New York: Las Américas Publishing Co., 1969. 667p. 3,179 items. Contents: I. Bibliografías. II. Ediciones. A. Obras. 1. Obras poéticas. 2. Obras completas. B. Obras sueltas o seleccionadas: libros y folletos. C. Poesías, escritos o selecciones en revistas y libros. III. Epistolarios y escritos de Rubén Darío sobre su vida y su obra. IV. Prólogos y prefacios. V. Traducciones. VI. Estudios y homenajes. VII. Indices alfabéticos. A. Onomástico. B. De temas. C. De revistas y periódicos.

Ellis, K. CRITICAL APPROACHES TO RUBEN DARIO. Toronto: University of Toronto Press, 1974. 170p. "Bibliography," pp. 118-133. Contents: I. Works by Rubén Darío. II. Collections. III. Some Recent Bibliographies. IV. Works on Darío.

Flores, BEH, pp. 100-104. Contents: I. Ediciones principales. II. Referencias. III. Bibliografía selecta (criticism).

Hebblethwaite, Frank P. "Una bibliografía de Rubén Darío (1945-1966)," REVISTA INTERAMERICANA DE BIBLIOGRAFIA, 17, Núm. 2 (abril/junio de 1967), 202-221. This partially annotated bibliography up-dates the "Bibliografía de Rubén

Darío," of Julio Saavedra Molina, published from 1944 to 1946 in the REVISTA CHILENA DE HISTORIA Y GEOGRAFIA. Contents: I. Obras de Rubén Darío. II. Escritos inéditos de Rubén Darío publicados en revistas. III. Libros y folletos sobre Rubén Darío. IV. Artículos sobre Rubén Darío.

Jirón Terán, José. "Bibliografía activa de Rubén Darío," CUADERNOS DE BIBLIOGRAFIA NICARAGUENSE, 2 (julio/diciembre de 1981), 1-40. Covers 1883 to 1980. 506 items. Includes individual volumes, complete works, anthologies, collections of previously unreprinted materials.

_______. "Bibliografía general de Rubén Darío (julio 1883 a enero 1967)," CUADERNOS UNIVERSITARIOS (Universidad Nacional Autónoma de Nicaragua, León), 2ª serie, Año 1, Núm. 2, vol. 2 (1967), 315-440. Also published as a monograph: Managua: Editorial San José, 1967. 128p. (Publicaciones del Centenario de Rubén Darío). An unannotated bibliography of 1,447 items of the compiler's and friends' personal holdings of Darío's works published between 1883 and 1967. Contents: I. Obras de Rubén Darío (Obras de Rubén Darío publicadas en vida. Libros y folletos): Tentativas de obras completas y colecciones. A. Editorial Mundo Latino. B. Ediciones Rubén Darío Sánchez. C. Ediciones Andrés González Blanco y Alberto Ghirald. D. Ediciones Afrodisio Aguado, S.A. E. Ediciones varias, 1916 a 1967. F. Poesía y prosa de Rubén Darío incluídas en obras de otros autores. II. Obras sobre Rubén Darío. A. Libros y folletos. B. Ensayos, poemas y estudios breves. There is not a subject or name index and some well known books and articles are missing. It contains, however, many Nicaraguan titles not found in other bibliographies.

_______. "Obras de Rubén Darío publicadas en vida," BOLETIN NICARAGUENSE DE BIBLIOGRAFIA Y DOCUMENTACION, Núm. 9 (enero/febrero de 1976), 7-9. The bibliography lists 55 works of Darío in chronological order.

Lozano, Carlos. RUBEN DARIO Y EL MODERNISMO EN ESPAÑA, 1888-1920. ENSAYO DE BIBLIOGRAFIA COMENTADA. New York: Las Américas Publishing Co., 1968. 158p. 947 entries under the following categories: I. Rubén Darío y el modernismo. A. Ensayos, artículos, conferencias y reseñas (By year, 1888-1919). B. Estudios (1888-1933). II. Composiciones varias de Darío (1890-1919). III. Obras de Darío. A. Obras completas. B. Obras varias. C. Primeras ediciones, etc. D. Traducciones por Darío. E. Traducciones por otros. 1888 the date of the publication of AZUL and 1920 "indica el momento en que el modernismo se devanecía, después de su máximo avance."

Mapes, Erwin Kempton. ESCRITOS INEDITOS DE RUBEN DARIO RECOGIDOS DE PERIODICOS DE BUENOS AIRES Y ANOTADOS. New York: Instituto de las Españas, 1938. 224p.

Moser, Gerald M. and Hensley C. Woodbridge. RUBEN DARIO Y "EL COJO ILUSTRADO." New York: Hispanic Institute, Columbia University, 1961-1964. 69p. This work first appeared in series form in the REVISTA HISPANICA MODERNA (1961-1964). The appendices list chronologically all Darío's contributions to El Cojo Ilustrado. The date and location of the first appearance of a work, previous to its existence in El Cojo Ilustrado, is provided, and for poetry, the important variants are noted.

Mota, Francisco. "Ensayo de una bibliografía cubana de y sobre Rubén Darío," L/L(Boletín del Instituto de Literatura y Lingüística, Academia de Ciencias de Cuba, La Habana), Año 1, Núm. 2 (abril/diciembre de 1967), 279-302. Contents: I. Bibliografía activa. II. Bibliografía pasiva. 228 entries.

Onís, Federico de. "Bibliografía de Rubén Darío," LA TORRE (Río Piedras, Puerto Rico), Año XV, Núm. 55/56 (enero/junio de 1967), 461-495. Contents: I. Ediciones. II. Obras inéditas y selecciones. III. Obras completas. IV. Traducciones. V. Estudios.

Pane, Remigio Ugo. "Rubén Darío, Nicaragua, 1867-1916; A Bibliography of His Poems and Short Stories in English Translations, together with a List of His Works," BULLETIN OF BIBLIOGRAPHY, 18, No. 3 (January/April 1944), 60-62.

Saavedra Molina, Julio. "Bibliografía De Ruben Dario," Núm. 105 (julio/diciembre de 1944), 3-23; REVISTA CHILENA DE HISTORIA Y GEOGRAFIA, Núm. 105 (julio/diciembre de 1944), 3-23; Núm. 106 (enero/diciembre de 1945), 24-66; Núm. 107 (enero/junio de 1946), 67-144. An annotated bibliography of Darío's books and pamphlets. The work is divided into four sections: I. Bibliografía de Rubén Darío. II. Obras completas de Rubén Darío. III. Libros y folletos publicados en vida de Rubén Darío. IV. Libros y folletos póstumos.

Silva Castro, Raúl. RUBEN DARIO Y CHILE; ANOTACIONES BIBLIOGRAFICAS PRECEDIDAS DE UNA INTRODUCCION SOBRE RUBEN DARIO EN CHILE. Santiago de Chile: Imprenta "La Tracción," 1930. 127p.

Susto, Juan Antonio. "Bibliografía de y sobre Rubén Darío en Panamá (1904-1907)," LOTERIA (PANAMA), Núm. 69 (febrero de 1947), 5-6.

Woodbridge, Hensley C. "Bibliografía de la literatura-nicaragüense traducida al inglés (segunda parte): Rubén Darío," BOLETIN NICARAGUENSE DE BIBLIOGRAFIA Y DOCUMENTACION, Núm. 18 (julio/agosto de 1977), 84-97.

______. "Rubén Darío: Una bibliografía selectiva, clasificada y anotada. Suplemento II para los años 1975-1978," CUADERNOS DE BIBLIOGRAFIA NICARAGUENSE, Núm. 2 (julio/diciembre de 1981), 71-96. Contents: I. Bibliografía. II. Estudios biográficos generales. III. Estudios biográficos especializados. IV. Darío y sus contemporáneos (casi todos españoles e hispanoamericanos). V. Poesía (general and then by title of poems). VI. Otros estudios sobre la poesía dariana (by topic). VII. Fuentes (of Darío's work). VIII. Estudios lingüísticos. IX. Darío como prosista. X. Darío, cuentista. XI. Azul. XII. Prólogos. XIII. Rubén Darío y el periodismo. XIV. Estudios sobre su fama, influencia y comparaciones con poetas posteriores. A few studies that appeared before 1975 are included in this supplement.

_______. "Rubén Darío: Bibliografía selectiva, clasificada y anotada. Suplemento para los años, 1974-76," CUADERNOS UNIVERSITARIOS (LEON, NICARAGUA), Núm. 20 (marzo de 1977), 35-66. Contents: I. Bibliografía. II. Estudios biográficos generales. III. Estudios biográficos. IV. Rubén Darío y sus contemporáneos hispanoamericanos. V. Rubén Darío y sus contemporáneos españoles. VI. Fuentes (of Darío's works). VII. Poesía (general and then by title of Darío's work). VIII. Otros estudios sobre la poesía dariana (by topic). IX. Darío como novelista. X. Los cuentos. X. Darío como ensayista. XI. Rubén Darío y el periodismo. XII. Prólogos. XIII. Fama e influencia. A few studies published prior to 1974 are also included in this bibliography.

_______. "Rubén Darío: A Critical Bibliography," HISPANIA, 50, No. 5 (December 1967), 982-995; 51, No. 1 (March 1968), 95-110. Woodbridge's bibliography based on some 400 items, are accompanied by very relevant comments. Contents: I. Bibliographies. II. Biographical Studies (General). III. Specialized Biographical Studies. IV. Darío and His Spanish American Contemporaries. V. Darío and His Spanish Contemporaries. VI. Critical Studies. A. Prose. B. Poetry. C. Sources. D. Stylistics. E. Miscellaneous. F. Influence and Reputation Studies. VII. Desiderata and Conclusions. VIII. Addenda. A. Bibliographies. B. General Biographies. C. Darío and His Spanish American Contemporaries. D. Darío and His Spanish Contemporaries. IX. Notes.

_______. RUBEN DARIO: A SELECTIVE, CLASSIFIED AND ANNOTATED BIBLIOGRAPHY. Metuchen, N.J.: Scarecrow Press, 1975. 245p. This bibliography of approximately 500 items serves as a guide to the important biographical and critical studies on Darío through 1973. Contents: Part I: Biographical Studies: General Biographical Studies; Specialized Biographical Studies; Paternity, Childhood and Adolescence, Education; Chile, El Salvador, etc.; Centennial Meetings; Seminario Archivo Rubén Darío; Iconography; Museo Archivo Rubén Darío; Rubén Darío and His Spanish American Contemporaries (by writer); Darío and His Spanish Contemporaries (by writer). Part II: Critical Studies: General Studies; Poetry (by work); Sources: Studies on Language, Asthetics, and Stylistics; Studies of Symbols in Darío's Works; Darío's Political and Social Ideas; Darío and Religion; Sexuality, Love and Eroticism in Darío's Works; Other Important Studies; AZUL; Darío as a Prose Writer; Darío as a Novelist (by work); Darío as a Short Story Writer (by work); Darío as Critic (by work); Darío as a Translator; Prologues; Darío as a Journalist (by journal); Studies on Darío's Influence and Reputation (by country); Index of Critics.

_______. RUBEN DARIO: BIBLIOGRAFIA SELECTIVA, CLASIFI-

CADA Y ANOTADA. León, Nicaragua: Editorial Universitaria (UNAM), 1975. 146p. Spanish edition of the Scarecrow Press edition with 40 additional entries.

_______. "Rubén Darío y EL PERU ARTISTICO: una bibliografía," BOLETIN NICARAGUENSE DE BIBLIOGRAFIA Y DOCUMENTACION (Managua), Núm. 9 (enero/febrero de 1976), 9-11. This bibliography lists the publications of Rubén Darío in this REVISTA, as well as works about him, and poems and stories dedicated to him. 19 entries. EL PERU ARTISTICO, Lima, 1893-1895, 48 nos.

DAVALOS, JUAN CARLOS (Argentina, 1887-1959)

Flores, BEH, pp. 214-215. Contents: I. Ediciones principales. II. Otras ediciones. III. Referencias. IV. Bibliografía selecta (criticism).

Rossi, Iris. CONTRIBUCION A LA BIBLIOGRAFIA DE JUAN CARLOS DAVALOS. Buenos Aires: Fondo Nacional de las Artes, 1966. 91p. (Bibliografía Argentina de Artes y Letras, Compilaciones Especiales, No. 23). Annotated contents: I. Obras del autor. A. Poesía. B. Teatro. C. Cuentos y relatos. D. Ensayos. E. Prólogos a obras de otros autores. F. Colaboraciones en publicaciones periódicas. 1. Poesía. 2. Teatro. 3. Cuentos y relatos. G. Discursos y conferencias. H. Encuestas y entrevistas. I. Prosa Varia. II. Traducciones de textos de otros autores. III. Traducciones de obras del autor. IV. Antologías de textos del autor. V. Textos del autor en diversas antologías. VI. Crítica y biografía. VII. Bibliografías. VIII. Textos inéditos. IX. Discografía. X. Cronología biobibliografía. Name, title, and illustration indexes are included for the 1,038 publications listed.

DAVALOS Y FIGUEROA, DIEGO (Peru, 1552/54-1608)

Lizaraso Sánchez, Amparo. "BIO-BIBLIOGRAFIA DE DIEGO DAVALOS Y FIGUEROA." Tesis. Lima: Biblioteca Nacional, Escuela de Bibliotecarios, 1959.

DAVILA, JOSE ANTONIO (Puerto Rico, 1898/99-1941)

Foster, P.R. Lit., pp. 97-98. Contents: I. Critical Monograph. II. Critical Essays.

DAVILA, VIRGILIO (Puerto Rico, 1869-1943)

Foster, P.R. Lit., pp. 98-100. Contents: I. Critical Monograph and Dissertation. II. Critical Essays.

DEBRAVO, JORGE (Costa Rica, 1938-)

Calvo Fajardo, Yadira. POESIA EN JORGE DEBRAVO. 7ª edición. San José. Costa Rica: Ministerio de Cultura, 1980. 287p. Contents: I. "Artículos de la prensa costarricense," pp. 272-274 (criticism on Debravo and his work). II. "Obras de Jorge Debravo consultada," p. 274.

DEGETAU Y GONZALEZ, FEDERICO (Puerto Rico, 1862-1914)
Foster, P.R. Lit., pp. 100-101. Contents: I. Critical Monographs. II. Critical Essays.

DELGADO, RAFAEL (Mexico, 1853-1914)
Flores, BEH, pp. 215-216. Contents: I. Ediciones principales. II. Otras ediciones. III. Referencias. IV. Bibliografía selecta (criticism).
Moore, Ernest R., and James G. Bickley. "Rafael Delgado, notas bibliográficas y críticas," EL LIBRO Y EL PUEBLO (México), 14, Núm. 4 (1941), 22-31.
_______. "Rafael Delgado, notas bibliográficas y críticas," REVISTA IBEROAMERICANA, 6 (1943), 155-201. Partially annotated works, with library locations listed for 28 U.S. and Mexican libraries. Contents: I. Delgado como novelista. II. Novelas, cuentos y notas. III. Poesías. IV. Estudios literarios y otros escritos. V. Teatro. VI. Obras inéditas. VII. Obras sobre Delgado.

DELGADO, WASHINGTON (Peru, 1927-)
Foster, Peruvian Lit., p. 101. Contents: I. Critical Monographs and Dissertations. II. Critical Essays.

DELGADO PASTOR, AMADEO (Peru, 1915-1951)
"Amadeo Delgado Pastor," ANUARIO BIBLIOGRAFICO PERUANO, 1951/1952, 292-296. Contents: I. Ediciones. II. Obras inéditas. III. Artículos. IV. Poesías. V. Notas bibliográficas. VI. Referencias.

DELIGNE, GASTON FERNANDO (Dominican Republic, 1861-1913)
Amiama Tió, Fernando A. CONTRIBUCION A LA BIBLIOGRAFIA DE GASTON FERNANDO DELIGNE. Ciudad Trujillo: Luis Sánchez Andújar Casa Editora, 1944. 28p. Contents: I. Nota biográfica. II. Bibliografía.

DELMONTE, RICARDO (Cuba, 1828-1909)
Figarola Caneda, Domingo. "Ricardo Delmonte," REVISTA DE LA BIBLIOTECA NACIONAL, 1 (enero/febrero de 1909), 66-69. Contents: I. Poesía. II. Prosa. The bibliography includes books, pamphlets, and articles (20 items in total).

DELMONTE Y APONTE, DOMINGO (Cuba, 1804-1853)
Foster, Cuban Lit., pp. 198-199. Contents: I. Critical Monographs and Dissertations. II. Critical Essays.

DENEVI, MARCO (Argentina, 1922-)
Denevi, Marco. PAGINAS DE MARCO DENEVI SELECCIONADAS POR EL AUTOR. ESTUDIO PRELIMINAR DE JUAN CARLOS MERLO. Buenos Aires: Editorial Celtia, 1983. 228p. Contents: I. "Bibliografía de Marco Denevi (1955-1982), p. 221 (monographs only). II. "Bibliografía sobre Marco Denevi," p. 223 (monographs only).

Flores, BEH, pp. 216-217. Contents: I. Ediciones. II. Bibliografía selecta (criticism).
Foster, Arg. Lit., pp. 344-345. Contents: I. Bibliography. II. Critical Monograph and Dissertations. III. Critical Essays.
Yates, Donald A. "Para una bibliografía de Marco Denevi," REVISTA IBEROAMERICANA, 33, Núm. 67 (enero/junio de 1967), 141-146. This bibliography is complete through December 1966. Arranged by work. Included in the bibliography are translations and movie, theatre, and television versions.

DIAS, ANTONIO GONÇALVES (Brazil, 1823-1864)
Ackermann, Fritz. "Bibliografia de Gonçalves Dias," BOLETIM BIBLIOGRAFICO (São Paulo, Biblioteca Municipal), Ano 1, Vol. 1 (outubro/dezembro 1943), 53-56. Contents: I. Edições dos cantos (inclusive traduções) e outras obras do poeta. II. Obras de alguns obras do poeta. III. Estudos biográficos e de história literária. IV. Artigos e conferências sôbre Gonçalves Dias e sua obra. V. Antologias. VI. Antologias e dicionários bibliográficos. VII. Tratados de versificação. VIII. Obras históricas e geográficas.
BIBLIOGRAFIA GONÇALVINA, CENTENARIO DE ANTONIO GONÇALVES DIAS. San Luís: Departamento de Cultura do Estado, 1964. 45p.
Dias, Gonçalves. POESIA COMPLETA E PROSA ESCOLHIDA. Rio de Janeiro: Editôra José Aguilar, Ltda., 1959. 926p. "Bibliografia," pp. 913-917. Updates M. Nogueira da Silva's: BIBLIOGRAFIA DE GONÇALVES DIAS. Rio de Janeiro: Imprensa Nacional, 1942. 203p. Contents: I. Obras. II. Crítica literal e teatral. III. Relatórios. IV. Diários. V. Poesias musicadas. VI. Estudos.
Montello, Josué. PARA CONHECER MELHOR GONÇALVES DIAS. Rio de Janeiro: Bloch Editores, 1973. 138p. "Bibliografia," pp. 19-21. Contents: I. Obras. II. Fontes para o estudo de Gonçalves Dias. A. Biografias. B. Bibliografia. C. Estudos literários.
Moraes, pp. 18-28. Major works by and about the author.
Rio de Janeiro. Biblioteca Nacional. EXPOSIÇAO COMEMORATIVA DO CENTENARIO DA MORTE DE GONÇALVES DIAS, 1864-1964. Rio de Janeiro: Biblioteca Nacional, 1964. 45p. Bibliography.
Silva, Manuel Nogueira da. BIBLIOGRAFIA DE GONÇALVES DIAS. Rio de Janeiro: Imprensa Nacional, 1942. 203p. 186 annotated entries, which include works by and about the author, are arranged chronologically, 1841-1941. Also includes poesias musicadas, trabalhos perdidos, and gravuras.
_______. AS EDIÇOES ALLEMAS DOS "CANTOS" DE GONÇALVES DIAS. Niterói: Officinas graphicas de Escola Profissional "Washington Luis," 1929. 34p.

DIAS, JOSE ERASMO (Brazil, 1916-)
Moraes, pp. 103-105. Major works by and about the author.

DIAS, TEOFILO (Brazil, 1857-1889)
Moraes, pp. 47-49. Major works by and about the author.

DIAZ, JESUS (Cuba, 1941/42-)
Foster, *Cuban Lit.*, p. 200. Critical Essays.

DIAZ, JORGE (Chile, 1930-)
Foster, *Chilean Lit.*, pp. 74-75. Contents: I. Critical Books and Theses. II. Critical Essays.

DIAZ ALFARO, ABELARDO MILTON (Puerto Rico, 1919-)
Foster, *P.R. Lit.*, pp. 101-102. Contents: I. Dissertation. II. Critical Essays.

DIAZ ARRIETA, HERNAN *see* ALONE

DIAZ CASANUEVA, HUMBERTO (Chile, 1906-)
Foster, *Chilean Lit.*, pp. 75-76. Contents: I. Critical Books and Theses. II. Critical Essays.

DIAZ CASTRO, EUGENIO (Colombia, 1804-1865)
Porras Collantes, pp. 199-207. Includes works of and critical studies about the author.

DIAZ DEL CASTILLO, BERNAL (1496-1584)
Villacorte Calderón, José Antonio. "Notas bibliográficas de la obra de Bernal Díaz del Castillo," *ANALES DE LA SOCIEDAD DE GEOGRAFIA E HISTORIA* (Guatemala), 10 (1934), 478-489. Contents: I. Original y copias. II. Ediciones impresas. III. Estudios.

DIAZ LOYOLA, CARLOS *see* ROKHA, PABLO DE

DIAZ MIRON, SALVADOR (Mexico, 1853-1928)
Anderson, pp. 62-65. Critical Essays.
Castro León, Antonio. *DIAZ MIRON; SU VIDA Y SU OBRA.* México: Editorial Porrúa, 1970. 270p. "Bibliografía general," pp. 225-269. Contents: I. Cronología de sus poemas. II. Ensayo de una cronología de sus poemas (por título, forma y metro, número de versos, fechada compuesta primera publicación). III. Bibliografía general. A. Obras (annotated). B. Biografía y crítica.
Flores, *BEH*, pp. 13-15. Contents: I. Ediciones principales. II. Otras ediciones. III. Referencias. IV. Bibliografía selecta (criticism).
Foster, *Mex. Lit.*, pp. 116-124. Contents: I. Bibliographies. II. Critical Monographs and Dissertations. III. Critical Essays.
Pasquel, Leonardo. *BIBLIOGRAFIA DIAZMIRONIANA.* México, D.F.: Editorial Citlaltépetl, 1966. 63p. Bibliography lists works both by and about Salvador Díaz Mirón in one alphabetical order.

DIAZ RODRIGUEZ, MANUEL (Venezuela, 1868-1927)

Anderson, pp. 66-67. Critical Essays.

Becco, Horacio Jorge. "Bibliografía," in Manuel Díaz Rodríguez's NARRATIVA Y ENSAYO. SELECCION Y PROLOGO: ORLANDO ARAUJO. CRONOLOGIA: MARIA BEATRIZ MEDINA (Caracas: Biblioteca Ayacucho, 1982), pp. 513-522. Contents: Obras de Manuel Díaz Rodríguez. A. Novela. B. Cuento. C. Ensayo. D. Antologías. II. Estudios sobre Manuel Díaz Rodríguez. A. Libros y folletos (selección). B. Hemerográfica (selección).

Caracas. Universidad Católica Andrés Bello. Seminario de Literatura Venezolana. CONTRIBUCION A LA BIBLIOGRAFIA DE MANUEL DIAZ RODRIGUEZ, 1871 (sic)-1927. Caracas: Gobernación del Distrito Federal, 1969? 157p. (Colección Bibliografías, 2). Contents: I. Bibliografía de Manuel Díaz Rodríguez. II. Fuentes bibliográficas. A. Obras mayores. 1. Novela. 2. Cuento. 3. Ensayo. B. Obra dispersa. 1. Novela. 2. Poesía. 3. Cuento. 4. Miscelánea. III. Bibliografía directa. IV. Epistolario. A. De Manuel Díaz Rodríguez. B. A Manuel Díaz Rodríguez. V. Biografía y crítica (libros, folletos, capítulos, artículos y referencias sobre el autor y su obra). 667 citings.

Dunham, Lowell. MANUEL DIAZ RODRIGUEZ: VIDA Y OBRA. México: Ediciones de Andrea, 1959. 93p. "Bibliografía," pp. 85-92. Contents: I. Obras. II. Crítica y documentación. III. Material no publicado.

Flores, BEH, pp. 218-219. Contents: I. Edición principal. II. Otras ediciones. III. Referencias. IV. Bibliografía selecta (criticism).

Foster, 20th Century, pp. 75-77. Contents: Critical Books. II. Critical Essays.

DIAZ SANCHEZ, RAMON (Venezuela, 1903-1968)

Caracas. Universidad Católica "Andrés Bello." Seminario de Literatura Venezolana. CONTRIBUCION A LA BIBLIOGRAFIA DE RAMON DIAZ SANCHEZ, 1903-1968. Caracas: Gobernación del Distrito Federal, 1970. 249p. (Colección bibliografías, 5). 1,126 citations. Contents: I. Referencias bibliográficas. II. Obras mayores. A. Novela. B. Cuento. C. Historia. D. Ensayo. E. Teatro. F. Discursos. G. Prólogos. III. Miscelánea. IV. Obra dispersa (mainly journal and newspaper articles). V. Epistolario. VI. Biografía y crítica (libros, folletos, capítulos, artículos y referencias sobre el autor y su obra).

DIAZ VALCARCEL, EMILIO (Puerto Rico, 1929-)

Dalmau de Sánchez, María Mercedes. "Bibliografía de Emilio Díaz Valcárcel," REVISTA DE ESTUDIOS HISPANICOS (PUERTO RICO), 3 (enero/junio de 1973), 81-89. Contents: I. Obra. A. Libros. B. En periódicos, revistas y antologías. C. Traducciones. D. Inédita. II. Crítica. III. Noticias. IV. Apéndice: Fichas suplidas por el autor que no pudieron ser cotejadas ni completadas.

Foster, P.R. Lit., pp. 102-103. Contents: I. Bibliography. II. Dissertation. III. Critical Essays.

DI BENEDETTO, ANTONIO (Argentina, 1922-1976)
Foster, Arg. Lit., pp. 179-180. Contents: I. Critical Monograph. II. Critical Essays.
Ricci, Graciela. LOS CIRCUITOS INTERIORES. "ZAMA" EN LA OBRA DE A. DI BENEDETTO. Buenos Aires: Fernando García Cambeiro, 1974. 109p. "Obra publicada por Antonio di Benedetto," pp. 100-101. I. Cuentos. II. Novelas. III. Ediciones bilingües (castellano e inglés). IV. Traducciones. V. Cuentos publicados en diarios, revistas y antologías. "Bibliografía general," pp. 102-104. I. Bibliografía de base sobre temas de análisis literario. II. Bibliografía de base sobre psicología y arte. III. Bibliografía sobre la narrativa en Hispanoamérica, donde se hace mención de ADB o de su obra. "Bibliografía específica," pp. 105-109. I. Testimonios provistos por el propio Di Benedetto. II. Bibliografía crítica existente en torno a ADB y su obra. A. Libros. B. Revistas. C. Diarios. D. Crónica no firmada. 1. Revistas. 2. Diarios.

DIEGO, ELISEO (Cuba, 1920-)
Foster, Cuban Lit., pp. 201-202. Contents: I. Bibliography. II. Critical Essays.
La Habana. Biblioteca Nacional "José Martí." BIBLIOGRAFIA DE ELISEO DIEGO. La Habana, 1970. 24p. Contents: I. Bibliografía activa. A. Cuento. B. Poesía. C. Prosa. D. Prosa poética. II. Traducciones, versiones, prólogos y selecciones. III. Bibliografía pasiva. A. De libros, folletos, publicaciones periódicas. B. Traducciones.

DIEGO, JOSE DE (Puerto Rico, 1866-1918)
Arce de Vázquez, Margot. "Bibliografía selecta," ASOMANTE, 22, Núm. 4 (octubre/diciembre de 1966), 79-83. "Se incluye aquí solamente la que de un modo u otro se refiere a su obra de escritos y se ha aprovechando en el texto del libro en prensa, LA OBRA LITERARIA DE JOSE DE DIEGO por Margot Arce de Vázquez." Contents: I. Poesía. II. Prosa. III. Estudios sobre José de Diego.
Foster, P.R. Lit., pp. 104-108. Contents: I. Bibliography. II. Critical Monographs and Dissertation. III. Critical Essays.

DIEGO PADRO, JOSE ISAAC DE (Puerto Rico, 1899-1974)
Foster, P.R. Lit., pp. 109-110. Contents: I. Bibliography. II. Critical Monographs and Dissertation. III. Critical Essays.
Rodríguez Torres, Carmelo. "Bibliografía mínima de José I. de Diego Padró," SIN NOMBRE, 6 (enero/marzo de 1976), 63-66. Contents: I. Ediciones. A. Poesías. B. Novelas. C. Ensayo. D. Publicaciones en antologías. II. Algunos artículos sueltos (periódicos y revistas). III. Estudios (criticism).

DIEGUEZ, JUAN (Guatemala, 1813-1866)
Carrera de Wever, Margarita, compiler. CORPUS POETICUM DE LA OBRA DE JUAN DIEGUEZ. Guatemala, C.A.: Universidad de San Carlos de Guatemala, 1959. 284p. (Colección de Autores Guatemalenses "Carlos Wyld Ospina," 3). "Fuentes bibliográficas," pp. 103-107. Contents: I. Bibliografía especial para el estudio de Juan Diéguez. II. Estudios publicados en diversos periódicos y revistas. III. Periódicos, revistas y libros que han reproducido poemas de Juan Diéguez.

DIEZ CANSECO, JOSE (Peru, 1904-1949)
"José Díez Canseco," ANUARIO BIBLIOGRAFICO PERUANO, 1949/1950, 323-344. Contents: I. Libros. II. Otras publicaciones. III. Artículos. IV. Referencias.

DIHIGO Y MESTRE, JUAN MIGUEL (Cuba, 1866-1952)
Dihigo y López-Trigo, Ernesto. BIBLIOGRAFIA DE JUAN MIGUEL DIHIGO Y MESTRE. Le Habana: Talleres del Archivo Nacional, 1964. 91p. 893 partially annotated entries. Contents: I. Lingüística. II. Etimología y Léxicos. III. Idiomas. IV. Consultas gramaticales y de otra índole. V. Filología clásica y arte. VI. Literatura. VII. Historia. VIII. Elogios y estudios sobre personas. IX. Notas bibliográficas (Book reviews). X. Notas necrológicas. XI. Universidad de La Habana. XII. Notas universitarias. XIII. Escuelas públicas y otros centros docentes. XIV. Congresos y viajes. XV. Miscelánea. XVI. Traducciones. XVII. Discursos varios. XVIII. Anejo A: Name index. XIX. Anejo B: Trabajos sobre Juan Miguel Dihigo y Mestre.

DISCEPOLO, ARMANDO (Argentina, 1887-1971)
Foster, Arg. Lit., pp. 346-347. Contents: I. Critical Monographs and Dissertation. II. Critical Essays.

DOMINGUEZ CAMARGO, HERNANDO (Colombia, 1606-1659)
Domínguez Camargo, Hernando. ANTOLOGIA POETICA. PROLOGO, SELECCION Y NOTAS DE EDUARDO MENDOZA VARELA. Medellín: Editorial Bedout, 1969. 223p. "Bibliografía," pp. 221-223. Includes works about the author and his work.
Flores, BEH, pp. 15-16. Contents: I. Ediciones. II. Bibliografía selecta (criticism).
Meo Zilio, Giovanni. ESTUDIO SOBRE HERNANDO DOMINGUEZ CAMARGO Y SU "IGNACIO DE LOYOLA," POEMA HEROICO. Messina-Firenze: G. D'Anna, 1967. 357p. "Principales referencias bibliográficas," pp. 333-342. I. Obras anónimas y colectivas. II. Obras nominativas. "Capítulo IV: la crítica sobre Camargo," pp. 168-196. Descriptive bibliographic survey.
Pérez Torres Quintero, Rafael. "Bibliografía sobre Hernando Domínguez Camargo," in Hernando Domínguez Camargo's OBRAS. EDICION A CARGO DE RAFAEL TORRES QUINTERO.... (Bogotá: Instituto Caro y Cuervo, 1960) pp. xiii-xxiv. (Biblioteca de Publicaciones del Instituto Caro y Cuervo, 15). 64 partially annotated entries.

DONOSO, JOSE (Chile, 1924-)

Cerezo, María del Carmen. "EL OBSCENO PAJARO DE LA NOCHE: EJERCICIO CREACIONAL." Ph.D., University of Toronto, 1984. The dissertation contains an extensive bibliography on Donoso and his work.

Flores, BEH, pp. 219-220. Contents: I. Ediciones. II. Bibliografía selecta (criticism).

Foster, Chilean Lit., pp. 76-82. Contents: I. Bibliographies. II. Critical Books and Theses. III. Critical Essays.

Foster, 20th Century, pp. 77-79. Contents: I. Bibliographies. II. Critical Books. III. Critical Essays.

Hassett, John J., Charles M. Tatum, and Kirsten Nigro. "Bibliography: José Donoso," CHASQUI, 2, Núm. 1 (noviembre de 1972), 15-30. Contents: I. Fiction by Donoso (in order of publication). II. Miscellaneous: Translations, Criticism, etc. by Donoso (in order of publication). III. Critical Articles and Interviews Regarding Donoso and His Work. IV. Reviews of Donoso's Fiction. V. Completed Theses and Dissertations. VI. Dissertations in Progress. VII. Critical Works. Not specifically Dedicated to a Study of Donoso but Which Contain Comments about Him and His Narrative. VIII. Works in Preparation.

McMurray, George R. "José Donoso: Bibliography-Addendum," CHASQUI, 3, Núm. 2 (febrero de 1974), 23-44. Addendum to the Hassett bibliography. Contents: I. Writings by Donoso (in order of publication). II. Books on José Donoso. III. Articles and Essays on Donoso and His Work. IV. Interviews. V. Recently Completed Doctoral Dissertations. VI. Theses and Dissertations in Progress. VII. Reviews of Donoso's Works. VIII. Books and Articles in which Donoso is Mentioned. IX. Bibliography.

Ocanto, Nancy. "Bio-bibliografía de José Donoso," ACTUALIDADES (CARACAS), 2 (1977), 191-215. Contents: I. Cuentos. II. Novelas. III. Ensayo-crítica. IV. Traducciones. V. Antologías. VI. Publicaciones periódicas en las que colaboró. VII. Prólogos. VIII. Bibliografía sobre datos bio-bibliográficos. IX. Bibliografía sobre José Donoso (383 items).

Quintero M., Isis. "Artículos publicados por José Donoso en la revista ERCILLA;" CHASQUI, 3, Núm. 2 (febrero de 1974), 45-52. By number of ERCILLA, número 1306 (1 de junio de 1960)-número 1549 (27 de enero de 1965).

_______. JOSE DONOSO: UNA INSURRECCION CONTRA LA REALIDAD. Madrid: Hispanova de Ediciones, 1978. 286p. "Bibliografía," pp. 259-282. Contents: I. Obra narrativa de José Donoso (cuento y novela; en orden de publicación, 1950-1977). II. Ensayos, prólogos, traducciones y otras publicaciones de Donoso (en orden de aparición, 1958-1977). III. Artículos periodísticos publicados por Donoso en la revista Ercilla (By year, 1960-1965). IV. Entrevistas. V. Libros sobre Donoso. VI. Artículos críticos y ensayos generales sobre Donoso y su obra. VII. Ensayos, artículos críticos y reseñas sobre Cuentos; Coronación; Este Domingo; El lugar sin límites; El obsceno pájaro de la noche; Historia personal del "Boom"; Tres novelitas burguesas. VIII. Libros y artículos críticos donde se menciona a Donoso.

Vidal, Hernán. JOSE DONOSO: SURREALISMO Y REBELION DE LOS INSTINTOS. Barcelona: Ediciones Aubí, 1972. 245p. Contents: I. "Contribución a la bibliografía de José Donoso," pp. 237-238. A. Cuento. B. Cuentos en revistas y antologías. C. Novela. D. Edición. E. Traducciones. II. "Bibliografía sobre José Donoso," pp. 238-242. A. Generales. B. Los cuentos. C. Coronación. D. Este Domingo. E. El lugar sin límites. F. El obsceno pájaro de la noche.

DORR, NICOLAS (Cuba, 1946/47-)

Foster, Cuban Lit., p. 203. Critical Essays.

DRAGUN, OSVALDO (Argentina, 1929-)

Foster, Arg. Lit., pp. 348-349. Critical Essays.

DROGUETT, CARLOS (Chile, 1912-)

Flores, BEH, pp. 220-222. Contents: I. Ediciones. II. Referencias. III. Bibliografía selecta (criticism).

Foster, Chilean Lit., pp. 82-84. Contents: I. Bibliographies. II. Critical Essays.

Foster, 20th Century, p. 80. Contents: I. Bibliographies. II. Critical Essays.

DUARTE, URBANO (Brazil, 1855-1902)

Mota, Artur. "Perfís acadêmicos, Cadeira, No. 12: Urbano Duarte," REVISTA DA ACADEMIA BRASILEIRA DE LETRAS, Núm. 83 (novembro de 1928), 327-331. Contents: I. "Bibliografia," pp. 327-328. II. "Fontes para o estudo crítico," pp. 328-329.

DUBLE URRUTIA, DIEGO (Chile, 1877-1970)

"Cartillas biobibliográficas de autores chilenos. Diego Dublé Urrutia. Angol, 1877. Poeta," BOLETIN DEL INSTITUTO DE LITERATURA CHILENA (Universidad de Chile, Santiago), Año 2, Núm. 4/5 (julio de 1963), 21-26. Contents: I. Obras en antologías poéticas. II. Traducciones de poemas. III. Referencias. IV. Tabla biográfica.

DUNCAN, QUINCE (Costa Rica, 1940-)

Jackson, Afro-Spanish, pp. 54-55. Contents: I. Works. II. Criticism.

"Quince Duncan (1940)," in Alfonso Chase's NARRATIVA CONTEMPORANEA DE COSTA RICA (San José, C.R.: Ministerio de Cultura, 1975), v. 2, pp. 333-353. Includes bibliography of Ducan's works and studies about him.

DUQUE SANCHEZ, EMIRO (Venezuela, 1915-)

Cardozo, Poesía, pp. 176-178. Includes the poetical works of and the critical studies about the author.

DURAND, LUIS (Chile, 1895-1954)
Decker, Donald M. "Bibliografía de y sobre Luis Durand," REVISTA IBEROAMERICANA, 30, Núm. 58 (1964), 313-317. Contents: I. Obras de Luis Durand. A. Libros. B. Cuentos y ensayos publicados en ATENEA. II. Sobre Luis Durand (Articles only from ATENEA).
Escudero, Alfonso M. "Fuentes consultadas sobre Luis Durand," REVISTA IBEROAMERICANA, 33, Núm. 61 (1966), 131-138. Supplements the Decker bibliography by adding other books and articles on Durand.
Flores, BEH, pp. 222-224. Contents: I. Ediciones. II. Referencias. III. Bibliografía selecta (criticism).
Foster, Chilean Lit., pp. 84-87. Contents: I. Bibliographies. II. Critical Books and Theses. III. Critical Essays.

- E -

ECHAGUE, JUAN PABLO (Argentina, 1875-1950)
"Bibliografía de don Juan Pablo Echagüe," BOLETIN DE LA ACADEMIA ARGENTINA DE LETRAS, 19, Núm. 73 (julio/setiembre de 1950), 303-306. 40 items, arranged by year, 1905-1950.

ECHEVERRIA, ESTEBAN (Argentina, 1805-1851)
Flores, BEH, pp. 16-17. Contents: I. Edición principal. II. Otras ediciones. III. Referencias. IV. Bibliografía selecta.
Flores, NH, v. 1, pp. 56-57. Contents: I. Ediciones principales. II. Referencias. III. Bibliografía selecta (criticism).
Foster, Arg. Lit., pp. 350-360. Contents: I. Bibliographies. II. Critical Monographs and Dissertations. III. Critical Essays.
Kisnerman, Natalio. CONTRIBUCION A LA BIBLIOGRAFIA DE ESTEBAN ECHEVERRIA (1805-1970). Buenos Aires: Universidad Nacional, Publicaciones de la Facultad de Filosofía y Letras, 1971. 123p. Contents: I. Bibliografía (Works and Criticism), pp. 5-105. 740 partially annotated entries. II. Iconografía de Estebán Echeverría (p. 106). III. Addenda a la bibliografía de obras (pp. 107-109). IV. Bibliografía general (pp. 110-115). V. Indice de autores y temas.
Weinberg, Félix. "Contribución a la bibliografía de Estebán Echeverría," UNIVERSIDAD, Núm. 45 (julio/setiembre de 1960), 159-226. The 159 annotated works are listed by year, 1830-1951, and translations from 1844-1957.

EDWARDS, JORGE (Chile, 1931-)
Foster, Chilean Lit., pp. 87-88. Critical Essays.

EDWARDS BELLO, JOAQUIN (Chile, 1877-1968)
"Cartillas biobibliográficas de autores chilenos: Joaquín Edwards Bello. Valparaíso, 1887. Novelista, cuentista, ensayista, periodista," BOLETIN DEL INSTITUTO DE LITERATURA CHILENA (Universidad de Chile, Santiago), Año 3, Núm. 7/8

(agosto de 1964), 7-17. Contents: I. Obra. II. Referencias. III. Vida.
Foster, Chilean Lit., pp. 88-90. Contents: I. Bibliographies. II. Critical Books and Theses. III. Critical Essays.
Orlandi Araya, Julio, and Alejandro Ramírez Cid. JOAQUIN EDWARDS BELLO (OBRA, ESTILO, TECNICA). Santiago de Chile: Editorial del Pacífico, 1960. 65p. "Bibliografía," pp. 59-64. Contents: I. Obras del autor (novelas, cuentos y crónicas). II. Referencias a sus obras.

EGANA, JUAN (Chile, 1768-1836)
Silva Castro, Raúl. BIBLIOGRAFIA DE DON JUAN EGANA, 1768-1836. Santiago de Chile: Imprenta Universitaria, 1949. 281p. "Bibliografía," pp. 7-163. Contents: I. El catálogo de Lizardi (poesías, pp. 17-18). II. Bibliografía rectificada (works arranged by year, 1802-1835). III. Colección (collected works). "Indice alfabético de nombres y seudónimos mencionadas en esta bibliografía," pp. 275-281.

EGUIARA Y EGUREN, JUAN JOSE (Mexico, 1695-1763)
Eguiara y Eguren, Juan José. PROLOGOS A LA BIBLIOTECA MEXICANA. EDICION DE AGUSTIN MILLARES CARLO. México, D.F.: Fondo de Cultura Económica, 1944. "Bibliografía," pp. 225-278. An annotated descriptive bibliographic approach for works published between 1712 and 1761. 244 titles are listed. Reprinted in Agustín Millares Carlo's DON JUAN JOSE DE EGUIARA Y EGUREN, 1695-1763 Y SU BIBLIOTECA MEXICANA (México, D.F.: UNAM, Facultad de Filosofía y Letras, 1957), pp. 89-171.

EGUREN, JOSE MARIA (Peru, 1874-1942)
Anderson, pp. 68-70. Critical Essays.
"Bio-bibliografía de José María Eguren," LETRAS (Lima), Núm. 47 (1952), 67-105. Annotated bibliography. Contents: I. Libros. II. Poemas en revistas y periódicos. III. Reportajes. IV. Antologías. V. Libros que tratan sobre J.M. Eguren. VI. Prólogos. VII. Inéditos. VIII. Iconografía. IX. Referencias. A. Libros y folletos. B. Artículos sobre José María Eguren. X. Notas necrológicos y homenajes. XI. Indice onomástico.
Eguren, José María. OBRAS COMPLETAS. Lima: Mosca Azul Editores, 1974. 550p. "Bibliografía," pp. 531-550. Contents: I. Obras de Eguren. II. Sobre Eguren. A. Libros íntegramente dedicados a Eguren. B. Libros parcialmente dedicados a Eguren. C. Antologías. III. Ensayos y artículos sobre Eguren en periódicos y revistas. IV. Poemas dedicados a Eguren. V. Tesis sobre Eguren. VI. Bibliografías.
Flores, BEH, pp. 224-226. Contents: I. Edición principal. II. Otras ediciones. III. Referencias. IV. Bibliografía selecta (criticism).
Foster, Peruvian Lit., pp. 102-111. Contents: I. Bibliographies.

II. Critical Monographs and Dissertations. III. Critical Essays.

Nuñez, Estuardo. "José María Eguren: vida y obra," REVISTA HISPANICA MODERNA, 27, Núm. 3/4 (junio/octubre de 1961), 197-298. Contents: I. Vida. II. Antología. III. Bibliografía. A. Obra. 1. Libros. 2. Poesías sueltas y selecciones. 3. Traducciones. 4. Prosa: artículos, notas y prólogos. B. Estudios y homenajes.

Paredes Ruiz, Eudoxio. "BIBLIOGRAFIA DE JOSE MARIA EGUREN." Tesis. Lima: Biblioteca Nacional, Escuela de Bibliotecarios, 1958.

EICHELBAUM, SAMUEL (Argentina, 1894-1967)

Foster, Arg. Lit., pp. 361-363. Contents: I. Critical Monographs and Dissertations. II. Critical Essays.

Karavellas, Panos D. DRAMATURGIA DE SAMUEL EICHELBAUM. Montevideo: Géminis, 1976. 188p. "Bibliografía," pp. 183-186. Contents: I. Obras dramáticas de Samuel Eichelbaum (arranged by year, 1912-1960). II. Obras escritas en colaboración con Pedro E. Pico. III. Obras escritas con colaboración con Agustín Remón. IV. Estudios consultados para la elaboración de este estudio (references to Eichelbaum and his work).

EIRO, PAULO (Brazil, 1836-1871)

Schmidt, Afonso. A VIDA DE PAULO EIRO. São Paulo: Companhia Editôra Nacional, 1940. 288p. (Bibliotheca Pedagogica Brasileira, Sér. 5.a., Brasiliana, v. 182). "Bibliografia," pp. 271-288. Contents: I. Obras de Paulo Eiró. A. Poesia. B. Teatro. C. História. D. Prosa. II. Escritos sôbre Paulo Eiró.

ELIS, BERNARDO (Brazil, 1915-)

Almeida, Nelly Alves de. PRESENÇA LITERARIA DE BERNARDO ELIS. Goiás: Oficinas Gráficas da Imprensa da Universidade Federal de Goiás, 1970. 263p. "Bibliografia," pp. 223-244. Contents: I. Produção do autor. A. Romance. B. Novela. C. Conto. II. Sôbre Bernardo Elis.

Elis, Bernardo. SELETA DE BERNARDO ELIS. ORGANIZAÇAO DE GILBERTO MENDONÇA TELES. ESTUDO E NOTAS DO PROF. EVANILDO BECHARA. Rio de Janeiro: Livraria José Olympio, 1974. 179p. "Bibliografia," pp. 176-177. Contents: I. De Bernardo Elis. II. Outros trabalhos (inéditos). III. Sôbre Bernardo Elis. IV. Antologias contendo conto de Bernardo Elis.

Porter, pp. 222-226. Contents: I. Writings. II. References, Critical and Biographical.

ELIZONDO, SALVADOR (Mexico, 1932-)

Foster, Mex. Lit., pp. 124-126. Contents: Critical Books. II. Critical Essays.

Foster, 20th Century, pp. 80-81. Contents: I. Critical Books. II. Critical Essays.

EMETH, OMER (Pseudonym of EMILIO VAISSE) (Chile, 1860-1935)

Feliú Cruz, Guillermo. "Emilio Vaïsse (Omer Emeth) y la bibliografía general de Chile," in his HISTORIA DE LAS FUENTES DE LA BIBLIOGRAFIA CHILENA (Santiago de Chile: Biblioteca Nacional, 1968), v. 3, pp. 122-204. The bibliography (pp. 201-204) supplements Yutronic Cruz's bibliography.

Yutronic Cruz, Marina. PRESENCIA DE OMER EMETH EN LA LITERATURA CHILENA Y SU MAGISTERIO CRITICO. Santiago de Chile: Imprenta Chilena, 1955. 117p. "Bibliografía de Emilio Vaïsse," pp. 37-108. 2,688 entries.

ENEIDA (Pseudonym of MORAIS, ENEIDA COSTA) (Brazil, 1903-1971)

Leão, Veloso. ENEIDA, SIMPLEMENTE ENEIDA: ENSAIO BIO-BIBLIOGRAFICO. Rio de Janeiro: Livraria São José, 1973. 74p. Contents: I. Biografia. II. Livros publicados. III. Livros inéditos.

ENRIQUETA, MARIA (Pseudonym of MARIA ENRIQUETA CAMARILLO ROA DE PEREYRA) (Mexico 1869/75-1968).

A bibliography of her works and critical studies about María Enriqueta appears in Sidonia Carmen Rosenbaum's MODERN WOMEN POETS OF SPANISH AMERICA (New York: Hispanic Institute in the United States, 1945), pp. 258-260.

ERCILLA Y ZUNIGA, ALONSO DE (Chile, 1533-1594)

Aquila, August J. ALONSO DE ERCILLA Y ZUNIGA: A BASIC BIBLIOGRAPHY. London: Grant and Cutler, Ltd., 1975. 96p. (Research Bibliographies and Checklists, 11). Annotated bibliography with brief critical commentaries for those items author examined. Except for three works, only material published before December 31, 1972 is included. Contents: I. Editions and Translations of LA ARAUCANA. A. Spanish Editions. B. English Translations. C. French Translations. D. German Translations. E. Dutch Translations. F. Italian Translations. II. Other Works by Ercilla. A. Ballads and glosas. B. Sonnets. C. Approbations by Ercilla. III. Critical Studies. A. Books, Periodicals and Theses Wholly or Substantially Devoted to Ercilla or to Some Aspect of LA ARAUCANA. B. Articles, References, and Sections of Books. IV. Related Material Based on LA ARAUCANA. A. Plays. B. Poems. C. Novels. V. Miscellaneous Material. VI. Index.

Dinamarca, Salvador. LOS ESTUDIOS DE MEDINA SOBRE ERCILLA. New York: Hispanic Institute in the United States, 1953. 86p. Reprinting of a bibliographical essay published in ATENEA (Santiago de Chile), Año 29, Núm. 107 (septiembre/octubre de 1952), 341-374. "Bibliografía de los estudios de Medina sobre Ercilla," pp. 73-83.

Ercilla y Zúñiga, Alonso de. LA ARAUCANA. EDICION DEL CENTENARIO ... LA PUBLICA JOSE TORIBIO MEDINA. Santiago de Chile, 1910-1918. 4 vs. "Bibliografía de la Araucana," v. 4, pp. 1-60.

_______. LA ARAUCANA. EDICION, INTRODUCCION Y NOTAS DE MARCOS A. MORINIGO E ISAIAS LERNER. Madrid: Clásicos Castalia, 1979. 2 vs. "Noticia bibliográfica: Ediciones," v. 1, pp. 98-99 (arranged by year, 1569-1968). "Bibliografía selecta sobre el autor," pp. 100-106.

Southern, Richard Cameron. "A CRITICAL EDITION OF CERTAIN CANTOS OF LA ARAUCANA BY ALONSO DE ERCILLA Y ZUNIGA, WITH A DESCRIPTIVE BIBLIOGRAPHY OF EDITIONS BEFORE 1800." Ph.D., University of Cambridge, 1968.

ESCARDO, ROLANDO (Cuba, 1925-1960)

Foster, Cuban Lit., p. 204. Critical Essays.

ESCOBAR, FEDERICO (Panama, 1861-1912)

Hernández, Octavio Augusto. "Bibliografía de Federico Escobar," LOTERIA (PANAMA), Núm. 232 (junio de 1975), 65-103. Part I of the bibliography of the poet contains a listing of 269 poems published separately; 56 prose compilations, including letters, speeches, prologues, and articles in periodicals; and Part II includes 18 critical studies about the poet and his work.

ESCRAGNOLLE TAUNAY, ALFREDO DE, VISCONDE DE TAUNAY (Brazil, 1843-1899)

Mota, Artur. "Perfís acadêmicos: Visconde Taunay," REVISTA DA ACADEMIA BRASILEIRA DE LETRAS, Núm. 85 (janeiro de 1929), 42-61. Contents: I. "Bibliografia," pp. 42-55. A. Romances. B. Contos e narrativos. C. Narrativos de campanha. D. Viagens e descripções da natureza brasileira. E. Memórias. F. Crítica literária e artística. G. Teatro. H. História, corografia e etnologia brasileiras. I. Discursos. J. Biografias. K. Traduções. L. Colaboração na imprensa. M. Composições musicais. II. "Fontes para o estudo crítico," pp. 53-55.

Serpa, Phocion. "Impressões de Inocência," CADERNO DA BIBLIOTECA DA ACADEMIA CARIOCA DE LETRAS, Núm. 11 (1944), 37-67.

_______. VISCONDE DE TAUNAY. ENSAIO BIO-BIBLIOGRAFICO Rio de Janeiro: Academia Brasileira de Letras, 1952. 136p.

ESPEJO, FRANCISCO JAVIER EUGENIO DE SANTA CRUZ (Ecuador, 1747-1795)

Flores, BEH, pp. 17-18. Contents: I. Ediciones. II. Bibliografía selecta (criticism).

ESPINOSA MEDRANO, JUAN DE "EL LUNAREJO" (Peru, 1632-1688)

Foster, Peruvian Lit., pp. 112-114. Contents: I. Critical Monographs and Dissertations. II. Critical Essays.

ESPINOSA POLIT, AURELIO (Ecuador, 1894-1961)

Romero Arteta, Oswaldo. BIBLIOGRAFIA DEL P. AURELIO ESPINOSA POLIT S.I. Y RESEÑA DE LOS CRITICOS DE SUS

OBRAS. Quito: Editorial "Don Bosco," 1961. 194p. Contents: I. Bibliografía cronológica (1917-1961; 578 heavily annotated entries). II. Bibliografía de consulta. III. Bibliografía necrológica (45 entries). IV. Bibliografía analítica (subject index to work). V. Indice onomástico.

ESTEVES, JOSE DE JESUS (Puerto Rico, 1881/82-1918)
Foster, P.R. Lit., pp. 110-111. Contents: I. Dissertation. II. Critical Essays.

ESTORINO, ABELARDO (Cuba, 1925-)
Foster, Cuban Lit., p. 205. Critical Essays.

ESTRADA, GENARO (Mexico, 1887-1937)
Valle, Rafael Heliodoro. "A Contribution toward the Bibliography of Genaro Estrada," HISPANIC AMERICAN HISTORICAL REVIEW, 18, No. 1 (May 1938), 243-248. Contents: I. Bibliographical titles, etc. A. Artículos sueltos. B. Bibliography. C. Critique. D. History. E. Periodicals and Reviews in which He Collaborated. F. Prefaces. G. Translations. H. Opinions and Judgments Relative to Estrada.
_______. "Additional Items toward a Bibliography of Genaro Estrada," HISPANIC AMERICAN HISTORICAL REVIEW, 18, No. 2 (August 1938), 424-425.

ESTRELLA GUTIERREZ, FERNAN (Argentina, 1900-)
Podestá, Edgar F., and Jorge Wilfredo Viera. FERNAN ESTRELLA GUTIERREZ. Buenos Aires: Ministerio de Educación y Justicia, Dirección General de Cultura, Ediciones Culturales Argentinas, 1962. 198p. I. Resumen biográfico, pp. 177-179. II. Bibliografía, pp. 181-191. A. Obras de Fernán Estrella Gutiérrez. 1. Libros. a. Poesía. b. Cuento. c. Crítica e historia literatura. d. Didáctica. B. Separatas, folletos y opúsculos. Ediciones anotadas y prologadas. C. Traducciones de textos de Fernán Estrella Gutiérrez a otras lenguas. D. Algunas antologías en que figuran textos de Fernán Estrella Gutiérrez. E. Algunos estudios y juicios sobre Fernán Estrella Gutiérrez y sus obras.

ESTUPINAN BASS, NELSON (Ecuador, 1915-)
Jackson, Afro-Spanish, pp. 55-57. Contents: I. Works. II. Criticism.

EVIA, JACINTO DE (Ecuador, 1629?- ?)
Flores, BEH, pp. 10-11. Contents: I. Ediciones. II. Bibliografía selecta (criticism).

- F -

FAGUNDES VARELA, LUIS NICOLAU (Brazil, 1841-1875)

Cavalheiro, Edgard. FAGUNDES VARELA. 3 ed. São Paulo: Livraria Martins, 1956. 325p. "Obras de Fagundes Varela," pp. 271-273.

Mota, Artur. "Perfis acadêmicos, Cadeira No. 11: Fagundes Varela," REVISTA DA ACADEMIA BRASILEIRA DE LETRAS, Núm. 81 (setembro de 1928), 49-58. Contents: I. "Bibliografia," pp. 49-51 (1861-1880s). II. "Fontes para o estudo crítico," pp. 51-53.

FARIA, OTAVIO DE (Brazil, 1908-)

Reichmann, Ernani. O TRAGICO DE OTAVIO DE FARIA: LIVRO COMEMORATIVO AO 70º ANIVERSARIO DE NASCIMIENTO DE OTAVIO DE FARIA, 15-10-1978. Curitiba: Editora Universidade Federal do Paraná, 1978. 321p. "Obras de Otávio de Faria," pp. 323-324.

FEIJOO, SAMUEL (Cuba, 1914-)

Foster, Cuban Lit., pp. 206-207. Critical Essays.

FELICIANO MENDOZA, ESTER (Puerto Rico, 1917-)

Foster, P.R. Lit., pp. 111-112. Contents: I. Bibliography. II. Critical Essays.

FELIPE, CARLOS (Cuba, 1914-1975)

Foster, Cuban Lit., pp. 208-209. Critical Essays.

FELIU CRUZ, GUILLERMO (Chile, 1901-1973)

Cifuentes A., Manuel, and M. Guillermo Fuenzalida. "Ensayo de una bibliografía de Guillermo Feliú Cruz (1916-1972)," in HOMENAJE AL PROFESOR GUILLERMO FELIU CRUZ (Santiago de Chile: Editorial Andrés Bello, 1974), pp. 1125-1200. Contents: I. Orden cronológico, 1916-1972 (545 entries). II. Orden temático. A. Catálogos. B. Colecciones documentales, reimpresiones y otras ediciones. C. Críticas, comentarios y reseñas de obras. D. Estudios bibliográficos. E. Estudios biográficos. F. Estudios críticos y ensayos. G. Prólogos. H. Conferencias, discursos, homenajes. I. Informe sobre memorias de pruebas de los licenciados en leyes y profesores de estado. J. Política bibliotecaria. K. La censura cinematográfica. L. Varios.

FERNAN CISNEROS, LUIS (Peru, 1882-1954)

"Luis Fernán Cisneros," ANUARIO BIBLIOGRAFICO PERUANO, 1953/1954, 360-372. Contents: I. Biografía. II. Libros y folletos. III. Otras publicaciones. IV. Artículos. V. Poesías. VI. Referencias. VII. Notas necrológicas.

FERNANDES, CARLOS D. (Brazil, 1875-1942)

Martins, Eduardo. CARLOS D. FERNANDES: NOTICIA BIOBIBLIOGRAFICO. João Pessoa: U União, 1976. 231p.

FERNANDEZ, MACEDONIO (Argentina, 1874-1952)

Becco, Horacio Jorge. "Bibliografía de Macedonio Fernández," in César Fernández Moreno's INTRODUCCION A MACEDONIO FERNANDEZ (Buenos Aires: Ed. Talía, 1960, pp. 39-46. 147 items. Contents: I. Libros (1928-1953). II. Poemas, ensayos y cuentos (by year, 1896-1953). III. Fragmentos recogidos en antologías. IV. Estudios. V. Bibliografía.

_______. "Contribución a la bibliografía de Macedonio Fernández," in Noé Jitrik's LA NOVELA FUTURA DE MACEDONIO FERNANDEZ (Caracas: Universidad Central de Venezuela, 1973), pp. 125-144. Contents: I. Introducción. II. Libros. III. Crítica. IV. Bibliografías.

Flammersfeld, Waltraut. MACEDONIO FERNANDEZ (1874-1952): REFLEXION UND NEGATION ALS BESTIMUNGEN D. MODERNITAT. Frankfurt am Main: Peter Lang; Bern: H. Lang, 1976. 278p. (Hispanistische Studien, 4). "Literaturverzeichnis," pp. 259-278. Contents: I. Primärtexte. A. Buchveröffentlichungen (by year, 1928-1974). B. Veröffentlichungen in Zeitschriften (soweit nicht in den Büchern abgedrucht; by year, 1892-1970). C. Unveröffentlichte Briefe (soweit hier zitiert), Archiv Adolf de Obieta. II. Sekundärliteratur zur Macedonio Fernández.

Flores, BEH, pp. 226-227. Contents: I. Ediciones. II. Referencias. III. Bibliografía selecta (criticism).

Foster, Arg. Lit., pp. 364-372. Contents: I. Bibliographies. II. Critical Monographs and Dissertations. III. Critical Essays.

Lindstrom, Naomi. MACEDONIO FERNANDEZ. Lincoln, Nebraska: Society of Spanish and Spanish-American Studies, 1981. 138p. "Selected Bibliography," pp. 129-135. Contents: I. Bibliographies. II. Books by Macedonio Fernández. III. Books on Macedonio Fernández. IV. Critical Articles and Discussions in Books.

FERNANDEZ, PABLO ARMANDO (Cuba, 1930-)

Foster, Cuban Literature, p. 210. Critical Essays.

FERNANDEZ DE CASTRO, JOSE ANTONIO (Cuba, 1897-1951)

Castro de Morales, Lilia. BIBLIOGRAFIA DE JOSE ANTONIO FERNANDEZ DE CASTRO. La Habana: Publicaciones de la Biblioteca Nacional, 1955. 48p. Contents: I. Síntesis Biográfica de José Antonio Fernández de Castro. II. Salvador Bueno: "José Antonio Fernández de Castro, periodista e investigador." III. Bibliografía pasiva. IV. Bibliografía activa. 251 entries in total.

Fernández de Castro, José Antonio. ORBITA DE JOSE ANTONIO FERNANDEZ DE CASTRO. INTRODUCCION Y SELECCION DE SALVADOR BUENO. La Habana: Colección Orbita, 1966. 356p. Contents: I. "Biografía activa, 1922-1952," pp. 337-350. II. "Biografía pasiva," pp. 335-336.

FERNANDEZ DE LIZARDI, JOSE JOAQUIN (Mexico, 1776-1827)

Beltrán Martínez, Román. "Bibliografía de José Joaquín Fernández de Lizardi. El pensador mexicano," BOLETIN BIBLIOGRAFICO DE LA SECRETARIA DE HACIENDA Y CREDITO PUBLICO (México), 25 (Dic. 15, 1954), suppl.; 26 (Enero 1, 1955), suppl.; 27 (Enero 15, 1955), suppl.; 29 (Febrero 15, 1955), suppl.; 30 (Marzo 1, 1955), suppl.; 31 (Marzo 15, 1955), suppl.; 32 (Abril 1, 1955), suppl.; 33 (Abril 15, 1955), suppl.; and 36 (Junio 1, 1955), suppl. Supplements the earlier works of Luis González Obregón and J. R. Spell, with illustrations from the early editions of Lizardi's work. Contents: I. Novelas. A. Periquillos. B. Quijotita. C. Noches tristes. D. Don Catrín. II. Fábulas. III. Piezas dramáticas y pastorales. IV. Calendarios o periódicos y misceláneas.

Flores, BEH, pp. 19-20. Contents: I. Obras principales. II. Referencias. III. Bibliografía selecta (criticism).

Flores, NH, v. 1, 32-34. Contents: I. Ediciones principales. II. Referencias. III. Bibliografía selecta (criticism).

Foster, Mex. Lit., pp. 126-134. Contents: I. Bibliographies. II. Critical Monographs and Dissertations. III. Critical Essays.

González Obregón, Luis. DON JOSE JOAQUIN FERNANDEZ DE LIZARDI (EL PENSADOR MEXICANO). México: Ediciones Botas, 1938. 223p. Reprint of the 1888 edition: DON JOSE JOAQUIN FERNANDEZ DE LIZARDI (EL PENSADOR MEXICANO): APUNTES BIOGRAFICOS Y BIBLIOGRAFICOS. México: Oficina Tip. de la Secretaría de Fomento, 1888. 91p. The 1938 edition also includes J. R. Spell items, and locations from Chilean, Mexican, and U.S. libraries, archives, etc. Contents: I. Novelas: ediciones. II. Fábulas. III. Piezas dramáticas y pastorales. IV. Calendarios, periódicos y misceláneas. V. Folletos.

McKegney, James C. "Obras de Fernández de Lizardi en el Museo Británico de Londres," HISTORIOGRAFIA Y BIBLIOGRAFIAS AMERICANISTAS, Núm. 21 (1971), 167-196.

Moore, Ernest R. "Una bibliografía descriptiva. El Periquillo Sarniento de José Joaquín de Lizardi," REVISTA IBEROAMERICANA, 10, Núm. 30 (marzo de 1946), 383-403. Locations from 26 U.S. and Mexican libraries are included. Editions of the work, including English translations are listed by year of publication.

Oviedo y Pérez Tudela, Rocio. "Los folletos de Fernández de Lizardi," CUADERNOS BIBLIOGRAFICOS, Núm. 44 (1982), 123-134. The folletos are listed chronologically, 1812-1881, and then alphabetically. Not an exhaustive list, since many folletos are still unknown.

Palacios Sierra, Margarita. "Indice cronológico de las obras de Lizardi," pp. 180-206 and "Bibliografía de referencias," pp. 207-215 in her ESTUDIOS PRELIMINARES Y INDICES DEL PERIODISMO DE JOSE JOAQUIN FERNANDEZ DE LIZARDI. México: UNAM, 1965. (Tesis licenciatura en lengua y literatura españolas. Universidad Nacional Autónoma de México). 220p.

Radin, Paul. "An Annotated Bibliography of the Poems and Pamphlets of Fernández de Lizardi, 1824-1827," HISPANIC AMERICAN HISTORICAL REVIEW, 26, No. 2 (May 1946), 284-291. Works are listed by year and are annotated. U.S. and Mexican library locations are also included.

_______. AN ANNOTATED BIBLIOGRAPHY OF THE POEMS AND PAMPHLETS OF J. J. FERNANDEZ DE LIZARDI. San Francisco: California State Library-Sutro Branch, 1940. 2 vs. (Occasional Papers, Mexican History Series, No. 2, Pts. I and II). Volume 1 covers the period 1808-1809 and volume 2 the period 1820-1823. Holdings are listed for private and public libraries in the U.S. and Mexico.

_______. THE OPPONENTS AND FRIENDS OF LIZARDI. San Francisco: California State Library, Sutro Branch, 1939. 134p. (Occasional Papers, Mexican History Series, No. 1). Bibliography-Part I: Luis Espino, Mariano Soto, el Papista, José María Aza. Bibliography-Part II: Special pamphlets, anonymous pamphlets.

_______. SOME NEWLY DISCOVERED POEMS AND PAMPHLETS OF J. J. FERNANDEZ DE LIZARDI (EL PENSADOR MEXICANO). Prepared by the Works Progress Administration. San Francisco: State Library, Sutro Branch, 1939. 78p. Contents: I. Poems and Prose Dialogues previously unknown to bibliographers. II. Poems and Prose Dialogues previously known but not seen. III. Rare periodicals. IV. Miscellaneous.

Spell, Jefferson Rea. THE LIFE AND WORKS OF JOSE JOAQUIN FERNANDEZ DE LIZARDI. Philadelphia: University of Pennsylvania, 1931. 141p. (Publications of the Series in Romantic Languages and Literatures, 23). "Bibliography," pp. 118-138. "This bibliography makes no pretence at being complete, but is intended merely to supplement the list of the various works of Lizardi published in 1888 and 1925 by González Obregón by giving: (1) works of Lizardi hitherto uncited; (2) all available material on Lizardi written by contemporaries; (3) the various studies concerning his life and works published since death; and (4) the general and bibliographical works which contain information about him." Contents: I. Works of Lizardi hitherto Unknown to Bibliographers. A. Manuscripts. B. Printed Material. C. Newspaper Articles. D. New Details Concerning Known Pamphlets. II. Material on Lizardi. A. Contemporary Material. 1. Official Documents. 2. Contemporary Pamphlets. 3. Newspaper Articles. 4. Announcements. B. Bibliographical Works. C. Articles and Studies. D. General Works. Library and archival locations for Mexican, Chilean, and U.S. holdings are given.

FERNANDEZ DE PALENCIA, DIEGO (Peru, fl. 1571)

Lostaunau, Alejandro. "Diego Fernández (El Palentino)," BOLETIN DE LA BIBLIOTECA NACIONAL (Lima), Año 16, No. 26

(segundo trimestre de 1963), 13-18. Biobibliography and descriptive bibliography of first editions.

FERNANDEZ JUNCOS, MANUEL (Puerto Rico, 1912-)
Foster, P.R. Lit., pp. 112-113. Contents: I. Critical Monograph and Dissertation. II. Critical Essays.

FERNANDEZ MORENO, BALDOMERO (Argentina, 1886-1950)
Fernández Moreno, César and Manrique. BIBLIOGRAFIA DE FERNANDEZ MORENO. CON UN APENDICE POR HORACIO JORGE BECCO. Buenos Aires: Universidad de Buenos Aires, Facultad de Filosofía y Letras, Instituto de Literatura Argentina "Ricardo Rojas," 1961. 105p. (Guías Bibliográficas, 5). Contents: I. Obra. A. Verso. 1. Obra originaria (Chronological 1910-1950). 2. Obra ordenada (by topic or theme). B. Prosa. C. Variedades. D. Traducciones. II. Antologías. A. Antologías generales. B. Antologías especiales. C. Antologías de su obra. D. Muestras periodísticas. III. Crítica. A. Juicios de ubicación. 1. En la literatura hispanoamericana. 2. En la literatura argentina. 3. En la poesía argentina. 4. En las generaciones de poetas argentinos. 5. En determinados años literarios argentinos. B. Juicios sobre el conjunto de su obra. 1. Estudios generales. 2. Otros juicios sobre el conjunto de su obra. C. Juicios sobre aspectos de su obra. 1. Expresados con motivo de otros temas. 2. Exclusivamente sobre aspectos de su obra. IV. Miscelánea. A. Poemas dedicados a Fernández Moreno. B. Reportajes y encuestas. C. Recuerdos y anécdotas. D. Crónica periodística. E. Miscelánea sobre determinados poemas. F. Miscelánea oral. G. Miscelánea pedagógica. H. Miscelánea final. V. Apéndice: 1953-1961. A. Obra. 1. Verso. 2. Prosa. B. Antología. 1. Antologías generales y especiales. 2. Antologías de su obra. C. Crítica y miscelánea. D. Bibliografía. VI. Indices: De nombres citados, de publicaciones y sus abreviaturas. 1,059 referencias in total.
Flores, BEH, pp. 104-105. Contents: I. Ediciones. II. Referencias. III. Bibliografía selecta (criticism).
Foster, Arg. Lit., pp. 373-378. Contents: I. Bibliographies. II. Critical Monographs and Dissertation. III. Critical Essays.

FERNANDEZ RETAMAR, ROBERTO (Cuba, 1930-)
Flores, BEH, p. 227. Contents: I. Ediciones. II. Bibliografía selecta (criticism).
Foster, Cuban Lit., pp. 211-213. Contents: I. Dissertation. II. Critical Essays.

FERNANDEZ Y SANTANA, CARLOS FELIPE (Cuba, 1914-1975)
"Carlos Felipe Fernández y Santiago (1914-1975): Bio-bibliografía," BIBLIOGRAFIA CUBANA, 1975, 206-207. Contents: I. Biografía. II. Bibliografía activa.

FERRANDO, JOSE D. (Peru, 1903-1947)
"José Ferrando: bibliografía," BOLETIN DE LA BIBLIOTECA NACIONAL (Lima), Años 11/12, Nos. 17/18 (1954/1955), 179-193. Contents: I. Novela. II. Artículos (by year).

FERREIRA, JOSE RIBAMAR (Brazil, 1930-)
Moraes, pp. 118-119. Major works by and about the author.

FIANSON SCHMIDT, JOSE (Peru, 1870-1952)
"José Fianson Schmidt," ANUARIO BIBLIOGRAFICO PERUANO, 1951/1952, 302-317. Contents: I. Antologías. II. Poesías. III. Referencias.

FIGAROLA-CANEDA, DOMINGO (Cuba, 1852-1926)
Foster, Cuban Lit., pp. 214-215. Contents: I. Bibliography. II. Critical Monograph. III. Critical Essays.

FIGUEIREDO, FIDELINO DE SOUSA (1888-1967)
IDEARIO CRITICO DE FIDELINO DE FIGUEIREDO. COMEMORAÇAO DO JUBILEU DE OURO DO PROFESSOR DOUTOR FIDELINO DE FIGUEREDO. ORGANIZAÇAO, PREFACIO E NOTAS DE CARLOS DE ASSIS PEREIRA. São Paulo, 1962. 529p. Apêndice II: "Bibliografia de Fidelino de Figueiredo por Neusa Dias de Macedo," pp. 447-485. 313 partially annotated entries arranged by year, 1905-1961. Apêndice III: "Bibliografia acêrca de Fidelino de Figueiredo por Neusa Dias de Macedo," pp. 489-495. 105 entries.

FIGUEIREDO, JACKSON (Brazil, 1891-1928)
Nogueira, Hamilton. JACKSON DE FIGUEIREDO. 2ed. Rio de Janeiro: Livraria Hachette; São Paulo: Edições Loyala, 1976. 146p. "Bibliografia," pp. 145-146. Includes the works of and about Jackson de Figueiredo.

FINGERIT, MARCOS (Argentina, 1904-)
Fernández Leys, Alberto. "Bibliografía de Marcos Fingerit," BOLETIN DEL INSTITUTO DE LITERATURA DE LA PROVINCIA DE BUENOS AIRES (La Plata), Núm. 2 (1971), 99-107. Partially annotated entries. Contents: I. Libros publicados. II. Folletos. III. Traducciones realizadas por Marcos Fingerit. IV. Traducciones de sus poemas. V. Libros y plaquettes con prólogos de Marcos Fingerit. VI. Ediciones de arte tipográfico. Plaquettes, fuera de comercio. Labor editorial y de arte gráfica. VII. Antologías donde figura la obra de Marcos Fingerit. VIII. Libros que contienen antecedentes de la obra literaria de Marcos Fingerit. IX. Colaboraciones de Marcos Fingerit en revistas y periódicos. X. Dirección de revistas y cuadernos literarios. XI. Estudios y ensayos sobre la obra de Marcos Fingerit. XII. Conferencias, charlas y cursillos. XIII. Cargos honoríficos.

FLORIT, EUGENIO (Cuba, 1903-)
Castellanos Collins, María. TIERRA, MAR Y CIELO EN LA POESIA

DE EUGENIO FLORIT. Miami: Ediciones Universal, 1976. 67p. "Bibliografía de Eugenio Florit," pp. 57-63. Contents: I. Obras de Florit. A. Libros. B. Artículos y reseñas de libros. C. Prólogos y palabras. D. Poemas sueltos. II. Libros y artículos sobre Eugenio Florit. Only citations to 1971 are included in the bibliography section.

Foster, Cuban Lit., pp. 216-219. Contents: I. Bibliographies. II. Critical Monographs and Dissertations. III. Critical Essays.

Parajón, Mario. EUGENIO FLORIT Y SU POESIA. Madrid: Impreso en Tordesillas, O.G., 1977. 206p. "Bibliografía," pp. 191-201. Contents: I. Libros. II. Artículos. III. Prólogos y palabras. IV. Poemas sueltos. V. Libros y artículos sobre Eugenio Florit. VI. Antologías y obras generales que incluyen estudios sobre Florit y selecciones de su obra.

FONSECA, CARLOS ALBERTO see FONSECA RECAVARREN, NELLY

FONSECA RECAVARREN, NELLY (Pseudonym of CARLOS ALBERTO FONSECA) (Peru, 1920-1963)

Ochoa Garzón, Carmen. "Nelly Fonseca Recavarrén," ANUARIO BIBLIOGRAFICO PERUANO, 1961/1963, 489-526. Contents: I. Cronobiografía. II. Libros, folletos. III. Otras publicaciones. IV. Artículos y ensayos. V. Poesías. VI. Leyendas. VII. Cartas. VIII. Notas críticas. IX. Traducciones. X. Reportajes. XI. Referencias. XII. Necrológicas.

FONTES, HERMES (Brazil, 1888-1930)

Porter, p. 215. Contents: I. Writings. II. References, Critical and Biographical.

FONTURA, ADELINO (Brazil, 1855-1884)

Moraes, pp. 49-51. Major works by and about the author.

FRANÇA JUNIOR, JOAQUIM JOSE DA (Brazil, 1838-1890)

Mota, Artur. "Perfís acadêmicos, Cadeira No. 12: França Júnior," REVISTA DA ACADEMIA BRASILEIRA DE LETRAS, Núm. 83 (novembro de 1928), pp. 320-327. Contents: I. "Bibliografia," pp. 321-323 (1861-1889). II. "Fontes para o estudo crítico," p. 324.

FRANCO, LUIS (Argentina, 1898-)

Panelas, Carlos. CONVERSACIONES CON LUIS FRANCO. Buenos Aires: Francisco Courbet, Ediciones de Poesía, 1978. 85p. "Obras de Luis Franco," pp. 81-84. Contents: I. Obra poética. II. Obra en prosa. III. En prensa.

FRANCO OPPENHEIMER, FELIX (Puerto Rico, 1912-)

Foster, P.R. Lit., pp. 113-114. Contents: I. Critical Monographs and Dissertation. II. Critical Essays.

González Torres, Rafael. LA OBRA POETICA DE FELIX FRANCO OPPENHEIMER: ESTUDIO TEMATICO-ANALITICO-ESTILISTICO.

Río Piedras: Editorial Universitaria, Universidad de Puerto Rico, 1981. 246p. "Bibliografía," pp. 181-192. Contents: I. Obras de Félix Franco Oppenheimer. A. Poesía. B. Antologías. C. Prosa. II. Estudios sobre la obra del autor. A. Libros. B. Ensayos y artículos.

"FRAY CANDIL" see BOBADILLA, EMILIO

"FRAY MOCHO" (Pseudonym of JOSE SIXTO ALVAREZ) (Argentina, 1858-1903)

Barcia, Pedro Luis. FRAY MOCHO DESCONOCIDO. Buenos Aires: Ediciones del Mar de Solís, 1979. 370p. "Fechación del material publicado en Caras y Caretas con los seudónimos de Fray Mocho y Fabio Carrizo," pp. 361-370. Covers Año 1 (1898) to año 6 (1903) of the journal Caras y Caretas.

Flores, BEH, pp. 57-58. Contents: I. Edición principal. II. Otras ediciones. III. Bibliografía selecta (criticism).

Foster, Arg. Lit., pp. 147-149. Contents: I. Critical Monographs. II. Critical Essays.

FREYRE, GILBERTO (Brazil, 1900-)

"Catálogo da exposição sôbre a obra de Gilberto Freyre," BOLETIM DA BIBLIOTECA DE CAMARA DOS DIPUTADOS (Brasília), 15, Núm. 3 (setembro/dezembro 1966), 489-516. A private collection of the works of Freyre which was exhibited in honor of his visit to Brasília. 133 entries, which include articles, books, speeches, essays. In addition, there are a few items concerning Freyre and his work.

Fonseca, Edson Nery da. UM LIVRO COMPLETA MEIO SECULO. Recife: Editôra Massangana, Fundação Joaquim Nabuco, 1983. 157p. "Referências bibliográficas," pp. 99-113. Contents: I. De Gilberto Freyre. A. Outras edições brasileiras (Casa-grande & senzala). B. Outras edições (translations, by language). C. Adaptações, paráfrases, etc. (Casa-grande & senzala). II. Sobre Gilberto Freyre. "Cronologia de Casa-grande & senzala," pp. 121-125 (bibliocronologia).

Freyre, Gilberto. TEMPO MORTE E OUTROS TEMPOS: TRECHOS DE UM DIARIO DE ADOLESCENCIA E PRIMEIRA MOCIDADE, 1915-1930. Rio de Janeiro: José Olympio, 1975. 267p. "Bibliografia de Gilberto Freyre," pp. 259-267. Contents: I. Prêmios. II. Livros (by year, 1933-1974). III. Alguns opúsculos (by year 1922-1972). IV. Adaptação teatral. V. Música. VI. Festejos populares. VII. Livros sôbre Gilberto Freyre.

FRIAS, HERBERTO (Mexico, 1870-1925)

Brown, James W. "Bibliografía de Heriberto Frías," BOLETIN DEL INSTITUTO DE INVESTIGACIONES BIBLIOGRAFICAS (Universidad Nacional Autónoma de México), 2, Núm. 1 (1970), 137-152. 16 library locations in the United States and Mexico are included for the 224 entries listed. Contents: I. Novelas, historias, colecciones, folletos. II. Artículos, cuentos y "vignettes" costumbristas. III. Versos. IV. Obras inéditas.

FUENTES, CARLOS (Mexico, 1928-)

Becco and Foster, pp. 106-118. Contents: I. Obras. II. Traducciones. III. Crítica.

Faris, Wendy B. CARLOS FUENTES. New York: Frederick Ungar, 1983. 241p. "Bibliography," pp. 225-233. Contents: I. Works by Carlos Fuentes; Translations. II. Works on Carlos Fuentes. A. Books. B. Interviews. C. Articles.

Flores, BEH, pp. 105-109, 182. Contents: I. Edición principal. II. Otras ediciones. III. Referencias. IV. Bibliografía selecta (criticism).

Flores, NH, v. 4, pp. 493-500. Contents: I. Ediciones principales. II. Referencias. III. Antología crítica. IV. Bibliografía selecta (criticism).

Foster, Mex. Lit., pp. 134-155. Contents: I. Bibliographies. II. Critical Monographs and Dissertations. III. Critical Essays.

Foster, 20th Century, pp. 81-89. Contents: I. Bibliographies. II. Critical Books. III. Critical Essays.

Jackson, Richard L. "Hacia una bibliografía de y sobre Carlos Fuentes," REVISTA IBEROAMERICANA, 31, Núm. 60 (julio/diciembre de 1965), 297-301. Includes 57 entries; however, very few of them are from Mexican journals. Contents: I. Obras de Carlos Fuentes. A. Cuentos. B. Novelas. C. Prólogos, artículos, reseñas y ensayos. II. Sobre Carlos Fuentes.

Reeve, Richard M. "An Annotated Bibliography on Carlos Fuentes: 1949-1969," HISPANIA, 53, No. 3 (September 1970), 597-652. This work focuses upon the criticism about Fuentes published in Mexico and in the U.S., and to a lesser degree in Latin America and Europe. Contents: I. Works by Fuentes. A. Books. B. Contributions to Periodicals and Newspapers. 1. Literary articles. 2. General cultural and political articles. 3. Short stories. 4. Fragments of unpublished novels. 5. Book reviews. 6. Motion picture scripts. 7. Motion picture reviews. C. Prologues about Fuentes. A. General studies exclusively on Fuentes. B. Briefer mention of Fuentes in books and periodicals. C. Bibliographies. D. Doctoral dissertations and Master's theses.

_______. "Carlos Fuentes y la novela: una bibliografía escogida," pp. 475-494, in HOMENAJE A CARLOS FUENTES. Long Island City, N.Y.: Las Américas Publishing Co., 1971. 494p. Contents: I. La novela de Carlos Fuentes (by work: editions, translations, and reviews). II. Otros libros de Carlos Fuentes. III. Crítica de Carlos Fuentes sobre la novela. A. La novela mexicana e hispanoamericana. B. La novela norteamericana y europea. IV. Una selección de estudios sobre Carlos Fuentes.

_______. "La narrativa y teatro de Carlos Fuentes: una bibliografía selecta," I, pp. 77-115 in Fuentes, Carlos. OBRAS COMPLETAS. México: Aguilar Editor, 1974. Contents: I. Cuentos y novelas cortas (by work; including editions, translations, studies, and reviews). II. Novelas (by work; including editions, translations, studies, and reviews). III. Teatro (by work; including editions, translations, studies, and reviews). IV. otros libros de Carlos Fuentes. V. Estudios generales sobre Carlos Fuentes.

FUENTES, NORBERTO (Cuba, 1943-)
Foster, Cuban Lit., p. 220. Critical Essays.

FUENTES BENAVIDES, RAFAEL DE LA see ADAN, MARTIN

- G -

GABALDONI, LUIS E. (Peru)
Lucero Nieto, Teodoro. SINTESIS BIBLIOGRAFICA DEL ESCRITOR LUIS E. GABALDONI. Lima: Perugraph Ed., 1982. 55p.

GAGINI CHAVARRIA, CARLOS (Costa Rica, 1865-1925)
Ureña de Molina, Cecilia. "Carlos Gagini Chavarría (1865-1925): Hechos y obras," REVISTA DE FILOLOGIA Y LINGUISTICA DE LA UNIVERSIDAD DE COSTA RICA, Núm. 5 (mayo de 1977), 3-4. Contents: I. Obras filológicas y didácticas. II. Obras inéditas. III. Obras literarias. A. De cuentos. B. De teatro. C. De novelas. IV. Obras de filosofía y psicología. V. Obras poéticas.

GALINDO, SERGIO (Mexico, 1926-)
Foster, Mex. Lit., pp. 155-156. Critical Essays.

GALLEGOS, ROMULO (Venezuela, 1884-1969)
Becco, Horacio Jorge. "Doña Bárbara de Rómulo Gallegos: bibliografía en su cincuentenario (1929-1979)," ACTUALIDADES (CARACAS), Núm. 5 (agosto de 1979), 49-87. Contents: I. Obras de referencia. II. Ediciones de Doña Bárbara (arranged chronologically, 1929-1979). III. Ediciones de obras completas. IV. Traducciones. V. Estudios galleguianos. VI. Addenda. The bibliography contains 357 entries, mostly annotated.
Caracas. Universidad Católica Andrés Bello. Seminario de Literatura Venezolana. CONTRIBUCION A LA BIBLIOGRAFIA DE ROMULO GALLEGOS. Caracas: Ediciones de la Gobernación del Distrito Federal, 1969. (Colección bibliografías, 1). 405p. 2,041 entries. Contents: I. Ficha bio-bibliográfica de Rómulo Gallegos. II. Referencias bibliográficas. III. Obras mayores. A. Novela. B. Cuento. C. Ensayo. D. Teatro. IV. Miscelánea. V. Epistolario. VI. Biografía y crítica (libros, folletos, capítulos, artículos y referencias sobre el autor y su obra).
Dunham, Lowell. ROMULO GALLEGOS: VIDA Y OBRA. México: De Andrea, 1957. 327p. "Bibliografía," pp. 301-327. Contents: I. Obras. A. Ensayos y artículos. B. Cuentos. C. Novelas. D. Discursos y correspondencia. E. Drama. F. Obras completas. II. Grabaciones. III. Crítica y documenta-

ción. A. Libros. B. Revistas. C. Periódicos. D. Material no publicado (mainly dissertations and theses).

Flores, BEH, pp. 109-112. Contents: I. Edición principal. II. Otras ediciones. III. Referencias. IV. Bibliografía selecta (criticism).

Foster, 20th Century, pp. 89-98. Contents: I. Bibliographies. II. Critical Books. III. Critical Essays.

Rivas Dugarte, Rafael Angel. "Rómulo Gallegos en publicaciones periódicas del exterior: una hemerografía," ACTUALIDADES (CARACAS), Núm. 5 (agosto de 1979), 89-130. Contents: I. Del autor. II. Sobre el autor. III. Indice temático. The bibliography includes 569 entries.

Shaw, Donald L. "Rómulo Gallegos: suplemento a una bibliografía," REVISTA IBEROAMERICANA, 37, Núm. 75 (abril/junio de 1971), 447-457. Supplements and updates the CONTRIBUCION A LA BIBLIOGRAFIA DE ROMULO GALLEGOS work. An alphabetical listing of critical works about Gallegos and his work.

Subero, Efraín. GALLEGOS: MATERIALES PARA EL ESTUDIO DE SU VIDA Y DE SU OBRA. Caracas: Ediciones del Congreso de la República, 1980. 4vs. The bibliography is contained in volumes 3 and 4. 3,644 partially annotated entries covering works to 1979 under the following categories: I. Referencias bibliográficas. II. Obras mayores. A. Novela. B. Cuento. C. Ensayo. D. Teatro. III. Miscelánea. IV. Obra dispersa. V. Biografía y crítica. There is also an índice onomástico.

GALVAO, PATRICIA REHDER (Brazil, 1910-1962)

Campos, Augusto de. PAGU: PATRICIA GALVAO: VIDA-OBRA. 2a edição. São Paulo: Editôra Brasiliense, 1982. 354p. "Bibliografia," pp. 349-351. Contents: I. Obras de Patrícia Galvão. II. Sôbre Patrícia Galvão. "Roteiro de uma vida-obra," pp. 319-347 (includes bibliographical information).

GALVAO, TRAJANO (Brazil, 1830-1864)

Moraes, pp. 30-32. Major works by and about the author.

GALVEZ, JOSE (Peru, 1885-1957)

Oliver Belmas, Antonio. JOSE GALVEZ Y EL MODERNISMO. Lima: Universidad Nacional Mayor de San Marcos, 1974. 173p. "Bibliografía," pp. 171-173. Contents: I. Bibliografía de José Gálvez. II. Bibliografía sobre José Gálvez.

GALVEZ, MANUEL (Argentina, 1882-1962)

Agresti, Mabel Susana. LITERATURA Y REALIDADES. LA VISION DEL PAIS EN ALGUNAS NOVELAS DE MANUEL GALVEZ. Mendoza: Universidad Nacional de Cuyo, 1981. 322p. Contents: Obras de Manuel Gálvez (4pp.) I. Novelas. II. Novelas históricas. III. Cuentos y relatos. IV. Poesía. V. Teatro. VI. Ensayo. VII. Biografías. VIII. Memorias.

Flores, BEH, pp. 228-230. Contents: I. Ediciones principales. II. Otras ediciones. III. Referencias. IV. Bibliografía selecta (criticism).

Foster, Arg. Lit., pp. 379-388. Contents: I. Bibliography. II. Critical Monographs and Dissertations. III. Critical Essays.

Foster, 20th Century, pp. 99-102. Contents: I. Bibliographies. II. Critical Books. III. Critical Essays.

Kisnerman, Natalio. BIBLIOGRAFIA DE MANUEL GALVEZ. Buenos Aires: Fondo Nacional de las Artes, 1964? 75p. (Bibliografía Argentina de Artes y Letras, Compilaciones Especiales, No. 17). Contents: I. Obras del autor. A. Poesía. B. Teatro. C. Novela y cuentos cortos. D. Ensayos. E. Biografías. F. Colaboraciones en publicaciones periódicas. G. Entrevistas, encuestas, reportajes. II. Prólogos y estudios de obras de otros autores. III. Textos del autor en diversas antologías. IV. Traducciones de obras del autor. V. Traducciones de obras de otros autores. VI. Crítica y biografía. Title, names, and illustration indexes are included for the 1,165 publications listed.

Roca Martínez, José Luis. "Contribución a la bibliografía literaria del dictador Juan Manuel Rosas," REVISTA DE INDIAS, Núm. 163/164 (enero/junio de 1981), 203-262. A bibliographic essay arranged under the following categories: I. Breves consideraciones sobre el dictador hispanoamericano como tema literario. II. Don Juan Manuel de Rosas (1793-1877) en la literatura argentina (by author). III. Manuel Gálvez (1882-1962) y sus escenas de la epoca de Rosas. IV. Cronología de la composición y del desarrollo de la acción de las novelas del ciclo rosito. V. Ideaología y estética del ciclo rosito. VI. Análisis y características de los personajes. VII. "El Gaucho de los cerridos." VIII. "El General Quiroga." IX. "La Ciudad pintada de rojo." X. "Tiempo de odio y angustia." XI. "Han tocado a degüello." XII. "Bajo la garra anglo-francesa." XIII. "Y así cayó Don Juan Manuel..."

GALVEZ BARRENECHEA, JOSE (Peru, 1885-1957)

"José Gálvez Barrenechea," ANUARIO BIBLIOGRAFICO PERUANO, 1955/1957, 471-514. Contents: I. Biografía. II. Libros y folletos. III. Artículos y ensayos. IV. Cuentos. V. Cartas, memorias, etc. VI. Discursos, conferencias. VII. Poesías. VIII. Notas bibliográficas. IX. Reportajes. X. Referencias. XI. Notas necrológicas.

GAMA, JOSE BASILIO DA (Brazil, 1740-1795)

Braga, Osvaldo. "O URUGUAI E SUAS EDIÇOES. Nota bibliográfica de Osvaldo Melo Braga," in José Basílio da Gama's O URAGUAI. EDIÇAO COMEMORATIVA DO SEGUNDO CENTENARIO, ANOTADA POR AFRANIO PEIXOTO, RODOLFO GARCIA E OSVALDO BRAGA (Rio de Janeiro, 1941), pp. 153-172. The work also includes a "Bibliografia de alguns estudos sôbre O URUGUAI."

Gama, José Basílio da. THE URUGUAY (A HISTORICAL ROMANCE OF SOUTH AMERICA). THE SIR RICHARD F. BURTON TRANSLATION. EDITED, WITH INTRODUCTION, NOTES, AND BIBLIOGRAPHY, BY FREDERICK C. H. GARCIA AND EDWARD F. STANTON. Berkeley: University of California Press, 1982. 264p. "Selected Bibliography," pp. 251-256. I. Edition of O Uruguai. II. Other Works by José Basílio de Gama. III. Works on José Basílio da Gama.

Porter, pp. 216-218. Contents: I. Writings. II. References, Critical and Biographical.

GAMA, LUIS "GETULINO" (Brazil, 1830-1882)

Porter, pp. 218-219. Contents: I. Writings. II. References, Critical and Biographical.

GAMBARO, GRISELDA (Argentina, 1928-)

Corvalán, p. 55. Contents: I. Works. II. Critical Works On.

Foster, Arg. Lit., pp. 389-391. Contents: I. Dissertations. II. Critical Essays.

GAMBOA, FEDERICO (Mexico, 1864-1939)

Flores, BEH, pp. 230-232. Contents: I. Edición principal. II. Otras ediciones. III. Referencias. IV. Bibliografía selecta (criticism).

Foster, Mex. Lit., pp. 156-161. Contents: I. Bibliographies. II. Critical Monographs and Dissertations. III. Critical Essays.

Foster, 20th Century, pp. 102-104. Contents: I. Bibliographies. II. Critical Books. III. Critical Essays.

Hooker, Alexander C. LA NOVELA DE FEDERICO GAMBOA. Madrid: Plaza Mayor, 1971. 141p. (Colección Scholar, 6). The work incorporates a bibliography (pp. 137-141), consisting not only of entries about Gamboa's novels but also of selective items related to the Spanish American novel in general.

Moore, Ernest R. "Bibliografía de obras y crítica de Federico Gamboa, 1864-1939," REVISTA IBEROAMERICANA, 2, Núm. 3 (Abril de 1940), 271-279. Contents: I. Novela. II. Teatro. III. Folletos y artículos. IV. Autobiografía. V. Traducciones. VI. Manuscritos. VII. Crítica. A. Libros. B. Artículos.

GANA, FEDERICO (Chile, 1867-1926)

"Cartillas biobibliográficas de autores chilenos: Federico Gana (Federico Gana y Gana). Santiago, 1867-1926. Cuentista," BOLETIN DEL INSTITUTO DE LITERATURA CHILENA (Universidad de Chile, Santiago), Año 1, Núm. 2 (mayo de 1962), 8-13. Contents: I. Obras. II. Publicaciones póstumas. III. Traducciones realizadas por Federico Gana. IV. Referencias. V. Tabla biográfica. VI. Otros datos.

Foster, Chilean Lit., pp. 91-92. Contents: I. Bibliographies. II. Critical Books and Theses. III. Critical Essays.

GANDARA, CARMEN (Argentina, 1903-)

Guasta, Eugenio. CARMEN GANDARA. Buenos Aires: Ediciones Culturales Argentinas, Ministerio de Educación y Justicia, Dirección General de Cultura, 1963. 75p. "Bibliografía de Carmen Gándara," pp. 71-73. 65 items. Contents: I. Novela. II. Cuento. III. Poesía. IV. Ensayos. V. Artículos y notas. VI. Crítica. VII. Notas y comentarios críticos sobre Carmen Gándara.

GARCIA CALDERON, FRANCISCO (Peru, 1883-1953)

"Francisco García Calderón Rey," ANUARIO BIBLIOGRAFICO PERUANO, 1953/1954, 379-399. Contents: I. Libros y folletos. II. Otras publicaciones. III. Artículos y ensayos. IV. Cartas y discursos. V. Notas bibliográficas. VI. Referencias.

Rodríguez, Carmen Rosa. "BIBLIOGRAFIA DE FRANCISCO GARCIA CALDERON." Tesis. Lima: Biblioteca Nacional, Escuela de Bibliotecarios, 1955.

GARCIA CALDERON, VENTURA (Peru, 1886-1959)

Flores, BEH, pp. 232-233. Contents: I. Ediciones principales. II. Otras ediciones. III. Bibliografía selecta (criticism).

Foster, Peruvian Lit., pp. 115-119. Contents: I. Bibliographies. II. Critical Monographs and Dissertations. III. Critical Essays.

Guijón, Ana María. "Ventura García Calderón Rey," ANUARIO BIBLIOGRAFICO PERUANO, 1958/1960, 509-532. Contents: I. Biografía. II. Libros y folletos. III. Otras publicaciones. IV. Poesías, cuentos, leyendas, etc. V. Cartas, discursos. VI. Reportajes. VII. Referencias. VIII. Notas necrológicas.

GARCIA GOYENA, RAFAEL (Guatemala, 1766-1823)

Flores, BEH, pp. 20-21. Contents: I. Ediciones. II. Bibliografía selecta (criticism).

García Goyena, Rafael. FABULAS. PROLOGO, BIBLIOGRAFIA Y NOTAS DE CARLOS SAMAYOA CHINCHILLA. Guatemala, C.A.: Ediciones del Gobierno de Guatemala, 1950. 167p. "Bibliografía," pp. liii-lvi. Contents: I. Ediciones de las fábulas del doctor Rafael García Goyena. II. Sobre García Goyena.

GARCIA MARQUEZ, GABRIEL (Colombia, 1928-)

Abenoza, Bianca Ossorio. "GABRIEL GARCIA MARQUEZ JUZGADO POR LA CRITICA: UNA BIBLIOGRAFIA ANALITICA Y COMENTADA." Ph.D., University of Virginia, 1979. 378p. "The main body of the dissertation presents, in chronological order, summaries of and commentaries on criticism devoted to García Márquez between 1955 and 1974. Books, theses, and essays are treated at greater length than journalistic writings. An appendix is also included that lists articles which appeared after 1975. Finally, there is an index of authors and an index of themes to make the dissertation useful as a research tool." (DISSERTATION ABSTRACTS INTERNATIONAL, 40 [December 1979], 3332A).

Benson, John. "García Márquez en Alternativa (1974-1979): una bibliografía comentada," CHASQUI, 8 (mayo de 1979), 69-81. Contents: I. Artículos escritos por García Márquez en Alternativa (1974-1979). 28 items listed chronologically. II. Artículos sobre García Márquez en Alternativa (1974-1979). 14 items.

Darío Carrillo, Germán. LA NARRATIVA DE GABRIEL GARCIA MARQUEZ (ENSAYOS DE INTERPRETACION). Madrid: Ediciones de Arte y Bibliofilia, 1975. 169p. "Bibliografía selecta," pp. 161-165. Contents: I. Cronología de la obra de García Márquez (Primeras ediciones, 1955-1975). II. Sobre García Márquez.

Fau, Margaret Eustella. GABRIEL GARCIA MARQUEZ: AN ANNOTATED BIBLIOGRAPHY, 1947-1979. Westport, Conn.: Greenwood Press, 1980. 198p. Contents: Primary Sources. A. The Narrative Works of Gabriel García Márquez. B. Nonfiction Articles and Books. C. Movie Picture Guides. D. Stories in Anthologies. E. Translations. II. Secondary Sources. A. Bibliographies on Gabriel García Márquez. B. Books and Doctoral Dissertations on Gabriel García Márquez. C. Chapters and Sections in Books. D. Critical Articles. E. Interviews. F. About Gabriel García Márquez: The Man, The Reporter, The Writer. G. Reviews of Gabriel García Márquez's Books and Stories (by work). III. Author Index.

Flores, BEH, pp. 112-115, 182-183. Contents: I. Ediciones. II. Referencias. III. Bibliografía selecta (criticism).

Foster, 20th Century, pp. 105-116. Contents: I. Bibliographies. II. Critical Books. III. Critical Essays.

García Márquez, Gabriel. ENTRE CACHACOS. RECOPILACION Y PROLOGO DE JACQUES GILARD. Barcelona: Burguera, 1982. 2vs. (Obra periodística, 2 and 3). "Cronología," v. 1 [12p.] is an index to articles that appeared in El Espectador (Bogotá), febrero de 1954-julio de 1955.

_______. TEXTOS COSTENOS. OBRA PERIODISTICA, TOMO I. RECOPILACION Y PROLOGO DE JACQUES GILARD. Barcelona: Bruguera, 1981. 891p. "Cronología," pp. 57-72. Indexes articles in El Universal (Cartagena, 1948-1949) and El Heraldo (Barranquilla, 1950-1952).

GABRIEL GARCIA MARQUEZ. EDICION DE PETER G. EARLE. Madrid: Ediciones Taurus, 1981. 294p. "Bibliografía," pp. 287-294. 83 entries. Contents: I. Libros: Primeras ediciones (1955-1981). II. Entrevistas. III. Bibliografía sobre G. García Márquez. A. Bibliografías. B. Libros. C. Recopilaciones críticas. D. Artículos y ensayos (no se incluyen los textos recogidos en esta antología).

Gilard, Jacques. "Cronología de los primeros textos literarios de García Márquez (1947-1955)," REVISTA DE CRITICA LITERARIA LATINOAMERICANA (Lima), Año 2, Núm. 3 (1976), 95-106. Analytical study of his work and the dating of the first appearance of his 21 stories.

_______. "La obra periodística de García Márquez, Cartagena,

1948-49," ECO (BOGOTA), Núm. 179 (setiembre de 1975), 525-534. A chronologically arranged bibliography of García Márquez's periodical writings for El Universal from Friday, May 21, 1948 to Friday, October 7, 1949.

_______. "La obra periodística de García Márquez, Barranquilla, 1950-1952," ECO (BOGOTA), Núm. 182 (diciembre de 1975), 168-198. A chronological listing of all the periodical articles of García Márquez from January 1950 to December 1952 which appeared in the column, "La jirafa" of El Heraldo under the pseudonymn of Septimus.

_______. "La obra periodística de García Márquez, 1954-1956," REVISTA DE CRITICA LITERARIA LATINOAMERICANA, Núm. 4 (1976), 151-176. "Bibliografía," pp. 163-176. The bibliography is an index to García Márquez's writings in El Espectador of Bogotá, febrero 1954-diciembre 1955 and El Independiente from marzo 1956-abril 1956. Articles are listed by year and then by month and day.

Lastra, Pedro. "Contribución a la bibliografía de Gabriel García Márquez," LETRAS (Lima), Núm. 78/79 (1967), 145-148. Contents: I. Obras (1955-1967). II. Referencias (annotated critical studies on García Márquez).

Levine, Suzanne Jill. EL ESPEJO HABLADO: UN ESTUDIO DE "CIEN ANOS DE SOLEDAD." Caracas: Monte Avila Editores, 1975. 162p. "Bibliografía," pp. 157-159. Contents: I. Obras de Gabriel García Márquez. II. Entrevistas a Gabriel García Márquez. III. Escritos sobre Gabriel García Márquez.

Lovera de Sola, Roberto J. "Referencias venezolanas de García Márquez," IMAGEN (CARACAS), Núm. 58/59 (1-15 de agosto de 1972), 30-32.

McMurray, George R. GABRIEL GARCIA MARQUEZ. New York: Frederick Ungar, 1977. 182p. "Bibliografía," pp. 169-174. Contents: I. Works by Gabriel García Márquez, in Spanish. II. Works by Gabriel García Márquez, Translated into English. III. Works about Gabriel García Márquez.

Mendoza, Roseanne B. de. "Bibliografía de y sobre Gabriel García Márquez," REVISTA IBEROAMERICANA, 41, Núm. 90 (enero/marzo de 1975), 107-143. Contents: I. Obras de Gabriel García Márquez ("Esta lista, que sigue un orden cronológico, incluye solamente las obras publicadas en forma de libro"). II. Traducciones de obras de García Márquez (Por orden cronológico de las traducciones). III. Gabriel García Márquez en periódicos literarios (includes his works and reviews about them, as well as articles about García Márquez).

Porras Collantes, pp. 251-289. Includes works of and critical studies about the author.

Porrata, Francisco E., ed. EXPLICACION DE "CIEN AÑOS DE SOLEDAD" (GARCIA MARQUEZ) INCLUYE UNA EXTENSA BIBLIOGRAFIA SOBRE EL AUTOR. Sacramento, Cal.: EXPLICACION DE TEXTOS LITERARIOS, 1975. 398p. "Bibliografía general," pp. 381-398. Criticism only.

Vargas Llosa, Mario. GABRIEL GARCIA MARQUEZ: HISTORIA DE UN DEICIDIO. Barcelona: Barral Editores, 1971. 667p.

"Bibliografía," pp. 643-664. Contents: I. Obras de García Márquez (1947-1970). II. Entrevistas, reportajes, declaraciones. III. Obras sobre García Márquez.

GARCIA PONCE, JUAN (Mexico, 1932-)

Foster, 20th Century, pp. 116-117. Contents: I. Critical Books. II. Critical Essays.

GARCIA VELLOSO, ENRIQUE (Argentina, 1880-1938)

Becco, Horacio Jorge. "Bibliografía de Enrique García Velloso," in Enrique García Velloso's MAMA CULEPINA. PROLOGO DE JUAN JOSE DE URQUIZA, EDICION, COMENTARIO Y NOTAS DE ALBERTO OSCAR BLASI (Buenos Aires: Librería Huemul, 1974), pp. 153-159. Contents: I. Novela. II. Teatro. III. Ensayo. IV. Antologías. V. Crítica.

Urquiza, Juan José. "Bibliografía de don Enrique García Velloso," BOLETIN DE LA ACADEMIA ARGENTINA DE LETRAS, 6, Núm. 21/22 (enero/junio de 1938), 13-20. 132 entries. Works are listed by year, 1896-1938.

_______. ENRIQUE GARCIA VELLOSO. Buenos Aires: Ediciones Culturales Argentinas, Ministerio de Educación y Justicia, Dirección General de Cultura, 1963. 141p. "Bibliografía teatral de Enrique García Velloso," pp. 134-137. "Otras obras," p. 139.

GARMENDIA, JULIO (Venezuela, 1898-1977)

Garmendia, Salvador. MEMORIAS DE ALTAGRACIA. EDICION DE OSCAR RODRIGUEZ ORTIZ. Madrid: Ediciones Cátedra, 1974. 232p. "Bibliografía," pp. 35-38. Contents: I. Obras de Salvador Garmendia. (primeras ediciones). II. Bibliografía fundamental sobre Salvador Garmendia y su obra. A. Monografías. B. Capítulos de libros. C. Principales trabajos en la prensa periódica. D. Entrevistas.

"Julio Garmendia," ANUARIO BIBLIOGRAFICO VENEZUELO, 1977, pp. 240-243. Biobibliography. The bibliography part includes listing of his monographic works and a list of necrologies.

Niño de Rivas, María Lya. "Julio Garmendia: una bibliografía," ACTUALIDADES (CARACAS), Núm. 3/4 (1977/1978), 141-155. Contents: I. Bibliografía del autor. A. Libros y folletos. B. Publicaciones en revistas y periódicos. C. Cuentos en antologías y otros libros. II. Bibliografía sobre el autor. A. En libros. B. En publicaciones periódicas. The work includes 305 unannotated entries.

GARRO, ELENA (Mexico, 1920-)

Corvalán, p. 56. Contents: I. Works. II. Critical Works On.

Foster, Mex. Lit., pp. 161-163. Critical Essays.

GAUTIER BENITEZ, JOSE (Puerto Rico, 1848-1880)

Curet de Anda, Miriam. LA POESIA DE JOSE GAUTIER BENITEZ. Río Piedras: Editorial Universitaria, Universidad de Puerto

Rico, 1980. 158p. "Bibliografía," pp. 155-158. Contents: I. Obra. II. Crítica.

Flores, NH, v. 4, pp. 426-427. Contents: I. Ediciones de su narrativa. II. Referencias. III. Bibliografía selecta (criticism).

Foster, P.R. Lit., pp. 115-117. Contents: I. Critical Monographs and Dissertations. II. Critical Essays.

JOSE GAUTIER BENITEZ: VIDA Y OBRA POETICA. INTRODUCCION AL TEXTO POR CESAREO ROSA NIEVES. Río Piedras: Editorial Edil, 1970. 293p. "Bibliografía esencial del poeta José Gautier Benítez para maestros y estudiantes," pp. 14-18; 31-32. Includes works by and about Gautier Benítez.

GAVIDIA, FRANCISCO ANTONIO (El Salvador, 1864-1955)

Armijo, Roberto and José Napoleón Rodríguez Ruiz. FRANCISCO GAVIDIA, LA ODISEA DE SU GENIO. San Salvador, El Salvador: Ministerio de Educación, Dirección General de Publicaciones, 1965. 2vs. Contents: I. "Traducciones de fragmentos de operas buscadas por Francisco Gavidia," v.2, pp. 192-193. II. "Guía bibliográfica para el estudio de Francisco Gavidia," v.2, pp. 195-203 (chronologically arranged).

"Francisco Gavidia. Bibliografía compilado por la Biblioteca Nacional," ANAQVELES (Biblioteca Nacional de El Salvador), Número extraordinario (1970). Bibliography covers 1882-1965. Contents: I. Primera parte: por año. A. Autor. B. Colaborador. C. Traductor. D. Materia (Criticism, reviews, etc. about Gavidia and his Work). II. Segunda parte: Orden alfabético. A. Autor. B. Colaborador. C. Traductor. D. Materia. III. Tercera Parte: Orden cronológico. A. Autor. B. Colaborador. C. Traductor. D. Materia.

Hernández-Aguirre, Mario. GAVIDIA: POESIA, LITERATURA, HUMANISMO. San Salvador, El Salvador: Ministerio de Educación, Dirección General de Cultura, Dirección de Publicaciones, 1965. 498p. Contents: I. "Cronografía gavidiana," pp. 13-40 (by year, 1865-1955). II. "Bibliografía gavidiana," pp. 43-55. A. Obra de Gavidia. A. Poesía. B. En antologías. C. Prosa. D. Ensayos. E. Historia. F. Teatro. II. Sobre Gavidia o con referencias directas sobre él. III. Lista de todos los artículos citados por Gavidia en sus obras.

Marroquín, Víctor. "Bibliografía general para el estudio de Francisco Gavidia," LA UNIVERSIDAD (Universidad de El Salvador), Año 90, Núm. 3/4 (mayo/agosto de 1965), 353-368. Covers his works, 1882-1960.

Mata Gavidia, José. MAGNIFICENCIA ESPIRITUAL DE FRANCISCO GAVIDIA. San Salvador, El Salvador: Ministerio de Educación, Dirección General de Cultura, Dirección de Publicaciones, 1965. 268p. "Obras consultadas," pp. 237-252. Contents: I. Obras de Francisco Gavidia. A. Colecciones básicas. B. Obras por separado. 1. Artes. 2. Educación. 3. Filología. 4. Filosofía. 5. Historia. 6. Humanidades. 7. Letras. 8. Teatro. 9. San Salvador. 10. Epicadramática. 11. Varia.

C. Publicaciones seriadas más importantes. II. Comentarios sobre Francisco Gavidia.

GAZDARU, DEMETRIO (Argentina, 1900-)

ESTUDIOS DEDICADOS A DEMETRIO GAZDARU. A CARGO DE JORGE DIAZ VELEZ; CESAR FERNANDEZ. La Plata: Instituto de Filología Románica. Facultad de Humanidades y Ciencias de la Educación, Universidad Nacional de La Plata, 1972. (Románica, 5). "Bibliografía de Demetrio Gazdaru," pp. 17-39.

Fernández Pereiro, Nydia G. B. de. "Bibliografía de las publicaciones de Demetrio Gazdaru," ROMANICA (UNIVERSIDAD NACIONAL DE LA PLATA), 5 (1972), 17-39. 385 entries, listed by year, 1916-1973.

GERCHUNOFF, ALBERTO (Argentina, 1883-1950)

Foster, Arg. Lit., pp. 392-398. Contents: I. Bibliographies. II. Critical Monographs and Dissertation. III. Critical Essays.

Gover de Nastasky, Miryam Esther. BIBLIOGRAFIA DE ALBERTO GERCHUNOFF. Buenos Aires: Fondo Nacional de las Artes y Sociedad Hebraica Argentina, 1976. 255p. Contents: I. Bibliografía de Alberto Gerchunoff. A. Libros (alphabetical). B. Colaboraciones en publicaciones periódicas (chronological). C. Colaboraciones en diarios y revistas sin verificar (chronological). D. Reportajes encuestas, entrevistas (chronological). E. Discursos y conferencias. F. Necrologías. G. Necrologías reconocidas por Manuel Kantor. H. Textos de Gerchunoff en diversas antologías (alphabetical). I. Prólogos y estudios de Gerchunoff en obras de otros autores (alphabetical). J. Traducciones de obras del autor. K. Traducción de obras de otros autores. II. Sobre Gerchunoff. A. Crítica y biografía (alphabetical). B. Artículos sin firmar (chronological). C. Artículos sin verificar (chronological). III. Apéndice; esta sección completa y actualiza datos. IV. Cuadro biográfico-cronológico. V. Indice onomástico. VI. Indice de títulos.

"GETULINO" see GAMA, LUIS

GIL, MARTIN (Argentina, 1868-1955)

"Bibliografía de don Martín Gil," BOLETIN DE LA ACADEMIA ARGENTINA DE LETRAS, 21, Núm. 79 (enero/marzo de 1956), 21-22. 13 books listed, 1900-1946.

GIRONDO, OLIVERIO (Argentina, 1891-1967)

Foster, Arg. Lit., pp. 399-402. Contents: I. Bibliography. II. Critical Monographs. III. Critical Essays.

Girondo, Oliverio. OBRAS COMPLETAS. Buenos Aires: Losada, 1968. 488p. "Bibliografía de Oliverio Girondo," pp. 461-478. Classified bibliography of 175 partially annotated entries. Contents: I. Libros. II. Antologías. III. Ensayos. IV. Discografía. V. Editor gráfico. VI. Traductor. VII. Crítica. VIII. Bibliografía.

Salvador, Nélida and Ilena Ardissone. "Contribución a la bibliografía de Oliverio Girondo," REVISTA IBEROAMERICANA, Núm. 102/103 (1978), 187-219. 228 entries, partially annotated. Contents: I. Obras del autor. A. Obras completas. B. Libros. C. Colaboraciones en publicaciones periódicas. 1. Prosa (orden cronológico). 2. Poesía (orden cronológico). D. Antologías de textos del autor. E. Textos del autor en diversas antologías. F. Prólogos y ediciones de obras de otros autores. G. Traducciones del autor. H. Traducciones de obras del autor (by language). I. Discos. II. Crítica y biografía. A. Libros. B. Capítulos sobre el autor incluídos en libros. C. Artículos en publicaciones periódicas. D. Artículos y menciones sobre el autor en historias de la literatura, enciclopedias y diccionarios. III. Indice alfabético de autores.

GIRRI, ALBERTO (Argentina, 1918-)

Foster, Arg. Lit., pp. 403-404. Contents: I. Dissertation. II. Critical Essays.

Girri, Alberto. OBRA POETICA. Buenos Aires: Corregidor, 1977. "Bibliografía," I, pp. 381-382. Contents: I. Poesía. II. Prosa. III. Traducciones, antologías, crítica. IV. Traducciones en colaboración.

GODOY ALCAYAGA, LUCILA see MISTRAL, GABRIEL

GOES, FERNANDO (Brazil,)

Porter, pp. 219-220. Contents: I. Writings. II. References, Critical and Biographical.

GOMES, JOSE TROBUZI PINHEIRO (Brazil, 1927-)

Moraes, pp. 113-115. Major works by and about the author.

GOMEZ, JUAN GUALBERTO (Cuba, 1854-1923)

Foster, Cuban Lit., pp. 221-222. Contents: I. Critical Monographs. II. Critical Essays.

GOMEZ CARRILLO, ENRIQUE (Guatemala, 1873-1927)

Abreu Gómez, Ermilo. "Clásicos de Guatemala: Enrique Gómez Carrillo (1873-1927)," BOLETIN DE LA BIBLIOTECA NACIONAL (Guatemala), 4 época, I, núm. 2 (1951), 93-107. 81 partially annotated entries are contained in the article's bibliografía, pp. 97-107. Contents: I. Obras principales de Gómez Carrillo (by title). II. Prólogos y prefacios por Gómez Carrillo. III. Obras sobre Gómez Carrillo. A. Libros. B. Revistas.

Enrique Barrientos, Alfonso. ENRIQUE GOMEZ CARRILLO. Guatemala: Editorial "José de Pineda Ibarra," 1973. 306p. Contents: I. "Cronología y bibliografía," pp. 269-281 (by year, 1873-1973). II. "Bibliografía sobre Gómez Carrillo," pp. 281-288. III. "El último recuento de su obra (alcanza 86 volúmenes)," pp. 288-291.

Torres, Edelberto. ENRIQUE GOMEZ CARRILLO: EL CRONISTA

ERRANTE. Guatemala, C.A.: Librería Escolar, 1956. 384p. Contents: I. "Cronología y bibliografía," pp. 371-380. II. "Bibliografía sobre Gómez Carrillo," pp. 380-384.

Ulner, Arnold Roland. "ENRIQUE GOMEZ CARRILLO EN EL MODERNISMO: 1889-1896." Ph.D., University of Missouri, 1972. 301p. "Bibliografía," pp. 266-301. Contents: I. Textos de Enrique Gómez Carrillo. A. Libros. B. Artículos y prólogos. II. Trabajos sobre Enrique Gómez Carrillo. A. Libros. B. Artículos y prólogos. III. Otras obras mencionadas o consultadas.

GOMEZ DE AVELLANEDA, GERTRUDIS (Cuba, 1814-1873)

"Contribución a la bibliografía de Gertrudis Gómez de Avellaneda," L/L (ANUARIO DEL INSTITUTO DE LITERATURA Y LINGUISTICA DE LA ACADEMIA DE CIENCIAS DE CUBA), 3/4 (1972/73), 25-39. Contents: I. Bibliografía activa. II. Bibliografía pasiva.

Corvalán, pp. 57-58. Contents: I. Works. II. Critical Works On.

Figarola Caneda, Domingo. GERTRUDIS GOMEZ DE AVELLANEDA. BIOGRAFIA, BIBLIOGRAFIA E ICONOGRAFIA, INCLUYENDO MUCHAS CARTAS INEDITAS O PUBLICADAS, ESCRITAS POR LA GRAN POETISA O DIRIGIDAS A ELLA, Y SUS MEMORIAS ... NOTAS ORDENADAS Y PUBLICADAS POR DONA EMILIA BOXHORN.... Madrid: Sociedad General Española de Librería, S.A., 1929. 292p. "Bibliografía," pp. 39-292. Contents: I. Teatro (by Work). II. Novelas (by Work). III. Varios (articles and poems). IV. Iconografía. V. Cartas a la Avellaneda. VI. Cartas de la Avellaneda. VII. Memorias.

Flores, BEH, pp. 21-22. Contents: I. Edición principal. II. Otras ediciones. III. Referencias. IV. Bibliografía selecta (criticism).

Foster, Cuban Lit., pp. 223-236. Contents: I. Bibliographies. II. Critical Monographs and Dissertations. III. Critical Essays.

García-Carrenza, Araceli. "Esquema bibliográfico de la Avellaneda en su centenario (1814-1873)," REVISTA DE LA BIBLIOTECA NACIONAL "JOSE MARTI", 3ª época, 15, Núm. 3 (setiembre/diciembre de 1973), 137-173. Critical comments. Contents: I. Bibliografía activa: en libros y folletos (1841-1965). II. Bibliografía activa: ediciones (1841-1914). III. Indice de títulos por materias.

Gómez de Avellaneda, Gertrudis. TEATRO. La Habana: Consejo Nacional de Cultura, 1965. 465p. "Bibliografía básica," pp. 449-464. Contents: I. Ediciones (by year, 1841-1953). II. Traducciones. III. Estudios (critical studies about the author and her work).

Harter, Hugh A. GERTRUDIS GOMEZ DE AVELLANEDA. Boston: Twayne, 1981. 182p. "Selected Bibliography," pp. 175-178. Contents: I. Primary Sources. A. Collected and Other Editions. B. Translations. II. Secondary Sources (briefly annotated).

Kelly, Edith L. "Bibliografía de la Avellaneda," REVISTA BIMESTRE CUBANA, 35, Núm. 1 (enero/febrero de 1935), 107-139; Núm. 2 (marzo/abril de 1935), 261-295. 362 items. Contents: I. Primera parte: A. Colecciones. B. Obras sueltas. C. Obras póstumas. D. Cartas, memorias, autobiografías. E. Notas suplementarias. 1. Obras dudosas. 2. Poemas sueltos. Primera parte is chronologically arranged. II. Segunda parte: A. Biógrafos y críticos (1841/42-1933). B. Lista suplementaria (1848-1932).

GOMEZ RESTREPO, ANTONIO (Colombia, 1869-1947)

Ortega Torres, José J., ed. EPISTOLARIO DE RUFINO JOSE CUERVO Y MIGUEL ANTONIO CARO CON ANTONIO GOMEZ RESTREPO. Bogotá: Instituto Caro y Cuervo, 1973. 295p. "Bibliografía de don Antonio Gómez Restrepo," pp. lv-cxx. The 539 entries are arranged chronologically, 1881-1952.

GONÇALVES, PAULO (Brazil, 1897-1927)

Porter, p. 221. Contents: I. Writings. II. References, Critical and Biographical.

GONZAGA, THOMAZ ANTONIO DE (Brazil, 1744-1807?)

Braga, Teofilo. FILINTO ELYSIO E OS DISSIDENTES DE ARCADIA. Porto: Livraria Chardron, 1901. 735p. "Bibliografia de Marília de Dirceu," pp. 620-628. Lists editions from 1792-1885 and translations from 1825-1890s.

Muricy, José Cândido de Andrade. "As edições de Marília de Dirceu," AUTORES E LIVROS (RIO DE JANEIRO), 1, Núm. 14 (1941), 267-277.

Oliveira, Osvaldo Melo Braga de. AS EDIÇOES DE "MARILIA DE DIRCEU": BIBLIOGRAFIA COMPLETA. Rio de Janeiro: Edição Benedicto de Souza, 1930. 58p. Contents: I. Cronologia. II. Edições em português. III. Traduções. IV. Fontes para um estudo completo.

Rio de Janeiro. Biblioteca Nacional. GONZAGUEANA DA BIBLIOTECA NACIONAL, CATALOGO ORGANIZADO PELO BIBLIOTECARIO EMMANUEL GAUDIE LEY. Rio de Janeiro, 1936. 76p. Bibliography.

GONZALEZ, JOAQUIN V. (Argentina, 1863-1923)

Pettoruti, Eduardo. "Síntesis cronológico de la vida y la obra de Joaquín V. González," REVISTA DE LA UNIVERSIDAD (Universidad Nacional de La Plata), 17 (1963), 177-215. 1863-1924.

GONZALEZ, JOSE LUIS (Puerto Rico, 1926-)

Foster, P.R. Lit., pp. 118-120. Contents: I. Bibliography. II. Critical Monograph. III. Critical Essays.

Ruscalleda Bercedóniz, Isabel. "Bibliografía de José Luis González," TEXTO CRITICO, Núm. 12 (1979), 115-127. Contents: I. Obras de José Luis González. A. Libros de cuentos. B.

Cuentos publicados en antologías y revistas. C. Novelas y fragmentos. D. Libros de versos. E. Artículos, autobiografías, cartas, conferencias, ensayos, monografías, notas, prólogos. II. Sobre José Luis González y su obra.

GONZALEZ, NATALICIO (Paraguay, 1897-1966)

González, Natalicio. ANTOLOGIA POETICA. EDICION, INTRODUCCION Y BIBLIOGRAFIA DE FRANCISCO PEREZ MERICEVICH. Asunción: Alcándara, 1984. 120p. "Bibliografía de J. Natalicio González," pp. 15-16.

GONZALEZ, PEDRO ANTONIO (Chile, 1863-1903)

"Cartillas biobibliográficas de autores chilenos: Pedro Antonio González Valenzuela. Coipúe, 1863-1903, Santiago. Poeta," BOLETIN DEL INSTITUTO DE LITERATURA CHILENA (Universidad de Chile, Santiago), Año 2, Núm. 4/5 (julio de 1963), 6-13. Contents: I. Obras. II. Ediciones y recopilaciones de sus obras. III. Referencias. IV. Tabla biográfica. V. Contribución para una iconografía de Pedro Antonio González.

GONZALEZ DEL VALLE Y RAMIREZ, FRANCISCO (Cuba, 1881-1942)

Peraza Sarausa, Fermín. BIBLIOGRAFIA DE FRANCISCO GONZALEZ DEL VALLE. 2ª edición. Gainesville, Florida, 1964. 15p. (Biblioteca del bibliotecario, 4). Contents: I. Noticia biográfica. II. Bibliografía activa. A. Obras. B. Ediciones. III. Bibliografía pasiva.

GONZALEZ GARCIA, MATIAS (Puerto Rico, 1866-1938)

Cuevas de Marcano, Concepción. MATIAS GONZALEZ GARCIA: VIDA Y OBRA. San Juan: Ediciones Borinquen, 1966. 96p. "Bibliografía," pp. 79-92. Contents: I. Obras de Matías González García. A. Cuentos publicados. 1. Libros de cuentos. 2. Cuentos en revistas y periódicos (by year, 1893-1934). B. Cuentos inéditos. C. Dramas publicados. D. Dramas inéditos. E. Novelas publicadas. F. Novelas inéditas. G. Poesías publicadas. H. Cuentos inéditos. II. Documentos sobre el autor. III. Estudios críticos.

Foster, P.R. Lit., pp. 120-121. Contents: I. Critical Monograph and Dissertation. II. Critical Essays.

GONZALEZ LANUZA, EDUARDO (Argentina, 1900-)

Foster, Arg. Lit., pp. 405-406. Contents: I. Dissertation. II. Critical Essays.

González Lanuza, Eduardo. PAGINAS. Buenos Aires: Editorial Celtia, 1983. 252p. Contents: I. "Bibliografía de Eduardo González Lanuza," pp. 245-246 (books only, arranged by year, 1924-1982). II. "Bibliografía sobre Eduardo González Lanuza," pp. 247-248.

GONZALEZ LEON, FRANCISCO (Mexico, 1862-1945)

Phillips, Allen W. FRANCISCO GONZALEZ LEON, EL POETA DE

LAGOS. México, D.F.: Instituto Nacional de Bellas Artes, Departamento de Literatura, 1964. 197p. "Apéndice I: Poemas no coleccionados en libro," pp. 163-174. 125 poems are listed which are not in any book by González León. "Bibliografía," pp. 187-192. Contents: I. Obras de Francisco González León. II. Obras sobre Lagos de Moreno. III. Sobre Francisco González León.

GONZALEZ MARTINEZ, ENRIQUE (Mexico, 1871-1952)

Anderson, pp. 71-76. Critical Essays.

Flores, BEH, pp. 233-235. Contents: I. Edición principal. II. Otras ediciones. III. Referencias. IV. Bibliografía selecta (criticism).

Foster, Mex. Lit., pp. 163-174. Contents: I. Bibliographies. II. Critical Monographs and Dissertations. III. Critical Essays.

González Martínez, Enrique. OBRAS COMPLETAS. México, D.F.: El Colegio Nacional, 1971. 862p. "Bibliografía," pp. 851-852. Contents: I. Poesía. II. Antologías. III. Prosa. IV. Prólogos.

Sánchez, Ana María. "Bibliografías mexicanas contemporáneas. V. Enrique González Martínez," BOLETIN DE LA BIBLIOTECA NACIONAL. (México), 2ª época, 8, Núm. 2 (abril/junio de 1957), 17-72. Contents: I. Obras de Enrique González Martínez. A. Poesía. B. Traducciones. C. Prosa. 1. Ensayos. 2. Cuentos. 3. Autobiografía. 4. Artículos. D. Prólogos. E. Epistolario de Enrique Martínez. IV. Crítica sobre Enrique González Martínez. A. Estudios. B. Artículos de revistas y periódicos. C. Reseñas.

GONZALEZ PACHECO, RODOLFO (Argentina, 1881-1949)

Guardia, Alfredo de la. RODOLFO GONZALEZ PACHECO. Buenos Aires: Ediciones Culturales Argentinas, 1963. 136p. Contents: "Colaboraciones con Pedro E. Pico," p. 133. "Cronología de las obras dramáticas," p. 135. "Ediciones de obras completas," p. 135.

GONZALEZ PRADA, MANUEL (Peru, 1848-1918)

Anderson, pp. 77-80. Critical Essays.

Flores, BEH, pp. 22-24. Contents: I. Ediciones. II. Referencias. III. Bibliografía selecta (criticism).

Foster, Peruvian Lit., pp. 141-153. Contents: I. Bibliographies. II. Critical Monographs and Dissertations. III. Critical Essays.

García Prada, Carlos. "Reseña bibliográfica de la obra poética de González Prada," in Manuel González Prada's ANTOLOGIA POETICA (México, D.F.: Cultura, 1940), pp. 345-359. Contents: I. Obras. II. Traducciones. III. Estudios (criticism, etc.).

Podesta, Bruno. "Bibliografía sobre Manuel González Prada: positivismo, anarquismo y crítica literaria," APUNTES (Universidad del Pacífico del Perú), Año 1, Núm. 2 (1974), 94-100.

GONZALEZ SUAREZ, FEDERICO (Ecuador, 1844-1917)
Davidson, Russ. "Federico González Suárez: Bio-Bibliographical Notes," REVISTA INTERAMERICANA DE BIBLIOGRAFIA, 33 (1983), 13-20. A selected and partially annotated bibliography of González Suárez's works, which are listed chronologically, 1875-1937, including literature and literary analysis.

GONZALEZ TUNON, RAUL (Argentina, 1905-1974)
Foster, Arg. Lit., pp. 407-408. Contents: I. Critical Monograph. II. Critical Essays.

GONZALEZ VERA, JOSE SANTOS (Chile, 1897-1970)
"Cartillas biobibliográficas de autores chilenos: José Santos González Vera. San Francisco del Monte, 1897. Novelista, cuentista, memorialista," BOLETIN DEL INSTITUTO DE LITERATURA CHILENA (Universidad de Chile, Santiago), Año 4, Núm. 9 (enero de 1965), 4-13. Contents: I. Obra. II. Referencias. III. Vida. IV. Otro dato.
Flores, BEH, pp. 235-236. Contents: I. Ediciones. II. Bibliografía selecta (criticism).
Foster, Chilean Lit., pp. 92-95. Contents: I. Bibliographies. II. Critical Books and Theses. III. Critical Essays.

GONZALEZ ZELEDON, MANUEL (Costa Rica, 1865-1936)
González Zeledón, Manuel. CUENTOS. ESTUDIO PRELIMINAR, EDICION Y GLOSARIO DE JOSE M. ARCE. San José, C.R.: Librería Antonio Lehmann, 1968. 416p. "Bibliografía," pp. xxxviii-xlv. Contents: I. Los cuentos. II. Los cuentos en antologías o en colecciones dispersas. III. Traducciones. IV. Poesía. V. Miscelánea. VI. Periodismo. VII. Obras no literarias. VIII. Cartas. IX. Apreciaciones y estudios en torno a su personalidad. X. Iconografía.

GONZALO PATRIZI, JUAN ANTONIO (Venezuela, 1911-1950)
Cardozo, Poesía, pp. 180-182. Includes poetical works of and critical studies about the author.

GONZALO SALAS, JUAN ANTONIO (Venezuela, 1887-1949)
Cardozo, Poesía, pp. 182-184. Includes the poetical works of and critical studies about the author.

GONZALO SALAS, TULIO (Venezuela, 1894-1916)
Cardozo, Poesía, pp. 184-186. Includes the poetical works and critical studies about the author.

GOROSTIZA, CARLOS (Argentina, 1920-)
Foster, Arg. Lit., p. 409. Critical Essays.

GOROSTIZA, CELESTINO (Mexico, 1904-1967)
Foster, Mex. Lit., pp. 174-176. Critical Essays.

GOROSTIZA, JOSE (Mexico, 1901-)
Flores, BEH, pp. 236-237. Contents: I. Ediciones. II. Bibliografía selecta (criticism).
Foster, Mex. Lit., pp. 176-180. Contents: Critical Books and Monographs. II. Critical Essays.
Gorostiza, José. PROSA. RECOPILACION, INTRODUCCION, BIBLIOGRAFIA Y NOTAS POR MIGUEL CAPISTRAN. EPILOGO DE ALFONSO REYES. Guanajuato: Universidad de Guanajuato, 1969. 285p. "Bibliografía de José Gorostiza," pp. 257-267. Contents: I. Obras. A. Poesía. B. Traducciones. C. Prólogos. D. Otros (selección y adaptación de textos). II. Poemas publicados en revistas y periódicos. III. Entrevistas y encuestas. "Bibliografía sobre José Gorostiza," pp. 268-279.

GOROSTIZA, MANUEL EDUARDO DE (Mexico, 1789-1851)
Aguilar M., María Esperanza. ESTUDIO BIO-BIBLIOGRAFICO DE DON MANUEL EDUARDO DE GOROSTIZA. México, D.F.: Renacimiento, 1932. 114p. Contents: I. "Bibliografía de don Manuel Eduardo de Gorostiza," pp. 101-107. II. "Bibliografía sobre don Manuel Eduardo de Gorostiza," pp. 108-114.
Foster, Mex. Lit., pp. 181-183. Contents: I. Bibliographies. II. Critical Monographs and Dissertations. III. Critical Essays.
Gorostiza, Manuel Eduardo de. TEATRO SELECTO. EDICION, PROLOGO Y NOTAS DE ARMANDO DE MARIA Y CAMPOS. México: Editorial Porrúa, 1957. 333p. "Nota bibliográfica," pp. xxi-xxiii. Includes a list of plays published and unpublished.

GORRITI, JUANA MANUELA (Argentina, 1818-1892)
Flores, NH, v. 1, p. 101. Contents: I. Obra narrativa. II. Bibliografía selecta (criticism).

GRANADA, NICOLAS (Argentina, 1840-1915)
Granada, Nicolás. LA GAVIOTA. CON UN ESTUDIO PRELIMINAR SOBRE LA EPOCA, LAS OBRAS Y SU INFLUENCIA LITERARIA; NOTAS EXPLICATIVAS Y ACLARACIONES LINGUISTICAS, BIBLIOGRAFIA FUNDAMENTAL, JUICIOS SOBRE EL AUTOR Y SU OBRA Y TEMAS DE ESTUDIO POR MARTA LENA PAZ. Buenos Aires: Editorial Plus Ultra, 1973. 180p. (Clásicos hispanoamericanos, 17). "Bibliografía fundamental," pp. 59-60. I. Ediciones. II. Estudios.

GRANATA, MARIA (Argentina, 1921/23-)
Corvalán, p. 59. Contents: I. Works. II. Critical Works On.

GRASES, PEDRO (Venezuela, 1909-)
Becco, Horacio Jorge. BIBLIOGRAFIA DE PEDRO GRASES. Caracas: Talleres Cromotip, 1984. 102p. 443 annotated entries. Contents: I. Libros y folletos. II. Ediciones, compilaciones y prólogos. III. Obras en colaboración. IV. Participa-

ción en obras colectivas. V. Obras de Pedro Grases (Edition of Editorial Seix Barral, Barcelona, 1981-1984). VI. Indice de ordenación cronológica. VII. Indice onomástico.

Grases, Pedro. LA OBRA DE PEDRO GRASES. Caracas: Editorial Arte, 1976. 303p. "Relación de publicaciones," pp. 269-298. I. Libros y folletos (listed by year, 1938-1975). II. Ediciones, compilaciones y prólogos.

GREIFF, LEON DE (Colombia, 1895-1976)

Mohler, Stephen Charles. EL ESTILO POETICO DE LEON DE GREIFF. Bogotá: Ediciones Tercer Mundo, 1975. 145p. "Bibliografía," pp. 139-145. Contents: I. Obras publicadas de León de Greiff (en orden cronológico). II. Traducciones. III. Crítica sobre León de Greiff. IV. Otras obras consultadas en la preparación de este estudio. V. Revistas y antologías colombianos que incluyen obras de León de Greiff. VI. Otras antologías poéticas.

Rodríguez Sardiñas, Orlando. LEON DE GREIFF: UNA POETICA DE VANGUARDIA. Madrid: Playor, S.A., 1975. 186p. "Bibliografía," pp. 181-186. A selected bibliography. Contents: I. Obras de León de Greiff. II. Obras en traducciones. III. Estudios. IV. Los siguientes trabajos han sido consultados en el Seminario Andrés Bello del Instituto Caro y Cuervo, Bogotá. V. Otras obras consultadas.

GRIECO, AGRIPPINO (Brazil, 1888-1973)

BIBLIOGRAFIA E CRITICA DE AGRIPPINO GRIECO: COLETANEA DE ESTUDOS PUBLICADOS POR OCASIAO DO NASCIMENTO DE ESCRITOR, COM TRANSCURSO EM 15 DE OUTUBRO DE 1968 E QUANDO DE SEU FALECIMENTO EM 25 DE AGOSTO DE 1973. ORGANIZADA POR DONATELLO GRIECO E FERNANDO SALES. Rio de Janeiro: Livraria Editôra José Olympio en convêncio com o Instituto Nacional do Livro, 1977. 233p. "Bibliografia crítica," pp. 17-20 (by year, 1968-1973).

Grieco, Donatello. BIBLIOGRAFIA E CRITICA DE AGRIPPINO GRIECO. COLETANEA ORGANIZADA EM COMEMORAÇAO DO OCTOGESIMO ANIVERSARIO DO NASCIMENTO DO ESCRITOR, COM TRANSCURSO EM 15 DE OUTUBRO DE 1968. Rio de Janeiro: Instituto Nacional do Livro, 1968. 401p. Works and critical studies, 1910-1968.

GROUSSAC, PAUL (Argentina, 1848-1929)

Canter, Juan. "Paul Groussac," BOLETIN DEL INSTITUTO DE INVESTIGACIONES HISTORICAS, Tomo IX, Año 8, Núm. 42 (octubre/diciembre de 1929), 484-710; Tomo X, Año 8, Núm. 43/44 (enero/junio de 1930), 260-353; Tomo XI, Año 9, Núm. 45 (julio/setiembre de 1930), 337-343. Partially annotated. Contents: I. Publicaciones que ha dirigido (22 items). II. Obras (by year, 1873-1928, 33 items). III. Artículos y otras publicaciones (by year, 1871-1927, 856 entries). IV. Adiciones.

GUANES, ALEJANDRO (Paraguay, 1872-1920)
Rodríguez-Alcalá, Hugo. "Alejandro Guanes, 1872-1920: vida y obra-bibliografía," REVISTA HISPANICA MODERNA, Año 14, Núm. 1/2 (enero/abril de 1948), 50. 13 items. Contents: I. Ediciones. II. Obras antológicas. III. Estudios.

GUARDIA, ALFREDO DE LA (Argentina, 1899-1974)
Becco, Horacio Jorge. "Bibliografía de don Alfredo de la Guardia," BOLETIN DE LA ACADEMIA ARGENTINA DE LETRAS, 39, Núm. 151/152 (enero/junio de 1974), 15-18. Contents: I. Ensayos. A. Libros. B. Folletos. II. Novela. III. Prólogos y ediciones.

GUERIOS, ROSARIO FARANI MANSUR (Brazil, 1907-)
Castagnola, Luigi. "Produção científica do linguista Rosário Farnâni Mansur Guérios," REVISTA LETRAS, 28 (1979), 33-60. Citations arranged by year, 1927-1977.

GUEVARA, (FRAY) MIGUEL DE (Mexico, 1585?-1646?)
Flores, BEH, p. 24. Contents: I. Ediciones. II. Bibliografía selecta (criticism).

GUIDO, BEATRIZ (Argentina, 1924/25-)
Corvalán, p. 60. Contents: I. Works. II. Critical Works On.
Foster, Arg. Lit., pp. 410-411. Contents: I. Critical Monographs and Dissertations. II. Critical Essays.
Foster, 20th Century, pp. 117-118. Contents: Critical Essays.

GUIDO Y SPANO, CARLOS (Argentina, 1827-1918)
Foster, Arg. Lit., pp. 412-415. Contents: I. Critical Monographs and Dissertation. II. Critical Essays.

GUILLEN, ALBERTO (Peru, 1897-1935)
Llasca, Hilda. "BIO-BIBLIOGRAFIA DE ALBERTO GUILLEN." Tesis. Lima: Biblioteca Nacional. Escuela de Bibliotecarios, 1958.

GUILLEN, NICOLAS (Cuba, 1904-)
Antuña, María Luisa, and Josefina García-Carranza. BIBLIOGRAFIA DE NICOLAS GUILLEN. La Habana: Biblioteca Nacional "José Martí," Instituto Nacional del Libro, 1975. (Colección Orbe). 2,737 citings divided into bibliografía activa and bibliografía pasiva sections. Contents: I. Bibliografía activa. A. Libros y folletos. B. Colaboraciones en volúmenes y folletería. C. Colaboraciones en publicaciones periódicas. D. Entrevistas. E. Prólogos. F. Traducciones. G. Partituras y discos. H. Misceláneas, programas, etc. I. Guillén en otros idiomas. II. Bibliografía pasiva (books, pamphlets, periodical publications). III. Author and title indices.
_______. "Bibliografía de Nicolás Guillén, Suplemento 1972-1977," REVISTA DE LA BIBLIOTECA NACIONAL "JOSE MARTI," 3a

época, 19 (setiembre/diciembre de 1977), 61-163. 530 partially annotated entries. Contents: I. Bibliografía activa (by year). A. Libros y folletos. B. Colaboraciones en libros y folletos. C. Colaboraciones en publicaciones seriadas. D. Entrevistas. E. Miscelánea. F. Guillén en otros idiomas. II. Bibliografía pasiva (by year). A. Libros y folletos. B. Publicaciones seriadas. III. Apéndice: asientos bibliográficos rezagados. IV. Indice de títulos. V. Indice onomástico.

"Bibliografía sumaria de Nicolás Guillén," REVISTA DE LITERATURA CUBANA (La Habana), Núm. 0 (julio de 1982), 91-103. Contents: I. Ediciones cubanas (by year, 1930-1981). II. Reediciones extranjeras en español (by year, 1950-1981). III. Traducciones a distintos idiomas (by language). IV. Antologías en español. V. Antologías en otras idiomas.

Flores, BEH, pp. 115-117, 183. Contents: I. Edición principal. II. Otras ediciones. III. Bibliografía selecta (criticism).

Foster, Cuban Lit., pp. 237-257. Contents: I. Bibliographies. II. Critical Monographs and Dissertations. III. Critical Essays.

García Carranza, Josefina. "Síntesis bio-bibliografía de Nicolás Guillén," UNIVERSIDAD DE LA HABANA, Núm. 216 (enero/abril de 1982), 55-121. 152 entries. Contents: I. Libros y folletos (by year, 1930-1980; annotated entries). II. Colaboraciones en libros y folletos (by year, 1922-1977). III. Indice de títulos.

Guillén, Nicolás. OBRA POETICA, 1920-1972. La Habana: Editorial de Arte y Literatura, 1974. 2vs. "Bibliografía," v. 2, pp. 537-553. Contents: I. Obras de poesía de Nicolás Guillén. II. Reediciones extranjeras. III. Traducciones a distintos idiomas (by language). IV. Antologías en español. V. Antologías en otros idiomas. VI. Algunos estudios críticos.

León, René. "Nicolás Guillén: bibliografía," EXPLICACION DE TEXTOS LITERARIOS, 7 (1978), 109-113. Contents: I. Obras de Nicolás Guillén (by year; only first editions of books are included). II. Artículos en revistas y periódicos sobre Guillén. III. Libros sobre Nicolás Guillén. IV. Obras generales relacionadas con género de poesía.

Morejón, Nancy. RECOPILACION DE TEXTOS SOBRE NICOLAS GUILLEN. La Habana: Casa de las Américas, 1974. 429p. "Bibliografía," pp. 375-420. Contents: I. Obras de Nicolás Guillén. II. Sobre Nicolás Guillén.

Perdomo, Omar. "Nicolás Guillén en la bibliografía de Angel Augier," SANTIAGO: REVISTA DE LA UNIVERSIDAD DE ORIENTE (Cuba), Núm. 50 (junio de 1983), 199-217.

RELACIONES DE OBRAS DE NICOLAS GUILLEN Y SUS TRADUCCIONES A DISTINTOS IDIOMAS. La Habana: Biblioteca Nacional "Jose Martí," 1962. 1v (unpaged). A booklet printed to accompany an exposition in honor of Guillén's 60th birthday. Its contents are a bibliography of his works and one of his poems translated into other languages.

Williams, Lorna V. SELF AND SOCIETY IN THE POETRY OF NICOLAS GUILLEN. Baltimore: Johns Hopkins Press, 1982.

177p. "Selected Bibliography," pp. 163-174. Contents: I. Works by Guillén. II. Anthologies and Translations. III. Secondary Sources (includes material on Cuban life and culture as well as on Guillén). A. Books. B. Unpublished sources (including dissertations). C. Articles.

GUIMARAENS, ALPHONSUS DE (Pseudonym of AFONSO HENRIQUES DA COSTA GUIMARAES) (Brazil, 1870-1921)

"Catálogo da exposição comemorativa do centenário de nascimento de Alphonsus de Guimaraens (1870-1970)," BOLETIM DA BIBLIOTECA DA CAMARA DOS DEPUTADOS (Brasília), 19, Núm. 2 (1970), 395-400.

Guimaraens, Alphonsus de. CONTOS DE AMOR. POEMAS ESCOLHIDOS. Rio de Janeiro: José Aguilar Editôra em convênio com o Instituto Nacional de Livro, 1972. 190p. (Biblioteca Manancial, 6). "Bibliografia," pp. 53-66. Contents: I. Obras. II. Estudos sôbre o autor.

_______. OBRA COMPLETA. ORGANIZAÇAO E PREPARAÇAO DO TEXTO POR ALPHONSUS DE GUIMARAENS FILHO. Rio de Janeiro: Editôra José Aguilar, Ltda., 1960. 764p. "Bibliografia," pp. 739-744. Contents: I. Obras. II. Estudos sôbre o autor.

Silva, Wilson Melo da. ALPHONSUS DE GUIMARAENS. Belo Horizonte: Imprensa Oficial, 1971. 416p. "Bibliografia," pp. 397-416 (includes critical works about Guimaraens and his work).

GUIMARAES, AFONSO HENRIQUES DA COSTA see GUIMARAENS, ALPHONSUS DE

GUIMARAES, LUIS, JR. (Brazil, 1845-1898)

Vilela, Iracema Guimarães. LUIZ GUIMARAES, JR. ENSAIO BIO-BIBLIOGRAFICO. Rio de Janeiro: Officina Industrial Graphica, 1934. 119p. (Publicações da Academia Brasileira III, Bibliografia, 5). Contents: I. Notas biográficas. II. Ensaio de bibliografia. A. Livros. B. Obras desaparecidas. III. Alguns escritos sôbre o poeta. IV. Alguns juizos sôbre o poeta.

GUIRALDES, RICARDO (Argentina, 1886-1927)

Amigos del Libro. CATALOGO DE LA EXPOSICION RICARDO GUIRALDES (1886-1927). HOMENAJE DE LA ASOCIACION AMIGOS DEL LIBRO EN EL XXV ANIVERSARIO DE LA MUERTE DEL POETA. Buenos Aires: Salón Kraft, Octubre de 1952. 74p. Contents: I. Manuscritos y pruebas de imprenta. II. Obras de Ricardo Güiraldes. Ediciones en idioma original. III. Fragmentos de obras de Ricardo Güiraldes en colecciones, antologías o publicadas en separatas. IV. Obras y fragmentos de Ricardo Güiraldes traducidos. V. Ensayos, críticas y comentarios de Ricardo Güiraldes, aparecidos en revistas y periódicos. VI. Notas, juicios y comentarios sobre Ricardo Güiraldes y su obra. VII. Oleos, croquis y dibujos por Ricardo

Güiraldes. VIII. Iconografía.

Becco, Horacio Jorge. "Bibliografía," in Ricardo Güiraldes' DON SEGUNDO SOMBRA, ILUSTRACIONES DE ALBERTO GUIRALDES (Buenos Aires: Compañía General Fabril Editora, S.A., 1961), no p. nos. Contents: I. Ediciones de DON SEGUNDO SOMBRA. II. Ediciones abreviadas de DON SEGUNDO SOMBRA. III. Ediciones no autorizadas de DON SEGUNDO SOMBRA. IV. Traducciones de DON SEGUNDO SOMBRA. V. Estudios sobre DON SEGUNDO SOMBRA. VI. Bibliografía.

_______. "Apéndice documental y bibliografía," in Ricardo Güiraldes's OBRAS COMPLETAS. PROLOGO DE FRANCISCO LUIS BERNARDEZ. 2ª EDICION HA ESTADO AL CUIDADO DE JUAN JOSE GUIRALDES Y AUGUSTO MARIO DELFINO. (Buenos Aires: Emecé, 1962), pp. 803-866. Contents: I. Sinopsis de la vida y la obra de Ricardo Güiraldes. II. Notas a las obras completas de Ricardo Güiraldes. III. Libros publicados en vida del autor (by title). IV. Libros de publicación póstuma. V. Poemas. VI. Cuentos y relatos. VII. Estudios comentarios. VIII. Notas y apuntes. IX. Del epistolario. X. Bibliografía. A. Obras de Ricardo Güiraldes. 1. Libros. 2. Obras completas. 3. Separatas y folletos especiales. 4. Ediciones no autorizadas. 5. Traducciones. 6. Selección en antologías y recopilaciones. a. Obra poética. b. Obras en prosa. B. Estudios críticos. C. Bibliografía.

_______. RICARDO GUIRALDES. Buenos Aires: Universidad de Buenos Aires, Facultad de Filosofía y Letras, Instituto de Literatura Argentina "Ricardo Rojas," 1959. 35p. (Guías bibliográficas, 1). A student guide. Contents: I. Libros. II. Separatas y folletos. III. Obras completas.

Blasi, Alberto Oscar. GUIRALDES Y LARBAUD: UNA AMISTAD CREADORA. Buenos Aires: Editorial Nova, 1969. 118p. "Indicación bibliográfica," pp. 113-118. Contents: I. Papeles de los protagonistas. II. Testimonios. III. Estudios de mayor contribución. IV. Lecturas complementarios. V. Crónica periodística. VI. Trabajos de edición posterior a 1965.

Curet de De Anda, Miriam. EL SISTEMA EXPRESIVO DE RICARDO GUIRALDES. Río Piedras: Editorial Universitaria, Universidad de Puerto Rico, 1976. 383p. "Bibliografía," pp. 368-383. Contents: I. Obras de Ricardo Güiraldes. A. Ediciones (selective). B. Sueltas. C. Cartas. D. Comentarios. E. Cuentos. F. Definiciones. G. Estudios. H. Notas. I. Poemas. J. Poemas en prosa. K. Semblanzas. II. Estudios sobre Güiraldes. A. Citados. B. No citados. III. Bibliografía general.

Flores, BEH, pp. 117-120. Contents: I. Edición principal. II. Otras ediciones. III. Referencias. IV. Bibliografía selecta (criticism).

Foster, Arg. Lit., pp. 416-437. Contents: I. Bibliographies. II. Critical Monographs and Dissertations. III. Critical Essays.

Foster, 20th Century, pp. 118-128. Contents: I. Bibliographies. II. Critical Books. III. Critical Essays.

Previtali, Giovanni. RICARDO GUIRALDES AND DON SEGUNDO SOMBRA: LIFE AND WORKS. FORWORD BY ADELINA DEL CARRIL DE GUIRALDES. PREFACE BY JORGE LUIS BORGES. New York: Hispanic Institute in the United States, 1963. 225p. "Bibliography," pp. 203-225. Contents: I. Works of Ricardo Güiraldes. A. Books. B. Other Writings. II. Translations. A. Translations of DON SEGUNDO SOMBRA. B. Translations from Other Books. III. Critical and Biographical Material. IV. Other Bibliographies. The Previtali work was translated into Spanish as: RICARDO GUIRALDES: BIOGRAFIA Y CRITICA. PREFACIO POR JORGE LUIS BORGES. TRADUCCION DEL INGLES POR PABLO MAX YNSFRAN. México D.F.; Ediciones De Andrea, 1965. 170p. (Colección Studium, 48). "Bibliografía," pp. 145-167.

GUIRAO, RAMON (Cuba, 1908-1949)
Foster, Cuban Lit., p. 258. Critical Essays.

GUTIERREZ, JUAN MARIA (Argentina, 1809-1879)
Becco, Horacio Jorge. "Bibliografía de Juan María Gutiérrez," REVISTA DE LA UNIVERSIDAD DE BUENOS AIRES, 5ª época, Año 4, Núm. 4 (octubre/diciembre de 1959), 604-620. The bibliography lists 54 works (excluding articles) by Gutiérrez and 212 works and articles on the author and his work. Contents: I. Libros. II. Otros trabajos. A. Ediciones. B. Traducciones. C. Prólogos. D. Participación en diarios y periódicos. III. Estudios críticos sobre Juan María Gutiérrez. IV. Bibliografías.
Schweistein de Reidel, María. "Contribución a la bibliografía de Juan María Gutiérrez," in her JUAN MARIA GUTIERREZ (La Plata: Universidad Nacional de La Plata, Facultad de Humanidades y Ciencias de la Educación, 1940), pp. 255-284. 503 unannotated titles in chronological order, 1833-1937. Includes books and newspaper and periodical articles.

GUTIERREZ NAJERA, MANUEL (Mexico, 1859-1895)
Anderson, pp. 81-85. Critical Essays.
Carter, Boyd G. EN TORNO A GUTIERREZ NAJERA Y LAS LETRAS MEXICANAS DEL SIGLO XIX. México: Ediciones Botas, 1960. 299p. "Bibliografía," pp. 291-299. Contents: I. Colecciones de obras y escritos diversos. II. Estudios, críticas, recuerdos y escritos diversos. A. Libros. B. Artículos. III. Poesías inéditas o recopilados completamente o en parte. IV. Revistas y periódicos consultados.
Contreras García, Irma. INDAGACIONES SOBRE GUTIERREZ NAJERA. México: Colección Metáfora, 1957. 173p. "Orden cronológico de las poesías publicadas en diversas periódicas," pp. 152-163. By year, 1876-1895.
_______. "Manuel Gutiérrez Nájera, 1859-1895: Apuntes para una bio-bibliografía," BOLETIN DE LA BIBLIOTECA NACIONAL (México), XIII, Núm. 1/2 (1962), 32-38. Contents: I. Bio-

bibliografía. II. Bibliografía del autor. III. Bibliografía sobre el autor.

Flores, BEH, pp. 24-26. Contents: I. Ediciones principales. II. Otras ediciones. III. Referencias. IV. Bibliografía selecta (criticism).

Foster, Mex. Lit., pp. 183-193. Contents: I. Bibliographies. II. Critical Monographs and Dissertations. III. Critical Essays.

Gómez Baños, Virginia. BIBLIOGRAFIA DE MANUEL GUTIERREZ NAJERA Y CUATRO CUENTOS INEDITOS. México, 1958. 88p. Contents: I. Poesía. II. Prosa. III. Prólogos. IV. Traducciones. A. El Republicano (1880). B. Publicaciones periodísticas. 1. El cronista de México (1880, 1881 y 1883). 2. El Demócrata (1893 y 1895). 3. Revista Azul (1894-1896). V. Traducciones al inglés por otros escritores. 271 total listings; partially annotated.

Mapes, E. K. "The First Published Writings of Manuel Gutiérrez Nájera," HISPANIC REVIEW, 5, No. 3 (July 1937), 225-240. Dates, pseudonyms, and other data, drawn from periodicals of the period.

_______. "Manuel Gutiérrez Nájera: seudónimos y bibliografía periodística," REVISTA HISPANICA MODERNA, 19, Núm. 1/4 (Enero/diciembre de 1953), 132-204. "Bibliografía periodística de Manuel Gutiérrez Nájera," pp. 161-204. The bibliography is alphabetical by periodical and within each periodical by date. Approximately 30 journals are indexed.

Mejía Sánchez, Ernesto, ed. EXPOSICION DOCUMENTAL DE MANUEL GUTIERREZ NAJERA, 1859-1959. México: Universidad Nacional Autónoma de México, Dirección General de Publicaciones, 1959. 53p. Contents: I. Documentos y fotografías (includes transcriptions). II. Manuscritos. III. Impresos (includes his works and autographed editions to Gutiérrez Nájera by other authors, e.g., Martí, Darío, etc.).

GUZMAN, MARTIN LUIS (Mexico, 1887-1977)

Abreu Gómez, Ermilo. MARTIN LUIS GUZMAN. México: Impresas Editoriales, S.A., 1968. 322p. "Bibliografía de Martín Luis Guzmán," pp. 311-319. Contents: I. Ediciones. II. Prosa publicada en revistas, periódicos y antologías. III. Artículos de crítica literaria. IV. Obras traducidas por Martín Luis Guzmán. V. Traducciones, a varios idiomas, de las obras de Martín Luis Guzmán. VI. Algunas opiniones de la crítica sobre Martín Luis Guzmán.

_______. "Martín Luis Guzmán." REVISTA INTERAMERICANA DE BIBLIOGRAFIA, 9, Núm. 2 (junio de 1959), 119-143. "Bibliografía de Martín Luis Guzmán," pp. 136-143. Contents: I. Obras, traducciones, colaboraciones. II. Bibliografía sobre Guzmán. III. Obras en prensa.

_______. "Martín Luis Guzmán: crítica y bibliografía," HISPANIA, 35, No. 1 (February 1952), 70-73. Contents: I. Obras, ediciones, traducciones. II. Estudios.

Flores, BEH, pp. 237-239. Contents: I. Edición principal. II.

Otras ediciones. III. Referencias. IV. Bibliografía selecta (criticism).

Foster, Mex. Lit., pp. 193-197. Contents: I. Bibliographies. II. Critical Books. III. Critical Essays.

Foster, 20th Century, pp. 128-129. Contents: I. Bibliographies. II. Critical Books. III. Critical Essays.

GUZMAN, NICOMEDES (Chile, 1914-1964)

Foster, Chilean Lit., pp. 95-96. Contents: I. Critical Books and Theses. II. Critical Essays.

Pearson, Lon. NICOMEDES GUZMAN: PROLETARIAN AUTHOR IN CHILE'S LITERARY GENERATION OF 1938. Columbia, Mo.: University of Missouri Press, 1976. 285p. "Selected Bibliography," pp. 267-275. Contents: I. Works by Nicomedes Guzmán. A. Literary. B. Critical. C. Editorial. II. Critical Appraisals of Nicomedes Guzmán and the Generation of 1938. III. General References.

GUZMAN CRUCHAGA, JUAN (Chile, 1895-)

"Cartillas biobibliográficas de autores chilenos: Juan Guzmán Cruchaga. Santiago, 1895. Poeta y dramaturgo," BOLETIN DEL INSTITUTO DE LITERATURA CHILENA (Universidad de Chile, Santiago), Año 2, Núm. 3 (octubre de 1962), 7-14. Contents: I. Obras en antologías poéticas. II. Referencias. III. Tabla biográfica.

Ivelić, Radoslav. JUAN GUZMAN CRUCHAGA. POEMAS, TEMATICAS, ANALISIS ESTILISTICO Y ESTETICO. Santiago de Chile: Editorial del Pacífico, S.A., 1963. 139?p. "Bibliografía de Juan Guzmán Cruchaga," pp. 132 (Unnumbered after p. 132). Contents: I. Obras de Juan Guzmán Cruchaga. A. En libros. 1. Poesía. 2. Teatro. B. En revistas y periódicos. 1. Poesía. 2. Prosa. a. cuentos. b. artículos. c. impresiones de viaje. II. Juicios sobre la obra de Juan Guzmán Cruchaga. A. En libros. B. En revistas. C. En periódicos.

- H -

HALMAR, AUGUSTO D' (Pseudonym of AUGUSTO THOMSON) (Chile, 1882-1950)

Acevedo, Ramón L. AUGUSTO D'HALMAR: NOVELISTA (ESTUDIO DE "PASION Y MUERTE DEL CURA DEUSTO"). Río Piedras, Puerto Rico: Editorial Universitaria, Universidad de Puerto Rico, 1976. 204p. "Bibliografía," pp. 195-202. Contents: I. Obras de Augusto d'Halmar. A. Novelas largas. B. Novelas cortas. C. Cuentos y esbozos. D. Ensayos. E. Artículos. F. Antologías. II. Referencias y estudios críticos sobre d'Halmar y LA PASION Y MUERTE DEL CURA DEUSTO. III. Bibliografía general.

"Cartillas biobibliográficas de autores chilenos: Augusto Goemine Thomson (seud. Augusto d'Halmar). Santiago, 1882-1950,

Santiago. Novelista, cuentista, poeta, periodista," BOLETIN DEL INSTITUTO DE LITERATURA CHILENA (Universidad de Chile, Santiago), Año 6, Núm. 13/14 (febrero de 1967), 15-35. Contents: I. Obra. II. Referencias. III. Vida.

Flores, BEH, pp. 217-218. Contents: I. Edición principal. II. Otras ediciones. III. Referencias. IV. Bibliografía selecta (criticism).

Foster, Chilean Lit., pp. 71-74. Contents: I. Bibliographies. II. Critical Books and Theses. III. Critical Essays.

Smith, George E. "Bibliografía de las obras de Augusto d'Halmar," REVISTA IBEROAMERICANA, 28, Núm. 54 (julio/diciembre de 1962), 365-382. Complete for the American publications, but it does not include any of the many articles published in Europe. The first section carries a listing of d'Halmar's books with their various editions published in Chile; the second, his writings in journals and newspapers.

HEIREMANS, LUIS ALBERTO (Chile, 1928-1964)

Cajano Salas, Teresa. TEMAS Y SIMBOLOS EN LA OBRA DE LUIS ALBERTO HEIREMANS. Santiago de Chile: "Fundación Luis Alberto Heiremans," 1970. 256p. "Apéndice I," pp. 235-256. Contents: I. Obras de Luis Alberto Heiremans. II. Obras estrenadas. III. Artículos escritos por Luis Alberto Heiremans. IV. Adaptaciones y traducciones de obras teatrales. V. Bibliografía: A. Libros. B. Obras y artículos publicados en revistas y diarios. C. Materiales inéditos. D. Otras fuentes. 1. Cartas. 2. Entrevistas.

Foster, Chilean Lit., pp. 97-98. Contents: I. Critical Books and Theses. II. Critical Essays.

HENRIQUEZ, CAMILO (Chile, 1769-1825)

Santana, Francisco. "Ensayo biobibliográfico sobre Camilo Henríquez y notas biográficas," ATENEA (Santiago de Chile), Año 15, Núm. 154, (abril de 1938), 92-118. "Solo se ha tenido en cuenta las monografías, estudios especiales y referencias encontradas en los libros. Se han excluído las publicaciones hechas en diarios y revistas.

HENRIQUEZ URENA, PEDRO (Dominican Republic, 1884-1946)

Speratti Piñero, Emma Susana. "Crono-bibliografía de don Pedro Henríquez Ureña," REVISTA IBEROAMERICANA, 21, Núm. 41/42 (enero/diciembre de 1956), 195-242. By year, 1894-1946.

HERAUD, JAVIER (Peru, 1942-1963)

Flores, BEH, p. 239. Contents: I. Ediciones. II. Bibliografía selecta (criticism).

Foster, Peruvian Lit., pp. 154-156. Contents: I. Critical Monographs and Dissertations. II. Critical Essays.

Heraud, Javier. JAVIER HERAUD: POESIAS COMPLETAS Y HOMENAJE. Lima: Ediciones de La Rama Florida, 1964. 242p. Contents: I. "Homenajes en revistas," pp. 222-224. II. "Poemas a Javier Heraud publicados en diversas revistas," pp. 227-228.

______. POESIAS COMPLETAS. EDICION PREPARADA Y REVISADA POR HILDEBRANDO PEREZ. Lima: Campodónico Ediciones, 1973. 382p. "Bibliografía," pp. 369-382. Contents: I. Libros de poesía. II. Poemas publicados en revistas y periódicos. III. Traducciones. IV. Sobre Javier Heraud.

______. POESIAS COMPLETAS Y CARTAS. Lima: Ediciones Peisa, 1976. 248p. "Bibliografía," pp. 237-248. Contents: I. Libros de poesía. II. Poemas publicados en revistas y periódicos. III. Traducciones. IV. Sobre Javier Heraud.

HEREDIA, JOSE MARIA (Cuba, 1803-1839)

Díaz, Lomberto. HEREDIA, PRIMER ROMANTICO HISPANOAMERICANO. Montevideo: Ediciones Géminis, 1973. 189p. "Bibliografía," pp. 181-188. Contents: I. Libros. II. Artículos.

Flores, BEH, pp. 26-27. Contents: I. Edición principal. II. Otras ediciones. III. Referencias. IV. Bibliografía selecta (criticism).

Flores, NH, v. 1, pp. 110-11. Contents: I. Edición principal. II. Otras ediciones. III. Bibliografía selecta (criticism).

Foster, Cuban Lit., pp. 259-273. Contents: I. Bibliographies. II. Critical Monographs and Dissertations. III. Critical Essays.

González del Valle y Ramírez, Francisco. CRONOLOGIA HEREDIANA 1803-1839. La Habana: Secretaría de Educación, Dirección de Cultura, 1938. 331p. The events and various writings of the Cuban poet during his life are listed in chronological order with biographical and bibliographical commentary. Includes an "Apéndice de trabajos de Heredia cuyas fechas no hemos encontrado."

Heredia, José María. POESIAS COMPLETAS. SELECCION, ESTUDIO Y NOTAS POR ANGEL APARICIO LAURENCIO. Miami: Ediciones Universal, 1970. 425p. (Clásicos cubana, 2). "Bibliografía," pp. 43-59. Contents: I. Ediciones (1820-1917). II. Estudios (critical studies on Heredia and his work).

Plasencia Moro, Aleida. "Los manuscritos de José María Heredia en la Biblioteca Nacional," REVISTA DE LA BIBLIOTECA NACIONAL (La Habana), 3ª serie, 1, Núm. 1/4 (enero/diciembre de 1959), 9-17. Contents: I. Poesía. II. Teatro. III. Historia. IV. Novela. V. Epistolario. VI. Cartas de familia, 1825-1833. VII. Catálogo de los libros que forman la biblioteca particular de José María Heredia, Toluca, 1833. VIII. Documentos biográficos.

Robaina, Tomás F. BIBLIOGRAFIA SOBRE JOSE MARIA HEREDIA. La Habana: Biblioteca Nacional "José Martí", 1970. 111p. This bibliography lists works found in the Biblioteca Nacional "José Martí" and in the Havana libraries of the Biblioteca Central de la Universidad de La Habana, Instituto de Literatura y Lingüística, Biblioteca "Gener y del Monte", and the Sociedad Económica de Amigos del País. 155 primary and 444 secondary sources are included under the following sections: I. Bibliografía activa. A. Obras generales. B. Correspondencia. C. Correspondencia-manuscritos. D. Cuentos, ensayos y prosa en general. E. Cuentos, ensayos y prosa en general-manuscritos. F. Poesías. G. Poesías-manuscritos. H. Poesías-traducciones. I. Teatro. J. Teatro-manuscritos. K. Teatro-traducciones. II. Bibliografía pasiva. A. Vida y obra. B. Bibliografías. C. Correspondencia a y sobre Heredia. D. Cuentos, ensayos y prosa en general. E. Poesías. F. Teatro. Author, subject and magazine indices are also included.

Toussaint, Manuel. BIBLIOGRAFIA MEXICANA DE HEREDIA. México: Secretaría de Relaciones Exteriores, Departamento de Información para el Extranjero, 1953. 146p. (Monografías bibliografías mexicanas, 2 serie, 5). An exhaustive annotated bibliography of 161 items concerning Heredia in Mexico. Contents: I. Obras originales. A. Pequeñas obras anteriores a 1832. B. Poesías. 1. Prospectos. 2. Ediciones críticas. C. Discursos. D. Lecciones de Historia Universal. E. Periódicos. F. Antologías. G. Traducciones. H. Teatro. I. Colaboraciones, remitidos y reproducciones. II. Acerca de Heredia. A. Biografías y estudios biográficos. B. Referencias personales y literarias. C. Referencias políticas. D. El centenario de su muerte. III. Indices.

HEREDIA, NICOLAS (Cuba, 1855-1901)

Collado y López, Olga. "Nicolás Heredia: Vida y obra," REVISTA DE LA BIBLIOTECA NACIONAL (La Habana), 2ª serie, 5, Núm. 3 (julio/setiembre de 1954), 103-197. "Bibliografía," pp. 190-197. Contents: I. Bibliografía general (includes critical studies about Heredia). II. Obras de Nicolás Heredia (listed by year, 1887-1930).

HERNANDEZ, EFREN (Mexico, 1903-1958)

Harmon, Mary M. EFREN HERNANDEZ, A POET DISCOVERED. Hattiesburg: University and College Press of Mississippi, 1972. 125p. "Bibliography," pp. 103-111. Contents: I. The Works of Efrén Hernández. A. Books. B. Articles. II. References. A. Books. B. Articles and Theses.

Hernández, Efrén. OBRAS: POESIA, NOVELA, CUENTOS. NOTA PRELIMINAR DE ALI CHUMACERO. BIBLIOGRAFIA DE EFREN HERNANDEZ POR LUIS MARIO SCHNEIDER. México, D.F.: Fondo de Cultura Económica, 1965. 429p. "Bibliografía de Efrén Hernández," pp. 415-423. Contents: I. Bibliografía directa. A. Obras publicadas. B. Prólogos. C. Hemerografía (by journal and then by year of publication). II. Bibliografía indirecta (criticism).

HERNANDEZ, FELISBERTO (Uruguay, 1902-1964)

Andreu, Jean L. "Para una bibliografía de Felisberto Hernández," in FELISBERTO HERNANDEZ ANTE LA CRITICA ACTUAL: EL SEMINARIO SOBRE FELISBERTO HERNANDEZ (1973-74) DEL CENTRO DE INVESTIGACIONES LATINOAMERICANAS DE LA

UNIVERSIDAD DE POITIERS, EDICION DE ALAIN SICARD (Caracas: Monte Avila, 1977), pp. 411-419. 111 entries. Contents: I. Textos de Felisberto Hernández. A. Libros. B. Obras completas. C. Colaboraciones en los diarios y revistas. D. Textos en antologías. II. Sobre Felisberto Hernández. A. Estudios generales. Testimonios biográficos. B. Reseñas y estudios particulares.

Echavarrén Welker, Roberto. ESPACIO DE LA VERDAD PRACTICA DEL TEXTO EN FELISBERTO HERNANDEZ. Buenos Aires: Editorial Sudamericana, 1981. 256p. "Bibliografía," pp. 247-256. Contents: I. Textos de Felisberto Hernández (arranged by year). A. Libros. B. Obras completas. C. Libros en traducción. D. Colaboraciones en diarios y revistas. E. Textos en antologías. II. Crítica sobre Felisberto Hernández.

Flores, BEH, pp. 239-240. Contents: I. Ediciones. II. Bibliografía selecta (criticism).

Hernández, Felisberto. 5 CUENTOS MAGISTRALES. CRITICA POR EXTRANJEROS. BIBLIOGRAFIA ANOTADA. Montevideo: Editorial Ciencias, 1979. 160p. Contents: I. "Bibliografía anotada, 1925-1979," pp. 111-121. A. Obras del autor. 1. Colaboraciones en diarios, periódicos y revistas. 2. Publicada en libros. 3. Antología individual. a. Libros. b. Folletos y revistas. 4. Textos incluídos en antologías. Libros. 5. Traducciones. 6. Obras completas. II. "Obra sobre el autor," pp. 129-134. A. Individual. Libros. B. Biocrítica. C. Ensayo y crítica. D. Miscelánea. E. Ensayo y crítica.

Lasarte, Francisco. FELISBERTO HERNANDEZ Y LA ESCRITURA DE "LO OTRO." Madrid: Insula, 1981. 198p. "Bibliografía," pp. 193-196. Contents: I. Obras completas. II. Selección de trabajos sobre Felisberto Hernández.

Rela, Walter. FELISBERTO HERNANDEZ: BIBLIOGRAFIA ANOTADA. Montevideo: Editorial Ciencias, 1979. 50p. "Bibliografía anotada, 1925-1979," pp. 15-44. I. Obras del autor. A. Colaboraciones en diarios, periódicos y revistas. B. Publicada en libros. C. Antología individual. Libros. D. Textos incluídos en antologías. Libros. E. Traducciones. F. Obras completas. II. Obra sobre el autor. A. Individual. Libros. 1. Biocrítica. 2. Ensayo y crítica. 3. Miscelánea. 4. Ensayo y crítica. 5. Miscelánea. B. General. Libros. 1. Ensayo y crítica. 2. Bibliografías. 3. Diccionarios. 4. General. Obras de referencia. Diarios, periódicos y revistas. III. Indices. A. Títulos. B. Nombres.

HERNANDEZ, GASPAR OCTAVIO (Panama, 1893-1918)

Hernández, Gaspar Octavio. OBRAS SELECTAS. COMPILACION, INTRODUCCION, NOTAS Y BIBLIOGRAFIA DE OCTAVIO AUGUSTO HERNANDEZ. Panamá: Imprenta Nacional, 1966. 589p. Contents: I. "Bibliografía de Gaspar Octavio Hernández," pp. 541-563. A. Poesías. B. Prosa. II. "Bibliografía sobre Gaspar Octavio Hernández," pp. 567-578.

Jackson, Afro-Spanish, pp. 84-87. Contents: I. Works. II.

Criticism. A. Bibliography. B. Books. C. Articles, Shorter Studies, and Dissertations. Annotated.

HERNANDEZ, JOSE (Argentina, 1834-1886)

Barbato, Martha J. "José Hernández y MARTIN FIERRO," LOGOS, Núm. 12 (1972), 259-313. The bibliography's 479 entries update the Cortázar and Becco (1966) bibliographies. Contents: I. Ediciones (1960's). A. Transcripciones al sistema braille. B. Traducciones. II. Otros escritos de Hernández. III. Obras inspiradas en la vida de Hernández y en MARTIN FIERRO. IV. Bibliografías. V. Estudios y ensayos. VI. A títulos. VII. Convergencias. VIII. Teatro. IX. Filmografía. X. Discografía. XI. Radiofonía. XII. Televisión. XIII. Críticas y reseñas.

Becco, Horacio Jorge. "Bibliografía hernandiana," in MARTIN FIERRO, UN SIGLO (Buenos Aires: Xerox Argentina, 1972), pp. 263-396. 1,220 entries through 1971. Contents: I. Ediciones. A. EL GAUCHO MARTIN FIERRO. B. LA VUELTA DE MARTIN FIERRO. C. MARTIN FIERRO (Unificación de las dos partes bajo este nombre a partir de 1910). D. Ediciones sin fecha. E. Ediciones sin editor ni fecha. II. Ediciones facsimilares. III. Traducciones. IV. Otras obras de José Hernández. A. Libros. B. Periódicos y artículos. C. Epistolario. D. Antologías. V. Crítica. A. Biografía. B. Homenajes. C. En la literatura gauchesca. D. Su Obra. Crítica general. VI. El poema MARTIN FIERRO. A. Crítica sobre el poema. B. Personajes. C. Lingüística. D. Aspectos sociales y políticos. E. Relaciones literarias. F. Teatralización. VII. Miscelánea de publicaciones no fundamentales sino complementarios como un artículo sobre una expresión plástica del poema, un número de CARAS Y CARETAS dedicado al gaucho, diversas revistas MARTIN FIERRO, etc. VIII. Bibliografías. IX. Index of names.

_______. "José Hernández: MARTIN FIERRO y su bibliografía-I," BIBLIOGRAFIA ARGENTINA DE ARTES Y LETRAS, Núm. 5 (1966), 123-145. Contents: I. Ediciones del MARTIN FIERRO. II. Ediciones sin fecha. III. Traducciones del MARTIN FIERRO (By language). IV. Otros trabajos de José Hernández.

_______. _______-II, CUADERNOS DEL IDIOMA (Buenos Aires), Año 2, Núm. 6 (octubre de 1966), 109-137. Contents: I. Crítica y biografía. II. Bibliografías. III. Discografía. IV. Filmografía.

Benson, Nettie Lee. "MARTIN FIERRO, at the University of Texas," LIBRARY CHRONICLE OF THE UNIVERSITY OF TEXAS, 8, No. 4 (Spring 1968), 13-27. Translated and published in CUADERNOS DEL SUR, Núm. 8/9 (julio de 1967/julio de 1968), 161-173. Survey of Texas holdings.

_______, ed. CATALOGUE OF "MARTIN FIERRO" MATERIALS IN THE UNIVERSITY OF TEXAS LIBRARY. Austin: The Institute of Latin American Studies, The University of Texas, 1972. 135p. (Guides and Bibliographies Series, No. 6).

Cortázar, Augusto Raúl. "José Hernández. MARTIN FIERRO y su

crítica: aportes para una bibliografía," BIBLIOGRAFIA ARGENTINA DE ARTES Y LETRAS, Núm. 5/6 (enero/julio de 1960), 51-126. Annotated entries. Contents: I. Ediciones de MARTIN FIERRO (1872-1960). II. Traducciones de MARTIN FIERRO. III. Otras obras de José Hernández. IV. Algunos poemas inspirados en MARTIN FIERRO o en personajes. V. Crítica y biografía (sobre el autor y su obra). VI. Indice alfabético (name index). VII. Cuadro biográfico-cronológico.

Flores, BEH, pp. 27-29. Contents: I. Ediciones principales. II. Otras ediciones. III. Referencias. IV. Bibliografía selecta (criticism).

Foster, Arg. Lit., pp. 438-475. Contents: I. Bibliographies. II. Critical Monographs and Dissertations. III. Critical Essays.

Maubé, José Carlos. ITINERARIO BIBLIOGRAFICO Y HEMEROGRAFICO DEL "MARTIN FIERRO." Buenos Aires: Editorial El Ombu, 1943. 179p. Contents: I. Ediciones. A. Proceso editorial. B. Ediciones facsimilares. C. Ediciones anotadas, comentadas o con explicaciones al texto. D. Ediciones de lujo e ilustradas. E. Ediciones económicas. F. Ediciones minúsculas (formato bolsillo). G. Ediciones para niños. H. Ediciones populares (costo ínfimo). I. Revistas. J. Ediciones de homenaje. K. Ediciones impresas en el interior del país. L. Ediciones impresas (temas marginales). N. Revistas y grupo literario MARTIN FIERRO. O. Antologías y parnasos (obras publicadas en el país y en el extranjero). P. Texto de estudio. Q. Antología miniatura. II. Epistolario de Hernández y primeros juicios críticos. III. Los prologuistas. IV. Ilustradores, grabadores, etc. V. Las traducciones realizadas en el extranjero y en nuestro país. VI. Itinerario bibliográfico (critical works, 1902-1943). VII. Exposiciones bibliográficas. VIII. Itinerario hemerográfico (1892-1943). Criticism mainly. IX. Conferencias y discursos. X. Escenificación del MARTIN FIERRO.

Rela, Walter, ed. ARTICULOS PERIODISTICOS DE JOSE HERNANDEZ EN "LA PATRIA" DE MONTEVIDEO, 1874. Montevideo: Editorial El Libro Argentino, 1967. 122p. This work lists Hernández's articles published during his exile in 1874 in the Uruguayan capital.

Sava, Walter. "José Hernández--cien años de bibliografía, aporte básico anotado," CHASQUI, 1, Núm. 3 (mayo/junio de 1972), 5-25. I. Libros. II. Periódicos y revistas. Annotated entries.

HERNANDEZ, JOSE P. H. (Puerto Rico, 1892-1922)

Foster, P.R. Lit., pp. 121-122. Contents: I. Critical Monograph. II. Critical Essays.

Hernández, José P. H. OBRA POETICA. CON UN ESTUDIO BIOGRAFICO-CRITICO DE MANUEL SIACA RIVERA. San Juan: Instituto de Cultura Puertorriqueña, 1966. 396p. "Bibliografía," pp. 119-124. Contents: I. Obra poética de José P. H. Hernández (1919-1949). II. Estudios sobre la obra de Hernández.

HERNANDEZ, LUISA JOSEFINA (Mexico, 1928-)
Brann, Sylvia Jean. "EL TEATRO Y LAS NOVELAS DE LUISA JOSEFINA HERNANDEZ." Ph.D., University of Illinois, 1969. 324p. "Bibliografía," pp. 316-323. Contents: I. Óbras publicadas de Luisa Josefina Hernández. A. Teatro. B. Fragmentos de las comedias. C. Novelas. D. Fragmentos de las novelas. E. Crítica. II. Traducciones por Luisa Josefina Hernández. III. Crítica sobre Luisa Josefina Hernández. A. Estudios y reseñas. B. Obras generales. C. Bibliografía.

HERNANDEZ AQUINO, LUIS (Puerto Rico, 1907-)
Foster, P.R. Lit., pp. 122-123. Critical Essays.

HERNANDEZ-CATA, ALFONSO (Cuba, 1885-1940)
Foster, Cuban Lit., pp. 274-277. Contents: I. Critical Monographs and Dissertations. II. Critical Essays.
Torriente, Gastón F. de la. LA NOVELA DE HERNANDEZ-CATA: UN ESTUDIO DESDE LA PSICOLOGIA. Madrid: Playor, 1976. 131p. "Bibliografía," pp. 121-131. Contents: I. Bibliografía activa. A. Novelas de Hernández-Catá. B. Novelas cortas de Hernández-Catá (colecciones). C. Cuentos de Hernández-Catá (colecciones). D. Teatro de Hernández-Catá. E. Obras poéticas de Hernández-Catá. II. Bibliografía pasiva.

HERNANDEZ PARDO F., JOSE ALFREDO (Peru, 1910-1962)
"José Alfredo Hernández Pardo F., ANUARIO BIBLIOGRAFICO PERUANO, 1961/1963, 530-543. Contents: I. Cronobiografía. II. Libros, folletos. III. Otras publicaciones. IV. Poesías. V. Cuentos leyendas. VI. Artículos, ensayos, etc. VII. Conferencias, discursos, etc. VIII. Notas bibliográficas. IX. Cartas. X. Referencias. XI. Necrológicas.

HERRERA, ERNESTO (Uruguay, 1889-1917)
Rela, Walter. "Ernesto Herrera: bibliografía," REVISTA DE LA BIBLIOTECA NACIONAL (Montevideo), 1, Núm. 1 (1966), 106-112. Contents: I. Obra de creación. A. Libros. B. Antologías. C. Periódicos. D. Revistas. II. Trabajos sobre el autor. A. Libros. 1. De referencia general. 2. Historias literarias. 3. Historias del teatro. 4. Biocrítica. 5. Ensayo y crítica. B. Revistas. C. Diarios y periódicos.

HERRERA, FLAVIO (Guatemala, 1894-1968)
Fecker, William. "Flavio Herrera: A Bibliography," REVISTA INTERAMERICANA DE BIBLIOGRAFIA, 28 (1978), 292-304. Contents: I. Bibliography. A. Works by Herrera. B. Novel in Manuscript. C. Short Stories: Books and Collections. D. Short Stories Published Separately. E. Short Stories: Updated Clippings from Magazines and Newspapers. F. Short Stories: Manuscripts. G. Nonficiton: Books. H. Nonfiction: Unpublished Duplicated Material. I. Nonfiction: Essays. J. Poetry: Books and Collections. II. Articles Related to the Life of

Flavio Herrera. III. Criticism on the Works of Flavio Herrera. A. Books on Flavio Herrera's Works. B. Books which Include Commentary on Flavio Herrera's Works. C. Unpublished Dissertations which Contain Commentary on Flavio Herrera's Works. D. Articles on Flavio Herrera's Works.

HERRERA Y REISSIG, JULIO (Uruguay, 1875-1910)

Anderson, pp. 86-90. Critical Essays.

Bula Píriz, Roberto. "Herrera y Reissig: vida y obra," REVISTA HISPANICA MODERNA, Año 17, Núm. 1/4 (enero/diciembre de 1951), 1-82. "Bibliografía," pp. 83-93. Contents: I. Ediciones. A. Obras publicadas en vida. 1. Poesía. 2. Prosa. 3. Prólogos. B. Obras publicadas después de su muerte. 1. Poesía. 2. Prosa. 3. Obras completas y selecciones. 4. Obras inéditas. C. Traducciones. II. Estudios. III. Poesías dedicadas.

_______. "Ediciones de poesías de Julio Herrera y Reissig," in Julio Herrera y Reissig's POESIAS COMPLETAS Y PAGINAS EN PROSA (Madrid: Aguilar, 1961), pp. 838-872. Contents: I. Ediciones de poesías de Herrera y Reissig. A. Recopilación de juicios críticos. B. Recopilación de poesías. II. La edición Aguilar. III. Poesías manuscritos por Julio Herrera y Reissig, que se conserva en su archivo. A. Poesías ordenadas por el autor. B. Poesías no ordenadas por el autor. IV. Copias manuscritas de poesías de Julio Herrera y Reissig hechas por otras personas que el autor, que contienen algunas correcciones de éste. A. Poesías ordenadas por el autor. B. Poesías no ordenadas por el autor. V. Copias manuscritas de poesías de Julio Herrera y Reissig hechas por otras personas. VI. "En este cuadro se reúnen las poesías publicadas por Herrera y Reissig durante su vida y total de manuscritos que figuren en su archivo, ordenadas de acuerdo al plan seguido en la edición Aguilar." A. Poesías ordenadas por el autor. B. Poesías no ordenadas por el autor.

Flores, BEH, pp. 120-122. Contents: I. Edición principal. II. Otras ediciones. III. Referencias. IV. Bibliografía selecta (criticism).

Herrera y Reissig, Julio. POESIA COMPLETA Y PROSA SELECTA. EDICION, NOTAS Y CRONOLOGIA: ALICIA MIGDAL. Caracas: Biblioteca Ayacucho, 1978. 441p. "Bibliografía," pp. 437-441. Contents: I. Poesía. II. Prosa. III. Obras completas y selecciones. IV. Estudios sobre Herrera y Reissig. V. Revistas de homenaje.

HIDALGO, ALBERTO (Peru, 1897-1967)

"Biobibliografía de Alberto Hidalgo," ANUARIO BIBLIOGRAFICO PERUANA, 1967/1969 (i.e., 1975), 190-193. Contents: I. Libros y folletos (1916-1967). II. Otras publicaciones. III. Artículos, ensayos. IV. Cuentos. V. Poesías. VI. Reportajes. VII. Referencias. VIII. Necrologías y homenajes póstumas.

Flores, BEH, pp. 240-241. Contents: I. Ediciones. II. Bibliografía selecta (criticism).

Foster, Peruvian Lit., pp. 157-159. Contents: I. Bibliographies. II. Critical Monographs and Dissertations. III. Critical Essays.

HOSTOS, EUGENIO MARIA DE (Puerto Rico, 1839-1903)

Flores, BEH, pp. 29-30. Contents: I. Edición principal. II. Otras ediciones. III. Referencias. IV. Bibliografía selecta (criticism).

Foster, P.R. Lit., pp. 124-143. Contents: I. Bibliographies. II. Critical Monographs and Dissertations. III. Critical Essays.

Hostos, Adolfo de. INDICE HEMERO-BIBLIOGRAFICO DE EUGENIO MARIA DE HOSTOS (INCLUYE MATERIAL INEDITO, ICONOGRAFIA Y HOSTOSIANA, 1863-1940). San Juan: Comisión Pro Celebración del Natalicio de Hostos, 1940. 756p. Contents: I. Libros, folletos, artículos periodísticos, escritos, reproducciones, metas, citas y referencias relativas a Hostos (pp. 1-657). Addenda a la primera parte (pp. 658-677). II. Libros, artículos periodísticos, cartas y escritos de Hostos (pp. 681-725). III. Iconografía (pp. 729-756).

Hostos, Eugenio María de. AMERICA: LA LUCHA POR LA LIBERTAD. ESTUDIO PRELIMINAR POR MANUEL MALDONADO-DENIS. México, D.F.: Siglo Veintiuno, 1980. 336p. "Bibliografía escogida," pp. 333-336. Contents: I. Obras completas de Hostos. II. Antologías de Hostos. III. Libros de Hostos. IV. Libros sobre Hostos. V. Traducciones de Hostos.

Oraa, Luis M. HOSTOS Y LA LITERATURA. Santo Domingo: Editorial Taller, 1982. 137p. "Bibliografía," pp. 133-137. Contents: I. Obras de Eugenio M. Hostos (Obras completas, 1939). II. Antologías de Hostos. III. Estudios sobre Eugenio M. de Hostos. IV. Colecciones de artículos sobre Hostos.

Rivera, Guillermo. "Special Bibliography: Eugenio María de Hostos, 1839-1903" in his A TENTATIVE BIBLIOGRAPHY OF THE BELLES-LETTRES OF PUERTO RICO (Cambridge: Harvard University Press, 1931), pp. 58-61. Works about Hostos arranged alphabetically.

HUDSON, WILLIAM HENRY (Argentina, 1841-1922)

Ara, Guillermo. "Libros de Hudson. Libros y artículos sobre Hudson," in his GUILLERMO E. HUDSON; EL PAISAJE PAMPEANO Y SU EXPRESION (Buenos Aires: Universidad de Buenos Aires, Facultad de Filosofía y Letras, Instituto de Literatura Argentina, 1954), pp. 319-324. The compiler lists 41 works by Hudson, 68 on Hudson, and 14 translations of his works.

Becco, Horacio Jorge. "Contribución a la bibliografía argentina: W. H. Hudson (1841-1922)," ALADA (Asociación Libreros Anticuarios de la Argentina), Año 3, Núm. 10 (octubre de 1955), 1+. Contents: I. Ediciones. II. Folletos. III. Antologías, selecciones, cartas. IV. Poemas. Artículos. Cuentos. V. Prólogos. VI. Traducciones. VII. Estudios. VIII. Bibliografía.

Payne, John R. W. H. HUDSON: BIBLIOGRAPHY. Folkestone, England: Dawson; Hamden, Conn.: Archon, 1977. 248p. Contents: I. Works by W. H. Hudson. A. Chronological Listing. B. Books and Pamphlets. C. Contributions to Books. D. Contributions to Periodicals. E. Translations. II. Books about W. H. Hudson. Compiler also lists the whereabouts of manuscripts and letters of Hudson.

Rosenbaum, Sidonia C. GUILLERMO ENRIQUE HUDSON (1841-1922): VIDA Y OBRA. New York: Hispanic Institute in the United States, 1946. "Bibliografía," pp. 37-45. Contents: I. Ediciones. II. Folletos. III. Poemas. IV. Artículos. V. Cuentos. VI. Antologías. VII. Selecciones. VIII. Cartas. IX. Traducciones. X. Estudios.

Wilson, George Francis. A BIBLIOGRAPHY OF THE WRITINGS OF W. H. HUDSON. London: The Bookman's Journal, 1922. 79p. Contents: I. First Editions, Pamphlets, Leaflets, etc. (42 titles). II. Contributions to Periodical Literature, Prefaces to Books, etc. which unless otherwise stated, have not been reprinted (15 titles).

HUERTA, EFRAIN (Mexico, 1914-)

Foster, Mex. Lit., pp. 197-198. Contents: I. Critical Monographs and Dissertations. II. Critical Essays.

HUIDOBRO, VICENTE (Chile, 1893-1948)

Flores, BEH, pp. 122-124. Contents: I. Edición principal. II. Otras ediciones. III. Bibliografía selecta (criticism).

Foster, Chilean Lit., pp. 98-108. Contents: I. Bibliographies. II. Critical Books and Theses. III. Critical Essays.

Goić, Çedomil. LA POESIA DE VICENTE HUIDOBRO. Santiago de Chile: Ediciones Nueva Universidad, Universidad Católica de Chile, 1974. 283p. Contents: I. "Bibliografía de Vicente Huidobro," pp. 261-269. A. Libros: poesía. B. Libros: narrativa. C. Libros: teatro. D. Libros: ensaysos. E. Traducciones. F. Antologías y obras completas de Huidobro. G. Artículos dispersos. H. Entrevistas. I. Antologías. II. "Bibliografía sobre Vicente Huidobro," pp. 271-283. A. Libros sobre Vicente Huidobro. B. Libros y compilaciones, capítulos o secciones sobre Huidobro. C. Libros de carácter general que se refieren a Huidobro. D. Prólogos. E. Artículos. F. Reseñas. G. Homenajes.

Hey, Nicholas. "Bibliografía de y sobre Vicente Huidobro," REVISTA IBEROAMERICANA, 41, Núm. 91 (abril/junio de 1975), 293-353. Contents: I. Bibliografía de Vicente Huidobro (exhaustive bibliography of 563 entries, partially annotated, and is especially strong in the inclusion of poems and other works in journals and newspapers). A. Antologías y compilaciones. B. Los libros de Huidobro. C. Otros poemas. D. Prosa dispersa. E. Entrevistas. II. Bibliografía sobre Vicente Huidobro. A. Libros y tesis. B. Estudios críticos. C. Homenajes a Vicente Huidobro. D. Reseñas de las publicaciones.

E. La biografía, la política, etc. F. Otros artículos. The above bibliography is reproduced in the following: Huidobro, Vicente. OBRAS COMPLETAS. PRIMERA EDICION COMPLETA DE LA OBRA LITERARIA DE V. HUIDOBRO PREPARADA, REVISADA Y PROLOGADA POR HUGO MONTES. CONTIENE UNA GUIA BIBLIOGRAFICA POR NICHOLAS HEY. Santiago de Chile: Editorial Andrés Bello, 1976. 2vs.

_______. "Adenda a la bibliografía de y sobre Vicente Huidobro," REVISTA IBEROAMERICANA, Núm. 106/107 (enero/junio de 1979), 387-398. Nos. 564-728. Contents: I. Bibliografía de Vicente Huidobro. A. Antologías y nuevas ediciones. B. Traducciones. C. Otros escritos de Huidobro. D. Entrevistas. II. Bibliografía sobre Vicente Huidobro. A. Libros y tesis. B. Estudios y artículos. III. Reseñas.

Wood, Cecil G. THE "CREACIONISMO" OF VICENTE HUIDOBRO. Fredericton: York Press, 1978. 300p. "Bibliography," pp. 290-297. Contents: I. Poetic Works of Vicente Huidobro. II. Selected Critical Works of Vicente Huidobro. III. Works on Vicente Huidobro. A. Books. B. Articles.

- I -

IBARBOUROU, JUANA DE (Argentina, 1895-1979)

Corvalán, pp. 62-64. Contents: I. Works. II. Critical Works On.

Feliciano Mendoza, Esther. JUANA DE IBARBOUROU: OFICIO DE POESIA. Río Piedras: Editorial Universitaria, Universidad de Puerto Rico, 1981. 284p. "Bibliografía," pp. 265-270. Contents: I. Obras de Juana de Ibarbourou. A. Poesía. B. Prosa. C. Teatro. II. Obra inédita. A. Poesía. B. Prosa. III. Antologías. IV. Estudios sobre Juana de Ibarbourou.

Flores, BEH, pp. 124-126. Contents: I. Edición principal. II. Otras ediciones. III. Bibliografía selecta (criticism).

IBARGUEREN (H), CARLOS (Argentina, 1897-1956)

"Bibliografía de don Carlos Ibargueren," BOLETIN DE LA ACADEMIA ARGENTINA DE LETRAS, 21, Núm. 80 (abril/junio de 1956), 187-207. 233 entries listed chronologically.

ICAZA, Jorge (Ecuador, 1906-1978)

Alarcón, Jorge N. "JORGE ICAZA Y SU CREACION LITERARIA." Ph.D., University of New Mexico, 1970. "Bibliografía," pp. 358-412.

"Bibliografía de Jorge Icaza," CULTURA (QUITO), 1 (mayo/agosto de 1978), 285-293.

"Bibliografía sobre Jorge Icaza," BIBLIOGRAFIA ECUATORIANA (QUITO), 7 (abril de 1977), 96-146.

Flores, BEH, pp. 126-128. Contents: I. Edición principal. II. Otras ediciones. III. Bibliografía selecta (criticism).

Flores, NH, v. 4, pp. 145-149. Contents: I. Edición principal. II. Referencias. III. Bibliografía selecta (criticism).

Foster, 20th Century, pp. 129-132. Contents: I. Critical Books. II. Critical Essays.

Sackett, Theodore A. EL ARTE EN LA NOVELISTICA DE JORGE ICAZA. Quito: Editorial Casa de la Cultura Ecuatoriana, 1974. 542p. "Bibliografía selecta," pp. 509-511. Contents: I. Ediciones de las novelas de Jorge Icaza. II. Bibliografías. III. Bibliografía selecta de los principales estudios icacianos de contenido estético.

Tijerina, Servando G. "A STUDY OF JORGE ICAZA AS A LITERARY FIGURE AND AS A SOCIAL REFORMER." Master's thesis, Columbia University, 1964. "Bibliography," pp. 114-164.

Vetrano, Anthony J. LA PROBLEMATICA PSICO-SOCIAL Y SU CORRELACION LINGUISTICA EN LAS NOVELAS DE JORGE ICAZA. Miami: Ediciones Universal, 1974. 154p. "Bibliografía," pp. 147, 151-152. Contents: I. Novelas de Jorge Icaza. II. Artículos relacionados con la novelística de Icaza.

INCHAUSTEGUI CABRAL, HECTOR (Dominican Republic, 1912-1979)

Núñez, Dulce María. "Bibliografía de y sobre Don Héctor Inchaustegui Cabral," EME-EME: ESTUDIOS DOMINICANOS (Santiago de los Caballeros), 9, Núm. 50 (setiembre/octubre de 1980), 117-124. Contents: I. Publicaciones de Héctor Inchaustegui Cabral. A. Libros. B. Artículos de revistas. C. Artículos o capítulos en libros. D. Artículos periódicos. II. Publicaciones sobre el doctor Héctor Inchaustegui Cabral. A. En libros. B. En revistas. C. En periódicos. D. Menciones en libros.

INCLAN, LUIS GONZAGA (Mexico, 1816-1875)

Porras Cruz, Jorge Luis. VIDA Y OBRA DE LUIS G. INCLAN. Río Piedras: Editorial Universitaria, Universidad de Puerto Rico, 1976. 230p. "Bibliografía," pp. 221-230. Contents: I. Obras de Luiz Gonzaga Inclán. II. Obras y estudios consultadas.

IRISARRI, ANTONIO JOSE DE (Guatemala, 1786-1868)

Flores, BEH, pp. 30-31. Contents: I. Ediciones. II. Referencias. III. Bibliografía selecta (criticism).

IRISARRI, HERMOGENES DE (Chile, 1819-1886)

Escudero, p. 298. Criticism.

ISAACS, JORGE (Colombia, 1837-1895)

Flores, BEH, pp. 60-63. Contents: I. Ediciones principales. II. Otras ediciones. III. Referencias. IV. Bibliografía selecta (criticism).

Flores, NH, v. 1, pp. 197-201. Contents: I. Ediciones principales. II. Referencias. III. Bibliografía selecta (criticism).

McGrady, Donald. BIBLIOGRAFIA SOBRE JORGE ISAACS. Bogotá: Instituto Caro y Cuervo, 1971. 75p. (Serie bibliográfica, 8). 490 items.

Porras Collantes, pp. 348-389. Includes works of and critical studies about the author.

Rodríguez Guerrero, Ignacio. "Jorge Isaacs: María. Noticia sobre algunas ediciones de la novela colombiana, 1867-1967," BOLETIN CULTURAL Y BIBLIOGRAFICO (BOGOTA), 10 (1967), 1063-1081. Bibliographic essay.

- J -

JAIMES FREYRE, RICARDO (Bolivia, 1870-1933)

Anderson, pp. 91-92. Critical Essays.

Flores, BEH, pp. 241-242. Contents: I. Edición principal. II. Otras ediciones. III. Bibliografía selecta (criticism).

JAMIS, FAYAD (Cuba, 1930-)

Foster, Cuban Lit., pp. 278-279. Critical essays.

JARA, MAX (Pseudonym of JOSE MAXIMILIANO JARA TRONCOSO) (Chile, 1886-1965)

"Cartillas biobibliográficas de autores chilenos: Max Jara. Yerbas Buenas, Prov. Linares, 1886-1956, Santiago. Poeta," BOLETIN DEL INSTITUTO DE LITERATURA CHILENA (Universidad de Chile, Santiago), Año 4, Núm. 11 (diciembre de 1965), 6-12. Contents: I. Obra. II. Referencias. III. Vida.

JARA TRONCOSO, JOSE MAXIMILIANO see JARA, MAX

JARAMILLO MEZA, J. B. (Honduras, 1892-)

"J. B. Jaramillo Meza: Síntesis biográfica y bibliografía," BOLETIN DE LA ACADEMIA HONDURENA DE LA LENGUA, 16 (julio de 1973), 129-131.

JARDIM, LUIS (Brazil, 1901-)

Jardim, Luís. SELETA. SELEÇAO DE PAULO RONAI. NOTAS, COMENTARIOS E ESTUDO CRITICO DE EUGENIO GOMES. Rio de Janeiro: José Olympio, 1974. 115p. "Bibliografia de Luís Jardim," pp. 113-114.

JEREZ VALERO, ERNESTO (Venezuela, 1923-)

Cardozo, Poesía, pp. 186-188. Includes the poetical works of and the critical studies about the author.

JOGLAR CACHO, MANUEL (Puerto Rico, 1898-)

Foster, P.R. Lit., pp. 143-144. Contents: I. Critical Monographs. II. Critical Essays.

JUARROZ, ROBERTO (Argentina, 1925-)

Foster, Arg. Lit., p. 476. Contents: I. Critical Monograph. II. Critical Essays.

JUCA FILHO, CANDIDO (Brazil, 1900-)
Barbadinho Neto, Raimundo. "Bibliografia de Cândido Jucá (filho)," in ESTUDOS EM HOMENAGEM A CANDIDO JUCA (FILHO) (Rio de Janeiro: Organização Simões Editôra, 1970?), pp. 13-27. By year, 1923-1968.

JUNQUEIRA FREIRE, LUIS JOSE (Brazil, 1832-1855)
Mota, Artur. "Perfis acadêmicos, Cadeira No. 25: Junqueira Freire," REVISTA DA ACADEMIA BRASILEIRA DE LETRAS, Núm. 168 (dezembro de 1935), 458-470. Contents: I. "Bibliografia," pp. 458-459. (1855-1869). II. "Fontes para o estudo crítico," pp. 459-461.
Pires, Homero. JUNQUEIRA FREIRE. ENSAIO BIO-BIBLIOGRAFICO. Rio de Janeiro: Officina Industrial Graphica, 1932. 91p. (Publicações da Academia Brasileira III, Bibliografia 4). Contents: I. Nota biográfica. II. Bibliografia. A. Manuscritos. B. Obras impressas. C. Estudos e opiniões sôbre Junqueira Freire. D. Depoimentos.
______. JUNQUEIRA FREIRE. SUA VIDA, SUA EPOCA, SUA OBRA. Rio de Janeiro: Edição de A ORDEM, orgão de Centro D. Vital, 1929. 343p. "Bibliografia," pp. 332-343. Contents: I. Manuscriptos de Junqueira Freire. II. Obras impressas de Junqueira Freire. III. Estudos e opiniões sôbre Junqueira Freire.
Rio de Janeiro. Biblioteca Nacional. LUIS JOSE JUNQUEIRA FREIRE, 1832-1855. BIBLIOGRAFIA ORGANIZADO PELA SEÇAO DE REFERENCIA DA BIBLIOTECA NACIONAL DO RIO DE JANEIRO, MAIO 1955. Rio de Janeiro, 1955. 15p.

JURANDIR, DALCIDIO (Brazil, 1909-)
Porter, pp. 226-227. Contents: I. Writings. II. References, Critical and Biographical.

"JUSTO DE LARA" see ARMAS Y CARDENAS, JOSE DE

- K -

KOZER, JOSE (Cuba, 1940-)
Foster, Cuban Lit., pp. 280-281. Critical Essays.

- L -

LABRADOR RUIZ, ENRIQUE (Cuba, 1902-)
Febres Cordero G., Julio. "Enrique Labrador Ruiz: contribución a una bibliografía," REVISTA DE LA BIBLIOTECA NACIONAL (LA HABANA), 2a. serie, 3, Núm. 2 (abril/junio de 1952), 93-135. Contents: I. Obras sobre el autor. II. Comentarios (citations to critical commentaries about Labrador Ruiz's individual works are listed under each work). III. Prosas y cuen-

tos. IV. Selección de artículos y crónicas. V. Poemas. VI. Viajes. VII. Premio Nacional, 1950. VIII. Sobre obras inéditas o en preparación.

Foster, Cuban Lit., pp. 282-284. Contents: I. Bibliography. II. Critical Monographs. III. Critical Essays.

Molinero, Rita. LA NARRATIVA DE ENRIQUE LABRADOR RUIZ. Madrid: Nova Scholar, 1977. 262p. "Bibliografía," pp. 249-257. Contents: I. Obras de Enrique Labrador Ruiz. A. Novelas. B. Cuentos. C. Libros de ensayos. D. Artículos (by year, 1938-1959). II. Estudios sobre Enrique Labrador.

LAFERRERE, GREGORIO DE (Argentina, 1867-1913)

Foster, Arg. Lit., pp. 477-479. Contents: I. Critical Monographs. II. Critical Essays.

Laferrère, Gregorio de. OBRAS ESCOGIDAS. PROLOGO Y NOTAS DE JOSE MARIA MONNER SANS. Buenos Aires: Angel Estrada y Cía., S.A., 1943. 331p. "Los estrenos de Laferrère," pp. 328-329. "Algunos trabajos sobre el autor," pp. 329-330.

LAFOURCADE, ENRIQUE (Chile, 1927-)

Foster, Chilean Lit., pp. 108-109. Critical Books and Theses.

LAGO, JESUS MARIA (Puerto Rico, 1873-1929)

Foster, P.R. Lit., pp. 144-145. Contents: I. Dissertation. II. Critical Essays.

LAGUERRE, ENRIQUE A. (Puerto Rico, 1906-)

Casonova Sánchez, Olga. LA CRITICA SOCIAL EN LA OBRA NOVELISTICA DE ENRIQUE A. LAGUERRE. Río Piedras, Editorial Cultural, 1975. 190p. "Bibliografía," pp. 171-184. Contents: I. Obra de Enrique A. Laguerre incluyendo parte de la labor periodística. A. Novelas. B. Teatro. C. Ensayos. D. Cuentos. E. Estudios, selecciones, prólogos y artículos de periódicos. II. Trabajos sobre Enrique Laguerre.

Foster, P.R. Lit., pp. 145-149. Contents: I. Critical Monographs and Dissertations. II. Critical Essays.

Irizarry, Estelle. ENRIQUE A. LAGUERRE. Boston: Twayne, 1982. 165p. "Selected Bibliography," pp. 157-161. Contents: I. Primary Sources. A. Novels (only first editions). B. Complete Works. C. Theater. D. Essays and Prologues Mentioned in this Study. E. Short Stories. II. Secondary Sources (briefly annotated). A. Books. B. Articles.

Zayas, Luis O. LO UNIVERSAL EN ENRIQUE A. LAGUERRE: ESTUDIO DE CONJUNTO DE SU OBRA. Río Piedras: Editorial Edil, 1974. 442p. "Bibliografía mínima," pp. 435-437. Contents: I. Obras de Enrique A. Laguerre. A. Novelas. B. Cuentos. C. Ensayos. D. Teatro. E. Antologías. F. Obras completas. II. Obras sobre el autor.

LAIR, CLARA (Puerto Rico, 1895-1973)

Foster, P.R. Lit., pp. 149-150. Contents: I. Critical Monograph. II. Critical Essays.

LANDIVAR, RAFAEL (Guatemala, 1731-1793)

Bendfeldt Rojas, Lourdes. "Tópicos en la bibliografía landivariana," UNIVERSIDAD DE SAN CARLOS DE GUATEMALA, Núm. 61 (setiembre/diciembre de 1963), 69-171. A critical bibliography of and about the works of Rafael Landívar. The bibliography is inclusive for the years, 1746-1962. 687 entries under the following categories: I. Opera Omnia. II. Traducciones. III. Obras y comentarios acerca de la RUSTICATIO. IV. Comentarios y referencias biográficos. V. Referencias menores. VI. Bibliografías. VII. Conmemoraciones landivarianas. VIII. Memorabilia landivariana. IX. Documentos landivarianos. X. Bibliografía (Reference).

Valle, Rafael Heliodoro. "Bibliografía de Rafael Landívar," THESAURUS, 8, Núm. 1/3 (1952), 35-80. Following a noticia biobibliográfica of the Guatemalan Jesuit poet, there is a two-part work with the first, "Bibliografía de Landívar," in chronological order, and the second, "Bibliografía sobre Landívar," in alphabetical order. Many items have brief critical commentary and quotations.

LARRABURE Y UNANUE, EUGENIO (Peru, 1844-1916)

Larrabure y Unánue, Eugenio. MANUSCRITOS Y PUBLICACIONES DE EUGENIO LARRABURE Y UNANUE. Lima: Imprenta Americana, 1934-1936. 3vs. Volume 1: Literatura y crítica literaria.

LARRETA, ENRIQUE (Argentina, 1875-1961)

Anderson, pp. 93-97. Critical essays.

Becco, Horacio Jorge. "Bibliografía de Enrique Larreta," BOLETIN DE LA ACADEMIA ARGENTINA DE LETRAS, 26, Núm. 101/102 (julio/diciembre de 1961), 585-591. 78 titles, which were published between 1903 and 1961, are registered under the following headings: I. Obras del autor. A. Obras completas. B. Poesía. C. Teatro. D. Novela y cuento. E. Discursos. F. Prosa varia (meditaciones-memorias-estampas). G. Prólogos a obras de otros autores. II. Tesis de doctorado. III. Colaboraciones en publicaciones periódicos. IV. Traducciones del autor. V. Antología de textos del autor. VI. Crítica y biografía. VII. Bibliografías. VIII. Cronología biobibliográfica. Title, name, and illustration indexes are also included.

Flores, BEH, pp. 242-244. Contents: I. Edición principal. II. Otras Ediciones. III. Referencias. IV. Bibliografía selecta (criticism).

Foster, Arg. Lit., pp. 480-488. Contents: I. Bibliographies. II. Critical Monographs and Dissertation. III. Critical Essays.

Foster, 20th Century, pp. 132-135. Contents: I. Bibliographies. II. Critical Books. III. Critical Essays.

Jansen, André. ENRIQUE LARRETA: NOVELISTA HISPANO-ARGENTINA, 1873-1961. PROLOGO DE ARTURO BERENGUER CARISMO. TRADUCCION DE FERNANDO MURRILLO RUBIERA. Madrid: Ediciones Cultura Hispánica, 1967. 349p. "Bibliografía," pp. 305-334. Contents: I. Obras de Enrique Larreta. A. Cuento. B. Novelas. C. Discursos, ensayos y memorias. D. Poesía. E. Teatro. F. Obras completas. II. Traducciones de las obras de Enrique Larreta. III. Obras generales de consulta. IV. Obras, manuales, tratados, estudios y artículos relativos a la literatura hispanoamericana. V. Estudio del movimiento modernista. VI. Estudio de la literatura española de fines del siglo XIX y del siglo XX. VII. Historia de la literatura argentina. VIII. Artículos y trabajos críticos relativos a la obra de Enrique Larreta. IX. Artículos y obras consultadas en relación con la biografía de Enrique Larreta.

Montero, María Luisa, and Angélica L. Tortola. CONTRIBUCION A LA BIBLIOGRAFIA DE ENRIQUE LARRETA. Buenos Aires: Fondo Nacional de las Artes, 1964. 59p. (Bibliografía Argentina de Artes y Letras, Compilaciones Especiales, 19). Contents: I. Obras del autor. A. Obras completas. B. Poesía. C. Teatro. D. Novela y cuento. E. Discursos. F. Prosa varia. II. Prólogos a obras de otros autores. III. Tesis de doctorado. IV. Colaboraciones en publicaciones periódicas. A. Poesía. B. Teatro. C. Novela y cuento. D. Discursos. E. Encuestas y entrevistas. F. Prosa varia. V. Traducciones de obras del autor. VI. Antología de textos del autor. VII. Textos del autor en diversas antologías. VIII. Crítica y biografía. A. Trabajos firmados. B. Artículos sin firmar. C. Notas necrológicas y homenajes póstumos. D. Reseñas. Notas bibliográficas. Crónicas de estreno. IX. Bibliografías. X. Tesis. XI. Cronología bio-bibliográfica. XII. Indices: De títulos, onomástico. XIII. Ilustraciones.

LARS, CLAUDIA (Pseudonym of CARMEN BRANNON BEERS) (El Salvador, 1899-1974)

Chavarría López, Mayra. "Bibliografía de Claudia Lars," REVISTA HISTORICO-CRITICA DE LITERATURA CENTROAMERICANA, 1 (enero/junio de 1975), 101-102.

Wycoff, Adriann Constantine. "THE LIFE AND WORKS OF CLAUDIA LARS." Ph.D., Northwestern University, 1984. 158p. The notes to Chapter 1 include a list of those libraries in the U.S. which have catalogued copies of Lars' volumes in their collections.

LASTARRIA, JOSE VICTORINO (Chile, 1817-1888)

Foster, Chilean Lit., pp. 109-112. Contents: I. Critical Books and Theses. II. Critical Essays.

Subercaseaux S., Bernardo. CULTURA Y SOCIEDAD LIBERAL EN EL SIGLO XIX (LASTARRIA, IDEOLOGIA Y LITERATURA). Santiago de Chile: Editorial Aconcagua, 1981. 325p. "José Victorino Lastarria," pp. 316-319. Contents: I. Obra. II.

Correspondencia. III. Algunas publicaciones en que colaboró (list of journals only). IV. Sobre Lastarria.

LATCHAM, RICARDO (Chile, 1903-1965)

"Cartillas biobibliográficas de autores chilenos: Ricardo Antonio Latcham Alfaro. La Serena, 1903-1965, La Habana (Cuba). Ensayista, cuentista y crítico literario," BOLETIN DEL INSTITUTO DE LITERATURA CHILENA (Universidad de Chile, Santiago), Año 4, Núm. 10 (julio de 1965), 23-36. Contents: I. Obra. II. Referencias. III. Vida. IV. Otros datos (diarios, periódicos y revistas). V. Homenajes.

Rojas Piña, Benjamín. "Don Ricardo A. Latcham en las páginas de ATENEA. Bibliografía," ATENEA (Santiago de Chile), Año 42, Tomo 158, Núm. 408 (abril/junio de 1965), 106-132. The compiler lists 22 comments on 66 contributions by the Chilean critic Ricardo Latcham, which appeared in the Chilean review ATENEA.

LATORRE, MARIANO (Chile, 1886-1955)

"Cartillas biobibliográficas de autores chilenos: Mariano Latorre Court. Cobquecura, Maule, 1886-1955, Santiago. Cuentista, novelista, crítico y ensayista," BOLETIN DEL INSTITUTO DE LITERATURA CHILENA (Universidad de Chile, Santiago), Años 7/8, Núm. 15/16 (diciembre de 1968), 15-44. Contents: I. Obra. II. Referencias. III. Vida.

Castilla, Homero. "Trayectoría bibliográfica de los cuentos de Latorre," REVISTA INTERAMERICANA DE BIBLIOGRAFIA, 9 (1959), 341-355. Annotated entries. Contents: I. Obras. II. Cuentos en antologías. III. Indice y trayectoría de los cuentos (Lista alfabética de los cuentos de Latorre, consignando el lugar en que aparecieron, las variantes de título y las traducciones que de ellos se conocen).

Flores, BEH, pp. 244-245. Contents: I. Ediciones. II. Referencias. III. Bibliografía selecta (criticism).

Foster, Chilean Lit., pp. 112-118. Contents: I. Bibliographies. II. Critical Books and Theses. III. Critical Essays.

Orlandi Araya, Julio and Alejandro Ramírez Cid. MARIANO LATORRE: OBRA, ESTILO, TECNICA. Santiago de Chile: Editorial del Pacífico, 1960. 63p. "Bibliografía de Mariano Latorre," pp. 53-62. Contents: I. Obras del autor. A. Novelas, cuentos y ensayos. B. Prólogos. II. Referencias a sus obras.

Santana, Francisco. MARIANO LATORRE. Santiago de Chile: Augusto Bello Editor, 1956. 72p. Contents: I. "Bibliografías y referencias críticas," pp. 65-68. II. "Prólogos," p. 68. III. "Entrevistas," p. 69. IV. "Cuentos publicados con diferentes títulos," pp. 69-71.

LAVARDEN, MANUEL JOSE DE (Argentina, 1754-1809)

Foster, Arg. Lit., pp. 489-490. Contents: I. Critical Monographs. II. Critical Essays.

LAZO, RAIMUNDO (Cuba, 1904-1976)
"Curriculum vitae de Raimundo Lazo," ANALES DE LITERATURA HISPANOAMERICANA (Madrid), Núm. 5 (1976), 15-19. A list of monographs published appears on pp. 17-19.
"Raimundo Lazo Baryolo: bío-bibliografía," BIBLIOGRAFIA CUBANA, 1976, 156-161. Contents: I. Biografía. II. Bibliografía activa. III. Prólogos.

LAZO BAEZA, OLEGARIO (Chile, 1878-1964)
"Cartillas biobibliográficas de autores chilenos: Olegario Lazo Baeza. San Fernando, 1878. Cuentista y novelista," BOLETIN DEL INSTITUTO DE LITERATURA CHILENA (Universidad de Chile, Santiago de Chile), Año 2, Núm. 4/5 (julio de 1963), 14-21.

LEAL, ANTONIO HENRIQUES (Brazil, 1828-1885)
Moraes, pp. 28-30. Major works by and about the author.

LEAL, LUIS (Mexico, 1907-)
HOMENAJE A LUIS LEAL: ESTUDIOS SOBRE LITERATURA HISPANOAMERICANA. Madrid: Insula, 1978. 216p. "Bibliografía de Luis Leal," pp. 15-25. Contents: I. Libros. II. Antologías y libros editados. III. Contribuciones en libros. IV. Prefacios a libros. V. Artículos y ensayos. VI. Reseñas.

LEANTE, CESAR (Cuba, 1928-)
Foster, Cuban Lit., pp. 285-286. Contents: I. Dissertation. II. Critical Essays.

LEAO, JOSE JOAQUIM DE CAMPOS see QORPO-SANTO

LEDESMA, ROBERTO (Argentina, 1901-1966)
Pereyra, Nicandro. ROBERTO LEDESMA. Buenos Aires: Ediciones Culturales Argentinas, Ministerio de Educación y Justicia, Dirección General de Cultura, 1964. 113p. "Bibliografía," pp. 103-110. 87 items. Contents: I. Ensayos. II. Conferencias. III. Reportajes. IV. Cuentos. V. Teatro. VI. Libros publicados. A. Poesía. B. Novela. C. Ensayos. VII. Juicios sobre Roberto Ledesma (trabajos firmados).

LENERO, VICENTE (Mexico, 1933-)
Flores, BEH, pp. 245-246. Contents: I. Ediciones. II. Bibliografía selecta (criticism).
Foster, Mex. Lit., pp. 219-221. Contents: I. Bibliographies. II. Critical Monographs and Dissertations. III. Critical Essays.
Foster, 20th Century, pp. 135-136. Contents: I. Critical Books. II. Critical Essays.

LENZ, RODOLFO (Chile, 1863-1939)
Escudero, Alfonso M. RODOLFO LENZ. Bogotá: Instituto Caro y Cuervo, 1963. 40p. "Bibliografía de Lenz," pp. 27-36. Re-

printed from THESAURUS (Bogotá), 18 (mayo/agosto de 1963), 471-480. The bibliography section annotates more than 104 titles, which are arranged chronologically, 1887-1940. There is also an "algunas fuentes consultables," section, pp. 480-484.

LEON, CARLOS AGUSTO (Venezuela, 1914-)

BENCOMO DE LEON, GUADALUPE. BIBLIOGRAFIA DE CARLOS AUGUSTO LEON Y OTRAS FUENTES PARA EL ESTUDIO DE SU OBRA. Caracas: Universidad Central de Venezuela, Ediciones del Rectorado, 1981. 189p. This bibliography lists separately the poetry and prose of León and references to him in dictionaries, histories, and other sources. Includes a name index.

LEONI, RAUL DE (Brazil, 1895-1926)

Leôni, Raul de. TRECHOS ESCOLHIDOS POR LUIZ SANTA CRUZ. Rio de Janeiro: Livraria Agir Editôra, 1961. 125p. "Bibliografia do autor," pp. 116-117 (arranged by year, 1919-1959). II. "Bibliografia sôbre o autor," pp. 118-121 (arranged by year, 1922-1956).

LESSA, PEDRO (Brazil, 1859-1921)

Mota, Artur. "Perfis acadêmicos, Cadeira No. 11: Pedro Lessa," REVISTA DA ACADEMIA BRASILEIRA DE LETRAS, Núm. 82 (outubro de 1928), pp. 241-248. Contents: I. "Bibliografia," pp. 241-242 (1871-1925). II. "Fontes para o estudo crítico," p. 243.

LEZAMA LIMA, JOSE (Cuba, 1910-1976)

Fernández, Luis Francisco. "JOSE LEZAMA LIMA Y LA CRITICA ANAGOGICA." Ph.D., University of Illinois, 1975. 316p. "Bibliografía," pp. 307-315. Contents: I. Obras de José Lezama Lima. A. Colecciones de poemas. B. Tomos de ensayos. C. Cuentos. D. Novela. E. Antologías de las obras de Lezama. F. Antologías preparadas por Lezama. II. Estudios sobre Lezama y otras obras consultadas.

Flores, BEH, pp. 246-248. Contents: I. Ediciones principales. II. Otras ediciones. III. Referencias. IV. Bibliografía selecta (criticism).

Foster, Cuban Lit., pp. 287-300. Contents: I. Bibliography. II. Critical Monographs and Dissertations. III. Critical Essays.

Foster, 20th Century, pp. 136-138. Contents: I. Bibliographies. II. Critical Books. III. Critical Essays.

"José Lezama Lima: bío-bibliografía," BIBLIOGRAFIA CUBANA, 1976, 161-165. Contents: I. Biografía. II. Bibliografía activa.

Ulloa, Justo C. JOSE LEZAMA LIMA: TEXTOS CRITICOS. Miami: Ediciones Universal, 1979. 156p. Contents: "Contribución a la bibliografía de y sobre José Lezama Lima (1937-1978)," pp. 115-156. 612 entries. I. Bibliografía de José Lezama Lima. A. Obras. B. Prólogos, antologías y compilaciones. C. Fragmentos. D. Colaboraciones en libros, revistas (by title) y periódicos (by title). E. Traducciones. II. Bibliografía sobre José Lezama Lima. A. Libros y tesis. C. Antologías, homenajes y compilaciones críticas. D. Encuestas. E. Entrevistas. F. Artículos, reseñas y menciones.

LIDA DE MALKIEL, MARIA ROSA (Argentina, 1910-1962)

Malkiel, Yakov. "Preliminary Bibliography of the Writings of María Rosa Lida de Malkiel," ROMANCE PHILOLOGY, 17, Nos. 1/2 (1963), 33-52. An annotated bibliography. Contents: I. General. II. Books. III. Articles. IV. Review Articles. V. Notes. VI. Prefaces. VII. Editions. VIII. Book Reviews. IX. Brief Book Reviews. X. Book Length Translations. XI. Shorter Translations. XII. Juvenilia. XIII. Writings Left Unpublished. XIV. Some Unpublished Lectures. XV. Addenda.

_______. "Supplement to the Preliminary María Rosa Lida de Malkiel Bibliography," ROMANCE PHILOLOGY, 20, No. 1 (August 1966), 44-52. Contents: I. Memorialization. A. Memorials. B. Writings Dedicated to the Memory of M.R.L. de M. 1. Books. 2. Articles and Chapters in Books. C. Necrologies. D. Appreciation. II. Addenda to Individual Entries.

LIHN, ENRIQUE (Chile, 1929-)

Flores, BEH, pp. 248-249. Contents: I. Ediciones. II. Bibliografía selecta (criticism).

Lihn, Enrique. CONVERSACIONES CON ENRIQUE LIHN. Xalapa, México: Centro de Investigaciones Lingüístico-Literarias, Instituto de Investigaciones Humanísticas, Universidad Veracruzana, 1980. 153p. (Cuadernos de texto crítico, 10). "Bibliografía," pp. 135-153. Includes works of and about the author.

LILLO, BALDOMERO (Chile, 1867-1923)

Flores, BEH, pp. 128-129. Contents: I. Edición principal. II. Otras ediciones. III. Referencias. IV. Bibliografía selecta (criticism).

Foster, Chilean Lit., pp. 118-121. Contents: I. Critical Books and Theses. II. Critical Essays.

LILLO, EUSEBIO (Chile, 1826-1910)

Escudero, pp. 298-300. Criticism.

LIMA, ALCEU AMOROSO (Brazil, 1893-)

Lima, Alceu Amoroso. ESTUDOS LITERARIOS. EDIÇAO ORGANIZADA POR AFRANIO COUTINHO COM ASSISTENCIA DO AUTOR. Rio de Janeiro: Companhia Aguilar Editôra, 1966. 1061p. "Bibliografia," pp. 43-49. Contents: I. Obras do autor. A. Edições brasileiras. B. Em língua castelhana. C. Em língua francesa. D. Traduções de outros autores. II. Obras sôbre o autor. A. Livros e folhetos. B. Fascículos e conferências. C. Revistas. D. Jornais.

LIMA, JORGE DE (Brazil, 1893-1953)
Lima, Jorge de. POESIA COMPLETA. SEGUNDA EDIÇAO. Rio de Janeiro: Nova Fronteira, 1980. 2vs. "Bibliografia," v. 1, pp. 31-33. Contents: I. Poesia. II. Romance. III. Ensaio. IV. Teatro e cinema. V. História e biografia. VI. Traduções. VII. Conferências. VIII. Traduções para outros idiomas. IX. Antologia. X. Pintura. XI. Música.
Porter, pp. 227-229. Contents: I. Writings. II. References, Critical and Biographical.

LINS, ALVARO (Brazil, 1912-)
Bolle, Adélia Bezerra de Meneses. A OBRA CRITICA DE ALVARO LINS E SUA FUNÇAO HISTORICA. Petrópolis: "Vozes," 1979. 117p. "Bibliografia," pp. 113-115. Contents: I. De Alvaro Lins. A. Livros. B. Artigos de jornal/revista. II. Sôbre Alvaro Lins. A. Artigos de livros. B. Artigos de jornal. III. Bibliografia geral consultada. A. Livros. B. Artigos de jornal/revista.
Fonseca, Edson Nery da. "Alvaro Lins: bibliografia com notas remissivos," REVISTA DO LIVRO (Rio), Núm. 43 (1970), 128-137. Contents: I. De Alvaro Lins. A. Livros. B. Colaboração em obras individuais e coletivas. C. Colaboração em revistas. D. Edições. II. Sôbre Alvaro Lins. 64 titles.

LIRA, MARTIN JOSE (Chile, 1835-1867)
Escudero, p. 301. Criticism.

LIRA, MIGUEL NICOLAS (Mexico, 1905-1961)
Arreola Cortés, Raúl. MIGUEL N. LIRA: EL POETA Y EL HOMBRE. México, D.F.: Editorial Jus, 1977. 308p. "Bibliografía de M.N.L.," pp. 293-308. The 231 entries are arranged by year, 1922-1961, and include books, journal articles, newspaper articles, and unedited works.

LISBOA, JOAO FRANCISCO (Brazil, 1812-1863)
Moraes, pp. 13-16. Major works by and about the author.
Mota, Artur. "Perfis acadêmicos, Cadeira No. 18: João Francisco Lisbôa," REVISTA DA ACADEMIA BRASILEIRA DE LETRAS, Núm. 96 (dezembro de 1929), 434-449. Contents: I. "Bibliografia," pp. 434-435 (1864-1891). "Fontes para o estudo crítico," pp. 435-436.
Peregrino Júnior, João. FRANCISCO LISBOA. HOMEM DA PROVINCIA. Rio de Janeiro: Publicações de Academia Brasileira, 1957. 97p. Contents: I. Estudo biográfico (pp. 7-73). II. Bibliografia (pp. 75-89). His works only.

LISPECTOR, CLARICE (Brazil, 1925-1977)
Corvalán, pp. 67-68. Contents: I. Works. II. Critical Works On.
Espejo Beshers, Olga. "Clarice Lispector: A Bibliography," REVISTA INTERAMERICANA DE BIBLIOGRAFIA, 34 (1984), 385-402. Contents: I. Works by Lispector (by year, 1944-1981;

monographs only). II. Stories by Lispector in Anthologies. III. Books and Dissertations about Lispector. IV. Chapters and Sections in Books about Lispector. V. Critical Articles about Lispector. VI. Writings about Clarice Lispector: The Woman, the Reporter, the Writer, Interviews. Briefly annotated entries.

Fitz, Earl F. "Bibliografia de y sôbre Clarice Lispector," REVISTA IBEROAMERICANA, Núm. 126 (enero/marzo de 1984), 293-304. Contents: I. Obras de Clarice Lispector (includes only first editions). II. Traduções. III. Livros sôbre Clarice Lispector. IV. Artigos e ensaios em tôrno de Clarice Lispector (newspaper articles not included).

Lispector, Clarice. SELETA DE CLARICE LISPECTOR. SELEÇAO E TEXTO-MONTAGEM DO PROF. RENATO CORDEIRO GOMES. ESTUDO E NOTAS DO PROF. AMARILES GUIMARAES HILL. Rio de Janeiro: Livraria José Olympio, 1975. 153p. "Bibliografia de Clarice Lispector," pp. 148-153. Contents: I. Romances. II. Contos. III. Livros infantis. IV. Alguns estudos sôbre Clarice Lispector.

Sá, Olga. A ESCRITURA DE CLARICE LISPECTOR. Petrópolis: Editôra Vozes, Ltda., 1979. 278p. Contents: I. "Bibliografia de Clarice Lispector," p. 267 (works arranged by year, p. 267). II. "Bibliografia sôbre Clarice Lispector," pp. 269-273.

LOBATO, JOSE BENTO MONTEIRO (Brazil, 1882-1948)

Athanázio, Enéas. 3 DIMENSÕES DE LOBATO. São Paulo: Editôra do Escritor, 1975. 81p. "Bibliografia lobatiana," pp. 73-75.

Cavalheiro, Edgard. MONTEIRO LOBATO: VIDA E OBRA. 3ª edição. São Paulo: Editôra Brasiliense, 1962. 2 vs. "Bibliografia," v. 2, pp. 277-292. Contents: I. Obras em livros. II. Obras em jornais e revistas.

Lobato, José Bento Monteiro. URUPES. São Paulo: Editôra Brasiliense, 1966. 300p. Contents: I. "Obras de Monteiro Lobato," pp. 61-62. II. "Fontes para o estudo de Monteiro Lobato e sua obra," pp. 63-78.

________. URUPES, OUTROS CONTOS E COISAS. EDIÇAO ONIBUS. ORGANIZADA E PREFACIADA POR ARTUR NEVES. São Paulo: Companhia Editôra Nacional, 1943. 663p. "Fontes para o estudo de Monteiro Lobato," pp. xlv-l.

Rio de Janeiro. Biblioteca Nacional. MONTEIRO LOBATO, 1882-1948. CATALOGO DA EXPOSIÇAO. Apresentação de Célia Ribeiro Zaher. Rio de Janeiro, 1982. 91p.

Silva, Maria do Carmo Fernandes da, and Eliana Floriano da Silva. "Bibliografia de e sôbre Monteiro Lobato (José Bento Monteiro Lobato, 1882-1948)," BOLETIM BIBLIOGRAFICO DA BIBLIOTECA MUNICIPAL "MARIO DE ANDRADE," 37 (julho/dezembro de 1976), 103-253. 1,674 entries. Contents: I. Produção literária de Monteiro Lobato. A. Literatura geral. 1. Obras (by work). 2. Conferências e entrevistas. 3. Prefácios e apresentações. 4. Traduções e versões. 5. Obras em coletâneas.

6. Transcrições em Braille. 7. Artigos de periódicos. a. Revistas. b. Jornais. B. Literatura infantil. 1. Obras (by work). 2. Traduções, adaptações e versões. 3. Obras coletâneas. 4. Transcrições em Braille. II. Publicações sôbre a obra de Monteiro Lobato. A. Crítica e interpretação (literatura geral). B. Crítica e interpretação (literatura infantil. C. Biografias gerais. D. Citações ao escritor. E. Homenagens. F. Filmografia.

Yunes, Eliana. PRESENÇA DE MONTEIRO LOBATO. Rio de Janeiro: Divulgação e Pesquisa, 1982. 67p. Contents: I. "Bibliografia infantil de Monteiro Lobato," pp. 65-66. II. "Bibliografia recente sôbre Monteiro Lobato," pp. 66-67.

LOBO, ANTONIO (Brazil, 1870-1916)
Moraes, pp. 81-83. Major works by and about the author.

LOPES, BERNARDINO DA COSTA (Brazil, 1859-1916)
Porter, pp. 232-233. Contents: I. Writings. II. References, Critical and Biographical.

LOPES NETO, JOAO SIMOES (Brazil, 1865-1916)
SIMOES LOPES NETO: A INVENÇAO, O MITO E A MENTIRA; UMA ABORDAGEM ESTRUTURALISTA. Porto Alegre: Movimento/I.E.L., 1973. 135p. Contents: I. "Bibliografia de Simões Lopes Neto (obras publicadas)," p. 24. II. "Bibliografia sôbre Simões Lopes Neto," pp. 25-26.

LOPEZ, LUCIO VICENTE (Argentina, 1848-1894)
Foster, Arg. Lit., pp. 491-492. Contents: I. Critical Monograph and Dissertation. II. Critical Essays.

LOPEZ, LUIS CARLOS (Colombia, 1883-1950)
Bazik, Martha S. THE LIFE AND WORKS OF LUIS CARLOS LOPEZ. Chapel Hill, N.C.: University of North Carolina, Department of Romance Languages, 1977. 147p. (North Carolina Studies in the Romance Languages and Literatures, 183). "Bibliography," pp. 111-115. Contents: I. Editions. II. Journal Publications. III. Anthologies. IV. Unpublished Poems. V. Anthologies Published in the United States. VI. Translations in English. VII. Critical References. VIII. Background Material.

Flores, BEH, pp. 129-130. Contents: I. Ediciones. II. Bibliografía selecta (criticism).

LOPEZ, RAFAEL (Mexico, 1873-1943)
Zaïtzeff, Serge I. "Más sobre Rafael López," BOLETIN DEL INSTITUTO DE INVESTIGACIONES BIBLIOGRAFICAS (México, D.F.), Núm. 14/15 (1977/78), 535-559. A bibliography. Contents: I. Libros. II. Prólogo. III. Hemerografía. IV. Bibliografía sobre Rafael López. A. Libros. B. Artículos. C. Encuestas. IV. Poemas desconocidos de Rafael López.

LOPEZ ALBUJAR, ENRIQUE (Peru, 1872-1966)

Cornejo, Raúl E. "Bibliografía general de López Albújar," in Enrique López Albújar's MEMORIAS. PROLOGO DE CIRO ALEGRIA. COLOFON Y BIBLIOGRAFIA DE RAUL ESTUARDO CORNEJO (Lima: P. L. Villanueva, 1963), pp. 129-212. Contents: I. Obra edita. A. Libros. B. Antología. C. Folletos. D. Prólogos y colofones. II. Obra inédita: libros. III. Publicaciones periodísticas (1892-1963). IV. Bibliografía sobre López Albújar. A. Libros. B. Tesis. C. Prólogos. D. Publicaciones periodísticas (1893-1963).

"Enrique López Albújar," ANUARIO BIBLIOGRAFICO PERUANO, 1964/1966, 565-612. Contents: I. Libros y folletos. II. Otras publicaciones. A. Cuentos. B. Novelas. C. Teatro. D. Poesías. E. Artículos y ensayos. F. Discursos. G. Conferencias. H. Cartas. I. Comunicaciones. J. Memorias. K. Reportajes. III. Referencias. IV. Homenajes. V. Homenajes y necrológicas póstumas.

Flores, BEH, pp. 130-131, 183-184. Contents: I. Ediciones. II. Referencias. III. Bibliografía selecta (criticism).

Foster, Peruvian Lit., pp. 160-162. Contents: I. Bibliographies. II. Critical Monographs. III. Critical Essays.

LOPEZ LOPEZ, JOAQUIN (Puerto Rico, 1900-1942)

Foster, P.R. Lit., pp. 155-156. Contents: I. Critical Monograph and Dissertation. II. Critical Essays.

LOPEZ PORTILLO Y ROJAS, JOSE (Mexico, 1850-1923)

Foster, Mex. Lit., pp. 221-222. Contents: I. Bibliographies. II. Critical Monographs and Dissertations. III. Critical Essays.

Villaseñor y Villaseñor, Ramiro. BIBLIOGRAFIA DE JOSE LOPEZ PORTILLO Y ROJAS, 1850-1923. Guadalajara, 1950. 20p. (Suplemento a Et Caetera, Año 1, Núm. 4 (Enero/diciembre de 1950). Contents: I. Libros y folletos (1870-1945). II. Traducciones. III. Artículos sueltos (1868-1935). IV. Periodismo (1866-1927). V. Crítica.

_______. "Bibliografía de D. José López-Portillo y Rojas," in José López-Portillo y Rojas' CUENTOS COMPLETOS (México: Ediciones I. T. G., 1952), v. 1, pp. xxxiii-xliii. Contents: I. Libros y folletos (1870-1945). II. Traducciones. III. Artículos sueltos (1868-1935). IV. Periodismo (1866-1927). V. Crítica.

Warner, Ralph E. "Aportaciones a la bibliografía de don José López Portillo y Rojas," REVISTA IBEROAMERICANA, 13, Núm. 25 (Octubre de 1947), 165-198. Not a comprehensive bibliography, but representative of the author's works and of writings about him. Chiefly lacking, according to the compiler, are early publications in newspapers and magazines of Guadalajara. Partially annotated entries under the following headings: I. Obras del autor. A. Novela. B. Poesía. C. Artículos literarios, etc. D. Obras dramáticas. E. Obras varias. F. Traducciones. II. Trabajos referentes a López Portillo.

LOPEZ SURIA, VIOLETA (Puerto Rico, 1926-)
Foster, P.R. Lit., pp. 156-157. Critical Essays.

LOPEZ VELARDE, RAMON (Mexico, 1888-1921)
Arce, David N. "Apuntes para la bibliografía de y sobre Ramón López Velarde," EL LIBRO Y EL PUEBLO, época 4, Núm. 2 (junio de 1963), 16-22 and 30. Contents: I. Obras. II. Crítica.
_______. "Bibliografías mexicanas contemporáneas. XIV. Obra y glosario de Ramón López Velarde," BOLETIN DE LA BIBLIOTECA NACIONAL (México), 14, Núm. 3/4 (julio/diciembre de 1963), 85-103. Contents: I. Obra original y antologías personales. II. Obra recogida en florilegios colectivos, homenajes, etc. III. Glosario (criticism).
Flores, BEH, pp. 249-251. Contents: I. Ediciones principales. II. Otras ediciones. III. Referencias. IV. Bibliografía selecta (criticism).
Foster, Mex. Lit., pp. 222-233. Contents: I. Bibliographies. II. Critical Monographs and Dissertations. III. Critical Essays.
Gálvez de Tovar, Concepción. RAMON LOPEZ VELARDE EN TRES TIEMPOS Y UN APENDICE SOBRE EL RITMO VELARDEANO. México: Editorial Porrúa, 1971. 314p. Contents: I. Bibliografía particular (obras), pp. 289-291. II. Bibliografía general, pp. 292-295. III. Hemerografía sobre Ramón López Velarde," pp. 297-312. IV. Hemerografía general, pp. 313-314.
Phillips, Allen W. RAMON LOPEZ VELARDE: EL POETA Y EL PROSISTA. México: Instituto Nacional de Bellas Artes, Departamento de Literatura, 1962. 354p. "Bibliografía," pp. 329-347. Contents: I. Sobre la época (bibliografía mínima y selecta). II. Algunos homenajes. III. Sobre Ramón López Velarde. A. Libros. B. Estudios, ensayos, etc.

LOPEZ Y FUENTES, GREGORIO (Mexico, 1897-1966)
Flores, BEH, pp. 251-252. Contents: I. Ediciones. II. Bibliografía selecta (criticism).
Foster, Mex. Lit., pp. 233-236. Contents: I. Critical Books. II. Critical Essays.
Foster, 20th Century, pp. 138-139. Contents: I. Critical Books. II. Critical Essays.

LOVEIRA Y CHIRINO, CARLOS (Cuba, 1882-1928)
Foster, Cuban Lit., pp. 302-304. Contents: I. Bibliographies. II. Critical Monographs and Dissertations. III. Critical Essays.

LOYNAZ, DULCE MARIA (Cuba, 1903-)
Foster, Cuban Lit., pp. 305-306. Contents: I. Critical Monographs. II. Critical Essays.

LUACES, JOAQUIN LORENZO (Cuba, 1826-1867)
Foster, Cuban Lit., pp. 307-308. Contents: I. Critical Monographs. II. Critical Essays.

LUGO, SAMUEL (Puerto Rico, 1905-)
Foster, P.R. Lit., p. 157. Critical Essays.

LUGONES, LEOPOLDO (Argentina, 1874-1938)
Anderson, pp. 98-106. Critical essays.
Becco, Horacio Jorge. "Indice cronológico de primeras ediciones de don Leopoldo Lugones," BOLETIN DE LA ACADEMIA ARGENTINA DE LETRAS, 39, Núm. 153/154 (julio/diciembre de 1974), 277-278. Contents: I. Primeras ediciones. II. Ediciones póstumas. III. Antologías.
_______. LEOPOLDO LUGONES: BIBLIOGRAFIA EN SU CENTENARIO (1874-1974). Buenos Aires: Ministerio de Cultura y Educación, Ediciones Culturales Argentinas, 1975. 250p.
Berg, Mary G. "Para la bibliografía de Lugones," HISPANIC REVIEW, 36, No. 4 (October 1968), 353-357. "Entre las muchas páginas de Leopoldo Lugones--verso y prosa--que se encuentran en CARAS Y CARETAS, la revista semanal que se publicó en Buenos Aires entre 1898 y 1939, hay por lo menos tres poemas que no entraron luego en la tercera edición de sus OBRAS POETICAS COMPLETAS, Madrid, Aguilar, 1959: TUS CUATRO ROMANZAS en el número 1369, 27 diciembre 1924; EL CONSUELO DE LA TARDE, número 1408, 26 setiembre 1925; and GRANZAS DE OTOÑO, número 1906, 13 abril 1935." Article also mentions a number of uncollected short stories that appeared in CARAS Y CARETAS between 1899-1935.
Flores, BEH, pp. 131-134. Contents: I. Ediciones principales. II. Otras ediciones. III. Referencias. IV. Bibliografía selecta (criticism).
Foster, Arg. Lit., pp. 493-524. Contents: I. Bibliographies. II. Critical Monographs and Dissertations. III. Critical Essays.
Lermon, Miguel. "Contribución a la bibliografía de Leopoldo Lugones. Su obra impresa hasta 1900," BOLETIN DE LA ACADEMIA ARGENTINA DE LETRAS, 25, Núm. 98 (octubre/diciembre de 1960), 502-541. Contents: I. Nota preliminar: firmas y seudónimos. II. Noticias bibliográficas (por orden cronológico).
_______. "Indice cronológico de las ediciones de los libros de Leopoldo Lugones," BOLETIN DEL INSTITUTO BONAERENSE DE NUMISMATICA Y ANTIGUEDADES (Buenos Aires), 2ª época, Núm. 7 (octubre de 1959), 167-170.
_______. CONTRIBUCION A LA BIBLIOGRAFIA DE LEOPOLDO LUGONES. CRONOLOGIA LUGONIANA POR NATALIO KISNERMAN. ORDENADA Y PREPARADA EN EL INSTITUTO DE LITERATURA DE LA FACULTAD DE FILOSOFIA Y LETRAS DE LA UNIVERSIDAD DE BUENOS AIRES, EN HOMENAJE AL XXV ANIVERSARIO DE SU MUERTE. Buenos Aires: Ediciones Maru, 1969. 255p. Contents: I. Obras: libros, folletos y antologías. II. Obras que forman parte de otros libros. III. Discursos y conferencias, cursos. IV. Varios: textos musicalizados, obras traducidas, etc.
Roggiano, Alfredo A. "Bibliografía de y sobre Leopoldo Lugones,"

REVISTA IBEROAMERICANA, 28, Núm. 53 (enero/julio de 1962), 155-213. Contents: I. Bibliografía de Leopoldo Lugones. A. Libros y folletos. B. Antologías, selecciones, poesías completas. C. Artículos, prólogos y otros publicaciones en periódicos. 1. Sobre literatura argentina e hispanoamericana. 2. Sobre ideas estéticas, literaturas y lenguaje. II. Bibliografía sobre Leopoldo Lugones.

LUJAN RIPOLL, ROGER (Peru, 1881-1962)
Ochoa Garzón, Carmen. "Róger Luján Ripoll," ANUARIO BIBLIOGRAFICO PERUANO, 1961/1963, 572-576. Contents: I. Cronobiografía. II. Artículos y ensayos. III. Cuentos. IV. Leyendas. V. Poesías. VI. Conferencias, discursos. VII. Cartas. VIII. Intervenciones parlamentarias. IX. Reportajes. X. Necrológicas.

LUSSICH, ANTONIO DIONISIO (Argentina, 1848-1928)
Ainsa, Fernando. "Antonio Dionisio Lussich: bibliografía," REVISTA IBEROAMERICANA, 40, Núm. 87/88 (abril/setiembre de 1974), 431-432. Contents: I. Obras de Antonio D. Lussich. A. Obras gauchescas. B. Otras obras de Lussich. C. Obras de Lussich incluídas en antologías. II. Crítica sobre Lussich (selección).

LUZ Y CABALLERO, JOSE DE LA (Cuba, 1800-1862)
Foster, Cuban Lit., pp. 309-314. Contents: I. Bibliography. II. Critical Monographs. III. Critical Essays.

LYNCH, BENITO (Argentina, 1885-1952)
Becco, Horacio Jorge, and Marshall R. Nason. "Bibliografía de Benito Lynch," BIBLIOGRAFIA ARGENTINA DE ARTES Y LETRAS, Núm. 8 (octubre/diciembre de 1960), 51-87. Contents: I. Obras del autor. A. Libros. B. Traducciones. C. Cuentos y relatos. D. Teatro. E. Colaboraciones en diarios y revistas. F. Textos inéditos. G. Antologías. H. Inéditos. I. Antologías de textos de Lynch. J. Textos de Lynch en diversas antologías. II. Crítica y biografía. III. Name, title, and illustration indexes.
Flores, BEH, pp. 252-254. Contents: I. Ediciones. II. Referencias. III. Bibliografía selecta (criticism).
Foster, Arg. Lit., pp. 525-531. Contents: I. Bibliographies. II. Critical Monographs and Dissertations. III. Critical Essays.
Foster, 20th Century, pp. 139-141. Contents: I. Bibliographies. II. Critical Books. III. Critical Essays.
Sonol, Albertina. "Bibliografía de Benito Lynch," in Julio Caillet-Bois's LA NOVELA RURAL DE BENITO LYNCH. (La Plata: Universidad Nacional de La Plata, Facultad de Humanidades y Ciencias de la Educación, Departamento de Letras, 1960), pp. 91-137. Contents: I. Novelas y cuentos publicados en libros y folletos. II. Novelas inéditas. III. Cuentos narraciones publicados exclusivamente en revistas y periódicos. IV. Teatro.

V. Antologías. VI. Bibliografía sobre el autor y su obra. VII. Crónicas periodísticas. VIII. Indice de títulos del autor.

LYNCH, MARTA (Argentina, 1929-1985)
Corvalán, p. 69. Contents: I. Works. II. Critical Works On.
Foster, Arg. Lit., pp. 532-533. Contents: I. Dissertations. II. Critical Essays.

- Ll -

LLANOS ALLENDE, VICTORIO (Peru, 1897-)
Jackson, Afro-Spanish, p. 88. Contents: I. Works. II. Criticism.

LLES Y BERDAYES, FERNANDO (Cuba, 1883-1949)
Foster, Cuban Lit., p. 301. Contents: I. Critical Monographs. II. Critical Essays.

LLONA, VICTOR (Peru, 1886-1953)
Nuñez, Estuardo. Víctor Llona (1886-1953). Bio-bibliografía. BOLETIN DE LA BIBLIOTECA NACIONAL (Lima), Años 17/18, Núms. 33/34 (1965), 3-6. Contents: I. Biografía. II. Bibliografía. A. Novelas. B. Obras críticas. C. Traducciones.

LLORENS TORRES, LUIS (Puerto Rico, 1878-1944)
Caraballo de Abreu, Daisy. "La prosa de Luis Lloréns Torres," REVISTA DE ESTUDIOS HISPANICOS (Río Piedras), Año 1, Núm. 3/4 (julio/diciembre de 1971), 81-91. Contents: I. Libros. II. Prólogos. III. Artículos. IV. Diálogos. V. Estudios (upon Lloréns Torres). Nearly 300 entries.
Foster, P.R. Lit., pp. 150-154. Contents: I. Bibliographies. II. Critical Monographs and Dissertations. III. Critical Essays.
Lloréns Torres, Luis. OBRAS COMPLETAS. San Juan: Instituto de Cultura Puertorriqueña, 1967. "Bibliografía," v. 1, pp. cxxv-cxxxi. Contents: I. Ediciones. II. Prólogos. III. Estudios (criticism). IV. Poesías dedicadas.
Ortiz García, Nilda S. VIDA Y OBRA DE LUIS LLORENS TORRES. San Juan: Instituto de Cultura Puertorriqueña, 1977. 302p. "Bibliografía," pp. 267-299. Contents: I. Obras de Luis Lloréns Torres. A. Ediciones. B. Poesías sueltas. C. Prólogos. D. Artículos. E. Poesías dedicadas a Lloréns Torres. F. Homenajes a Lloréns Torres. G. Traducciones (English only). II. Estudios (criticism).

LLUCH MORA, FRANCISCO (Puerto Rico, 1924-)
Foster, P.R. Lit., p. 155. Critical Essays.

- M -

MACEDO, JOAQUIM MANUEL DE (Brazil, 1820-1882)

Mota, Artur. "Perfis acadêmicos, Cadeira No. 20: Joaquim Manuel de Macedo," REVISTA DA ACADEMIA BRASILEIRA DE LETRAS, Núm. 113 (maio de 1931), 80-99. Contents: I. "Bibliografia," pp. 80-88. (1844-1880s). II. "Fontes para o estudo crítico," pp. 88-89.

MACHADO, NAURO (Brazil, 1935-)
Moraes, pp. 119-122. Major works of and about the author.

MACHADO DE ASSIS, JOAQUIM MARIA (Brazil, 1839-1908)
Bagby Junior, Alberto I. "Eighteen Years of Machado de Assis: A Critical Annotated Bibliography for 1956-1974," HISPANIA, 58 (October 1975), 648-683. Critical commentaries on works, as well as reviews, are listed whenever applicable. Contents: I. Works by Assis. A. Anthologies, including excerpts from Assis' Works. B. Translations. 1. Novels. 2. Short Stories. 3. Poetry. 4. Drama. II. Works about Assis. A. Biography. B. Criticism. (16 topics). C. Some Commemorative Articles in the Fiftieth Anniversary of Assis' Death, 1958. III. Addendum: 1972-1974. A. Works by Assis: Anthologies. B. Works about Assis.

Fleiuss, Max. PAGINAS DE HISTORIA. 2.ed. Rio de Janeiro: Imprensa Nacional, 1930. 930p. "Chronicas de Machado de Assis na Illustração brasileira (1876-1878)."

Gomes, Celuta Moreira. "Machado de Assis: Bibliografia de livros e trechos esparsos de poesia e prosa vertidos para outras línguas," REVISTA DO LIVRO (Rio), Núm. 2 (dezembro de 1958), 281-287. Contents: I. Livros (by title and then by language). II. Antologias e periódicos. III. Poesia (by title and language).

Machado de Assis, Joaquim Maria. DOM CASMURRO. Rio de Janeiro: Civilização Brasileira; Brasília: Instituto Nacional do Livro, 1975. 267p. (Edições críticas de obras de Machado de Assis, 12). Contents: I. "Cronologia biobibliográfica," pp. 18-22. II. "Bibliografia," pp. 23-38. A. Edições. B. Traduções. C. Obra inspirada. D. Estudos referentes ao romance.

________. MEMORIAS POSTUMAS DE BRAS CUBAS. Rio de Janeiro: Civilização Brasileira; Brasília: Instituto Nacional do Livro, 1975. 301p. (Edições críticas de obras de Machado de Assis, 13). Contents: I. "Cronologia biobibliográfica," pp. 16-20. II. "Bibliografia," pp. 21-41. A. Edições. B. Estudos referentes ao romance. C. Traduções.

________. POESIAS COMPLETAS. Rio de Janeiro: Civilização Brasileira; Brasília: Instituto Nacional do Livro, 1976. 520p. (Edições críticas de obras de Machado de Assis, 7). Contents: I. "Cronologia biobibliográfica," pp. 18-22. II. "Bibliografia," pp. 23-30. A. Edições. B. Estudos referentes às poesias.

Masa, Jean-Michel. BIBLIOGRAPHIE DESCRIPTIVE, ANALYTIQUE ET CRITIQUE DE MACHADO DE ASSIS. IV: 1957-1958. Rio de Janeiro: Livraria São José, 1965. 225p. Only volume ever published. The work was conceived as a supplement to José Galante de Sousa's: FONTES PARA O ESTUDO DE MACHADO

DE ASSIS. Each item is analyzed, and a critical comment accompanies the more significant ones. A code indicates the relative originality of each contribution as well as the topics treated. Order is chronological; no alphabetical index of authors. 713 items.

_______. "LA JEUNESSE DE MACHADO DE ASSIS (1839-1870): ESSAI DE BIOGRAPHIE INTELLECTUELLE." Thèse pour le doctorat ès-lettres présentée à la Faculté des Lettres et Sciences Humaines de Poitiers, 1969. 2vs. Contents: I. "Bibliographie," v. 2, pp. 673-696. A. Ouvrages de référence. B. Documents sur Machado de Assis et sa famille. 1. Manuscrits. 2. Documents. C. Oeuvres de Machado de Assis. 1. Obras completas. 2. Publications partielles de textes retrouvés. 3. Bibliographie chronologique des oeuvres de Machado de Assis (1855-1869). II. "Critique," v. 2, pp. 709-712.

_______. "Machado de Assis traduzido," VERITAS, 25, Núm. 97 (março de 1980), 89-102. Contents: I. Novelas (includes reviews). II. Contos (includes reviews). III. Poesia. IV. Teatro.

Montello, José. MACHADO DE ASSIS. Lisboa: Verbo, 1972. 135p. Contents: I. "Bibliografia de Machado de Assis," pp. 130-132. A. Livros publicados durante a vida do autor. B. Obras completas. C. Edições de dispersos e antologias. II. "Bibliografia sôbre Machado de Assis," pp. 132-133.

Nunes, Maria Luisa. THE CRAFT OF AN ABSOLUTE WINNER: CHARACTERIZATION AND NARRATOLOGY IN THE NOVELS OF MACHADO DE ASSIS. Westport, Conn.: Greenwood Press, 1983. 158p. "Critical Works on Machado de Assis," pp. 145-148.

Porter, pp. 234-243. Contents: I. Writings. II. References, Critical and Biographical.

Rio de Janeiro. Instituto Nacional do Livro. EXPOSIÇAO MACHADO DE ASSIS. CENTENARIO DO NASCIMENTO DE MACHADO DE ASSIS, 1839-1939. Rio de Janeiro, 1939. Contents: I. "Edições originais," pp. 211-214. II. "Bibliografia do centenário," pp. 215-235.

Sousa, José Galante de. BIBLIOGRAFIA DE MACHADO DE ASSIS. Rio de Janeiro: Instituto Nacional do Livro, 1955. 772p. (Coleção B1, Bibliografia 10). An analytical bibliography of Machado de Assis' works. Contents: I. Pseudônimos, iniciais e anônimos. II. Edições. III. Versões. A. De conjunto. B. Em coletâneas. C. Em obras diversas. D. Em periódicos. E. Em separata. IV. Prefácios. V. Manuscritos. VI. Facsímiles. VII. Poesias musicadas. VIII. Discos. IX. Peça filmada. X. Adaptações radiofônicas. XI. Teatro representado. XII. Peças perdidas. XIII. Peças atribuídas. XIV. Obras de inspiração machadiana. XV. Colaboração. A. Em periódicos. B. Em obras diversas. XVI. Transcripções. A. Em periódicos. B. Em antologias. C. Em obras diversas. XVII. Indice cronológico (works listed by year, 1855-1909). XVIII. Indice alfabético. XIV. Facsímiles (reproductions of title pages from first editions).

______. FONTES PARA O ESTUDO DE MACHADO DE ASSIS. 2 ED. AMPLIADA. Rio de Janeiro: Ministério da Educação e Cultura, Instituto Nacional do Livro, 1969. 326p. (Coleção brasileira, Série bibliográfica, 1). Contents: I. By year, 1857-1957: annotated works, criticism, biographical sketches, manuscripts, etc. II. Indice onomástico. III. Suplemento (pp. 311-326). "Este suplemento inclui apenas trabalhos publicados em livro, no período 1958-1968, e alguns anteriores que escaparam a primeira edição" (by author).

MAGALHAES, ADELINO (Brazil, 1887-1969)
Magalhães, Adelino. OBRA COMPLETA. Rio de Janeiro: Companhia Aguilar Editôra, 1963. 1054p. "Bibliografia," pp. 1047-1052. Contents: I. Obras do autor. A. Livros. B. Diversos. II. Estudos sôbre o autor. A. Livros. B. Revistas. C. Jornais.

MAGALHAES, CELSO (Brazil, 1849-1879)
Moraes, pp. 45-47. Major works by and about the author.

MAGALHAES, DOMINGOS JOSE GONÇALVES DE, VISCONDE DE ARAGUAIA (Brazil, 1811-1882)
Mota, Artur. "Perfis acadêmicos, Cadeira, No. 9: Gonçalves de Magalhães," REVISTA DA ACADEMIA BRASILEIRA DE LETRAS, Núm. 77 (maio de 1928), 57-70. Contents: I. "Bibliografia," pp. 58-62. (1832-1880). II. "Fontes para o estudo crítico," pp. 63-65.

MAGALLANES MOURE, MANUEL (Chile, 1878-1924)
"Cartillas biobibliográficas de autores chilenos: Manuel Magallanes Moure. La Serena, 1878-1924, Santiago. Poeta, comediógrafo, cuentista y crítica de arte," BOLETIN DEL INSTITUTO DE LITERATURA CHILENA (Universidad de Chile, Santiago), Año 1, Núm. 2 (mayo de 1962), 13-18. Contents: I. Obras. II. En antologías poéticas. III. En antologías de cuentos. IV. Traducciones. V. Referencias. VI. Tabla biográfica.
Foster, Chilean Lit., p. 122. Contents: I. Bibliographies. II. Critical Books and Theses. III. Critical Essays.

MAGDALENO, MAURICIO (Mexico, 1906-)
Flores, BEH, pp. 254-255. Contents: I. Ediciones. II. Referencias. III. Bibliografía selecta (criticism).

MAIA, ALVARO (Brazil, 1893-1969)
Braga, Genesino. "Bibliografia de Alvaro Maia," REVISTA DA ACADEMIA AMAZONENSE DE LETRAS (MANAUS), Ano 49, v. 14 (1969), 126-130. Works are arranged by year, 1923-1967. A selected bibliography.

MALARET, AUGUSTO (Puerto Rico, 1878-1967)
Foster, P.R. Lit., pp. 158-159. Contents: I. Critical Monographs. II. Critical Essays.

MALLEA, EDUARDO (Argentina, 1903-1982)

Becco, Horacio Jorge. EDUARDO MALLEA. Buenos Aires: Universidad de Buenos Aires, Facultad de Filosofía y Letras, Instituto de Literatura "Ricardo Rojas," 1959. 24p. (Guías bibliográficas, 3). Partially annotated student guide. Contents: I. Libros, 1926-1958. II. Prólogos. III. Crítica.

Cohen, Howard R. "CRITICAL APPROACHES TO MALLEA AND SABATO: AN ANNOTATED BIBLIOGRAPHY." Ph.D., University of Virginia, 1977. 288p. Includes bibliographies of their works as well as bibliographies about them, through 1970. A cross-reference index, alphabetized by author, is also provided.

_______. "Eduardo Mallea: A Selective Annotated Bibliography of Criticism," HISPANIA, 62 (October 1979), 444-467. "This work annotates many of the important critical works on Mallea published in English and Spanish through 1978. Every attempt has been made to provide a synthesis of the scholarly books and articles cited that is faithful to the intent of each critic" (p. 444). The bibliography contains 134 entries listed chronologically, 1935-1978. Author and title indices are also included.

Flores, BEH, pp. 255-257. Contents: I. Edición principal. II. Otras ediciones. III. Referencias. IV. Bibliografía selecta (criticism).

Foster, Arg. Lit., pp. 534-548. Contents: I. Bibliographies. II. Critical Monographs and Dissertations. III. Critical Essays.

Foster, 20th Century, pp. 142-147. Contents: I. Bibliographies. II. Critical Books. III. Critical Essays.

Mallea, Eduardo. "HISTORY OF AN ARGENTINE PASSION." TRANSLATED, WITH AN INTRODUCTION AND ANNOTATIONS BY MYRON I. LICHTBLAU. Pittsburgh: Latin American Literary Review Press, 1983. 184p. "Bibliography," pp. xix-xxi. Contents: I. On History of an Argentine Passion. II. On Eduardo Mallea.

_______. OBRAS COMPLETAS. NOTA BIOBIBLIOGRAFICA Y PROLOGO DE MARIANO PICON-SALAS. Buenos Aires: Emecé Editores, 1961. "Bibliografía," por Horacio Jorge Becco, I, 1227-1244. Contents: I. Libros. II. Teatro. III. Prólogos. IV. Traducciones. V. Crítica sobre su obra.

Pinkerton, Marjorie J. "Eduardo Mallea: suplemento a una bibliografía," REVISTA IBEROAMERICANA, 30, Núm. 58 (julio/diciembre de 1964), 319-323. Updates and makes additions to Becco's Section V (Crítica sobre su obra) contained in Mallea's OBRAS COMPLETAS.

Pintor Genaro, Mercedes. EDUARDO MALLEA, NOVELISTA. Río Piedras: Editorial Universitaria, Universidad de Puerto Rico, 1976. 277p. "Bibliografía," pp. 265-277. The extensive bibliography includes all of Mallea's works and the major criticism written during the past fifty years. There is also a useful listing of general titles dealing with Spanish American literature.

MALUENDA LABARCA, RAFAEL (Chile, 1885-1963)

"Cartillas biobibliográficas de autores chilenos: Rafael Maluenda Labarca. Santiago de Chile, 1885. Novelista, cuentista, dramaturgo y periodista," BOLETIN DEL INSTITUTO DE LITERATURA CHILENA (Universidad de Chile, Santiago), Año 2, Núm. 3 (octubre de 1962), 24-34. Contents: I. Obras. II. Referencias. III. Tabla biográfica.

Foster, Chilean Lit., pp. 123-124. Contents: I. Bibliographies. II. Critical Books and Theses. III. Critical Essays.

MANACH, JORGE (Cuba, 1898-1961)

Alvarez, Nicolás Emilio. LA OBRA LITERARIA DE JORGE MANACH. Potomac, Md.: Porrúa Turanzas, 1979. 279p. "Bibliografía," pp. 265-270. Contents: I. Obra de Jorge Mañach. A. Libros, por orden cronológico (1924-1975). B. Artículos, estudios y opúsculos, por orden alfabético de títulos. II. Obras críticas sobre Mañach.

Foster, Cuban Lit., pp. 315-319. Contents: I. Bibliography. II. Critical Monographs and Dissertations. III. Critical Essays.

Martí, Jorge Luis. EL PERIODISMO LITERARIO DE JORGE MANACH. San Juan: Editorial Universitaria, Universidad de Puerto Rico, 1977. 333p. "Bibliografías," pp. 253-321. Contents: I. Bibliografía activa (no política). A. Libros. B. Folletos. C. Publicaciones literarias. 1. Ficción. 2. Arte. 3. Cultura. 4. Filosofía. 5. Literatura. D. Periodismo literario y literatura en periódicos. 1. Arte. 2. Costumbrismo. 3. Cultura. 4. Filosofía. 5. Literatura. 6. Periodismo. 7. Viajes. 8. Semblanzas. 9. Dibujos. II. Bibliografía pasiva (criticism).

Rovirosa, Dolores F. JORGE MANACH: BIBLIOGRAFIA. Madison, Wisc.: Seminar on the Acquisitions of Latin American Library Materials Secretariat, 1985. 259p. (SALALM Bibliography and Reference Series, 13). Contains 2,516 entries on the life and works of Mañach as well as listings of his works.

Torre, Amalia María V. de la. JORGE MANACH, MAESTRO DEL ENSAYO. Miami: Ediciones Universal, 1978. 259p. Contents: I. "Trabajos sobre Mañach," pp. 254-255. II. "Obras de Jorge Mañach," pp. 255-256.

Valdespino, Andrés. JORGE MANACH Y SU GENERACION EN LAS LETRAS CUBANAS. Miami: Ediciones Universal, 1971. 266p. "Bibliografía," pp. 245-253. Contents: I. Trabajos de Jorge Mañach. A. Libros y opúsculos. B. Artículos y estudios sobre temas literarios o relacionados con la literatura. II. Trabajos sobre Jorge Mañach.

MANRIQUE CABRERA, FRANCISCO (Puerto Rico, 1908-)

Foster, P.R. Lit., pp. 159-160. Contents: I. Critical Monographs and Dissertations. II. Critical Essays.

MANZANO, JUAN FRANCISCO (Cuba, 1797-1854)

Foster, Cuban Lit., pp. 320-321. Critical Essays.

Jackson, Afro-Spanish, pp. 88-90. Contents: I. Works. II. Criticism. Annotated entries.

MAPLES ARCE, MANUEL (Mexico, 1898-)
Foster, Mex. Lit., pp. 236-237. Contents: I. Critical Monographs and Dissertations. II. Critical Essays.

MARANHAO SOBRINHO, JOSE (Brazil, 1879-1916)
Moraes, pp. 83-85. Major works by and about the author.

MARASSO, ARTURO (Argentina, 1890-1970)
Becco, Horacio Jorge. "Bibliografía de don Arturo Marasso, 1890-1970," BOLETIN DE LA ACADEMIA ARGENTINA DE LETRAS, 35, Núm. 135/136 (enero/junio de 1970), 15-22. Contents: I. Poesía. II. Estudios críticos. Obras varias. III. Prólogos y ediciones. IV. Antología. Reprinted: CUADERNOS DEL SUR, Núm. 11 (julio 1969/junio de 1971), 457-466.

MARECHAL, LEOPOLDO (Argentina, 1900-1970)
Coulson, Graciela. MARECHAL: LA PASION METAFISICA. Buenos Aires: Fernando García Cambeiro, 1974. 159p. Contents: "Contribución a la bibliografía de Leopoldo Marechal (en colaboración con William Hardy)," pp. 141-159. 329 entries. I. Obras de Leopoldo Marechal. A. Poesía. B. Narrativa. C. Prosa. D. Prosa varia. E. Entrevistas y diálogos. II. Referencias.
_______, and William Hardy. "Contribución a la bibliografía de Leopoldo Marechal," REVISTA CHILENA DE LITERATURA, Núm. 5/6 (1972), 313-333.
Flores, BEH, pp. 257-259. Contents: I. Ediciones. II. Referencias. III. Bibliografía selecta (criticism).
Foster, Arg. Lit., pp. 549-559. Contents: I. Bibliography. II. Critical Monographs and Dissertations. III. Critical Essays.
Foster, 20th Century, pp. 147-149. Contents: I. Bibliographies. II. Critical Books. III. Critical Essays.

MARIA Y CAMPOS, ARMANDO (Mexico, 1897-1967)
Viruegas Hernández, Alfredo. "Bibliografías mexicanas contemporáneas. XIII. Periodismo y libros de Armando de María y Campos," BOLETIN DE LA BIBLIOTECA NACIONAL (México), 2ª época, 11, Núm. 2 (abril/junio de 1960), 9-17. Contents: I. Published Works. II. Works in preparation.

MARIATEGUI, JOSE CARLOS (Peru, 1894/95-1930)
Chang Rodríguez, Eugenio. POETICA E IDEOLOGIA EN JOSE CARLOS MARIATEGUI. Madrid: Porrúa Turanzas, 1983. 238p. "Bibliografía," pp. 205-230. Contents: I. Libros por José Carlos Mariátegui. II. Crónicas y artículos por José Carlos Mariátegui. III. Poemas por José Mariátegui. IV. Piezas teatrales. V. Cartas. VI. Antologías y selecciones. VII. Estudios sobre José Carlos Mariátegui.

Dessau, Adalbert. "Neuere lateinamerikanische Publikationen über José Carlos Mariátegui," LATEINAMERIKA (Rostock, D.D.R.), Frühjahrssemester 1967, 157-173. This work presents and comments on a number of Latin American publications on the life and work of José Carlos Mariátegui published during the sixties.

Foster, David W. "A Checklist of Criticism on José Carlos Mariátegui," LOS ENSAYISTAS, Núm. 10/11 (1981), 231-257.

Foster, Peruvian Lit., pp. 163-179. Contents: I. Bibliographies. II. Critical Monographs and Dissertations. III. Critical Essays.

Mead, Robert G. "Bibliografía crítica de José Carlos Mariátegui," REVISTA HISPANICA MODERNA, Año 27, Núm. 2 (abril de 1961), 138-142. Article does not pretend to be exhaustive.

Rouillon, Guillermo. "Bio-bibliografía de José Carlos Mariátegui," BOLETIN BIBLIOGRAFICO (Biblioteca de la Universidad de San Marcos), Año 25, Vol. 22, Núm. 1/4 (diciembre de 1952), 102-221. 1,696 briefly annotated entries. Contents: I. Biografía. II. Bibliografía. A. Libros. B. Prólogos. C. Antologías. D. Ensayos y artículos. E. Inéditos. F. Artículos y ensayos en revistas y periódicos (by year, 1914-1952).

_______. BIO-BIBLIOGRAFIA DE JOSE CARLOS MARIATEGUI. Lima: Universidad Nacional Mayor de San Marcos, 1963. 345p. 3,462 fully annotated items. Contents: I. "Obras," pp. 17-169. A. Libros, folletos. B. Antologías, prólogos, y otros. C. Ensayos, artículos y otras colaboraciones. All entries under the Obras section are arranged by year. II. "Estudios críticos y biográficos sobre José Carlos Mariátegui," pp. 173-255. A. Libros, selecciones, folletos. B. Ensayos, artículos y crónicas. All entries under section II are arranged by year. III. "Referencias," pp. 259-306. IV. "Iconografía," pp. 309-328. V. "Indice de autores," pp. 329-345.

Vanden, Harry E. "Mariátegui: Marxismo, Comunismo, and Other Bibliographic Notes," LATIN AMERICAN RESEARCH REVIEW, 14, No. 3 (1979), 61-86. "Bibliography," pp. 79-86. Emphasizes 1960 to 1977. Contents: I. Obras completas de José Carlos Mariátegui. II. Reprints of Mariátegui's Newspaper and Magazine Articles. III. Other Editions of Mariátegui's Works. IV. Secondary Works.

MARIN, FRANCISCO GONZALO (Puerto Rico, 1863-1897)

Foster, P.R. Lit., pp. 160-162. Contents: I. Critical Monographs. II. Critical Essays.

MARIN, JUAN (Chile, 1900-1963)

Foster, Chilean Lit., pp. 124-125. Contents: I. Bibliographies. II. Critical Books and Theses. III. Critical Essays.

Swain, James O. JUAN MARIN-CHILEAN: THE MAN AND HIS WRITINGS. Cleveland, Tenn.: Pathway Press, 1971. 224p. "Selected Bibliographies," pp. 206-214. Contents: I. Book Length Publications by Juan Marín, Listed Chronologically. II. Shorter Publications by Juan Marín: Pamphlets, Lectures,

Reprints, etc. (listed alphabetically). III. Secondary Sources. IV. Unpublished Studies Concerning Juan Marín. V. Short List of Works by Juan Marín Published in Anthologies and in Foreign Language Magazines.

MARINELLO, JUAN (Cuba, 1898-1977)

Antuña, María Luisa, and Josefina García-Carranza. "Bibliografía de Juan Marinello," REVISTA DE LA BIBLIOTECA NACIONAL "JOSE MARTI" (La Habana), 3ª época, XVI, Núm. 3 (septiembre/diciembre de 1974), 25-473. 2,638 partially annotated entries under the following categories: I. Activa. A. Libros y folletos (by year, 1919-1973). B. Prólogos (1928-1974). C. Colaboración en libros (1918-1974). D. Colaboraciones en publicaciones periódicas (1917-1974). E. Entrevistas (1925-1974). F. Hojas sueltas (1935-1946). G. Marinello en otros idiomas. II. Pasiva. A. Libros. B. Publicaciones periódicas (by year 1923-1974). III. Indice de títulos. IV. Indice onomástico. V. Cronología.

_______, and _______. BIBLIOGRAFIA DE JUAN MARINELLO. La Habana: Editorial Orbe, Instituto Cubano del Libro, 1975. 473p. Contents: I. Bibliografía activa (chronologically arranged). A. Libros y folletos. B. Prólogos. C. Colaboraciones en libros. D. Colaboraciones en publicaciones periódicas. E. Entrevistas. F. Hojas sueltas. G. Marinello en otros idiomas. II. Bibliografía pasiva (chronologically arranged). A. Libros. B. Publicaciones periódicas. III. Indice de títulos. IV. Indice onomástico.

Foster, Cuban Lit., pp. 322-324. Contents: I. Bibliographies. II. Critical Essays.

"Juan Marinello Vidaurreta: bío-bibliografía," BIBLIOGRAFIA CUBANA, 1977, 226-235. Contents: I. Biografía. II. Bibliografía activa. III. Colaboraciones con otros autores.

MARMOL, JOSE (Argentina, 1817-1871)

Blasi Brambilla, Alberto. JOSE MARMOL Y LA SOMBRA DE ROSAS. Buenos Aires: Editorial Pleamar, 1970. 285p. Contents: I. "Bibliografía de José Mármol," pp. 261-263. A. Poesía. B. Narrativa. C. Teatro. D. Crítica literaria. E. Ensayo. F. Oratoria. G. Periodismo. II. "Bibliografía sobre José Mármol," pp. 265-270.

Flores, BEH, pp. 31-32. Contents: I. Ediciones principales. II. Otras ediciones. III. Bibliografía selecta (criticism).

Foster, Arg. Lit., pp. 560-564. Contents: I. Bibliography. II. Critical Monographs. III. Critical Essays.

Giannangeli, Liliana. CONTRIBUCION A LA BIBLIOGRAFIA DE JOSE MARMOL. LA FAMA DE JOSE MARMOL POR JUAN CARLOS GHIANO. La Plata: Universidad Nacional de La Plata, Facultad de Humanidades y Ciencias de la Educación, Departamento de Letras, Instituto de Literatura Argentina e Iberoamericana, 1972. 254p. (Textos, Documentos y Bibliografía, 5). Contents: I. Obras del autor. A. Obras en libros y folletos. 1. Poesía. Ordenación cronológica. 2. Teatro. 3. Prosa. a. Novela: AMALIA. Ordenación cronológica. b. Prosa varia. Ordenación cronológica. c. Cartas aparecidas en publicaciones periódicas y libros. Ordenación cronológica epistolar. B. Hemerografía de José Mármol: nómina de las publicaciones más importantes que fundó o en las que actuó como colaborador o redactor. Ordenación cronológica. 1. Redacción y colaboraciones. a. Prosa. Ordenación cronológica: publicada en diversos periódicos; índice del periódico LA SEMANA. 2. Seudónimos y alfónimos usados por José Mármol. Trabajos firmados con seudónimos, alfónimos y sin firma. Ordenación cronológica y por periódico. C. Prólogo a obra de otro autor. D. Textos de Mármol en diversas antologías. Ordenación cronológica. E. Traducciones de obras de José Mármol. 1. Novela: AMALIA. 2. Poesía. F. Plagio de AMALIA. 1. Traducción al español. 2. Traducción al ruso. G. Discografía. H. Adaptaciones de AMALIA. 1. Poesía. 2. Adaptación musical y discografía. 3. Adaptación para teatros. Ordenación cronológica. 4. Adaptaciones para cine. I. Obra parlamentaria. J. Discursos. II. Sobre José Mármol. Crítica y biografía sobre el autor en ensayos generales, nacionales e historias de la literatura. A. Trabajos en libro de José Mármol. Ordenación alfabética. B. Hemerografía sobre José Mármol, con firma. Ordenación alfabética. C. Hemerografía sin firma sobre José Mármol. Ordenación alfabética. D. Crónicas de estreno. Ordenación cronológica. E. Iconografía. Ordenación cronológica. F. Poesías dedicadas a Mármol por otros autores. Ordenación cronológica. G. Noticias sobre su enfermedad, notas necrológicas, homenajes póstumas, aniversarios. Ordenación alfabética. H. Bibliografías auxiliares. Ordenación alfabética. III. Indice onomástico.

MARQUES, OSWALDINO (Brazil, 1916-)
Moraes, pp. 105-107. Major works by and about the author.

MARQUES, RENE (Puerto Rico, 1919-1979)
Foster, P.R. Lit., pp. 162-168. Contents: I. Bibliography. II. Critical Monographs and Dissertations. III. Critical Essays.
Martin, Eleanor. RENE MARQUES. Boston: Twayne, 1979. 168p. "Selected Bibliography," pp. 158-163. Contents: I. Primary Sources. A. Drama. B. Short Stories. C. Novel. D. Essays. E. Poetry. F. Translations. II. Secondary Sources (briefly annotated). A. Drama. B. Short Stories. C. Novel. D. General.
Rodríguez Ramos, Esther. "Aproximación a una bibliografía: René Marqués," SIN NOMBRE, 10 (octubre/diciembre de 1979), 121-148. Contents: I. Obras de René Marqués (all arranged by year). A. Poesía. B. Cuentos. C. Teatro. 1. Obras publicadas. 2. Obras inéditas. D. Ensayos. E. Artículos. F. Reseñas. G. Novelas. H. Trabajos para el Departamento de Instrucción Pública. 1. Libros para el pueblo. 2. Guiones cinematográficos. I. Antología. II. Estudios, artículos, comen-

tarios críticos y noticias firmados sobre René Marqués. III. Noticias anónimas sobre René Marqués.

_______. LOS CUENTOS DE RENE MARQUES. San Juan: Editorial Universitaria, Universidad de Puerto Rico, 1976. 202p. "Bibliografía," pp. 185-200. Contents: I. Obras de René Marqués. A. Teatro. 1. Obras publicadas. 2. Obras inéditas. B. Cuentos. C. Ensayos y artículos. D. Reseñas. E. Novela. F. Poesía. G. Antología. II. Estudios críticos sobre René Marqués.

MARQUES, XAVIER (Brazil, 1861-1942)

Salles, David. O FICCIONISTA XAVIER MARQUES. UM ESTUDO DA TRANSIÇAO ORNAMENTAL. Rio de Janeiro: Civilzação Brasileira, 1977. 223p. (Coleção Vera Cruz, 242). "Bibliografia," pp. 197-208. Contents: I. Fontes primárias (by year, 1886-1932). II. Específica sôbre o autor. A. Obras de referência biobibliográfica. B. Estudos analíticos da obra. C. Artigos de abordagem genérica sôbre o autor e sua obra. D. Artigos e recensões relativos a livros individualizados. 1. Relativos a livros de ficção. 2. Relativos a livros de poesia. 3. Relativos a livros de ensaio. E. Discursos, alusoẽs, circunstâncias, etc. F. Recensões não assinados notícias literárias sôbre Xavier Marques no período literário.

MARRERO, CARMEN (Puerto Rico, 1907-)

Foster, P.R. Lit., p. 169. Critical Essays.

MARROQUIN, JOSE MANUEL (Colombia, 1827-1908)

Porras Collantes, pp. 442-452. Includes works of and critical studies about the author.

MARTES DE OCA, MARCO ANTONIO (Mexico, 1932-)

Foster, Mex. Lit., pp. 237-239. Contents: I. Critical Monographs and Dissertations. II. Critical Essays.

MARTI, JOSE (Cuba, 1853-1895)

Anderson pp. 107-128. Contents: Critical Essays.

Benítez, María. "Bibliografía martiana de Emilio Roig de Leuchsenring," ANUARIO DEL CENTRO DE ESTUDIOS MARTIANOS, 2 (1979), 310-324.

Blanch y Blanco, Celestino. BIBLIOGRAFIA MARTIANA, 1954-1963. La Habana: Biblioteca Nacional "José Martí," Departamento de Colección Cubana, 1965. 111p. An exhaustive, partially annotated bibliography of 1,008 entries. Includes titles from Cuba and other countries. Contents: I. Bibliografía activa (libros, folletos, revistas--by year, and then alphabetical). II. Bibliografía pasiva (by year, and then alphabetical). III. Suplemento. IV. Indice analítico.

_______. "Bibliografía martiana: enero de 1964-agosto de 1968," ANUARIO MARTIANO (Biblioteca Nacional "José Martí", Sala Martí), Núm. 1 (1969), 361-373. A continuation of the 1954-1963 bibliography. Same format with an apéndice section:

"Fichas rezagadas, 1954- ."
Flores, BEH, pp. 32-35. Contents: I. Ediciones principales. II. Otras ediciones. III. Referencias. IV. Bibliografía selecta (criticism).
Foster, Cuban Lit., pp. 325-402. Contents: I. Bibliographies. II. Critical Monographs and Dissertations. III. Critical Essays.
García-Carranza, Araceli. "Bibliografía martiana: setiembre de 1968-agosto de 1969," ANUARIO MARTIANO, Núm. 2 (1970), 587-626. Same format as Blanch y Blanco.
_______. "Bibliografía martiana: setiembre de 1969-agosto de 1970," ANUARIO MARTIANO, Núm. 3 (1971), 341-384. 358 items. Same format.
_______. "Bibliografía martiana: setiembre de 1970-mayo de 1971," ANUARIO MARTIANO, Núm. 4 (1971), 401-441. 397 items. Same format.
_______. "Bibliografía martiana, enero-diciembre de 1975," ANUARIO MARTIANO, 7 (1977), 423-490. Contents: I. Bibliografía activa. II. Bibliografía pasiva. Also includes an apéndice section for bibliografía activa (1967-1974) and bibliografía pasiva (1962-1974).
_______. "Bibliografía martiana (1976 y 1977)," ANUARIO DEL CENTRO DE ESTUDIOS MARTIANOS, 1 (1978), 346-402.
_______. "Bibliografía martiana (enero-diciembre de 1978)," ANUARIO DEL CENTRO DE ESTUDIOS MARTIANOS, 2 (1979), 325-370.
González, Manuel Pedro. FUENTES PARA EL ESTUDIO DE JOSE MARTI: ENSAYO DE BIBLIOGRAFIA CLASIFICADA. La Habana: Publicaciones del Ministerio de Educación, Dirección de Cultura, 1950. (Bibliografía cubana, 1). 517p. Contents: I. Bibliografía activa. A. Bibliografía selecta de los escritos de José Martí publicados hasta 1895. B. Colecciones en varios volúmenes y obras completas. C. Miscelánea de recopilaciones o reimpresiones en un volumen. D. Versos. 1. Ediciones. 2. Epistolarios-colecciones. E. Discursos-ediciones y colecciones. F. Antologías, crestomatías. G. Ediciones de LA EDAD DE ORO. H. Traducciones de prosas y versos de Martí a otros idiomas. I. Traducciones al español hechas por Martí. J. Lista de periódicos y revistas en que colaboró Martí. K. Iconografía de Martí. II. Bibliografía pasiva. A. El hombre y su "role" histórica. B. Sus ideas. C. El artista de la palabra. D. Miscelánea.
"José Martí," BIBLIOGRAFIA CUBANA, 1979, v. 1, 19-20. Contents: I. Bibliografía activa. II. Bibliografía pasiva. Includes items for 1979 only.
Martí, José. NUEVAS CARTAS DE NUEVA YORK. INVESTIGACION, INTRODUCCION Y INDICE POR ERNESTO MEJIA SANCHEZ. Madrid: Siglo Veintiuno Editores, 1980. 268p. Work includes an index to all the letters written to El Partido Liberal (Mexico) and La Nación (Buenos Aires), along with a summary of each letter's contents.
Peraza Sarausa, Fermín. BIBLIOGRAFIA MARTIANA, 1853-1955. La Habana: Ediciones Anuario Bibliográfico Cubano, 1956.

720p. Contents: I. Bibliografia activa. II. Bibliografia pasiva. III. Complemento (Que contiene adiciones a los años anteriores y la bibliografia--libros y folletos--correspondiente a los años 1954-1955). Over 10,000 items.

_______. "Bibliografia martiana, 1956-1968," REVISTA CUBANA (New York), Año 1, Núm. 2 (julio/diciembre de 1968), 485-499. Contents: I. Compilaciones bibliográficas. II. Obras completas. III. Bibliografia activa. IV. Bibliografia pasiva.

Perdomo Correa, Omar. BIBLIOGRAFIA MARTIANA DE ANGEL AUGIER. La Habana: Dirección de Cultura de La Habana Vieja, 1980. 46p.

Quintana, Jorge. CRONOLOGIA BIOBIBLIOGRAFICA DE JOSE MARTI. Caracas, 1964. 262p. 1852-1951.

MARTINEZ, FERNANDO ANTONIO (Colombia, 1917-1972)

Romero Rojas, Francisco. "Bibliografia de y sobre Fernando Antonio Martínez," in HOMENAJE A FERNANDO ANTONIO MARTINEZ: ESTUDIOS DE LINGUISTICA, FILOLOGIA, LITERATURA E HISTORIA CULTURAL (Bogotá: Instituto Caro y Cuervo, 1979), pp. 745-765. Contents: I. Diccionario. II. Libros. III. Traducciones. IV. Ensayos y artículos. V. Reseñas. A. Libros y ensayos. B. De revistas. VI. Varia. VII. Bibliografia sobre Fernando Antonio Martínez.

MARTINEZ DE NAVARRETE, MANUEL (Mexico, 1768-1809)

Flores, BEH, p. 63. Contents: I. Ediciones. II. Bibliografia selecta (criticism).

MARTINEZ ESTRADA, EZEQUIEL (Argentina, 1895-1964)

Adam, Carlos. BIBLIOGRAFIA Y DOCUMENTOS DE EZEQUIEL MARTINEZ ESTRADA. ADVERTENCIA PRELIMINAR POR JUAN CARLOS GHIANO. La Plata: Universidad Nacional de La Plata, Facultad de Humanidades y Ciencias de la Educación, 1968. 247p. (Departamento de Letras, Instituto de Letras, Textos, Documentos y Bibliografias, 3). Lists 1,056 items. Contents: I. Obras. A. Indice cronológica. B. Indice temático. 1. Poesía. 2. Teatro. 3. Cuento. 4. Ensayos (literarios, histórico-sociológicos, polémicos). 5. Antología. C. Colaboraciones en publicaciones periódicas. Ordenación cronológica. D. Entrevistas, encuestas, reportajes. Ordenación cronológica. E. Prólogos y estudios de obras de otros autores. Ordenación cronológica. F. Textos del autor en diversas antologías. Ordenación cronológica. G. Traducciones de obras de otros autores. H. Transcripciones del autor. II. Crítica y biografía. A. Trabajos firmados. B. Comentarios y reseñas de las obras de Martínez Estrada. Sin firmar. C. Artículos periodísticos. Ordenación cronológica. D. Tésis inédita. E. Indice de autores. F. Libros, artículos y reseñas aparecidos o localizados, ya en prensa el presente volumen. III. Marginalia. A. Premios obtenidos por Martínez Estrada. B. Números especiales de publicaciones periódicas dedicadas a

Ezequiel Martínez Estrada. C. Material existente que no ha podido verificarse. D. Material inédita. IV. Documentos. A. Epistolario. B. Comentarios sobre la obra. V. Cronología básica. (S. R. Wilson's review of the Adam bibliography, which appeared in HISPANIC REVIEW (38, October 1970, 446-451), corrects entries and adds titles.)

Becco, Horacio Jorge. "Cronología y bibliografía de Ezequiel Martínez Estrada," in Ezequiel Martínez Estrada's LOS INVARIANTES HISTORICOS EN EL FACUNDO (Buenos Aires: Casa Pardo 1974), pp. 84-90. Coverage: 1895-1973.

Earle, Peter G. PROPHET IN THE WILDERNESS: THE WORKS OF EZEQUIEL MARTINEZ ESTRADA. Austin: University of Texas Press, 1971. 254p. "Bibliography," pp. 227-242. Contents: I. Books by Martínez Estrada. II. Articles by Martínez Estrada. III. Critical and Related Writings.

Echevarría, Israel. "Don Ezequiel Martínez Estrada en Cuba: contribución a su bibliografía," REVISTA DE LA FACULTAD DE CIENCIAS ECONOMICAS (Universidad Nacional de Colombia, Bogotá), 10, Núm. 2 (mayo/agosto de 1968), 113-165. Divided into two phases, before and after the Cuban Revolution; the first consisting of five entries, whereas the second totals 143, largely attributable to the two years Martínez Estrada spent on the island giving lectures, being interviewed, and collaborating in diverse publications.

Fernández Moreno, César. "Ficha de Ezequiel," DIALOGOS (México), 10, Núm. 5 (setiembre/octubre de 1974), 23-28. Contents: I. El escritor. II. La persona. III. Bibliografía básica (extensive commentaries of his works). A. Obras. B. Introducción crítica. IV. Ampliación de lecturas. A. Obras. B. Más crítica.

Flores, BEH, pp. 259-262. Contents: I. Ediciones. II. Referencias. III. Bibliografia selecta (criticism).

Flores, NH, v. 4, pp. 38-42. Contents: I. Ediciones de su narrativa. II. Referencias. III. Homenajes. IV. Bibliografía selecta (criticism).

Foster, Arg. Lit., pp. 565-575. Contents: I. Bibliographies. II. Critical Monographs and Dissertations. III. Critical Essays.

Prior, Aldo. "Bibliografía de Martínez Estrada," SUR (Buenos Aires), Núm. 295 (julio/agosto de 1965), 73-78. Incomplete bibliography. Contents: I. Obras. II. Sobre la vida y la obra.

MARTINEZ MORENO, CARLOS (Uruguay, 1917-)

Foster, 20th Century, pp. 149-150. Critical essays.

Orthmann, Nora Gladys. "LIFE AND WORKS OF CARLOS MARTINEZ MORENO." Ph.D., University of Toronto, 1976. "An exhaustive bibliography of works by and about Martínez Moreno follows the Appendix."

MARTINEZ VILLENA, RUBEN (Cuba, 1899-1934)

Martínez Villena, Rubén. ORBITA DE RUBEN MARTINEZ VIL-

LENA. ESBOZO BIOGRAFICO DE RAUL ROA. SELECCION Y NOTA FINAL DE ROBERTO FERNANDEZ RETAMAR. La Habana: Colección Orbita, 1964. 244p. "Bibliografía," pp. 237-242. Contents: I. Obras publicadas de Rubén Martínez Villena. II. Escritos sobre Rubén.

Núñez Machín, Ana. RUBEN MARTINEZ VILLENA. La Habana: UNEAC, 1971. 458p. "Bibliografía," pp. 285-311. Contents: I. Bibliografía activa. A. Verso. B. Otros. C. Publicado después de su muerte. D. Prosa. E. Obra orgánica publicada después de su muerte. II. Bibliografía pasiva (critical studies about Martínez Villena and his work).

MARTINEZ ZUVIRIA, GUSTAVO ADOLFO see WAST, HUGO

MARTINS JUNIOR, JOSE ISIDORO (Brazil, 1860-1904)

Mota, Artur. "Perfis acadêmicos, Cadeira No. 13: José Isidoro Martins Júnior," REVISTA DA ACADEMIA BRASILEIRA DE LETRAS, Núm. 86 (fevereiro de 1929), pp. 157-172. Contents: I. "Bibliografia," pp. 157-160 (1879-1903). II. "Fontes para o estudo crítico," pp. 161-162.

Porter, p. 244. Contents: I. Writings. II. References, Critical and Biographical.

MASFERRER, ALBERTO (El Salvador, 1868-1932)

Masferrer, Alberto. OBRAS ESCOGIDAS. SELECCION Y PROLOGO DE LA DRA. MATILDE ELENA LOPEZ. San Salvador, El Salvador: Editorial Universitaria, 1971. 531p. Contents: I. "Bibliografía de Alberto Masferrer," pp. 85-88. II. "Indice cronológico de trabajos del maestro Don Alberto Masferrer, publicados en Patria entre los años, 1928-1937," pp. 89-120 (bibliographic information is incomplete).

MASTRONARDI, CARLOS (Argentina, 1901-1976)

Becco, Horacio Jorge. "Bibliografía de don Carlos Mastronardi (1901-1976)," BOLETIN DE LA ACADEMIA ARGENTINA DE LETRAS, 41, Núm. 159/160 (enero/junio de 1977), 135-137. Contents: I. Poesía. II. Ensayo. III. Prólogos y ediciones. IV. Antología. V. Traducción.

MATAMOROS, MERCEDES (Cuba, 1858-1906)

Pichardo, Hortensia. "Mercedes Matamoros, su vida y su obra," REVISTA BIMESTRE CUBANA, 68 (julio/diciembre de 1951), 21-90. Contents: I. "Relación de la poesías de Mercedes Matamoros no incluídos en el volumen de sus Poesías completas ni en el folleto de sus Sonetos, con expresión de las publicaciones en que aparecieron," pp. 83-85 (listed by year). II. "Bibliografía," pp. 85-87. A. Libros. B. Periódicos.

MATIENZO CINTRON, ROSENDO (Puerto Rico, 1855-1913)

Foster, P.R. Lit., pp. 169-170. Contents: I. Critical Monographs. II. Critical Essays.

MATOS, GREGORIO DE (Brazil, 1636-1696)
Pólvora, Hélio. PARA CONHECER MELHOR: GREGORIO DE MATOS. Rio de Janeiro: Bloch Editores, 1974. 108p. "Bibliografia," pp. 27-31. Contents: I. Obras. II. Fontes para o estudo de Gregório de Matos.
Porter, p. 226. Contents: I. Writings. II. References, Critical and Biographical.
Salles, Fritz Teixeira de. POESIA E PROTESTO EM GREGORIO DE MATOS: ESTUDO CRITICO E SELEÇAO DE POEMAS. Belo Horizonte: Interlivros, 1975. 202p. "Bibliografia," pp. 197-202.

MATOS BERNIER, FELIX (Puerto Rico, 1869-1937)
Foster, P.R. Lit., pp. 170-171. Contents: I. Dissertation. II. Critical Essays.

MATOS PAOLI, FRANCISCO (Puerto Rico, 1915-)
Foster, P.R. Lit., pp. 171-172. Contents: I. Critical Monograph. II. Critical Essays.

MATTA, GUILLERMO (Chile, 1829-1899)
Escudero, pp. 300-301. Criticism.

MATTO DE TURNER, CLORINDA (Peru, 1854-1909)
Corvalán, p. 71. Contents: I. Works. II. Criticism.
Flores, BEH, pp. 63-64. Contents: I. Ediciones. II. Bibliografía selecta (criticism).
Flores, NH, v. 2, pp. 51-53. Contents: I. Ediciones. II. Referencias. III. Bibliografía selecta (criticism).
Foster, Peruvian Lit., pp. 180-184. Contents: I. Critical Monographs and Dissertations. II. Critical Essays.

MEDINA, JOSE TORIBIO (Chile, 1852-1930)
Feliú Cruz, Guillermo. "Bibliografía de don José Toribio Medina," BOLETIN DEL INSTITUTO DE INVESTIGACIONES HISTORICAS (Buenos Aires), Año 10, Tomo 13 (1931), 220-492. Contents: I. Catálogo formado por Víctor M. Chiappa, 1873-1914 (Nos. 1-226). II. Continuación ... por Guillermo Feliú Cruz, 1910-1923 (Nos. 227-307). III. Bibliografía de Medina hasta su muerte, por Guillermo Feliú Cruz, con una lista de obras póstumas, 1923-1930 (Nos. 308-408).
"José Toribio Medina," in Guillermo Feliú Cruz's HISTORIA DE LAS FUENTES DE LA BIBLIOGRAFIA CHILENA: ENSAYO CRITICO (Santiago de Chile: Biblioteca Nacional, 1967), II, pp. 183-409. A descriptive bibliography. Contents: I. José Toribio Medina, el bibliógrafo. II. Estudios bibliográficos relativos a Chile (1884-1929). III. Estudios bibliográficos menores de Medina. IV. Los estudios bibliográficos de Medina relativos a América y a Oceanía y a los dominios que integraron el imperio español: nota bibliográfica, 1888-1958. V. Notas bibliográficas sobre Medina, 1907-1965. A. Fuentes básicas. B.

Estudios del autor sobre su vida y obra. C. Otras fuentes bibliográficas para el estudio de la vida de Medina.

MEIRELES, CECILIA (Brazil, 1901-1964)

Corvalán, pp. 72-74. Contents: I. Works. II. Critical Works On.

Damasceno, Darcy. "Notícia biográfica e bibliografia," in Cecília Meireles' OBRA POETICA (Rio de Janeiro: Editôra Nova Aguilar, 1983), pp. 51-76. Contents: I. Obras da autora. A. Em língua portuguesa (by year, 1919-1972). B. Poesia traduzida. 1. Em antologias estrangeiras. 2. Em revistas e jornais literários. C. Teatro. D. Ficção. E. Prosa poética. F. Crônica. G. Ensaios e conferências. H. Artigos. I. Livros didáticos. J. Traduções. 1. Publicadas. 2. Não publicadas. II. Estudos, artigos e reportagens sôbre a autora. III. Composições musicais sôbre poemas da autora.

Meireles, Cecília. FLOR DE POEMAS. SEGUNDA EDIÇAO. Rio de Janeiro: Companhia José Aguilar Editôra, 1972. 308p. "Bibliografia," pp. 49-57. Contents: I. Obras de autora. A. Em língua portuguesa. B. Poesia traduzida. 1. Em antologias estrangeiras. C. Teatro. D. Ficção. E. Prosa poética. F. Crônica; em antologias. G. Ensaios e conferências. H. Artigos. I. Livros didáticos. J. Traduções. II. Estudos, artigos e reportagens sôbre o autor. III. Composições musicais sôbre poemas da autora.

________. OBRA POETICA. Rio de Janeiro: Companhia José Aguilar Editôra, 1967. 894p. "Bibliografia," pp. 91-98. Contents: I. Obras. II. Teatro. III. Traduções. A. Publicadas. B. Ainda não publicadas. IV. Conferências. V. Artigos. VI. Traduções para outros idiomas. VII. Músicas. VIII. Estudos, reportagens, homenagens.

Zagury, Elaine. CECILIA MEIRELES: NOTICIA BIOGRAFICA, ESTUDO CRITICO, ANTOLOGIA, BIBLIOGRAFICO, DISCOGRAFIA, PARTITURAS. Petropolis: Vozes, 1973. 181p. "Bibliografia," pp. 167-181. Contents: I. Poesia. II. Poesia traduzida. A. Em antologias estrangeiras. B. Em revistas e jornais literários. III. Teatro. IV. Ficção. V. Prosa poética. VI. Crônica. VII. Ensaio e conferências. VIII. Livros didáticos. IX. Traduções. X. Bibliografia da crítica (abreviada). A. Livros. B. Ensaios em livros e folhetos. C. Ensaios em revistas. D. Em jornais. XI. Discografia. XII. Partituras.

MEJIA SANCHEZ, ERNESTO (Nicaragua, 1923-)

Valle-Castillo, Julio. "Bibliografía de Ernesto Mejía Sánchez," BOLETIN NICARAGUENSE DE BIBLIOGRAFIA Y DOCUMENTACION, Núm. 2 (octubre/diciembre de 1974), 22-27. Contents: I. Libros y ensayos personales publicados en revistas especializadas o en volúmenes colectivos de los cuales se han hecho tirada aparte. II. Ediciones críticas, antologías, recopilaciones, con prólogo, estudios preliminares y notas.

MEJIA VALLEJO, MANUEL (Colombia, 1923-)

Flores, BEH, p. 262. Contents: I. Ediciones. II. Bibliografía selecta (criticism).
Porras Collantes, pp. 465-471. Includes works of and about the author.

MELENDEZ, CONCHA (Puerto Rico, 1895/96-)
Arnaldi de Olmeda, Cecilia. CONCHA MELENDEZ: VIDA Y OBRA. San Juan: Editorial Universitaria, Universidad de Puerto Rico, 1972. 187p. "Bibliografía," pp. 165-178. Contents: I. Obras de Concha Meléndez. A. Poesía. B. Ensayos (de crítica y creación). C. Publicaciones dispersas en revistas y periódicos. 1. Ensayos y estudios críticos. 2. Reseñas y comentos sobre libros o personas. 3. Ensayos de creación. 4. Prólogos. 5. Biografías, bocetos y semblanzas. II. Crítica sobre su obra. A. Estudios críticos. B. Apuntes biográficos o semblanzas de Concha Meléndez.
Foster, P.R. Lit., pp. 172-174. Contents: I. Critical Monograph. II. Critical Essays.

MELENDEZ MUNOZ, MIGUEL (Puerto Rico, 1884-1966)
Foster, P.R. Lit., pp. 174-176. Contents: I. Critical Monographs and Dissertations. II. Critical Essays.

MELGAR, MARIANO (Peru, 1791-1815)
Flores, BEH, pp. 35-36. Contents: I. Ediciones. II. Referencias. III. Bibliografía selecta (criticism).
Foster, Peruvian Lit., pp. 185-189. Contents: I. Bibliographies. II. Critical Monographs and Dissertations. III. Critical Essays.
Mostajo, Francisco. "Panorama bibliográfico de las poesías de Melgar," REVISTA DE LA UNIVERSIDAD DE SAN AGUSTIN (Arequipa, Peru), Núm. 38 (1953), 144-151.
Núñez, Estuardo. "Bibliografía," in Mariano Melgar's POESIAS COMPLETAS (Lima: Academia Peruana de la Lengua, 1971), pp. 519-534. Contents: I. Obras de Mariano Melgar. II. Manuscritos. III. Música. IV. Fotografía. V. Artículos y ensayos sobre Melgar.

MELIAN LAFINUR, ALVARO (Argentina, 1889-1958)
"Bibliografía de Alvaro Melián Lafinur," BOLETIN DE LA ACADEMIA ARGENTINA DE LETRAS, 24, Núm. 91/92 (enero/junio de 1959), 11. 12 items; libros, folletos.

MELLO, MANDEL CAETANO BANDEIRA DE (Brazil, 1918-)
Moraes, p. 109. Major works by and about the author.

MELO NETO, JOAO CABRAL DE (Brazil, 1920-)
Nunes, Benedito. JOAO CABRAL DE MELO NETO. NOTA BIOGRAFICA, INTRODUÇAO CRITICA, ANTOLOGIA E BIBLIOGRAFIA. Petrópolis, Brazil: Editôra Vozes em convênio com o Instituto Nacional do Livro, Brasília, 1971. 217p. (Coleção Poetas Modernos do Brasil, 1). "Bibliografia," pp. 205-217.

Contents: I. Bibliografia do autor. A. Poesias. B. Poesia traduzida. C. Prosa. D. Traduções do autor. E. Antologias com poemas do autor (by language). F. Principais entrevistas e depoimentos. II. Bibliografia sôbre o autor. III. Discografia.

MENDA, AMERICO (Venezuela, 1887-1946)
Cardozo, Poesía, pp. 188-189. Includes the poetical works of and the critical studies about the author.

MENDES, MANDEL ODORICO (Brazil, 1799-1864)
Moraes, pp. 9-11. Major works by and about the author.

MENDEZ, MANUEL ISIDRO (Cuba, 1884-)
García-Carranza, Araceli. "Citas para una bibliografía de Manuel Isidro Méndez," ANUARIO MARTIANO, 5 (1974), 343-376. Contents: I. Bibliografía activa. A. Libros y folletos. B. Colaboraciones en libros. C. Colaboraciones en publicaciones periódicas. II. Bibliografía pasiva. The bibliography contains 205 partially annotated entries.

MENDEZ PEREIRA, OCTAVIO (Panama, 1887-1954)
Herrera, Carmen D. OCTAVIO MENDEZ PEREIRA: BIOGRAFIA, PENSAMIENTO Y BIBLIOGRAFIA. Panamá: Universidad de Panamá, Biblioteca, 1969. 28p. Contents: I. "Bibliografía del Dr. Octavio Méndez Pereira," pp. 15-25. II. "Bibliografía sobre el Dr. Octavio Méndez Pereira," pp. 25-28.

MENDONÇA, LUCIO DE (Brazil, 1854-1909)
Mendonça, Edgar de, and Carlos Süssekind. LUCIO DE MENDONÇA. ENSAIO BIO-BIBLIOGRAFICO. Rio de Janeiro: Civilização Brasileira, S.A., 1934. 134p. (Publicações da Academia Brasileira III, Bibliografia 6). Contents: I. Notas biográficas. II. Ensaio de bibliografia. Livros publicados. III. Apócrifo. IV. Livros inéditos. V. Trabalhos sôbre Lúcio de Mendonça. VI. Juízos e depoimentos.
Mota, Artur. "Perfís acadêmicos, Cadeira No. 11: Lúcio de Mendonça," REVISTA DA ACADEMIA BRASILEIRA DE LETRAS, Núm. 81 (setembro de 1928), pp. 59-69. Contents: I. "Bibliografia," pp. 59-69 (1869-1905). II. "Fontes para o estudo crítico," pp. 61-62.

MENESES, GUILLERMO (Venezuela, 1911-1979)
Becco, Horacio Jorge. "Bibliografía," in Guillermo Meneses' ESPEJOS Y DISFRACES. SELECCION Y PROLOGO: JOSE BAEZA. CRONOLOGIA: SALVADOR TENREIRO. (Caracas: Biblioteca Ayacucho, 1981), pp. 645-652. Contents: I. Obras de Guillermo Meneses. A. Libros y folletos. B. Antologías, prólogos, discursos. II. Obras sobre Guillermo Meneses. A. Libros y folletos. B. Hemerográfica (selectiva).
García Riera, Gladys. GUILLERMO MENESES: UNA BIBLIOGRAFIA. Caracas: Instituto Universitario Pedagógico de Caracas,

1981. 169p. This bibliography contains Meneses' works and critical studies about him and his work.

MENEZES, EMILIO DE (Brazil, 1866-1918)
Menezes, Emilio de. OBRA REUNIDA. ORGANIZAÇAO POR CASSIANA LACERDA CAROLLO. Rio de Janeiro: Livraria José Olympio, 1980. 424p. Contents: "Bibliografia," pp. 470-474. I. Do autor. II. Sôbre o autor.

MERA, JUAN LEON (Ecuador, 1832-1894)
Flores, BEH, p. 65. Contents: I. Ediciones. II. Bibliografía selecta (criticism).
Flores, NH, v. 1, pp. 162-163. Contents: I. Ediciones de la narrativa. II. Referencias. III. Bibliografía selecta (criticism).
Guevara, Darío. JUAN LEON MERA O EL HOMBRE DE CIMAS. SEGUNDA EDICION, REVISADA Y AUMENTADA CON NUEVAS NOTAS. Quito, 1965. 296p. Contents: I. "Obras de Juan León Mera (1858-1933)," pp. 287-289. II. "Obras de referencia y de crítica acerca de Juan León Mera," pp. 290-291.

MERCADO, JOSE RAMON (Puerto Rico, 1863-1911)
Foster, P.R. Lit., pp. 176-177. Contents: I. Dissertation. II. Critical Essays.

MERCHAN, RAFAEL MARIA (Cuba, 1844-1905)
Figarola-Caneda, Domingo. BIBLIOGRAFIA DE RAFAEL M. MERCHAN. Segunda edición, corregida y aumentada. La Habana: Imprenta y Papelería "La Universal de Ruiz y Hno.," 1905. 48p. Annotated entries. Contents: I. Biografía. II. Bibliografía (by year, 1867-1903). III. Tabla metódica (dictionary index).

MERINO REYES, LUIS (Chile, 1912-)
Valjalo, David. "Luis Merino Reyes: bibliografía," LITERATURA CHILENA: CREACION Y CRITICA, Núm. 28 (abril/junio/primavera de 1984), 27. Contents: I. Poesía. II. Cuentos. III. Novelas. IV. Sobre el autor (en libros). V. Sobre el autor (en diarios y revistas). Every section is arranged chronologically.

MESQUITA, ODERICO (Brazil, 1854-1889)
Porter, p. 213. Contents: I. Writings. II. References, Critical and Biographical.

MEYER, AUGUSTO (Brazil, 1902-1970)
Carvalhal, Tânia Franco. O CRITICO A SOMBRA DA ESTANTE: LEVANTAMENTO E ANALISE DA OBRA DE AUGUSTO MEYER. Porto Alegre: Editôra Globo, 1976. 155p. "Bibliografia," pp. 135-151. Contents: I. Textos de autor. A. Livros. B. Traduções. C. Em jornais (by newspaper). D. Em revistas (by review). E. Prefácios. II. Testos sôbre o autor. A. Em

livros. B. Em revistas e periódicos.

Meyer, Augusto. SELETA EM PROSA E VERSO. SELEÇAO E NOTAS DE DARCY DAMASCENO. Rio de Janeiro: Livraria José Olympio Editôra, 1973. 163p. Contents: I. "Bibliografia de Augusto Meyer," pp. xii-xiii. II. "Trabalhos sôbre o autor," pp. xiii-xiv.

MILANES, JOSE JACINTO (Cuba, 1814-1863)

Foster, Cuban Lit., pp. 403-404. Critical Essays.

Milanés, José Jacinto. OBRAS COMPLETAS. La Habana: Editorial del Consejo Nacional de Cultura, 1963. 2vs. (Biblioteca Básica de Autores Cubanos). "Ediciones y bibliografía de José Jacinto Milanés," II, 418-436. Contents: I. Ediciones de las obras de José Jacinto Milanés. II. Cronología de José Jacinto Milanés (1814-1863). III. Bibliografía activa (libros y folletos) de José Jacinto Milanés. IV. Bibliografía pasiva (selección).

MILLA Y VIDAURRE, JOSE (Guatemala, 1822-1882)

Flores, BEH, p. 36. Contents: I. Edición principal. II. Otras ediciones. III. Bibliografía selecta (criticism).

MILLIET, SERGIO (Brazil, 1898-1966)

"Sérgio Milliet: bibliografia," BOLETIM BIBLIOGRAFICO (Biblioteca Municipal "Mário de Andrade," São Paulo), 31 (julho/setembro de 1972), 97-172. Contents: I. Produção literária de Sérgio Milliet. A. Obras. B. Conferências e entrevistas. C. Prefácios e apresentações. D. Traduções. E. Compilações. F. Artigos de periódicos (revistas, jornais). II. Publicações sôbre Sérgio Milliet. III. Homenagens. 1,014 items.

MIRANDA, LUIS ANTONIO (Puerto Rico, 1896-)

Foster, P.R. Lit., pp. 177-178. Critical Essays.

MIRO, RICARDO (Panama, 1883-1940)

Alvarado de Ricord, Elsie. APROXIMACION A LA POESIA DE RICARDO MIRO: ENSAYO. Panamá: INCUDE, 1973. 216p. "Bibliografía sobre Ricardo Miró," pp. 205-210. "Bibliografía de Ricardo Miró," p. 211.

MIRO, RODRIGO (Panama, 1912-)

Menéndez Franco, Alvaro. "La literatura panameña de Rodrigo Miró: breve apuntamiento y noticia," LOTERIA (Panamá), Núm. 182 (enero de 1971), 75-80. Includes an extensive bibliography.

MISTRAL, GABRIELA (Pseudonym of LUCILA GODOY ALCAYAGA) (Chile, 1889-1957)

Albanell, Norah, and Nancy Mango. "Los escritos de Gabriela Mistral y estudios sobre su obra," in GABRIELA MISTRAL, 1889-1957 (Washington, D.C.: Pan American Union, 1958), pp. 49-90. 506 entries. Contents: I. Obra. A. Poesía. B. Prosa.

C. Poesías y artículos publicados en antologías, revistas, etc. 1. Poesía. 2. Prosa. D. Traducciones de su obra. 1. Poesía. 2. Prosa. II. Estudios críticos y biográficos. III. Bibliografías. A useful but not complete bibliography.

Caimano, Sister Rose Aquin. MYSTICISM IN GABRIELA MISTRAL. New York: Pageant Press International, 1969. 328p. "Bibliography," pp. 284-308. Contents: I. Bibliographies. II. Selected Works of Gabriela Mistral. A. Poetry. B. Prose. III. Critical Studies on Gabriela Mistral.

Corvalán, pp. 75-83. Contents: I. Works. II. Critical Works On.

Escudero, Alfonso M. LA PROSA DE GABRIELA MISTRAL; FICHAS DE CONTRIBUCION A SU INVENTARIO. Segunda edición. Santiago de Chile: EDICIONES DE LOS ANALES DE UNIVERSIDAD DE CHILE. 1957. 62p. An annotated listing of 549 entries from books, periodicals, and newspapers. Emphasis is on Chilean publications, but also included are sources from Spain, Mexico, Argentina, Colombia, and Costa Rica. Covers 1909-1957.

Flores, BEH, pp. 134-139. Contents: I. Edición principal. II. Otras ediciones. III. Referencias. IV. Bibliografía selecta (criticism).

Foster, Chilean Lit., pp. 125-147. Contents: I. Bibliographies. II. Critical Books and Theses. III. Critical Essays.

Jiménez, Onilda A. CRITICA LITERARIA EN LA OBRA DE GABRIELA MISTRAL. Miami: Universal, 1983. 303p. "Bibliografía," pp. 227-277. Contents: I. Obras de Gabriela Mistral. A. Poesía. B. Libros de poesía y prosa. C. Prosa. D. Cartas. E. Prólogos. F. Artículos (por orden alfabético). II. Bibliografía selecta sobre Gabriela Mistral.

Mistral, Gabriela. GABRIELA MISTRAL EN EL "REPERTORIO AMERICANO." PROLOGO, SELECCION Y NOTAS: MARIO CESPEDES. San José, Costa Rica: Editorial Universidad de Costa Rica: Editorial Universidad de Costa Rica, 1978. 310p. "Indice de los trabajos de Gabriela en el Repertorio Americano," pp. 301-308 (arranged by year, 1919-1951).

Pane, Remigio Ugo. "Gabriela Mistral (Lucila Godoy Alcayaga), Chile, b. 1889; A Bibliography of Her Poems in English Translation, Together with a List of Her Works," BULLETIN OF BIBLIOGRAPHY, 18, No. 5 (September/December 1944), 104-105. Contents: I. Translations. A. Collections. B. Individual Poems. II. Works (1908-1941)--only books are included.

Pinilla, Norberto. BIBLIOGRAFIA CRITICA SOBRE GABRIELA MISTRAL. Santiago de Chile: Universidad de Chile, 1940. 69p. 433 referencias; not an exhaustive bibliography. Contents: I. Obras de Gabriela Mistral. II. Prólogos de Gabriela Mistral. III. Poesías puestas en música. IV. Traducciones. V. Antologías en que figura. VI. Estudios y biografías. VII. Publicaciones en que hacen referencias o alusiones a Gabriela Mistral. VIII. Artículos sobre libros acerca de Gabriela Mistral; Acerca del premio Nobel para Gabriela Mistral.

Taylor, Martin C. GABRIELA MISTRAL'S RELIGIOUS SENSI-

BILITY. Berkeley and Los Angeles: University of California Press, 1968. 191p. "Bibliography," pp. 163-178. Contents: I. Unpublished Materials. II. Selected Works by Gabriela Mistral. III. Bibliographical Sources. IV. Critical Studies on Gabriela Mistral.

Zamudio, José. "Primera producción de Gabriela Mistral 1904-1914," in HOMENAJE AL PROFESOR GUILLERMO FELIU CRUZ (Editorial Andrés Bello, 1974), pp. 1111-1124. Contents: I. Revistas y periódicos revisados. A. Con colaboraciones de Gabriela Mistral. B. Sin colaboraciones de Gabriela Mistral. II. Publicaciones periódicas con posibles colaboraciones de Gabriela Mistral. III. Gabriela Mistral y otros seudónimos.

MOHANA, JOAO (Brazil, 1925-)

Moraes, pp. 111-113. Major works by and about the author.

MOLINA, ENRIQUE (Argentina, 1910-)

Foster, Arg. Lit., pp. 579-580. Contents: I. Dissertation. II. Critical Essays.

Molina, Enrique. OBRAS COMPLETAS. TOMO 1: PROSA. Buenos Aires: Ediciones Corregidor, 1984. 357p. "Bibliografía de Enrique Molina," pp. 355-356. Contents: I. Poesía. II. Narrativa. III. Antologías. IV. Ensayos. V. Traducciones.

MOLINA, JUAN RAMON (Honduras, 1875-1908)

Molina, Juan Ramón. TIERRAS, MARES Y CIELOS: POESIAS. PROLOGO DE ARGENTINA DIAZ LOZANO. BIBLIOGRAFIA DE RAFAEL HELIODORO VALLE. Guatemala, C.A.: Ediciones del Gobierno de Guatemala, 1947. 235p. Contents: I. "Bibliografía de Juan Ramón Molina," pp. 217-222. II. "Sobre Molina," pp. 222-230. III. "Iconografía," pp. 230-231.

_______. _______. SELECCION, INTRODUCCION Y NOTAS DE JULIO ESCOTO. San José, C.R.: EDUCA, 1977. 238p. Contents: I. "Cronología de Juan Ramón Molina," pp. 227-229. II. "Bibliografía de Juan Ramón Molina," pp. 231-232. III. "Bibliografía sobre Juan Ramón Molina," pp. 232-234.

MOLINARI, RICARDO E. (Argentina, 1898-)

Flores, BEH, pp. 262-264. Contents: I. Ediciones principales. II. Otras ediciones. III. Referencias. IV. Bibliografía selecta.

Foster, Arg. Lit., pp. 581-584. Contents: I. Bibliography. II. Critical Monographs and Dissertation. III. Critical Essays.

Pousa, Narciso. RICARDO E. MOLINARI. Buenos Aires: Ediciones Culturales Argentinas, Ministerio de Educación y Justicia, Dirección General de Cultura, 1961. 115p. "Bibliografía," pp. 103-112. 100 entries. Works arranged by year, 1927-1960 (annotated), and a "bibliografía de las obras y artículos referentes a Ricardo E. Molinari."

MONTALVO, JUAN (Ecuador, 1832-1889)

Flores, BEH, pp. 36-38. Contents: I. Ediciones. II. Antologías. III. Referencias. IV. Bibliografía selecta (criticism).

Naranjo, Plutarco. JUAN MONTALVO. TOMO 2: ESTUDIO BIBLIOGRAFICO. Quito: Editorial Casa de la Cultura Ecuatoriana, 1966. Reprinted: Puebla, México: Editorial J. M. Cájica, Jr., 1971. (Biblioteca Cájica de Cultura Universal, 75). Contents: I. Obras de Juan Montalvo. II. Escritos cortos y hojas sueltas de Juan Montalvo. III. Obras con lecturas o trozos selectos de Juan Montalvo. IV. Epistolarios de Juan Montalvo. V. Trozos reproducidos en revistas y periódicos. VI. Biografías y estudios críticos sobre Juan Montalvo. VII. Obras que tratan de Juan Montalvo. VIII. Publicaciones de revistas sobre Juan Montalvo. IX. Revistas con ediciones especiales y otras publicaciones conmemorativas dedicadas a Montalvo. X. Ediciones conmemorativas de los principales periódicos del Ecuador a partir de 1932. XI. Otras publicaciones aparecidas en diarios del país y del exterior. XII. Principales obras de Montalvo. XIII. Indice de ediciones de obras de Juan Montalvo. XIV. Indice geográfico. A. Obras de Juan Montalvo. B. Obras y artículos que tratan sobre Montalvo. C. Indice de autores. D. Indice general.

MONTANER, CARLOS ALBERTO (Cuba, 1943-)

Foster, Cuban Lit., pp. 405-406. Contents: I. Bibliography. II. Critical Monographs. III. Critical Essays.

Goodyear, Russell Howard. "Bibliografía de la narrativa de Carlos Alberto Montaner," in LA NARRATIVA DE CARLOS ALBERTO MONTANER: ESTUDIOS SOBRE LA NUEVA LITERATURA HISPANOAMERICANA, EDICION A CARGO DE GASTON FERNANDEZ DE LA TORRIENTE (Madrid: CUPSA, 1978), pp. 253-260. Bibliography lists critical studies about Montaner and his work.

MONTEAGUDO RODRIGUEZ, JOAQUIN (Puerto Rico, 1890-1966)

Foster, P.R. Lit., p. 178. Critical Essays.

MONTELLO, JOSUE (Brazil, 1917-)

Moraes, pp. 107-109. Major works by and about the author.

Montello, Josué. ALELUIA: ROMANCE. Rio de Janeiro: Nova Fronteira, 1982. 188p. Contents: I. "Bibliografia de Josué Montello," pp. 181-183. A. Romances. B. Ensayo. C. História. D. Biografia. E. História literária. F. Discursos. G. Antologia. H. Educação. I. Educação cívica. J. Crônicas. K. Novelas. L. Teatro. M. Biblioteconomia. N. Literatura infantil. O. Prefácios. P. Antologias. Q. Traduções. R. Livro falado. S. Cinema. T. Televisão. II. "Estudos sôbre Josué Montello publicados em livros," pp. 184-187.

_______. LARGO DO DESTERRO: ROMANCE. Rio de Janeiro: Nova Fronteira, 1981. 330p. Contents: I. "Bibliografia de Josué Montello," pp. 323-325. Same type of index as in his ALELUIA. II. "Estudos sôbre Josué Montello publicados en livros," pp. 326-329. III. "Enciclopédias e dicionários," p. 330.

MONTES HUIDOBRO, MATIAS (Cuba, 1931-)
Foster, Cuban Lit., p. 407. Critical Essays.

MOOCK, ARMANDO (Chile, 1894-1942)
Foster, Chilean Lit., pp. 147-149. Contents: I. Critical Books and Theses. II. Critical Essays.
Silva Cáceres, Raúl. LA DRAMATURGIA DE ARMANDO MOOCK. Santiago de Chile: Sociedad de Escritores de Chile-Editorial Universitaria, 1964. 110p. "Bibliografía de y sobre Armando Moock," pp. 99-109. Contents: I. Bibliografía de Armando Moock. II. Bibliografía sobre el autor. A. Estudios y ensayos críticos. B. Referencias y críticas menores.

MORAES, JOSE DO NASCIMENTO (Brazil, 1882-1958)
Moraes, pp. 87-88. Major works by and about the author.

MORAES, VINICIUS DE (Brazil, 1913-)
Moraes, Vinicius de. POESIA COMPLETA E PROSA. Rio de Janeiro: Companhia José Aguilar Editôra, 1974. 787p. "Bibliografia," pp. 769-772. Contents: I. Obras do autor. II. Traduções. II. Estudos, reportagens, homenagens.

MORAIS, ENEIDA COSTA DA see ENEIDA

MORAIS FILHO, JOSE NASCIMENTO (Brazil, 1922-)
Moraes, pp. 110-111. Major works by and about the author.

MORALES, JORGE LUIS (Puerto Rico, 1930-)
Foster, P.R. Lit., p. 179. Critical Essays.

MORALES, JOSE RICARDO (Chile, 1915-)
Morales, José Ricardo. TEATRO INICIAL. Santiago de Chile: Ediciones de la Universidad de Chile, 1976. 167p. "Obras de José Ricardo Morales," p. 167. Contents: I. Teatro. II. Adaptaciones. III. Crítica y antología. IV. Ensayo.

MORE, FEDERICO (Peru, 1889-1955)
More, Anabelle. "Federico More," ANUARIO BIBLIOGRAFICO PERUANO, 1955/1957, 545-589. Contents: I. Biografía. II. Libros y folletos. III. Obras publicaciones. IV. Artículos y ensayos. V. Cuentos. VI. Poesías. VII. Biografías. VIII. Conferencias, discursos. IX. Cartas, circulares, memorias, etc. X. Reportajes. XI. Referencias. XII. Notas necrológicas.

MOREJON, NANCY (Cuba, 1944-)
Jackson, Afro-Spanish, pp. 90-91. Contents: I. Works. II. Criticism.

MORO, CESAR (Pseudonym of CESAR QUISPES ASIU) (Peru, 1906-1956)

Foster, Peruvian Lit., pp. 190-191. Contents: I. Critical Monographs. II. Critical Essays.

Moro, César. OBRA POETICA. Lima: Instituto Nacional de Cultura, 1980. "Bibliografía de y sobre César Moro," v. 1, pp. 259-269. Contents: I. Obras de César Moro (by year; books only). II. Sobre César Moro.

MORUA DELGADO, MARTIN (Cuba, 1856-1909/10)

Foster, Cuban Lit., pp. 408-409. Contents: I. Critical Monographs. II. Critical Essays.

Jackson, Afro-Spanish, pp. 91. Contents: I. Works. II. Criticism. A. Books. B. Articles, Shorter Studies, and Dissertations. Annotated entries.

MOSTAJO, FRANCISCO (Peru, 1874-1953)

"Francisco Mostajo," ANUARIO BIBLIOGRAFICO PERUANO, 1953/1954, 434-462. Contents: I. Biografía. II. Libros y folletos. III. Otras publicaciones. IV. Poesías. V. Artículos y ensayos. VI. Conferencias y discursos. VII. Cartas, circulares, informes y memorias. VIII. Notas bibliográficas. IX. Referencias.

MOURA, CAETANO DE LOPES (Brazil, 1780-1860)

Porter, pp. 233-234. Contents: I. Writings. II. References, Critical and Biographical.

MOYANO, DANIEL (Argentina, 1928-)

Foster, Arg. Lit., pp. 585-586. Critical Essays.

Foster, 20th Century, p. 150. Contents: Critical Essays.

MUJICA LAINEZ, MANUEL (Argentina, 1910-1984)

Carsuzán, María Emma. MANUEL MUJICA LAINEZ. Buenos Aires: Ediciones Culturales Argentinas, Ministerio de Educación y Justicia, Dirección General de Cultura, 1962. 157p. 164 entries. "Biobibliografía," pp. 145-156. Contents: I. Biografía literaria de Manuel Mujica Láinez. II. La obra (published books). III. Estudios literarios, de arte y otros escritos. IV. Algunas publicaciones periodísticas firmadas. V. Traducciones. VI. Libreto cinematográfico. VII. Bibliografía referente a la obra de Manuel Mujica Láinez (obra, artículos generales, traducciones de la obra).

Font, Eduardo. "The Narrative of Manuel Mujica Láinez." Ph.D., University of California, Los Angeles, 1971. 229p. "Bibliografía," pp. 222-229. Contents: I. Obras de Mujica Láinez. II. Estudios sobre el autor. III. Bibliografía general. Minor works, such as crónicas periodísticas, artículos ocasionales and reseñas of Mujica Láinez are not included. Only selected lists of critical works are included.

Foster, Arg. Lit., pp. 587-590. Contents: I. Critical Monographs and Dissertations. II. Critical Essays.

Foster, 20th Century, pp. 151-152. Contents: I. Critical Books. II. Critical Essays.

MUNOZ, RAFAEL FELIPE (Mexico, 1899-)
Flores, BEH, pp. 264-265. Contents: I. Ediciones. II. Bibliografía selecta (criticism).

MUNOZ RIVERA, LUIS (Puerto Rico, 1859-1916)
Foster, P.R. Lit., pp. 179-182. Contents: I. Critical Monographs. II. Critical Essays.

MURENA, H. A. (Argentina, 1923-1975)
Foster, Arg. Lit., pp. 591-593. Critical Essays.
Foster, 20th Century, p. 152. Contents: Critical Essays.

MURILLO, JOSEFA (Mexico, 1860-1898)
Dehesa y Gómez Farías, María Teresa. OBRA POETICA DE JOSEFA MURILLO. México, D.F.: Editorial Citlaltepetl, 1970. 379p. "Bibliografía," pp. 365-368. Contents: I. Obras de Josefa Murillo. II. Obras sobre Josefa Murillo.

- N -

NABUCO, JOAQUIM (Brazil, 1849-1910)
Braga, Oswaldo Melo. BIBLIOGRAFIA DE JOAQUIM NABUCO. Rio de Janeiro: Ministério da Educação e Saúde, Instituto Nacional do Livro, 1952. 265p. (Coleção B1, Bibliografia 8). Annotated bibliography. Contents: I. Obras publicadas. II. Discursos. A. Na Câmara dos Deputados. B. Na Academia de Letras. C. No Instituto Histórico. III. Trabalhos diversos. A. Em jornais e revistas. B. Cartas. IV. Trabalhos manuscritos. A. Poesia. B. Prosa. V. Fontes para um estudo sôbre Joaquim Nabuco. VI. Anexos (documents reproduced).

NALE ROXLO, CONRADO (Argentina, 1898-1971)
Becco, Horacio Jorge. "Bibliografía de don Conrado Nalé Roxlo," BOLETIN DE LA ACADEMIA ARGENTINA DE LETRAS, 36, Núm. 141/142 (julio/diciembre de 1971), 263-267. Contents: I. Poesía. II. Teatro. III. Obras varias. IV. Humorismo. A. Antologías. VI. Prólogos. VII. Traducciones. VIII. Bibliografías.
Flores, BEH, pp. 139-140. Contents: I. Ediciones. II. Bibliografía selecta (criticism).
Foster, Arg. Lit., pp. 594-597. Contents: I. Bibliography. II. Critical Monographs and Dissertation. III. Critical Essays.
Lacau, María Hortensia. TIEMPO Y VIDA DE CONRADO NALE ROXLO ENTRE EL ANGEL Y EL DUENDE. Buenos Aires: Editorial Plus Ultra, 1976. 351p. Contents: I. "Obras de Conrado Nalé Roxlo (primeras ediciones)," pp. 345-346. Listed by year, 1923-1969. II. "Bibliografía," pp. 347-349. Includes works about Nalé Roxlo.

NARANJO, CARMEN (Costa Rica, 1931-)
Corvalán, p. 84. Contents: I. Works. II. Critical Works On.

NASCENTES, ANTENOR (Brazil, 1886-1972)
Porter, p. 247. Contents: I. Writings. II. References, Critical and Biographical.

NAVARRO LUNA, MANUEL (Cuba, 1894-)
Foster, Cuban Lit., pp. 410-412. Contents: I. Critical Monograph. II. Critical Essays.

NAZOA, AQUILES (Venezuela, 1920-)
Rivas, Rafael. "Contribución a la bibliografía de Aquiles Nazoa," LETRAS (CARACAS), Núm. 34/35 (octubre/diciembre de 1977-enero/marzo de 1978), 165-175. Contents: I. Bibliografía directa (works of Nazoa). II. Bibliografía indirecta (works about the author and his work). The bibliography comprises 150 citations.

NEJAR, CARLOS (Brazil, 1939-)
Nejar, Carlos. DE "SELESIS" A DANAÇOES. São Paulo: Edições Quíron em convênio com o Ministério da Educação e Cultura, Instituto Nacional do Livro, 1975. 265p. "Bibliografia acerca do autor," pp. 263-266. Contents: I. Livros. II. Estudos en livros. III. Alguns estudos em periódicos e revistas.
______. OBRA POETICA: I. Rio de Janeiro: Nova Fronteira, 1980. 474p. "Bibliografia de e sôbre Carlos Néjar," pp. 463-474. Contents: I. Obras do autor. A. Livros. B. Antologias. C. Composições musicais (sôbre poemas do autor). D. Traduções (realizadas pelo autor). E. Sôbre o autor. 1. Livros. 2. Estudos em livros. 3. Alguns estudos em periódicos e revistas.

NERUDA, PABLO (Pseudonym of NEFTALI RICARDO REYES) (Chile, 1904-1973)
Becco, Horacio Jorge. PABLO NERUDA: BIBLIOGRAFIA. Buenos Aires: Casa Pardo, 1975. 261p. 1,057 annotated titles. Contents: I. Bibliografía cronológica de Pablo Neruda. II. Cronología de su obra orgánica. A. Obras completas. B. Obra poética. C. Obra dispersa. D. Antología. E. Neruda traductor. F. Neruda editor. G. Memorias. II. Crítica. III. Indice de títulos. IV. Indice onomástico.
Beckett, Bonnie A. THE RECEPTION OF PABLO NERUDA'S WORKS IN THE GERMAN DEMOCRATIC REPUBLIC. Berne: Peter Lang, 1981. 251p. (Germanic Studies in America, 42). "Selective Bibliography," pp. 215-249. Contents: I. The Reception of Latin American Literature in German-Speaking Areas Prior to 1949. II. German Exile Literature. III. GDR Kulturpolitik. IV. Bibliographies on Pablo Neruda. A. German Democratic Republic. B. Federal Republic of Germany. C.

Miscellaneous. V. Primary Works by Pablo Neruda. A. Spanish. B. German Democratic Republic. C. Other German Editions. D. Other Editions. VI. Secondary Literature on Pablo Neruda. A. GDR Criticism. B. Other German language criticism.

Berchenko, Pablo. "El impacto póstumo de Neruda: el caso de un muerto indocil," VENTANAL, 6 (1983), 89-118. "Bibliografía," pp. 97-114. Contents: I. Obras póstumas de Pablo Neruda (noviembre 1973-octubre de 1982). II. Recopilaciones de obras y documentos (1974-1982). III. Antologías (1974-1981). IV. Libros y monografías (1975-1981). V. Simposio y coloquio. VI. Compilaciones de estudios y documentos (1974-1980). VII. Homenajes de revistas y libros (1974-1981). VIII. Memorias y tesis. IX. Estudios y artículos (1974-1982). 100 items. "Discografía," pp. 115-117. 25 records listed. "Filmografía," p. 118. 3 films.

BIBLIOGRAFISK OVERSIKT OVER PABLO NERUDA: BOCKER UR "COLECCION NERUDA" FRAN BIBLIOTEKET VID CHILES UNIVERSITET, SOM PRESENTERAS AV CHILES UTRIKESMINISTERUM; EXPOSICION BIBLIOGRAFICA DE PABLO NERUDA: LIBROS DE LA "COLECCION NERUDA" DE LA BIBLIOTECA CENTRAL DE LA UNIVERSIDAD DE CHILE, QUE SE PRESENTAN BAJO EL PATROCINIO DEL MINISTERIO DE RELACIONES EXTERIORES DE CHILE. Stockholm, 1966. 55p. The 202 works by Neruda are arranged in this catalog by language. A description of the "Colección Neruda" is provided in both Spanish and Swedish on pp. 8-13.

Cohen, Jonathan I. "NERUDA IN ENGLISH: A CRITICAL HISTORY OF THE VERSE TRANSLATIONS AND THEIR IMPACT ON AMERICAN POETRY. Ph.D., State University of New York at Stony Brook, 1980. 234p. The dissertation includes a "Selected Bibliography, divided in four parts: the first offers a chronological list of books of Neruda's poetry in English translation; the second, a list of anthologies that include Neruda; the third, a list of reviews and articles about the translations; the fourth, a list of biographical and critical works about Neruda that are available in English." (DISSERTATION ABSTRACTS INTERNATIONAL, 41 [May 1981], 4712-A).

Escudero, Alfonso. "Fuentes para el conocimiento de Pablo Neruda," TALLER DE LETRAS (Revista del Instituto de Letras de la Universidad Católica de Chile, Santiago), Núm. 2 (1972), 1,253 entries by year, 1919-1972. Books, newspapers, and periodicals indexed. Heavy emphasis on Chilean, Mexican, and Argentinean materials. Author index included.

Figueroa, Esperanza. "Pablo Neruda en inglés," REVISTA IBEROAMERICANA, 39, Núm. 82/83 (enero/junio de 1973), 301-347. Bibliographic essay. Contents: I. Neruda en revistas académicas. II. Revistas y periódicas de carácter general. III. El New York Times Book Review. IV. Los libros. V. Traducciones sueltas. VI. Antologías. VII. Libros (traducciones). VIII. Los traductores. IX. Anotaciones complementarias.

Flores, BEH, pp. 140-145, 184. Contents: I. Edición principal. II. Otras ediciones. III. Referencias. IV. Bibliografía selecta (criticism).

_______. APROXIMACIONES A PABLO NERUDA. SIMPOSIO DIRIGIO POR ANGEL FLORES. Barcelona: Ocnos/Llibres de Sinera, 1974. 255p. "Bibliografía," pp. 245-255. Contents: I. Edición principal. II. Otras ediciones (1921-1973). III. Crítica.

Foster, Chilean Lit., pp. 149-185. Contents: I. Bibliographies. II. Critical Books and Theses. III. Critical Essays.

Loyola, Hernán. "La obra de Pablo Neruda, guía bibliográfica," in Pablo Neruda: OBRAS COMPLETAS (Buenos Aires: Editorial Losada, 1968), II, pp. 1317-1501. 1,345 items are listed under the following categories: I. Publicaciones en español. A. Antologías y compilaciones. B. Nerudiana orgánica. Los libros de Neruda. C. Nerudiana dispersa. D. Neruda traductor. E. Neruda editor. II. Publicaciones en otros idiomas. III. Addenda. A. Publicaciones en español. B. Publicaciones en otros idiomas. Entries through May 1968 are included. This bibliography is reprinted with additions in: Pablo Neruda, OBRAS COMPLETAS (Buenos Aires: Editorial Losada, 1973), III, 911-1106.

_______. "Summa bibliográfica de la obra nerudiana," MAPOCHO (Santiago de Chile), Tomo 3, Núm. 3, Vol. 9 (1965), 178-213. An annotated bibliography of books and articles by Neruda, chronologically arranged for the period of 1920-1964. 433 entries under the following categories: I. Los libros de Neruda y su contenido. II. Nerudiana dispersa ("Una cantidad, impresionante de trabajos de Pablo Neruda, en prosa y en verso, no han sido incluídos en ninguno de los libros de Neruda"). Included sources are newspapers, magazines, hojas sueltas, carteles, and pamphlets.

Morelli, Gabriele. "Bibliografía de Neruda en Italia," REVISTA IBEROAMERICANA, 39, Núm. 82/83 (enero/junio de 1973), 369-371. Contents: I. Traducciones. II. Antologías (en que aparecen poemas de Pablo Neruda). III. Crítica. 26 items.

Pane, Remigio Ugo. "Pablo Neruda (Neftalí Ricardo Reyes), Chile, b. 1904; a Bibliography of His Poems in English Translation," BULLETIN OF BIBLIOGRAPHY, 20, No. 1 (January/April 1950), 6-7. Contents: I. Collections. II. Individual Poems.

Pring-Mill, Robert D. F. "Pablo Neruda: A Brief Bibliographical Guide," BULLETIN OF THE SOCIETY FOR LATIN AMERICAN STUDIES, 22 (January 1975), 19-27. A most useful short annotated bibliography the purpose of which is "to help those who wish to read or teach poetry" (p. 19). Contents: I. The Period Prior to the Spanish Civil War. II. Other Books by 1957 Obras completas. III. Other Books by 1962 Obras completas. IV. Other Books by 1968 Obras completas. V. Other Books in Period Covered by 1973 Obras completas. VI. Subsequent Publications in Book Form.

Sanhueza, Jorge. "Catálogo de la exposición bibliográfica de Pablo Neruda," ANALES DE LA UNIVERSIDAD DE CHILE (Santiago de Chile), 122, Núm. 131 (julio/septiembre de 1964), 173-207. Exposición bibliográfico de Pablo Neruda, organizada con ocasión del 60º aniversario de nacimiento del poeta. Contents: I. Ediciones hispanoamericanas y españoles. II. Traducciones (by language). III. Volantes--carteles, hojas sueltas, etc. IV. Discos (interpretados por el autor; otros intérpretes). V. Apéndice (adiciones de la obra de Pablo Neruda no exhibidas en esta oportunidad) and a list of translations (by language).

_______. "Nota bibliográfica sobre Tentativa del hombre infinito," in Pablo Neruda's TENTATIVA DEL HOMBRE INFINITO (Santiago de Chile: Talleres de Arancibia Hnos., 1964), n.p. Sanhueza was the conservator of the "Colección Neruda" de la Universidad de Chile.

_______. "Pablo Neruda y las ediciones de sus obras," PRO-ARTE, Núm. 174/175 (1954), 15-31.

Servicio de Extensión de Cultura Chilena. BIBLIOGRAFIA DE PABLO NERUDA, POETA CHILENO, 1917-1975. Santiago de Chile, 1976. 54p. Contents: I. "Obras de Pablo Neruda," pp. 1-44 (entries arranged in reverse chronological order, 1975-1917). Only books, journal, and pamphlet works are listed. II. "Referencias a la obra de Pablo Neruda," pp. 44-54.

Shur, Leonid Avel'evich, comp. PABLO NERUDA: BIO-BIBLIOGRAFICHESKII UKAZATEL'. Moscow: Izdatel'stvo Vsesoiuznoi Knizknoi Palaty, 1960. 74p. Major importance of the bibliography lies in its listing of the Russian translations of Neruda's works and of the Russian critical studies about them.

SIMPOSIO PABLO NERUDA. EDITED BY ISAAC LEVY AND JUAN LOVELUCK. Columbia, S.C.: University of South Carolina, Department of Languages and Literatures, 1975. 427p. "Fuentes para el conocimineto de Pablo Neruda, 1967-1974" por Enrique-Mario Santí, pp. 366-382. Contents: I. Homenajes. II. Libros. III. Menciones en libros. IV. Artículos. V. Material anterior a 1967 (no incluído en otras bibliografías).

Volek, Emil. "Pablo Neruda y algunos países socialistas de Europa," REVISTA IBEROAMERICANA, 39, Núm. 82/83 (enero/junio de 1973), 349-368. Article includes a "Bibliografía complementaria" section (by country).

NERVO, AMADO (Mexico, 1870-1919)

Anderson, pp. 129-133. Critical Essays.

Estrada, Genaro. BIBLIOGRAFIA DE AMADO NERVO. México: Imprenta de la Secretaría de Relaciones Exteriores, 1925. 36p. (Monografías bibliográficas mexicanas, 1). Contents: I. Libros de Amado Nervo (1895-1922). II. Publicaciones especiales sobre Amado Nervo. III. Estudios y opiniones sobre Amado Nervo, publicados en libros, revistas y periódicos. Comprende hasta 1919. The bibliography has many incomplete citings.

Flores, BEH, pp. 265-268. Contents: I. Edición principal. II. Otras ediciones. III. Referencias. IV. Bibliografía selecta (criticism).

Foster, Mex. Lit., pp. 239-252. Contents: I. Bibliographies. II. Critical Monographs and Dissertations. III. Critical Essays.

Herrera y Sierra, Amanda Marcela. AMADO NERVO: SU VIDA, SU PROSA CON DATOS INEDITOS. México, D.F.: Centro Cultural Universitario incorporado a la Universidad Nacional Autónoma de México, 1952. 235p. "Bibliografía," pp. 223-232 (includes books and journal and newspaper articles about Nervo).

Pane, Remigio Ugo. "Amado Nervo, Mexico, 1870-1919: A Bibliography of His Poems in English Translation, Together with a List of His Works," BULLETIN OF BIBLIOGRAPHY, 18, No. 6 (January/April 1945), 126-128. Contents: I. Translations. A. Collections. B. Individual Poems. II. Works. The works are arranged chronologically, 1895-1933.

NODA MARTINEZ, TRANQUILINO SANDALIO (Cuba, 1808-1866)

Febres Cordero G., Julio. "Las cosas de Noda," REVISTA DE LA BIBLIOTECA NACIONAL (La Habana), 2a serie, 4, Núm. 2 (abril/junio de 1953), 190-276. "Bibliografía," pp. 209-276. Contents: I. Obras (listed by title). II. Sobre el autor. III. Cronología de Noda.

NOGALES, LYDIA (El Salvador)

Ayala, Juan Antonio. LYDIA NOGALES: UN SUCESO EN LA HISTORIA DE EL SALVADOR. San Salvador, El Salvador: Ministerio de Cultura, Departmento Editorial, 1956. 299p. "Principales referencias bibliográficas acerca de Lydia Nogales," pp. 295-299.

NOVAS CALVO, LINO (Cuba, 1905-1985)

Foster, Cuban Lit., pp. 413-415. Contents: I. Critical Monographs and Dissertations. II. Critical Essays.

Souza, Raymond D. LINO NOVAS CALVO. Boston: Twayne, 1981. 146p. Selected Bibliography," pp. 134-143. Contents: I. Primary Sources. A. Books. B. Periodicals. II. Secondary sources (briefly annotated). A. Books. B. Articles.

NOVO, SALVADOR (Mexico, 1904-1974)

Arce, David N. BIBLIOGRAFIAS MEXICANAS CONTEMPORANEAS, XII. NOMINA BIBLIOGRAFICA DE SALVADOR NOVO. México, D.F.: Biblioteca Nacional, 1963. 37p. (Publicación de la Biblioteca Nacional, 9; BMC, 13). Contents: I. Adaptaciones. II. Compilaciones. III. Obra original. IV. Su producción recogida en antologías, etc. V. Prólogos, etc. VI. Traducciones. VII. En publicaciones periódicas.

Foster, Mex. Lit., pp. 252-255. Contents: I. Bibliographies. II. Critical Monographs and Dissertations. III. Critical Essays.

Magaña-Esquivel, Antonio. SALVADOR NOVO. México, D.F.: Empresas Editoriales, S.A., 1971. 318p. "Bibliografía directa," pp. 301-310. Contents: I. La creación. A. Poesía. B. Ensayos. C. Teatro. D. Historia. E. Prólogos. G. En antologías. H. Traducciones. "Bibliografía indirecta," pp. 311-316 (criticism).

NUCETE, JOSE VICENTE (Venezuela, 1827-1888)
Cardozo, Poesía, pp. 189-191. Includes the poetical works of and the critical studies about the author.

NUNEZ, ENRIQUE BERNARDO (Venezuela, 1895-1964)
Caracas. Universidad Católica "Andrés Bello." Seminario de Literatura Venezolana. CONTRIBUCION A LA BIBLIOGRAFIA DE ENRIQUE BERNARDO NUNEZ, 1895-1964. Caracas: Facultad de Humanidades y Educación, Escuela de Letras; Ediciones de la Gobernación del Distrito Federal, 1970. 203p. (Colección bibliografías, 6). 962 citations. Contents: I. Referencias bibliográficas. II. Obras mayores. A. Novela. B. Ensayo. III. Miscelánea. IV. Obra dispersa (mainly journal and newspaper articles). V. Biografía y crítica (libros, folletos, capítulos, artículos y referencias) sobre el autor y su obra.
ENRIQUE BERNARDO NUNEZ. INDICE DE SUS TRABAJOS PUBLICADOS. Caracas: Imprenta Municipal de la Lotería de Caracas, 1963. 19p. Contents: I. Ficción (temas de geografía e historia de Venezuela). II. Figuras y episodios de la guerra federal. III. Escritos venezolanos. IV. Periodismo. V. Caracas: cronista de la ciudad.
Larrazabal Henríquez, Osvaldo. ENRIQUE BERNARDO NUNEZ. Caracas: Ediciones de la Biblioteca de la Universidad Central de Venezuela, 1969. 98p. "Bibliografía," pp. 95-98. Contents: I. Bibliografía directa (obras del autor). II. Bibliografía indirecta (obras sobre el autor).

NUNEZ DE PINEDA Y BASCUNAN, FRANCISCO (Chile, 1607-1682)
Flores, BEH, p. 38. Contents: I. Ediciones. II. Bibliografía selecta (criticism).

- O -

OBESO, CANDELARIO (Colombia, 1849-1884)
Jackson, Afro-Spanish, p. 95. Contents: I. Works. II. Criticism. A. Books. B. Articles, Shorter Studies, and Dissertations.

OBLIGADO, PEDRO MIGUEL (Argentina, 1890-1967)
Becco, Horacio Jorge. "Bibliografía de Pedro Miguel Obligado, 1890-1967," BOLETIN DE LA ACADEMIA ARGENTINA DE LETRAS, 32, Núm. 123/124 (enero/junio de 1967), 169-173. Contents: I. Poesía. II. Prosa. III. Prólogos. IV. Traducciones. V. Bibliografía.

OBLIGADO, RAFAEL (Argentina, 1851-1920)
Foster, Arg. Lit., pp. 598-603. Contents: I. Critical Monographs. II. Critical Essays.

OCAMPO, SILVINA (Argentina, 1906-)
Foster, Arg. Lit., p. 604. Critical Essays.
Klingenberg, Patricia Nisbet. "EL INFIEL ESPEJO: THE SHORT STORIES OF SILVINA OCAMPO." Ph.D., University of Illinois/Urbana-Champaign, 1981. 195p. "Bibliography," pp. 182-184. Contents: I. Primary Sources. A. Works by Silvina Ocampo. B. Works by Silvina Ocampo Done in Collaboration with Others. II. Secondary Sources. A. Works about Silvina Ocampo. B. Theoretical and Critical Works Consulted.
Ocampo, Silvina. PAGINAS DE SILVINA OCAMPO SELECCIONADO POR LA AUTORA. ESTUDIO PRELIMINAR DE ENRIQUE PEZZONI. Buenos Aires: Editorial Celtia, 1984. 256p. Contents: I. "Bibliografía de Silvina Ocampo (1937-1979)," p. 250. II. "Bibliografía sobre la autora," pp. 251-253.

OCAMPO, VICTORIA (Argentina, 1890-1979)
Corvalán, p. 85. Contents: I. Works. II. Critical Works On.
Foster, Arg. Lit., pp. 605-609. Contents: I. Bibliographies. II. Critical Monographs. III. Critical Essays.
_______. "Bibliography of Writings by and about Victoria Ocampo (1890-1979)," REVISTA INTERAMERICANA DE BIBLIOGRAFIA, 30 (1980), 51-58. Contents: I. Works by Victoria Ocampo. II. Criticism about Victoria Ocampo. A. Bibliographies. B. Critical Monographs and Dissertations. C. Critical Essays. III. Writings about Sur. "Excluded are Ocampo's essays in journals, magazines, and newspapers not gathered in her collections of essays, or are review notes on her works published in journals or newspapers. Excluded also are the numerous materials published on Ocampo in the literary supplements of newspapers..." (p. 52).
Meyer, Doris. VICTORIA OCAMPO: AGAINST THE WIND AND THE TIDE. New York: G. Braziller, 1979. 314p. "Selected Bibliography," pp. 303-305. Contents: I. Works by Victoria Ocampo (in chronological order, 1924-1977; books only). II. Works about Victoria Ocampo. A. Books. B. Articles. III. Works by Victoria Ocampo Published in English.
Schultz de Mantovani, Fryda. VICTORIA OCAMPO. Buenos Aires: Ediciones Culturales Argentinos, 1963. 113p. Contents: I. "Bibliografía," pp. 103-107. A. Libros. B. Traducciones. C. Artículos, cartas, conferencias, discursos, folletos. II. "Bibliografía sobre Victoria Ocampo (según fichero de La Prensa)," p. 109. III. "Bibliografía sobre Victoria Ocampo (según fichero de La Nación y noticias sobre su actuación)," p. 111.
Tuninetti, Beatriz T. CONTRIBUCION A LA BIBLIOGRAFIA DE VICTORIA OCAMPO. Buenos Aires: Universidad de Buenos

Aires, Facultad de Filosofía y Letras, Instituto Argentina "Ricardo Rojas," 1962. 26p. (Guías bibliográficas, 6). An incomplete student guide. The bibliography contains few entries from U.S., France, Chile, Mexico, or Spain. Contents: I. Libros. A. Originales. B. Traducciones. C. Traducciones en colaboración. D. Colaboración en libros de otros autores. II. Colaboraciones en publicaciones periódicas. A. Originales. B. Traducciones. III. Conferencias y disertaciones. IV. Entrevistas. V. Crítica y biografía. VI. Indice alfabético de títulos. VII. Indice alfabético de autores y críticos. 304 references.

OCANTOS, CARLOS MARIA (Argentina, 1860-1949)

Andersson, Theodore. CARLOS MARIA OCANTOS, ARGENTINE NOVELIST; A STUDY OF INDIGENOUS, FRENCH, AND SPANISH ELEMENTS IN HIS WORK. New Haven: Yale University Press, 1934. 136p. (Yale Romantic Studies, 8). "Bibliography," pp. 130-136. Contents: I. Chronological Bibliography of Ocantos' works, 1883-1933. II. Criticism. A. Books. B. Periodicals. III. General Bibliography.

OCTAVIANO, FRANCISCO (Brazil, 1825-1889)

Mota, Artur. "Academia Brasileira de Letras: Francisco Octaviano," REVISTA DO BRASIL. Núm. 62 (fevereiro de 1921), 155-160. Biobibliography.

________. "Perfís acadêmicos, Cadeira No. 13: Francisco Octaviano de Almeida Rosa," REVISTA DA ACADEMIA BRASILEIRA DE LETRAS, Núm. 84 (dezembro de 1928), 498-506. Contents: I. "Bibliografia," pp. 498-500 (1841-1925). II. "Fontes para o estudo crítico," pp. 500-501.

ODIO, EUNICE (Costa Rica, 1922-1974)

Vallbona, Rima. "Bibliografía de Eunice Odio, 1945-1978," REVISTA INTERAMERICANA DE BIBLIOGRAFIA, 31 (1981), 207-214. Contents: I. Obras de Eunice Odio. A. Libros. B. Antologías de Eunice Odio. C. Publicaciones en revistas, periódicos y antologías. 1. Poesía. 2. Prosa. 3. Obra inédita. II. Estudios, ensayos y otros escritos sobre Eunice Odio y referencias a su obra.

OLAVIDE Y JAUREGUI, PABLO DE (Peru, 1725-1803)

Foster, Peruvian Lit., pp. 192-195. Contents: I. Critical Monographs and Dissertations. II. Critical Essays.

OLIVEIRA, ALBERTO DE (Brazil, 1857-1937)

Serpa, Phocion. ALBERTO DE OLIVEIRA, 1857-1957; ENSAIO BIOBIBLIOGRAFICO. Rio de Janeiro: Livraria São José, 1957. 196p.

OLIVEIRA, FRANKLIN DE (Brazil, 1916-)

Moraes, pp. 102-103. Major works by and about the author.

OLMEDO, JOSE JOAQUIN (Ecuador, 1780-1847)

Castillo, Abel Romeo. "Las ediciones del Canto a Junín," BOLETIN DE LA ACADEMIA NACIONAL DE LA HISTORIA (Caracas), 29 (1946), 55-60.

Flores, BEH, pp. 38-39. Contents: I. Edición principal. II. Otras ediciones. III. Referencias. IV. Bibliografía selecta (criticism).

Olmedo, José Joaquín. POESIAS COMPLETAS. México, D.F.: F.C.E., 1947. 317p. "Bibliografía," por Aurelio Espinosa Pólit, pp. 221-309. A descriptive, annotated bibliography. Contents: I. La obra poética de Olmedo: Ediciones. II. Composiciones que figura en esta edición. III. Los fragmentos. IV. Décima improvisada. V. Composiciones de Olmedo de las que sólo se conocen los títulos. VI. Tradiciones. VII. Principales estudios acerca de Olmedo por orden cronológico.

ONA, PEDRO DE (Chile, 1570-1643)

Flores, BEH, pp. 39-40. Contents: I. Ediciones. II. Referencias. III. Bibliografía selecta (criticism).

Román Lagunas, Jorge. "Obras de Pedro de Oña y bibliografía sobre él," REVISTA INTERAMERICANA DE BIBLIOGRAFIA, 31 (1981), 345-365. 145 partially annotated entries. Contents: I. "Bibliografía de Pedro de Oña," pp. 347-349 (chronologically arranged, 1596-1630). II. "Bibliografía sobre Pedro de Oña," pp. 349-365. A. Bibliografías. B. Libros. C. Ensayos críticos y artículos. D. Notas y referencias.

ONETTI, JUAN CARLOS (Uruguay, 1909-)

Flores, BEH, pp. 145-148, 184. Contents: I. Edición principal. II. Otras ediciones. III. Referencias. IV. Bibliografía selecta (criticism).

Foster, 20th Century, pp. 153-159. Contents: I. Bibliographies. II. Critical Books. III. Critical Essays.

Frankenthaler, Marilyn. "Complemento a la bibliografía de y sobre Juan Carlos Onetti," REVISTA IBEROAMERICANA, 41, Núm. 91 (abril/junio de 1975), 355-365. Up-dates and supplements the Verani bibliographies. Contents: I. Cuentos. II. Novelas. III. Colecciones de cuentos y novelas. IV. Fragmentos de novelas. V. Artículos periodísticos. VI. Miscelánea. VII. Entrevistas, reportajes y encuestas. VIII. Libros, tesis y colecciones de ensayos sobre Onetti. IX. Estudios, notas y reseñas.

_______. J. C. ONETTI: LA SALVACION POR LA FORMA. New York: ABRA Ediciones, 1977. 184p. "Bibliografía," pp. 161-181. Contents: I. Bibliografía cronológica directa, 1933-1974 (Onetti's works). II. Bibliografía indirecta (works about Onetti).

Kadir, Djelal. JUAN CARLOS ONETTI. Boston: Twayne Publishers, 1977. 160p. "Selected Bibliography," pp. 155-157. Contents: I. Primary Sources. A. Novels. B. Collections of Short Stories and Novels. C. Collected Articles and Essays.

D. English Translations. II. Secondary Sources. A. Books and Articles. B. Collected Studies.

Ocampo, Aurora M. "Bibliografía de Onetti," TEXTO CRITICO, Núm. 18/19 (julio/diciembre de 1980), 276-294. Contents: I. Obras: artículos, ensayos y prólogos. II. Narrativa. III. Poesía. IV. Traducción. V. Referencias (criticism).

Prego, Omar. JUAN CARLOS ONETTI, O LA SALVACION POR LA ESCRITURA. Alcobendas, Madrid: S.G.E.L., 1981. 246p. (Colección Clásicos y Modernos, 6). Contents: I. "Cronología comparada de la narrativa de Juan Carlos Onetti," pp. 240-241 (works listed by year, 1933-1979). II. "Bibliografía sumaria," pp. 244-246. A. Compilaciones críticas sobre la obra de Juan Carlos Onetti. B. Estudios, tesis, memorias y reportajes.

Verani, Hugo J. "Contribución a la bibliografía de Juan Carlos Onetti," REVISTA IBEROAMERICANA, 38, Núm. 80 (julio/diciembre de 1972), 523-548. Contents: I. Obras de Onetti. A. Cuentos. B. Novelas. C. Colecciones de cuentos y novelas. D. Fragmentos de novelas. E. Traducciones de sus obras. F. Artículos periodísticos. G. Miscelánea. 1. Prólogos. 2. Traducciones del inglés. H. Disco, película. I. Entrevistas, reportajes y encuestas. II. Crítica sobre la obra de Onetti. A. Libros, tesis y colecciones de ensayos. B. Estudios, notas y reseñas. C. Menciones breves.

_______. _______. CUADERNOS HISPANOAMERICANOS, Núm. 292/294 (octubre/diciembre de 1974), 731-750. Same contents as above entry.

_______. _______, in Juan Carlos Onetti's ONETTI: SELECCION, CRONOLOGIA Y PRESENTACION DE JORGE RUFINELLI (Montevideo: Biblioteca de Marcha, 1973), pp. 267-291. Same contents as first entry.

_______. ONETTI: EL RITUAL DE LA IMPOSTURA. Caracas: Monte Avila, 1982. 333p. "Bibliografía," pp. 281-333. Contents: I. Obras de Onetti. A. Cuentos (by year, 1933-1976). B. Novelas (by year, 1939-1973). C. Colecciones de cuentos y novelas (by year, 1951-1976). D. Fragmentos de novelas. E. Poemas. F. Traducciones de sus obras (by language). G. Artículos periodísticos (by year, 1939-1976). H. Miscelánea. 1. Prólogos. 2. Disco. 3. Película. 4. Guion cinematográfico. 5. Traducciones del inglés. I. Entrevistas, reportajes y encuestas. II. Crítica sobre la obra de Onetti. A. Libros, tesis y colecciones de ensayos. B. Estudios, notas y reseñas.

OQUENDO DE AMAT, CARLOS (Peru, 1905-1936)

Foster, Peruvian Lit., pp. 196-197. Contents: I. Critical Monographs and Dissertations. II. Critical Essays.

OREAMUNO, YOLANDA (Costa Rica, 1916-1956)

Urbano, Victoria. UNA ESCRITURA COSTARRICENSE: YOLANDA OREAMUNO: ENSAYO CRITICO. Madrid: Coleccion Orosí, 1968. 246p. Contents: I. "Su obra: ficha bibliográfica," pp. 28-30 (by year, 1936-1961). II. "Obra inédita o dispersa," pp. 31-39.

Valbona, Rima de. YOLANDA OREAMUNO. San José, C.R.: Ministerio de Cultura, Juventud y Deportes, Departamento de Publicaciones, 1972. 159p. Contents: I. "Obras," pp. 109-112 (by year, 1936-1971). II. "Bibliografía: artículos, comentarios y crítica sobre la obra," pp. 112-114.

ORIA, JOSE A. (Argentina, 1892-1970)

Becco, Horacio Jorge. "Bibliografía de don José A. Oría," BOLETIN DE LA ACADEMIA ARGENTINA DE LETRAS, 35, Núm. 135/136 (enero/junio de 1970), 33-37. Contents: I. Estudios críticos. II. Prólogos y ediciones.

OROZ, RODOLFO (Chile, 1895-)

Contreras, Lidia. "Bibliografía cronológica de las obras de Rodolfo Oroz," in LENGUA, LITERATURA, FOLKLORE: ESTUDIOS DEDICADOS A RODOLFO OROZ (Santiago de Chile: Editorial Universitaria, 1967), pp. 1-11. Work lists 140 titles, 1922-1965.

ORREGO ESPINOZA, ANTENOR (Peru, 1892-1960)

Otero, María Teresa. "Atenor Orrego Espinoza," ANUARIO BIBLIOGRAFICO PERUANO, 1958/1960, 613-623. Contents: I. Biografía. II. Libros y folletos. III. Otras publicaciones. IV. Artículos y ensayos. V. Cartas, discursos. VI. Notas bibliográficas. VII. Reportajes. VIII. Referencias. IX. Notas necrológicas.

ORREGO LUCO, LUIS (Chile, 1866-1948)

Foster, Chilean Lit., pp. 185-187. Contents: I. Bibliographies. II. Critical Books and Theses. III. Critical Essays.

Rojas Piña, Benjamín. "Cartillas biobibliográficas de autores chilenos: Luis Orrego Luco. Santiago, 1866-1948. Santiago. Novelista y cuentista," BOLETIN DEL INSTITUTO DE LITERATURA CHILENA (Universidad de Chile, Santiago), Año 1, Núm. 1 (septiembre de 1961), 26-30. Contents: I. Obras. II. Referencias. III. Tabla biográfica. IV. Otras publicaciones.

ORTIZ, ADALBERTO (Ecuador, 1914-)

Jackson, Afro-Spanish, pp. 96-100. Contents: I. Works. II. Criticism. Annotated entries.

ORTIZ, FERNANDO (Cuba, 1881-1969)

Fernández de la Vega, Oscar, and Alberto N. Pamies. "Bibliografía primordial de Fernando Ortiz relacionada con la literatura negrista," in their INICIACION A LA POESIA AFRO-AMERICANA (Miami: Ediciones Universal, 1973), pp. 152-155. Contents: I. Libros y folletos. II. Artículos y ensayos en revistas.

Foster, Cuban Lit., pp. 416-419. Contents: I. Bibliographies. II. Critical Monograph. III. Critical Essays.

García-Carranza, Araceli. BIO-BIBLIOGRAFIA DE DON FERNANDO ORTIZ. La Habana: Biblioteca Nacional, "José Martí," 1972. 250p. Contents: I. Bibliografía activa. A. Libros y folletos. B. Prólogos e introducciones. C. Traducciones. D. Colaboraciones en libros. E. Colaboraciones en publicaciones periódicas. II. Bibliografía pasiva. A. Libros y folletos. B. Colaboraciones en publicaciones periódicas. III. Indice de títulos. IV. Indice analítico.

León, René. "Fernando Ortiz: Bibliografía sobre el tema negro," EXPLICACION DE TEXTOS LITERARIOS, 12, Núm. 1 (1983), 19-25. Contents: I. Libros y folletos. II. Colaboraciones en revistas.

OSORIO, LUIS ENRIQUE (Colombia, 1896-1966)

Porras Collantes, pp. 507-512. Includes works of and critical studies about the author.

OSORIO, MIGUEL ANGEL see BARBA-JACOB, PORFIRIO

OSORIO LIZARAZO, JOSE ANTONIO (Colombia, 1900-1964)

Porras Collantes, pp. 513-519. Includes works of and critical studies about the author.

OTERO, LISANDRO (Cuba, 1932-)

Foster, Cuban Lit., pp. 420-421. Critical Essays.

OTERO SILVA, MIGUEL (Venezuela, 1908-1985)

Flores, BEH, pp. 268-269. Contents: I. Ediciones. II. Bibliografía selecta (criticism).

López de Valdivieso, Miriam and Olga Santéliz. "Contribución a la bibliografía de Miguel Otero," in Efraín Subero's CERCANIA DE MIGUEL OTERO SILVA (Caracas: Oficina Central de Información, 1975), pp. 60-69. Contents: I. Poesía. II. Novela. III. Teatro. IV. Miscelánea. This title's "Cronología vital de Miguel Otero Silva" section is biobibliographical in nature.

OTHON, MANUEL JOSE (Mexico, 1858-1906)

Flores, BEH, pp. 269-271. Contents: I. Ediciones principales. II. Otras ediciones. III. Referencias. IV. Bibliografía selecta (criticism).

Foster, Mex. Lit., pp. 255-261. Contents: I. Bibliographies. II. Critical Monographs and Dissertations. III. Critical Essays.

Meade, Joaquín. "Othón en periódicos potosinos," ABSIDE (México), 22, Núm. 4 (octubre/diciembre de 1958), 441-469. The article indexes works by and about Othón which appeared in La Voz de San Luis (1883-1884) and El Estandarte (1885-1912). The works are listed by year and issue.

Montejano y Aguiñaga, Rafael. LO QUE ESCRIBIO MANUEL JOSE OTHON: BIBLIOGRAFIA ESENCIAL. San Luis Potosí, México: Universidad Autónoma, 1959. 46p. Annotated 130 entries.

Contents: I. Colecciones. A. Impresas. B. Inéditas. II. Poesía. A. Impresas. B. Inéditas. III. Cuentos y novelas cortas. A. Impresas. B. Inéditas (en volumen, trabajos sueltos). IV. Teatro. A. Impresos. B. Inéditos. V. Crítica. A. Impresas. B. Inéditas. VI. Discursos. A. Impresos. B. Inéditos. VII. Prosa varia. A. Impresas. B. Inéditas (en volumen, trabajos sueltos). VIII. Jurisprudencia. A. Impresas. B. Inéditas.

Udick, Bernice. "Adiciones a la bibliografía de Manuel José Othón," ABSIDE, 15, Núm. 2 (abril/junio de 1951), 279-294. Updates and supplements the Warner bibliography. Contents: I. Obras de Manuel José Othón. A. Poesía. 1. Colecciones. 2. Poesías sueltas. B. Teatro. C. Prosa. 1. Cuentos y novelas cartas. 2. Cartas. II. Estudios sobre Othón. 107 entries.

Warner, Ralph. "Bibliografía de Manuel José Othón (1858-1906)," REVISTA IBEROAMERICANA, 11, Núm. 21 (15 de junio de 1946), 351-378. This work is not comprehensive; e.g., it does not include the numerous anthologies in which Othón's poetry appears. Contents: I. Obras de Manuel José Othón. A. Poesía. 1. Colecciones. 2. Poesías sueltas. B. Teatro. C. Prosa. 1. Cuentos y novelas cortas. 2. Miscelánea. II. Estudios críticos y biográficos. 208 items.

________. "Los poemas rústicos de Manuel José Othón: estudio bibliográfico analítico," ABSIDE, 19, Núm. 4 (septiembre/diciembre de 1955), 438-447.

OVALLE, ALONSO DE (Chile, 1601-1651)

Foster, Chilean Lit., pp. 187-188. Contents: I. Critical Books and Theses. II. Critical Essays.

OWEN, GILBERTO (Mexico, 1905-1952)

Foster, Mex. Lit., pp. 261-262. Contents: I. Critical Monographs and Essays. II. Critical Essays.

Owen, Gilberto. OBRAS. EDICION DE JOSEFINA PROCOPIO. SEGUNDA EDICION AUMENTADA. México, D.F.: Fondo de Cultura, 1979. 318p. Contents: I. "Bibliografía directa," pp. 295-304. A. Poesía. B. Narración. C. Otras ediciones. D. Prólogos. E. Traducciones. F. Hemerografía (by journal). G. Antologías. II. "Bibliografía indirecta," pp. 305-310 (critical studies).

OYUELA, CALIXTO (Argentina, 1857-1935)

Sordelli, Víctor O. "Bibliografía de Calixto Oyuela," BOLETIN DE LA ACADEMIA ARGENTINA DE LETRAS, 3, Núm. 10 (abril/junio de 1935), 117-122. 81 entries. Works are listed by year, 1881-1934.

- P -

PACHECHO, CARLOS MAURICIO (Argentina, 1881-1924)
Lena Paz, Marta A. BIBLIOGRAFIA CRITICA DE CARLOS MAURICIO PACHECHO, APORTE PARA UN ESTUDIO. Buenos Aires: Fondo Nacional de las Artes, 1963. 94p. (Bibliografía Argentina de Artes y Letras, Compilaciones Especiales, 14). Contents: I. Obras del autor. A. Obra dramática. B. Colaboraciones en publicaciones periódicas. II. Crítica y biografía. III. Compañías que estrenaron las obras del autor. IV. Indices (names and titles).

PACHECO, JOSE EMILIO (Mexico, 1939-)
Foster, Mex. Lit., pp. 262-265. Contents: I. Critical Monographs and Dissertations. II. Critical Essays.

PADILLA, HERBERTO (Cuba, 1932-)
Foster, Cuban Lit., pp. 422-423. Contents: I. Critical Monograph. II. Critical Essays.

PADILLA, JOSE GUALBERTO (Puerto Rico, 1829-1896)
Foster, P.R. Lit., pp. 182-183. Contents: I. Critical Monograph. II. Critical Essays.

PAGANO, JOSE LEON (Argentina, 1875-1964)
"Bibliografía de don José León Pagano," BOLETIN DE LA ACADEMIA ARGENTINA DE LETRAS, 20, Núm. 114 (octubre/diciembre de 1964), 365-367. 44 entries. I. Obras. II. Historia. III. Arte. IV. Cuentos. V. Novela. VI. Teatro.

PAGES LARRAYA, ANTONIO (Argentina, 1918-)
Kisnerman, Natalio. BIBLIOGRAFIA DE ANTONIO PAGES LARRAYA. Buenos Aires: Grupo Editor Argentino, 1963. 25p. 301 entries.

PAIVA, MANUEL DE OLIVEIRA (Brazil, 1861-1892)
Pinto, Rolando Morel. EXPERIENCIA E FICÇAO DE OLIVEIRA PAIVA. São Paulo: Publicação do Instituto de Estudos Brasileiros, 1967. 189p. "Bibliografia," pp. 185-187. Contents: I. Bibliografia do autor. II. Bibliografia sôbre o autor.

PALACIOS, ARNOLDO (Colombia, 1924-)
Jackson, Afro-Spanish, p. 100. Contents: I. Works. II. Criticism.

PALACIOS, EUSTAQUIO (Colombia, 1830-1898)
Porras Collantes, pp. 524-528. Includes works of and critical studies about the author.

PALACIOS, PEDRO B. see "ALMAFUERTE"

PALES MATOS, LUIS (Puerto Rico, 1898-1959)

"Bibliografía de Luis Palés Matos," LA TORRE, Año 8, Núm. 29/30 (enero/junio de 1960), 331-336. The bibliography includes a list of studies about the poet but, unfortunately, does not include any of his contributions to periodicals.

Flores, BEH, pp. 148-149. Contents: I. Ediciones. II. Bibliografía selecta (criticism).

Foster, P.R. Lit., pp. 183-193. Contents: I. Bibliographies. II. Critical Monographs and Dissertations. III. Critical Essays.

Onís, Federico de. LUIS PALES MATOS (1898-1959): VIDA Y OBRA, BIBLIOGRAFIA, ANTOLOGIA, POESIAS INEDITAS. San Juan: Ediciones Ateneo Puertorriqueño, 1960. 91p. "Bibliografía," pp. 57-62. Contents: I. Obras de Palés. II. Estudios sobre Palés.

Palés Matos, Luis. POESIA COMPLETA Y PROSA SELECTA. EDICION, PROLOGO Y CRONOLOGIA POR MARGOT ARCE DE VAZQUEZ. Caracas: Biblioteca Ayacucho, 1978. 429p. "Bibliografía," pp. 409-416. Contents: I. Poesía. A. Libros. B. Poemas sueltos publicados. C. Poemas en antologías. II. Prosa. A. Prosa publicada. B. Prosa inédita. III. Obras inéditas. IV. Estudios selectos (criticism).

Puebla, Manuel de la. "Notas en torno a la bibliografía sobre Palés," MAIRENA (Río Piedras, P.R.). Núm. 1 (primavera de 1979), 77-91.

Romero García, Luz Virginia. EL ALDEANISMO EN LA POESIA DE LUIS PALES MATOS. San Juan: Editorial Universitaria, Universidad de Puerto Rico, 1973. 123p. "Bibliografía," pp. 105-114. Contents: I. Obras de Luis Palés Matos. A. Poesías. B. Novela. II. Estudios sobre el autor.

Ward, James H. "Bibliografía de Luis Palés Matos," LA TORRE, Año 21, Núm. 79/80 (enero/junio de 1973), 221-230. Contents: Obras publicadas de Luis Palés Matos. I. Antologías poéticas. II. Poemas. III. Prosa.

PALHARES, VICTORIANO JOSE MARINHO (Brazil, 1840-1890)

Porter, p. 249. Contents: I. Writings. II. References, Critical and Biographical.

PALLAIS, AZARIAS H. (Nicaragua, 1885-1954)

Arellano, Jorge Eduardo. "Pallais en el Repertorio Americano y bibliografía básica," BOLETIN NICARAGUENSE DE BIBLIOGRAFIA Y DOCUMENTACION, Núm. 44/45 (noviembre 1981/febrero de 1982), 139-141. Contents: I. Repertorio Americano (entries are arranged by title). II. Bibliografía básica. A. Poesía. B. Prosa.

"Azarías H. Pallais en el REPERTORIO AMERICANO," BOLETIN NICARAGUENSE DE BIBLIOGRAFIA Y DOCUMENTACION (Managua), Núm. 8 (noviembre/diciembre de 1975), 6-8.

PALMA, RICARDO (Peru, 1833-1919)

Compton, Merlin D. RICARDO PALMA. Boston: Twayne, 1982.

168p. "Selected Bibliography," pp. 161-165. Contents: I. Primary Sources. A. Poetry. B. Prose. II. Secondary Sources.

_______. "Las tradiciones peruanas de Ricardo Palma: bibliografía y lista cronológica tentativas," DUQUESNE HISPANIC REVIEW, 8, No. 3 (Spring 1969), 1-24. Work is arranged by title of the tradition, year, and other publication data under the following categories: I. Publicaciones periódicas. II. Libros. III. Otros colecciones (no publicados en series). 529 entries.

Feliú Cruz, Guillermo. EN TORNO DE RICARDO PALMA. Tomo 1: LA ESTANCIA EN CHILE. Tomo 2: ENSAYO CRITICO-BIBLIOGRAFICO. Santiago de Chile: Prensas de la Universidad de Chile, 1933. Contents: I. Ensayo crítico-bibliográfico (annotated, 1848-1933). II. Notas biobibliográficas (1860-1933). III. Indice alfabético de nombres citados en la bibliografía.

Flores, BEH, pp. 40-44. Contents: I. Ediciones principales. II. Otras ediciones. III. Antologías. IV. Bibliografía selecta (criticism).

_______. "Bibliografía," in ORIGENES DEL CUENTO HISPANOAMERICANO: RICARDO PALMA Y SUS "TRADICIONES." (México, D.F.: Premia, 1979), pp. 141-146. Contents: I. Ediciones principales. II. Primeras ediciones. III. Antologías. IV. Referencias. V. Libros, artículos y comentarios sobre Palma y su obra (few citations after 1968, however).

Foster, Peruvian Lit., pp. 198-214. Contents: I. Bibliographies. II. Critical Monographs and Dissertations. III. Critical Essays.

Palma, Edith. "Bibliografía," in Ricardo Palma: TRADICIONES PERUANAS COMPLETAS. EDICION Y PROLOGO DE EDITH PALMA (Madrid: Aguilar, 1953), pp. 1730-1760. Contents: I. Fuentes y documentos de información de que se sirvió el autor. II. Bibliografía de Ricardo Palma. A. Obras publicadas bajo la dirección de Ricardo Palma. B. Antologías. C. Obras en los ANALES se encuentran tradiciones y poemas de Ricardo Palma. D. Traducciones. III. Bibliografía sobre Ricardo Palma. A. Artículos que aparecen en la edición oficial editada por Calpe, Madrid, 1943-1946. B. Artículos, notas críticas y poemas sobre Ricardo Palma (aparecidos en otras ediciones, revistas y diarios). C. Homenajes a Ricardo Palma.

Porras Barrenechea, Raúl. "Bibliografía de Ricardo Palma," in Ricardo Palma's TRADICIONES PERUANAS (Lima: Editorial Cultural Antártica, 1951), v. 1, pp. xi-lxxxi. Contents: I. Tradiciones peruanas (by year and edition, 1872-1923/25). II. Ediciones parciales de las Tradiciones y antologías (by year, 1891-1950/51). III. Obras en coloboración (by year, 1857-1877/78). IV. Obras inéditas perdidas y clandestinas. A. Obras dramáticas (1850-1854). B. Obras perdidas en el incendio de Miraflores de 1881. C. Tradiciones en Salsa Verde. V. Catálogo y memorias bibliográficas. VI. Biografía de Palma. VII. Bibliografía sobre Palma (by year, 1891-1943). VIII. Ensayos y críticas (by year, 1862-1952).

Suárez Osorio, Miguel. REGISTRO BIBLIOGRAFICO DE ARTICULOS PERIODISTICOS DE DON RICARDO PALMA. ALGUNAS TRANSCRIPCIONES DE SU PLUMA PERIODISTICA. Huancayo, Perú: Talls. Mimeográficos "Amauta," 1969. 43p. Indexes Palma's work in the following journals: El Burro, El Liberal, La Campana, Revista Peruana, La Broma, El Ateneo de Lima.

PARDO Y ALIAGA, FELIPE (Peru, 1806-1868)

Cachy Díaz, Roselina. "Felipe Pardo y Aliaga, 1806-1868, biobibliografía," BOLETIN DE LA BIBLIOTECA NACIONAL (Lima), Años 22/23, Núms. 45/48 (primer y segundo semestres de 1968), 3-27. Contents: I. Biobibliografía. II. Homobibliografía. A. Inéditos. B. Editos. III. Heterobibliografía (criticism). IV. Indice onomástico.

Flores, BEH, p. 44. Contents: I. Ediciones. II. Referencias. III. Bibliografía selecta (criticism).

Flores, NH, v. 1, pp. 78-79. Contents: I. Ediciones. II. Referencias. III. Bibliografía selecta (criticism).

Foster, Peruvian Lit., pp. 215-217. Contents: I. Bibliographies. II. Critical Monographs and Dissertations. III. Critical Essays.

PARRA, NICANOR (Chile, 1914-)

Escudero, Alfonso M. "Fuentes de consulta sobre Nicanor Parra," AISTHESIS: REVISTA CHILENA DE INVESTIGACIONES ESTETICAS, Núm. 5 (1970), 307-312. Entries arranged by year, 1951-1970.

Fernández F., Maximino. "Fichas bibliográficas sobre Nicanor Parra," REVISTA CHILENA DE LITERATURA, Núm. 15 (abril de 1980), 107-131. 583 unannotated entries. Contents: I. Libros. II. Bibliografías. III. Artículos con nombre de autor. IV. Artículos anónimos.

________. "Fichas bibliográficas sobre Nicanor Parra-II," REVISTA CHILENA DE LITERATURA, abril 1984.

Flores, BEH, pp. 150-152. Contents: I. Edición principal. II. Otras ediciones. III. Bibliografía selecta (criticism).

Foster, Chilean Lit., pp. 188-193. Contents: I. Bibliographies. II. Critical Books and Theses. III. Critical Essays.

Gottlieb, Marlene. NO SE TERMINA NUNCA DE NACER: LA POESIA DE NICANOR PARRA. Madrid: Playor, 1977. 167p. Contents: I. "Bibliografía: obras de Nicanor Parra," p. 147 (books only). II. "Bibliografía de artículos sobre Nicanor Parra," pp. 149-165. III. "Libros sobre Nicanor Parra," p. 167.

Grossman, Edith. THE ANTIPOETRY OF NICANOR PARRA. New York: New York University Press, 1975. 201p. "Bibliography," pp. 191-195. Very selected bibliography of works by and about Parra.

Montes, Hugo, and Mario Rodríguez. NICANOR PARRA Y LA POESIA DE LO COTIDIANO. 2ª edición. Santiago de Chile: Editorial del Pacífico, S.A., 1974. 149p. "Bibliografía," pp.

139-148. Contents: I. De Nicanor Parra. II. Sobre Nicanor Parra.

PARRA, TERESA DE LA (Venezuela, 1895-1936)

Caracas. Universidad Católica "Andrés Bello." Seminario de Literatura Venezolana. CONTRIBUCION A LA BIBLIOGRAFIA DE TERESA DE LA PARRA, 1895-1936. Caracas: Gobernación del Distrito Federal, 1972. 133p. (Colección bibliografías, 7). 473 references. Contents: I. Referencias bibliográficas. II. Obras mayores. A. Novela. B. Cuento. III. Miscelánea. IV. Obra dispersa (mainly journal and newspaper articles). V. Epistolario. A. De Teresa de la Parra. B. A Teresa de la Parra. VI. Biografía y crítica (libros, folletos, capítulos, artículos y referencias sobre el autor y su obra).

Corvalán, p. 88. Contents: I. Works. II. Critical Works On.

Flores, BEH, pp. 271-273. Contents: I. Edición principal. II. Otras ediciones. III. Bibliografía selecta (criticism).

Parra, Teresa de la. OBRA (NARRATIVA-ENSAYOS-CARTAS). SELECCION, ESTUDIO CRITICO Y CRONOLOGIA POR VELIA BOSCH. Caracas: Biblioteca Ayacucho, 1982. 752p. "Bibliografía," pp. 745-752. Contents: I. Obras de Teresa de la Parra. II. Estudios sobre Teresa de la Parra. A. Libros y folletos. B. Hemerografía (selectiva). C. Bibliografías.

PARRA, VIOLETA (Chile, 1917-1967)

Agosin, Marjorie. "Bibliografía de Violeta Parra," REVISTA INTERAMERICANA DE BIBLIOGRAFIA, 32 (1982), 179-190. Contents: I. Bibliografía de Violeta Parra--obras de Violeta Parra. II. Bibliografía sobre Violeta Parra. A. Artículos, libros y notas. B. Referencias breves sobre Violeta Parra. Partially annotated entries.

PASO, FERNANDO DEL (Mexico, 1935-)

Foster, Mex. Lit., pp. 265-266. Contents: I. Critical Monographs and Dissertations. II. Critical Essays.

PATROCINIO, JOSE CARLOS DO (Brazil, 1854-1905)

Mota, Artur. "Perfís acadêmicos, Cadeira No. 21: José Carlos do Patrocinio," REVISTA DA ACADEMIA BRASILEIRA DE LETRAS, Núm. 119 (novembro de 1931), 308-331. Contents: I. "Bibliografia," pp. 308-309 (1875-1905). II. "Fontes para o estudo crítico," pp. 309-310.

Reis, Antônio Simões dos. "José Carlos do Patrocinio: Notas para uma bibliografia," EUCLYDES, Núm. 10 (15 janeiro de 1941), 154-158; Núm. 11 (1 fevereiro de 1941), 175-176.

PAYRO, ROBERTO J. (Argentina, 1867-1928)

Flores, BEH, pp. 152-154. Contents: I. Ediciones principales. II. Referencias. III. Bibliografía selecta (criticism).

Foster, Arg. Lit., pp. 615-622. Contents: I. Bibliographies. II. Critical Monographs and Dissertation. III. Critical Essays.

PAZ, OCTAVIO (Mexico, 1914-)

Flores, BEH, pp. 154-158. Contents: I. Ediciones. II. Referencias. III. Bibliografía selecta (criticism).

Foster, Mex. Lit., pp. 266-288. Contents: I. Bibliographies. II. Critical Monographs and Dissertations. III. Critical Essays.

Martínez Torrón, Diego. VARIABLES POETICAS DE OCTAVIO PAZ. Madrid: Impreso en la Cooperativa Industrial T.C., 1979. 287p. "Bibliografía," pp. 267-277. Contents: I. Bibliografía de Octavio Paz. A. Obras de creación poética. B. Obras de crítica y ensayo. C. Poemas. D. Artículos. E. Antologías preparadas por Octavio Paz. II. Bibliografía sobre Octavio Paz.

Roggiano, Alfredo. "Bibliografía de y sobre Octavio Paz," in Octavio Paz (Madrid: Editorial Fundamentos, 1979), pp. 371-395. Contents: I. Obras de Octavio Paz. A. Poesía (by year, monographs only). B. Prosa (by year). C. Teatro. D. Ediciones, antologías, prólogos y traducciones. E. Octavio Paz en periódicos literarios (selected). F. Traducciones de obras de Octavio Paz (by year, 1957-1974). II. Sobre Octavio Paz (selección).

Verani, Hugo J. "Hacia la bibliografía de Octavio Paz," CUADERNOS HISPANOAMERICANOS, Núm. 343/345 (enero/marzo de 1979), 752-791. Contents: I. Obras de Octavio Paz. A. Poesía. B. Prosa. C. Teatro. D. Ediciones, antologías, prólogos y traducciones. E. Miscelánea. F. Ensayos dispersos. G. Traducciones de obras de Octavio Paz (by language, books only). II. Sobre Octavio Paz. A. Libros, tesis, homenajes. B. Estudios, notas, entrevistas, reseñas.

_______. OCTAVIO PAZ: BIBLIOGRAFIA CRITICA. México, D.F.: Universidad Nacional Autónoma de México, 1983. 257p. Contents: I. Obras de Octavio Paz. A. Poesía. B. Prosa. C. Teatro. D. Ediciones, traducciones, prólogo. E. Primeras publicaciones. 1. Poemas. 2. Ensayos, artículos, reseñas. F. Miscelánea. 1. Revistas fundadas por Octavio Paz. 2. Película. 3. Disco. 4. Grabaciones magnetofónicas. 5. Premios y distinciones. G. Traducciones de obras de Octavio Paz. II. Obras sobre Octavio Paz. A. Libros. B. Tesis universitarias. C. Publicaciones colectivas. D. Ensayos y estudios. 1. Estudios de carácter general. a. Poesía. b. Prosa. 2. Estudios de carácter particular. a. Libros. b. Poemas. c. Aspectos. E. Entrevistas y diálogos. F. Biografías y semblanzas. G. Bibliografías. H. Notas, comentarios, homenajes. 1. Notas de carácter general. a. Poesía. b. Prosa. 2. Notas de carácter particular. a. Libros. b. Poemas. c. Biobibliografías. d. Miscelánea. I. Reseñas. J. Indices. 1. Indice de revistas y periódicos. 2. Indice alfabético de autores.

Wilson, Jason. OCTAVIO PAZ: A STUDY OF HIS POETICS. Cambridge: Cambridge University Press, 1979. 192p. "Bibliography," pp. 185-188. Contents: I. Bibliographies. II. Works by Octavio Paz. III. Octavio Paz in English. IV. Works on Octavio Paz. V. Interviews with Octavio Paz. VI. Records.

PAZ CASTILLO, FERNANDO (Venezuela, 1893-)
Caracas. Universidad Católica "Andrés Bello." Seminario de Literatura Venezolana. CONTRIBUCION A LA BIBLIOGRAFIA DE FERNANDO PAZ CASTILLO, 1893. Caracas: Gobernación del Distrito Federal, 1974. 332p. (Colección bibliografías, 11). 1,477 references. Contents: I. Referencias bibliográficas. II. Obras mayores. A. Ensayo. B. Poesía. C. Cuento. III. Miscelánea. IV. Obra dispersa (mainly journal and newspaper articles). V. Epistolario. VI. Biografía y crítica (libros, folletos, capítulos, artículos y referencias sobre el autor y su obra). VII. Apéndice. A. Fichas incompletas. B. Ultimas referencias bibliográficas y hemerográficas.

PAZ SOLDAN Y UNANUE, PEDRO see ARONA, JUAN DE

PEDREIRA, ANTONIO S. (Puerto Rico, 1898-1939)
Foster, P.R. Lit., pp. 193-197. Contents: I. Critical Monographs and Dissertation. II. Critical Essays.

PEDRONI, JOSE BARTOLOME (Argentina, 1899-1968)
Pedroni, José Bartolomé. OBRA POETICA. Rosario, Argentina: Editorial Biblioteca, 1969. 2vs. "Bibliografía," v. 2, no p. nos. Contents: I. Obra poética (1920-1967). II. Labor cultural y social del poeta: su actividad gremial y ciudadana. A. Teatro. B. Periodismo. C. Acción gremial. D. Actividad cívica. E. Conferencias. F. Correspondencia. G. Discursos, declaraciones, reportajes, etc. H. En función pública. III. Premios-homenajes. IV. Crítica-valoración. V. Significativos artículos en prensa. VI. Traducciones-versones. VII. Tablilla. A. Algunas antologías. B. Diccionario de la materia. C. Indice. VIII. Obras muscicales para orquesta y canto. IX. Dedicatoria lírica.

PEDROSO, REGINO (Cuba, 1896/98-1983)
Foster, Cuban Lit., pp. 424-425. Contents: I. Bibliography. II. Critical Essays.
Jackson, Afro-Spanish, pp. 100-102. Contents: I. Works. II. Criticism. Annotated entries.

PEIXOTO, AFRANIO (Brazil, 1876-1947)
Peixoto, Afrânio. CARTAS, 1894-1937. Salvador: Fundação Cultural do Estado, 1977. 102p. (Inventário de Casa de Cultura Afrânio Peixoto, 1). Inventory of the correspondence received by Brazilian writer Afrânio Peixoto between 1894 and 1937 and which is in the holdings of the Casa de Cultura Afrânio Peixoto in Bahia.
_______. ROMANCES COMPLETOS. ORGANIZAÇAO, INTRODUCÇAO E NOTAS DE AFRANIO COUTINHO. Rio de Janeiro: Editôra José Aguilar Ltda., 1962. 950p. "Bibliografia," pp. 945-948. Contents: I. Fontes. II. Obras de autor. III. Estudos sôbre o autor.

PELLICER, CARLOS (Mexico, 1899-1977)

Andrea, Pedro F. de, and George Melnykovich. "Carlos Pellicer: aportación bibliográfica," BOLETIN DE LA COMUNIDAD LATINOAMERICANA DE ESCRITORES (México), 4 (1969), 8-26. Contents: I. Enfoques sobre su obra. II. Y lo que opina Carlos Pellicer de su poesía. III. Bibliografía activa (47 items). IV. Referencias (122 items).

Foster, Mex. Lit., pp. 288-292. Contents: I. Bibliographies. II. Critical Monographs and Dissertations. III. Critical Essays.

Lara Barba, Othón. "Carlos Pellicer: Testimonio (Ensayo biblioiconográfico ilustrado con textos)," BOLETIN DEL INSTITUTO DE INVESTIGACIONES BIBLIOGRAFICAS (Universidad Nacional Autónoma de México), Núm. 5 (enero/junio de 1971), 9-103. 300 entries partially annotated. Contents: I. Bibliografía de Carlos Pellicer. A. Poesía. B. La poesía en las revistas literarias. C. Prosa. 1. Artículos. 2. Discursos. 3. Prólogos. D. Antologías. II. Bibliografía sobre Carlos Pellicer. A. Bibliografías. B. Gacetillas. C. Homenajes poemáticos. D. Entrevistas a Carlos Pellicer. E. Imágenes biográficas sobre Carlos Pellicer. F. Referencias a la obra de Carlos Pellicer. G. Reportajes y crónicas sobre Carlos Pellicer.

Mullen, Edward J. POESIA DE CARLOS PELLICER: INTERPRETACIONES CRITICAS. México, D.F.: UNAM, 1979. 239p. "Bibliohemerografía," pp. 235-239. Contents: I. Obra poética de Carlos Pellicer (by year, 1916-1976). II. Estudios sobre Pellicer. A. Libros. B. Ensayos. C. Documentos. D. Traducciones.

Melnykovich, George. REALITY AND EXPRESSION IN THE POETRY OF CARLOS PELLICER. Chapel Hill, N.C.: Department of Romance Languages, 1979. 150p. (University of North Carolina Studies in the Romance Languages and Literatures, 211). Contents: I. "Works by Carlos Pellicer," pp. 143-144 (arranged by year, 1916-1969). II. "Studies on Pellicer," pp. 144-150.

Ponce de Hurtado, María Teresa. EL RUISENOR LLENO DE MUERTE: APROXIMACION A CARLOS PELLICER. México, D.F.: Editorial Meridiano, 1970. 218p. "Bibliografía," pp. 209-216. Contents: I. Bibliografía directa (obras de Carlos Pellicer). II. Bibliografía indirecta (obras sobre Carlos Pellicer).

PENA, CORNELIO (Brazil, 1896-1958)

Pena, Cornélio. ROMANCES COMPLETOS. Rio de Janeiro: Editôra José Aguilar, 1958. 1388p. "Bibliografia," pp. 1373-1376. Contents: I. Obras. II. Estudos, reportagens, homenagens.

PENA, LUIS CARLOS MARTINS (Brazil, 1815-1848)

Pena, Luís Carlos Martins. COMEDIAS DE MARTINS PENA. EDIÇAO CRITICA POR DARCY DAMASCENO. Rio de Janeiro: Edições de Ouro, 1983. 639p. "Bibliografia," pp. 13-22. Contents: I. Obra dramática. II. Edições. III. Edições coletivas.

Veiga, Luís Francisco da. "Carlos Martins Pena, o criador da comédia nacional," REVISTA DO INSTITUTO HISTORICO E GEOGRAFICO BRASILEIRO, 40, pt. 2 (1877), 375-407. A bibliographic essay on Martins Pena's works appears between pages 375 and 407.

PENA FILHO, CARLOS (Brazil, 1929-1960)

Coutinho, Edilberto. O LIVRO DE CARLOS: CARLOS PENA FILHO, POESIA E VIDA. Rio de Janeiro: Livraria José Olympio Editôra, 1983. 152p. "Bibliografia," pp. 148-152. Includes works by and about Carlos Pena Filho.

PERALTA, ARTURO see CHURATA, GAMALIEL

PERALTA BARNUEVO ROCHA Y BENAVIDES, PEDRO DE (Peru, 1663-1743)

Burga, Alicia. "BIBLIOGRAFIA DE PEDRO DE PERALTA Y BARNUEVO." Tesis. Lima: Biblioteca Nacional, Escuela de Bibliotecarios, 1957.

Carpio Cuba, José Efraín del. "Datos bibliográficos," in Pedro de Peralta Barnuevo's OBRAS DRAMATICAS CORTAS (Lima: Biblioteca Universitaria, 1964), pp. 47-54. Works are listed by year, 1688-1742.

Chavez, Erlinda. "BIBLIOGRAFIA DE PEDRO DE PERALTA Y BARNUEVO." Tesis. Lima: Biblioteca Nacional, Escuela de Bibliotecarios, 1954.

Foster, Peruvian Lit., pp. 218-222. Contents: I. Bibliographies. II. Critical Monographs and Dissertations. III. Critical Essays.

PEREZ, FELIPE (Colombia, 1836-1891)

Porras Collantes, pp. 532-541. Includes works of and critical studies about the author.

PEREZ, JOSE JOAQUIN (Dominican Republic, 1845-1900)

Pérez, José Joaquín. OBRA POETICA. SELECCION Y NOTAS DE CARLOS FEDERICO PEREZ. Santo Domingo: Universidad Nacional "Pedro Henríquez Ureña," 1970. 350p. "Bibliografía," pp. 16-18. Lists brief studies about the work and life of the author.

PEREZ BONALDE, JUAN ANTONIO (Venezuela, 1846-1892)

Johnson, Ernest A. JUAN ANTONIO PEREZ BONALDE. LOS ANOS DE FORMACION, 1846-1870. DOCUMENTOS. PROLOGO POR PEDRO GRASES. Mérida, Venezuela: Universidad de los Andes, Facultad de Humanidades y Educación, Escuela de Letras, 1971. 315p. "Bibliografía," pp. 301-309. Contents: I. Publicaciones de Juan A. Pérez Bonalde (orden cronológico, 1864-1964). II. Fuentes inéditas. III. Artículos (critical studies about Pérez Bonalde and his work).

PEREZ DE VARGAS, JOSE (Peru, 1776-1855)

Tauro, Alberto. "José Pérez de Vargas, maestro y poeta," FENIX

(Biblioteca Nacional, Lima), Núm. 1 (1944), 104-120; Núm. 2 (1945), 249-263; Núm. 3 (1945), 515-540; Núm. 4 (1946), 839-865. Contents: I. Noticia biográfica. Apéndice: documentos. II. Proyecciones de su labor pedagógica. III. Poeta. IV. Antología. V. Bibliografía de José Pérez de Vargas. A. Prelusions académicos y composiciones escolares (by year). B. Obra didáctica (by year). C. Poesías diversas. D. Traducciones. VI. Bibliografía sobre José Pérez de Vargas.

PEREZ DE ZAMBRANA, LUISA (Cuba, 1835-1922)
Tejera y Horta, María Luisa de la. BIBLIOGRAFIA DE LUISA PEREZ DE ZAMBRANA. Tesis de grado para optar al título de técnica bibliotecaria. La Habana: Imprenta Fernández y Cía., 1958. 32p. Contents: I. Bibliografía activa. A. Verso. B. Prosa. II. Bibliografía pasiva.

PEREZ LUGO, J. see RAMIREZ CABANAS, JOAQUIN

PEREZ PIERRET, ANTONIO (Puerto Rico, 1885-1937)
Foster, P.R. Lit., p. 198. Contents: I. Critical Monograph and Dissertation. II. Critical Essays.

PEREZ ROSALES, VICENTE (Chile, 1807-1886)
Foster, Chilean Lit., pp. 193-194. Contents: I. Critical Books and Theses. II. Critical Essays.

PESADO, JOSE JOAQUIN (Mexico, 1801-1861)
Flores, BEH, pp. 65-66. Contents: I. Ediciones. II. Bibliografía selecta (criticism).

PEYROU, MANUEL (Argentina, 1902-1974)
Becco, Horacio Jorge. "Bibliografía de don Manuel Peyrou (1902-1974)," BOLETIN DE LA ACADEMIA ARGENTINA DE LETRAS, 39, Núm. 151/152 (enero/junio de 1974), 9-10. Contents: I. Narrativa. A. Cuentos. B. Novelas. II. Traducciones. III. Bibliografías.

PEZA, JUAN DE DIOS (Mexico, 1852-1910)
Contreras García, Irma. "En torno a Juan de Dios Peza," BOLETIN DEL INSTITUTO DE INVESTIGACIONES BIBLIOGRAFICAS (México, D.F.), Núm. 4 (julio/diciembre de 1970), 85-106. Contents: I. "Poemas de los Cartas del hogar que fueron publicados en el Album de la mujer," pp. 100-106 (arranged by year, 1884-1889. II. "Ediciones del libro: Cantos del hogar," p. 106 (by year, 1881?-1966).
Valle, Rafael Heliodoro. "Bibliografía de Juan de Dios Peza," BOLETIN DE LA BIBLIOTECA NACIONAL (México), 2a época, 5, Núm. 3 (julio/septiembre de 1954), 3-20. Contents: I. Obras sobre Juan de Dios Peza. II. Obras de Juan de Dios Peza (by year, 1873-1954).

PEZOA VELIZ, CARLOS (Chile, 1879-1908)

Flores, BEH, pp. 158-159. Contents: I. Ediciones. II. Referencias. III. Bibliografía selecta (criticism).

Foster, Chilean Lit., pp. 194-198. Contents: I. Bibliographies. II. Critical Books and Theses. III. Critical Essays.

Pinilla, Norberto. "Bibliografía crítica sobre Carlos Pezoa Véliz," REVISTA IBEROAMERICANA, 4, Núm. 8 (febrero de 1942), 473-482. Contents: I. Obras del poeta. II. Libros antológías en que aparecen poemas de Carlos Pezoa Véliz. III. Estudios sobre el poeta. IV. Textos en que se hacen referencias o alusiones a Carlos Pezoa Véliz.

PICON FEBRES, GABRIEL (Venezuela, 1890-1969)

Cardozo, Poesía, pp. 191-193. Includes the poetical works of and the critical studies about the author.

PICON FEBRES, GONZALO (Venezuela, 1860-1918)

Cardozo, Poesía, pp. 193-197. Includes the poetical works of and the critical studies about the author.

_______. "Gonzalo Picón-Febres, el gran desterrado," ALMANAQUE LITERARIO VENEZOLANO, 3 (1968/1969), 83-87. "Bibliografía," pp. 85-87. Lists books only by title of work. Bibliography includes literary criticism, biographies, novels, and poems of the author.

_______. "Gonzalo Picón Febres: vida y poesía," REVISTA NACIONAL DE CULTURA (Caracas), Núm. 196 (1971), 13-26. "Bibliografía," pp. 22-26. Contents: I. Sobre el autor. II. Del autor. Sólo en poesía.

PICON LARES, EDUARDO (Venezuela, 1889-1960)

Cardozo, Poesía, pp. 197-199. Includes the poetical works of and the critical studies about the author.

PICON LARES, ROBERTO (Venezuela, 1891-1950)

Cardozo, Poesía, pp. 199-202. Includes the poetical works of and the critical studies about the author.

PICON SALAS, MARIANO (Venezuela, 1901-1965)

Grases, Pedro. "Contribución a la bibliografía de Mariano Picón Salas (1901-1965)," MAPOCHO (Santiago de Chile), Vol. 13, Tomo 5, Núm. 1 (1966), 227-232. Contents: I. Esquema biográfico. II. Publicaciones. A. Compilaciones antologías. B. Obras (libros y folletos). 1. Historia. 2. Ensayos. 3. Creación. III. Publicaciones periódicas (editor of). The bibliography contains a total of 87 items.

Lovera de Sola, Roberto. "Mariano Picón Salas: cronología biobibliográfica," IMAGEN (Caracas), Núm. 103/104 (1975), 158-161.

Morin, Thomas D. MARIANO PICON SALAS. Boston: Twayne, 1979. 155p. "Selected Bibliography," pp. 140-152. Contents: I. Primary Sources. A. Books and Editions. B. Essays in

El Nacional (listed by year, 1944-1965). C. Anthologies. D. Books Edited with Other Authors. II. Secondary Sources (briefly annotated).

PINERA, VIRGILIO (Cuba, 1912-1979)
Foster, Cuban Lit., pp. 426-427. Contents: I. Dissertation. II. Critical Essays.
"Virgilio Piñera Llera, 1912-1979," BIBLIOGRAFIA CUBANA, 1979, v. 1, 531-537. Contents: I. Cronología. II. Bibliografía activa. III. Traducciones más importantes.

PINEYRO, ENRIQUE (Cuba, 1839-1911)
"Bibliografía de Enrique Piñeyro," pp. 217-321, in ENRIQUE PIÑEYRO'S VIDA Y ESCRITOS DE JUAN CLIMENTE ZENEA. La Habana: Consejo Nacional de Cultura, 1964. 329p. Contents: I. Nota biográfica preliminar (pp. 219-229). II. Bibliografía de Enrique Piñeyro (pp. 217-296; by date 1856-1907). III. Complemento (pp. 296-305; by date 1868-1927). IV. Biografías y citaciones (pp. 305-311; by date 1868-1917). V. Necrología (pp. 311-313). VI. Juicios de obras de Peñeyro (pp. 313-321; by work and covers the period 1871-1912).
Foster, Cuban Lit., pp. 428-429. Contents: I. Bibliography. II. Critical Monographs. III. Critical Essays.

PITA RODRIGUEZ, FELIX (Cuba, 1909-)
Foster, Cuban Lit., pp. 430-431. Critical Essays.
Rodríguez H., Luis M. "Cronología de la vida y la obra de Félix Pita Rodríguez," ISLAS, Núm. 62 (enero/abril de 1979), 3-74. Contents: I. "Bibliografía cronológica de Félix Pita Rodríguez," pp. 39-47 (works are arranged by year, 1926-1977). II. "Bibliografía consultada," pp. 47-50 (includes critical studies upon Pita Rodríguez).

PITOL, SERGIO (Mexico, 1933-)
Ocampo, Aurora M. "Bibliografía de Sergio Pitol," TEXTO CRITICO, Núm. 21 (1981), 63-67. Contents: I. Obras. A. Cuento. B. Ensayo. C. Novela. D. Traducción. E. Hemerografía. 1. Cuento. 2. Novela. 3. Traducción. II. Referencias.

PIZARNIK, ALEJANDRA (Argentina, 1936/37-)
Foster, Arg. Lit., p. 623. Critical Essays.
Piña, Cristina. PALABRA COMO DESTINO. UN ACERCAMIENTO A LA POESIA DE ALEJANDRA PIZARNIK. Buenos Aires: Botella al Mar, 1981. 95p. "Bibliografía," pp. 94-95. Contents: Obras de Alejandra Pizarnik.

"PLACIDO" (Pseudonym of GABRIEL DE LA CONCEPCION VALDES) (Cuba, 1809-1844).
Cervantes, Carlos A. "Bibliografía placidiana," REVISTA CUBANA, 8, Núm. 22/24 (abril/junio de 1937), 155-186. This bib-

liography lists works about Plácido and his work.
Flores, BEH, pp. 44-45. Contents: I. Ediciones. II. Referencias. III. Bibliografía selecta (criticism).
Foster, Cuban Lit., pp. 460-464. Contents: I. Bibliographies. II. Critical Monographs and Dissertation. III. Critical Essays.
García, Enildo Alberto. "CUBA EN LA OBRA DE PLACIDO (1809-1844): ANALISIS Y BIBLIOGRAFIA COMENTADA." Ph.D., New York University, 1982. 426p. "Bibliografía." Contents: I. Obras y ediciones. II. Bibliografía general. III. Bibliografía anotada (includes critical studies about Plácido and his work).
Jackson, Afro-Spanish, pp. 106-114. Contents: I. Works. II. Criticism. A. Bibliography. B. Books. C. Articles, Shorter Studies, and Dissertations. Annotated entries.
"Plácido: Bibliografía pasiva (selección)," REVISTA DE LA BIBLIOTECA NACIONAL "JOSE MARTI", 3a época, 6, Núm. 3/4 (junio/diciembre de 1964), 117-124.
Plasencia, Aleida. "Bibliografía activa de Gabriel de la Concepción Valdés, Plácido," REVISTA DE LA BIBLIOTECA NACIONAL "JOSE MARTI", 3a época, 6, Núm. 3/4 (julio/diciembre de 1964), 77-116. By year, 1838-1930. Extensive commentaries.
Stimson, Frederick S. CUBA'S ROMANTIC POET: THE STORY OF PLACIDO. Chapel Hill: The University of North Carolina Press, 1964. 150p. (Studies in the Romance Languages and Literatures, 47). "A Selected Bibliography," pp. 146-150. Contents: I. Biographies and Anthologies in Spanish. II. Unpublished Letters and Miscellany. III. Outstanding Editions. IV. CONSPIRACION DE LA ESCALERA. V. Stylistic Studies. VI. North American Biographers and Translations. VII. Nineteenth-Century Travel Literature Pertaining to Cuba. VIII. Miscellaneous.

POCATERRA, JOSE RAFAEL (Venezuela, 1890-1955)
Caracas. Universidad Católica "Andrés Bello." Seminario de Literatura Venezolana. CONTRIBUCION A LA BIBLIOGRAFIA DE JOSE RAFAEL POCATERRA, 1890-1955. Caracas: Gobernación del Distrito Federal, 1970. 96p. (Colección bibliografías, 4). 360 references. Contents: I. Referencias bibliográficas. II. Bibliografía directa. A. Obras mayores (by year, 1913-1965). B. Obra dispersa (mainly journal and newspaper articles). III. Bibliografía crítica.
Flores, BEH, pp. 273-274. Contents: I. Edición principal. II. Otras ediciones. III. Bibliografía selecta (criticism).
Tejera, María Josefa. JOSE RAFAEL POCATERRA: FICCION Y DENUNCIA Caracas: Monte Avila Editores, 1976. 470p. "Bibliografía de José Rafael Pocaterra," pp. 433-470. Contents: I. Novelas, cuentos, memorias y otras obras. A. Diversas ediciones. B. Prólogos y traducciones. C. Cuentos grotescos. D. Primeras apariciones en revistas y diarios. E. Obras dispersas: artículos publicados en diarios y periódicos nacionales y extranjeros. F. Versiones. G. Obras inéditas o inconclusas.

H. Traducciones. I. Reportajes y entrevistas. I. Correspondencia. J. Obras publicadas en La Lectura Semanal. II. Bibliografía sobre Pocaterra.

POLETTI, SYRIA (Argentina, 1922-)
Corvalán, p. 92. Critical Works On.

POMPEIA, RAUL (Brazil, 1863-1895)
López Heredia, José. MATERIA E FORMA NARRATIVA DE "O ATENEU." São Paulo: Quíron, 1979. 145p. (Coleção Logos, 12). "Bibliografia," pp. 139-145. Contents: I. Edições de O Ateneu de Raúl Pompéia (by year, 1888-1974). II. Edições e escritos de Raúl Pompéia utilizados. III. Bibliografia auxiliar (includes critical studies about Pompéia and his work).
Rio de Janeiro. Biblioteca Nacional. EXPOSIÇAO COMEMORATIVA DO CENTENARIO DE NASCIMENTO DE RAUL POMPEIA. Rio de Janeiro, 1963. 40p. Bibliography.

PONDAL RIOS, SIXTO (Argentina, 1907-1968)
Petit de Murat, Ulyses. SIXTO PONDAL RIOS. Buenos Aires: Ediciones Culturales Argentinas, Ministerio de Cultura y Educación, 1981. 153p. "Noticia bibliográfica," pp. 145-150. Contents: I. Poesías. II. Obras de teatro (en colaboración con Carlos Alberto Olivari). III. Películas.

PONIATOWSKA, ELENA (Mexico, 1932-)
Corvalán, pp. 92-93. Contents: I. Work. II. Critical Works On.
Foster, Mex. Lit., pp. 292-294. Critical Essays.

PORTO-ALEGRE, MANUEL JOSE DE ARAUJO, BARAO DE SANTO ANGELO (Brazil, 1806-1879)
Lôbo, Hélio. MANOEL DE ARAUJO PORTO-ALEGRE. ENSAIO BIOBIBLIOGRAFICO. Rio de Janeiro: Empresa A.B.C., 1938. 180p. (Publicações da Academia Brasileira III, Bibliografia 9). Contents: I. Nota biográfica. II. Ensaio de bibliografia. A. Principais escritos sôbre o poeta. B. Depoimentos sôbre o poeta.

PORTUONDO, JOSE ANTONIO (Cuba, 1911-)
Foster, Cuban Lit., p. 432. Critical Essays.

POVEDA, JOSE MANUEL (Cuba, 1888-1926)
Foster, Cuban Lit., p. 433. Critical Essays.

PRADO, PEDRO (Chile, 1886-1952)
Blondet, Olga. "Pedro Prado: bibliografía," REVISTA HISPANICA MODERNA, Año 26, Núm. 1/2 (enero/abril de 1960), 81-84. Contents: I. Ediciones. A. Cuento y novela. B. Ensayo. C. Poesía. D. Artículos y obra suelta. E. Prólogos, discursos. F. Antologías. G. Traducciones. II. Estudios.
De Costa, George René. "THE EVOLUTION OF FORM AND STYLE

IN THE EARLY POETRY OF PEDRO PRADO, 1908-1926." Ph.D., Washington University (St. Louis), 1970. 236p. "Working Bibliography," pp. 219-227. "This working bibliography not only up-dates Blondet's bibliography, but also adds many new Pedro Prado items recently discovered in the libraries and archives of Santiago."

Flores, BEH, pp. 274-275. Contents: I. Ediciones. II. Referencias. III. Bibliografía selecta (criticism).

Foster, Chilean Lit., pp. 198-202. Contents: I. Bibliographies. II. Critical Books. III. Critical Essays.

Foster, 20th Century, pp. 159-160. Contents: I. Bibliographies. II. Critical Books. III. Critical Essays.

PRATA, RANULFO HORA (Brazil, 1896-1942)

Carvalho-Neto, Paulo. "Um lugar para Ranulfo Prata: contribuição bibliográfica," REVISTA INTERAMERICANA DE BIBLIOGRAFIA, 24 (enero/marzo de 1974), 3-30. "Bibliografía," pp. 11-30. Includes both works by and about the author.

PRECIADO, ANTONIO (Ecuador)

Jackson, Afro-Spanish, p. 102. Contents: Works.

PRIETO, GUILLERMO (Mexico, 1818-1897)

McLean, Malcolm D. BIBLIOGRAPHY ON GUILLERMO PRIETO: MEXICAN POET-STATESMAN. Fort Worth, Texas: Texas Christian University Press, 1968. 399p. Includes library locations in the U.S., England, and Mexico. Contents: I. Obras de Prieto. II. Lo que se ha escrito sobre Prieto. III. Indice onomástico.

PUGA DE LOSADA, AMALIA (Peru, 1866-1963)

"Amalia Puga de Losada," ANUARIO BIBLIOGRAFICO PERUANO, 1961/1963, 594-600. Contents: I. Libros y folletos. II. Otras publicaciones. III. Artículos y ensayos. IV. Cuentos, traducciones, etc. V. Poesías, discursos, conferencias. VI. Traducciones. VII. Cartas, reportajes. VIII. Referencias. IX. Necrologías.

PUIG, MANUEL (Argentina, 1932-)

Corbatta, Jorgelina. "Bibliografía sobre Manuel Puig," DISCURSO LITERARIO, 2 (otoño 1984), 245-250. Alphabetically arranged entries.

Epple, Juan Armando. "Bibliografía de Manuel Puig y sobre él," REVISTA INTERAMERICANA DE BIBLIOGRAFIA, 28 (1978), 165-168. Contents: I. Obras de Manuel Puig. II. Bibliografía sobre Manuel Puig. A. Referencias. B. Artículos sobre Manuel Puig.

Flores, BEH, pp. 275-277. Contents: I. Ediciones. II. Bibliografía selecta (criticism).

Foster, Arg. Lit., pp. 624-630. Contents: I. Bibliographies. II. Critical Monograph and Dissertations. III. Critical Essays.

Foster, 20th Century, pp. 161-162. Contents: Critical Essays.

- Q -

QORPO-SANTO (Pseudonym of JOSE JOAQUIM DE CAMPOS LEAO) (Brazil, 1829-1883)

Aguiar, Flávio. OS HOMENS PRECARIOS: INOVAÇAO E CONVENÇAO NA DRAMATURGIA DE QORPO-SANTO. Porto Alegre: Instituto Estadual do Livro-DAC/SEC, 1975. 262p. Contents: I. "Os fascículos da ensiqlopèdia: Descrição dos volumes e do sistema de notação empregado para a localização dos textos," pp. 235-244. II. "Fortuna crítica de Qorpo-Santo: Relação bibliográfica," pp. 253-262. A. Em livros. B. Em revistas. 1. Artigos e entrevistas. 2. Noticiário e reportagens. C. Em volantes. D. Em jornais. 1. Artigos, entrevistas e notas assinados. 2. Cartas. 3. Poemas. 4. Notícias e reportagens.

Qorpo-Santo. QORPO-SANTO: "AS RELAÇOES NATURAIS" E OUTROS COMEDIAS. FIXAÇAO DO TEXTO, ESTUDO CRITICO E NOTAS POR GUILHERMINO CESAR. Porto Alegre: Edições da Faculdade de Filosofia, Universidade Federal do Rio Grande do Sul, 1969. 299p. "Bibliografia sôbre Qorpo-Santo," pp. 287-298. Contents: I. Jornais, periódicos e volantes. II. Em livros. III. Noticiário de imprensa.

_______. "AS RELAÇOES NATURAIS" E OUTRAS COMEDIAS. SEGUNDA EDIÇAO. FIXAÇAO DO TEXTO, ESTUDIO CRITICO E NOTAS POR GUIHERMANO CESAR. Porto Alegre: Editôra Movimento, 1976. 244p. "Bibliografia," pp. 240-246. Contents: I. Livros. II. Periódicos e volantes. Artigos assinados. Entrevistas. III. Periódicos. Noticiário. IV. Adaptação ao cinema. V. Poesia. VI. Tradução para o inglês.

_______. TEATRO COMPLETO. FIXAÇAO DO TEXTO, ESTUDO CRITICO E NOTAS POR GUILHERMINO CESAR. Rio de Janeiro: Serviço Nacional de Teatro, Fundação Nacional de Arte, 1980. 404p. "Bibliografia sôbre Qorpo-Santo," pp. 395-404. Contents: I. Livros. II. Periódicos e volantes. Artigos assinados. Entrevistas. III. Periódicos. Noticiário. IV. Adaptação ao cinema. V. Poesia. VI. Tradução para o inglês.

QUEIROS, AMADEU DE (Brazil, 1897-)

"O atual ocupante da Cadeira No. 5: Amadeu de Queirós," REVISTA DA ACADEMIA PAULISTA DE LETRAS, Núm. 89 (março de 1977), 13-16. Contents: I. Traduções. II. Obras originais.

QUEIROZ, DINAH SILVEIRA DE (Brazil, 1911-1982)

Queiroz, Dinah Silveira de. SELETA DE DINAH SILVEIRA DE QUEIROZ. APRESENTAÇAO E NOTAS DA PROFESSORA BELLA JOZEF. Rio de Janeiro: Livraria José Olympio Editôra, 1974. 176p. Contents: I. "Obras de Dinah Silveira de Queiroz," p. 174. II. "Sucinta bibliográfica sôbre Dinah Silveira de Queiroz," pp. 175-176. A. Em livros. B. Em jornais (por ordem cronológica).

QUEIROZ, RACHEL DE (Brazil, 1910-)

Queiroz, Rachel de. SELETA DE RACHEL DE QUEIROZ. ORGANIZADA PELO PROF. PAULO RONAI. Rio de Janeiro: Livraria José Olympio Editôra, 1973. 204p. Contents: I. "Obras de Rachel de Queiroz," [p. 202]. A. Romances. B. Teatro. C. Crônica. D. Literatura infantil. E. Seleta. II. "Bibliografia resumida sôbre Rachel de Queiroz," [p. 203].

QUESADA Y MIRANDA, GONZALO (Cuba, 1900-1976)

"Gonzalo de Quesada y Miranda: Bío-bibliografía," BIBLIOGRAFIA CUBANA, 1976, 168-173. Contents: I. Biografía. II. Bibliografía activa.

Graupern, Elena. "Bibliografía de Gonzalo de Quesada y Miranda, 1900-1976," ANUARIO DEL CENTRO DE ESTUDIOS MARTIANOS, 1 (1978), 339-345.

QUEZADA, JAIME (Chile, 1942-)

Quezada, Jaime. ASTROLABIO. Santiago de Chile: Editorial Nascimento, 1976. 126p. "Referencias críticas importantes," pp. 113-117. Alphabetically arranged critical studies about the author and his work.

QUIROGA, HORACIO (Uruguay and Argentina, 1879-1937)

Becco, Horacio Jorge. "Bibliografía de Horacio Quiroga," in Noé Jitrik's HORACIO QUIROGA: UNA OBRA DE EXPERIENCIA Y RIESGO (Buenos Aires: Ministerio de Educación y Justicia, Ediciones Culturales Argentinas, 1959), pp. 141-159. Contents: I. Ediciones. A. Libros. B. Folletos. C. Antologías y recopilaciones. D. Traducciones. E. Traducciones en antologías. II. Estudios. A. Bibliografía. B. Biografía.

Boulé-Christauflour, Annie. "Proyecto para obras completas de Horacio Quiroga," BULLETIN HISPANIQUE, 67, Num. 1/2 (janvier/juin 1965), 91-128. Continues the Speratti Piñero and Rodríguez Monegal articles. Contents: I. List by title, journal name, date, volumes of cuentos y series de artículos signed or unsigned. II. Lista cronológica de las publicaciones de Horacio Quiroga (1897-1937, by date, title, journal, volume, etc.). III. Repartición cronológica de las publicaciones de Quiroga en la prensa.

Flores, BEH, pp. 160-164. Contents: I. Ediciones principales. II. Otras ediciones. III. Referencias. IV. Bibliografía selecta (criticism).

________. APROXIMACIONES A HORACIO QUIROGA. Caracas: Monte Avila Editores, 1976. 296p. "Bibliografía," pp. 283-296. Contents: I. Ediciones principales. II. Otras ediciones. III. Referencia. IV. Bibliografía selecta (criticism).

Quiroga, Horacio. CUENTOS COMPLETOS. EDICION AL CUIDADO DE ALFONSO LLAMBIAS DE AZEVEDO. Montevideo: Ediciones de la Plata, 1978. 2vs. "Bibliografía fundamental," v. 2, pp. 905-913. Contents: I. Bibliografías. II. Estudios críticos.

Rela, Walter. HORACIO QUIROGA; GUIA BIBLIOGRAFICA. Montevideo: Ulises, 1967. 138p. 795 partially annotated entries.

Contents: I. Cuadro biográfico-cronológico. II. Obras del autor. A. Cuento y novela. B. Teatro. C. Ediciones parciales. D. Colaboraciones en diarios, periódicos y revistas (incomplete). E. Publicaciones póstumas. F. Antologías de textos de autor. G. Textos del autor en diversas antologías y recopilaciones. H. Traducciones individuales de textos del autor. III. Obras sobre el autor. A. Biocrítica. B. Historias literarias. C. Ensayo y crítica. D. Artículos en diarios, periódicos y revistas. E. Varios. 1. Bibliografía individual. 2. Referencia general. 3. Diccionarios. IV. Indice onomástico.

______. HORACIO QUIROGA: REPERTORIO BIBLIOGRAFICO ANOTADO, 1897-1971. Buenos Aires: Casa Pardo, 1972. 145p. Contents: I. Cuadro biográfico-cronológico. II. Obra del autor. A. Colaboraciones en diarios, periódicos y revistas. B. Publicada en libros. C. Apéndice primero: textos póstumos, notas. D. Apéndice segundo: 1. Antologías de textos del autor-notas. 2. Textos incluídos en diversas antologías y recopilaciones. 3. Traducciones individuales de textos. III. Obra sobre el autor. A. Individual. Libros: bibliografía, biocrítica, ensayos y crítica. B. Individual. Diarios, periódicos y revistas (firmados). Bibliografía, ensayo y crítica. C. Individual. Diarios, periódicos y revistas (sin firma). D. General. Libros: bibliografía, historias literarias, ensayo y crítica. E. General. Diarios, periódicos y revistas. IV. Diccionarios. V. Addenda: veintitrés ejemplos de variantes del Archivo Horacio Quiroga. VI. Indice alfabético de títulos correlacionados (obra del autor). VII. Indice analítico de nombres. VIII. Indice por materias.

Rodríguez Monegal, Emir. "Horacio Quiroga en el Uruguay: una contribución bibliográfica," NUEVA REVISTA DE FILOLOGIA HISPANICA, 11, Núm. 3/4 (julio/diciembre de 1957), 392-394. 47 items, 1897-1901. Contents: I. Artículos. II. Poemas (en verso y prosa). III. Esbozos de cuentos.

Speratti Piñero, Emma Susana. "Hacia la cronología de Horacio Quiroga," NUEVA REVISTA DE FILOLOGIA HISPANICA, 9, Núm. 4 (octubre/diciembre de 1955), 367-382. 267 items, 1903-1935. Emphasis on Quiroga's short stories.

QUIROGA, MALVINA ROSA (Argentina, 1900-)

"Bio-bibliografía," in Dolores Villa's BIBLIOGRAFIA CRITICA DE LA LITERATURA DE CORDOBA (Córdoba: Instituto de Literatura e Iberoamericana, Facultad de Filosofía y Humanidades, Universidad Nacional de Córdoba, 1981), pp. 65-79. Contents: I. Reseña biográfica. II. Libros de poesía. III. Algunos poemas aparecidos en periódicos y antologías. IV. Publicaciones en prosa (ensayos, artículos, estudios críticos). V. Acerca de la autora y su obra.

Torres de Peralta, Elba. LA TEMATICA DE MALVINA ROSA QUIROGA. Córdoba: Subsecretaría de Cultura, 1970. 121p. Contents: "Bibliografía de Malvina Rosa Quiroga," [pp. 115-

117]. I. Libros. II. Algunos poemas sueltos. III. Prosa. IV. Obras inéditas.

QUIROS, ANGEL FERNANDO DE (Peru, 1799-1862)
Araujo Ruiz, Graciela. "BIO-BIBLIOGRAFIA DE ANGEL FERNANDO DE QUIROS (1799-1862)." Tesis. Lima: Biblioteca Nacional, Escuela de Bibliotecarios, 1957.

QUISPES ASIU, CESAR see MORO, CESAR

QUISPEZ ASIN ROCA, FERNANDO (Peru, 1937-1963)
Ochoa Garzón, Carmen. "Fernando Quíspez Asín Roca," ANUARIO BIBLIOGRAFICO PERUANO, 1961/1963, 601-602. Contents: I. Libros y folletos. II. Artículos y ensayos. III. Referencias. IV. Necrológicas.

- R -

RABANALES, AMBROSIO (Chile, 1917-)
Contreras, Lidia. "Bibliografía de Ambrosio Rabanales, 1930-1979," BOLETIN DE FILOLOGIA, 31 (1980/1981), 61-95. "Bibliografía cronológica," pp. 68-95. Includes title and subject indices.

RABASA, EMILIO (Mexico, 1856-1930)
Flores, BEH, pp. 164-165. Contents: I. Ediciones principales. II. Otras ediciones. III. Referencias. IV. Bibliografía selecta (criticism).
Glass, Elliot S. MEXICO EN LAS OBRAS DE EMILIO RABASA. México, D.F.: Editorial Diana, 1975. 164p. Translation of the author's dissertation: "Mexico in the Work of Emilio Rabasa" (Columbia University, 1972). "Bibliografía selecta," pp. 151-160. Contents: I. Obras de Emilio Rabasa (by year, 1873-1955; includes both books and journal and newspaper articles). II. Obras con referencias específicas a Emilio Rabasa.
Hakala, Marcia A. EMILIO RABASA: NOVELISTA INNOVADOR MEXICANO EN EL SIGLO XIX. México, D.F.: Editorial Porrúa, 1974. 204p. "Bibliografía," pp. 195-202. Contents: I. Fuentes primarias. A. Lista cronológica de las obras de Rabasa. B. Entrevistas y cartas. II. Fuentes secundarias (criticism, biographies, etc.).

RABELO, LAURINDO JOSE DA SILVA (Brazil, 1826-1864)
Porter, pp. 267-268. Contents: I. Writings. II. References, Critical and Biographical.
Rabelo, Laurindo José da Silva. OBRAS COMPLETAS: POESIA, PROSA E GRAMATICA. ORGANIZAÇAO, INTRODUÇAO E NOTAS POR OSVALDO MELO BRAGA. São Paulo: Companhia Editôra Nacional, 1946. 548p. Contents: I. "Bibliografia de Laurindo José da Silva Rabelo," pp. 11-13. II. "Algumas fontes para um estudo sobre Laurindo," pp. 15-17.

RAGGI Y AGEO, CARLOS M. (Cuba, 1910-1975)

Raggi, Ana H. "Ficha bío-bibliográfico: Dr. Carlos M. Raggi y Ageo," in ESTUDIOS LITERARIOS SOBRE HISPANOAMERICA: HOMENAJE A CARLOS M. RAGGI Y AGEO (Miami: Hispanova de Ediciones, 1976), pp. 19-26. Contents: I. Publicaciones sobre crítica o investigación literaria. II. Obras. III. Reseñas de obras. A. En periódicos. B. En revistas. IV. Gramática, lingüística, filología, etc. V. Publicaciones de cualquier otra materia. VI. Divulgación histórica. Raggi y Ageo's archeological, ethnological, sociological, statistical, and economic articles and studies are excluded from this bibliography.

RAGUCCI, RODOLFO MARIA (Argentina, 1887-1973)

Becco, Horacio Jorge. "Bibliografía del Prbo. Don Rodolfo María Ragucci, S.D.B.," BOLETIN DE LA ACADEMIA ARGENTINA DE LETRAS, 38, Núm. 147/148 (enero/junio de 1973), 19-23. Contents: I. Ensayos. II. Poesía. III. Prólogos.

RAMIREZ CABANAS, JOAQUIN (Mexico, 1886-1945)

Yarza C., Ofelia. "Ensayo biobibliográfico de don Joaquín Ramírez Cabañas (J. Pérez Lugo, seudónimo); 23 de agosto de 1886-2 de enero de 1945)," BOLETIN DEL INSTITUTO DE INVESTIGACIONES BIBLIOGRAFICAS (México, D.F.), Núm. 14/15 (1977/78), 562-581. Contents: I. "Referencias," pp. 574-576. II. "Obra literaria," pp. 576-577 (arranged by year, 1914-1976). III. "Obra histórica y periodística," pp. 578-581 (arranged by year, 1920-1967).

RAMOS, EDUARDO (Brazil, 1854-1923)

Mota, Artur. "Perfís acadêmicos, Cadeira No. 11: Eduardo Ramos," REVISTA DA ACADEMIA BRASILEIRA DE LETRAS, Núm. 83 (Novembro de 1928), pp. 305-313. Contents: I. "Bibliografia," pp. 305-306 (1909-1923). II. "Fontes para o estudo crítico," p. 306.

RAMOS, GRACILIANO (Brazil, 1892-1953)

Cristóvão, Fernando Alves. GRACILIANO RAMOS: ESTRUCTURA E VALORES DE UM MODO DE NARRAR. Rio de Janeiro: Instituto Nacional do Livro, 1975. 330p. (Coleção Leturas, 3). Contents: I. "Bibliografia ativa," pp. 311-314. A. Primeiros escritos. B. Escritos de intenção ñao literária mas com importância histórico-literária. C. Romance. D. Conto. E. Teatro. F. Memórias. G. História e crônica regional. H. Jornalismo. I. Traduções. J. Inéditos. II. "Bibliografia passiva," pp. 314-324 (criticism).

Cunha, Antonio C. R. "GRACILIANO RAMOS: AN ANNOTATED BIBLIOGRAPHY." Master's thesis, San Diego State University, 1970.

Mourão, Rui. ESTRUTURAS: ENSAIO SOBRE O ROMANCE DE GRACILIANO. Belo Horizonte: Edições Tendência, 1969. 211p. "Bibliografia sôbre Graciliano," pp. 199-209.

Rio de Janeiro. Biblioteca Nacional. EXPOSIÇAO GRACILIANO RAMOS, 1892-1953. Rio de Janeiro, 1963. 24p. Bibliography.
Sant'ana, Moacir Medeiros de. GRACILIANO RAMOS: ACHEGAS BIBLIOGRAFICAS. Maceió: Arquivo Público de Alagoas, SENEC, 1973. 92p. "Graciliano Ramos no estrangeiro," pp. 51-54. "Edições brasileiros," pp. 55-59. "Bibliografia sôbre Graciliano Ramos," pp. 63-74 (124 entries).

RAMOS, JOSE ANTONIO (Cuba, 1885-1946)
Flores, BEH, pp. 277-278. Contents: I. Ediciones. II. Referencias. III. Bibliografía selecta (criticism).
Foster, Cuban Lit., pp. 434-437. Contents: I. Bibliographies. II. Dissertation. III. Critical Essays.
Peraza Sarausa, Fermín. "Bibliografía de José Antonio Ramos," REVISTA IBEROAMERICANA, 12, Núm. 24 (junio de 1947), 335-400. An extensive bibliography of 529 items of the author's works and of writings about him, followed by an analytical index.
_______. BIBLIOGRAFIA DE JOSE ANTONIO RAMOS. 2ª edición. La Habana: Ediciones Anuario Bibliográfico Cubano, 1956. 69p. (Biblioteca del Bibliotecario, 18). Contents: I. Noticia biográfica. II. Bibliografía activa. III. Bibliografía pasiva.
Ramos, José Antonio. CANIQUI, TRINIDAD, 1830. La Habana: Consejo Nacional de Cultura, 1963. 371p. "Bibliografía," pp. 315-371. Contents: I. Bibliografía activa (arranged by title). II. Bibliografía pasiva. 530 entries in the bibliography.

RAMOS, JUAN PEDRO (Argentina, 1878-1959)
"Bibliografía de don Juan Pedro Ramos," BOLETIN DE LA ACADEMIA ARGENTINA DE LETRAS, 25, Núm. 95 (enero/marzo de 1960), 15-37. 247 items listed by year, 1910-1958.

RAMOS, PERICLES EUGENIO DA SILVA (Brazil, 1919-)
Ramos, Péricles Eugenio da Silva. POESIA QUASE COMPLETO. Rio de Janeiro: Livraria José Olympio Editôra, 1972. 158p. "Do autor," pp. x-xi. Contents: I. Poesia. II. Ensaio. III. Edições e antologias. IV. Traduções. A. Em verso. B. Em prosa.

RAMOS, VESPASIANO (Brazil, 1884-1916)
Moraes, pp. 90-92. Major works by and about the author.

RAMOS SUCRE, JOSE ANTONIO (Venezuela, 1890-1930)
Ramos Sucre, José Antonio. OBRA COMPLETA. PROLOGO DE JOSE RAMON MEDINA; CRONOLOGICA:SONIA GARCIA. Caracas: Biblioteca Ayacucho, 1980. 589p. (Biblioteca Ayacucho, 197). "Bibliografía de Ramos Sucre," pp. 583-589. Contents: I. Obras de José Antonio Ramos Sucre (does not include journal or newspaper articles). II. Antologías y selecciones. III. Escritos sobre J. A. Ramos Sucre.

REBOLLEDO, EFREN (Mexico, 1877-1929)

Rebolledo, Efrén. OBRAS COMPLETAS. INTRODUCCION, EDICION Y BIBLIOGRAFIA POR LUIS MARIO SCHNEIDER. México, D.F.: Instituto Nacional de Bellas Artes, Departamento de Literatura, 1968. 315p. "Bibliografía," pp. 303-310. Contents: I. Bibliografía directa. A. Poesía. B. Prosa. C. Traducciones. II. Bibliografía indirecta (criticism). III. Hemerografía (by journal or newspaper, then by issue).

REGO, JOAO DE DEUS DO (Brazil, 1867-1902)

Porter, pp. 258-259. Contents: I. Writings. II. References, Critical and Biographical.

REGO, JOSE LINS DO (1901-1957)

Brazil. Biblioteca Nacional. Seção de Promoções Culturais. JOSE LINS DO REGO, 1901-1957: CATALOGO DA EXPOSIÇAO. APRESENTAÇAO DE PLINIO DOYLE; PREFACIO DE JOSUE MONTELLO. Rio de Janeiro: A Biblioteca, 1981. 95p. Based upon the holdings of the Biblioteca Nacional, this bibliography lists writings by and about José Lins do Rêgo.

Castelo, José Aderaldo. JOSE LINS DO REGO: MODERNISMO E REGIONALISMO. São Paulo: EdArt, 1961. 210p. "Bibliografia," pp. 203-210. Contents: I. Fontes primarias. II. Principais referências sôbre José Lins do Rêgo. III. Referências gerais, notadamente sôbre o modernismo. A selected bibliography.

Kelly, John R. "An Annotated Bibliography of the Early Writings of José Lins do Rêgo," LUSO-BRAZILIAN REVIEW, 9 (June 1972), 72-85. Lists 88 newspaper articles written between 1921 and 1932, and according to the compiler, are contained nowhere else. The newspapers indexed are: JORNAL DO RECIFE, JORNAL DE ALAGOAS, A PROVINCIA (Recife), O SEMEADOR (Maceió), and NOVIDADE (Maceió).

Martins, Eduardo. JOSE LINS DO REGO: O HOMEM E A OBRA. Recife: Secretaria da Educação e Cultura, 1980. 425p. "Notas bibliográficas," pp. 129-159. Contents: I. Obras de José Lins do Rêgo (works arranged by year and includes all editions). II. Obras de José Lins do Rêgo no estrangeiro. III. Obra reunida de ficção. IV. Filmografia. V. Fogo morto. Peça teatral. Apreciada pelo própio romanicista. VI. Classificação, por assunto, das obras de José Lins do Rêgo (first editions only). VII. Algumas obras e estudos sobre José Lins do Rêgo (arranged by year, 1932-1980).

Porter, pp. 259-261. Contents: I. Writings. II. References, Critical and Biographical.

Rêgo, José Lins do. ANTOLOGIA E CRITICA. INTRODUÇAO E NOTAS DE EDILBERTO COUTINHO. Brasília: Coordenada-Editôra de Brasília, 1971. 101p. Contents: I. "Bibliografia de José Lins do Rêgo," pp. 93-96. A. Romances. B. Memórias. C. Literatura infantil. D. Cronicas. E. Conferências. F. Viagens. G. Tradução. H. Obras traduzidas. II. "Bibliografia sôbre José Lins do Rêgo," pp. 97-100.

______. DIAS IDOS E VIVIDOS: ANTOLOGIA. SELEÇAO, ORGANIZAÇAO E ESTUDOS CRITICOS DE IVAN JUNQUEIRA. Rio de Janeiro: Nova Fronteira, 1981. 460p. Contents: I. "Obras de José Lins do Rêgo," pp. 449-551. A. Ficção. B. Ensaio. C. Crônica. D. Memórias. E. Conferências. F. Literatura infantil. G. Ficção reunida. II. "Bibliografia sôbre o autor," pp. 453-460.

______. FICÇAO COMPLETA. Rio de Janeiro: Editôra Nova Aguilar, 1976. 2vs. "Bibliografia," v. 2, pp. 1317-1322. Contents: I. Do autor. A. Romances. B. Obra reunida de ficção. C. Memórias. D. Leitura infantil. E. Crônicas. F. Conferências. G. Viagem. H. No estrangeiro. I. Filmografia. II. Sôbre o autor. A. Livros. B. Artigos em jornal.

REIS, FRANCISCO SOTERO DOS (Brazil, 1800-1871)

Moraes, pp. 11-13. Major works by and about the author.

REMOS, JUAN J. (Cuba, 1896-1969)

Inclán, Josefina. CUBA EN EL DESTIERRO DE JUAN J. REMOS. Miami: Ediciones Universal, 1971. 172p. (Colección Polymita, 1). Contents: I. "Obras publicadas," p. 13. II. "Folletos, discursos y conferencias," pp. 14-16. III. "Obras teatrales," p. 16. IV. "Condecoraciones," p. 16. V. "Colaboraciones especiales," p. 16. VI. Principales referencias," pp. 16-17.

RENDON, FRANCISCO DE PAULA (Colombia, 1857-1917)

Porras Collantes, pp. 562-568. Includes works of and critical studies about the author.

RESTREPO, FELIX (Colombia, 1887-1965)

Kimsa, Antanas. "Bibliografía del R.P. Félix Restrepo, S.J.," BOLETIN DEL INSTITUTO CARO Y CUERVO (Bogotá), 5 (1949), 478-548. Sobretiro: Bogotá: Instituto Caro y Cuervo, 1950. 79p. 707 references, 1911-1950.

REVUELTAS, JOSE (Mexico, 1914-1976)

"Bibliografía de José Revueltas," TEXTO CRITICO, Núm. 2 (julio/diciembre de 1975), 88-90. Contents: I. Novelas y libros de cuentos. II. Teatro. III. Traducciones. IV. Otros. V. Cuentos, ensayos, prólogos.

Flores, BEH, pp. 278-279. Contents: I. Edición principal. II. Otras ediciones. III. Bibliografía selecta (criticism).

Foster, Mex. Lit., pp. 294-300. Contents: I. Bibliographies. II. Critical Monographs and Dissertations. III. Critical Essays.

Foster, 20th Century, pp. 162-163. Contents: Critical Essays.

Frankenthaler, Marilyn N. "Bibliografía de y sobre José Revueltas," CHASQUI, 7 (febrero de 1978), 46-86. 504 partially annotated entries. Contents: I. Cronología. A. Obra narrativa recogida en libro. 1. Cuentos y fragmentos de novelas. 2. Poesía. 3. Libros de ensayos. B. Artículos (artículos periodísticos, fragmentos de libros, estudios, ensayos, prólogos, cartas y memorias). C. Obras teatrales. D. Colaboraciones cinematográficas. E. Miscelánea. F. José Revueltas en otros idiomas. G. Diálogos, entrevistas y reportajes. II. Bibliografía sobre José Revueltas. A. Tesis. B. Estudios, ensayos, artículos y fragmentos de libros.

Revueltas, José. CONVERSACIONES CON JOSE REVUELTAS. ENTREVISTA DE GUSTAVO SAINZ. INTRODUCCION DE JORGE RUFFINELLI. BIBLIOGRAFIA DE Y SOBRE JOSE REVUELTAS DE MARILYN R. FRANKENTHALER. Xalapa: Universidad Veracruzana, Centro de Investigaciones Lingüístico-Literarias, 1977. 153p. (Cuadernos de Texto Crítico, 3). "Bibliografía," pp. 115-153.

Slick, Sam L. JOSE REVUELTAS. Boston: Twayne Publishers, 1983. 226p. "Selected Bibliography," pp. 209-215. Contents: I. Primary Sources. A. Collected Works. B. Novels and Short Story Collections. C. Theater Works. D. Major Essays. II. Secondary Sources. Partially annotated entries.

REYES, ALFONSO (Mexico, 1889-1959)

Arce, David N. "Bibliografías mexicanas contemporáneas, III. Estos y 'aquellos días' de Alfonso Reyes," BOLETIN DE LA BIBLIOTECA NACIONAL (México), 2ª época, 7, Núm. 4 (octubre/diciembre de 1956), 7-51. In alphabetical order, the work lists 237 works, translations, prologues, etc. of Alfonso Reyes. Periodical publications are excluded.

Blondet, Olga. "Alfonso Reyes, bibliografía," REVISTA HISPANICA MODERNA, Año 22, Núm. 3/4 (julio/octubre de 1956), 248-269. Contents: I. Ediciones. A. Ensayo. B. Poesía. C. Novelística. D. Archivo de Alfonso Reyes. E. Artículos y poesía suelta. F. Epistolario. G. Prólogos y ediciones comentadas. H. Traductor. I. Traducciones. II. Estudios.

Flores, BEH, pp. 280-282. Contents: I. Edición principal. II. Otras ediciones. III. Referencias. IV. Bibliografía selecta (criticism).

González, Manuel Pedro. "Ficha bibliográfica de Alfonso Reyes," REVISTA IBEROAMERICANA, 15, Núm. 29 (febrero/julio de 1949), 13-28. Contents: I. Datos biográficos. A. Estudios, cargos, comisiones y grados. B. Condecoraciones. C. Otros títulos honoríficos. II. Datos bibliográficos. A. Verso. B. Prosa. 1. Crítica, ensayos y memorias. 2. Novelística. 3. Prólogos y ediciones comentadas. 4. Traducciones. 5. Trabajos no literarios (se prescinde de los recogidos en edición aparte). Periodical articles are excluded.

Morales, Jorge Luis. ALFONSO REYES Y LA LITERATURA ESPANOLA. Río Piedras: Editorial Universitaria, Universidad de Puerto Rico, 1980. 193p. "Bibliografía," pp. 169-193. Contents: I. Obras de Alfonso Reyes. A. Ensayo. B. Prosa. C. Novelística. D. Obras completas. E. Traducciones. F. "Archivo de Alfonso Reyes." II. Estudios sobre Alfonso Reyes. 412 entries.

Patout, Paulette. ALFONSO REYES ET LA FRANCE. Paris: Klincksieck, 1978. 687p. "Bibliographie," pp. 619-648. Contents: I. Oeuvres d'Alfonso Reyes. A. Vers (poésie et théâtre; oeuvres posthumes; all arranged by year, 1922-1954). B. Prose (arranged by year, 1907-1959). C. Préfaces et éditions critiques (arranged by year, 1917-1960). D. Collection "Archivo de Alfonso Reyes." E. Anthologies et selections. F. Oeuvres completes d'Alfonso Reyes. G. "Historia documental de mis libros." H. Inédits. I. Principales correspondances publiées. J. Traductions. II. Oeuvres d'Alfonso Reyes parues en France (arranged by year, 1910-1972). III. Bibliographie française d'Alfonso Reyes (les écrits consacrés a Alfonso Reyes et a son oeuvre; d'auteur français ou de langue française, ou ayant paru en France ou dans des revues françaises a l'étranger, 1911-1978). IV. Etudes generales sur Alfonso Reyes. V. Livres d'hommage.

Rangel Guerra, Alfonso. CATALOGO DE INDICES DE LOS LIBROS DE ALFONSO REYES. Monterrey: Universidad de Nuevo León, 1955. 89p. (Biblioteca universitaria).

Rendón Hernández, José Angel. ALFONSO REYES, INSTRUMENTOS PARA SU ESTUDIO. Monterrey: Universidad Autonóma de Nuevo León, Biblioteca Central, 1980. 173p. (Serie Capilla Alfonsina, 1). Contents: I. "Bibliografía de Alfonso Reyes," pp. 63-104. A. Verso: Poesía lírica. B. Verso: poesía lírico-dramática. C. Obra narrativa: cuentos, relatos, ficciones, novelas cortas. D. Prosa ensayística: ensayos, monografías, memorias. E. Obras completas. F. Archivo. G. Antologías. H. Prólogos y ediciones comentadas. I. Epistolarios. J. Grabaciones. K. Trabajos no literarios. L. Adiciones y curiosidades (miscellaneous writings, etc.). M. Traducciones. 1. Verso (by language). 2. Prosa (by language). All entries in section I are arranged by year. II. "Bibliografía sobre Alfonso Reyes," pp. 105-171 (entries are arranged alphabetically by author).

Robb, James Willis. EL ESTILO DE ALFONSO REYES. 2ª edición, revista y aumentada. México, D.F.: Fondo de Cultura Económica, 1978. 303p. "Bibliografía selecta," pp. 287-300. Contents: I. Obras principales de Alfonso Reyes. A. Verso: poesía lírica. B. Verso: poesía lírico-dramática. C. Obra narrativa: cuentos, relatos, ficciones, novelas cortas. D. Prosa ensayística (ensayos, monografías, memorias). E. Obras completas de Alfonso Reyes. F. Antologías de la obra de Alfonso Reyes. G. Epistolarios publicados: libros. II. Estudios y escritos varios sobre Alfonso Reyes (selección de bibligrafía reciente). A. Bibliografías. B. Volúmenes de homenaje a Alfonso Reyes. C. Estudios sobre Alfonso Reyes (libros). D. Otros estudios, artículos, críticas, crónicas, poemas sobre Alfonso Reyes.

________. REPERTORIO BIBLIOGRAFICO DE ALFONSO REYES. México, D.F.: UNAM. Instituto de Investigaciones Bibliográficas, Biblioteca Nacional de México, 1974. 294p. (Serie bibliografías, 2). Contents: I. Obras literarias de Alfonso Reyes. A. Obras en verso (poesía y teatro). B. Prosa narrativa (cuentos y ficciones). C. Obras ensayísticas (ensayos, monografías, memorias). D. Prólogos y ediciones comentadas. E. Archivo de Alfonso Reyes. F. Epistolario. G. Traducciones. H. Antologías y colecciones. I. Obras completas. II. Sobre Alfonso Reyes: Bibliografía selecta. A. Bibliografías. B. Volúmenes de homenaje. C. Libros, artículos, estudios, críticas, crónicas sobre Alfonso Reyes. D. Suplemento núm. 1. E. Suplemento núm. 2 (hasta julio de 1970). F. Suplemento núm. 3 (agosto de 1970). III. Indice analítico.

_______. "Repertorio bibliográfico de Alfonso Reyes: Suplemento 1975-1977," BOLETIN DEL INSTITUTO DE INVESTIGACIONES BIBLIOGRAFICAS (México, D.F.), Núm. 14/15 (1977/78), 611-626. Contents: I. Obras literarias de Alfonso Reyes. A. Obras en verso (poesía y teatro). B. Epistolario (Adiciones). II. Sobre Alfonso Reyes: bibliografía selecta. (Libros, artículos, estudios, poemas, críticos, crónicas sobre Alfonso Reyes).

REYES, NEFTALI RICARDO see NERUDA, PABLO

REYES, SALVADOR (Chile, 1899-)

"Cartillas biobibliográficas de autores chilenos: Salvador Reyes Figueroa. Copiapó, 1899. Poeta, cuentista, periódista, novelista y ensayista," BOLETIN DEL INSTITUTO DE LITERATURA CHILENA (Universidad de Chile, Santiago), Años 7/8, Núms. 15/16 (diciembre de 1968), 5-15. Contents: I. Obra. II. Referencias. III. Vida.

REYLES, CARLOS (Uruguay, 1868-1938)

Flores, BEH, pp. 282-284. Contents: I. Ediciones. II. Referencias. III. Bibliografía selecta (criticism).

Foster, 20th Century, pp. 163-166. Contents: I. Bibliographies. II. Critical Books. III. Critical Essays.

Rela, Walter. CARLOS REYLES; GUIA BIBLIOGRAFICA. Montevideo: Editorial Ulises, 1967. 67p. Contents: I. Cuadro biográfico-cronológico. II. Obras del autor. A. Novela y cuento. B. Ensayo. C. Conferencias y discursos. D. Colaboraciones en diarios, periódicos y revistas. E. Antologías del textos del autor. F. Textos del autor en diversas antologías. G. Traducciones del obras del autor. H. Prólogos del autor. II. Obras sobre el autor. A. Biocrítica. B. Historias literarias. C. Ensayos y crítico. D. Artículos en diarios, periódicos y revistas. E. Varios. III. Indice onomástico. IV. Indices de títulos, ediciones, reseñas.

RIBEIRO, JOAO (Brazil, 1860-1934)

Leão, Múcio. JOAO RIBEIRO: ENSAIO BIOBIBLIOGRAFICO. Rio de Janeiro: Academia Brasileira de Letras, 1965. 89p.

"Bibliografia," pp. 49-59. Contents: I. Poesia. II. Filologia. Obras didáticas. III. Historia. IV. Memórias. V. Crítica. VI. Antologias. VII. Ensaios. VIII. Ficção. IX. Traduções. X. Almanaques. XI. Dicionários. "Plano das obras completas de João Ribeiro," pp. 61-64. "Algumas opiniões sôbre João Ribeiro," pp. 65-81 (excerpts from original works). "Algumas fontes sôbre João Ribeiro," pp. 83-89.

Reis, Antônio Simões dos. JOÃO RIBEIRO: BIBLIOGRAFIA SOBRE A SUA OBRA. Rio de Janeiro: Ministério da Educação e Cultura, Instituto Nacional do Livro, 1960. 45p. (REVISTA DO LIVRO, Suplemento 4). 288 annotated entries by year, 1881-1960. There is an appendix entitled: Bibliografia de João Ribeiro, na imprensa (achêgas), 1885-1928. 232 entries.

RIBEIRO, JULIO CESAR (Brazil, 1845-1890)

Mota, Artur. "Perfis acadêmicos, Cadeira No. 24: Júlio César Ribeiro," REVISTA DA ACADEMIA BRASILEIRA DE LETRAS, Núm. 166 (outubro de 1935), 165-173. Contents: I. "Bibliografia," pp. 165-166. II. "Fontes para o estudo crítico," pp. 166-167.

RIBERA CHEVREMONT, EVARISTO (Puerto Rico, 1896-)

Foster, P.R. Lit., pp. 199-202. Contents: I. Critical Monographs and Dissertation. II. Critical Essays.

Ribera Chevremont, Evaristo. ANTOLOGIA POETICA, 1924-1950. INTRODUCCION POR FEDERICO DE ONIS. San Juan: Ediciones de la Universidad de Puerto Rico, 1957. 301p. "Bibliografía," pp. 28-34. Contents: I. Ediciones. A. Poesía. B. Prosa. II. Estudios (criticism).

_______. OBRA POETICA. Río Piedras: Editorial Universitaria, Universidad de Puerto Rico, 1980. 2vs. "Bibliografía mínima sobre Evaristo Ribera Chevremont," v. 1, pp. xxxvii-xxxviii.

RIBEYRO, JULIO RAMON (Peru, 1929-)

Foster, Peruvian Lit., pp. 223-226. Contents: I. Bibliographies. II. Critical Monographs and Dissertations. III. Critical Essays.

Vidal, Luis Fernando. "Apuntes para una bibliografía de Julio Ramón Ribeyro," in Julio Ramón Ribeyro's LA CAZA SUTIL: ENSAYOS Y ARTICULOS DE CRITICA LITERARIA (Lima: Milla Batres, 1975), pp. 159-168. Contents: I. Obra del autor. A. Cuentos, novela. B. Antologías. C. Ensayo. D. Teatro. E. Artículos, estudios en publicaciones periódicos. II. Obra acerca del autor. A. Entrevistas, referencias. B. Crítica, comentario. C. Tesis.

RICARDO, CASSIANO (Brazil, 1895-1974)

Ricardo, Cassiano. SELTA EM PROSA E VERSO. ORGANIZAÇAO, ESTUDO E NOTAS DA PROFESSORA NELLY NOVAES COELHO. 2. ed. Rio de Janeiro: José Olympio, 1975. 161p. Contents: I. "Bibliografia de Cassiano Ricardo," pp. 159-160. A. Poesia. B. No estrangeiro (translations). C. Prosa. II. "Bibliografia acerca de Cassiano Ricardo (publicada em livros)," p. 161.

_______. VIAGEM NO TEMPO E NO ESPAÇO (MEMORIAS). Rio de Janeiro: Livraria José Olympio, 1970. 333p. (Coleção Documentos Brasileiros, 145). Contents: I. Obras de Cassiano Ricardo," pp. x-xi. II. "Bibliografia sôbre Cassiano Ricardo," pp. xii-xiii. (This section is incomplete bibliographically).

RIO, JOAO DO (Pseudonym of PAULO BARRETO) (Brazil, 1881-1921)

PAULO BARRETO, 1881-1921: CATALOGO DA EXPOSIÇAO COMEMORATIVA DO CENTENARIO DE NASCIMENTO. ORGANIZADO PELA SEÇAO DE PROMOÇOES CULTURAIS; APRESENTAÇAO DE PLINIO DOYLE; PREFACIO DE HOMERO SENNA. Rio de Janeiro: Biblioteca Nacional, 1981. 47p. A selected bibliography, based upon the holdings of the Biblioteca Nacional, of writings by and about João do Rio.

Porter, pp. 185-186. Contents: I. Writings. II. References, Critical and Biographical.

RIOS, JUAN (Peru, 1914-)

Adler, Heidrun. JUAN RIOS: EIN PERUANISCHER LYRIKER. Bern: Herbert Lang Verlag, 1972. 131p. (Europaische Hochschulschriften, 24; Ibero-Romanischen Sprachen und Literaturen, 3). "Bibliographie," pp. 120-131.

RIQUELME, DANIEL (Chile, 1857-1912)

Flores, BEH, p. 45. Contents: I. Ediciones. II. Bibliografía selecta (criticism).

Foster, Chilean Lit., p. 203. Contents: I. Critical Books and Theses. II. Critical Essays.

RIVAS GROOT, JOSE MARIA (Colombia, 1863-1923)

Ortega Torres, José J. "Anotaciones bibliográficas sobre don José María Rivas Groot," ANUARIO DE LA ACADEMIA COLOMBIANA, 10 (1942/1943), 516-560. Descriptive bibliography.

Porras Collantes, pp. 580-592. Includes works of and critical studies about the author.

RIVERA, JOSE EUSTACIO (Colombia, 1888-1928)

Flores, BEH, pp. 165-167. Contents: I. Edición principal. II. Otras ediciones. III. Bibliografía selecta (criticism).

Foster, 20th Century, pp. 166-169. Contents: I. Critical Books. II. Critical Essays.

Herrera Molina, Luis Carlos. JOSE EUSTACIO RIVERA: POETA DE PROMISION. Bogotá: Imprenta Patriótica del Instituto Caro y Cuervo, 1968. 262p. "Bibliografía de José Eustacio Rivera," pp. 253-257. Contents: I. Libros. II. Otros escritos. III. Bibliografía sobre José Eustacio Rivera. A. Libros. B. Ensayos.

_______. RIVERA: LIRICO Y PINTOR. Bogotá: Instituto

Colombiano de Cultura, 1972. 146p. Contents: I. "Bibliografía de José Eustacio Rivera," pp. 141-142. A. Libros. B. Otros escritos. II. "Bibliografía sobre José Eustacio Rivera," pp. 143-146.

Porras Collantes, pp. 593-627. Includes works of and critical studies about the author.

ROA BARCENA, JOSE MARIA (Mexico, 1827-1908)

Flores, BEH, pp. 66-67. Contents: Ediciones. II. Referencias. III. Bibliografía selecta (criticism).

Flores, NH, v. 1, pp. 120-121. Contents: I. Ediciones. II. Referencias. III. Bibliografía selecta (criticism).

Rosaldo, Renato. "Notas bibliográficas sobre la obra poética de José María Roa Bárcena," REVISTA IBEROAMERICANA, 9, Núm. 18 (Mayo de 1945), 381-389. Contents: "Cronología de las obras poéticas de don José María Roa Bárcena"; lists 14 books published between 1856-1913.

ROA BASTOS, AUGUSTO (Paraguay, 1918-)

Aldana, Adolfo L. LA CUENTISTA DE AUGUSTO ROA BASTOS. Montevideo: Ediciones Géminis, 1975. 220p. "Bibliografía," pp. 215-218. Includes works by and about Roa Bastos.

Flores, BEH, pp. 284-286. Contents: I. Ediciones. II. Referencias. III. Bibliografía selecta (criticism).

Flores, NH, v. 4, pp. 292-296. Contents: I. Ediciones de su narrativa. II. Referencias. III. Antologías críticas dedicados a Augusto Roa Bastos. IV. Bibliografía selecta (criticism).

Foster, 20th Century, pp. 169-172. Contents: I. Bibliographies. II. Critical Books. III. Critical Essays.

Lechner, Jan. "Augusto Roa Bastos: Datos biográficos," in CUADERNO DE NORTE (Amsterdam: Norte, Revista Hispánica de Amsterdam, 1976), pp. 68-70. Contents: I. Obras originales. II. Traducciones. III. Textos varios. IV. Sobre la obra de Roa Bastos.

RODO, JOSE ENRIQUE (Uruguay, 1871-1917)

Anderson, pp. 134-143. Critical Essays.

Flores, BEH, pp. 167-169. Contents: I. Edición principal. II. Otras ediciones. III. Referencias. IV. Bibliografía selecta (criticism).

ORIGINALES Y DOCUMENTOS DE JOSE ENRIQUE RODO. EXPOSICION INAUGURADA EL 19 DE DICIEMBRE DE 1947, SALON DE ACTOS DEL TEATRO SOLIS. Montevideo: Ministerio de Instrucción Pública y Provisión Social, Comisión de Investigaciones Literarias, 1947. N.p. Contents: I. Manuscritos. A. Serie I: Manuscritos literarios (Items 1-80). B. Serie II: Manuscritos de carácter político (Items 81-86). C. Serie III: Manuscritos de carácter periodístico (Items 87-91). D. Serie IV: Manuscritos de carácter didáctico (Items 92-98). E. Serie V: Manuscritos de valor literario indiferente y clasificación indecisa (Items 99-100). F. Serie VI: Manuscrito de carácter autobiográfico (Items 101-119). II. Correspondencia. A. Serie I: Cartas de Rodó (Items 120-150). B. Serie II: Cartas a Rodó (Items 151-183). III. Impresos. A. Serie I: Obras de Rodó (Ediciones realizadas en vida del maestro): 1. Ediciones originales y reediciones. 2. Folletos consistentes en páginas o fragmentos de obras mayores. 3. Obras ajenas-individuales y colectivas-con páginas de Rodó. B. Serie II: Obras de Rodó (Ediciones posteriores a la muerte del maestro). 1. Recopilaciones póstumas (bibliograficamente perfectibles de páginas inéditas). C. Serie III: Obras de Rodó: Traducciones en diversas lenguas. D. Serie IV: Obras que integraron la biblioteca de Rodó. 1. Obras con dedicatorias autografiadas recibidas por el maestro. 2. Obras de estudio (con anotaciones manuscritas). E. Serie V: Páginas sueltas. 1. Escritos del maestro. 2. Escritos ajenos relacionados con su vida y su obra. IV. Documentos. A. Serie I: Documentos personales testimonios. B. Serie II: Testimonios directos. V. La coordinación temática y la indagación estilística: una muestra aislada, hecha con la base de ARIEL. A. La gesta de la forma. B. La publicación. C. El éxito. D. Reimpresiones de ARIEL en vida del maestro (acompañadas de un complemento ilustrativo). E. Traducciones de ARIEL (con los antecedentes documentales correspondientes a la primera versión francesa).

Rodó, José Enrique. OBRAS COMPLETAS. EDITADAS, CON INTRODUCCION, PROLOGOS Y NOTAS, POR EMIR RODRIGUEZ MONEGAL. Madrid: Aguilar, 1957. 1481p. "Cronología y bibliografía de José Enrique Rodó," pp. 1417-1447. Contents: I. Cronología de Rodó. II. Bibliografía crítica. A. Fuentes manuscritas. 1. Oficiales. 2. Particulares. B. Fuentes impresas. 1. Obras de José Enrique Rodó. a. Obras completas. b. Obra original. c. Obra póstuma. d. Obras ajenas o colectivas que contienen páginas de Rodó. e. Páginas de Rodó en publicaciones periódicas. f. Intervenciones parlamentarias. g. Traducciones de obras o artículos de José Enrique Rodó. 2. Estudios sobre José Enrique Rodó. a. Estudios generales que contienen referencias a Rodó. b. Estudios particulares.

Scarone, Arturo. BIBLIOGRAFIA DE RODO. EL ESCRITOR. LAS OBRAS. LA CRITICA. Montevideo: Imprenta Nacional, 1936. 2 vs. (Publicaciones de la Biblioteca Nacional de Montevideo). Volume 1, Parte primera: La producción de Rodó. Contents: I. Rodó: su bibliografía y sus críticos, estudio preliminar por Ariosto D. González. II. Obras fundamentales (fragmentos). III. Obras fundamentales de Rodó. IV. Artículos, juicios, críticos, cartas, pensamientos, etc., publicados en libros, revistas y diarios nacionales y extranjeros. V. Labor parlamentaria. VI. Oratoria (discursos, proyectos, informes, etc.). VII. Discursos pronunciados en distintos actos, no parlamentarios ni políticos. VIII. Actuación política de Rodó (discursos, manifiestos, cartas, etc.) IX. Apéndice de la primera parte (escritos diversos de Rodó). Volume 2, parte segunda: Escritos sobre la personalidad y labor cultural de Rodó. I. Crítica sobre la personalidad y la obra de Rodó (nacionales). II. Crítica sobre la personalidad y la obra de Rodó (extranjeros). III. La partida de Rodó para Europa-actos realizados con ese motivo. IV. La muerte de Rodó-homenajes tributados a su memoria. V. El repatrio de los restos del maestro. VI. Homenajes realizados en los aniversarios de su muerte y en distintas fechas. VII. Escritos diversos sobre Rodó y su obra y datos para su biografía. VIII. Segundo apéndice a la parte primera (references found after the first volume was published). IX. Apéndice a esta segunda parte. X. Indice alfabético de los autores de trabajos citados en esta segunda parte. XI. Indice de grabados.

RODRIGUEZ, LUIS FELIPE (Cuba, 1888-1947)
Foster, Cuban Lit., pp. 438-439. Contents: I. Critical Monograph and Dissertation. II. Critical Essays.

RODRIGUEZ, SIMON (Venezuela, 1771-1854)
Grases, Pedro. LA PERIPECIA BIBLIOGRAFICA DE SIMON RODRIGUEZ. Caracas: Publicación de la Universidad Nacional "Simón Rodríguez," 1979. 47p. Contents: I. La obra de Simón Rodríguez. II. Esquema bibliográfico. III. Desventura de las ediciones. IV. Referencias a otros escritos. V. La primera versión castellana de Atala.
Pérez Vila, Manuel. "Contribución a la bibliografía de Simón Rodríguez," LIBROS AL DIA (CARACAS), Año 1, Núm. 1 (15 de agosto de 1975), 23-28. Contents: I. Escritos de Simón Rodríguez. II. Bibliografía relativa a Simón Rodríguez. A. Biografía y ensayos de interpretación. B. Estudios monográficos sobre aspectos de la vida de Simón Rodríguez. C. Compilaciones de trabajos sobre Simón Rodríguez. The bibliography contains a total of 72 items.

RODRIGUEZ-ALCALA, HUGO (Paraguay, 1918-)
Galbis, Ignacio R. M. HUGO RODRIGUEZ-ALCALA: A BIBLIOGRAPHY, 1937-1981. Syracuse, N.Y.: Centro de Estudios Hispánicos, Syracuse University, 1982. 45p. (Bibliotheca Hispana Novissima, 6). Provides listing of publications on and by the author.

RODRIGUEZ CERNA, JOSE (Guatemala, 1885-1952)
Dardón Córdova, Gonzalo. BIBLIOGRAFIA DE AUTORES GUATEMALTECOS. VOLUMEN 1: JOSE RODRIGUEZ CERNA. Guatemala: Universidad de San Carlos de Guatemala, Facultad de Humanidades, Escuela de Bibliotecología, 1962. 28p. (Publicaciones de la Escuela de Bibliotecología, 3). Contents: I. Obras literarias. II. Otras. III. Artículos de divulgación literaria. IV. Crónicas. V. Poemas. VI. El autor y sus obras.

RODRIGUEZ DE TIO, LOLA (Puerto Rico, 1843-1924)
Foster, P.R. Lit., pp. 202-204. Contents: I. Critical Monograph. II. Critical Essays.

RODRIGUEZ FREYLE, JUAN (Colombia, 1566-c. 1640)
Flores, BEH, p. 45. Contents: I. Ediciones. II. Bibliografía selecta (criticism).

RODRIGUEZ GALVAN, IGNACIO (Mexico, 1816-1842)
Moore, Ernest R. "Bibliografía de Ignacio Rodríguez Galván," REVISTA IBEROAMERICANA, 8, Núm. 15 (mayo de 1944), 167-191. Contents: I. Colecciones. A. Obra que editó. B. Obras dramáticas. C. Poesías. D. Novelas y cuentos. E. Artículos varios. F. Traducciones. II. Obras críticas y biográficas referentes a Rodríguez Galván. Twenty library locations are included from U.S. and Mexican libraries.

RODRIGUEZ VELASCO, LUIS (Chile, 1838-1919)
Escudero, pp. 302-303. Criticism.

ROIG DE LEUCHSENRING, EMILIO (Cuba, 1889-1964)
Foster, Cuban Lit., p. 440. Critical Essays.

ROJAS, ARISTIDES (Venezuela, 1826-1894)
Grases, Pedro. BIBLIOGRAFIA DE DON ARISTIDES ROJAS, 1826-1894. 2ª edición ampliada. Caracas: Fundación para el Rescate del Acervo Documental Venezolano, 1977. 169p. 1,088 fully annotated entries. Contents: I. Libros y folletos de don Arístides Rojas. II. Publicaciones monográficas de don Arístides Rojas. III. Publicaciones en las que don Arístides Rojas figura como editor, compilador, arreglador, traductor, colaborador o coleccionista. IV. Noticias de obras inéditas de don Arístides Rojas. V. Obras de otros autores donde aparecen escritos de don Arístides Rojas; y obras relativos a él. VI. Indice temático y onomástico.

ROJAS, GONZALO (Chile, 1917-)
Coddou, Marcelo. "Gonzalo Rojas: Bibliografía," LITERATURA CHILENA: CREACION Y CRITICA, Núm. 29 (julio/setiembre/verano de 1984), 31-32. Contents: I. Libros. II. Sobre el autor (en libros). III. Entrevistas. IV. Sobre el autor (en diarios y revistas).

ROJAS, JORGE (Colombia, 1911-)
Rojas, Jorge. SUMA POETICA, 1939-1976. Bogotá: Instituto Colombiano de Cultura, 1977. 512p. "Obras publicadas del autor," pp. 507-508. Only books published between 1939 and 1976 are included.

ROJAS, RICARDO (Argentina, 1882-1957)
Becco, Horacio Jorge. "Bibliografía de Ricardo Rojas," REVISTA IBEROAMERICANA, 23, Núm. 46 (julio/diciembre de 1958), 335-350. Contents: I. Poesías. II. Prosa. III. Teatro. IV. Folletos. V. Otros trabajos (materiales folklóricos). VI. Estudios preliminares y prólogos. VII. Discografía. VIII. Tra-

ducciones. A. Libros. B. Fragmentos.

Salvador, Nelida. "Ensayo de bibliografía de Ricardo Rojas," REVISTA DE LA UNIVERSIDAD DE BUENOS AIRES, 5ª época, Año III, Núm. 3 (julio/setiembre de 1958), 479-490. 169 entries are listed chronologically, 1901-1956.

ROJAS SEPULVEDA, MANUEL (Chile, 1896-1973)

"Cartillas biobibliográficas de autores chilenos: Manuel Rojas Sepúlveda. Buenos Aires, 1896. Novelista, cuentista, poeta y ensayista," BOLETIN DEL INSTITUTO DE LITERATURA CHILENA (Universidad de Chile), Año 6, Núm. 13/14 (febrero de 1967), 2-15. Contents: I. Obra. II. Referencias. III. Vida.

Cortés, Darío A. "Bibliografía de Manuel Rojas (Cuentos)," LITERATURA CHILENA: CREACION Y CRITICA, Núm. 30 (octubre/diciembre/otoño de 1984), 30-31. Contents: I. Cuentos (publicación inicial). II. Antologías de sus cuentos. III. Cuentos incluídos en volúmenes de sus obras. IV. Antologías generales que incluyen sus cuentos. V. Traducciones. All sections are arranged chronologically.

________. "Bibliografía del cuento y ensayo de Manuel Rojas Sepúlveda," CHASQUI, 10 (noviembre de 1980), 43-70. Contents: I. Escritos de Manuel Rojas Sepúlveda. A. Cuentos: Publicación inicial. B. Antologías de los cuentos rojianos. C. Cuentos incluídos en volúmenes de sus obras. D. Cuentos de Rojas incluídos en antologías generales, revistas y periódicos. E. Traducciones. F. Ensayos. 1. Publicados en revistas. 2. Ensayos coleccionados. 3. Artículos y reseñas de prensa. G. Obras de erudición. H. Poesía. I. Novelas. II. Escritos sobre Manuel Rojas Sepúlveda. A. Libros. B. Artículos y reseñas dedicados exclusivamente o en parte a los cuentos. C. Artículos y reseñas dedicados a los ensayos, y otros, a su poesía y teatro. D. Estudios sobre su obra en general. E. Tesis.

Foster, Chilean Lit., pp. 203-207. Contents: I. Bibliographies. II. Critical Books and Theses. III. Critical Essays.

Foster, 20th Century, pp. 172-174. Contents: Critical Essays.

Rodríguez Reeves, Rosa. "Bibliografía de y sobre Manuel Rojas," REVISTA IBEROAMERICANA, 42, Núm. 95 (abril/junio de 1976), 285-313. Contents: I. Bibliografía de Manuel Rojas. A. Novelas; traducciones de sus novelas. B. Cuentos. C. Ensayos. D. Poesía. E. Artículos y otras publicaciones. II. Bibliografía sobre Manuel Rojas. A. Libros. B. Artículos. C. Material que no está publicado (theses mainly).

Rojas Sepúlveda, Manuel. MARES LIBRES Y OTROS CUENTOS. PROLOGO, NOTAS Y BIBLIOGRAFIA DE NORMAN CORTES. Valparaíso: Ediciones Universitarias de Valparaíso, Universidad Católica de Valparaíso, 1975. 159p. "Bibliografía," pp. 147-157. Contents: I. Cuentos de Manuel Rojas. II. Referencias sobre los cuentos de Manuel Rojas. Partially annotated entries.

ROKHA, PABLO DE (Chile, 1894-1968)
Foster, Chilean Lit., pp. 208-209. Contents: I. Critical Books and Theses. II. Critical Essays.

ROMERO, FRANCISCO (Argentina, 1891-1962)
Becco, Horacio Jorge. "Bibliografía de Francisco Romero," BOLETIN DE LA ACADEMIA ARGENTINA DE LETRAS, 27, Núm. 105/106 (julio/diciembre de 1962), 351-353. Only Romero's works are included.
_______. _______, CIUDAD (Buenos Aires), Num. 4/5 (1956), 66-88. The compiler lists 37 books and pamphlets, 353 articles and prologues, and 211 works on Romero.
Rodríguez-Alcalá, Hugo. "Bibliografía de Francisco Romero," REVISTA HISPANICA MODERNA, 20, Núm. 1/2 (enero/abril de 1954), 39-44. 211 entries. Contents: I. Ediciones. A. Libros. B. Artículos y prólogos. II. Estudios (criticism).

ROMERO, JOSE RUBEN (Mexico, 1890-1952)
Cooper, William F. "La obra escrita de Francisco Romero," in HOMENAJE A FRANCISCO ROMERO (Buenos Aires: Universidad de Buenos Aires, Facultad de Filosofía y Letras, Departamento de Filosofía, 1964), pp. 221-322. 685 entries of his work listed by year, 1916-1962. Names, title, and works in preparation indexes.
Cord, William O. JOSE RUBEN ROMERO. CUENTOS Y POESIAS INEDITOS. ESTUDIO Y BIBLIOGRAFIA SELECTA. México: Ediciones de Andrea, 1964. 111p. "Bibliografía selecta," pp. 95-104. Contents: I. Reseñas. II. Estudios (revistas y diarios). III. Entrevistas. IV. Libros. V. Tesis (de maestro, doctoral). VI. Obras generales.
Flores, BEH, pp. 286-288. Contents: I. Ediciones principales. II. Otras ediciones. III. Referencias. IV. Bibliografía selecta (criticism).
Foster, Mex. Lit., pp. 300-306. Contents: I. Bibliographies. II. Critical Monographs and Dissertations. III. Critical Essays.
Foster, 20th Century, pp. 174-176. Contents: I. Bibliographies. II. Critical Books. III. Critical Essays.
Moore, Ernest R. "José Rubén Romero: bibliografía," REVISTA HISPANICA MODERNA, Año 12, Núm. 1 (enero/abril de 1946), 35-40. Contents: I. Ediciones. A. Poesías. B. Poesías sueltas. C. Prosa. D. Suelta. E. Prólogos. F. Traducciones. II. Estudios.
Romero, José Rubén. OBRAS COMPLETAS. PROLOGO DE ANTONIO CASTRO LEAL. México, D.F.: Editorial Porrúa, 1970. 837p. "Bibliografía," pp. 835-837. Contents: I. Bibliografía de Romero. A. Poesía. B. Prosa. II. Estudios sobre José Rubén Romero.

ROMERO, SILVIO (Brazil, 1851-1914)
Mendonça, Carlos Süssekind de. SILVIO ROMERO: SUA FORMAÇAO INTELECTUAL, 1851-1880: COM INDICAÇAO BIBLIOGRAFICA. São Paulo: Companha Editôra Nacional, 1938.

(Biblioteca Pedagógica Brasileira. Sér. 5ª: Brasiliana, v. 114). "Indicação bibliográfica de Sílvio Romero (1869-1914)," pp. 305-319. Contents: I. Por ordem cronológica. II. Por ordem alfabética.

Rabelo, Sylvio. ITINERARIO DE SILVIO ROMERO. Rio de Janeiro: Editôra Civilização Brasileira, 1967. 240p. Reprint of 1944 edition. "Bibliografia," pp. 233-240. Includes both works by and about Romero.

ROSA, JOAO GUIMARAES (Brazil, 1908-1967)

Brayner, Sônia. "A crítica rosiana," REVISTA BRASILEIRA DE LINGUA E LITERATURA, 2 (1979), 60-62. An annotated bibliography.

Doyle, Plínio. "Bibliografia sôbre João Guimarães Rosa," in EM MEMORIA DE JOÃO GUIMARÃES ROSA. Rio de Janeiro: Livraria José Olympio Editora, 1968), pp. 199-255. Contents: I. Livros. II. Prefácios. III. Discursos. IV. Correspondência publicada. V. Traduções. VI. Trabalhos em publicações brasileiras. A. Publicações diversas. B. Em LETRAS E ARTES, A MANHÃ (Suplemento), O GLOBO-RIO, PULSO. C. Obras de João Guimarães Rosa adaptadas para teatro, ciência e literatura infantil. D. Trabalhos incluídos em antologias nacionais e estrangeiras. E. Traduções. 1. Livros. 2. Contos e estórias divulgadas em publicações periódicas. VII. Bibliografia sôbre João Guimarães Rosa. A. Em jornais e periódicos brasileiros. B. Em jornais e periódicos estrangeiros.

Leonel, Maria Célia de Moraes, and Sandra Guardini Teixeira Vasconcelos. "Arquivo Guimarães Rosa," REVISTA DO INSTITUTO DE ESTUDOS BRASILEIROS (São Paulo), Núm. 24 (1982), 178-180. Description of the Guimarães Rosa collection of manuscripts and published works given to the Instituto.

Porter, pp. 173-174. Contents: I. Writings. II. References, Critical and Biographical.

Reis, Roberto. "Bibliografia de João Guimarães Rosa," TEXTO CRITICO, Núm. 12 (enero/marzo de 1979), 182-184. Contents: I. De Guimarães Rosa. II. Sobre Guimarães Rosa. III. Obras de J. G. R. adaptadas para teatro, cine, ballet y literatura infantil.

Rosa, João Guimarães. COLETANEA ORGANIZADA POR EDUARDO F. COUTINHO. Rio de Janeiro: Civilização Brasileira, 1983. 579p. (Coleção Fortuna Crítica, 6). Contents: I. "Bibliografia ativa," pp. 19-20. II. "Bibliografia passiva (seleção)," pp. 21-33. III. "Edições e periódicos especiais sôbre Guimarães Rosa (seleção)," p. 34.

_______. PRIMEIRAS ESTORIAS DE JOAO GUIMARAES ROSA. 8. ed. Rio de Janeiro: Livraria José Olympio, 1975. 179p. 179p. "Bibliografia de e sôbre João Guimarães Rosa," pp. xxiv-xxvii. Contents: I. Livros (by work). II. Adaptações para teatro, cinema e literatura infantil. III. Livros no estrangeiro. IV. Alguns livros sôbre João Guimarães Rosa.

Sperber, Suzi Frankl. CAOS E COSMOS: LEITURAS DE GUI-

MARAES ROSA. São Paulo: Livraria Duas Cidades, 1976. 210p. "Biblioteca de João Guimarães Rosa," pp. 159-201.

Vincent, Jon S. JOAO GUIMARAES ROSA. Boston: Twayne Publishers, 1978. 182p. "Selected Bibliography," pp. 173-178. Contents: I. Primary Sources. A. Works in Order of Publication (editions are those used in this study). B. Translations. II. Secondary Sources (briefly annotated).

ROSA-NIEVES, CESAREO (Puerto Rico, 1901-1974)

Figueroa de Cifredo, Patricia. APUNTES BIOGRAFICOS EN TORNO A LA VIDA Y OBRA DE CESAREO ROSA-NIEVES. San Juan: Editorial Cordillera, 1965. 319p. "Bibliografía," pp. 309-317. Contents: I. Obras. A. Poesías. B. Teatro. C. Ensayos. D. Antologías. E. Cuentos. II. Crítica sobre el autor.

Foster, P.R. Lit., pp. 204-205. Contents: I. Critical Monographs. II. Critical Essays.

ROSENBLAT, ANGEL (Venezuela, 1903-1984)

Alvar, Manuel. "Nuestros filólogos," BOLETIN DE FILOLOGIA ESPAÑOLA, Núm. 36/37 (julio/diciembre de 1970), 3-9. "Algunos títulos de la bibliografía de Angel Rosenblat," pp. 7-9.

Tejera, María Josefina. ANGEL ROSENBLAT. Caracas: Facultad de Humanidades y Educación, Escuela de Biblioteconomía y Archivos, 1967. 82p. (Serie bibliográfica, 3). The partially annotated works are listed by year, 1930-1967.

ROSSI, VICENTE (Argentina, 1871-1945)

Becco, Horacio Jorge. "Bibliografía de Vicente Rossi," in Vicente Rossi's COSAS DE NEGROS (Buenos Aires: Editorial Hachette, 1958), pp. 28-35. Contents: I. Libros. II. Ensayos y artículos. III. Teatro.

RUBIAO, MURILO (Brazil, 1916-)

Schwartz, Jorge. MURILO RUBIAO: A POETICA DO UROBORO. São Paulo: Editôra Atica, 1981. 113p. "Bibliografia," pp. 97-110. Contents: I. Obras do autor (by year, 1947-1981). II. Contos publicados em jornais e revistas (by title). III. Contos publicados em jornais e revistas estrangeiros (traduções). IV. Bibliografia sôbre Murilo Rubião (by his individual work). VI. Entrevistas. VII. Estudos em livros. VIII. Em antologias.

RULFO, JUAN (Mexico, 1918-1986)

Alvarez, Nicolás Emilio. ANALISIS ARQUETIPICO, MITICO Y SIMBOLOGICO DE "PEDRO PARAMO." Miami: Ediciones Universal, 1983. 140p. "Bibliografía selecta," pp. 127-132. Contents: I. Ediciones de Pedro Páramo. II. Colecciones críticas sobre la obra de Juan Rulfo o con artículos variados sobre la misma. III. Obras críticas seleccionadas especialmente sobre Pedro Páramo.

Becco and Foster, pp. 161-171. Contents: I. Obras. II. Traducciones. III. Crítica.

Fernández-Cuesta, Marino. "JUAN RULFO: BIBLIOGRAFIA ANOTADA." Ph.D., University of New Mexico, 1983. 320p. "The Dissertation is divided into four chapters. The first categories more than two hundred critical studies according to the theoretical focus used in each one.... The second chapter forms the main corpus of the dissertation; in it the bibliographical entries of the secondary source material on Rulfo's works are organized chronologically and critical annotations of selected works are included. The third chapter provides an alphabetically-listed bibliography of the same critical material, and the last chapter consists of name index that facilitates the identification of the critical material as it relates to each of Rulfo's works. In this way the critical studies have been cross-indexed (1) by the type of criticism used, (2) the year each study was published, (3) in alphabetical order and, finally, (4) according to the narrative works that each study analizes." (DISSERTATION ABSTRACTS INTERNATIONAL, 45 (December 1984), 1768A-1769A).

Foster, Mex. Lit., pp. 306-323. Contents: I. Bibliographies. II. Critical Monographs and Dissertations. III. Critical Essays.

Foster, 20th Century, pp. 176-181. Contents: I. Bibliographies. II. Critical Books. III. Critical Essays.

Gordon, Donald K. LOS CUENTOS DE JUAN RULFO. Madrid: Playor, 1976. 196p. "Bibliografía," pp. 189-192. Contents: I. Obras de Rulfo. II. Recientes ediciones. III. Estudios sobre Rulfo y El llano en llamas. IV. Artículos anónimos.

Gutiérrez Marrone, Nila. EL ESTILO DE JUAN RULFO: ESTUDIO LINGUISTICO. New York: Bilingual Press, 1978. 176p. "Bibliografía," pp. 137-169. Contents: I. Obras y traducciones de obras de Juan Rulfo. A. Cuentos. 1. Antologías y revistas que contienen varios cuentos de Juan Rulfo. 2. Cuentos publicados individualmente. 3. Colecciones de cuentos. B. Fragmentos de novelas y novela. C. Otras publicaciones. 1. Disco. 2. Guiones cinematográficos. 3. Ediciones, prólogos, reseñas, etc. II. Crítica sobre la obra de Rulfo. A. Antologías de ensayos sobre Rulfo y colecciones que contienen más de un ensayo sobre Rulfo. B. Libros y ensayos críticos sobre la obra de Rulfo. C. Libros y ensayos generales que se refieren a la obra de Rulfo.

Juzyn, Olga. "Bibliografía actualizada sobre Juan Rulfo," INTI: REVISTA DE LITERATURA HISPANICA, Núm. 13/14 (primavera/otoño de 1981), 128-151. Contents: I. Colecciones de ensayos sobre Rulfo. II. Bibliografía sobre Rulfo (alphabetical arrangement of critical studies). III. Tesis inéditas.

Kent Lloret, E. "Continuación a una bibliografía de y sobre Juan Rulfo," REVISTA IBEROAMERICANA, 40, Núm. 89 (octubre/diciembre de 1974), 693-705. Supplements and updates the Ramírez bibliography. Contents: I. Obras de Juan Rulfo. II. Materia bibliográfica. III. Entrevistas y materia de interés biográfico. IV. Referencias en general a la obra de Rulfo. V. Reseñas y artículos sobre El llano en llamas o sus cuentos. VI. Reseñas y artículos sobre Pedro Páramo.

Leal, Luis. JUAN RULFO. Boston: Twayne Publishers, 1983. 132p. "Selected Bibliography," pp. 116-125. Contents: I. Primary Sources. A. Novels. B. Fragments of Novels. C. Short Stories. D. Anthologies. E. Other Prose Writings. F. Translations (English only). II. Secondary Sources. A. Bibliographies. B. Criticism. Partially annotated entries in this bibliography.

Ramírez, Arthur. "Hacia una bibliografía de y sobre Juan Rulfo," REVISTA IBEROAMERICANA, 40, Núm. 86 (enero/marzo de 1974), 135-171. 517 items. Contents: I. Obras de Juan Rulfo. A. Libros. B. Cuentos. C. Fragmentos. D. Traducciones a otras lenguas extranjeras. E. Antologías. F. Miscelánea. II. Estudios bibliográficas. III. Entrevistas y material biográfico. IV. Referencias en general a la obra de Rulfo. V. Reseñas y artículos sobre El llano en llamas. VI. Reseñas y artículos sobre Pedro Páramo.

Rulfo, Juan. AUTOBIOGRAFIA ARMADA. RECOPILACION DE REINA ROFFE. Buenos Aires: Corregidor, 1973. 100p. "Bibliografía," pp. 91-100. Contents: I. Obra de Rulfo. II. Sobre Rulfo.

- S -

SA, ANTONIO JOAQUIM FRANCO DE (Brazil, 1836-1856)

Moraes, pp. 39-40. Major works by and about the author.

SABAT ERCASTY, CARLOS (Uruguay, 1887-1982)

Flores, BEH, pp. 288-289. Contents: I. Ediciones. II. Bibliografía selecta (criticism).

SABATO, ERNESTO (Argentina, 1911-)

Cohen, Howard R. "CRITICAL APPROACHES TO MALLEA AND SABATO: AN ANNOTATED BIBLIOGRAPHY." Ph.D., University of Virginia, 1977. 288p. Includes bibliographies of their works as well as bibliographies about them, through 1970. A cross-reference index, alphabetized by author, is also provided.

Dellepiane, Angela B. ERNESTO SABATO: EL HOMBRE Y SU OBRA (ENSAYO DE INTERPRETACION Y ANALISIS LITERARIO). Long Island City, N.Y.: Las Américas Publishing Co., 1968. 358p. "Contribución a la bibliografía de Ernesto Sábato," pp. 337-358. 253 entries. Contents: I. Obras del autor. A. Novelas y cuentos (ordenación alfabética). B. Ensayos (ordenación alfabética). C. Miscelánea (ordenación cronológica). D. Colaboraciones en publicaciones periódicas. 1. Fragmentos y capítulos de novelas (ordenación cronológica). 2. Artículos (ordenación cronológica). 3. Entrevistas, encuestas, reportajes (ordenación cronológica). 4. Reseñas (ordenación cronológica). 5. Comentario de noticias. II. Traducciones de obras del autor (by language). III. Crítica sobre el autor. A. Libros (ordenación alfabética). B. Artículos (ordenación alfabética). IV. Notas bibliográficas (ordenación alfabética). Supplemented in her SABATO: UN ANALISIS DE SU NARRATIVA. Buenos Aires: Editorial Nova, 1970, pp. 309-340.

Flores, BEH, pp. 289-292. Contents: I. Edición principal. II. Otras ediciones. III. Referencias. IV. Bibliografía selecta (criticism).

Foster, Arg. Lit., pp. 631-647. Contents: I. Bibliographies. II. Critical Monographs and Dissertations. III. Critical Essays.

Foster, 20th Century, pp. 182-189. Contents: I. Bibliographies. II. Critical Books. III. Critical Essays.

Predmore, James R. ESTUDIO CRITICO DE LAS NOVELAS DE ERNESTO SABATO. Madrid: José Porrúa, 1981. 168p. "Bibliografía," pp. 151-156. Contents: I. Ficción y ensayos de Sabato. II. Estudios sobre Sábato y sus obras. III. Otras obras consultadas.

SABINES, JAIME (Mexico, 1925-)

Foster, Mex. Lit., pp. 323-325. Contents: I. Critical Monographs and Dissertations. II. Critical Essays.

SAENZ, JAIME (Bolivia, 1921-)

Sáenz, Jaime. OBRA POETICA. La Paz: Biblioteca del Sesquicentenario de la República, 1975. 437p. "Bibliografía," pp. 423-424. Works of Jaime Sáenz only.

SAENZ HAYES, RICARDO (Argentina, 1888-1976)

Becco, Horacio Jorge. "Bibliografía de don Ricardo Saénz-Hayes," BOLETIN DE LA ACADEMIA ARGENTINA DE LETRAS, 41, Núm. 159/160 (enero/junio de 1976), 125-128. Contents: I. Ensayo. II. Cuento. III. Novela. IV. Separatas y folletos.

SAEZ, ANTONIA (Puerto Rico, 1889-1964)

Foster, P.R. Lit., pp. 206-207. Critical Essays.

SAID ALI, MANUEL (Brazil, 1861-1953)

"Bibliografia de Manuel Said Ali," in MISCELANEA DE ESTUDOS EM HONRA DE MANUEL SAID ALI, PROFESSOR DE COLEGIO PEDRO II. Rio de Janeiro, 1938. 142p. Works are arranged by year, 1893-1938.

SAINZ, GUSTAVO (Mexico, 1940-)

Foster, Mex. Lit., pp. 325-327. Contents: I. Critical Monographs and Dissertations. II. Critical Essays.

Foster, 20th Century, pp. 189-190. Contents: I. Critical Books. II. Critical Essays.

SALARRUE (Pseudonym of SALVADOR SALAZAR ARRUE) (El Salvador, 1899-1975)

Cherry, Sharon Ann Young. "FANTASY AND REALITY IN SALAR-

RUE." Ph.D., Northwestern University, 1977. 290p. "The bibliography contains a complete list of all editions of Salarrué's major works, a partial list of his stories, essays, and poems not printed in collections, thirteen anthologies that include his stories, and fifty-one items about the author." (Abs.).

SALAVERRY, CARLOS AUGUSTO (Peru, 1830-1891)
Foster, Peruvian Lit., pp. 227-228. Contents: I. Critical Monographs. II. Critical Essays.

SALAZAR ARRUE, SALVADOR see SALARRUE

SALAZAR BONDY, AUGUSTO (Peru, 1925-1974)
"Bibliografía de Augusto Salazar Bondy," (TEXTUAL) (Lima, Instituto Nacional de Cultura), Núm. 9 (diciembre de 1974), 143-152. 300 items. Contents: I. Libros y folletos. II. Artículos, ensayos y separatas. III. Antologías, prólogos y traducciones. IV. Informes y proyectos. V. Entrevistas, declaraciones y intervenciones.
Rivera de Tuesta, María Luisa. "Augusto Salazar Bondy, 1925-1975 (sic)," SAN MARCOS, Núm. 12 (julio/septiembre de 1975), 165-185. "Bibliografía de Augusto Salazar Bondy," pp. 168-185. Contents: I. Filosofía. A. Libros, folletos, ensayos, artículos periodísticos, separatas, prólogos y reseñas bibliográficas. B. Textos. C. Traducciones. II. Filosofía y historia de las ideas en le Perú y en Latinoamérica. A. Libros, folletos, ensayos, artículos periodísticos, separatas, prólogos y reseñas bibliográficas. III. Educación. A. Libros, folletos, ensayos, artículos periodísticos, entrevistas, discursos, informes y proyectos. B. Textos. IV. Filosofía política, cultura, economía y sociedad. A. Libros, folletos, ensayos, artículos periodísticos, prólogos y reseñas bibliográficas. B. Traducciones.

SALAZAR BONDY, SEBASTIAN (Peru, 1924-1965)
Foster, Peruvian Lit., pp. 229-231. Contents: I. Bibliographies. II. Critical Monographs and Dissertations. III. Critical Essays.
Tello de Medina, Luzmilla. "Sebastian Salazar Bondy," ANUARIO BIBLIOGRAFICO PERUANO, 1964/1966, 618-684. Contents: I. Biografía. II. Libros y folletos. III. Otras publicaciones. IV. Artículos y ensayos. V. Cuentos, poesías. VI. Teatro. VII. Notas bibliográficas. VIII. Referencias.

SALDANHA, JOSE DA NATIVIDADE (Brazil, 1796-1830)
Porter, p. 261. Contents: I. Writings. II. References, Critical and Biographical.

SALES, HERBERTO (Brazil, 1917-)
Alves, Ivia Iracema. HERBERTO SALES: BIOGRAFIA. Salvador: Faculdade Cultural do Estado da Bahia, 1979. 121p. (Coleção Cabrália, 7). "Bibliografia selecionada sôbre Herberto Sales," pp. 113-115. "Bibliografia de Herberto Sales," pp. 117-119 (works arranged by year, 1944-1978).

Sales, Herberto. EU, HERBERTO SALES. DEPOIMENTO TOMADO EM GRACAÇAO POR ENEIDA LEAL. Rio de Janeiro: Editôra Cátedra, 1978. 82p. (Série Escritor ao Vivo, 1). "Bibliografia de Herberto Sales," pp. 75-78. Contents: I. Romance. II. Conto. III. Literatura infantil. IV. Outros trabalhos. V. Em colaboração. VI. No exterior. VII. Adaptações, condensações e traduções (Edições do ouro). VIII. Antologias (organização). "Fontes para o estudo da vida e obra de Herberto Sales," pp. 79-82.

SAMPER, JOSE MARIA (Colombia, 1828-1888)
Porras Collantes, pp. 650-660. Includes works of and critical studies about the author.

SAMPER ORTEGA, DANIEL (Colombia, 1895-1943)
Porras Collantes, pp. 661-665. Includes works of and critical studies about the author.

SANCHEZ, FLORENCIO (Argentina, 1875-1910)
FLORENCIO SANCHEZ; CENTENARIO DE SU NACIMIENTO: BIBLIOGRAFIA. Montevideo: Biblioteca Nacional, 1975. 53p. A homenaje exposition. Contents: I. Testimonios personales. A. Manuscritos de obras. B. Correspondencia. 1. Manuscritos originales. 2. Facsímiles. C. Programas. D. Objetos. E. Varios. II. Obras. A. Obras (todas las ediciones). B. Traducciones. C. Publicaciones en diarios y revistas. III. Bio-crítica. A. Libros. B. Ensayos en otros libros. C. Artículos en diarios y revistas. IV. Iconografía. A. Del autor. B. Caricaturas, retratos y dibujos. C. El autor con otras personas. D. De familiares. E. Otras fotografías.
Flores, BEH, pp. 292-294. Contents: I. Ediciones principales. II. Referencias. III. Bibliografía selecta (criticism).
Rela, Walter. FLORENCIO SANCHEZ: GUIA BIBLIOGRAFICA. Montevideo: Ulises, 1967. 104p. 541 items. Contents: I. Cuadro biográfico-cronológico. II. Indice cronológico de estrenos. III. Obras del autor. A. Teatro. 1. Obras completas. 2. Ediciones parciales. a. Libros. b. Folletos. c. Antologías en textos del autor. d. Recompilaciones de textos del autor. (1). Libros. (2). Folletos. e. Textos del autor en diversas antologías. f. Traducciones de textos del autor. B. Ensayo. 1. Libros. 2. Revistas y folletos. III. Colaboraciones en diarios, periódicos y revistas (compilación parcial). IV. Obras sobre el autor. A. Biografía. B. Biocrítica. C. Historias literarias. D. Historia del teatro. E. Ensayo y crítica individual. F. Ensayo y crítica general. G. Memorias y comentarios sobre temas teatrales. H. Artículos en diarios, periódicos y revistas. 1. Firmados. 2. Sin firma. I. Varios. 1. Bibliografía individual. 2. De referencia general. 3. Diccionarios. 4. Folletos. V. Indice onomástico.
Richardson, Ruth. FLORENCIO SANCHEZ AND THE ARGENTINE THEATRE. New York: Instituto de las Españas, 1933. 243p.

"Bibliography," pp. 229-243. Contents: I. Plays with Place and Date of Initial Performances, 1903-1909. II. Editions. III. Studies. A. Biographical. B. Critical (on works in general). C. Criticism of Specific Works, General. D. Bibliography of the Argentine Theatre.

Sánchez, Florencio. TEATRO. SELECCION Y PROLOGO DE WALTER RELA. Montevideo: Ministerio de Cultura, 1967. (Biblioteca Artigas, 121). "Addenda," pp. lvi-lxxv. Contents: I. Indice cronológico de estrenos. II. Algunos críticos sobre las obras seleccionadas. C. Influencia probable de obras dramáticas europeas sobre las que figuran en esta antología. D. Tabla cronológica de las principales obras teatrales europeas representadas en Buenos Aires durante la permanencia de Florencio Sánchez en esa ciudad. E. Bibliografía. Ediciones fundamentales de la obra teatral de Florencio Sánchez. 1. Obras completas. 2. Ediciones parciales. 3. Antologías. a. Obra personal. b. En obras colectivas. 4. Traducciones.

Uruguay. Ministerio de Educación. Biblioteca Nacional. FLORENCIO SANCHEZ: CENTENARIO DE SU NACIMIENTO, 1875-1975: BIBLIOGRAFIA. Montevideo, 1975. 53p. Bibliography of the exposition commemorating Sanchez's birth.

SANCHEZ, LUIS ALBERTO (Peru, 1900-)

Galindo Vera, Vidal. "Contribución a la bibliografía de Luis Alberto Sánchez," BOLETIN BIBLIOGRAFICO (Universidad Nacional de San Marcos, Biblioteca), Año 35, Vol. 33, Núm. 3/4 (diciembre de 1962), 7-86; Año 36, Vol. 34, Núm. 1/2 (junio de 1963), 3-98. The first part lists 186 books and pamphlets (1918-1962) and 703 articles (1909-1962). The second part registers 1,482 articles. Contents: I. Cronología biográfica del doctor Luis Alberto Sánchez. II. Libros y folletos por orden cronológico (1919-1962). III. Libros y folletos por materias. A. Literatura. B. Historia. C. Ciencias sociales. D. Educación. E. Otros asuntos. IV. Artículos publicados en la revista MUNDIAL DE LIMA (1921-1933). VI. Artículos publicados en otras revistas y periódicos (1916-1962). A name index is also included.

HOMENAJE A LUIS ALBERTO SANCHEZ. Madrid: Insula, 1983. 537p. "Obras de Luis Alberto Sánchez," pp. 527-536.

Sánchez, Luis Alberto. PASOS DE UN PEREGRINO SON ERRANTE ... (ANTOLOGIA, 1919-1968). SELECCION Y PROLOGO DE JORGE PUCCINELLI. Lima, n.p., 1968. 448p. "Bibliografía," pp. 3-9 (entries arranged by year, 1918-1967). Only books and pamphlets are included, however.

SANCHEZ, LUIS RAFAEL (Puerto Rico, 1936-)

Foster, P.R. Lit., pp. 207-209. Contents: I. Bibliography. II. Dissertation. III. Critical Essays.

SANCHEZ BOUDY, JOSE (Cuba, 1927-)

Foster, Cuban Lit., p. 441. Critical Essays

SANCHEZ GOMEZ, GREGORIO (Colombia, 1895-1942)
Porras Collantes, pp. 667-675. Includes works of and critical studies about the author.

SANDOVAL Y ZAPATA, LUIS DE (Mexico, Fl. 1645-1683)
Flores, BEH, pp. 46-47. Contents: I. Ediciones. II. Bibliografía selecta (criticism).

SANFUENTES, SALVADOR (Chile, 1817-1860)
Escudero, pp. 297-298. Criticism.

SANIN CANO, BALDOMERO (Colombia, 1861-1957)
Hebblethwaite, Frank P. "Bibliografía de Baldomero Sanín Cano," REVISTA INTERAMERICANA DE BIBLIOGRAFIA, 2ª época, Núm. 16 (octubre/diciembre de 1961), 320-328. Work lists 83 titles under the following categories: I. Obra. A. Libros, selecciones, folletos. B. Artículos y otras colaboraciones. II. Estudios críticos y biográficos sobre Sanín Cano. III. Traducciones.
Sanín Cano, Baldomero. EL OFICIO DE LECTOR. COMPILACION, PROLOGO Y CRONOLOGIA: J. G. COBO BORDA. Caracas: Biblioteca Ayacucho, 1978. 505p. "Bibliografía," pp. 497-499. Contents: I. Libros de B. Sanín Cano. II. Estudios sobre B. Sanín Cano.

SANTA CRUZ, MARIA MERCEDES, CONDESA DE MERLIN (Cuba, 1789-1852)
Foster, Cuban Lit., pp. 442-443. Contents: I. Critical Monographs. II. Critical Essays.

SANTA CRUZ, NICOMEDES (Peru, 1925-)
Jackson, Afro-Spanish, pp. 102-104. Contents: I. Works. II. Criticism. Annotated.

SANTIBANEZ PUGA, FERNANDO see SANTIVAN, FERNANDO

SANTIVAN, FERNANDO (Pseudonym of FERNANDO SANTIBANEZ PUGA) (Chile, 1886-1973)
"Cartillas biobibliográficas de autores chilenos: Fernando Santiván (Fernando Santibáñez Puga). Arauco, 1886. Novelista, cuentista y memorialista," BOLETIN DEL INSTITUTO DE LITERATURA CHILENA (Universidad de Chile, Santiago), Año 1, Núm. 2 (mayo de 1962), 4-8. Contents: I. Obras. II. Referencias. III. Tabla biográfica.
Foster, Chilean Lit., pp. 209-211. Contents: I. Bibliographies. II. Critical Books and Theses. III. Critical Essays.

SANTOS, LUIS DELFINO DOS (Brazil, 1834-1910)
Porter, pp. 212-213. Contents: I. Writings. II. References, Critical and Biographical.

SANTOS MOLANO, ENRIQUE (Colombia, 1942-)
Porras Collantes, pp. 682-686. Includes works of and critical studies about the author.

SARDUY, SEVERO (Cuba, 1937-)
Flores, BEH, pp. 294-296. Contents: I. Ediciones. II. Referencias. III. Bibliografía selecta (criticism).
Foster, Cuban Lit., pp. 444-450. Contents: I. Bibliographies. II. Critical Monograph and Dissertations. III. Critical Essays.
Foster, 20th Century, pp. 190-191. Contents: I. Bibliographies. II. Critical Essays.
González Echevarría, Roberto. "Para una bibliografía de y sobre Severo Sarduy," REVISTA IBEROAMERICANA, 38, Núm. 79 (abril/junio de 1972), 333-343. Contents: I. Libros. II. Traducciones de las novelas. III. Colaboraciones en libros, periódicos y revistas. IV. Bibliografía sobre Severo Sarduy. A. Entrevistas. B. Estudios. C. Reseñas. D. Memorias. 140 items.
_______. "Para una bibliografía de y sobre Severo Sarduy (1955-1974)," in SEVERO SARDUY (Madrid: Editorial Fundamentos, 1976), pp. 177-192. 212 unannotated entries. Contents: I. Bibliografía de Severo Sarduy. A. Libros. B. Traducciones de novelas (by work). C. Colaboraciones en libros, periódicos y revistas (by title). D. Prólogos y ensayos breves en catálogos de exposiciones de arte. II. Bibliografía sobre Severo Sarduy. A. Entrevistas. B. Estudios reseñas y menciones.

SARMIENTO, DOMINGO FAUSTINO (Argentina, 1811-1888)
Amaral Insiarte, Alfredo. BIBLIOGRAFIA SOBRE SARMIENTO. PIEZAS BIBLIOGRAFICAS EXISTENTES EN LA BIBLIOTECA PUBLICA DE LA UNIVERSIDAD. CON UN NOMINA DE LAS OBRAS DE SARMIENTO PERTENECIENTES A LA INSTITUCION). La Plata: Universidad Nacional, Biblioteca Pública, 1938. 62p. 484 entries.
Ara, Guillermo. "Las ediciones del FACUNDO," REVISTA IBEROAMERICANA, 23, Núm. 46 (julio/diciembre de 1958), 375-394. Contents: I. Primera edición (1845)-sexta edición (1889). II. Otras ediciones en castellano. III. La traducción inglesa de Mrs. Mann. IV. Otras traducciones.
Becco, Horacio Jorge. "Bibliografía de Sarmiento," HUMANIDADES (La Plata, Argentina), 37, Núm. 2 (1961), 119-144. Lists 437 works by and on Sarmiento. Contents: I. Libros y folletos. II. Otras ediciones. III. Antologías. IV. Crítica y biografía.
Flores, BEH, pp. 47-49. Contents: I. Edición principal. II. Otras ediciones de sus obras principales. III. Referencias. IV. Bibliografía selecta (criticism).
Foster, Arg. Lit., pp. 648-704. Contents: I. Bibliographies. II. Critical Monographs and Dissertations. III. Critical Essays.
_______. "Domingo Faustino Sarmiento: A Bibliography of Critical Monographs and Articles on Domingo Faustino Sarmiento,"

BULLETIN OF BIBLIOGRAPHY, 39 (1982), 26-48. Contents: I. Bibliographies. II. Monographs and Dissertations. III. Critical Essays. A. General Essays. B. Biography and Memorabilia. C. Sarmiento Abroad and His International Relations. D. Sarmiento and Sociopolitical Issues. E. Sarmiento and Education. F. Sarmiento and Literature and the Arts; Sarmiento and Other Writers. G. Facundo. H. Recuerdos de provincia. I. Other Works. "Excluded are materials published on Sarmiento in literary supplements and general interest magazines..." (p. 26).

La Plata. Universidad Nacional. Facultad de Ciencias Jurídicas y Sociales. Sección de Filosofía y Letras. BIBLIOGRAFIA DE SARMIENTO. PROLOGO DE RICARDO ROJAS. TRABAJO REALIZADO POR LOS ALUMNOS DE LETRAS. Buenos Aires: Imprenta Coni Hermanos, 1911. 582p. An index to his OBRAS COMPLETAS (edición oficial).

Moglia, Raul, and Miguel García. "Catálogo de la exposición bibliográfica," in SARMIENTO; EDUCADOR, SOCIOLOGO, ESCRITOR, POLITICO (Buenos Aires: Universidad Nacional de Buenos Aires, Facultad de Filosofía y Letras, 1963), pp. 155-230. Enumerates with annotations the 237 entries in the exposition, Sept. 12-22, 1961. Contents: I. Obras completas. II. FACUNDO. III. El tigre de los Llanos. IV. Educación. V. Recuerdos de Provincia. VI. Campaña en el ejército. VII. Chile. VIII. Biografías. IX. Presidencia. X. Conflictos y armonías. XI. La vejés. XII. Varia. XIII. Juicios. XIV. Bibliografía sobre Sarmiento.

Montt, Luis. NOTICIAS DE LAS PUBLICACIONES HECHAS EN CHILE POR DON DOMINGO F. SARMIENTO (1841-1871). Santiago de Chile: Imprenta Gutenberg, 1884. 83p. Also published in OBRAS DE SARMIENTO, tomo 1 (Santiago de Chile, 1887).

Ottolenghi, Julia. VIDA Y OBRA DE SARMIENTO EN SINTESIS CRONOLOGICA. Buenos Aires: Editorial Kapelusz, 1950. 387p. I. 1811-1888 (setiembre). II. Los seudónimos de Sarmiento. III. Bibliografía de Sarmiento (upon Sarmiento, by subject).

SARNLY, JOSE (Brazil, 1930-)

Moraes, pp. 117-118. Major works by and about the author.

SASSONE SUAREZ, FELIPE (Peru, 1884-1959)

Birimisa, Martha. "Felipe Sassone Suárez," ANUARIO BIBLIOGRAFICO PERUANA; 1958/1960, 624-639. Contents: I. Biografía. II. Libros y folletos. III. Artículos y ensayos. IV. Cuentos, poesías. V. Cartas. VI. Discursos, conferencias. VII. Reportajes. VIII. Notas bibliográficas. IX. Referencias. X. Notas necrológicas.

SCHMIDT, AUGUSTO FREDERICO (Brazil, 1906-1965)

Schmidt, Augusto Frederico. SELTA EM PROSA E VERSO DE

AUGUSTO FREDERICO SCHMIDT. ORGANIZAÇAO, ESTUDO E NOTAS DO PROF. SILVIO ELIA. Rio de Janeiro: Instituto Nacional do Livro; Brasília: Ministério da Educação e Cultura, 1975. 182p. "Bibliografia," pp. 179-180. Contents: I. Obras do autor. A. Poesia. B. Prosa. II. Sôbre o autor.

Tolman, Jon M. AUGUSTO FREDERICO SCHMIDT. São Paulo: Edição Quíron Limitada, 1976. 273p. Contents: I. "Bibliografia," pp. 263-264. II. "Bibliografia acerca de A. F. Schmidt," pp. 264-273.

SCORZA, MANUEL (Peru, 1928-1983)

Foster, Peruvian Lit., pp. 232-233. Critical Essays.

SEGURA, MANUEL ASCENSIO (Peru, 1805-1871)

Fernández Dávila V., Pablo; J. Ramón Mariátegui V. G.; and César Larrabure G. "Bibliografía," in Manuel Ascenio Segura's LAS TRES VIDAS: COMEDIA DE COSTUMBRES (Lima: Ediciones Markham, 1963), pp. 150-156. Contents: I. De Segura. II. Sobre Segura.

Foster, Peruvian Lit., pp. 234-236. Contents: I. Bibliographies. II. Critical Monographs and Dissertations. III. Critical Essays.

SELVA, SALOMON DE LA (Nicaragua, 1893-1959)

Arellano, Jorge Eduardo. "Bibliografía fundamental de Salomón de la Selva," CUADERNOS UNIVERSITARIOS (Universidad Nacional Autónoma de Nicaragua), 2ª serie, Núm. 5 (agosto de 1969), 153-160. 77 entries. Contents: I. Antologías y selecciones que incluyen poemas de Salomón de la Selva. II. Obras y artículos generales sobre Salomón de la Selva. III. Obras en verso y prosa de Salomón de la Selva. IV. Estudios y artículos particulares sobre Salomón de la Selva.

_______. "Salomón de la Selva en el REPERTORIO AMERICANO," BOLETIN NICARAGUENSE DE BIBLIOGRAFIA Y DOCUMENTACION, Número 5 (mayo/junio de 1975), 23-27. 145 entries which are arranged alphabetically by title.

SERRA, JOAQUIM MARIA (Brazil, 1838-1888)

Moraes, pp. 40-42. Major works by and about the author.

Mota, Artur. "Perfis acadêmicos: Joaquim Maria Serra," REVISTA DA ACADEMIA BRASILEIRA DE LETRAS, Núm. 118 (1931), 155-168. Contents: I. "Bibliografia," pp. 155-157 (1862-1884). II. "Fontes para o estudo crítico," p. 158.

SIERRA, JUSTO (Mexico, 1848-1912)

Mantecón Navasal, José Ignacio; Irma Contreras García; and Ignacio Osorio Romero. BIBLIOGRAFIA GENERAL DE DON JUSTO SIERRA. México, D.F.: UNAM, Instituto de Investigaciones Bibliográficas, Biblioteca Nacional de México, 1969. 273p. The bibliography is divided into three parts: list of Sierra's work arranged chronologically (1865-1912), with comments on contents; bibliographies about him; essays and studies concerned with him and his writings. Comments about each one of 1,451 entries of his writings are taken from 45 different journals. An "índice analítico" is also included.

SIGUENZA Y GONGORA, CARLOS DE (Mexico, 1645-1700)

Flores, BEH, pp. 49-50. Contents: I. Ediciones. II. Referencias. III. Bibliografía selecta (criticism).

Foster, Mex. Lit., pp. 327-330. Contents: I. Bibliographies. II. Critical Monographs and Dissertations. III. Critical Essays.

Leonard, Irving Albert. ENSAYO BIBLIOGRAFICO DE DON CARLOS DE SIGUENZA Y GONGORA. México, 1929. (Monografías bibliográficas mexicanas, 15). Contents: I. Libros, impresos, folletos. II. Manuscritos. III. Cartas e informes. IV. Estudios sobre Sigüenza y Góngora. V. Adiciones.

Sigüenza y Góngora, Carlos de. PIEDAD HEROYCA DE DON FERNANDO CORTES. EDICION Y ESTUDIO POR JAIME DELGADO. Madrid: Colección Chimalistac de Libros y Documentos acerca de la Nueva España, 1960. 108p. "La obra," pp. liv-cviii. A descriptive bibliography of Sigüenza y Góngora's works and their various editions.

SILVA, ANTONIO JOSE DA (Brazil, 1705-1739)

Basseches, Bruno. "Achêgas a uma bio-bibliografia de Antônio José da Silva," COMENTARIO (RIO DE JANEIRO), Ano 2, v.2, Núm. 1 (janeiro/março 1961), 84-90. Contents: I. Obra. II. Sôbre Antônio José da Silva.

Kohut, George Alexander. JEWISH MARTYRS OF THE INQUISITION IN SOUTH AMERICA. Baltimore: The Friedewald Co., 1895. 87p. Contents: I. "Bibliography of Works Relating to Antônio José da Silva," pp. 81-84. II. "Bibliography of Don Antônio's Compositions," pp. 84-87.

Silva, Antônio José da. OBRAS COMPLETAS. Lisboa: Livraria Sá da Costa-Editôra, 1957-1958. 4vs. Contents: I. "O teatro de Antônio José da Silva," pp. xxvi-xxxvi. II. "As edições setecentistas das composições dramáticas de Antônio José da Silva," pp. xxxvii-xli. III. "As edições dos séculos XIX e XX--a presente edição," pp. xlii-xlvii.

SILVA, DOMINGOS CARVALHO DA (Brazil, 1915-)

Silva, Domingos Carvalho da. MULTIPLA ESCOLHA. INTRODUÇAO: DIANA BERNARDES. Rio de Janeiro: Livraria José Olympio com convênio do Instituto Nacional do Livro, Ministério da Educação e Cultura, Brasília, 1980. 160p. "Bibliografia de e sôbre Domingos Carvalho da Silva," pp. 11-19. Contents: I. Obras do autor. A. Poesia. B. Poesia traduzida. C. Traduções de poesia em livros alheios. D. Colaboração em antologias e coletâneas. E. Ficção. F. Ensaio e crítica. G. Principais ensaios publicados em periódicos. H. Prefácios e introduções. I. Edições de obra alheia. J. Antologias. K. Colaboração em dicionários e histórias da literatura. II. Fontes para o estudo da obra do autor. A. Dicionários e enciclopédias.

B. Livros de história literária, ensaio e crítica. C. Periódicos (artigos principais; by work).

SILVA, JOSE ASUNCION (Colombia, 1865-1896)
Anderson, pp. 144-148. Contents: Critical Essays.
Flores, BEH, pp. 50-53. Contents: I. Ediciones. II. Otras ediciones. III. Bibliografía selecta (criticism).
Osiek, Betty Tyree. JOSE ASUNCION SILVA: ESTUDIO ESTILISTICO DE SU POESIA. México: De Andrea, 1968. 204p. "Bibliografía," pp. 186-202. Contents: I. Obras de José Asunción Silva. A. Obras. B. Poemas y prosa publicados. Antes de la muerte de Silva, en antologías y colecciones. C. Prosa publicada, antes de la muerte de Silva, en periódicos. D. Poemas en periódicos ("...solo la primera aparición de los poemas publicados en periódicos."). E. Versiones en periódicos. II. Estudios sobre Silva.
Porras Collantes, pp. 689-695. Includes works of and critical studies about the author.
Silva, José Asunción. OBRA COMPLETA. EDICION, NOTAS Y CRONOLOGIA: EDUARDO CAMACHO GUIZADO Y GUSTAVO MEJIA. Caracas: Biblioteca Ayacucho, 1977. 325p. "Bibliografía," pp. 317-325. Contents: I. Obras de José Asunción Silva. II. Estudios (criticism, etc.).

SILVA, JOSE BONIFACIO DE ANDRADA E (Brazil, 1763-1838)
Neiva, Venâncio de Figueiredo. REZUMO BIOGRAFICO DE JOSE BONIFACIO DE ANDRADA E SILVA: O PATRIARCA DA INDEPENDENCIA DO BRASIL. Rio de Janeiro: Irmãos Pongetti, 1938. 305p. Contents: I. "Obras de José Bonifácio," pp. 285-292. II. "Obras consultadas," pp. 293-299.
Sousa, Octávio Tarquínio de. JOSE BONIFACIO (HISTORIA DOS FUNDADORES DO IMPERIO DO BRASIL). Rio de Janeiro: Livraria José Olympio, 1972. 287p. (Coleção Documentos Brasileiros, 51). "Trabalhos de José Bonifácio," pp. xi-xix. Contents: I. Livros, opúsculos e manifestos. II. Colaboração em publicações periódicas. III. Trabalhos escritos em colaboração com outros autores. IV. Tradução.

SILVA, MANUEL CICERO PEREGRMO DA (Brazil, 1866-1956)
Rio de Janeiro. Biblioteca Nacional. MANUEL CICERO PEREGRMO DA SILVA, 1866-1966: EXPOSIÇAO COMEMORATIVA DO CENTENARIO DE NASCIMENTO. Rio de Janeiro: Biblioteca Nacional, Divisão de Publicações e Divulgação, Seção de Exposições, 1968. 22p. Contents: I. "Bibliografia de Manuel Cícero," pp. 7-12. II. "Bibliografia sôbre Manuel Cícero," pp. 12-13.

SILVA, MEDARDO ANGEL (Ecuador, 1898-1919)
Silva, Medardo Angel. OBRA COMPLETA. N.p., 1966. 331p. Contents: I. "Obras de Medardo Angel Silva," pp. 319-320. II. "Antologías nacionales y extranjeras (en los que figura

Medardo Angel Silva, por orden cronológico)," pp. 320-321. III. "Historias literarias o estudios sobre literatura ecuatoriana en las que figura Medardo Angel Silva, por orden cronológico," pp. 322-323. IV. "Artículos, ensayos y conferencias (con estudios dedicados a Medardo Angel Silva, por orden cronológico)," pp. 323-326. V. "Revistas literarias (en las que colaboró o se publicaron en época de Medardo Angel Silva)," pp. 326-329.

SILVA, VICTOR DOMINGO (Chile, 1882-1960)
Foster, Chilean Lit., pp. 211-212. Contents: I. Critical Books and Theses. II. Critical Essays.

SILVA CASTRO, RAUL (Chile, 1903-1970)
Decker, Donald M. RAUL SILVA CASTRO, HISTORIADOR-CRITICO DE LAS LETRAS CHILENAS. Santiago de Chile: Ediciones de la revista MAPOCHO, 1965, pp. 214-225. Offprint from MAPOCHO, 3, Núm. 3 (1965), 214-225. "Bibliografía de Raúl Silva Castro." Contents: I. Libros y folletos. II. Obras de colaboración. III. Obras de terceros editas en introducciones, notas, etc. IV. Prólogos e introducciones. V. Traducciones de obras de terceros. 152 items.
Escudero, Alfonso María. "Apuntes para una bibliografía de Raúl Silva Castro," EL BIBLIOFILO CHILENO (Santiago), 2, Núm. 11 (julio de 1971), 6-26. Lists 208 publications among essays, editions, anthologies, prologues, introductions, and translations for the period 1926-1970. In addition, there are 294 articles published between 1923 and 1969.
Mac Hale, Tomás P. "Bibliografia de Raúl Silva Castro (1903-1970)," REVISTA INTERAMERICANA DE BIBLIOGRAFIA, 22, Núm. 1 (enero/marzo de 1972), 30-44. Contents: I. Libros, folletos, separatas (by year, 1930-1969). II. Antologías, recopilaciones (by year, 1931-1970). III. Prólogos (by year, 1926-1969). IV. Traducciones (by year, 1933-1969). 190 total items.

SILVEIRA, ALVARO FERNANDO SOUSA DA (Brazil, 1883-1967)
Pereira Filho, Emmanuel. "Bibliografia do professor Sousa da Silveira," IBERIDA (Rio), Núm. 3 (dezembro de 1959), 209-229. Entries are arranged by year, 1908-1960. Reprinted (pp. 21-45) in 3º CONGRESSO BRASILEIRO DE LINGUA E LITERATURA (DE 5 A 16 DE JULHO DE 1971). "Homenagem ao professor Sousa da Silveira." Rio de Janeiro: Edições Gernasa e Artes Gráficas, Ltda., 1972. 344p.

SKARMETA, ANTONIO (Chile, 1940-)
Foster, Chilean Lit., pp. 212-213. Critical Essays.

SOFFIA, JOSE ANTONIO (Chile, 1843-1886)
Escudero, pp. 305-306. Criticism.
Silva Castro, Raúl. JOSE ANTONIO SOFFIA, 1843-1886. Santiago

de Chile: Editorial Andrés Bello, 1968. 183p. (Ensayos, 15). "Apéndice bibliográfico," pp. 149-160. Contents: I. Guerra de España en el Pacífico. II. Guerra del Pacífico. III. La voz de Chile (articles are listed by date). IV. Polémica de la aurora poética. V. Colaboración dispersa (articles by journal and then by issue).

SOJO, JUAN PABLO (Venezuela, 1908-1948)
Jackson, Afro-Spanish, pp. 104-105. Contents: I. Works. II. Criticism. A. Books. B. Articles, Shorter Studies, and Dissertations. Annotated.

SOLAR, ENRIQUE DEL (Chile, 1844-1893)
Escudero, p. 306. Criticism.

SOLARI SWAYNE, ENRIQUE (Peru, 1915-)
Foster, Peruvian Lit., p. 237. Critical Essays.

SOLER PUIG, JOSE (Cuba, 1916-)
Foster, Cuban Lit., pp. 451-452. Critical Essays.

SOLIS FOLCH DE CARDONA, JOSE (Colombia, ?-1770)
Lyday, León F. "El Virrey Solís en las letras colombianas (bibliografía)," BOLETIN CULTURAL Y BIBLIOGRAFIA (Bogotá), 12, Núm. 3 (1969), 53-63. Contents: I. Estudios históricos. II. Estudios de literatura y leyenda.

SOLORZANO, CARLOS (Guatemala and Mexico, 1922-)
Andrea, Pedro F. de. CARLOS SOLORZANO, BIBLIOGRAFIA. México: Hojas volantes de la CLE, 1970. 37p. 356 entries. Contents: I. Enfoques sobre su vida y obra (cronología bibliográfica mínima). II. Obra de Carlos Solórzano. III. Referencias sobre Carlos Solórzano. Entries are partially annotated.
Rodríguez, Orlando. "Carlos Solórzano: cronología bibliográfica mínima," CHASQUI (Madison, Wisconsin), 1, Núm. 1 (1972), 12-19. Contents: I. Biobibliografía. II. Obra de Carlos Solórzano. 63 titles.

SOTILLO, PEDRO (Venezuela, 1909-1977)
"Pedro Sotillo," ANUARIO BIBLIOGRAFICO VENEZOLANO, 1977, 272-279. Biobibliography.

SOTO, PEDRO JUAN (Puerto Rico, 1926-)
Foster, P.R. Lit., pp. 210-211. Contents: I. Bibliography. II. Critical Monographs and Dissertations. III. Critical Essays.
Ortiz Guzmán, Rosaura. "Pedro Juan Soto: Treinta años de producción literaria (1948-1978): Guía bibliográfica," REVISTA DE ESTUDIOS HISPANICOS (Puerto Rico), 6 (1979), 251-283. "Bibliografía," pp. 256-283. Contents: I. Ediciones. A. Cuentos. B. Novela. C. Teatro. D. Autobiobibliografía.

II. Obra suelta. A. Cuento. B. Novela. C. Teatro. D. Prosa varia. III. Argumentos y guiones cinematográficos. IV. Traducciones. V. Obras traducidas. A. Cuento. B. Novela. C. Teatro. VI. Obra inédita. A. Novela. B. Teatro. C. Prosa. VII. Antología. VIII. Representaciones. IX. Tesis. X. Estudios de conjunto (criticism). XI. Estudios generales (criticism). XII. Miscelánea. A. Biografías. B. Biobibliografías. C. Entrevistas. XIII. Actividades y noticias. XIV. Apéndice. Tareas varias.

SOTO APARICIO, FERNANDO (Colombia, 1933-)

Porras Collantes, pp. 702-708. Includes works of and critical studies about the author.

SOUSA, JOAO CARDOSO DE MENESES E, BARAO DE PARANAPIACABA (Brazil, 1827-1915)

Sousa, João Cardoso de Meneses e. POESIAS ESCOLHIDAS. INTRODUÇAO, SELEÇAO E NOTAS DE PERICLES EUGENIO DA SILVA RAMOS. São Paulo: Conselho Estadual de Cultura, 1965. 171p. Contents: I. "Bibliografia," pp. 16-17. II. "Bibliografia sôbre o autor," p. 18.

SOUSANDRADE, JOAQUIM DE (Brazil, 1832-1902)

Campos, Augusto and Haroldo de. REVISAO DE SOUSANDRADE. São Paulo: Edições Invenção, 1964. 275p. "Bibliografia de Sousândrade," pp. 266-271. Contents: I. Obras de autor. II. Colaboração em antologias e periódicos. III. Sôbre o autor (arranged by year, 1860-1963).

Moraes, pp. 33-37. Major works by and about the author.

Souza, Erthos A. de. "Bibliografia de Joaquim de Sousândrade (1833-1902)," ESTUDOS UNIVERSITARIOS (Revista de Cultura da Universidade do Recife), 2 (outubro/dezembro de 1962), 41-43. Contents: I. Obras de Sousândrade. II. Sôbre a vida e a obra de Sousândrade.

William, Frederick G. SOUSANDRADE: VIDA E OBRA. São Luís, Maranhão: Edições SIOGE, 1976. 277p. Contents: I. "Cronologia da vida e da obra," pp. 41-52. II. "Bibliografia crítica do autor," pp. 61-67. A. Livros de poesia. B. Poesia publicada em periódicos. C. Participação na antologias. D. Prosa de ficção. E. Artigos em jornais. 1. Literatura. 2. Política. 3. Universidade. 4. Assuntos vários. III. "Bibliografia sôbre Sousândrade," pp. 211-232. A. Referências contemporâneas (1857-1902). B. Referências anteriores a 1960 (arranged chronologically, 1903-1959). C. Referências depois de 1960 (arranged chronologically, 1960-1976).

SOUZA, AFONSO FELIX DE (Brazil, 1925-)

Souza, Afonso Félix de. ANTOLOGIA POETICA. 2ª ed., revista e ampliada. Goiânia, Goiás: Oriente, 1979. 172p. "Bibliografia," pp. 169-172. Contents: I. Obras. II. Algumas traduções. III. Antologias em que figura. A. No Brasil. B. No exterior. IV. O autor e o crítica.

SOUZA, ANTONIO GONÇALVES TEIXEIRA E (Brazil, 1812-1861)
Porter, pp. 268-269. Contents: I. Writings. II. References, Critical and Biographical.

SOUZA, JOAO DA CRUZ E (Brazil, 1862-1898)
Porter, pp. 209-211. Contents: I. Writings. II. References, Critical and Biographical.
Souza, João da Cruz e. OBRA COMPLETA. ORGANIZAÇAO GERAL, INTRODUÇAO, NOTAS, CRONOLOGIA E BIBLIOGRAFIA POR ANDRADE MURICY. EDIÇAO COMEMORATIVO DO CENTENARIO. Rio de Janeiro: José Aguilar Editora, 1961. 837p. (Bibliografia Luso-Brasileira, Série brasileira, 22-A). "Bibliografia," pp. 811-820. Contents: I. Obras. II. Livros, artigos, conferências.

SPERONI, ROBERTO THEMIS (Argentina, 1922-1967)
Arrastua de Muños, Esther. "Bibliografía de Roberto Themis Speroni," BOLETIN DEL INSTITUTO DE LITERATURA DE LA PROVINCIA DE BUENOS AIRES (La Plata), I (1970), 99-102. Partially annotated entries. Contents: I. Edita. A. Poesía. B. Prosa. II. Inédita. A. Poesía. B. Prosa. III. Sobre Roberto Themis Speroni.

SPINETTI DINI, ANTONIO (Venezuela, 1900-1941)
Cardozo, Poesía, pp. 203-207. Includes the poetical works of and the critical studies about the author.

SPOSITO, EMILIO MENOTTI (Venezuela, 1891-1951)
Cardozo, Poesía, pp. 207-210. Includes the poetical works of and critical studies about the author.

SPOTA, LUIS (Mexico, 1925-1985)
Foster, 20th Century, pp. 191-192. Contents: Critical Essays.

STORNI, ALFONSINA (Argentina, 1892-1938)
Baralis, Marta. CONTRIBUCION A LA BIBLIOGRAFIA DE ALFONSINA STORNI. Buenos Aires: Fondo Nacional de las Artes, 1964. 64p. (Bibliografía Argentina de Artes y Letras, Compilaciones Especiales, 18). Contents: I. Obras de la autora. A. Poesía. B. Poemas en prosa. C. Prosa. D. Teatro. E. Discurso. II. Colaboraciones en publicaciones periódicas. A. Poesía. B. Poemas en prosa. C. Teatro en prosa. D. Novela corta. E. Cuentos. F. Artículos y notas. G. Estudios sobre otros autores. H. Discurso. I. Entrevistas y encuestas. III. Traducciones de obras de otros autores. IV. Traducciones de obras de la autora. V. Antología de poesías de la autora. VI. Obras de la autora en diversas antologías. A. Poesía. B. Teatro. VII. Crítica y biografía. VIII. Nota biográfica. IX. Indices. A. De títulos. B. Onomástico.
Corvalán, pp. 99-101. Contents: I. Works. II. Critical Works

On.

Flores, BEH, pp. 171-173. Contents: I. Ediciones principales. II. Otras ediciones. III. Referencias. IV. Bibliografía selecta (criticism).

Foster, Arg. Lit., pp. 705-713. Contents: I. Bibliographies. II. Critical Monographs and Dissertations. III. Critical Essays.

Pérez Blanco, Lucrecio. LA POESIA DE ALFONSINA STORNI. Madrid: El autor, 1975. 402p. "Bibliografía," pp. 387-392. Contents: I. Obras de la autora. A. Poesía. B. Poemas en prosa. C. Prosa. D. Teatro. E. Discurso. II. Colaboraciones, traducciones de otros autores y traducciones de su obra en otras lenguas. III. Antologías de poesía de la autora. IV. Obras de la autora en diversas antologías. V. Estudios sobre la autora.

SUAREZ, ARTURO (Colombia, 1887-1956)

Porras Collantes, pp. 710-717. Includes works of and critical studies about the author.

SUAREZ, MARCO FIDEL (Colombia, 1855-1927)

Ortega Torres, Jorge. MARCO FIDEL SUAREZ: BIBLIOGRAFIA. Bogotá: Instituto Caro y Cuervo, 1956. 547p. (Filólogos colombianos, 2). Contents: I. Bibliografía de don Marco Fidel Suárez (by work). II. Bibliografía sobre don Marco Fidel Suárez (by author or title). III. Guión bio-bibliográfico de don Marco Fidel Suárez.

SUAREZ, Y ROMERO, ANSELMO (Cuba, 1818-1878)

Foster, Cuban Lit., pp. 453-455. Contents: I. Bibliography. II. Critical Monograph. III. Critical Essays.

Moreno Fraginales, Manuel. "Indice de los manuscritos de Anselmo Suárez y Romero que se conservan en la Biblioteca Nacional," REVISTA DE LA BIBLIOTECA NACIONAL (La Habana), 2ª serie, 1, Núm. 2 (febrero de 1950), 73-121. 166 manuscripts are enumerated under the following headings: I. Literatura. II. Derecho, educación. III. Otros asuntos (cartas diversas, misceláneas).

SUASSUNA, ARIANO (Brazil, 1927-)

Mertin, Ray-Güde. ARIANO SUASSUNA: "ROMANCE D'A PEDRA DO REINO": ZUR VERARBEITUNG VON VOLKS-UND HOCH-LITERATUR IM ZITAT. Genève: Librairie Droz, 1979. 285p. "Bibliographie," pp. 262-266. Contents: Ariano Suassuna. I. Werke. II. Interviews und Aufsätze in Zeitungen und Zeitschriften, Beiträge zu anderen Werken (Auswahl). III. Darstellungen über Ariano Suassuna.

Suassuna, Ariano. SELETA EM PROSA E VERSO DE ARIANO SUASSUNA. ESTUDO, COMENTARIOS E NOTAS DO PROF. SILVIANO SANTIAGO. Rio de Janeiro: Livraria José Olympio, 1974. 195p. "Obras de Ariano Suassuna," pp. 191-193. Contents: I. Teatro (by year, 1947-1974). II. Prosa de ficção (by year, 1956-1972). III. Poesia (by year, 1946-1970). IV. Outros atividades artísticas. V. Alguns estudos sôbre a obra de Ariano Suassuna.

SUBERCASEAUX ZANARTU, BENJAMIN (Chile, 1902-1973)
"Cartillas biobibliográficas de autores chilenos: Benjamín Subercaseaux Zañartu. Santiago, 1902. Ensayista, novelista, cuentista y periodística," BOLETIN DEL INSTITUTO DE LITERATURA CHILENA (Universidad de Chile, Santiago), Año 3, Núm. 6 (diciembre de 1963), 12-20. Contents: I. Obra. II. Traducciones. III. Referencias. IV. Tabla biográfica. V. Otros datos.
Foster, Chilean Lit., pp. 213-214. Contents: I. Bibliographies. II. Critical Books and Theses. III. Critical Essays.

- T -

TABLADA, JOSE JUAN (Mexico, 1871-1945)
Foster, Mex. Lit., pp. 330-333. Contents: I. Bibliographies. II. Critical Monographs and Dissertations. III. Critical Essays.
Tablada, José Juan. OBRAS. I. Poesía. México: UNAM, 1971. Contents: "Bibliografía publicada de José Juan Tablada," pp. 629-630. I. Poesía. II. Prosa. III. Teatro. "Bibliografía consultada," pp. 631-634.

TACCONI, EMILIO CARLOS (Uruguay, 1895-)
Tacconi, Emilio Carlos. PERSONAJES DE MI PUEBLO. Montevideo: Ediciones de Agadu, 1978. 163p. "Obras de Emilio Carlos Tacconi," n.p. Contents: I. Teatro. II. Poesía. III. Prosa. IV. Discos. V. En preparación.

TALLET, JOSE ZACARIAS (Cuba, 1893-)
Foster, Cuban Lit., p. 456. Critical Essays.
Tallet, José Z. ORBITA DE JOSE Z. TALLET. La Habana: Colección Orbita, 1969. 329p. "Bibliografía," pp. 321-329. Contents: I. Antologías. II. Referencias (libros). III. Referencias (artículos).

TAMAYO, FRANZ (Bolivia, 1879-1956)
Tamayo, Franz. OBRA ESCOGIDA. SELECCION, PROLOGO Y CRONOLOGIA: MARIANO BAPTISTA GUMUCIO. Caracas: Biblioteca Ayacucho, 1979. 359p. "Bibliografía," pp. 349-353. Contents: I. Obras de Franz Tamayo. II. Obras sobre Franz Tamayo.

TAPIA Y RIVERA, ALEJANDRO (Puerto Rico, 1826-1882)
Foster, P.R. Lit., pp. 212-214. Contents: I. Critical Monographs and Dissertations. II. Critical Essays.

TAVORA, FRANKLIN (Brazil, 1842-1888)

Mota, Artur. "Perfis acadêmicos: Franklin Távora," REVISTA DA ACADEMIA BRASILEIRA DE LETRAS, Núm. 87 (março de 1929), 279-287. Contents: I. "Bibliografia," pp. 279-281 (1861-1882). II. "Fontes para o estudo crítico," p. 281.

TEIXEIRA, BENTO (Brazil, ?-1600?)
Sousa, José Galante de. EM TORNO DO POETA BENTO TEIXEIRA. São Paulo: Instituto de Estudos Brasileiros, 1972. 115p. (Its Publicações, 24). "Bibliografia e referências," pp. 85-106. Contents: I. Edições conjuntas. II. Naufrágio. III. Prosopopéia. IV. Diálogos. V. Referências.

TEJERA, DIEGO VICENTE (Cuba, 1848-1903)
Tejera, Eduardo J. DIEGO VICENTE TEJERA: PATRIA-POETA Y PENSADOR CUBANO. ENSAYO BIOGRAFICO Y RECOPILACION PARCIAL DE SU OBRA POETICA Y POLITICA. Madrid: Compañía de Impresores Reunidos, 1981. 300p. "Bibliografía comentada," pp. 113-116. Contents: I. Libros, poesías y prosa del mismo D. V. Tejera. II. Libros, ensayos o artículos en el cual se trata sobre D. V. Tejera.

TEJERA, HUMBERTO (Venezuela, 1892-1971)
Cardozo, Poesía, pp. 210-212. Includes the poetical works of and the critical studies about the author.

TELLES, LYGIA FAGUNDES (Brazil, 1923-)
Telles, Lygia Fagundes. SELETA DE LYGIA FAGUNDES TELLES. ORGANIZAÇAO, ESTUDO E NOTAS DA PROFESSORA NELLY NOVAES COELHO. 2. ed. Rio de Janeiro: José Olympio, 1975. 151p. "Bibliografia," pp. 144-145. Contents: I. Livros. II. Estudos sôbre a autora.

THOMSON, AUGUSTO see HALMAR, AUGUSTO D'

TIGRE, MANUEL BASTOS (Brazil, 1882-1957)
Menezes, Raimundo de. BASTOS TIGRE E "LA BELLE EPOQUE." São Paulo: Edart, 1966. 395p. "Obras de Bastos Tigre," pp. 389-391. "Fontes sôbre Bastos Tigre," pp. 393-395. Bastos Tigre's "pseudônimos," are included on p. 391.

TISCORNIA, ELEUTERIO FELIPE (Argentina, 1878-1945)
"Bibliografía de don Eleuterio F. Tiscornia," BOLETIN DE LA ACADEMIA ARGENTINA DE LETRAS, 14, Núm. 52 (julio/setiembre de 1945), 373-374. Books and pamphlets only.

TORRES, ANTONIO (Brazil, 1885-1934)
ANTONIO TORRES E SEUS AMIGOS: NOTAS BIO-BIBLIOGRAFICOS SEGUIDAS DE CORRESPONDENCIA POR GASTAO CRULS. São Paulo: Companhia Editôra Nacional, 1950. 352p. "Antônio Tôrres, notas bio-bibliográficos," pp. 1-80.

TORRES, CARLOS ARTURO (Colombia, 1867-1911)
Torres, Carlos Arturo. HACIA EL FUTURO. PROLOGO Y NOTAS DE ERMILO ABREU GOMEZ. Washington, D.C.: Unión Panamericana, 1949. 58p. (Escritos de América). Contents: I. Obras de Carlos Arturo Torres, pp. 55-56. II. Selecciones de su obra, pp. 57-58. III. Estudios sobre Carlos Arturo Torres, p. 58.

TORRES, VICTOR (Chile, 1847-)
Escudero, p. 307. Criticism.

TORRES BODET, JAIME (Mexico, 1902-1974)
Arce, David N. SIN TREGUA Y CON FERVOR: LA OBRA DE JAIME TORRES BODET. México: Biblioteca Nacional, 1958. 23p. (Bibliografías mexicanas contemporáneas, 7). "Obras," pp. 15-18. Coverage is 1918-1958.
Carballo, Emmanuel. JAIME TORRES BODET. México, D.F.: Empresas Editoriales, S.A., 1968. 323p. "Bibliografía directa," pp. 289-293. I. Poesía. II. Prosa narrativa. III. Ensayo, crítica y memorias. IV. Discursos. V. Antologías. VI. En antologías. VII. Prólogos. VIII. Traducciones. "Bibliografía indirecta," pp. 293-321. Criticism.
Flores, BEH, pp. 296-297. Contents: I. Edición principal. II. Otras ediciones. III. Referencias. IV. Bibliografía selecta (criticism).
Foster, Mex. Lit., pp. 333-340. Contents: I. Bibliographies. II. Critical Monographs and Dissertations. III. Critical Essays.

TORRES RIOSECO, ARTURO (Chile, 1897-1971)
Escudero, Alfonso M., and Elena Castedo. "Arturo Torres Rioseco," ATENEA, (Santiago de Chile), Año 43, Tomo 164, Núm. 414 (octubre/diciembre de 1966), 145-159. "Lista de libros y folletos," pp. 153-156. The list is by year, 1921-1965.

TORRES RUBIO, DIEGO DE (Peru, 1547-1638)
San Román, Amanda. "BIOBIBLIOGRAFIA DE DIEGO TORRES RUBIO." Tesis. Lima: Biblioteca Nacional, Escuela de Bibliotecarios, 1960.

TORRIENTE BRAU, PABLO DE LA (Cuba and Puerto Rico, 1901-1936)
Abad, Diana. "Pablo de la Torriente-Brau: Bibliografía activa," UNIVERSIDAD DE LA HABANA, Núm. 206 (abril/diciembre de 1977), 157-194. 261 items. Contents: I. Bibliografía activa," pp. 163-190 (by year, 1925-1936). II. "Ediciones de sus obras," pp. 191-194 (by year, 1938-1975).
Foster, Cuban Lit., p. 457. Critical Essays.

TORUNO, JUAN FELIPE (Nicaragua, 1898-)
Jirón Terán, José. "Bibliografía de Juan Felipe Toruño," BOLETIN NICARAGUENSE DE BIBLIOGRAFIA Y DOCUMENTA-

CION, Núm. 16 (marzo/abril de 1977), 57-59. 35 items. Contents: I. Poesía. II. Novela. III. Cuento. IV. Ensayo. V. Crónica. VI. Crítica. Periodical and newspaper articles are excluded from the bibliography.

TOUSSAINT, MANUEL (Mexico, 1890-1955)
Carrera Stampa, Manuel. "Bibliografías mexicanas contemporáneas. I. Don Manuel Toussaint y Ritter (1890-1955)," BOLETIN DE LA BIBLIOTECA NACIONAL (México), 2ª época, 7, Núm. 2 (abril/junio de 1956), 3-52. 283 entries. Contents: I. Obras literarias. II. Poesías. III. Estudios de crítica literaria. IV. Artículos de crítica literaria. V. Reseñas de crítica literaria. VI. Obras acerca de historia. VII. Artículos acerca de historia del arte en México. VIII. Estudios en colaboraciones acerca de historia del arte en México. IX. Reseñas de crítica sobre arte. X. Prólogos en obras de arte. XI. Obras y artículos históricos y bibliográficos. XII. Crítica histórica. XIII. Estudios biográficos. XIV. Estudios acerca de tipografía y periodismo en México. XV. Estudios folklóricos. XVI. Reimpresión de libros y documentos. XVII. Varios. XVIII. Obras inéditas. XIX. Obras en prensa. XX. Estudios y artículos sobre don Manuel.
Mantecón, José Ignacio. BIBLIOGRAFIA DE MANUEL TOUSSAINT. México, D.F.: UNAM, 1957. 36p. (ANALES DEL INSTITUTO DE INVESTIGACIONES ESTETICAS, Núm. 25, 1957, suplemento 1). "Bibliografía," pp. 9-31 (works are arranged by year, 1914-1956). "Indice de materias," pp. 35-36.

TRIANA, JOSE (Cuba, 1931/33-)
Foster, Cuban Lit., pp. 458-459. Contents: I. Critical Monograph and Dissertation. II. Critical Essays.

TRINIDADE, SOLANO (Brazil, 1908-1973)
Porter, p. 270. Contents: I. Writings. II. References, Critical and Biographical.

- U -

URBANEJA ACHELPOHL, LUIS MANUEL (Venezuela, 1873-1937)
Caracas. Universidad Católica "Andrés Bello." Seminario de Literatura Venezolana. CONTRIBUCION A LA BIBLIOGRAFIA DE LUIS MANUEL URBANEJA ACHELPOHL, 1873-1937. Caracas: Gobernación del Distrito Federal, 1971. 113p. (Colección bibliografías, 8). 335 citations. Contents: I. Referencias bibliográficas. II. Obras mayores. A. Novela. B. Cuento. III. Miscelánea. IV. Obra dispersa (mainly journal and newspaper articles). V. Biografía y crítica (libros, folletos, capítulos, artículos y referencias sobre el autor y su obra).

URBINA, LUIS G. (Mexico, 1868-1934)
Flores, BEH, pp. 297-299. Contents: I. Ediciones principales. II. Otras ediciones. III. Referencias. IV. Bibliografía selecta (criticism).
Rosenbaum, Sidonia C. "Luis G. Urbina: bibliografía," REVISTA HISPANICA MODERNA, Año 1, Núm. 1 (octubre de 1934), 101-102. Contents: I. Ediciones. A. Poesía. B. Prosa. C. Artículos y prólogos. II. Estudios.

URETA, ALBERTO (Peru, 1885-1966)
Corcurra, Arturo. "Biobibliografía de Alberto Ureta," REVISTA PERUANA DE CULTURA (Lima), Núm. 3 (1964), 15-17. Works, by year, 1885-1964.
Prieto Celi, Pilar. "Alberto Ureta," ANUARIO BIBLIOGRAFICO PERUANO, 1964/1966, 688-718. Contents: I. Biografía. II. Otras publicaciones. III. Libros y folletos. IV. Poesías. V. Artículos y ensayos. VI. Traducciones. VII. Cartas, oficios, etc. VIII. Reportajes. IX. Recitales. X. Referencias, retratos, caricaturas. XI. Necrológicas y homenajes póstumas.

URUETA, MARGARITA (Mexico, 1918-)
Corvalán, p. 103. Includes critical studies on the author.

USIGLI, RODOLFO (Mexico, 1905-1979)
Flores, BEH, pp. 299-301. Contents: I. Edición principal. II. Otras ediciones. III. Referencias. IV. Bibliografía selecta.
Foster, Mex. Lit., pp. 340-344. Contents: I. Bibliographies. II. Critical Monographs and Dissertations. III. Critical Essays.
Scott, Wilder P. "Toward an Usigli Bibliography (1931-1971)," LATIN AMERICAN THEATRE REVIEW, 6, No. 1 (1972), 53-62. 237 entries. Contents: I. Plays by Usigli. II. Other Writings by Usigli. III. Translations by Usigli. IV. Published Translations of Usigli's Plays. V. Critical Writings about Usigli (includes Ph.D. dissertations).

USLAR PIETRI, ARTURO (Venezuela, 1906-)
Caracas. Universidad Católica Andrés Bello. Escuela de Letras. Centro de Investigaciones Literarias. CONTRIBUCION A LA BIBLIOGRAFIA DE ARTURO USLAR PIETRI. Caracas, 1973 or 1974. 396p. (Colección Bibliografías, 10). 1,882 references. Contents: I. Referencias bibliográficas. II. Obras mayores. A. Novela. B. Cuento. C. Ensayo. D. Biografías. E. Teatro. III. Miscelánea. IV. Obras dispersas. V. Biografía y crítica (libros, folletos, artículos y referencias sobre el autor y su obra).
Flores, BEH, pp. 301-303. Contents: I. Edición principal. II. Otras ediciones. III. Bibliografía selecta (criticism).
Foster, 20th Century, pp. 193-194. Contents: I. Critical Books. II. Critical Essays.
García G., Dunia. "Contribución a la bibliografía del doctor Arturo Uslar Pietri," BOLETIN DE LA BIBLIOTECA GENERAL

(Universidad del Zulia, Maracaibo), Años 10/11, Núm. 17-18 (Agosto 1970-junio 1971), 287-317. Bibliography does not pretend to be a definitive work; only most important works are included under the following categories: I. Curriculum Vitae: Arturo Uslar Pietri. II. Obras del autor. A. Cuentos. B. Novelas. C. Descripciones y viajes. D. Ensayos y estudios. E. Teatro. F. Selecciones. G. Reediciones de conjunto. H. Discursos-conferencias. I. Introducciones, prólogos, orientaciones. II. Obras sobre el autor.

Lovera de Sola, Roberto J. "Los 70 años de Uslar Pietri (Intento de ordenación bibliográfica), LIBROS AL DIA (Caracas), Año 1, Núm. 20 (1/15 de junio de 1976), 21-29. Contents: I. Compilaciones generales. II. Cuento. III. Novela. IV. Poesía. V. Teatro. VI. Ensayo. A. Misceláneas. B. Arte. C. Economía. D. Educación. E. Política. F. Literario. G. Historia.

Miliani, Domingo. USLAR PIETRI: RENOVADOR DEL CUENTO VENEZOLANO. Caracas: Monte Avila Editores, 1969. 183p. "Aportación a la bibliografía de Arturo Uslar Pietri," pp. 165-177. Contents: I. Obra narrativa. A. Cuento. B. Novela. II. Obra ensayística. III. Teatro. IV. Discursos y conferencias. V. Compilaciones y antologías. VI. Hemerografía (algunos ensayos publicados en revistas y periódicos). "Estudios y ensayos sobre su obra," pp. 179-183.

Uslar Pietri, Arturo. LAS LANZAS COLORADAS Y CUENTOS SELECTOS. PROLOGO Y CRONOLOGIA: DOMINGO MILIANI. Caracas: Biblioteca Ayacucho, 1979. 477p. "Bibliografía," pp. 471-477. Contents: I. Obras de Arturo Uslar Pietri. II. Estudios sobre Antonio Uslar Pietri.

Vivas, José Luis. LA CUENTISTICA DE ARTURO USLAR PIETRI. Caracas: Universidad Central de Venezuela, Facultad de Humanidades y Educación, 1963. 153p. Contents: I. "Obras de Arturo Uslar Pietri," pp. 145-150. A. Libros de cuentos. B. Novelas (includes translations). C. Antologías. D. Ensayos y artículos (sueltos o en libros). E. Introducciones, prólogos, orientaciones. F. Teatro. G. Discursos. II. "Obras sobre Arturo Uslar Pietri," pp. 151-153.

- V -

VACAREZZA, ALBERTO (Argentina, 1888-1957)

Franco, Lily. ALBERTO VACAREZZA. Buenos Aires: Ediciones Culturales Argentinas, 1975. 113p. "Obras de Alberto Vacarezza," pp. 107-113. Contents: I. Teatro (Chronologically arranged). II. Canciones populares.

VAISSE, EMILIO see EMETH, OMER

VALDELOMAR, ABRAHAM (Peru, 1888-1919)

Angeles Caballero, César A. VALDELOMAR: VIDA Y OBRA.

Lima: P. L. Villanueva, 1964. 188p. "Derrotero bibliográfico," pp. 179-188. Contents: I. Prosa. A. Cuento. B. Novela. C. Crónica. D. Biografía novelada. E. Ensayo. F. Prosas cívico-patrióticas. II. Poesía. III. Antología. IV. Sobre Abraham Valdelomar. A. Libros y folletos. B. Artículos en publicaciones periódicas.

Flores, BEH, pp. 303-305. Contents: I. Ediciones. II. Referencias. III. Bibliografía selecta (criticism).

Foster, Peruvian Lit., pp. 238-244. Contents: I. Bibliographies. II. Critical Monographs and Dissertations. III. Critical Essays.

Tamayo Vargas, Augusto. "Abraham Valdelomar: bibliografía," REVISTA HISPANICA MODERNA, 35, Núm. 1/2 (1969), 45-71. Contents: I. Ediciones. A. Antologías. II. Estudios. III. Colaboración periodística (by title of the newspaper or journal).

Valdelomar, Abraham. OBRAS. TEXTOS Y DIBUJOS REUNIDOS POR WILLY F. PINTO GAMBOA. PROLOGO DE LUIS ALBERTO SANCHEZ. Lima: Editorial Pizarro, 1979. 913p. "Bibliografía de Abraham Valdelomar," pp. 889-913. Contents: I. Diarios y revistas de Lima y provincias (works are listed by newspaper or journal title and then by year). II. Diarios de provincias (same format as part I). III. Revistas extranjeras (same format as part I).

Xammar, Luis Fabbio. VALDELOMAR: SIGNO. Lima: Ediciones Sphinx, 1940. 106p. "Contribución a la bibliografía de Abraham Valdelomar," pp. 95-106. Contents: I. Diarios y revistas de Lima (by journal or paper, date, title of work, and genre of work). II. Diarios de provincias (same format as in section I).

VALDES, GABRIEL DE LA CONCEPCION see "PLACIDO"

VALDES, JOSE MANUEL (Peru, 1767-1844)

Jackson, Afro-Spanish, pp. 114-115. Contents: I. Works. II. Criticism. Annotated.

Romero, Fernando. "José Manuel Valdés, Great Peruvian Mulatto," PHYLON, 3 (1942), 297-319. "Bibliography of José Manuel Valdés," pp. 317-319. Contents: I. Works by Valdés. A. Medical Works. B. Literary Works. II. Works about Valdés.

VALENCIA, GUILLERMO (Colombia, 1873-1943)

Anderson, pp. 149-152. Critical Essays.

ESTUDIOS: EDICION EN HOMENAJE A GUILLERMO VALENCIA, 1873-1973. A CARGO DE HERNAN TORRES. Cali: Carvajal y Cía., 1976. 438p. "Bibliografía selecta," pp. 403-420. Includes only works about Valencia and his writings.

Flores, BEH, pp. 305-306. Contents: I. Ediciones principales. II. Otras ediciones. III. Referencias. IV. Bibliografía selecta (criticism).

Karsen, Sonja. GUILLERMO VALENCIA: COLOMBIAN POET, 1873-1943. New York: Hispanic Institute in the United States,

1951. 269p. Bibliography of Guillermo Valencia. A. Books and Pamphlets. B. Poetry in Periodicals--Original and Translations. C. Speeches. D. Articles. E. Unedited Works. II. Studies. A. Poems on Valencia. B. Valencia in Translations. III. General Works. A. Studies. B. Anthologies.

Romero Rojas, Francisco José. "Bibliografía de Guillermo Valencia," NOTICIAS CULTURALES (Instituto Caro y Cuervo, Bogotá), Núm. 153 (octubre de 1973), 13-18. Does not try to be exhaustive but attempts to supplement and update the Karsen bibliographic material. Contents: I. Escritos de Guillermo Valencia (books only). II. Escritos sobre Guillermo Valencia (books and articles).

VALLE, FELIX (Peru, 1892-1950)

"Félix del Valle," ANUARIO BIBLIOGRAFICO PERUANO, 1949/1950, 367-372. Contents: I. Libros y folletos. II. Otras ediciones. III. Artículos. IV. Referencias. V. Artículos necrológicos.

VALLE, JOSE CECILIO DEL (Guatemala, 1777-1834)

Valle, José Cecilio del. ESCRITOS DE JOSE CECILIO DEL VALLE: UNA SELECCION. Washington, D.C.: Secretaría General, Organización de los Estados Americanos, 1981. 255p. Contents: "Bibliografía básica comentada de y sobre José Cecilio del Valle," pp. 242-253. Contents: I. La Ilustración en el Reino de Guatemala. II. Biografías de Valle. III. Escritos y proyecciones. IV. Bibliografía especial de Valle. V. Periódicos en que Valle tuvo activa participación.

VALLE, JUVENCIO (Pseudonym of GILBERTO CONCHA RIFFO) (Chile, 1900-)

"Cartillas biobibliográficas de autores chilenos: Juvencio Valle, seud. Gilberto Concha Riffo. Villa-Almagro, 1900. Poeta," BOLETIN DEL INSTITUTO DE LITERATURA CHILENA (Universidad de Chile, Santiago), Año 4, Núm. 11 (diciembre de 1965), 12-17. Contents: I. Obra. II. Referencias. III. Vida.

Foster, Chilean Lit., pp. 214-215. Contents: I. Bibliographies. II. Critical Books and Theses. III. Critical Essays.

VALLE, RAFAEL HELIODORO (Honduras, 1891-1959)

Romero de Valle, Emilia. "Bibliografía sumaria de Rafael Heliodoro Valle," in Oscar Acosta's RAFAEL HELIODORO VALLE: VIDA Y OBRA. BIOGRAFIA, ESTUDIO CRITICO, BIBLIOGRAFIA Y ANTOLOGIA DE UN INTELECTUAL HONDURENO (Tegucigalpa, Honduras: Universidad Nacional Autónoma de Honduras, 1964), pp. 130-133. Contents: I. Poemas. II. Relatos. III. Historia. IV. Bibliografía. V. Antología. VI. Política. VII. Libros en prensa. VIII. En preparación. Newspaper and periodical articles are not included.

Spell, Lota M. "Rafael Heliodoro Valle (1891-1959)," HISPANIC AMERICAN HISTORICAL REVIEW, 40 (1960), 424-430. Includes a selected bibliography of his works.

VALLE GOYCOCHEA, LUIS (Peru, 1911-1953)

Córdova Carrasco, Jorge. "BIBLIOGRAFIA DE LUIS VALLE GOYCOCHEA." Tesis. Lima: Biblioteca Nacional, Escuela de Bibliotecarios, 1958.

"Luis Valle Goycochea," ANUARIO BIBLIOGRAFICO PERUANO 1953/1954, 400-405. Contents: I. Biografía. II. Libros y folletos. III. Otras publicaciones. IV. Poesía. V. Prosa. VI. Referencias.

VALLE Y CAVIEDES, JUAN DEL (Peru, 1651?-1697?)

Cáceres Sánchez, María Leticia. LA PERSONALIDAD Y OBRA DE D. JUAN DEL VALLE Y CAVIEDES. Arequipa: Imp. Editorial "El Sol," 1975. 280p. "Selecciones bibliográficas sobre Caviedes (incluye los códices de la obra del Caviedes), pp. 269-280.

Flores, BEH, pp. 53-54. Contents: I. Ediciones. II. Bibliografía selecta (criticism).

Foster, Peruvian Lit., pp. 245-248. Contents: I. Bibliographies. II. Critical Monographs and Dissertations. III. Critical Essays.

Reedy, Daniel R. THE POETIC ART OF JUAN DEL VALLE Y CAVIEDES. Chapel Hill, N.C.: University of North Carolina Press, 1964. 170p. (Studies in the Romance Languages and Literature, 46). Appendix I, pp. 150-157: Alphabetical Listing of All of the Poems Written by Caviedes (265 items). A. Amorous Poetry. B. Poetry of Social Satire. 1. Medical Satire. 2. Satire of Other Professions and Types. 3. Feminine Satire. C. Religious Poetry. D. Miscellaneous Poetry. Appendix II, pp. 158-165: Descriptions of 8 Known Mss. of Caviedes' Works. List of Works Consulted, pp. 166-170.

VALLEJO, CESAR (Peru, 1892-1938)

Flores, BEH, pp. 174-176, 184. Contents: I. Ediciones principales. II. Otras ediciones. III. Referencias. IV. Bibliografía selecta (criticism).

_______. APROXIMACIONES A CESAR VALLEJO. SIMPOSIO DIRIGIDO POR ANGEL FLORES. New York: Las Américas Pub. Co., 1971. 2vs. "Bibliografía," II, pp. 429-442. Contents: I. Obras de César Vallejo. II. Estudios y artículos acerca de Vallejo y su obra.

_______. CESAR VALLEJO: SINTESIS BIOGRAFICA, BIBLIOGRAFIA E INDICE DE POEMAS. México, D.F.: La Red de Jonas, 1982. 148p. "Bibliografía," pp. 121-131. Contents: I. Ediciones principales. II. Otras ediciones. III. Bibliografía selecta (criticism).

Foster, Peruvian Lit., pp. 249-282. Contents: I. Bibliographies. II. Critical Monographs and Dissertations. III. Critical Essays.

Foti, Luis. "Bibliografía vallejiana," AULA VALLEJO (Córdoba, Argentina), Núm. 1 (1961), 137-144. Contents: I. Ediciones. A. Libros. B. Artículos y prosa suelta. C. Teatro. D. Cuento. E. Poesías sueltas. F. Antologías. II. Traducciones. III. Correspondencia.

______. ______. AULA VALLEJO, Núm. 5/7 (1963/1965), 444-497. Contents: I. Libros. II. Estudios, ensayos, prólogos. III. Homenajes colectivos. IV. Artículos, discursos. V. Reportajes sobre o en relación con Vallejo. VI. Reseñas y comentarios de libros y publicaciones de y sobre Vallejo. VII. Juicios y menciones de Vallejo en trabajos panorámicos o do otro género. VIII. Notas, noticias, incidencias, polémicas.... IX. Libros, ensayos, artículos ... en otros idiomas. X. Poemas dedicados a César Vallejo.

Monguió, Luis. CESAR VALLEJO: VIDA Y OBRA. Lima: Editor Perú Nuevo, 1971. 252p. "Bibliografía," pp. 167-196. Reprinted from REVISTA HISPANICA MODERNA, Año 16, Núm. 1/4 (enero/diciembre de 1950), 83-98. Contents: I. Ediciones. A. Libros, poesías sueltas: recogidas después en libros, no recogidas en libros, reproducidas de libros. B. Artículos y prosa suelta. C. Obras inéditas. D. Traducciones, traductor. II. Estudios. III. Iconografía.

Roggiano, Alfredo. "Mínima guía bibliográfica: César Vallejo," REVISTA IBEROAMERICANA, 36, Núm. 71 (abril/junio de 1970), 353-358. Contents: I. Bibliografía. II. Vida y persona. III. Textos vallejianos. IV. Crítica vallejiana (selección). A descriptive bibliography.

Sobrevilla, David. "Las ediciones y estudios vallejianos, 1971-1979," in CESAR VALLEJO: ACTAS DEL COLOQUIO INTERNACIONAL FREIE UNIVERSITAT BERLIN, 7-9 JUNIO 1979 (Tübingen: Niemeyer, 1981), pp. 64-94. Bibliographic essay.

Vallejo, César. OBRA POETICA COMPLETA. EDICION, PROLOGO Y CRONOLOGIA: ENRIQUE BALLON AGUIRRE. Caracas: Biblioteca Ayacucho, 1979. 329p. "Bibliografía," pp. 315-329. Contents: I. Obras de César Vallejo. A. Poesía. 1. Poemas no recogidos en libro. 2. Versiones primeras. a. De Los heraldos negros. b. De Trilce. c. De Poemas humanos. 3. Poemarios. B. Prosa. 1. Narración. 2. Teatro. 3. Tesis y ensayos. D. Crónicas. (by journal or newspaper). E. Varia. F. Traducciones. G. Obras completas. II. Estudios sobre César Vallejo. A. Libros y artículos. B. Crestomatías y revistas especializadas.

Villanueva de Puccinelli, Elsa. "Bibliografía selecta de César Vallejo," VISION DEL PERU, Núm. 4 (julio de 1969), 58-65. Contents: I. La obra de Vallejo. II. Artículos y crónicas de Vallejo. III. Libros y folletos sobre Vallejo.

VALLEJO, JOSE JOAQUIN (Chile, 1809/11-1858)

Foster, Chilean Lit., pp. 215-216. Contents: I. Critical Books and Theses. II. Critical Essays.

VARELA, JUAN DE LA CRUZ (Argentina, 1794-1839)

Foster, Arg. Lit., pp. 714-716. Contents: I. Critical Monographs. II. Critical Essays.

VARGAS LLOSA, MARIO (Peru, 1936-)

Flores, BEH, pp. 176-180. Contents: I. Ediciones. II. Referencias. III. Bibliografía selecta (criticism).

Flores, NH, v. 4, pp. 517-521. Contents: I. Ediciones de su narrativa. II. Referencias. III. Antologías críticas. IV. Bibliografía selecta (criticism).

Foster, Peruvian Lit., pp. 283-303. Contents: I. Bibliographies. II. Critical Monographs and Dissertations. III. Critical Essays.

Foster, 20th Century, pp. 194-203. Contents: I. Critical Books. II. Critical Essays.

Haraszti, Zsuzsa. A MEGALAZAS PROBLEMATIKAJA MARIO VARGAS REGENYEIBEN. Budapest: Akadémiai Kiadó, 1977. 111p. An appendix includes a complete list of Vargas Llosa's works in Hungarian.

"Mario Vargas Llosa in BOOKS ABROAD/WORLD LITERATURE TODAY (1965-1968)," WORLD LITERATURE TODAY, 52 (1978), 75.

Martín, José Luis. LA NARRATIVA DE VARGAS LLOSA: ACERCAMIENTO ESTILISTICO. Madrid: Editorial Gredos, 1974. 281p. "Bibliografía selecta," pp. 265-272. 99 items. Contents: I. Obra narrativa de Mario Vargas Llosa. II. Crítica sobre Mario Vargas Llosa (lista mínima). A. Obras de conjunto. B. Estudios y artículos fundamentales. C. Algunas reseñas y otros trabajos.

Oviedo, José Miguel. MARIO VARGAS LLOSA: LA INVENCION DE UNA REALIDAD. Barcelona: Barral Editores, 1970. 272p. "Bibliografía," pp. 251-272. Contents: I. Obra del autor. A. Obra narrativa. B. Otras obras recogidas en libros. C. Crónicas, notas y artículos dispersos del autor. D. Reportajes. E. Mesas redondas y encuestas. II. Otras sobre el autor. A. Obras y artículos de referencia. B. Trabajos artículos y reseñas. III. Addenda bibliográfica (1970).

_______. "Selected Bibliography (1959-1977)," WORLD LITERATURE TODAY, 52 (1978), 71-75. Contents: I. Narrative Works by Mario Vargas Llosa. II. Other Books by the Author. III. Essays and Critical Articles by the Author. IV. Discussions, Interviews, Addresses. V. English Translations of Vargas Llosa's Works. VI. Translation into other Languages (by language). VII. Works and Selected Articles (criticism).

Vargas Llosa, Mario. CONTRA VIENTO Y MAREA (1962-1982). TESTIMONIO DE LA VIGILANTE ACTITUD MORAL DEL ESCRITOR ANTE LA HISTORIA. Buenos Aires: Sudamericana/Planeta, 1984. 462p. "Bibliografía," pp. 449-452. List of essays in journals, by year, 1962-1981.

VARGAS VILA, JOSE MARIA (Colombia, 1860-1933)

Porras Collantes, pp. 743-786. Includes works of and critical studies about the author.

VARNHAGEN, FRANCISCO ADOLFO DE (Brazil, 1816-1878)

Fleiuss, Max. PAGINAS DE HISTORIA. 2. ed. Rio de Janeiro:

Impresa Nacional, 1930. 930p. "Bibliografia de Varnhagen," pp. 423-436.

Fontes, Armando Ortega. BIBLIOGRAFIA DE VARNHAGEN. Rio de Janeiro: Ministério das Relações Exteriores, 1945. 42p. 141 entries by year, 1839-1938.

Horch, Hans. FRANCISCO ADOLFO DE VARNHAGEN: SUBSIDIOS PARA UMA BIBLIOGRAFIA. São Paulo: Editôras Unidas, 1982. 454p. A descriptive bibliography containing 505 entries. Contents: I. Livros e publicações avulsas," pp. 25-216. II. Colaboração na Revista do Instituto Histórico e Geográfico Brasileiro," pp. 217-298. III. Colaboração na imprensa periódica," pp. 299-359. IV. Correspondência, discursos e relatório de carácter diplomático," pp. 361-413. The work includes the following indices: name, title, language, biographical, chronological, place of publication, publishers and printers, periodical, and geographic.

Lessa, Clado Ribeiro de. "Colaboração de Varnhagen no O Panorama," REVISTA DO INSTITUTO HISTORICO E GEOGRAFICO BRASILEIRO, Núm. 193 (1946), 105-109.

Magalhães, Basílio de. "Bibliografia varnhageniana," REVISTA DA ACADEMIA BRASILEIRA DE LETRAS, Núm. 83 (novembro de 1928), 332-374. Contents: I. "Literatura," pp. 354-358. A. Livros. B. Em revistas. II. "Crítica e polêmica," pp. 362-365. A. Livros. B. Na Revista do Instituto Histórico e Geográfico Brasileiro. C. Em jornaes de Lisbôa. III. "Publicações referentes a Varnhagen," pp. 369-374. A. De edições brasileiras. 1. Em livros. 2. Na Revista do Instituto Geográfico e Histórico Brasileiro. 3. Em outras revistas, jornaes e relatórios. B. De autores estrangeiros. 1. Em livros. 2. Em publicações periódicas. C. Iconografia. D. Homenagens especiaes.

VARONA, ENRIQUE JOSE (Cuba, 1849-1933)

Ferrer Canales, José. IMAGEN DE VARONA. Santiago de Cuba: Universidad de Oriente, 1964. 350p. "Bibliografía de Varona," pp. 337-348. Contents: I. Obras (newspaper and periodical articles excluded). II. Antologías. III. Estudios (including studies about Varona and his work).

Foster, Cuban Lit., pp. 465-478. Contents: I. Bibliographies. II. Critical Monographs and Dissertations. III. Critical Essays.

Peraza y Sarausa, Fermín. "Bibliografía de Enrique José Varona," REVISTA BIMESTRE CUBANA (1930-1932), 26, pp. 161-177; 27, pp. 100-116, 226-250, 427-454; 28, pp. 94-131, 278-315, 459-473; 29, pp. 130-157, 306-313, 425-474; 30, pp. 120-158, 302-307. Reprinted as a monograph; La Habana: Molína y Cía., 1932. 299p. (Colección cubana de libros y documentos inéditos o raros, dirigida por Fernando Ortiz, 11). This annotated bibliography consists of 1,880 titles published in books, pamphlets, periodicals and newspapers.

_______. "Bibliografía de Enrique José Varona (Complemento)," REVISTA BIMESTRE CUBANA, 39, pp. 240-272, 460-476; 40, pp. 133-146, 310-319; 41, pp. 113-122, 304-316; 1937/38. 570 titles; same format as above.

_______. "Bibliografía del Primer Centenario del Nacimiento de Enrique José Varona," in HOMENAJE A ENRIQUE JOSE VARONA EN EL CENTENARIO DE SU NATALICIO (La Habana: Publicaciones del Ministerio de Educación, Dirección de Cultura, 1951), v. 2, pp. 177-189. Annotated bibliography for 1949-1950. Contents: I. Bibliografía activa. II. Bibliografía pasiva.

VASCONCELOS, JOSE (Mexico, 1882-1959)

Arce, David N. "Bibliografías mexicanas contemporáneas. VI. José Vasconcelos," BOLETIN DE LA BIBLIOTECA NACIONAL (México), 2ª época, 8, Núm. 4 (octubre/diciembre de 1957), 31-44. Only Vasconcelos' books are listed.

Bar-Lewan, Itzhak. INTRODUCCION CRITICO-BIBLIOGRAFICO A JOSE VASCONCELOS (1882-1959). Madrid: Ediciones Latinoamericanos, 1965. 209p. Contents: I. Bibliografía cronológico de José Vasconcelos, pp. 201-204. II. Bibliografía selecta sobre José Vasconcelos, pp. 205-207. Books only. Reprinted in his: José Vasconcelos. Vida y obra. México, D.F.: Clásica Selecta Editora Librera, Editora Intercontinental, 1965. 248p.

Beer, Gabriella de. JOSE VASCONCELOS AND HIS WORLD. New York: Las Américas Publishing Co., 1966. 450p. "Bibliography," pp. 387-450. Contents: I. Books by José Vasconcelos. II. Newspaper and Magazine Articles by José Vasconcelos. III. Prologues and Introductions. IV. General Studies and References. V. Particular Studies on Vasconcelos.

Foster, David W. "A Checklist of Criticism on José Vasconcelos," LOS ENSAYISTAS, Núm. 14/15 (1983), 177-212.

Sierra, Carlos J. "José Vasconcelos: Hemerografía," BOLETIN BIBLIOGRAFICO DE LA SECRETARIA DE HACIENDA Y CREDITO PUBLICO, 11, Núm. 311 (15 de junio de 1965), 6-34. 1,526 items.

VASCONCELOS, JOSE ("EL NEGRITO POETA") (Mexico, 1722?-1760?)

Jackson, Afro-Spanish, pp. 115-116. Contents: I. Works. II. Criticism. Annotated entries.

VAZ FERREIRA, CARLOS (Uruguay, 1872-1958)

MacColl, Norah Albanell. "Bibliografía de Vaz Ferreira," REVISTA INTERAMERICANA DE BIBLIOGRAFIA, 8, Núm. 3 (julio/setiembre de 1958), 245-255. Contents: I. Obras. A. Libros y folletos. B. Colaboraciones en revistas y otras publicaciones. C. Obras completas. II. Estudios críticos sobre Vaz Ferreira. III. Bibliografía sobre Vaz Ferreira. 117 entries are listed.

VAZ FERREIRA, MARIA EUGENIA (Uruguay, 1875-1924)

MARIA EUGENIA VAZ FERREIRA, 1875-1975: BIBLIOGRAFIA. Montevideo: Biblioteca Nacional, 1975. 48p. A homenaje exposition. Contents: I. Testimonios personales. A. Manuscritos. B. Correspondencia. C. Varios. II. Obras. A. Obras (todas las ediciones). B. Publicaciones en libros, diarios y revistas. C. Traducciones. III. Crítica. A. Ensayos críticos publicados en libros. B. Ensayos críticos publicados en diarios y revistas. C. Otros artículos. IV. Iconografía. A. Del autor. B. Retratos y dibujos. C. El autor con otras personas. D. Familiares. E. Otras fotografías.

VEDIA, LEONIDAS DE (Argentina, 1901-1975)

Becco, Horacio Jorge. "Bibliografía de don Léonidas de Vedia, 1901-1975," BOLETIN DE LA ACADEMIA ARGENTINA DE LETRAS, 40, Núm. 157/158 (julio/diciembre de 1975), 313-315. Contents: I. Libros. II. Discursos. III. Prólogos.

VEGA, "EL INCA" GARCILASO DE LA (Peru, 1539-1616)

Castanien, Donald G. "EL INCA" GARCILASO DE LA VEGA. New York: Twayne Publishers, 1969. 154p. "Selected Bibliography," pp. 149-150. Contents: I. Primary Sources (principal editions of the works of Garcilaso). II. Secondary Sources.

Durand, José. "Ediciones de La Florida," in "El Inca" Garcilaso de la Vega's LA FLORIDA DEL INCA (México, D.F.: Fondo de Cultura Económica, 1956), pp. lxxvii-lxxxv. Contents: I. Ediciones en español (1605-1829). II. Antologías en español (1910-1938). III. Traducciones al francés (1670-1751). IV. Traducciones al alemán (1753-1796). V. Traducciones inglesas (1881-1951). VI. Traducción flamenca (1930).

Flores, BEH, pp. 54-56. Contents: I. Edición principal. II. Otras ediciones. III. Antologías. IV. Bibliografía selecta (criticism).

Foster, Peruvian Lit., pp. 120-140. Contents: I. Bibliographies. II. Critical Monographs and Dissertations. III. Critical Essays.

Gerzenstein, Ana. "Bibliografía," in "El Inca" Garcilaso de la Vega's LOS COMENTARIOS REALES (Buenos Aires: Plus Ultra, 1967), pp. 66-73. Contents: Obras del Inca Garcilaso de la Vega. A. Ediciones principales. B. Algunas ediciones posteriores. C. Algunas traducciones. D. Selecciones y antologías. II. Obras sobre el Inca Garcilaso de la Vega.

Jákfalvi-Leiva, Susana. TRADUCCION, ESCRITURA Y VIOLENCIA COLONIZADORA: UN ESTUDIO DE LA OBRA DEL INCA GARCILASO. Syracuse, N.Y.: FAES, 1984. 134p. (Colonial Latin America Series, 7). "Bibliografía consultada," pp. 121-124. Contents: I. Obras completas. II. Estudios críticos sobre el Inca Garcilaso y su obra.

Porras Barrenechea, Raúl. "EL INCA" GARCILASO EN MONTILLA (1561-1614). Lima: Universidad Nacional Mayor de San Marcos, 1955. "Bibliografía sobre Garcilaso," pp. 297-300. Entries are by year, 1847-1955.

Tauro, Alberto. "Bibliografía del Inca Garcilaso de la Vega," DOCUMENTA (Lima), 4 (1965), 393-437. Contents: I. Obra del Inca Garcilaso (Editions for 1590-1964). II. Estudios sobre la personalidad y la obra del Inca Garcilaso. III. Garcilaso y Blas Valera. IV. Indice onomástico.

Varner, John Grier. "EL INCA:" THE LIFE AND TIMES OF GARCILASO DE LA VEGA. Austin: University of Texas Press, 1968. 413p. "A Selected Bibliography," pp. 391-400. Contents: I. Archives and Libraries Consulted. II. Collections. III. Books. IV. Periodicals.

VEGA URIBE, DANIEL EMILIANO DE LA (Chile, 1892-1971)

"Cartillas biobibliográficas de autores chilenos: Daniel Emiliano de la Vega Uribe. Quilpe, 1892. Poeta, dramaturgo, novelista, cuentista, y periódista," BOLETIN DEL INSTITUTO DE LITERATURA CHILENA (Universidad de Chile, Santiago), Año 5, Núm. 12 (julio de 1966), 18-27. Contents: I. Obra. II. Referencia. III. Vida. IV. Otros datos (entrevistas literaria).

VERACRUZ, (FRAY) ALONSO DE LA (Mexico, ca. 1504-1584)

Bolaño e Isla, Amancio. CONTRIBUCION AL ESTUDIO BIOBIBLIOGRAFICO DE FRAY ALONSO DE LA VERA CRUZ. PROLOGO DE AGUSTIN MILLARES CARLO. México, D.F.: Antigua Librería Robredo, 1947. 156p. (Biblioteca Histórico Mexicana de Obras Inéditas, 21). "Descripción bibliográfica de las obras de Fray Alonso de la Vera Cruz," pp. 45-73. A descriptive bibliography of books, manuscripts, and parts of works published later in other publications.

VERBITSKY, BERNARDO (Argentina, 1907-1978)

Foster, Arg. Lit., pp. 717-718. Critical Essays.

VERISSIMO, ERICO (Brazil, 1905-1975)

Chaves, Flávio Loureiro. ERICO VERISSIMO: REALISMO E SOCIEDADE. Porto Alegre: Editôra Globo, 1976. 185p. "Bibliografia de e sôbre Erico Veríssimo," pp. 159-183. Contents: I. Textos de ficção. A. Livros. B. Em jornais e revistas. C. Textos de literatura infantil e infante-juvenil. D. Livros de viagem. E. Autobiografia. F. Memórias. G. Ensaio. H. Artigos. I. Prefácios. J. Entrevistas e depoimentos. II. "Publicações: livros, ensaios e crônicas sôbre Erico Veríssimo.

Veríssimo, Erico. FICÇÃO COMPLETA. Rio de Janeiro: Companhia José Aguilar Editôra, 1966. 5vs. "Bibliografia," v.1, pp. 33-39. Contents: I. Obras do autor. A. Ficção. B. Viagens. C. Literatura infantil. II. Traducções. A. Em inglês. B. Em castelhano. C. Em francês. D. Em alemão. E. Em italiano. F. Em holandês. G. Em norueguês. III. Estudos, artigos e reportagens sôbre o autor.

VERISSIMO, JOSE (Brazil, 1857-1916)

Veríssimo, José. JOSE VERISSIMO: TEORIA, CRITICA E HISTORIA LITERARIA. SELEÇAO E APRESENTAÇAO DE JOAO ALEXANDRE BARBOSA. Rio de Janeiro: Livros Técnicos e

Científicos; São Paulo: Edição da Universidade de São Paulo, 1977. 287p. Contents: I. "Bibliografia de José Veríssimo," pp. 277-278. II. "Bibliografia sôbre José Veríssimo," pp. 278-279.

VIANA, JAVIER DE (Uruguay, 1868-1926)

Flores, BEH, pp. 306-308. Contents: I. Edición principal. II. Otras ediciones. III. Bibliografía selecta (criticism).

Garganigo, John F. JAVIER DE VIANA. New York: Twayne Publishers, Inc., 1972. 185p. "Selected Bibliography," pp. 174-176. Contents: I. Primary Sources. A. Books by Javier de Viana. B. Newspaper Articles. C. Poetry. D. Anthologies of Viana's Stories. II. Secondary Sources.

VICUNA CIFUENTES, JULIO (Chile, 1865-1936)

"Cartillas biobibliográficas de autores chilenos: Julio Vicuña Cifuentes. La Serena, 1865-1936, Santiago. Poeta, cuentista e investigador," BOLETIN DEL INSTITUTO DE LITERATURA CHILENA (Universidad de Chile, Santiago), Año 4, Núm. 10 (julio de 1965), 11-23. Contents: I. Obra. II. Referencias. III. Vida. IV. Otros datos.

Escudero, Alfonso M. "Don Julio Vicuña Cifuentes (1865-1936)" ATENEA (Santiago de Chile), Año 42, Tomo 160, Núm. 410 (octubre/diciembre de 1965), 229-256. "Principales obras y fuentes consultables," pp. 248-256. Contents: I. Principales obras suyas. II. Fuentes consultables (por orden cronológico). 14 items registered for I; 141 items for II.

Rojas Piña, Benjamín. "Julio Vicuña Cifuentes en LA REVISTA COMICA (1895-1898): notas bibliográficas," BOLETIN DEL INSTITUTO DE LITERATURA CHILENA (Universidad de Chile, Santiago), Año 4, Núm. 10 (julio de 1965), 2-11. 97 annotated entries.

VICUNA MACKENNA, BENJAMIN (Chile, 1831-1886)

Benelli, Alejandro. BIBLIOGRAFIA GENERAL DE VICUNA MACKENNA INTEGRADA EN LOS TRABAJOS DE RAMON BRISENO, CARLOS VICUNA MACKENNA, GUILLERMO FELIU CRUZ Y EUGENIO ORREGO VICUNA. Santiago de Chile: Prensas de la Universidad de Chile, 1940. 279p. Contents: I. E. Orrego Vicuña, "Bibliógrafos y bibliografías principales de Vicuña Mackenna," pp. 9-12; Benelli B., A., "Obras de Vicuña Mackenna," pp. 13-59; Orrega Vicuña, E., "Bibliografía de Vicuña Mackenna en la Universidad de Chile," pp. 61-68; Vicuña Mackenna, C., "Bibliografía parlamentaria de Vicuña Mackenna," pp. 69-99; Benelli B., A., C. Vicuña Mackenna, Guillermo Feliú Cruz, "Bibliografía periodística de Vicuña Mackenna," pp. 101-164. In the appendix is reproduced the "bibliografías primitivas de Vicuña Mackenna," or, rather, those works of P. Moliné, Jover, and Briseño.

Donoso, Ricardo. DON BENJAMIN VICUNA MACKENNA. SU VIDA, SUS ESCRITOS Y SU TIEMPO, 1831-1886. Santiago:

Imprenta Universitaria, 1925. 671p. Bibliografía de don Benjamín Vicuña Mackenna." pp. 525-656. A very complete bibliography of Vicuña Mackenna's books, pamphlet literature, and periodical articles.

Feliú Cruz, Guillermo. LAS OBRAS DE VICUNA MACKENNA. ESTUDIO BIBLIOGRAFICO PRECEDIDO DE UN PANORAMA DE LA LABOR LITERARIA DEL ESCRITOR. Santiago de Chile: Prensas de la Universidad de Chile, 1932. 226p. Contents: I. Panorama de la labor literaria del escritor, pp. 13-49. II. Bibliografía (by year, 1850-1932, partially annotated), pp. 51-119. III. Vicuña Mackenna, Carlos: "Bibliografía parlamentaria de Vicuña Mackenna," pp. 121-147. IV. Vicuña Mackenna, Carlos: "Bibliografía periodística de Vicuña Mackenna," pp. 149-178. V. Bibliográfos y bibliografías de Vicuña Mackenna, pp. 179-219. A. Fuentes generales. B. Fuentes especiales.

VIDARTE, SANTIAGO (Puerto Rico, 1827-1848)

Foster, P.R. Lit., p. 215. Contents: I. Dissertation. II. Critical Essays.

VIEIRA, ANTONIO (Brazil, 1608-1697)

Frota, Guilherme de Andréa. "Padre Antônio Vieira. Ensaio bibliográfico relativo ao Brasil," OCIDENTE, 71, Núm. 340 (agosto 1966), 76-96. 191 items. Contents: I. Edições de Vieira no Brasil. II. Livros e opúsculos. III. Artigos em publicações seriadas e jornais.

Porter, pp. 272-275. Contents: I. Writings. II. References, Critical and Biographical.

Vieira, Antônio. HISTORIA DO FUTURO (LIVRO ANTEPRIMEIRO). EDIÇAO CRITICA PREFACIADA E COMENTADA POR JOSE VAN DEN BESSELAAR. Münster: Aschendorfische Verlagsbuchhandlung, 1972. 2 vs. (Portugiesische Forschungen der Görresgesellschaft, Dritte Reihe, 3, Band 1). "Bibliografia," v. 1, pp. ix-xii. Contents: Obras de Antônio Vieira. A. Edições do Livro Anteprimeiro. B. Obras relacionadas com o Quinto Império e o Processo de Vieira. C. Sermões. D. Outros escritos.

VIGIL, JOSE MARIA (Mexico, 1829-1909)

Agraz García de Alba, Gabriel. BIOBIBLIOGRAFIA GENERAL DE DON JOSE MARIA VIGIL. México, D.F.: Instituto de Investigaciones Bibliográficas, UNAM, 1981. 286p. (Serie bibliografías, 7).

VILLAR-BUCETA, MARIA (Cuba, 1899-1977)

García-Carranza, Araceli. "Bio-bibliografía de María Villar-Buceta," REVISTA DE LA BIBLIOTECA NACIONAL "JOSE MARTI" 20, Núm. 3 (setiembre/diciembre de 1978), 149-180. Contents: I. "Bibliografía activa. Libros, folletos y colaboraciones en libros," pp. 157-160 (arranged by year, 1919-1978). II. "Bibliografía activa. Colaboraciones en publicaciones seriadas," pp. 160-168 (arranged by year, 1915-1977). III. "Bibliografía pasiva," pp. 168-174 (arranged by year, 1919-1978). IV. "Indice de títulos," pp. 174-178. V. "Indice onomástico," pp. 178-180.

"María Villar Buceta: bío-bibliografía," BIBLIOGRAFIA CUBANA, 1977, 236-238. Contents: I. Biografía. II. Bibliografía activa.

VILLARAN, ACISCLO (Peru, 1841-1927)

Roda, María Isable. "BIO-BIBLIOGRAFIA DE ACISCLO VILLARAN." Tesis. Lima: Biblioteca Nacional, Escuela de Bibliotecarios, 1955.

VILLARROEL, GASPAR DE (Ecuador, c.1587-1665)

Flores, BEH, p. 56. Contents: I. Ediciones. II. Bibliografía selecta (criticism).

VILLAURRUTIA, XAVIER (Mexico, 1903-1950)

Flores, BEH, pp. 308-310. Contents: I. Ediciones principales. II. Otras ediciones. III. Referencias. IV. Bibliografía selecta (criticism).

Foster, Mex. Lit., pp. 344-350. Contents: I. Bibliographies. II. Critical Monographs and Dissertations. III. Critical Essays.

Schneider, Luis Mario. "Bibliografía de Xavier Villaurrutia," pp. xxxi-lxxi in Xavier Villaurrutia's OBRAS. Editada por Miguel Capistrán, Alí Chumacero y Luis Mario Schneider. 2. ed. aumentada. México: FCE, 1966. 1096p. Contents: I. Bibliografía directa. A. Poesía. B. Teatro. C. Relato. D. Ensayo. E. Epistolario. F. Conferencias. G. Prólogos. H. Traducciones. I. Ediciones. All chronological entries. J. Hemerografía (by journal; then article). II. Bibliografía indirecta (criticism).

Snaidas, Adolf. EL TEATRO DE XAVIER VILLAURRUTIA. México, D.F.: Secretaría de Educación Pública, 1973. 207p. "Bibliografía," pp. 198-206. Contents: I. Obras de Xavier Villaurrutia. A. Colecciones. B. Poesía. C. Teatro. D. Relato. E. Ensayo. F. Epistolario. G. Traducciones. H. Ediciones. II. Obras consultadas (includes criticism on Villaurrutia).

VILLAVERDE, CIRILO (Cuba, 1812-1894)

ACERCA DE CIRILO VILLAVERDE. SELECCION, PROLOGO Y NOTAS DE IMELDO ALVAREZ. La Habana: Ed. Letras Cubanas, 1982. 430p. Includes a bibliografía activa (works of the author) and a bibliografía inactiva (works about the author), pp. 419-430.

Fernández, Tomás. "Bibliografía de Cecilia Valdés," REVISTA DE LITERATURA CUBANA, (La Habana), Núm. 2/3 (enero/julio de 1984), 102-127. Contents: I. Bibliografía activa (editions are arranged by year, 1839-1982; includes translations). II. Bibliografía pasiva (criticism on Cecilia Valdés). A. Siglo

XIX (arranged by year, 1839-1894). B. Siglo XX: 1900-1958. C. Siglo XX: 1959-1982. III. Algunas críticas a versiones y adaptaciones de Cecilia Valdés.

Flores, BEH, pp. 310-311. Contents: I. Ediciones. II. Referencias. III. Bibliografía selecta (criticism).

Foster, Cuban Lit., pp. 479-483. Contents: I. Bibliographies. II. Critical Monographs and Dissertations. III. Critical Essays.

Villaverde, Cirilo. CECILIA VALDES O LA LOMA DEL ANGEL. La Habana: Consejo Nacional de Cultura, 1964. 666p. "Bibliografía-ediciones," pp. 653-664. Contents: I. Narraciones. II. Artículos en revistas. III. Artículos en el diario Faro Industrial de La Habana (1841-1847). IV. Obras de texto. V. Folletos. VI. Traducciones. VII. Adaptaciones. VIII. Estudios.

______. CECILIA VALDES O LA LOMA DEL ANGEL (NOVELA DE COSTUMBRES CUBANAS). EDICION, PROLOGO Y NOTAS POR OLGA BLONDET TUDISCO Y ANTONIO TUDISCO. New York: Anaya Book Co., 1971. 2vs. "Cirilo Villaverde: bibliografía," v. 1, pp. 45-54. Contents: I. Ediciones. A. Novelas (by year, 1837-1925). B. Artículos y cuentos. C. Traductor. D. Traducciones. II. Estudios.

______. LA JOVEN DE LA FLECHA DE ORO. La Habana: Comisión Nacional Cubana de la UNESCO, 1962. "Bibliografía," pp. 381-384. Bibliografía activa only.

Ximeno, Manuel de. "Papeletas bibliográficas de Cirilo Villaverde," REVISTA DE LA BIBLIOTECA NACIONAL (La Habana), 2ª serie, IV, Núm. 2 (1953), 133-153.

VINAS, DAVID (Argentina, 1929-)

Foster, Arg. Lit., pp. 719-723. Contents: I. Bibliography. II. Dissertations. III. Critical Essays.

Valdes, Gustavo. "David Viñas y la generación del 55," VORTICE (Stanford University, Stanford, Cal.), Núm. 1 (Primera 1974), 93-102. Article includes a bibliography. Contents: I. David Viñas: una bibliografía de su obra. A. Cuentos. B. Ensayo. C. Guiones cinematográficos. D. Novelas. E. Teatro. F. En preparación. G. En artículos. (All these sections are arranged by year.) II. Sobre David Viñas. III. La Generación del "55."

VINCENZI, MOISES (Costa Rica, 1895-1964)

Cordero, Rodrigo, ed. MOISES VINCENZI. San José: Ministerio de Cultura, Juventud y Deportes, Departamento de Publicaciones, 1975. 307p. Contents: I. "Bibliografía sobre Moisés Vincenzi," p. 129. II. "Obras de Moisés Vincenzi," pp. 301-303.

VITIER, CINTIO (Cuba, 1921-)

Foster, Cuban Lit., pp. 484-485. Contents: I. Critical Monograph. II. Critical Essays.

HOMENAJE A CINTIO VITIER, 30 AÑOS CON LA POESIA. La

Habana: Biblioteca Nacional "José Martí," 1968. Contents: I. Bibliografía activa. A. Libros, folletos, separatas. B. Traducciones. C. Colaboraciones en publicaciones periódicas. II. Bibliografía pasiva.

VITOR, NESTOR (Brazil, 1868-1932)
Sousa, José Galante de. "Nestor Vítor," REVISTA DO LIVRO, Núm. 34 (júlio/setembro de 1968), 55-62. "Bibliografia," pp. 58-62. Includes works by and about the author.

VIVAS BRICENO, CLARA (Venezuela, 1897-)
Cardozo, Poesía, pp. 213-215. Includes the poetical works of and the critical studies about the author.

VIZCARRONDO, CARMELINA (Puerto Rico, 1906-)
Foster, P.R. Lit., pp. 216-217. Contents: I. Critical Monograph and Dissertation. II. Critical Essays.

- W -

WALKER MARTINEZ, CARLOS (Chile, 1842-1905)
Escudero, pp. 304-305. Criticism.

WAST, HUGO (Pseudonym of GUSTAVO ADOLFO MARTINEZ ZUVIRIA) (Argentina, 1883-1962)
Becco, Horacio Jorge. "Bibliografía de Gustavo A. Martínez Zuviría," BOLETIN DE LA ACADEMIA ARGENTINA DE LETRAS, 27, Núm. 103 (enero/marzo de 1962), 7-13. In chronological order (1902-1960), lists 63 first editions and a number of other editions authorized by author. Articles, speeches, and translations into other languages are excluded.
"Bibliografía de don Gustavo A. Martínez Zuviría," BOLETIN DE LA ACADEMIA ARGENTINA DE LETRAS, 48, Núm. 189/190 (julio/diciembre de 1983), 307-313. Includes only books, arranged by year, 1902-1960. 60 items. There is also an "obras completas" section.
Foster, Arg. Lit., pp. 576-578. Contents: I. Bibliographies. II. Critical Monographs. III. Critical Essays.
Moreno, Juan Carlos. GUSTAVO MARTINEZ ZUVIRIA. Buenos Aires: Ediciones Culturales Argentinas, 1962. 107p. Contents: "Obras de Hugo West," pp. 101-102 (1904-1960). "Antologías," p. 102. "Traducciones," pp. 103-105 (arranged by language).

WESTPHALEN, EMILIO ADOLFO (Peru, 1910-)
Silva-Santisteban, Ricardo. "Bibliografía de Emilio Adolfo Westphalen," CREACION Y CRITICA (Lima), Núm. 20 (agosto de 1977), 73-79. Contents: I. Libros. II. Poemas no recogidos en libros. III. Versiones poéticas. IV. Artículos, ensayos y prosa diversa no recogidos en libros. V. Sobre Emilio Adolfo

Westphalen. A. En libros. B. En publicaciones periódicas. C. Tesis sobre Westphalen.

WIESSE DE SABOGAL, MARIA (Peru, 1894-1964)
Márquez P., María Antonieta. "María Wiesse de Sabogal," ANUARIO BIBLIOGRAFICO PERUANO, 1964/1966, 719-732. Contents: I. Biografía. II. Libros y folletos. III. Artículos y ensayos. IV. Traducciones. V. Cartas. VI. Reportajes. VII. Notas bibliográficas. VIII. Referencias. IX. Necrológicas y homenajes póstumos.

WILDE, EDUARDO (Argentina, 1844-1913)
Buffa Peyrot, Yolanda H. CONTRIBUCION A LA BIBLIOGRAFIA DE EDUARDO WILDE. Buenos Aires: Fondo Nacional de las Artes, 1967. (Bibliografía Argentina de Artes y Letras, Compilaciones Especiales, 31). Contents: I. Obras del autor. A. Obras completas. B. Prosa varia. C. Discursos. D. Tesis de doctorado. II. Colaboraciones en publicaciones periódicas. III. Discursos y memorias. A. Discursos parlamentarios y políticos. B. Otros discursos. C. Memorias ministeriales. IV. Antologías de textos del autor. V. Textos del autor en diversas antologías. VI. Problemas de atribución. VII. Crítica y biografía. A. Trabajos firmados. B. Trabajos firmados con seudónimos no escalrecidos. C. Trabajos sin firma. VIII. Anécdotas. IX. Cuadro biográfico-cronológico. X. Indices. A. De títulos. B. Onomástico. 933 entries.
Flores, BEH, pp. 67-69. Contents: I. Ediciones principales. II. Otras ediciones. III. Referencias. IV. Bibliografía selecta (criticism).
Foster, Arg. Lit., pp. 724-727. Contents: I. Bibliography. II. Critical Monographs. III. Critical Essays.

WILSON, CARLOS GUILLERMO (Panama, 1941-)
Jackson, Afro-Spanish, pp. 116-117. Contents: I. Works. II. Criticism. Annotated.

WOOLF, EGON (Chile, 1926-)
Foster, Chilean Lit., pp. 216-217. Critical Essays.

- X -

XAMMAR, LUIS FABIO (Peru, 1911-1947)
Chirinos Rodríguez, Ruth. "BIO-BIBLIOGRAFIA DE LUIS FABIO XAMMAR (1911-1947)." Tesis. Lima: Biblioteca Nacional, Escuela de Bibliotecarios, 1957.
Delgado Pastor, Amadeo. "Bio-bibliografía de Luis Fabio Xammar," BOLETIN DE LA BIBLIOTECA NACIONAL (Lima), Año 4, Núm. 10 (junio de 1947), 123-152. Contents: I. Libros y folletos. II. Otras ediciones. III. Prólogos. IV. Antologías. V. Poesías. VI. Cuentos. VII. Ensayos. VIII. Correspon-

dencia noticiosa. IX. Notas bibliográficas (Critical reviews). X. Inéditos. XI. Referencias sobre Luis Fabio Xammar. XII. Conferencias. XIII. Homenajes y necrologías. Reprinted as "Luis Fabio Xammar," in ANUARIO BIBLIOGRAFICO PERUANO, 1947, 256-287.

- Y -

YANEZ, AGUSTIN (Mexico, 1904-1980)

"Agustín Yáñez: curriculum vitae (hasta 1975)," MEMORIAS DE LA ACADEMIA MEXICANA, 22 (1975), 250-273. "Bibliografía," pp. 266-273. Contents: I. Obras (by year, 1931-1975; monographs mainly). II. Principales traducciones. III. Algunos prólogos. IV. Actividades editoriales. V. Crítica y bibliografía indirecta (critical studies about Yáñez and his work).

Flores, BEH, pp. 311-314. Contents: I. Ediciones. II. Referencias. III. Bibliografía selecta (criticism).

Foster, Mex. Lit., pp. 350-359. Contents: I. Bibliographies. II. Critical Monographs and Dissertations. III. Critical Essays.

Foster, 20th Century, pp. 203-207. Contents: I. Critical Books. II. Critical Essays.

Gamiochipi de Liguori, Gloria. YAÑEZ Y LA REALIDAD MEXICANA. México, D.F.: 1970. 196p. "Bibliografía," pp. 171-194. Contents: I. Obras de Agustín Yáñez. A. Traducciones. B. Hemerografía (by year). II. Obras consultadas. III. Estudios sobre Agustín Yáñez.

Rangel Guerra, Alfonso. AGUSTIN YAÑEZ. México, D.F.: Empresas Editoriales, S.A., 1969. 320p. "Bibliografía directa," pp. 293-302. Contents: I. Novelas, cuentos, relatos y crónicas. II. Ensayos, artículos, estudios, reseñas y textos diversos. III. Discursos. IV. Prólogos y ediciones. V. Biografías. VI. Traducciones de algunas obras de Agustín Yáñez. "Bibliografía indirecta," pp. 303-317 (criticism).

- Z -

ZAPATA OLIVELLA, JUAN (Colombia, 1922-)

Jackson, Afro-Spanish, p. 118. Contents: I. Works. II. Criticism.

ZAPATA OLIVELLA, MANUEL (Colombia, 1920-)

Jackson, Afro-Spanish, pp. 118-121. Contents: I. Works. II. Criticism.

Porras Collantes, pp. 813-818. Includes works of and critical studies about the author.

ZEGARRA BALLON, EDILBERTO (Peru, 1867-1956)

Seminario, Angelica. "Edilberto Zegarra Ballón," ANUARIO BIBLIOGRAFICO PERUANO, 1955/1957, 637-742. Contents: I.

Biografía. II. Libros y folletos. III. Artículos y ensayos. IV. Cuentos. V. Poesías. VI. Discursos. VII. Cartas. VIII. Reportajes. IX. Referencias. X. Notas necrológicas.

ZENEA, JUAN CLEMENTE (Cuba, 1832-1871)
Foster, Cuban Lit., pp. 486-488. Contents: I. Critical Monographs. II. Critical Essays.

ZENO GANDIA, MANUEL (Puerto Rico, 1885-1930)
Arce de Vázquez, Margot. "Bibliografía de Manuel Zeno Gandía," ASOMANTE, 11 (octubre/diciembre de 1955), 72-74. A selective bibliography which has many entries that are incomplete bibliographically. Contents: I. Obras literarias. A. Cuentos. B. Novela. C. Poesía (poemas). D. Prosa. 1. Conferencias. 2. Crítica. 3. Crónicas. 4. Meditaciones filosóficas. E. Teatro.
Flores, NH, v. 2, pp. 84-85. Contents: I. Ediciones de su narrativa. II. Referencias. III. Bibliografía selecta (criticism).
Foster, P.R. Lit., pp. 217-220. Contents: I. Bibliography. II. Critical Monographs and Dissertations. II. Critical Essays.
Gardón Franceschi, Margarita. MANUEL ZENO GANDIA: VIDA Y POESIA. San Juan, Puerto Rico: Ed. Coqui, 1969. 175p. "Bibliografía," pp. 165-171. Contents: I. Obras de autor. A. Artículos (juicios críticos). B. Cuentos. C. Gramática. D. Novela. E. Teatro. F. Poesía.
Palmer de Dueño, Rosa M. SENTIDO, FORMA Y ESTILO DE "REDENTORES" DE MANUEL ZENO GANDIA. Río Piedras: Editorial Universitaria, Universidad de Puerto Rico, 1974. 119p. "Bibliografía," pp. 113-115. Contents: I. Obras del autor. A. Novelas. B. Cuentos. C. Poesías. D. Editoriales. E. Prólogos. F. Juicios críticos. II. Bibliografía del autor (criticism).

ZORRILLA DE SAN MARTIN, JUAN (Uruguay, 1855-1931)
Flores, BEH, pp. 69-70. Contents: I. Edición principal. II. Otras ediciones. III. Referencias. IV. Bibliografía selecta (criticism).
Ibañez, Roberto. ORIGINALES Y DOCUMENTOS DE ZORRILLA DE SAN MARTIN. Montevideo: Ministerio de Instrucción Pública y Previsión Social. Instituto Nacional de Investigaciones y Archivos Literarios, 1956. 102p. (Exposición 28 de diciembre 1955-5 de enero de 1956--Salón de Actos de Teatro Solís). The work enumerates more than 251 works, manuscripts, etc., under the following headings: I. Iconografía. II. Manuscritos literarios (poesía, prosa). III. Correspondencia. IV. Miscelánea documental. V. Bibliografía crítica.
Xalambri, Arturo E. BIBLIOGRAFIA FRAGMENTARIA Y SINTETICA DEL DOCTOR JUAN ZORRILLA DE SAN MARTIN. Montevideo, 1956. 40p. (Separata de "Tribuna Católica," Año 21, Núm. 3 [1955], aumentada con intercalaciones, escritos y adiciones). The work is based on the author's private col-

lection. Contents: I. La leyenda patria. A. La leyenda patria inserta con TABARE. B. La leyenda patria en antologías. C. La leyenda patria en música. D. TABARE. E. Otras estampaciones tabareanas. F. Traducciones de TABARE. G. Obras musicales y teatrales inspiradas en TABARE. II. Otras obras poéticas de Zorrilla. III. Obras puestas en música. IV. Obras en prosa de Zorrilla. V. Obras completas. A. Edición del Banco de la República Oriental del Uruguay. VI. Poesías dedicadas a Zorrilla.

ZUM FELDE, ALBERTO (Uruguay, 1887-1976)

Montevideo. Biblioteca Nacional. EXPOSICION BIBLIOGRAFICA Y DOCUMENTAL: ALBERTO ZUM FELDE EN EL CINCUENTENARIO DE LA PUBLICACION DEL "PROCESO INTELECTUAL DEL URUGUAY" Y CRITICA DE SU LITERATURA. Montevideo, 1980. 71p.

ADDITIONAL BIOBIBLIOGRAPHIC SOURCES
(Arranged by country or region)

GENERAL LATIN AMERICAN SOURCES

Acuña, René. EL TEATRO POPULAR EN HISPANOAMERICA: UNA BIBLIOGRAFIA ANOTADA. México, D.F.: Universidad Nacional Autónoma de México, 1979. 111p. "Hispanoamérica," pp. 51-101. Contents: I. El teatro nativo. A. Estudios generales. B. México y Centroamérica. II. Influencia y desarrollo del teatro peninsular en América. A. Obras generales. B. El teatro en lenguas indígenas. C. Algo sobre el South y el Southwest norteamericano. D. Teatro navideño, autos, loas y la pasión en la Nueva España. E. Algo del corpus y otros juegos escénicos. III. Los Moros y Cristianos y Los Bailes de la Conquista. A. Obras generales. B. Algunos textos de bailes. IV. Suramérica a vista de pájaro (by country). 380 partially annotated entries.

Alarcón, Norma, and Sylvia Kossnar. BIBLIOGRAPHY OF HISPANIC WOMEN WRITERS. Bloomington, Ind.: Chicano-Riqueño Studies, 1980. 96p. (Chicano-Riqueño Studies, Bibliography Series, 1). This bibliography provides bibliographic information, somewhat inconsistent at times, for about 150 women authors who appeared in MLA International Bibliography, 1922-1978.

Anderson, Robert Roland. SPANISH AMERICAN MODERNISM: A SELECTED BIBLIOGRAPHY. Tucson, Ariz.: The University of Arizona Press, 1970. 167p. Contents: I. General References. II. Authors. A. Julián del Casal. B. José Santos Chocano. C. Rubén Darío. D. Salvador Díaz Mirón. E. Manuel Díaz Rodríguez. F. José María Eguren. G. Enrique González Martínez. H. Manuel González Prada. I. Manuel Gutiérrez Nájera. J. Julio Herrera y Reissig. K. Ricardo Jaimes Freyre. L. Enrique Larreta. M. Leopoldo Lugones. N. José Martí. O. Amado Nervo. P. José Enrique Rodó. Q. José Asunción Silva. R. Guillermo Valencia. III. Index. This work is indexed in the preceding GUIDE.

Becco, Jorge Horacio. DICCIONARIO DE LITERATURA HISPANOAMERICANA: AUTORES. Buenos Aires: Huemul, 1984. 313p. Includes biobibliographies.

_______, and Alberto Amengual. "Antologías poéticas americanas y venezolanas en el siglo XIX," in III SIMPOSIO DE DOCENTES E INVESTIGADORES DE LA LITERATURA VENEZOLANA, MERIDA, 24-26 DE NOVIEMBRE DE 1977 (Mérida, Venezuela: Universidad de los Andes, Facultad de Humanidades y Educación, 1978), v. 1, pp. 238-249. Anthologies are arranged chronologically, 1846-1895. Each entry lists which authors appear in each volume.

_______, and David William Foster. LA NUEVA NARRATIVA HISPANO-AMERICANA: BIBLIOGRAFIA. Buenos Aires: Casa Pardo, S.A., 1976. 226p. Contents: I. Referencias generales; Estudios comprensivos sobre la nueva narrativa hispanoamericana. II. Referencias nacionales. A. Argentina. B. Chile. C. Colombia. D. Cuba. E. México. F. Paraguay. G. Perú. H. Uruguay. III. Autores. A. Mario Benedetti. B. Guillermo Cabrera Infante. C. Alejo Carpentier. D. Julio Cortázar. E. José Donoso. F. Carlos Fuentes. G. Gabriel García Márquez. H. José Lezama Lima. I. Juan Carlos Onetti. J. Manuel Puig. K. Augusto Roa Bastos. L. Juan Rulfo. M. Ernesto Sábato. N. Severo Sarduy. O. Mario Vargas Llosa. IV. Anexo. A. Referencias generales. B. Referencias nacionales. C. Autores. V. Indice onomástico. Most entries for authors include obras, traducciones, and crítica. Dissertations are also given. The bibliography includes a total of 2,257 unannotated items and is indexed in the preceding GUIDE.

Bellini, Giuseppe. BIBLIOGRAFIA DELL'ISPANOAMERICANISMO ITALIANO: CONTRIBUTI CRITICA. Milano: Istituto Editoriale Cisalpino-La Goliardica, 1981. 100p. Contents: I. Repertori e studi bibliografici. II. Storie della cultura, letterarie e studi settoriali. III. Relazioni culturali. IV. Cronaca: studi su opere e autori. V. Narrativa: studi generali. VI. Narrativa: studi su opere e autori. VII. Poesia: studi generali. VIII. Poesia: studi su opere e autori. IX. Saggistica. X. Teatro. XI. Studi linguistici. XII. Storia e vita economico-sociale e religiosa. XIII. Problemi dell'America contemporanea. XIV. Relazioni politiche, emigrazione, viaggi. XV. Indice delle materie. XVI. Indice degli autori. 1,191 items covering the period, 1940-1980. Unfortunately, page numbers were not included in any bibliographic citation.

_______. "Bibliografia dell'ispanoamericanismo italiano: Le traduzioni," RASSEGNA IBERISTICA, No. 6 (1979), 3-42. Contents: I. Antologie generali (subdivided by genre). II. Autori. III. Testi originali. 585 items.

Billick, David J. "Women in Hispanic Literature: A Checklist of Doctoral Dissertations and Master's Theses, 1905-1975," WOMEN STUDIES ABSTRACTS, 6, No. 2 (1977), 1-11. Supplement 1: Ibid., 7, No. 2/3 (1978), 1-3; Supplement 2: Ibid., 9, No. 3 (1980), 1-4. Supplement 3: LETRAS FEMENINAS, 8, No. 2 (1982), 54-57.

Boyd, Robert. "Bibliography of Translations on the Latin American Novel, 1900-1970," REVISTA DE ESTUDIOS HISPANICOS, 7, Núm. 1 (enero de 1973), 139-144. Entries are arranged by author under country divisions.

Carpenter, Charles A. "Latin American Theater Criticism, 1966-1974: Some Addenda to Lyday and Woodyard," REVISTA INTER-AMERICANA DE BIBLIOGRAFIA, 30 (1980), 246-253. 97 items.

Christensen, George K. "A Bibliography of Latin American Plays in English Translation," LATIN AMERICAN THEATRE REVIEW, 6 (Spring 1973), 29-39. "This bibliography is an attempt to list both the published and the manuscript copies for the benefit of scholars, future translators and theatre directors." (p. 29). It contains materials relating to Argentina, Brazil, Colombia, Cuba, Nicaragua, Panamá, Paraguay, Perú, Puerto Rico, and Venezuela.

Coll, Edna. INDICE INFORMATIVO DE LA NOVELA HISPANOAMERICANA. Río Piedras: Editorial Universitaria, Universidad de Puerto Rico, 1974- (in progress). Volume 1: Las Antillas (1974); Volume 2: Centroamericana (1977); Volume 3: Venezuela (1978); Volume 4: Colombia (1980). Within each country section the listing is alphabetical by novelist's surname. Most entries include a biographical note on the author, together with a list of novels (often a critical commentary is included) and bibliographic references which include biographical and critical studies.

Cortina, Lynn Ellen Rice. SPANISH-AMERICAN WOMEN WRITERS: A BIBLIOGRAPHICAL RESEARCH CHECKLIST. New York: Garland, 1983. 292p. (Garland Reference Library of the Humanities, 356). Organized by country, this bibliography includes the author's name and a list of her works, with occasional other details about her literary activities. Unfortunately, often such basic bibliographic information as dates, publishers, page numbers, and other data is missing from the entries. There is only a name index. 1,994 author entries are included in the bibliography; however, some are only a name and a country.

Corvalán, Graciela N.V. LATIN AMERICAN WOMEN WRITERS IN ENGLISH TRANSLATION: A BIBLIOGRAPHY. Los Angeles: California State University, Latin American Studies Center, 1980. 109p. (Latin American Bibliography Series, 9). Contents: I. Bibliographies and Bibliographies of Bibliographies. II. Bibliography of Anthologies. III. General Bibliography of Women Writers: A Selection. IV. Latin American Women Writers in English Translation (282 women writers are alphabetically arranged by author; genre listed as well as critical works when available in English). Section IV of Corvalán's work is indexed in the preceding GUIDE.

Finch, Mark Steven. "AN ANNOTATED BIBLIOGRAPHY OF RECENT

SOURCES ON LATIN AMERICAN THEATER: GENERAL SECTION, ARGENTINA, CHILE, MEXICO, AND PERU." Ph.D., University of Cincinnati, 1978. 372p. "The eight hundred eighty-four items of this document are, then, a supplement, extension and clarification of such sources as the PMLA annual bibliography, the Hebblethwaite bibliography, the Dauster 'recent research' article, the Woodyard-Lyday bibliography and The Handbook of Latin American Studies." The general section chapter as well those on Argentina, Chile, México and Perú are divided into the following sections: books and reviews, articles, anthologies, bibliographies and miscellaneous items. (Dissertation Abstracts International, 39 [1979], 5502A.)

Flores, Angel. BIBLIOGRAFIA DE ESCRITORES HISPANOAMERICANOS. A BIBLIOGRAPHY OF SPANISH-AMERICAN WRITERS, 1609-1974. New York: Gordian Press, 1975. 319p. Alphabetical listing of 190 writers. Each author entry usually includes: "edición principal," "otras ediciones," "referencias," and "bibliografía selecta." Unfortunately, many entries are incomplete bibliographically and, at times, inaccurate. This work is indexed in the preceding GUIDE.

Forster, Merlin H. HISTORIA DE LA POESIA HISPANOAMERICANA. Clear Creek, Ind.: The American Hispanist, 1981. 329p. "Bibliografía," pp. 209-324. Contents: I. Estudios críticos y bibliografías. A. Estudios generales. B. Estudios por época. 1. Precolombina. 2. Siglo XIX. 3. Modernismo y postmodernismo. C. Estudios nacionales (alphabetical by country). II. Antologías. A. Antologías generales. B. Antologías nacionales (by country). III. Época precolombina. A. Poesía náhuatl. B. Poesía maya-quiché. C. Poesía quechua. IV. Poetas principales (obras; recopilaciones y antologías; estudios).

Foster, David William. A DICTIONARY OF CONTEMPORARY LATIN AMERICAN AUTHORS. Tempe, Ariz.: Centre for Latin American Studies, 1975. 110p. A biobibliographical dictionary of living authors only, with each author entry containing a list of the principal works of the author. The focus of the work is on younger writers.

______. THE 20TH CENTURY SPANISH-AMERICAN NOVEL: A BIBLIOGRAPHIC GUIDE. Metuchen, N.J.: Scarecrow Press, 1975. 227p. "Our goal here has been first to provide for the first time a working bibliography on the criticism pertaining to the fifty-six Spanish-American novelists most commonly studied in the U.S...." (p. vi). Bibliographies, critical books, and/or critical essays are included for most author entries. The work is unannotated and is indexed in the preceding GUIDE.

Foster, Jerald. "Towards a Bibliography of Latin American Short Story Anthologies," LATIN AMERICAN RESEARCH REVIEW, 12,

No. 2 (1977), 103-108. "The bibliography presented here is an effort to describe the content of these anthologies as an aid to course preparation and research. Over fifty anthologies of all types are given, including short stories in English translation" [p. 103]. All anthologies are critically annotated.

Fretes, Hilda Gladys, and Esther Bárbara. BIBLIOGRAFIA ANOTADA DEL MODERNISMO. Mendoza, Argentina: Universidad Central de Cuyo, Biblioteca Central, 1970 (c. 1973). 138p. (Cuadernos de la Biblioteca, 5). The modernismo movement rather than individual author's contributions are emphasized in this bibliography, which contains 245 annotated entries.

Freudenthal, Juan R., and Patricia M. Freudenthal. INDEX TO ANTHOLOGIES OF LATIN AMERICAN LITERATURE IN ENGLISH TRANSLATION. Boston: G. K. Hall, 1977. 199p. An index to English translation of some 1,128 Spanish-American and Brazilian authors' works in 116 anthologies. Arranged by author, with translator and geographic indexes. Genre is indicated. Original titles of works are, however, not given. Appended to main work is a "Further Reading" list: I. Histories, essays, criticism. II. Bibliographies, Dictionaries, Encyclopedias. III. Articles, Reviews.

Hebblethwaite, Frank P. A BIBLIOGRAPHICAL GUIDE TO THE SPANISH AMERICAN THEATRE. Washington, D.C.: Pan American Union, 1969. 84p. (Basic Bibliographies, 6). Contents: I. Books (General Sources and Sources by Country). II. Articles (General Sources and Sources by Country). III. Bibliography of Bibliographies.

Herrera Pamies, Alberto. "Bibliografía específica," in Oscar Fernández de la Vega and Alberto N. Pamies' INICIACION A LA POESIA AFRO-AMERICANA (Miami: Ediciones Universal, 1973), pp. 203-212. Alphabetical, arranged by author.

Hoffman, Herbert H. LATIN AMERICAN PLAY INDEX: 1920-1980. Metuchen, N.J.: Scarecrow Press, 1983-1984. 2 vs. "Access provided to about 3,300 South American plays published between 1920 and 1980, by some 1,000 authors." (v.1, p. iv). This bibliography uses the HANDBOOK OF LATIN AMERICAN STUDIES volume and entry numbers and periodical codes whenever possible. It includes both Spanish-American and Brazilian playwrights. Although the bibliography is limited to works published in South America, it includes the works of playwrights born outside the area. The following indices are included: I. Playwrights Included. II. Author Index. III. Title Index. IV. List of Collections and Anthologies. V. List of Periodicals Indexed.

Horl, Sabine. DER ESSAY ALS LITERARISCHE GATTUNG IN LATEINAMERIKA. Frankfurt-am-Main: Peter Lang, 1980. 100p.

Contents: I. Lateinamerika allgemein. II. Einzelne Länder. III. Amerikanität und nationale Identität. IV. Einzelne Essayisten. V. Literaturkritik und "periodismo." VI. Europäische Einflüsse. 722 entries.

Hulet, Claude L. LATIN AMERICAN POETRY IN ENGLISH TRANSLATION: A BIBLIOGRAPHY. Washington, D.C.: Pan American Union, 1965. 192p. (Basic Bibliographies, 2). Entries are listed under country and then by author. Also includes anthologies, collections, and miscellaneous works containing poetry.

_______ LATIN AMERICAN PROSE IN ENGLISH TRANSLATION: A BIBLIOGRAPHY. Washington, D.C.: Pan American Union, 1964. 191p. (Basic Bibliographies, 1). Contents: I. Biography (by country). II. Discourses, Wills and Letters. III. Drama. IV. Essay. V. Literary Criticism. VI. Novel. VII. Philosophy. VIII. History. IX. Short Story Anthologies and Other Works Containing Translations. X. Bibliography of Bibliography of Translations. Sections II-VIII are arranged by country and then by author.

Jackson, Richard L. THE AFRO-SPANISH AMERICAN AUTHOR: AN ANNOTATED BIBLIOGRAPHY OF CRITICISM. New York: Garland, 1980. 129p. Contents: I. Introduction: Trends in Afro-Spanish American Literary Criticism. II. List of Authors by Country. III. List of Authors by Period. IV. General Bibliographies. V. General Studies and Anthologies. A. Full-length Studies and Anthologies. B. Articles, Shorter Studies, and Dissertations. VI. Authors and Criticism (arranged alphabetically by author; entries include works and criticism). Section VI of this work is indexed in the preceding GUIDE.

_______ "Research on Black Themes in Spanish American Literature: A Bibliographic Guide to Recent Trends," LATIN AMERICAN RESEARCH REVIEW, 12, No. 1 (1977), 87-103. "A Select Listing of Creative and Critical Writings," pp. 94-103. Contents: I. Literary Works and Anthologies. II. Critical Studies and References.

Jones, William Knapp. LATIN AMERICAN WRITERS IN ENGLISH TRANSLATION: A CLASSIFIED BIBLIOGRAPHY. Washington, D.C.: Pan American Union, 1944. 140p. (Bibliography Series, No. 30). Reprinted: Detroit: Blaine Ethridge Books, 1972. "This bibliography is intended to list all Latin American writing from the time of Columbus and Cortés to the present that has been translated into English." Contents: 1. History and Travel. 2. Essays (Historical Place and Peoples, Customs, Criticism, etc.). 3. Poetry. 4. Drama. 5. Fiction (Short Stories and Novels). 6. Essays. 7. Poetry. 8. Author Index. Work is arranged under subject by country and then by author.

______ MEN AND ANGELS: THREE SOUTH AMERICAN PLAYS. Carbondale, Ill.: Southern Illinois University Press, 1970. 191p. "Checklist of Translations of Spanish American Plays," pp. 181-191. This checklist, arranged alphabetically by country and then by name of playwright, identifies sources for translations. Most of them are not published but are in manuscript form in several repositories. Included in the bibliography are the following countries: Argentina, Bolivia, Chile, Colombia, Cuba, Ecuador, Guatemala, México, Nicaragua, Perú, Puerto Rico, Uruguay, Venezuela, Philippines, and the state of New Mexico.

Larsen, Jurgen Ingemann. BIBLIOGRAFI OVER LATINAMERIKANSK SKØNLITTERATUR PAA DANSK SAMT OVER DANSKE BIDRAS TIL DEN LATINAMERIKANSEK LITTERATURS HISTORIE. København: The Author, 1982. 122p. The Latin American literature section is arranged by country. Includes literary history and translations of Latin American authors into Danish.

Levine, Suzanne Jill. LATIN AMERICA: FICTION AND POETRY IN TRANSLATION. New York: Center for Inter-American Relations, 1970. 72p. Includes both authors from Spanish America and Brazil. Only titles in English published in the United States are listed, however. Thirty-three anthologies are identified by Levine.

Lozano, Stella. SELECTED BIBLIOGRAPHY OF CONTEMPORARY SPANISH-AMERICAN WRITERS. Los Angeles: California State University, Latin American Studies Center, 1979. 149p. (Latin American Bibliography Series, 8). 1,361 entries. This bibliography "...contains critical books, critical essays, dissertations, interviews, and book reviews covering literary production of 47 Spanish-American writers of the XX Century.... It was not my intention to pass judgment on the quality of the entries listed here; I simply wanted to acknowledge material available on those authors covering criticism published from 1974 to 1978, except for the women writers in which case material is listed regardless of date." (p. iii). How the author decided which authors to choose for the bibliography is not told. For example, Jorge Luis Borges is not included.

Medina, José Toribio. DICCIONARIO DE ANONIMOS Y SEUDONIMOS HISPANOAMERICANOS, APUNTACIONES REUNIDAS. Buenos Aires: Imprenta de la Universidad Nacional de Buenos Aires, 1925. 2 vs. (Publicaciones del Instituto de Investigaciones Históricas de la Universidad Nacional de Buenos Aires, 26-27). Alphabetically arranged entries with "Indice de iniciales," "Indice de seudónimos" and "Indice de anónimos" sections. Corrections and additions supplied by Ricardo Victorica's ERRORES Y OMISIONES DEL "DICCIONARIO DE ANONIMOS Y SEUDONIMOS HISPANOAMERICANOS" DE JOSE TORIBIO MEDINA (Buenos Aires: Viau & Zona, 1928), which is alphabetically arranged, and his

NUEVA EPANORTOSIS AL "DICCIONARIO DE ANONIMOS Y SEUDONIMOS" DE JOSE TORIBIO MEDINA (Buenos Aires: L. J. Rosso, 1929), which is also alphabetically arranged.

Molloy, Sylvia. LA DIFFUSION DE LA LITTERATURA HISPANO-AMERICAINE EN FRANCE AU XXe SIECLE. Paris: Presses Universitaires de France, 1972. 356p. (Publications de la Faculté des Lettres et Sciences Humaines de Paris-Sorbonne, Série Recherches, 68). "Ouvrages hispano-américains traduits ou écrits directement en français," pp. 271-273 (by author). "Anthologies," pp. 273-287. Contents: I. Classement alphabétique par nom de compilateur. II. Classement alphabétique par nom d'auteur. "Textes d'auteurs hispano-américaines parus dans des publications périodiques," pp. 287-308 (by author). "Etudes critiques parues en France sur la littérature hispano-américaine," pp. 309-342. Contents: I. Etudes generales (classement chronologique). II. Etudes sur les littératures nationales (classement alphabétique par nom de pays). III. Etudes sur les écrivains hispano-américains (classement alphabétique par nom d'écrivain étudié).

Neglia, Erminio, and Luis Ordaz. REPERTORIO SELECTO DEL TEATRO HISPANOAMERICANO CONTEMPORANEO. Tempe, Ariz.: Center for Latin American Studies, Arizona State University, 1980. 110p. This bibliography provides two listings of general sources and an alphabetical listing of Spanish American dramatists by country. For each author a chronological listing of his or her dramas is given and, for those that have been published, appropriate bibliographic information is included. 168 playwrights are included. The bibliography also provides "Lista parcial de fuentes bibliográficas," "Antologías de teatro," and "Indice de autores" sections.

Núñez, Benjamín. DICTIONARY OF AFRO-LATIN AMERICAN CIVILIZATION. Westport, Conn.: Greenwood Press, 1980. 525p. More than 4,500 entries pertinent to the study of Africans in Latin America and the Caribbean are included in this dictionary. Literary authors are given notice.

O'Brien, Robert. SPANISH PLAYS IN ENGLISH TRANSLATION. New York: Las Américas Publishing Co., 1963. 82p. Brief descriptions of each author and play.

Ocampo de Gómez, Aurora M. NOVELISTAS IBEROAMERICANOS CONTEMPORANEOS: OBRAS Y BIBLIOGRAFIA CRITICA. México, D.F.: Universidad Nacional Autónoma de México, 1979-1981. 5 parts. (Cuadernos del Centro de Estudios Literarios, 2, 4, 6, 10, 11). Bibliography is arranged alphabetically by author with brief biographies and selected lists of authors' works and criticism about them provided.

Parks, George B., and Ruth Z. Temple, eds. THE LITERATURE OF

THE WORKS IN ENGLISH TRANSLATION: A BIBLIOGRAPHY. New York: Frederick Ungar Publishing Co., 1970. Vol. 3: The Romance Literatures. Spanish American literature, pp. 329-453, which includes background, literary studies, collections, colonial Spanish American literature, and individual authors by countries.

Reichardt, Dieter. LATEINAMERIKANISCHE AUTOREN: LITERATUR-LEXIKON UND BIBLIOGRAPHIE DER DEUTSCHEN UBERSETZUNGEN. Tübingen und Basel: Horst Erdmann Verlag, 1972. 719p. Bibliography lists German translations of Latin American authors' works that appeared individually and in anthologies. Arrangement is by country and then by author. Biographical information is included.

Rela, Walter. GUIA BIBLIOGRAFICA DE LA LITERATURA HISPANO-AMERICANA DESDE EL SIGLO XIX HASTA 1970. Buenos Aires: Casa Pardo, 1971. 613p. 6,023 unannotated entries. General and country subdivisions. The following categories are used: Bibliografías generales; Bibliografías nacionales; Bibliografías individuales; Historias literarias generales; Historias literarias nacionales; Ensayo, historia y crítica; Ensayo, historia y crítica individual; Antologías generales; Antologías nacionales; Antologías individuales; Biografías colectivas; Diccionarios; Biografías individuales; Misceláneas de literatura; Varias.

_______. SPANISH AMERICAN LITERATURE: A SELECTED BIBLIOGRAPHY; LITERATURA HISPANOAMERICANA: BIBLIOGRAFIA SELECTA, 1970-1980. East Lansing, Mich., Department of Romance and Classical Languages, Michigan State University, 1982. 231p. Contents: I. Bibliographies. A. General. B. National. C. Individual Authors. II. Dictionaries. A. General. B. National. III. Literary Criticism and History. A. General Studies. B. National Studies. C. Individual Authors. IV. Anthologies. A. General. B. National. C. Individual Authors. V. Congresses. A. Instituto Internacional de Literatura Iberoamericana. B. Other Institutions. VI. Author Index. VII. Index of Critics. VIII. Index of Translators.

Resnick, Margery, and Isabelle de Courtivron. WOMEN WRITERS IN TRANSLATION: AN ANNOTATED BIBLIOGRAPHY, 1945-1982. New York: Garland, 1984. 272p. "Brazil," pp. 5-7 (arrangement of surnames incorrectly listed). "Spanish America," pp. 231-246. English translations of only books and pamphlets are listed by author. Entries are annotated.

Sáinz de Robles, Federico Carlos. ENSAYO DE UN DICCIONARIO DE LA LITERATURA. 3. ed., corr. y aumentada. Madrid: Aguilar, 1964-1967. 3 vs. vol. 2: ESCRITORES ESPAÑOLES Y HISPANO-AMERICANOS. Alphabetical biobibliographic entries. Most useful reference tool, but should be used with caution because of its selection and incomplete entry information.

Samurović-Pavlović, Liliana. LES LETTRES HISPANO-AMERICAINES AU "MERCURE DE FRANCE" (1897-1915). Beograd: Filološki Fakulted Beogradskog Univerziteta, 1969. 183p. (Monografije, 27). Contents: I. "Bibliographie: Mercure de France," pp. 165-169. (entries arranged chronologically, 1897-1915). II. "Oeuvres hispano-américaines publiées en France (1897-1915)," pp. 173-178 (arranged by Latin American author).

Sarnacki, John. LATIN AMERICAN LITERATURE AND HISTORY IN POLISH TRANSLATION: A BIBLIOGRAPHY. Port Huron, Michigan: Author, 1973. 84p. Translations are arranged by country. Bibliography includes biographical and critical studies, book reviews, and, in most cases, the title of the translated work as well as that of the Polish title.

Shaw, Bradley A. LATIN AMERICAN LITERATURE IN ENGLISH TRANSLATION: AN ANNOTATED BIBLIOGRAPHY. New York: New York University Press for the Center for Inter-American Relations, 1976. 144p. Includes books and anthologies published both in the United States and England (selected titles). Organization of the bibliography is by genre and then by country. In most instances, the title of the original work is given.

_______. LATIN AMERICAN LITERATURE IN ENGLISH, 1975-1978. SUPPLEMENT TO REVIEW (Center for Inter-American Relations), No. 24 (1979). 23p. Contents: I. Anthologies (by editor). II. Individual Works (by author). III. Additions to Original Volume (items published before 1975). IV. Reprints (published before 1975).

Shimose, Pedro. DICCIONARIO DE AUTORES IBEROAMERICANOS. Madrid: Instituto de Cooperación Iberoamericana de Madrid, Dirección General de Relaciones Culturales, Ministerio de Asuntos Exteriores, 1982. 459p. Biobibliographies of 20th-century authors.

Thompson, Lawrence S. A BIBLIOGRAPHY OF SPANISH PLAYS ON MICROCARDS. Hamden, Conn.: Shoe String Press, 1968. 490p. Six thousand Spanish, Catalonian, and Spanish-American plays from the sixteenth century to the present are recorded. The plays form part of an ongoing commercial microform project edited by the author. The original texts are in the University of Kentucky Library. Arrangement is alphabetical by author or by title in the case of anonymous works.

Toro, Josefina del. A BIBLIOGRAPHY OF THE COLLECTIVE BIOGRAPHY OF SPANISH AMERICA. Río Piedras, Puerto Rico: The University of Puerto Rico, 1938. 140p. (The University of Puerto Rico Bulletin, Series IX, No. 1, September, 1938). Classified by author, with an author index.

Trenti Rocamora, José Luis. EL REPERTORIO DE LA DRAMATICA COLONIAL HISPANO-AMERICANA. Buenos Aires: Talleres Gráficos ALEA, 1950. 110p. Contents: I. Piezas en lenguas indias. II. Piezas en lengua española (listing is by country and then by author). III. Notas (contains supplementary bibliographical data).

Uribe Muñoz, Bernardo. MUJERES DE AMERICA. Medellín: Imprenta Oficial, 1934. 460p. Brief biographies or autobiographies are included for 130 prominent women authors (at the time) of Spanish America. Arrangement is by country.

Vecchiola, Raffaele. "ENSAYO BIBLIOGRAFICO-CRITICO SOBRE TRADUCCIONES ITALIANAS DE NOVELAS HISPANOAMERICANOS." Ph.D., Facoltà di Magistero, Università degli Studi di Firenze, 1967.

Woodbridge, Hensley C. SPANISH AND SPANISH-AMERICAN LITERATURE: AN ANNOTATED BIBLIOGRAPHY TO SELECTED BIBLIOGRAPHIES. New York: The Modern Language Association of America, 1983. 74p. "Spanish-American Literature," pp. 35-70. Contents: I. Current and Retrospective Periodical Indexes and Book Review Index. II. General. III. By country (current bibliographies; bibliographies of a country's literature; and bibliographies of poetry, plays, fiction, and miscellaneous works). IV. Translations. V. Dissertations. VI. National Bibliographies. VII. Bibliographies of Bibliographies. VIII. Library Catalogs and Union Lists. IX. Author Index. Entries 159-374 cover Spanish-America.

Woodyard, George W., and Leon F. Lyday. "Studies on the Latin American Theatre, 1960-1969," THEATRE DOCUMENTATION, 2 (Fall 1969/Spring 1970), 49-84. This bibliography contains 694 "references to studies published between 1960 and 1969 on the Latin American theatre, including critical references from scholarly and specialized journals, book-length studies, Ph.D. dissertations, and reviews of books cited. Primary sources are not included, except in those cases in which an anthology or collection contains a valuable introduction or prologue" [p. 49]. An index to 117 dramatists is also included.

Zeitz, Eileen M., and Richard A. Seybolt. "Hacia una bibliografía sobre el realismo mágico," HISPANIC JOURNAL, 3 (Fall 1981), 159-167. Contents: I. El realismo mágico en la literatura hispanoamericana. II. El realismo mágico en José María Arguedas. III. El realismo mágico en Miguel Angel Asturias. IV. El realismo mágico en Alejo Carpentier. V. El realismo mágico en Gabriel García Márquez. VI. El realismo mágico en Augusto Roa Bastos. VII. El realismo mágico en Juan Rulfo. VIII. El realismo mágico en Arturo Uslar Pietri.

ANDEAN COUNTRIES

Mundo Lo, Sara de. INDEX TO SPANISH AMERICAN COLLECTIVE BIOGRAPHY. VOLUME 1: THE ANDEAN COUNTRIES. Boston: G. K. Hall, 1981. 466p. Contains some 1,100 annotated entries for biographical works ranging in date from the seventeenth century to the present, arranged alphabetically by author within major disciplines or fields of activity. Complete author, title, geographic, and biographee indexes supplement the main listings. Covers Bolivia, Colombia, Chile, Ecuador, Peru, and Venezuela. U.S. library locations are given.

ARGENTINA

Becco, Horacio Jorge. ANTOLOGIA DE LA POESIA GAUCHESCA CON INTRODUCCION, NOTAS, VOCABULARIO Y BIBLIOGRAFIA. Madrid: Aguilar, 1972. 1779p. "La literatura gauchesca," pp. 1737-1765. Contents: I. El Gaucho. II. Literatura gauchesca. III. Bibliografía de los autores incluídos.

Caraffa, Pedro I. HOMBRES NOTABLES DE CUYO. 2ª edición. La Plata: Taller Gráfico de J. Sesé y Cía., 1912. 315p.

Coester, Alfred. A TENTATIVE BIBLIOGRAPHY OF THE BELLES-LETTRES OF THE ARGENTINE REPUBLIC. Cambridge, Mass.: Harvard University Press, 1933. 94p. Contents: I. Authors, alphabetically arranged. II. Anthologies. III. Bibliographies. IV. Periodicals. V. Pseudonyms. VI. Plays (by author).

LA CRITICA TEATRAL ARGENTINA (1880-1962). Buenos Aires: Bibliografía Argentina de Artes y Letras, 1966. 78p. (Compilaciones especiales, 27/28). Contents: I. Obras de referencia. Diccionarios. Anuarios. II. Historia del teatro. Orígenes. Circo. Sainete. III. Crítica. Estudios. Ensayos. Comentarios. A. Crítica sobre un autor. B. Crítica sobre dos o más autores. C. Comentarios sobre puestas en escena. IV. Teatro infantil. Teatro escolar. Títeres. V. Actores. Directores. VI. Aspectos técnicos y escenográficos. VII. Notas sobre teatros argentinos.

Cutolo, Vicente Osvaldo. DICCIONARIO DE ALFONIMOS Y SEUDONIMOS DE LA ARGENTINA, 1800-1930. Buenos Aires: Ediciones Elche, 1962. 160p. Reprinted from: BOLETIN DE LA ACADEMIA NACIONAL DE LA HISTORIA (Buenos Aires), 32 (1961), 417-563. 1,100 items are listed in alphabetical order (including articles). In most cases, sources for the entries are given.

______. NUEVO DICCIONARIO BIOGRAFICO ARGENTINO (1750-

1930). Buenos Aires: Ediciones Elche, 1968- (In progress of publication). Biobibliographical entries.

Durán, Leopoldo. CONTRIBUCION A UN DICCIONARIO DE SEUDONIMOS EN LA ARGENTINA. Buenos Aires: Huemul, 1961. 60p. 678 items are given in two alphabetical arrangements: first, pseudonyms; second, true names.

Foppa, Tito Livio. DICCIONARIO TEATRAL DEL RIO DE LA PLATA. Buenos Aires: Argentores, Ed. del Carro de Tespis, 1961. 1046p. Divided into two sections; Part I, in alphabetical arrangement, contains a bibliographical survey of artists, writers, and critics of the theater.

Foster, David William. ARGENTINE LITERATURE: A RESEARCH GUIDE. 2nd Edition, Revised and Expanded. New York: Garland, 1982. 778p. Contents: I. Bibliography of Criticism: General References. A. Bibliographies. B. General Histories and Literature. C. Collected Essays of Criticism. D. Studies on Criticism, Including Reviews, Journals, and Critics. E. Literature and Other Subjects. F. Argentine Literature and Foreign Literatures. G. Special Literary Topics: Gaucho and Rural Themes. H. Special Literary Topics: Other (including Folklore and Literary Language). I. Special Literary Topics: Urban (including Immigrant) Themes. J. Women Authors. K. General Studies on Colonial Literature. L. General Studies on 19th Century Literature (including modernismo). M. General Studies on 20th Century Literature. N. General Studies on Poetry. O. Colonial Poetry. P. 19th Century Poetry. Q. 20th Century Poetry (including martinfierrismo and ultraísmo). R. Special Topics in Poetry. S. General Studies on Drama. T. Colonial Drama. U. 19th Century Drama. V. 20th Century Drama. T. Colonial Drama. U. 19th Century Drama. V. 20th Century Drama. W. Special Topics in Drama. X. General Studies on Prose Fiction. Y. 19th Century Prose Fiction. Z. 20th Century Prose Fiction. AA. Special Topics in Prose Fiction. BB. General Studies on the Essay. CC. Wit and Humor. DD. Regional and Local Literature. II. Bibliography of Criticism: Authors. The author section (73 authors) is arranged alphabetically, and includes entries for bibliographies, critical monographs and dissertations, and/or critical essays. Section II is indexed in the preceding GUIDE.

Foster, Virginia Ramos. "Contemporary Argentine Dramatists: A Bibliography," THEATRE DOCUMENTATION, 4 (1971/72), 13-20.

Frugoni de Fritzsche, Teresita. INDICE DE POETAS ARGENTINOS. Buenos Aires: Universidad de Buenos Aires, Facultad de Filosofía y Letras, Instituto de Literatura Argentina "Ricardo Rojas," 1963-1968. 4vs. (Guías bibliográficas, 8). "Ordena alfabéticamente a los poetas argentinos de todos los tiempos y da la lista [cronológica] de sus obras."

GRANDES HOMBRES DE NUESTRA PATRIA. Buenos Aires: Editorial Pleamar, 1968. 3 vs. Biographical dictionary.

Lagmanovich, David. BIBLIOGRAFIA DE LA PAGINA LITERARIA DE "LA GACETA," DE S. M. DE TUCUMAN (1956-1961). Buenos Aires: Fondo Nacional de las Artes, 1963. 48p. (Bibliografía Argentina de Artes y Letras, Compilaciones Especiales, 15).

Muzzio, Julio A. DICCIONARIO HISTORICO Y BIOGRAFICO DE LA REPUBLICA ARGENTINA. Buenos Aires: J. Roldán, 1920. 2 vs. Alphabetically arranged biobibliographic entries.

LA NACION. Buenos Aires. ARTES Y LETRAS EN "LA NACION" DE BUENOS AIRES, 4 ENERO 1870-31 DICIEMBRE 1889. Buenos Aires: Fondo Nacional de las Artes, 1968. 552p. (Bibliografía Argentina de Artes y Letras, Compilación Especial, Nos. 32/35). 8,796 entries arranged by Dewey Decimal Classification. There are author and subject indexes.

Orgambide, Pedro, and Roberto Yahni. ENCICLOPEDIA DE LA LITERATURA ARGENTINA. Buenos Aires: Editorial Sudamericana, 1970. 639p. Alphabetically arranged biobibliographies.

QUIENES SON LOS ESCRITORES ARGENTINOS. Buenos Aires: Ediciones Crisol, 1980. 206p. Biographical sketches of contemporary Argentinian writers. Some bibliographical information is included.

Roca Martínez, José Luis. "Contribución a la bibliografía literaria del dictador Juan Manuel Rosas," REVISTA DE INDIAS, Núm. 163/164 (enero/junio de 1981), 203-262. A bibliographic essay arranged under the following categories: I. Breves consideraciones sobre el dictador hispanoamericano como tema literario. II. Don Juan Manuel de Rosas (1793-1877) en la literatura argentina (by author). III. Manuel Gálvez (1882-1962) y sus escenas de la epoca de Rosas. IV. Cronología de la composición y del desarrollo de la acción de las novelas del ciclo rosito. V. Ideaología y estética del ciclo rosito. VI. Análisis y características de los personajes. VII. "El Gaucho de los cerridos." VIII. "El General Quiroga." IX. "La Ciudad pintada de rojo." X. "Tiempo de odio y angustia." XI. "Han tocado a degüello." XII. "Bajo la garra anglo-francesa." XIII. "Y así cayó Don Juan Manuel...."

Sansone de Martínez, Eneida. "Pequeño diccionario de seudónimos de poetas gauchescos," in LA IMAGEN DE LA POESIA ARGENTINA (Montevideo: Universidad de la República, Facultad de Humanidades y Ciencias, 1962), pp. 391-394. Pseudonym followed by true name. Based mainly on Scarone's works.

Scotto, José Antonio. "Los pseudónimos en el periodismo argentino," REVISTA NACIONAL (Buenos Aires), 25 (1898), 259-262, 28 (1899), 206-207, 29 (1900), 172-173.

Sosa de Newton, Lily. DICCIONARIO BIOGRAFICO DE MUJERES ARGENTINAS: AUMENTADO Y ACTUALIZADO. 2. ed. Buenos Aires: Plus Ultra, 1980. 533p. Provides biographical information of contemporary and famous women in Argentine history. A useful bibliography of pertinent sources is also included (pp. 507-523).

Trevia Paz, Susana N. CONTRIBUCION A LA BIBLIOGRAFIA DEL CUENTO FANTASTICO ARGENTINO EN EL SIGLO XX. Buenos Aires: Fondo Nacional de las Artes, 1966. 49p. (Bibliografía Argentina de Artes y Letras, Compilaciones Especiales, Nos. 29/30). The following authors are included: Enrique Anderson Imbert, Adolfo Bioy Casares, Jorge Luis Borges, Julio Córtazar, Santiago Dabove, Macedonio Fernández, Alberto Girri, Leopoldo Lugones, Silvina Ocampo, Manuel Peyrou, Juan Pinto, Horacio Quiroga. Most author entries include: Libros, antologías de sus cuentos, colaboraciones en publicaciones periódicas, crítica (when they apply). Name and title indexes are also included.

Udaondo, Enrique. DICCIONARIO BIOGRAFICO ARGENTINO. Buenos Aires: Institución Mitre, 1938. 1,151p. Alphabetical by individual.

______. DICCIONARIO COLONIAL ARGENTINO. Buenos Aires: Huarpes, 1945. 980p. Entries are listed in alphabetical order.

Unión Panamericana, Washington, D.C. Sección Letras. DICCIONARIO DE LA LITERATURA LATINOAMERICANA. VOL. 4: ARGENTINA. 1960-1961. 2vs. Volume 1: Deceased authors, from the colonial period to the time of publication. Volume 2: Living authors, at the time of publication. Each entry includes the following information: biografía; valoración; bibliografía (del autor); sobre de autor.

Villa, Dolores. BIBLIOGRAFIA CRITICA DE LA LITERATURA DE CORDOBA. Córdoba: Instituto de Literatura Argentina e Iberoamericana, Facultad de Filosofía y Humanidades, Universidad Nacional de Córdoba, 1981. 90p. (Cuaderno 2). Brief bio-bibliographies of the following writers (only books and pamphlets of the authors are included, however): Oscar Guiñazu Alvarez (1916-); Mario Edgardo Altamirano (1943-); Rafael Mario Altamirano (1943-); María Nélida Astrada; Lida Argentina Balkenende (1934-); Genaro Barcía García (1927-); Honorario Humberto Bastos (1935-); Rafael Horacio López (1931-); Bienvenido Marcos (h); Manuel Ernesto Molinari Romero (1915-); Nora Nani (1946-); Rodolfo Rivarola (1933-); Salomón Sabas (1901-1978); Amelia Sailg (1937-); María Meleck Vivanco (1926-).

Yaben, Jacinto R. BIOGRAFIAS ARGENTINAS Y SUDAMERICANAS. Buenos Aires: Metrópolis, 1938-1940. 5 vs. Alphabetically arranged biobibliographies. There is a supplement in Volume 5.

Zayas de Lima, Perla. DICCIONARIO DE AUTORES TEATRALES ARGENTINOS, 1950-1980. Buenos Aires: Editorial R. Alonso, 1981. 188p. Alphabetically arranged biobibliographies. Includes information on productions inside and outside of Argentina.

BOLIVIA

Arze, José Roberto. ENSAYO DE UNA BIBLIOGRAFIA BIOGRAFIA BOLIVIANA. La Paz: Cochabamba: Editorial Los Amigos del Libro, 1981. 71p. Includes biographical studies of Bolivians published as separates and arranged by author, with an index of the biographees. Collective biographies of Bolivians are also included.

Barnadas, Josep M., and Juan José Coy. REALIDAD SOCIOHISTORICA Y EXPRESION LITERARIA EN BOLIVIA: INTRODUCCION GENERAL Y BIBLIOGRAFIA. Cochabamba: Los Amigos del Libro, 1977. 122p. "Bibliografía," pp. 33-122.

Costa de la Torre, Arturo. CATALOGO DE LA BIBLIOGRAFIA BOLIVIANA. La Paz. Universidad Mayor de San Andrés, 1968-1973. 2 vs. Volume 1: Escritores bolivianos: libros y folletos, 1908-1963. Continues chronologically René-Moreno's BIBLIOTECA BOLIVIANA and its supplements. In volume 2: ADICIONES AL SEGUNDO SUPLEMENTO DE LA BIBLIOGRAFIA BOLIVIANA DE GABRIEL RENE-MORENO (1900-1908) y FOLLETOS ANONIMOS EN GENERAL, 1908-1963. Volume 1 provides an alphabetical listing of more than 3,000 Bolivian authors with some 8,700 bibliographical entries. An extensive introductory section (pp. 1-237) provides a comprehensive survey of Bolivian bibliography. Volume 2 lists the adiciones by author and the folletos anónimos en general section chronologically.

Díaz Arguedas, Julio. PACENOS CELEBRES: ESBOZOS BIOGRAFICOS. La Paz: Isla, 1974. 224p.

DICCIONARIO DE LA LITERATURA LATINOAMERICANA: BOLIVIA. Washington, D.C.: Unión Panamericana, 1958. 121p. Alphabetical arrangement. Each entry usually includes: "Biografía," "Valoración," "Bibliografía," and "Sobre el Autor" sections.

Echevarría, Evelio. "Panorama y bibliografía de la novela social boliviana," REVISTA INTERAMERICANA DE BIBLIOGRAFIA, 27 (1977), 143-152. "Bibliografía," pp. 149-152. Contents: I. 1904-1952 (by author). II. 1952-1970 (by author).

Gutiérrez, José Rosendo. DATOS PARA LA BIBLIOGRAFIA BOLIVIANA: LIBROS Y FOLLETOS DE AUTORES BOLIVIANOS O RELATIVOS A BOLIVIA. La Paz, 1875. 225p. Supplement:

La Paz, 1880. 126p. Covers period 1825-1875 and includes 2,203 titles, listed by author alphabetically. The supplement lists 886 editions.

Guzmán, Augusto. BIOGRAFIAS DE LA LITERATURA BOLIVIANA: BIOGRAFIA, EVALUACION, BIBLIOGRAFIA. Cochabamba: Editorial Los Amigos del Libro, 1982. 307p. Biobibliographies of Bolivian authors. The author entries are arranged by the generation in which they were born: colonial (1520-1825), 1825-1884, 1884-1925.

_______. BIOGRAFIAS DE LA NUEVA LITERATURA BOLIVIANA. Cochabamba: Los Amigos del Libro, 1982. 151p. Biobibliographies of Bolivian authors born 1925 and after.

Leavitt, Sturgis E. A TENTATIVE BIBLIOGRAPHY OF BOLIVIAN LITERATURE. Cambridge: Mass.: Harvard University Press, 1933. 23p. This volume is one alphabetical listing by author.

Montenegro, Edmundo. DICCIONARIO BIOGRAFICO DE PERSONALIDES EN BOLIVIA. La Paz: Librería e Imprenta Renovación, 1968. 152p.

Mundo Lo, Sara de. INDEX TO SPANISH AMERICAN COLLECTIVE BIOGRAPHY. VOLUME 1: THE ANDEAN COUNTRIES. Boston: G. K. Hall, 1981. 466p. Contains some 1,100 annotated entries for biographical works ranging in date from the seventeenth century to the present, arranged alphabetically by author within major disciplines or fields of activity. Complete author, title, geographic, and biographic indexes supplement the main listings. Covers Bolivia, Colombia, Chile, Ecuador, Peru, and Venezuela. U.S. library locations are given.

Muñoz Cadima, W. Oscar. TEATRO BOLIVIANO CONTEMPORANEO. La Paz: Casa Municipal de la Cultura "Franz Tamayo," 1981. 214p. "Bibliografía," pp. 203-214. Contents: I. Fuentes primarias (teatro boliviano selecto). II. Fuentes secundarias. A. Literatura e historia boliviana. B. Teatro boliviano. C. Teatro latinoamericano. D. Teatro y teoría teatral.

Ortega, José. "Bibliografía selecta de la literatura boliviana (1969-1974)," REVISTA DE CRITICA LITERARIA LATINOAMERICANA, Núm. 1 (1975), 159-169. Classified annotated bibliography.

_______. LETRAS BOLIVIANAS DE HOY: RENATO PRADA Y PEDRO SHIMOSE; MANUAL DE BIBLIOGRAFIA DE LA LITERATURA BOLIVIANA. Buenos Aires: Fernando García Cambeiro, 1973. 115p. "Manual de bibliografía de literatura boliviana," pp. 89-113. Contents: I. Historia y crítica literarias. II. Antologías y colecciones literarias. III. Obras bibliográficas y catálogos bolivianos. IV. Revistas y periódicos bolivianos. V. Fuentes generales.

_______. "Manual de bibliografía de la literatura boliviana," CUADERNOS HISPANOAMERICANOS, Núm. 263/264 (1972), 657-671. Contents: I. Historia y crítica literarias. II. Antologías y colecciones literarias. III. Obras bibliográficas y catálogos bolivianos. IV. Revistas y periódicos bolivianos. V. Fuentes generales.

_______, and Adolfo Cáceres Romero. DICCIONARIO DE LA LITERATURA BOLIVIANA. La Paz: Editorial Los Amigos del Libro, 1977. 337p. Biobibliographies of Bolivian writers.

Paredes de Salazar, Elsa. DICCIONARIO BIOGRAFICO DE LA MUJER BOLIVIANA. La Paz: Isla, 1965. 309p.

Poppe, René. INDICE DEL CUENTO MINERO BOLIVIANO. La Paz: Instituto Boliviano de Cultura, Instituto Nacional de Historia y Literatura, Departamento de Literatura, 1979. 16p. (Serie Cuadernillos de Investigación, 1).

_______. INDICE DE LOS LIBROS DE CUENTOS BOLIVIANOS. PRIMERA PARTE. La Paz: Instituto Boliviano de Cultura, Instituto Nacional de Historia y Literatura, Departamento de Literatura, 1979. 13p. (Serie de Cuadernillos de Investigación, 2).

René-Moreno, Gabriel. BIBLIOTECA BOLIVIANA. CATALOGO DE LA SECCION DE LIBROS Y FOLLETOS. Santiago de Chile: Guttenberg, 1879. 888p. Two main sections--printed works and manuscripts. Alphabetical listing by title with annotations giving the contents. General alphabetical listing of authors, chief translators, and editions. PRIMER SUPLEMENTO A LA BIBLIOTECA BOLIVIANA, 1879-1899. Santiago de Chile: Barcelona, 1900. 359p. SEGUNDO SUPLEMENTO A LA BIBLIOTECA BOLIVIANA, 1900-1908. Santiago de Chile: Universitaria, 1908. 349p.

Abecía, Valentín. ADICIONES A LA BIBLIOTECA BOLIVIANA DE GABRIEL RENE-MORENO ... CON APENDICE DEL EDITOR, 1602-1879. Santiago de Chile: Barcelona, 1899. 440p. 571 entries; Nos. 1-350 are the work of Abecía; Nos. 351-571 form part of the appendix by the publishers.

Soria, Mario T. TEATRO BOLIVIANO EN EL SIGLO XX. La Paz: Biblioteca Popular Boliviana de "Ultima Hora," 1980. 237p. "Bibliografía de teatro boliviano del siglo XX," pp. 211-226. Bibliography is alphabetically arranged by author, with their plays listed chronologically. Pages 227-230 lists articles and essays on the Bolivian theatre and Bolivian dramatists.

BRAZIL

Alves, Henrique L. BIBLIOGRAFIA AFRO-BRASILEIRA: ESTUDOS SOBRE O NEGRO. APRESENTAÇAO DE JOSE HONORIO RODRIGUES. 2. ed., rev. e ampliada. Rio de Janeiro: Livraria Editôra Cátedra, 1979. 181p. Entries are alphabetically arranged by author or anonymous title. Language and literature citations are included.

ANUARIO BRASILEIRO DE LITERATURA. Rio de Janeiro, 1937-1943/44? Each yearly volume contains a "Movimento bibliográfico de ..." section, which lists by broad subject works published during the past year. Emphasis on literature and the arts. "Pseudônimos de escritores brasileiros," in 1938, pp. 2-5.

Autori, Luiz. OS QUARENTA IMORTAIS. Rio de Janeiro: Borsoi, 1945. 432p. Contains biobibliographies of past and then current members of the Academia Brasileira de Letras.

Basseches, Bruno. A BIBLIOGRAPHY OF BRAZILIAN BIBLIOGRAPHIES; UMA BIBLIOGRAFIA DAS BIBLIOGRAFIAS BRASILEIRAS. Detroit: Blaine Ethridge Books, 1978. 185p. All subjects are included. Entries are alphabetically arranged.

Behar, Ely. VULTOS DO BRASIL: DICIONARIO BIO-BRASILEIRO ILUSTRADO. São Paulo: Livraria Exposição do Livro, 1963? 222p. A biobibliographical dictionary of the important figures of Brazil, including of letters. All periods of Brazilian literature are covered. Entries are alphabetically arranged.

BIBLIOGRAFIA DE DRAMATURGIA BRASILEIRA. São Paulo: Escola de Comunicações e Artes da Universidade de São Paulo; Associação Museu Lasar Segall, 1981- . V. 1: A-M. Contents: I. "Bibliografia," pp. 1-142 (1,471 items listed by playwright). II. "Indice de títulos," pp. 143-184. III. "Indice de personagens," pp. 185-224. Library locations are included.

Bittencourt, Adalzira. DICIONARIO BIO-BIBLIOGRAFICO DE MULHERES ILUSTRES, NOTAVEIS E INTELECTUAIS DO BRASIL. Rio de Janeiro: Ed. Pongetti, 1969-1972. 3 vs. (No more published?)

Bittencourt, Agnello. DICIONARIO AMAZONENSE DE BIOGRAFIAS: VULTOS DO PASSADO. Rio de Janeiro: Conquista, 1973. (Academia amazonense, 4). Who-was-who of Amazônia.

Blake, Augusto Vitorino Alves Sacramento. DICCIONARIO BIBLIOGRAPHICO BRAZILEIRO. Rio de Janeiro: Typographia Nacional e Imprensa Nacional, 1883-1902. 7 vs. Arranged alphabetically by first name; an author approach by surname is available

through the following indexes: 1. Fischer, Jango. INDICE ALPHABETICO DO DICCIONARIO BIBLIOGRAPHICO BRASILEIRA de Sacramento Blake. Rio de Janeiro: Imprensa Nacional, 1937. 127p. 2. Eulálio, Alexandre. "Indice do DICCIONARIO BIBLIOGRAPHICO BRAZILEIRO, de A.V.A. Sacramento Blake," REVISTA DO LIVRO (Rio), Nos. 5 (março de 1957), 213-236; 6 (junho de 1957), 219-232; 7 (setembro de 1957), 225-242; 8 (dezembro de 1957), 265-284. The latter not only is arranged by surname but, unlike the Fischer index, also includes titles of persons and pseudonyms.
3. Torres, Octávio. INDICE DE "DICIONARIO BIBLIOGRAFICO BRASILEIRO" DO DR. AUGUSTO VICTORINO ALVES DO SACRAMENTO BLAKE, POR ORDEM ALFABETICO DOS SOBRENOMBRES E POR ESTADOS, COM ANEXOS DOS ESTRANGEIROS QUE VIVERAM NO BRASIL. Salvador: Fundação Gonçalo Moniz, 1961. 194p.

Brazil. Ministério das Relações Exteriores. Serviço de Documentação. Biblioteca. TRADUÇOES DE AUTORES BRASILEIROS E LIVROS SOBRE O BRASIL ESCRITOS EM IDIOMA ESTRANGEIRO. Rio de Janeiro, 1960 or 1961, 92p. Both sections of this bibliography are arranged by language and then by author.

Brinches, Victor. DICIONARIO BIOBIBLIOGRAFICO LUSO-BRASILEIRO. Lisboa, Rio de Janeiro, São Paulo: Editôra Fondo de Cultura, 1965. 509p. Biobibliography, alphabetical by author. Two sections: Portugal and Brazil.

Carmo, José Arimatéia Pinto do. NOVELAS E NOVELISTAS BRASILEIROS: INDICAÇOES BIBLIOGRAFICAS. Rio de Janeiro: Organização Simões, 1957. 67p. Bibliography is arranged by year, 1826-1956. Only well-known novelists are included. Partially annotated.

Carpeaux, Otto Maria. PEQUENA BIBLIOGRAFIA CRITICA DA LITERATURA BRASILEIRA. 4. edição. Rio de Janeiro: Tecnoprint Gráficas, S.A., 1968. 335p. Bibliography of each literary period is followed by an outstanding author listing and selected bibliography.

Carvalho, José Lopes Pereira de. OS MEMBROS DA ACADEMIA BRASILEIRA EM 1915. (TRAÇOS BIO-BIBLIOGRAFICOS ACOMPANHADOS DE EXCERPTOS DE SUAS PRODUÇOES). Rio de Janeiro, N.p., 1917? 630p.

Coelho, Jacinto do Prado. DICIONARIO DE LITERATURA: LITERATURA PORTUGUESA, LITERATURA BRASILEIRA, LITERATURA GALEGA, ESTILISTICA LITERARIA. 3a. edição. Porto: Livraria Figuerinhas, 1978. 5 vs. Includes biobibliographies of Brazilian authors.

Coelho, Nelly Novaes. DICIONARIO CRITICO DA LITERATURA INFANTIL JUVENIL BRASILEIRA. São Paulo: Quíron, 1983. 963p. Dictionary is arranged by the first name of authors. Entries include a discussion of the author and a listing of his or her work with commentaries. "Bibliografia geral de literatura infantil," pp. 937-960. Dictionary covers the period of 1882-1982.

Costa, Francisco Augusto Pereira da. DICCIONARIO BIOGRAPHICO DE PERNAMBUCANOS CELEBRES. Recife: Typ. Universal, 1882. 804p. Dictionary is arranged alphabetically by first name; index arranged the same way.

Coutinho, Afrânio. BRASIL E BRASILEIROS DE HOJE (ENCICLOPEDIA DE BIOGRAFIAS). Rio de Janeiro: Editorial Sul Americana, 1961. 2 vs. This work contains about 7,000 biographies arranged by surname.

Ford, Jeremiah Denis Matthias; Arthur F. Whittem; and Maxwell I. Raphael. A TENTATIVE BIBLIOGRAPHY OF BRAZILIAN BELLES-LETTRES. Cambridge: Harvard University Press, 1931. 201p. Contents: I. General Works: Bibliographies, Catalogues, etc., pp. 1-2; Bibliography of Brazilian Literature (by author), pp. 3-184; III. Periodicals, pp. 187-201.

Foster, David William, and Roberto Reis. A DICTIONARY OF CONTEMPORARY BRAZILIAN AUTHORS. Tempe, Ariz.: Arizona State University, Center for Latin American Studies, 1981. 152p. At the end of each biographical sketch is a listing of principal works of the author.

Freitas, Edna Gondim de. "Repertórios biográficos brasileiros; bibliografia, cronologia e índice onomástico, geográfico e temático," REVISTA DO LIVRO (Rio de Janeiro), 39 (1969), 127-166. This bibliography of biographical compilations covers 1847-1967.

Fundação Nacional do Livro Infantil e Juvenil, São Paulo. BIBLIOGRAFIA ANALITICA DA LITERATURA INFANTIL E JUVENIL PUBLICADA NO BRASIL, 1965-1974. São Paulo, 1977. 384p.

Gomes, Celeuta Moreira, and Thereza da Silva Aguiar. BIBLIOGRAFIA DO CONTO BRASILEIRA: 1841-1967. Rio de Janeiro: Biblioteca Nacional, 1968. 2 vs. (Anais da Biblioteca Nacional, v. 87). Arranged by author.

Griffin, William J. "Brazilian Literature in English Translation," REVISTA INTERAMERICANA DE BIBLIOGRAFIA (5 (1/2), enero/junio de 1955, 21-37. 207 unannotated titles. "A Checklist of Brazilian Literature Translated into English," pp. 24-37. Contents: I. Books and Pamphlets containing Translations of Selected Items. II. Poetry (entries by author). III. Novels (entries by author). IV. Short Fiction (by author). V. Drama (by author).

Grupo Gente Nova. DICIONARIO CRITICO DO MODERNO ROMANCE BRASILEIRO. Belo Horizonte: Editôra São Vicente, 1970-1971. 3 vs. Biobibliographies. Arrangement is alphabetical by author.

Guaraná, Armindo. DICIONARIO BIO-BIBLIOGRAPHICO SERGIPANO. Rio de Janeiro: Empreza Graphica Editôra Paulo Pongetti & Co., 1925. 282p. For index, see: Maria Helena de Castro Horta's INDICE DO DICIONARIO BIO-BIBLIOGRAPHICO SERGIPANO DO DR. ARMINDO GUARANA (Aracaju: Governo do Estado de Sergipe, Secretaria da Educação e Cultura, Departamento de Cultura e Patrimônio Histórico, 1975, 45p.).

Johnson, Harvey L. "The Brazilian Mirror: Some Brazilian Writings in English Translations," The Americas, 21 (1965), 274-294. A bibliographic survey. Contents and critical commentary follow each title listed.

Lima, Alceu Amoroso. "Bibliografia sucinta do neo-modernismo (1945-1965)," REVISTA INTERAMERICANA DE BIBLIOGRAFIA, 17 (4), octubre/diciembre de 1967, 408-413. Contents: I. Prosa de ficção (1945-1965, by author). II. Selecção de poetas e poemas (1945-1965, by author).

Luyten, Joseph Maria. BIBLIOGRAFIA ESPECIALIZADA SOBRE LITERATURA POPULAR EM VERSO. São Paulo: Escola de Comunicações e Artes da Universidade de São Paulo, 1981. 104p. Under each letter of the alphabet are included the following categories: livros, monografias, artigos (revistas) and/or periódicos (articles).

Marília, Brazil. Faculdade de Filosofia, Ciências e Letras. CATALOGO DA COLEÇAO DE LITERATURA DE CORDEL, FACULDADE DE FILOSOFIA, CIENCIAS E LETRAS DE MARILIA. Marília, 1970. 79p.

Martins Mendes, Deoceli Regina. "Les Ecrivains brésiliens traduits en France (1945-1975)," RECHERCHES ET ETUDES COMPARATISTES IBERO-FRANÇAISES DE LA SORBONNE, 1 (1979), 57-60.

Melo, Joaquim Antônio. BIOGRAPHIAS DE ALGUNS POETAS E HOMENS ILLUSTROS DA PROVINCIA DE PERNAMBUCO. Recife: Typ. Universal, 1858-1860. 3 vs.

Melo, Luís Correia de. DICIONARIO DE AUTORES PAULISTAS. São Paulo: Comissão do IV Centenário da Cidade de São Paulo, Serviço de Comemorações Culturais, 1954. 674p. Biobibliographies, arranged by surname.

______. SUBSIDIOS PARA UM DICIONARIO DOS INTELECTUAIS RIOGRANDENSES. Rio de Janeiro: Civ. Brasileira, 1944. 136p.

Mendonça, Rubens de. DICIONARIO BIOGRAFICO MATO-GROSSENSE. 2. ed. Goiânia, Goiás: Editôra Rio Bonito, 1971. 165p. Entries are alphabetically arranged.

Menezes, Raimundo de. DICIONARIO LITERARIO BRASILEIRO ILUSTRADO. PREF. DO PROFESSOR ANTONIO CANDIDO. São Paulo: Edição Saraiva, 1969. 5 vs. A biobibliographical dictionary of Brazilian literature.

Moraes, Jomar. BIBLIOGRAFIA CRITICA DA LITERATURA MARANHENSE. São Luís: Departamento de Cultura do Maranhão, 1972. 122p. Contents: I. Obras gerais sôbre a literatura maranhense. II. O groupo maranhense neoclássicos e românticos. III. Naturalistas e parnasianos, 1870-1890. IV. Os novos atenienses, 1899-1930. V. Quarto ciclo. Under sections II-V, the principal works by and about a group of representative authors are listed by author. Sections II-V are indexed in the preceding GUIDE.

Paiva, Tancredo de Barros. ACHEGAS A UM DICCIONARIO DE PSEUDONYMOS, INICIAES, ABREVIATURAS E OBRAS ANONYMAS DE AUCTORES BRASILEIROS E DE ESTRANGEIROS, SOBRE O BRASIL OU NO MESMO IMPRESSAS. Rio de Janeiro: J. Leite & Co., 1929. 248p. Contents: I. Pseudonymos, iniciaes e abreviaturas. II. Obras anonymas. III. Indice e indicações bio-bibliographicas.

Parks, George Brenner, and Ruth Z. Temple. THE LITERATURES OF THE WORLD IN ENGLISH TRANSLATION: A BIBLIOGRAPHY. New York: Frederick Ungar, 1970. V.3: Brazilian Literature, pp. 193-212. A selected listing. Contents: I. Background. II. Bibliography. III. Literary Studies. IV. Collections. V. Eighteenth and Nineteenth Centuries (individual authors). VI. Twentieth Century (individual authors).

Placer, Xavier. MODERNISMO BRASILEIRO: BIBLIOGRAFIA, 1918-1971. Rio de Janeiro: Biblioteca Nacional, Divisão de Publicações e Divulgação, 1972. 401p. (Coleção Rodolfo Garcia. Serie B: Catálogos e Bibliografias). "Biografias e biobibliografias," pp. 151-162; "Homenagens," pp. 163-170.

Porter, Dorothy B. AFRO-BRAZILIANA: A WORKING BIBLIOGRAPHY. Boston: G. K. Hall, 1978. 294p. "Bibliographies, Bibliographies of Bibliography, Biographical Dictionaries and Encyclopedias," pp. 3-9. "Literature," pp. 135-170. Contents: I. Anthologies. A. General Works. B. Poetry. C. Short Stories. D. Essays. II. History and Criticism. III. Poetry with Afro-Brazilian Theme. IV. Prose with Afro-Brazilian Theme. V. Dramas and Plays with Afro-Brazilian Themes and Characters.

VI. Individual and Collective Biography. "Writings of Selected Authors, with Critical and Biographical References," pp. 173-276 (by author). This section is indexed in the preceding GUIDE.

Prisco, Francisco. "Pseudônimos de Imortais," REVISTA DA ACADEMIA BRASILEIRA DE LETRAS, Núm. 101 (maio de 1930), 80-94. Includes both living and deceased writers. Arrangement is by first name of the author.

_______. PSEUDONIMOS BRASILEIRAS. PEQUENOS VERBETES PARA UM DICIONARIO. Rio de Janeiro: Z. Valverde, 1941-1945. 5 vs. The index is volume 5.

Reis, Antonio Simões dos. BIBLIOGRAFIA DAS BIBLIOGRAFIAS BRASILEIRAS. Rio de Janeiro: Instituto Nacional do Livro, 1942. 186p. (Coleção B1: Bibliografia 1). Works are listed by year, 1741-1941, and there is an author index and a subject index.

_______. POETAS DO BRASIL (BIBLIOGRAFIA). Rio de Janeiro: Organizações Simões, 1949. 2 vs. (His Bibliografia brasileira, 3). A biobibliography of Brazilian poets.

_______, and Regina Lúcia de Lemos Gill. INDICE DE BIOBIBLIOGRAFIA BRASILEIRA. Rio de Janeiro: Instituto Nacional do Livro, Ministério da Educação e Cultura, 1963. 440p. Alphabetically arranged, this work indexes names in 29 reference works.

Rela, Walter. "Contribución a la bibliografía del teatro brasileño," CEBELA (REVISTA DO CENTRO BRASILEIRO DE ESTUDOS LATINO-AMERICANOS, UNIVERSIDADE DO RIO GRANDE DO SUL, Porto Alegre), 1 (junho de 1966), 105-127. List of individual authors' works is complemented by bibliography of criticism. Within each classification, items are listed chronologically, except periodicals, which appear in alphabetical order.

Ribeiro, João de Souza. DICIONARIO BIOBIBLIOGRAFICO DE ESCRITORES CARIOCOS (1565-1965). Rio de Janeiro: Livraria Brasiliana, 1965. 285p. Brief biobibliographies of writers from Rio de Janeiro and surrounding area. Arrangement is alphabetical by surname.

São Paulo, Brazil (City). Universidade. Departamento de Biblioteconomia e Documentação. BIBLIOGRAFIA SOBRE TEATRO PAULISTA. EDIÇAO PRELIMINAR. São Paulo: Escola de Comunicações e Artes, Departamento de Jornalismo e Editoração, 1972. 103p. (Serie Biblioteconomia e Documentação, 2). Contents: I. Obras (monographs), nos. 1-62. II. Revistas (articles published in reviews), nos. 63-176. III. Jornais (articles published in newspapers), nos. 177-337. IV. Bienais de teatro, nos.

338-346. V. Congressos de teatro, nos. 347-350. V. Indice, pp. 98-103. A. Peças. B. Bienais. C. Congressos. 350 annotated entries.

Souza, José Galante de. O TEATRO NO BRASIL. VOL. 2: SUBSIDIOS PARA UMA BIOBIBLIOGRAFIA DO TEATRO NO BRASIL. Rio de Janeiro: Instituto Nacional do Livro, 1960. Bibliography is arranged by surname of the playwrights. Pseudonyms are included.

Studart, Guilherme, Barão de. DICIONARIO BIO-BIBLIOGRAFICO CEARENSE. Fortaleza: Typo-Lithographia a Vapor e Typ. Minerva, de Assis Bezerra, 1910-1915. 3 vs. Indexes: Nery, Paulo Sérgio. "Indice geral do DICIONARIO BIOBIBLIOGRAFICO CEARENSE de Guilherme Studart," REVISTA DO LIVRO, Nos. 3/4 (dezembro de 1956), 264-284. (This is a surname index with titles of persons, etc.); Teixeira, Regina Lopes. "Indice alfabético e remissivo para o Dicionário bio-bibliográfico cearense de Guilherme Studart," BOLETIM BIBLIOGRAFICO (São Paulo), Núm. 12 (1949), 55-108. A dictionary index (author-title-subject-name).

Velho Sobrinho, João Francisco. DICIONARIO BIO-BIBLIOGRAFICO BRASILEIRO. Rio de Janeiro: Pongetti, 1937-1940. 2 vs. Arranged alphabetically by first name. Index is in second volume.

Vieira, Nelson H. "A Brazilian Biographical Bibliography," BIOGRAPHY, 5 (Fall 1982), 351-364. The bibliography is a selected listing of "various types of memoirs, autobiographies and biographies..." [p. 353]. Collections of correspondence are also included. Items that appeared in periodicals as well as crônicas are excluded. Arrangement is alphabetical by surname.

Villas-Bôas, Pedro. NOTAS DE BIBLIOGRAFIA SUL-RIO-GRANDENSE: AUTORES. Porto Alegre: A. Nação, 1974. 615p. Biobibliographies.

_______. PSEUDONIMOS DE REGIONALISTAS E ABREVIATURAS. Porto Alegre: Impressora Moliterni, 1967. 26p. Listing is by pseudonym or abbreviation followed by real name of writer.

CARIBBEAN COUNTRIES

CARIBBEAN WRITERS: A BIO-BIBLIOGRAPHICAL-CRITICAL ENCYCLOPEDIA. Washington, D.C.: Three Continents Press, 1979. 943p. Contains biographical data on some 2,000 creative writers (both current and deceased writers) and bibliographical detail on nearly 15,000 works. Lists of authors by country, by language used, and by sociopolitical entity are provided. There are separate sections on English, French, Spanish, and Dutch Caribbean writers. Each section contains essays on national literature and listings of pertinent literary journals. Cuba, Dominican Republic, and Puerto Rico are covered on pp. 599-943.

Mundo Lo, Sara de. INDEX TO SPANISH AMERICAN COLLECTIVE BIOGRAPHY. VOLUME 3: THE CENTRAL AMERICAN AND CARIBBEAN COUNTRIES. Boston: G. K. Hall, 1984. 360p. This volume contains approximately 1,000 annotated listings for collective biographical works that contain biographical information about individuals from Costa Rica, Cuba, the Dominican Republic, El Salvador, Guatemala, Honduras, Nicaragua, Panamá, and Puerto Rico. Arrangement is by author within major disciplines or fields of activity. Complete author, title, geographic, and biographee indexes supplement the main listings. U.S. library locations are given.

Thompson, Donald. "Music, Theater, and Dance in Central America and the Caribbean: An Annotated Bibliography of Dissertations and Theses," REVISTA/REVIEW INTERAMERICANA, 9, No. 1 (Spring 1979), 113-140. 126 entries arranged by author. A subject index appears on pp. 118-119.

CENTRAL AMERICA

Acevedo, Ramón Luis. LA NOVELA CENTROAMERICANA (DESDE EL POPOLVUH HASTA LOS UMBRALES DE LA NOVELA ACTUAL). San Juan: Editorial Universitaria, Universidad de Puerto Rico, 1982. 503p. "Bibliografía: autores y crítica," pp. 461-491. Alphabetical by author.

Arellano, Jorge Eduardo. "Bibliografía general de la literatura centroamericana," BOLETIN NICARAGUENSE DE BIBLIOGRAFIA Y DOCUMENTACION, Núm. 29 (1979), 1-5. Contents: I. Obras de referencia. II. Antologías. III. Estudios. "... esta guía de estudio comprende aquellos títulos de carácter centroamericanos--los que abarcan en conjunto al Istmo ..." [p. 1]. Fifty-five unannotated entries.

Doyle, Henry Grattan. A TENTATIVE BIBLIOGRAPHY OF THE BELLES-LETTRES OF THE REPUBLICS OF CENTRAL AMERICA. Cambridge, Mass.: Harvard University Press, 1935. 136p. Contents: I. General Works. II. Costa Rica. III. Guatemala. IV. Honduras. V. Nicaragua. VI. El Salvador. VII. Current Newspapers and Periodicals of Central America.

Mundo Lo, Sara de. INDEX TO SPANISH AMERICAN COLLECTIVE

BIOGRAPHY. VOLUME 3: THE CENTRAL AMERICAN AND CARIBBEAN COUNTRIES. Boston: G. K. Hall, 1984. 360p. This volume contains approximately 1,000 annotated listings for collective biographical works that contain biographical information about individuals from Costa Rica, Cuba, the Dominican Republic, El Salvador, Guatemala, Honduras, Nicaragua, Panamá, and Puerto Rico. Arrangement is by author within major disciplines or fields of activity. Complete author, title, geographic, and biographee indexes supplement the main listings. U.S. library locations are given.

Thompson, Donald. "Music, Theater, and Dance in Central America and the Caribbean: An Annotated Bibliography of Dissertations and Theses," REVISTA/REVIEW INTERAMERICANA, 9, No. 1 (Spring 1979), 113-140. 126 entries arranged by author. A subject index appears on pp. 118-119.

CHILE

Anrique Reyes, Nicolás. ENSAYO DE UNA BIBLIOGRAFIA DRAMATICA CHILENA. Santiago de Chile: Imprenta Cervantes, 1899. 184p. Contents: I. Teatro extranjero relativo a Chile, 1612-1886 (descriptive bibliography, entries are arranged by year). II. Teatro nacional, 1693-1899 (same format as in part I).

BIBLIOGRAFIA DE ESCRITORES DE CHILE, 1569-1975. Santiago de Chile: Servicio de Extensión Chilena, 1976. 60p. Contents: I. "Escritores chilenos," pp. 1-20 (arranged by major generation periods; then by major author and a selected list of his/her works). II. "Otros escritores," pp. 20-25 (alphabetically arranged by author). III. "Poetas chilenos," pp. 26-34 (chronologically arranged listing of works by major Chilean poets). IV. "Otros poetas chilenos," pp. 35-38 (chronologically arranged). V. "Escritores chilenos de teatro," pp. 38-42 (chronologically arranged listing of works by the major Chilean dramatists). VI. "Otros escritores chilenos de teatro," pp. 42-43 (chronologically arranged). VII. "Críticos y ensayistas chilenos," pp. 44-48 (chronologically arranged listing of works by the major Chilean critics and essayists). VIII. "Otras ensayistas y críticos chilenos," pp. 48-50 (chronologically arranged). IX. "Indice onomástico," pp. 56-60.

California. University. Library. CONTEMPORARY CHILEAN LITERATURE IN THE UNIVERSITY LIBRARY AT BERKELEY: A BIBLIOGRAPHY WITH INTRODUCTION, BIOGRAPHICAL NOTES, AND COMMENTARIES BY GASTON SOMOSHEGYI-SZOKOL. Berkeley: Center for Latin American Studies, University of California, 1975. 161p. Contents: I. Bibliography of

Selected 20th-Century Authors. II. Bibliographical Guide to Histories of Chilean Literature. III. Biographical Sketches of "Selected Contemporary Chilean Writers Whose Works are Considered to Be the Most Significant in Chilean Letters." The bibliography includes an index of authors.

Castillo, Homero, and Raúl Silva Castro. HISTORIA BIBLIOGRAFICA DE LA NOVELA CHILENA. Charlottesville: Bibliographical Society of the University of Virginia; México: Ediciones De Andrea, 1961, 214p. Arranged alphabetically by author. Titles are listed in chronological order, and imprint information is given.

Chile. Biblioteca Nacional. REFERENCIAS CRITICAS SOBRE AUTORES CHILENOS. Santiago de Chile, v. 1- ; 1968- . An irregularly published annual volume divided into two sections: "Referencias críticas sobre autores" (arranged by author) and "Los críticos" (arranged by critic). Studies in books, newspapers, and periodicals published in Chile are included.

DICCIONARIO DE LA LITERATURA LATINOAMERICANA: CHILE. Washington, D.C.: Unión Panamericana, 1958. 234p. Alphabetical arrangement. Each author entry usually includes: "Biografía," "Valoración," "Bibliografía," and "Sobre el autor" sections.

Dolz Henry, Inés. LOS ROMANCES TRADICIONALES CHILENOS: TEMATICA Y TECNICA. Santiago de Chile: Editorial Nascimento, 1976. 270p. "Bibliografía," pp. 261-267. Alphabetically arranged entries.

Durán Cerda, Julio. REPERTORIO DEL TEATRO CHILENO: BIBLIOGRAFIA, OBRAS INEDITAS Y ESTRENADAS. Santiago de Chile: Prensas de Editorial Universitaria, 1962. 247p. A partially annotated bibliography of 1,710 entries by author in alphabetical arrangement. Part II gives fundamental studies concerning the theater in Chile since 1910; entries are by author in alphabetical order. Part III includes alphabetical listing of authors. Part IV is an alphabetical index of works.

Escudero, Alfonso M. "Fuentes de consulta sobre los poetas románticos chilenos," AISTHEIS (PONTIFICIA UNIVERSIDAD CATOLICA DE CHILE, SANTIAGO), Núm. 5 (1970), 295-307. Contents: I. Obras generales (41 unannotated titles). II. Autores (titles about the following poets' works and lives are listed): Salvador Sanfuentes; Hermogenes de Irisarri; Eusebio Lillo, Guillermo Matta; Guillermo Blest Gana; Martín José Lira; Domingo Arteaga Alemparte; Luis Rodríguez Velasco; Eduardo de la Barra; Carlos Walker Martínez; José Antonio Soffia; Enrique del Solar; and Víctor Torres. Section II is indexed in the preceding GUIDE.

Figueroa, Pedro Pablo. DICCIONARIO BIOGRAFICO DE CHILE. 4.

edición. Santiago de Chile: Imprenta y Encuadernación Barcelona, 1897-1902. 3 vs. Primarily 19th-century biographees.

Figueroa, Virgilio. DICCIONARIO HISTORICO, BIOGRAFICO Y BIBLIOGRAFICO DE CHILE, 1800-1930. Santiago de Chile: Barcells & Co., 1925-1931. 5 vs. in 4. Most biographies concluded with bibliographies of source materials.

Finch, Mark Steven. "AN ANNOTATED BIBLIOGRAPHY OF RECENT SOURCES ON LATIN AMERICAN THEATER: GENERAL SECTION, ARGENTINA, CHILE, MEXICO, AND PERU." Ph.D., University of Cincinnati, 1978. 372p. "The eight hundred eighty-four items of this document are, then, a supplement, extension and clarification of such sources as the PMLA annual bibliography, the Hebblethwaite bibliography, the Dauster 'recent research' article, the Woodyard-Lyday bibliography and The Handbook of Latin American Studies." The general section chapter, as well those on Argentina, Chile, Mexico and Peru, are divided into the following sections: books and reviews, articles, anthologies, bibliographies, and miscellaneous items. (Dissertation Abstracts International, 39 [1979], 5502A.)

Fleak, Kenneth. "The Chilean Generation of 1950: An Introduction and a Bibliography to Its Original Works," CHASQUI, 10, Núm. 2/3 (febrero/mayo de 1981), 26-36. The original works of the following authors are listed: Margarita Aguirre (1925-); Guillermo Blanco (1926-); Armando Cassígoli (1928-); José Donoso (1924-); Alfonso Echeverría (1922-1969); Jorge Edwards (1931-); Félix Emerich; Mario Espinoso; Pablo García (1919-); María Elena Gertner (1927-); Claudio Giaconi (1927-); César Ricardo Guerra; Yolanda Gutiérrez; Luis Alberto Heiremans (1928-1964); Alejandro Jodorowsky; Enrique Lafourcade (1927-); Pilar Larraín; Jaime Laso (1926-1969); Enrique Lihn (1929-); Enrique Moletto (1923-); Gloria Montaldo; Herbert Müller (1923-); Alberto Rubio (1928-); María Eugenia Sanhueza (1925-); José Manuel Vergara (1928-); Waldo Vila (1925-); José Zañartu. Only books and pamphlets are included; genre listed after titles.

Foster, David William. CHILEAN LITERATURE: A WORKING BIBLIOGRAPHY OF SECONDARY SOURCES. Boston: G. K. Hall, 1978. 236p. Contents: I. Critical References on Chilean Literature: General References. A. Bibliographies. B. General History and Criticism. C. Collected Essays of Criticism. D. Studies on Criticism, Including Reviews and Journals. E. Literature and Other Subjects. F. Chilean Literature and Foreign Literatures. G. Special Literary Topics. H. Women Authors. I. General Studies on Colonial Literature. J. General Studies on 19th Century Literature. K. General Studies on 20th Century Literature. L. General Studies on Poetry. M. Colonial and 19th Century Poetry. N. 20th Century Poetry. O. Special Topics in

Poetry. P. General Studies on Drama. Q. Colonial Drama. R. 19th Century Drama. S. 20th Century Drama. T. Special Topics in Drama. U. General Studies on Prose Fiction. V. 19th Century Prose Fiction. W. 20th Century Prose Fiction. X. Special Topics in Prose Fiction. Y. General Studies on the Essay. Z. Wit and Humor. AA. Folk and Local Literature. BB. Regional and Local Literature. II. Critical References on Chilean Literature: Authors (46 authors; each author entry contains critical monographs, bibliographies, dissertations, and/or critical essays). Section II is indexed in the preceding GUIDE.

Goić, Cedomil. "Bibliografía de la novela chilena del siglo XX," BOLETIN DE FILOLOGIA DE LA UNIVERSIDAD DE CHILE, 14 (1962), 51-168. Tirada aparte: Santiago de Chile: Editorial Universitaria, 1962. 168p. This study embraces the Chilean novel from 1910 to 1961, as well as works of novelists born from 1860 to date. Its scope is broad and arrangement is by chronological order.

Guerra-Cunningham, Lucia. "Fuentes bibliográficas para el estudio de la novela chilena (1843-1960)," REVISTA IBEROAMERICANA, 42, Núm. 96/97 (julio/diciembre de 1976), 601-619. Contents: I. Literatura chilena en general. II. Movimientos literarios y tendencias en particular. III. Autores y novelas. IV. Espacios, temas y motivos en la novela chilena. V. Material bibliográfico.

Lastro, Pedro. "Registro bibliográfico de antologías del cuento chileno, 1876-1976," REVISTA DE CRITICA LITERARIA LATINOAMERICANA (Lima), Año 3, Núm. 5 (1977), 89-111. Bibliographic introduction followed by the list chronologically. Contents of the anthologies are included.

López L., Guillermo. INDICE DE SEUDONIMOS. Santiago de Chile: Universidad de Chile, 1939. 108p. Reprinted from ANALES DE LA UNIVERSIDAD DE CHILE, 3a serie, Año 97, Nos. 33/34 (1939), 56-159. A list of 1,224 pseudonyms are indexed along with a list of true names. There is also a list of "Impresos seudónimos chilenos, anteriores a 1926, no incluídos en el DICCIONARIO DE ANONIMOS Y SEUDONIMOS HISPANOAMERICANOS, de José Toribio Medina," pp. 130-156.

Matta Vial, Enrique. "Apuntes Para un diccionario biográfico," REVISTA CHILENA DE HISTORIA Y GEOGRAFIA, 43 (1922), 300-532. Alphabetically arranged by surname; some entries contain bibliographical material. Emphasis is on colonial and early independence periods.

Medina, José Toribio. DICCIONARIO BIOGRAFICO COLONIAL DE CHILE. Santiago de Chile: Imprenta Elzeviriana, 1906. 1004p. Covers through the 18th century. Corrections are supplied by: Luis Francisco Prieto del Río, MUESTRAS DE ERRORES Y DEFECTOS DEL "DICCIONARIO BIOGRAFICO COLONIAL DE CHILE,"

POR JOSE TORIBIO MEDINA. Santiago de Chile: Imprenta y Encuadernación Chile, 1907. 124p.

______. LA LITERATURA FEMININA EN CHILE (NOTAS BIBLIOGRAFICAS Y EN PARTE CRITICAS). Santiago de Chile: Universitaria, 1923. 334p. "Poesía," pp. 15-65. "La novela," pp. 143-180. "Teatro," pp. 189-202. "Periodismo," pp. 217-224 (list of women's journals). Under each of these subject headings, entries are arranged chronologically and then by author's work. Lengthy bibliographical information is given for each entry.

Mundo Lo, Sara de. INDEX TO SPANISH AMERICAN COLLECTIVE BIOGRAPHY. VOLUME 1: THE ANDEAN COUNTRIES. Boston: G. K. Hall, 1981. 466p. Contains some 1,100 annotated entries for biographical works ranging in date from the seventeenth century to the present arranged alphabetically by author within major disciplines or fields of activity. Complete author, title, geographic, and biographee indexes supplement the main listings. Covers Bolivia, Colombia, Chile, Ecuador, Peru, and Venezuela. U.S. library locations are given.

Rela, Walter. CONTRIBUCION A LA BIBLIOGRAFIA DEL TEATRO CHILENO, 1804-1960. NOTICIA PRELIMINAR DE RICARDO LATCHAM. Montevideo: Universidad de la República, 1960, 51p. Covers the period indicated in the title, listing 895 items with an author and title index. The bibliography is divided into two sections: the first history and criticism ("obras generales," "artículos de crítica," "revistas,") and the second a listing of individual plays. The introduction by Ricardo A. Latcham (pp. 7-16), is a succinct outline history of the Chilean theatre.

Santana, Fracisco. EVOLUCION DE LA POESIA CHILENA. Santiago, de Chile: Editorial Nascimiento, 1976. 342p. "Antologías de poesía chilena," pp. 309-314. 113 works are listed by year, 1846-1975.

Silva Castro, Raúl. EL CUENTO CHILENO: BIBLIOGRAFIA. Santiago de Chile: Prensas de la Universidad de Chile, 1936. 62p. This is a very extensive listing of Chilean short stories from the late nineteenth century through the mid 1930's. Arrangement is alphabetical by author. Information includes titles and where published originally.

______. "Indice de seudónimos," ANALES DE LA UNIVERSIDAD DE CHILE, 3ª serie, Núm. 33/34 (1939), 56-159. An index of pseudonyms used by Chilean authors. The bibliography includes a section of pseudonyms not included in Medina's DICCIONARIO DE ANONIMOS Y SEUDONIMOS HISPANOAMERICANOS.

______. "Notas bibliográficas para el estudio de la poesía vulgar en Chile," ANALES DE LA UNIVERSIDAD DE CHILE, Núm. 79

(1950), 69-86. The fully annotated entries are arranged by year, 1866-1938.

Szmulewicz, Efraín. DICCIONARIO DE LA LITERATURA CHILENA. Santiago de Chile: Selecciones Lautaro, 1977. 563p. Brief biobibliographies of both deceased and living writers. The bibliographies include books and pamphlets only. The work also includes an excellent "bibliografía general sobre literatura chilena" section (pp. 535-560).

Torres-Rioseco, Arturo, and Raúl Silva Castro. ENSAYO DE BIBLIOGRAFIA DE LA LITERATURA CHILENA. Cambridge, Mass.: Harvard University Press, 1935. 71p. Contents: I. Novela. II. Poesía. III. Drama. IV. Crítica y fuentes bibliográficas. Arrangement within each section is alphabetical by author.

Villacura Fernández, Maúd. "Bibliografía de narradores chilenos nacidos entre 1935-1949," REVISTA CHILENA DE LITERATURA, Núm. 4 (1973), 109-128. "En este bibliografía se incluye la producción completa de los narradores chilenos nacidos entre 1935 y 1949.... Los límites cronológicos de este registro comprenden desde la primera publicación de 1956 hasta el 31 de diciembre de 1970 en que la bibliografía se cierra" [p. 109]. Contents: I. Novelas. II. Novelas cortas y cuentos. III. Antologís citadas. IV. Indice de autores. V. Indice de títulos. The entries were derived from books, anthologies, reviews and newspapers (both published in Chile and abroad), and translations.

COLOMBIA

Acosta Hoyos, Luis Eduardo. BIBLIOGRAFIA ANOTADA DEL DEPARTAMENTO DE NARIÑO. Pasto: Imprenta del Departamento, 1966. 226p. 805 (1869-1966) entries listed alphabetically by author with subject, title, and chronological indexes.

Alvarez Retrespo, Mary. BIBLIOGRAFIA DE AUTORES ANTIOQUEÑOS. Antioquía: Universidad de Antioquía, 1960. 691-838p. "Separata de la Revista UNIVERSIDAD DE ANTIOQUIA, No. 146." Arrangement is by subject matter; a bibliography of bibliographies is given. An author index concludes the study.

Arboleda, Gustavo. DICCIONARIO BIOGRAFICO Y GENEALOGICO DEL ANTIGUO DEPARTAMENTO DEL CAUCA. 3. ed. Bogotá: Biblioteca Horizontes, Librería Horizontes, 1962. 488p. Entries are arranged alphabetically.

Bronx, Humberto. LA NOVELA Y EL CUENTO EN ANTIOQUIA. Medellín: Academia Antioqueña de Historia, 1975. 108p. (Colección Academia Antioqueña de Historia, 33). "Bibliografía de la novela en Antioquia," pp. 101-108. Entries are arranged by author.

Cobo Borda, J. G. "La nueva poesía colombiana: una década, 1970-1980," BOLETIN CULTURAL Y BIBLIOGRAFIO (Bogotá), 16, Núm. 9/10 (1979), 75-122. "Bibliografía," pp. 77-80.

Curcio Altamar, Antonio. EVOLUCION DE LA NOVELA EN COLOMBIA. Bogotá: Instituto Caro y Cuervo, 1957. 339p. (Its Publicaciones, 11). "Bibliografía de la novela," pp. 267-323 (alphabetically arranged by author of the novel).

DICCIONARIO DE LA LITERATURA LATINOAMERICANA: COLOMBIA. Washington, D.C.: Unión Panamericana, Secretaría General, Organización de los Estados Unidos, División de Filosofía y Letras, Departamento de Asuntos Culturales, 1959. 179p. Contents: I. Clásicos colombianos de la colonia al presente. II. Autores colombianos vivos. III. Bibliografía de las letras colombianas. Each author entry under I. and II. includes biografía, valoración, and bibliografía sections.

Englekirk, John Eugene, and Gerald E. Wade. "Bibliografía de la novela colombiana," REVISTA IBEROAMERICANA, 15, Núm. 30 (1949/1950), 309-411. 19th and 20th centuries. A bibliographical essay is followed by the bibliographical listing. Entries are alphabetical by author with many commentaries. Library location is given for about 650 items.

Giraldo Jaramillo, Gabriel. BIBLIOGRAFIA DE BIBLIOGRAFIAS COLOMBIANAS. 2ª EDICION, CORR. Y PUESTA AL DIA POR RUBEN PEREZ ORTIZ. Bogotá: Instituto Caro y Cuervo, 1960. 204p. (Publicaciones del Instituto Caro y Cuervo. Serie bibliográfica, 1). "Filología y lingüística," pp. 102-104; "Literatura," pp. 126-134.

Laverde Amaya, Isidoro. APUNTES SOBRE BIBLIOGRAFIA COLOMBIANA CON MUESTROS ESCOGIDOS EN PROSA Y EN VERSO CON UN APENDICE QUE CONTIENE LA LISTA DE LAS ESCRITORES COLOMBIANAS, LAS PIEZAS DRAMATICAS, NOVELAS, LIBROS DE HISTORIA Y DE VIAJES ESCRITOS POR COLOMRIANOS [sic]. Bogotá: Imprenta de Vapor de Zalamea Hermanos, 1842. 254p. Alphabetical by author. Many anthological excerpts of obscure, early Colombian poets and prose writers. Pseudonyms on pp. 237-240. Pseudonym first, followed by real name. "Escritores colombianas," pp. 209-214 (brief biobibliographies). "Teatro colombiano," pp. 214-222 (works arranged by playwright). "Novelas de autores colombianos," pp. 223-229 (arranged by author).

______. BIBLIOGRAFIA COLOMBIANA. Bogotá: M. Rivas, 1895. 296p. Tomo I: Abadía Méndez-Ovalle only published. Colombian biobibliography; covers 19th-century authors mainly.

Leavitt, Sturgis E., and Carlos García Prada. A TENTATIVE BIBLIOGRAPHY OF COLOMBIAN LITERATURE. Cambridge: Harvard University Press, 1934. 80p. The bibliography lists works by grammarians, linguists, bibliographers, novelists, poets, and prose writers. Travel accounts, chronicles, biographies and public addresses of literary significance are included. Contents: I. List of bibliographies, catalogues, histories of literature, etc. II. A Tentative bibliography of Colombian literature (alphabetical listing by author).

McGrady, Donald. "Ediciones a la bibliografía de la novela colombiana: 1856-1962," THESAURUS, 20 (1965), 120-137. Supplements Englekirk, Laverde Amaya, and Leavitt. Items are arranged alphabetically by author and include more than 70 new novels and more than 190 editions of known titles.

Mena, Lucila Inés. "Bibliografía anotada sobre el ciclo de la violencia en la literatura colombiana," LATIN AMERICAN RESEARCH REVIEW, 13, No. 3 (1978), 95-107. Contents: I. "Novelas sobre la violencia," pp. 100-101 (74 novels, arranged by author; unannotated). II. "Crítica sobre la novela de la violencia," pp. 101-107.

Mundo Lo, Sara de. INDEX TO SPANISH AMERICAN COLLECTIVE BIOGRAPHY. VOLUME 1: THE ANDEAN COUNTRIES. Boston: G. K. Hall, 1981. 466p. Contains some 1,100 annotated entries for biographical works ranging in date from the seventeenth century to the present, arranged alphabetically by author within major disciplines or fields of activity. Complete author, title, geographic, and biographee indexes supplement the main listings. Covers Bolivia, Colombia, Chile, Ecuador, Peru, and Venezuela. U.S. library locations are given.

Orjuela, Héctor H. LAS ANTOLOGIAS POETICAS DE COLOMBIA; ESTUDIO Y BIBLIOGRAFIA. Bogotá: Instituto Caro y Cuervo, 1966. 514p. (Publicaciones del Instituto Caro y Cuervo. Serie bibliográfica, 6). The bibliographic section lists 389 items; entries are listed alphabetically by author or title. Contents: I. Bibliografía de antologías poéticas de Colombia," pp. 253-355. II. "Bibliografía de antologías poéticas generales," pp. 357-458.

_______. BIBLIOGRAFIA DE LA POESIA COLOMBIANA. Bogotá: Instituto Caro y Cuervo, 1971. 486p. (Publicaciones del Instituto Caro y Cuervo. Serie bibliográfica, 9). Entries alphabetically arranged; library locations noted; some contents notes; books and anthologies only.

_______. BIBLIOGRAFIA DEL TEATRO COLOMBIANO. Bogotá: Instituto Caro y Cuervo, 1974. 312p. (Serie bibliográfica, 10). The main part of the bibliography is an annotated alphabetical listing by author of dramatic works. "Secciones complementares," pp. 209-276, contains lists of sources for the study of the Colombian theater, for the study of the Latin American theater, and for the study of theater in general. Library locations are frequently given, including a selected number of U.S. libraries.

_______. FUENTES GENERALES PARA EL ESTUDIO DE LA LITERATURA COLOMBIANA; GUIA BIBLIOGRAFICA. Bogotá: Instituto Caro y Cuervo, 1968. 863p. (Publicaciones del Instituto Caro y Cuervo. Serie bibliográfica, 7). Work is arranged by subject; then listings by author. Contents notes as well as quotes from reviewers are included. Locations of titles from major U.S., Colombian, and other libraries are included.

Ortega Ricaurte, José Vicente. HISTORIA CRITICA DEL TEATRO EN BOGOTA. Bogotá: Ediciones Colombia, 1927. 318p. "Lista detallada de las obras estrenadas en Bogotá, por orden alfabético de sus autores (1620-1927)," pp. 183-195. An annotated list of the published and unpublished plays by 102 playwrights. Some bibliographic data are missing from the published titles.

Ospina, Joaquín. DICCIONARIO BIOGRAFICO Y BIBLIOGRAFICO DE COLOMBIA. Bogotá: Editorial Cromos, 1927-1939. 3 vs. Alphabetically arranged entries covering from the conquest to the time of publication.

Otero Muñoz, Gustavo. SEMBLANZAS COLOMBIANAS. Bogotá: Editorial ABC, 1938. 2 vs. Contents: I. Cronistas primitivos. II. Escritores coloniales. III. Literatos de la Revolución. IV. Escritores de la Gran Colombia.

_______. "Seudónimos de escritores colombianos," THESAURUS, 13 (1958), 112-131. One alphabetical list by pseudonym, with parallel indication of true name.

Pachón Padilla, Eduardo. EL CUENTO COLOMBIANO: ANTOLOGIA, ESTUDIO HISTORICO Y ANALITICO. Bogotá: Plaza y Janes Editores-Colombia, Ltda., 1980. 2 vs. "Bibliografía del cuento colombiano," v. 2, pp. 307-334. Contents: I. Textos. II. Antologías y selecciones. III. Teoría y crítica.

Pérez Ortiz, Rubén. SEUDONIMOS COLOMBIANOS. Bogotá: Instituto Caro y Cuervo, 1961. 276p. (Publicaciones del Instituto Caro y Cuervo. Serie Bibliográfica, 2). Divided into two main parts: (1) lists each pseudonym in alphabetical order followed by the real name of the author and in many cases the publications where the pseudonym appears; (2) lists the real names followed by the author's pseudonym or pseudonyms.

Porras Collantes, Ernesto. BIBLIOGRAFIA DE LA NOVELA EN COLOMBIA, CON NOTAS DE CONTENIDO Y CRITICA DE LAS OBRAS Y GUIAS DE COMENTARIOS SOBRE LOS AUTORES. Bogotá: Instituto Caro y Cuervo, 1976. 888p. (Serie bibliográfica, 11).

The bibliography contains more than 2,326 entries and is arranged by author with title and chronological indexes. Bibliographical information is full with numerous notes on contents and excerpts from critical evaluations. In addition, library locations are given, including a number from outside Colombia. There is a "Lista de seudónimos." The major novelists are indexed in the preceding GUIDE.

Posada, Eduardo. BIBLIOGRAFIA BOGOTANA. Bogotá: Arboleda y Valencia, 1917-1925. 2 vs. (Biblioteca de Historia Nacional, v. 16; v. 36). Chronological arrangement covering from 1731 to 1831. Over 1,400 entries with annotations and occasional excerpts. Indexes give chronological listings of title, author and additions.

Romero Castañeda, Rafael. AUTORES MAGDALENENSES. Bogotá: Instituto de Ciencias Naturales, Universidad Nacional de Colombia, 1968. 115p. Alphabetically arranged; emphasis is on twentieth century.

Salazar, Hernando; Luis Darío González; and Gustavo Arbeláez. BIBLIOGRAFIA DE AUTORES ANTIOQUEÑOS (DESDE 1822 HASTA 1974). SE PUBLICA CON MOTIVO DE LOS 300 AÑOS DE LA FUNDACION DE MEDELLIN. Medellín: Hernando Salazar M., Editor, 1975. 427p. 33p. of index. By author under each subject heading. The following subject headings are pertinent: "Lingüística en general," pp. 122-126; "Literatura, ensayos, cuento," pp. 160-209; "Poesía," pp. 269-327; "Teatro," pp. 327-372; and "Biografías," pp. 381-417.

Sánchez López, Luis María. DICCIONARIO DE ESCRITORES ANTIOQUENOS. N.p.: Imprenta San Martín, 1982? 130p. Biobibliographies of writers from the Department of Antioquia, Colombia.

________. DICCIONARIO DE ESCRITORES COLOMBIANOS. Barcelona: Plaza y Janés, 1978. 548p. Brief biobibliographies. Includes a "Lista de seudónimos," pp. 531-546.

Valle, Francisco. BIBLIOGRAFIA DE AUTORES ANTIOQUEÑOS, 1960-1969. Medellín: Editorial Universidad de Antioquía, 1971. 102p. (Publicaciones de la Escuela Interamericana de Bibliotecología, Serie bibliográfica, 29). Updates Mary Alvarez Restrepo's work. Work excludes periodical articles. "Literatura," pp. 50-69; "Lingüística," pp. 40-41. Authors are listed under each genre.

Viloria Bermúdez, Jorge Enrique. "Indice biobibliográfico de autores colombianos de teatro hasta el siglo XIX," LOGOS (CALI), Núm. 10 (1974), 7-22.

Williams, Raymond L. "La novela Colombiana, 1960-1974," CHASQUI, 5, Núm. 3 (mayo de 1976), 27-39. Arrangement is alphabetical by author.

COSTA RICA

Dobles Segreda, Luis. INDICE BIBLIOGRAFICO DE COSTA RICA. San José: Lehmann, 1927-1936. 16 sections in 9 volumes. Sección XII: novela, cuento y artículo literario. Sección XV: Teatro. Sección XVI: Poesía. Each section is a chronological listing of works with critical commentaries, and library locations are given.

Kargleder, Charles L., and Warren H. Mory. BIBLIOGRAFIA SELECTA DE LA LITERATURA COSTARRICENSE. San José: Editorial Costa Rica, 1978. 109p. Contents: I. Antologías. II. Obras (works listed by author and then title). Works that appeared in anthologies, newspapers, or periodicals are not included.

Menton, Seymour. EL CUENTO COSTARRICENSE: ESTUDIO, ANTOLOGIA Y BIBLIOGRAFIA. México, D.F.: Ediciones De Andrea, 1964. 184p. (Antologías Studium, 8). "Indice bibliográfico del cuento costarricense," pp. 163-182.

Portuguez de Bolaños, Elizabeth. EL CUENTO EN COSTA RICA: ESTUDIO, BIBLIOGRAFIA Y ANTOLOGIA. San José: Antonio Lehmann, 1964. "Indice de autores del cuento costarricense," pp. 309-338.

Salas, Germán. "Bibliografía de poetas costarricenses," ANAQUELES (San Salvador), 2ª época, 1 (julio de 1971/diciembre de 1972), 43-67. Brief biobibliographies of Costa Rican poets.

CUBA

Abella, Rosa. "Bibliografía de la novela publicada en Cuba y en el extranjero por cubanos desde 1959 hasta 1965," REVISTA IBEROAMERICANA, 32, Núm. 62 (julio/diciembre de 1966), 307-318. By author.

_______. "Cinco años de la novela cubana," CUADERNOS DE HOMBRE LIBRE (Miami, Florida), Núm. 1 (julio/septiembre de 1966), 9-14. Translation into English: "Five Years of the Cuban Novel," THE CARREL (University of Miami Library, 7, No. 1

[June 1966], 17-21). Includes a selected list of Cuban novels, 1960-1965, in the University of Miami Library.

Alonso, Modesto. OBRAS EPIGRAMATICAS Y BUFAS EN UN ACTO. La Habana: Imprenta La Nueva, 1898. 1 v. Entries by author or anonymous title.

Antuña, María Luisa, and Josefina García Carranza. "Bibliografía de teatro cubano," REVISTA DE LA BIBLIOTECA NACIONAL "JOSE MARTI," 3a Serie, 13, Núm. 3 (1971), 87-154. Arrangement of bibliography is by playwright. Also includes an "índice de títulos" section. Unannotated.

Arrom, José Juan. HISTORIA DE LA LITERATURA DRAMATICA CUBANA. New Haven: Yale University Press, 1944. 132p. "Apéndice bibliográfico de obras dramáticas cubanas," pp. 95-127. Entries are alphabetically arranged by author and includes library locations in U.S. (Harvard, Library of Congress, New York Public Library, and Yale) and Cuba.

"Bibliografía de la crítica literaria cubana-1981," REVISTA DE LITERATURA CUBANA (La Habana), Núm. 1 (julio de 1983), 101-121. Contents: I. Siglos XVII-XIX (by critic). II. Siglo XX (by critic).

"Bibliografía de la crítica literaria cubana de 1982," REVISTA DE LITERATURA CUBANA (La Habana), Núm. 2/3 (enero/julio de 1984), 229-247. Arranged by author.

BIBLIOGRAFIA DE LA POESIA CUBANA EN EL SIGLO XIX. La Habana: Departamento de Publicaciones de la Biblioteca Nacional "José Martí," 1965. 89p. 1,111 entries are arranged by year, 1800-1899. Also includes "índice de autores" and "índice de anónimos" sections.

"Bibliografía sobre el teatro manuscrito de la Colección Biblioteca Coronado," ISLAS, 11 (i.e., 10), Núm. 4 (octubre/diciembre de 1968), 323-335. Bibliography lists the authors and titles of the "teatro bufo." Arrangement is by author or anonymous title.

Bueno, Salvador. FIGURAS CUBANAS: BREVES BIOGRAFIAS DE GRANDES CUBANOS DEL SIGLO XIX. La Habana: Comisión Nacional Cubana de la UNESCO, 1964. 390p.

Calcagno, Francisco. DICCIONARIO BIOGRAFICO CUBANO (COMPRENDE HASTA 1878). New York: N. Ponce de León, 1878. 727p. Includes life and works of Cubans up to 1878. Arrangement is alphabetical by name and includes notable Cubans in other countries as well as those in residence in Cuba.

Casal, Lourdes. "A Bibliography of Cuban Creative Literature:

1958-1971," CUBAN STUDIES NEWSLETTER (Pittsburgh), 2, No. 2 (June 1972), 2-29. The bibliography lists novels and short stories, plays, and poetry by Cuban authors residing in Cuba or emigrées published in Cuba or abroad during the period 1959-1971.

________. "The Cuban Novel, 1959-1969: An Annotated Bibliography," ABRAXAS, 1 (1970), 77-92. The bibliography briefly summarizes seventy-seven novels with critical articles sometimes noted after the summaries. Pages 91-92 includes a "Selected Reference Works, Testimonies, and Articles" section that deals with the Cuban novel.

DICCIONARIO DE LA LITERATURA CUBANA. VOLUME 1: A-LL. La Habana: Editorial Letras Cubanas, 1980. 537p. There are entries for literary themes, movements, biographies of authors, etc. The author biographies include bibliographies of their works and studies about their work and lives. Major writers living outside of Cuba, e.g., Carlos Franqui and Guillermo Cabrera Infante, are not included.

Fernández, José B. and Roberto G. Fernández. INDICE BIBLIOGRAFICO DE AUTORES CUBANOS: DIASPORA, 1959-1979: LITERATURA. Miami: Ediciones Universal, 1983. 106p. 971 entries. Contents: I. Cuento. II. Poesía. III. Teatro. IV. Folklore. V. Crítica literaria. VI. Lingüística. Each section under parts I-VI are arranged by author. VII. Indice de autores cubanos.

Fernández Robaina, Tomás. BIBLIOGRAFIA DE BIBLIOGRAFIAS CUBANAS: 1859-1972. La Habana: Biblioteca Nacional "José Martí," 1973. 340p. Partially annotated listing of over 1,300 entries divided into 19th-and 20th-century works. A supplementary section of 75 titles published after 1972 is included. An informative essay on Cuban bibliography appears before the main listing of bibliography.

________. BIBLIOGRAFIA SOBRE ESTUDIOS AFRO-AMERICANOS. La Habana: Biblioteca Nacional" José Martí," 1968. 96p. Entries include works on Cuban, Latin American, and African blacks found in the Biblioteca Nacional "José Martí." The bibliography is organized alphabetically by author, including also a thematic listing of topics in many fields, including literature.

Figarola-Caneda, Domingo. DICCIONARIO CUBANO DE SEUDONIMOS. La Habana: Imprenta "El Siglo XX," 1922. 182p. Alphabetically arranged listing of pseudonyms with an index of authors.

Ford, Jeremiah D. M., and Maxwell I. Raphael. A BIBLIOGRAPHY OF CUBAN BELLES-LETTRES. Cambridge, Mass.: Harvard University Press, 1933. 204p. Work is divided into four sections: general works, bibliography of Cuban literature (listed by author), anonymous and collective works, and periodicals.

Fort, Gilberto V. THE CUBAN REVOLUTION OF FIDEL CASTRO VIEWED FROM ABROAD. Lawrence, Kan.: University of Kansas Libraries, 1969. 140p. Section 14: Fiction and Poetry, pp. 125-131. Annotated entries.

Foster, David William. CUBAN LITERATURE: A RESEARCH GUIDE. New York: Garland, 1985. 522p. Contents: I. Bibliography of Criticism: General References. A. Bibliographies. B. General Literary Histories. C. Collected Essays. D. Literary Criticism, Reviews, and Journals. E. Literature and Other Subjects. F. Relations with Foreign Literatures. G. Women Authors. H. Special Topics. I. General Studies on Colonial Literature. J. General Studies on 19th-Century Literature. K. General Studies on 20th-Century Literature. L. General Studies on Poetry. M. Colonial and 19th-Century Poetry. N. 20th-Century Poetry. O. Special Topics in Poetry. P. General Studies on Drama. Q. Colonial and 19th-Century Drama. R. 20th-Century Drama. S. Special Topics in Drama. T. General Studies on Prose Fiction. U. 19th-Century Prose Fiction. V. 20th-Century Prose Fiction. W. Special Topics in Prose Fiction. X. General Studies on the Essay. Y. Regional and Local Literature. Z. Periodical Indexes. II. Bibliography of Criticism: Authors (98 authors are listed; bibliographies, critical monographs, dissertations, and/or critical essays are included under each author entry). III. Index of Critics. Section II is indexed in the preceding GUIDE.

García Garofalo, and Manuel Mesa. DICCIONARIO OF PSEUDONIMOS DE ESCRITORES, POETAS Y PERIODISTAS VILLACLARENOS. La Habana: J. Arroyo, 1926. 61p. Listing is by author's pseudonym followed by his or her real name.

Graupera Arango, Elena. BIBLIOGRAFIA SOBRE TEATRO CUBANO: LIBROS Y FOLLETOS. La Habana: Biblioteca Nacional "José Martí," Departamento Información y Documentación de la Cultura, 1981. 27p. Covers the period 1959-1981. Contents: I. Bibliografía activa (works are listed by playwright; contents listed where applicable). II. Bibliografía pasiva (critical studies).

Hernández-Miyares, Julio. "The Cuban Short Story in Exile: A Selected Bibliography," HISPANIA, 54 (May 1971), 384-385.

Inerarity Romero, Zayda. "Ensayo de una bibliografía para un estudio del teatro cubano hasta el siglo XIX," ISLAS, Núm. 36 (mayo/agosto de 1970), 151-171. Contents: I. Bibliografías generales. II. Bibliografías particulares. III. Historias. A. Historias de la literatura cubana. B. Historias del teatro cubano. IV. Biografías. A. Biografías de autores. B. Biografías de actores, directores, etc. V. Antologías. VI. Aspectos materiales del teatro. A. Historias o descripciones de teatros. B. Cronologías. VII. Representaciones y actuaciones. VIII. La crítica teatral. IX. La censura. X. Arte y teatro. XI. Música y vestuario. XII. Indice de títulos. XIII. Indice de autores. 100 annotated items.

Le Riverand, Julio. "Notas para una bibliografía cubana de los siglos XVII y XVIII," UNIVERSIDAD DE LA HABANA, Núm. 88/90 (1950), 128-231. A descriptive bibliography.

"Literatura cubana en la revolución (1959-1983)," REVISTA DE LITERATURA CUBANA (La Habana), Núm. 2/3 (enero/julio de 1984), 153-207. Contents: I. Poesía. II. Novela. III. Cuento. IV. Dramaturgia. All of these sections are arranged by author.

López Barrero, Olga L. "Cronología de la novela cubana: 1850-1900," ISLAS, Núm. 48 (mayo/agosto de 1974), 187-212. A literary period survey is followed by a selected chronological listing (pp. 199-212).

Menton, Seymour. PROSE FICTION OF THE CUBAN REVOLUTION. Austin: University of Texas Press, 1975. 344p. (Latin American Monographs, 37). "Bibliography," pp. 284-317. Contents: I. Chronology of Novels and Short Stories. II. Cuban Novels of the Revolution. III. Annotated Bibliography of Anthologies of the Cuban Short Story. IV. Cuban Short Stories of the Revolution. V. Antirevolutionary Cuban Novels. VI. Short Stories by Cubans in Exile. VII. Foreign Prose Fiction of the Cuban Revolution. VIII. Works Consulted.

Montes Huidobro, Matías, and Yara González. BIBLIOGRAFIA CRITICA DE LA POESIA CUBANA (EXILIO: 1959-1971). Madrid, Nueva York: Plaza Mayor Ediciones, 1972. 137p. (Colección Scholar, 15). By author. Extensive descriptions of contents and significance of work.

Muriedas, Mercedes. BIBLIOGRAFIA DE LA LITERATURA INFANTIL CUBANA, SIGLO XIX: TOMO I. La Habana: Biblioteca Nacional "José Martí," Departamento Juvenil, 1969. 102p. Contents: I. Orden alfabético (author listing). II. Orden cronológico (works listed by year, 1812-1899). III. Publicaciones periódicas.

Palls, Terry L. "Annotated Bibliographical Guide to the Study of Cuban Theatre after 1959," MODERN DRAMA, 22 (1979), 391-408. Contents: I. Books. II. Articles. 121 items.

Pane, Remigio U. "Cuban Poetry in English: A Bibliography of English Translations from Casal, Florit, Gómez de Avellaneda, Guillén, Heredia, Pedroso and 'Plácido,'" BULLETIN OF BIBLIOGRAPHY AND DRAMATIC INDEX, 18 (1946), 199-201. Includes a list of the collections of translations used to compile this bibliography.

Peavler, Terry J. "Prose Fiction Criticism and Theory in Cuban Journals: An Annotated Bibliography," CUBAN STUDIES, 7 (1977), 58-118. Annotated bibliography of 632 entries. Contents: I. Specific Authors and Literary Works. II. Literature, Literary Criticism, Literary Theory. A. Special Issues. B. Encuestas. C. Articles. III. Non-Hispanic Literatures (excluding the U.S.). A. Special Issues. B. Articles. IV. United States Literature. A. Special Issues. B. Articles. V. Index of Names.

Peraza Sarausa, Fermín. DICCIONARIO BIOGRAFICO CUBANO. La Habana and Gainesville, Fla.: Ed. Anuario Bibliográfico Cubano, 1951-1968. 14 vs. Only persons no longer living are included.

_______. PERSONALIDADES CUBANAS. La Habana, and Gainesville, Fla.: Ed. Anuario Bibliográfico Cubano, 1957-1968. 8 vs. Work gives brief sketches of living persons.

Perrier, José Luis. BIBLIOGRAFIA DRAMATICA CUBANA, INCLUYE A PUERTO RICO Y SANTO DOMINGO. New York: Phos Press, 1926. 115p. Alphabetical listing by authors of their plays. No separate listing by country.

Rivero Muñiz, José. BIBLIOGRAFIA DEL TEATRO CUBANO. PROLOGO DE LILIA CASTRO DE MORALES. La Habana: Publicaciones de la Biblioteca Nacional, 1957. 120p. Arranged alphabetically by authors, from the early 1800's to the present century. Lists the dramatic works, including unpublished manuscripts, found in the library which belonged to Francisco de Paula Coronado.

Sánchez, Julio C. "Bibliografía de la novela cubana," ISLAS 3, Núm. 1 (setiembre/diciembre de 1960), 321-356. 800 titles arranged by author. Bibliography does not pretend to be complete.

Skinner, Eugene R. "Research Guide to Post-Revolutionary Cuban Drama," LATIN AMERICAN THEATRE REVIEW, 7, No. 2 (1974), 59-68. "This bibliography represents an attempt to construct, from existing general bibliographies and from personal research in the Cuban journals ... a specialized guide to post-Revolutionary Cuban theatre" [p. 59]. Contents: I. Bibliographies. II. Articles and Books. III. Reviews.

Trelles y Govín, Carlos Manuel. BIBLIOGRAFIA CUBANA DE LOS SIGLOS XVII Y XVIII. 2ª edición. La Habana: Imprenta del Ejército, 1927. 463p.

_______. BIBLIOGRAFIA CUBANA DEL SIGLO XIX. Matanzas: Imprenta de Quirós y Estrada, 1911-1915. 8 vs. Chronologically arranged.

_______. BIBLIOGRAFIA CUBANA DEL SIGLO XX. Matanzas: Imprenta de Quirós y Estrada, 1916-1917. 2 vs. Alphabetically arranged by author; contains about 8,000 entries.

_______. "Bibliografía de autores de la raza de color en Cuba," CUBA CONTEMPORANEA, 43 (1927), 30-78. 402 entries; includes literary, journalistic, and political writings. Contents: I. En la época de la esclavitud (chronologically arranged and then by author). II. Después de la esclavitud (alphabetically arranged). III. Periódicos de la raza de color.

_______. "Los poetas cubanos de los siglos XVII y XVIII agrupados por regiones," REVISTA CUBANA, 1 (abril/junio de 1935), 173-180. Bibliographical information is included. Entries are listed under: Camagüey, Habana, Villaclara, Mantanzas, España, Indeterminados, and Conquista de La Habana.

Valdés, Nelson P., and Edwin Lieuwen. THE CUBAN REVOLUTION, 1959-1969: A RESEARCH GUIDE. Albuquerque: The University of New Mexico Press, 1971. 230p. "Essay, pp. 187-188" and "Literature and Fine Arts, pp. 188-202."

DOMINICAN REPUBLIC

Alfau Durán, Vetilio. "Apuntes para la bibliografía de la novela en Santo Domingo," ANALES DE LA UNIVERSIDAD DE SANTO DOMINGO, 23 (enero/junio de 1958), 203-224; 24 (julio/diciembre de 1958), 405-435; 26 (1960), 87-100. This bibliography was never completed; covers only authors through the letter "F." Brief biographies of authors are provided as well as summaries of the novels listed.

_______. "Apuntes para la bibliografía poética dominicana," CLIO (Santo Domingo), Núm. 122 (enero/abril de 1965), 34-60; Núm. 123 (enero/agosto de 1968), 107-119; Núm. 124 (enero/agosto de 1969), 53-68; Núm. 125 (enero/agosto de 1970), 50-77. Biobibliographies; excludes, however, poems that appeared in periodicals. Núm. 122, pp. 41-57 lists anthologies. Entries are arranged alphabetically by author.

Boggs, Ralph Steele. "A Selected Bibliography of Dominican Literature," BULLETIN HISPANIQUE, 32 (1930), 404-410. 176 publications are listed by author.

Florén Lozano, Luis. "Algunos seudónimos dominicanos. Aportaciones a un diccionario de seudónimos de escritores nacionales," ANALES DE LA UNIVERSIDAD DE SANTO DOMINGO, 14 (1949), 95-122.

_______. BIBLIOGRAFIA DE LAS BELLAS ARTES EN SANTO DOMINGO. Bogotá: Antares, 1956. 53p. (Materiales para el estudio de la cultura dominicana, v. 8).

_______. "Contribuciones a la bibliografía dominicana: libros, folletos y artículos de autores dominicanos o relativos a Santo Domingo," REVISTA DE EDUCACION, VI época, Núm. 91 (1948), 35-72; Núm. 92 (1948), 51-68; Núm. 93 (1949), 38-55.

Rodríguez Demorizi, Emilio. SEUDONIMOS DOMINICANOS. 2. ed. Santo Domingo: Editora Taller, 1982. 280p. (Publicaciones de la Fundación Rodríguez Demorizi, 14). Reprint of the 1956 edition. Contains identifications to Dominican nicknames and pseudonyms.

Romero, Guadalupe. "Bibliografía comentada de la literatura dominicana," EME EME, Núm. 14 (septiembre/octubre de 1974), 104-156. After a brief historical review, the bibliography contains the following sections: I. Antologías. A. Generales. B. Poesía. C. Prosa. II. Bibliografías. A. General. B. Poesías. C. Prosa. D. Teatro. III. Historias literarias. A. Generales. B. Poesía. IV. Estudios. 173 annotated items.

Waxman, Samuel Montefiore. A BIBLIOGRAPHY OF THE BELLES-LETTRES OF SANTO DOMINGO. Cambridge, Mass.: Harvard University Press, 1931. 31p. Arrangement is alphabetical by author. Work is supplemented and corrected by Vetilio Alfau Durán's "Apuntes de bibliografía dominicana en torno a las rectificaciones hechas a la obra del Prof. Waxman," CLIO (Santo Domingo), Num. 108, (julio/diciembre de 1956) and Pedro Henríquez Ureña and Gilberto Sánchez Lustrino's review in the REVISTA DE FILOLOGIA ESPANOLA, 21 (1934), 293-309.

ECUADOR

Barriga López, Franklin, and Leonardo Barriga López. DICCIONARIO DE LA LITERATURA ECUATORIANA. 2. edición, corregida y aumentada. Guayaquil: Núcleo del Guyas, Casa de la Cultura Ecuatoriana, 1980. 5 vs. Primarily a biographical dictionary of Ecuadorian writers with entries for literary societies, movements, and institutions.

Biblioteca Nacional del Ecuador. BIBLIOGRAFIA DE AUTORES ECUATORIANOS. Quito: Editorial Casa de la Cultura Ecuatoriana, 1977. 474p. Contents: I. "Literatura de la colonia," pp. 7-10. II. "Literatura," pp. 258-275. III. "Poesía," pp. 276-324. IV. "Teatro," pp. 325-333. V. "Novela-cuento," pp. 334-365. VI. "Biografía," pp. 414-446.

DICCIONARIO DE LA LITERATURA LATINOAMERICANA: ECUADOR. Washington, D.C.: Unión Panamericana, 1962. 172p. Contents: I. Clásicos ecuatorianos de la colonia al presente. II. Autores ecuatorianos vivos. III. Bibliografía de letras ecuatorianas. Each author entry under I. and II. includes biografía, valoración, and bibliografía sections.

Luzuriaga, Gerardo. BIBLIOGRAFIA DEL TEATRO ECUATORIANO, 1900-1982. Quito: Editorial Casa de la Cultura Ecuatoriana, 1984. 132p.

Mundo Lo, Sara de. INDEX TO SPANISH AMERICAN COLLECTIVE BIOGRAPHY. VOLUME 1: THE ANDEAN COUNTRIES. Boston: G. K. Hall, 1981. 466p. Contains some 1,100 annotated entries for biographical works ranging in date from the seventeenth century to the present, arranged alphabetically by author within major disciplines or fields of activity. Complete author, title, geographic, and biographee indexes supplement the main listings. Covers Bolivia, Colombia, Chile, Ecuador, Peru, and Venezuela. U.S. library locations are given.

Pérez Marchant, Braulio. DICCIONARIO BIOGRAFICO DEL ECUADOR. Quito: Escuela de Artes y Oficios, 1928. 515p. Covers all periods of Ecuadorian culture, but it mainly emphasizes the 19th century.

Rivera, Guillermo. A TENTATIVE BIBLIOGRAPHY OF THE BELLES-LETTRES OF ECUADOR. Cambridge: Harvard University Press, 1934. 76p. Alphabetical listing by author, with a brief supplement of addenda.

Rojas, Angel F. LA NOVELA ECUATORIANA. México: Fondo de Cultura Económica, 1948. 234p. A chronological list of Ecuadorian novels, pp. 220-225, is included.

Rolando, Carlos A. LAS BELLAS LETRAS EN EL ECUADOR. Guayaquil: Imprenta i Talleres Municipales, 1944. 157p. A bibliography of literary works printed in Ecuador from colonial period to time of compilation. Arranged by the Dewey Decimal System, including bibliography, library science, periodicals, poetry, fiction, drama, essays, etc. Author index is included.

_______. CRONOLOGIA DEL PERIODISMO ECUATORIANO. PSEUDONIMOS DE LA PRENSA NACIONAL. Guayaquil: Imprenta y Papeleria Mercantil Monteverde y Velarde, 1920. 166p. The pseudonym sections contains 1,250 pseudonyms in alphabetical order by the real name of the person, followed by pseudonyms. There is, however, no alphabetical index to the pseudonyms.

_______. _______: Suplemento. Guayaquil: Tip. y Lit. de la Sociedad Filantrópica del Guayas, 1934. 87p. Adds additional pseudonyms from November 1920.

GUATEMALA

Ciruti, Joan. "THE GUATEMALAN NOVEL: A CRITICAL BIBLIOGRAPHY." Ph.D., Tulane University, 1959. 263p. "A Critical Bibliography of the Guatemalan Novel," pp. 106-253. "The materials listed in this bibliography have been arranged under three headings. Under Section A, 'General Critical Studies,' the user will find listed in alphabetical order references which deal with the Guatemalan novel in general. In Sections B and C, 'The Novel before 1920' and 'The Novel Since 1920,' he will find material on the individual novelists and their novels" [p. 106]. 558 annotated items.

Valenzuela, Gilberto, and Gilberto Valenzuela Reyna. BIBLIOGRAFIA GUATEMALTECA Y CATALOGO GENERAL DE LIBROS, FOLLETOS, PERIODICOS, REVISTAS, 1821-1960. Guatemala: Tipografía Nacional, 1961-1964. 8 vs. (Colección Bibliográfica del Tercer Centenario de la Fundación de la Primera Imprenta en Centro América). A chronological listing of Guatemalan publications, with alphabetical indices in each volume.

HONDURAS

Durón, Jorge. INDICE DE LA BIBLIOGRAFIA HONDUREÑA. Tegucigalpa: Imprenta Calderón, 1946. 211p. More than 3,000 entries by author or anonymous author or title.

MEXICO

Agraz García de Alba, Gabri. BIOBIBLIOGRAFIA DE LOS ESCRITORES DE JALISCO. México, D.F.: Universidad Nacional Autónoma de México, 1980- (in progress). This work also includes seudónimos, anagramas, and iniciales.

Almada, Francisco R. DICCIONARIO DE HISTORIA, GEOGRAFIA Y BIOGRAFIA CHIHUAHUENSES. 2. ed. Chihuahua: Universidad de Chihuahua, Departamento de Investigaciones Sociales, Sección de Historia, 1968. 578p.

_______. DICCIONARIO DE HISTORIA, GEOGRAFIA Y BIOGRAFIA DEL ESTADO DEL COLIMA. Chihuahua: Talleres Tipográficos de Ecos de la Costa, 1937. 109p. Alphabetically arranged entries.

_______. DICCIONARIO DE HISTORIA, GEOGRAFIA Y BIOGRAFIA

SONORENSES. Chihuahua, 1952. 860p. Alphabetically arranged entries.

Aranda Pamplona, Hugo. BIOBIBLIOGRAFIA DE LOS ESCRITORES DEL ESTADO DE MEXICO. México, D.F.: Universidad Nacional Autónoma de México, 1978. 105p. (Instituto de Investigaciones Bibliográficas, Biblioteca Nacional, Serie Bibliográfias, 5). Entries are arranged by surname.

Bolio Ontiveros, Edmundo. DICCIONARIO HISTORICO, GEOGRAFICO Y BIOGRAFICO DE YUCATAN. México, D.F.: I.C.D., 1944. 250p. Entries are arranged alphabetically.

Gordillo, Ignacio B. del. "Catálogo de seudónimos, anagramas, iniciales, etc. de escritores mexicanos y extranjeros incorporados a las letras mexicanas," BOLETIN DE LA BIBLIOTECA NACIONAL (Mexico), 2a época, 4, Núm. 4 (1953), 31-48. Supplements the work of Juan Iguíniz and Juana Manrique de Lara.

CATALOGO DEL TEATRO MEXICANO CONTEMPORANEO. México, D.F.: Instituto Nacional de Bellas Artes, 1956-1960. 3 vs. A series of three catalogs, including one devoted to "teatro infantil, escolar y guinol." Listings are arranged alphabetically by author. Each item is described: synopsis of the play, scene designs, price, and whereabouts of the work. An alphabetical list of authors, as well as works, is provided in the 1960 catalog.

DICCIONARIO PORRUA DE HISTORIA, BIOGRAFIA Y GEOGRAFIA DE MEXICO. 4. edición, corregida y aumentada. México, D.F.: Editora Porrúa, 1976. 2 vs. The biographical entries for authors contain bibliographies.

Finch, Mark Steven. "AN ANNOTATED BIBLIOGRAPHY OF RECENT SOURCES ON LATIN AMERICAN THEATER: GENERAL SECTION, ARGENTINA, CHILE, MEXICO, AND PERU." Ph.D., University of Cincinnati, 1978. 372p. "The eight hundred eighty-four items of this document are, then, a supplement, extension and clarification of such sources as the PMLA annual bibliography, the Hebblethwaite bibliography, the Dauster 'recent research' article, the Woodyard-Lyday bibliography and The Handbook of Latin American Studies." The general section chapter, as well those on Argentina, Chile, Mexico and Peru, are divided into the following sections: books and reviews, articles, anthologies, bibliographies, and miscellaneous items. (Dissertation Abstracts International, 39 [1979], 5502A.)

Foster, David William. MEXICAN LITERATURE: A BIBLIOGRAPHY OF SECONDARY SOURCES. Metuchen, N.J.: Scarecrow Press, 1981. 386p. Contents: I. General References. A. Bibliographies. B. General Histories. C. Collected Essays. D. Literary Criticism, Reviews and Journals. E. Literature and Other

Subjects. F. Relations with Foreign Literatures. G. Women Authors. H. Special Literary Topics. I. General Studies on Colonial Literature. J. General Studies on 19th-Century Literature. K. General Studies on 20th-Century Literature. L. General Studies on Poetry. M. Colonial Poetry. N. 19th-Century Poetry. O. 20th-Century Poetry. P. Special Topics in Poetry. Q. General Studies on Drama. R. Colonial Drama. S. 19th-Century Drama. T. 20th-Century Drama. U. Special Topics in Drama. V. General Studies on Prose Fiction. W. Colonial Prose Fiction. X. 19th-Century Prose Fiction. Y. 20th-Century Prose Fiction. Z. Special Topics in Prose Fiction. AA. General Studies on the Essay. BB. Regional Literature (excluding Mexico City). II. Authors (50) (alphabetically arranged). The author section includes bibliographies, critical monographs, dissertations, and/or critical essays. Section II is indexed in the preceding GUIDE.

García Icazbalceta, Joaquín. BIBLIOGRAFIA MEXICANA DEL SIGLO XVI. CATALOGO RAZONADO DE LIBROS IMPRESOS EN MEXICO DE 1539 A 1600. CON BIOGRAFIAS DE AUTORES Y OTRAS ILUSTRACIONES.... México, D.F.: Andrade y Morales, 1886. 508p. Reprinted with additions and corrections by Agustín Millares Carlo: México: Fondo de Cultura Económica, 1954. 481p. Chronological arrangement of work with descriptions and many excerpts.

Gordillo y Ortiz, Octavio. DICCIONARIO BIOGRAFICO DE CHIAPAS. México, D.F.: B. Costa-Amic Editor, 1977. 295p. Alphabetically arranged biobibliographies.

Hoffman, Herbert H. CUENTO MEXICANO INDEX. Newport Beach, Cal.: Headway Publications, 1978. 600p. "This index covers 7,230 short stories by 400 Mexican authors born after 1870 or so. Only books published since 1945 have been analysed" (see tipped-in errata page). Some 674 collections (a few of them in English) are analyzed. Contents: I. Directory of Authors. II. Author-Title Index. III. Title-Author Index. IV. List of Books Analyzed. V. Books Not Available for Analysis. VI. List of Publishers.

Iguíniz, Juan Bautista. BIBLIOGRAFIA DE NOVELISTAS MEXICANOS. ENSAYO BIOGRAFICO, BIBLIOGRAFICO Y CRITICO, PRECEDIDO DE UN ESTUDIO HISTORICO DE LA NOVELA MEXICANA POR FRANCISCO MONTERDE GARCIA ICAZBALCETA. México, D.F.: Imprenta de la Secretaría de Relaciones Exteriores, 1926. 432p. (Monografías bibliográficas mexicanas, 3). Reprinted: New York: Burt Franklin, 1970. 432p. (Burt Franklin Bibliography and Reference Series, 397. Essays in Literature and Criticism, 110).

_______. BIBLIOGRAFIA BIOGRAFICA MEXICANA. México, D.F.: Universidad Nacional Autónoma de México, Instituto de Investigaciones Históricas, 1969. 431p. (Serie bibliográfica, 5). Alphabetically arranged. Part 1 contains collective biographies; part 2, individual ones. An index of proper names lists entries with information on biographees.

_______. CATALOGO DE SEUDONIMOS, ANAGRAMAS E INICIALES DE ESCRITORES MEXICANOS. Paris: Charles Bouret, 1913. 62p. An alphabetical listing of about 300 pseudonymous names with only the individual's true name provided for each entry.

Lamb, Ruth S. BIBLIOGRAFIA DEL TEATRO MEXICANO DEL SIGLO XX. México, D.F.: Ediciones de Andrea, 1962. 141p. A brief history of the Mexican theatre introduces the work. Alphabetical arrangement by author.

Langle Ramírez, Arturo. VOCABULARIO, APODOS, SEUDONIMOS, SOBRENOMBRES Y HEMEROGRAFIA DE LA REVOLUCION. México, D.F.: Universidad Nacional Autónoma de Mexico, Instituto de Investigaciones Históricas, 1966. 151p. (Serie de Historia Moderna y Contemporánea, 6). "Apodos, seudónimos y sobrenombres," pp. 77-130. References are from pseudonyms, etc. to real name, followed by biographical sketches.

Leal, Luis. BIBLIOGRAFIA DEL CUENTO MEXICANO. México, D.F.: Ediciones de Andrea, 1958. 162p. Alphabetical author listing of the Mexican short story since the eighteenth century. Work includes titles of books as well as short stories published in newspapers and magazines.

López de Escalera, Juan. DICCIONARIO BIOGRAFICO Y DE HISTORIA DE HISTORIA DE MEXICO. México, D.F.: Editorial del Magisterio, 1964. 1200p.

López Mena, Héctor F. DICCIONARIO GEOGRAFICO, HISTORICO, BIOGRAFICO Y LINGUISTICO DEL ESTADO DE GUERRO. México, D.F.: Editorial Pluma y Lápiz de México, 1942. 461p. Entries are arranged alphabetically.

Manrique de Larra, Juana, and Guadalupe Monroy. SEUDONIMOS, ANAGRAMAS, INICIALES, ETC. DE AUTORES MEXICANOS Y EXTRANJEROS. México, D.F.: Secretaría de Educación Pública, 1943. 78p. An alphabetical listing by initials, anagram, or pseudonym, followed by a true name. Divided into three parts: Parts I and II concern Mexican writers, with arrangement first by pseudonym and second by true name; Part III is a brief listing of some foreign pseudonyms, with nationality indicated after the true name.

Montejano y Aguiñaga, Rafael. DICCIONARIO BIBLIOGRAFICO DE ESCRITORES POTOSINOS. México, D.F.: Universidad Nacional Autonoma de Mexico, 1978.

Monterde García Icazbalceta, Francisco. BIBLIOGRAFIA DEL TEATRO EN MEXICO. México, D.F.: Imprenta de la Secretaría de Relaciones Exteriores, 1933, i.e., 1934. 649p. (Monografías bibliográficas mexicanas, 28). Reprint: New York, Burt Franklin, 1970 (Theater and Drama Series, 11). This bibliography includes dramas by Mexicans, those on Mexican subjects, and those printed in México; translations of foreign dramas by Mexicans, and of Mexican drama into foreign languages; works about the Mexican drama, dramatists, and theater. An appendix lists operas and popular and patriotic dialogues. Includes books, periodical articles, and some manuscripts. The bibliography also includes sections for "obras del teatro regional yucateco" and "índice alfabético de autores y traductores."

Moore, Ernest Richard. BIBLIOGRAFIA DE NOVELISTAS DE LA REVOLUCION MEXICANA. México: Fondo de Cultura Económica, 1941. 190p. A listing by author with critical commentaries. Location of most items in libraries or private collections is indicated.

_______. "Obras críticas y bibliográficas referentes a la novela mexicana anterior al siglo XX." REVISTA IBEROAMERICANA, 3 (1941), 235-264. 380 entries in alphabetical order by author.

Mondo Lo, Sara de. INDEX TO SPANISH AMERICAN COLLECTIVE BIOGRAPHY: VOLUME 2: MEXICO. Boston: G. K. Hall, 1982. 374p. 922 entries from biographical works from the sixteenth century to the present are arranged alphabetically by author within major disciplines or fields of activity. Complete author, title, geographic, and biographee indexes supplement the main listings. U.S. library locations are included.

Ocampo de Gómez, Aurora Maura. LITERATURA MEXICANA CONTEMPORANEA. BIO-BIBLIOGRAFIA CRITICA. México, D.F.: Universidad Nacional Autónoma de México, 1965. 329p. Work is an alphabetical arrangement by author, giving biographical and bibliographical information for each author; then a bibliography of authors by genre and by place of birth.

_______, and Ernesto Prado Velázquez. DICCIONARIO DE ESCRITORES MEXICANOS. México, D.F.: Universidad Nacional Autónoma de México, 1967. 422p. Biobibliographical dictionary which deals with 542 authors. Basic reference work. Coverage is from the pre-Hispanic period through the twentieth century. The dictionary itself contains biographical data, works, and a bibliography of criticism.

Palacios Beltrán, Miguel. "Resumen bibliográfico del cuento mexicano 1958-1967," BIBLIOTECAS Y ARCHIVOS (México), Núm. 2 (1971), 119-133.

Pasquel, Leonardo. BIOGRAFIAS DE VERACRUZANOS PORTENOS.

México, D.F.: Editorial Citlaltepetl, 1981. 418p. Contains brief descriptions of nearly 200 individuals who were prominent in Vera Cruz from the 17th to 20th century.

Peral, Miguel Angel. DICCIONARIO BIOGRAFICO MEXICANO. México, D.F.: Ed. P.A.C., 1944. 2 vs and Apéndice. Covers 544 to 1944. No bibliographical data or references to sources are given, however.

Reyes de la Maza, Luis. EL TEATRO EN MEXICO DURANTE EL PORFIRISMO. México, D.F.: Imprenta Universitaria, 1964. 3 vs. Volume 1: "Indice alfabético de obras representadas en los años de 1880-1887," pp. 347-369; "Indice alfabético de nombres," pp. 371-379. Volume II: "Indice de obras representadas en los años 1888 a 1899," pp. 387-420; "Indice alfabético de nombres," pp. 421-433. Volume III: "Indice de obras representadas en los años 1900 a 1910," pp. 465-519; "Indice alfabético de nombres," pp. 521-545.

_______. EL TEATRO EN MEXICO DURANTE EL SEGUNDO IMPERIO (1862-1867). México, D.F.: Imprenta Universitaria, 1959. 241p. "Lista alfabética de obras representadas en años de 1862-1867," pp. 209-226; "Indice alfabético de nombres," pp. 227-239.

_______. EL TEATRO EN MEXICO DURANTE LA INDEPENDENCIA (1810-1839). México, D.F.: UNAM, 1969. 429p. "Indice alfabético de obras representadas entre 1810 y 1840," pp. 401-421. "Indice alfabético de nombres," pp. 423-428.

_______. EL TEATRO EN MEXICO CON LERDO Y DIAZ, 1873-1879. México, D.F.: Imprenta Universitaria, 1963. 345p. "Indice alfabético de nombres," pp. 329-344; "Indice alfabético de obras representadas en los años de 1873 a 1879," pp. 309-328.

_______. EL TEATRO EN MEXICO EN LA EPOCA DE JUAREZ, 1868-1872. México, D.F.: Universitaria, 1961. 249p. A bibliographical essay is followed by a history of programas and crónicas of the Mexican theatre. Division is by year.

_______. EL TEATRO EN MEXICO EN 1857 Y SUS ANTECEDENTES (1855-1856). México, D.F.: Instituto de Investigaciones Estéticas, Imprenta Universitaria, 1956. 433p. "Catálogo alfabético de las obras presentadas en los años de 1855, 56 y 57," pp. 425-433.

_______. EL TEATRO EN MEXICO ENTRE LA REFORMA Y EL IMPERIO, 1858-1861. México, D.F.: Imprenta Universitaria, 1958. 197p. "Indice onomástico de personas, relacionadas con el teatro," pp. 173-181; "Indice alfabético de obras representadas durante 1858-1861," pp. 183-196.

Rouaix, Pastor. DICCIONARIO GEOGRAFICO, HISTORICO Y BIO-

GRAFICO DEL ESTADO DE DURANGO. México, D.F.: Editorial Cultura, 1946. 518p. (Publicación del Instituto Panamericano de Geografía e Historia, 80). Alphabetically arranged entries.

Rutherford, John David. AN ANNOTATED BIBLIOGRAPHY OF THE NOVELS OF THE MEXICAN REVOLUTION OF 1910-1917 IN ENGLISH AND SPANISH. Troy, New York: Whitston, 1972. 180p. General survey and arrangement is by author.

Torrea, Juan Manual. DICCIONARIO GEOGRAFICO, HISTORICO, BIOGRAFICO Y ESTADISTICA DE LA REPUBLICA MEXICANA: ESTADO DE TAMAULIPAS. México, D.F.: Sociedad Mexicana de Geografía y Estadística, 1940. 608p. Entries are arranged alphabetically.

Torres Rioseco, Arturo. BIBLIOGRAFIA DE LA NOVELA MEJICANA. Cambridge, Mass.: Harvard University Press, 1933. 58p. Introductory survey with a bibliography arranged by author.

_______. BIBLIOGRAFIA DE LA POESIA MEJICANA. Cambridge, Mass.: Harvard University Press, 1934. 86p. Introductory survey with a bibliography of Mexican poetry under such subject headings as antologías, colecciones, crítica, etc.

Wright de Kleinhaus, Laureana. MUJERES NOTABLES MEXICANAS. México, D.F.: Tip. Económica, 1910. 246 (i.e., 546) p. 124 biographies of famous Mexican women.

NICARAGUA

Arellano, Jorge Eduardo. "Bibliografía general de Nicaragua, primera entrega: 1674-1900," CUADERNOS DE BIBLIOGRAFIA NICARAGUENSE, 1 (enero/junio de 1981), 1-87.

_______. "Cien novelas de autores nicaragüenses," LA PRENSA LITERARIA (Managua), 7 de diciembre de 1975, p. 4.

_______. DICCIONARIO DE LAS LETRAS NICARAGUENSE. Managua: Biblioteca Nacional "Rubén Darío," Ministerio de Cultura, 1982. (Cuadernos de Bibliografía Nicaragüense, 3-4).

_______. PANORAMA DE LA LITERATURA NICARAGUENSE. 4. edición. Managua: Editorial Nueva Nicaragua, 1982. 197p. "Bibliografía fundamental," pp. 191-197. Contents: I. Estudios. A. Libros y folletos. B. Ensayos y artículos (arranged by year; 1878-1976). II. Antologías. A. Generales. B. Particulares (provincianas o de temas, grupos o períodos determinados; arranged by year, 1927-1980). 85 entries in total.

Cuadra Downing, Orlando. SEUDONIMOS Y APODOS NICARAGUENSES. Managua, 1967. 341p. Alphabetically arranged by pseudonym or apodo.

White, Steven F., ed. POETS OF NICARAGUA: A BILINGUAL ANTHOLOGY, 1918-1979. Greensboro, N.C.: Unicorn Press, 1982. 209p. "Selected Bibliography," pp. 203-208. Includes works of authors, anthologies, and critical studies.

PANAMA

Beleño C., Joaquín. "La novela panameña: guía cronológica de la novelas publicadas en Panamá y sus autores (1920-1963)," LOTERIA (Panamá), Núm. 97 (diciembre de 1963), 32-38.

BIBLIOGRAFIA DE OBRAS ESCRITAS POR MUJERES PANAMENAS, 1970-1974. Panamá: Asociación Panameña de Bibliotecarios, 1976. 112p. "Obras de mujeres panameñas," pp. 102-111. Entries listed alphabetically; literary criticism and language studies included.

Conte Porras, J. Indice general bio-bibliográfico de panameños ilustres en la revista "Lotería," 1941-1974. Panamá: Academia Panameña de la Historia, 1975. 62p.

_______. ITINERARIO DE LA POESIA EN PANAMA (1502-1974). Panamá: Editorial Universitaria, 1974. 735p. "Bibliografía complementaria para la historia de la poesía en Panamá," pp. 721-724. Contents: I. Antologías, índices, parnasos. II. Historia y crítica. III. Reflexiones acerca de la poesía.

Doyle, Henry Grattan. A TENTATIVE BIBLIOGRAPHY OF THE BELLES-LETTRES OF PANAMA. Cambridge, Mass.: Harvard University Press, 1934. 21p. Divided into three sections: general works, list of authors, and current periodicals of Panamá.

King, Charles A. "Apuntes para una bibliografía de la literatura de Panamá," REVISTA INTERAMERICANA DE BIBLIOGRAFIA, 14, Núm. 3 (julio/setiembre de 1964), 262-302. Divided into sections by genre: poesía, novela, cuento, teatro.

Miró, Rodrigo. BIBLIOGRAFIA POETICA PANAMEÑA. Panamá: Imprenta Nacional, 1942. 61p. Lists works from 1872 to 1942 by author and the entries are annotated.

_______. EL CUENTO EN PANAMA (ESTUDIO, SELECCION, BIBLIOGRAFIA). Panamá, n.p., 1950. 203p. "Bibliografía del cuento y la novela panameñas," pp. 189-201. Contents: I.

Autores nacionales (arranged by author). II. Libros de material vario, que incluyen cuentos. III. Novelas de tema o ambiente panameño.

PARAGUAY

Fernández-Caballero, Carlos F. S. ARANDUKA HA KUATIAÑEE PARAGUAI REMBIAPOCURE. THE PARAGUAYAN BIBLIOGRAPHY: A RETROSPECTIVE AND ENUMERATIVE BIBLIOGRAPHY OF PRINTED WORKS OF PARAGUAYAN AUTHORS. Asunción: Washington, D.C.: Arandú Books, 1970. 143p. 1,423 items. Author listing of works published between 1724 and 1969, most of which are monographs. There is no subject or title index. This work is continued by: PARAGUAI TAI HŨME: TOVE PARAGUAI ARANDU TAISARAMBI KO YUY APERE= THE PARAGUAYAN BIBLIOGRAPHY. Vol. 2. Amherst, Mass.: Seminar on The Acquisition of Latin American Library Materials, University of Massachusetts Library, 1975. 221p. This second volume of 2,363 entries records additional authors and titles identified since the first volume was published and includes works published from the eighteenth century to 1974, by: (1) Paraguayans and non-Paraguayans on any topic. Identification of Paraguayan authors are noted by an asterisk (*) before their names. Entries are arranged alphabetically by author. Subject indexes to both volumes are also included.

Jones, David Lewis. PARAGUAY: A BIBLIOGRAPHY. New York: Garland, 1979. 499p. "Literature," pp. 372-415. Contents: I. General Studies. II. The Period before 1935: Individual Writers. III. The Period after 1935: Individual Writers.

Pérez-Maricevich, Francisco. DICCIONARIO DE LA LITERARIA PARAGUAYA. Asunción: Instituto Colorado de Cultura, 1983- (in progress). Tomo 1: A-El cuento paraguayo. Includes biobibliographies of Paraguayan authors.

Raphael, Maxwell I. A TENTATIVE BIBLIOGRAPHY OF PARAGUAYAN LITERATURE. Cambridge, Mass.: Harvard University Press, 1934. 25p. Two sections of "General Works Relative to Paraguay" and "Paraguayan Periodicals" precede the bibliography, which is arranged alphabetically by author.

PERU

Angeles Caballero, César Augusto. "Diccionario de seudónimos peruanos," BOLETIN BIBLIOGRAFICO (Biblioteca de la Universidad de San Marcos), Año 35, Vol. 32, Nos. 1/2 (enero/junio de 1962), 37-90. 1,449 pseudonyms are listed by pseudonym and then by true name. Contents: I. Introducción. II. Bibliografía básica para el estudio de los seudónimos peruanos. III. Seudónimos peruanos. IV. Indice de autores.

_______. "Diccionario de seudónimos peruanos," BOLETIN BIBLIOGRAFICO (Biblioteca de la Universidad de San Marcos), Año 35, Vol. 33, Nos. 3/4 (diciembre de 1962), 162-164. Despite its title, this is a brief supplement to original article.

_______. "Diccionario de sobre-nombres literarios peruanos," BOLETIN BIBLIOGRAFICO (Biblioteca de la Universidad de San Marcos), Año 36, Vol. 34, No. 1/2 (enero/junio de 1963), 134-142. Contents: I. Introducción. II. Clasificación de los sobrenombres que puntualizan cualidades. III. Sobre-nombres que apuntan a rasgos físicos. IV. Sobre-nombres que guardan sabor familiar. V. Sobre-nombres que encierran comicidad en la expresión. VI. Indice de autores. 115 names listed first by sobrenombre and then by real name.

Arriola Grande, F. Maurilio. DICCIONARIO LITERARIO DEL PERU: NOMENCLATURA POR AUTORES. Barcelona: Comercial y Artes Gráficas, 1968. 546p. Brief biobibliographies. Both living and deceased authors are included.

Basarde, Jorge. "Una bibliografía de la literatura peruana," BOLETIN BIBLIOGRAFICO (Biblioteca de la Universidad de San Marcos), Año 9, Vol. 6, No. 2 (junio de 1936), 28-38. Corrects and supplements Leavitt's bibliography.

Bermejo, Vladimiro. AREQUIPA (BIO-BIBLIOGRAFIA DE AREQUIPEÑOS CONTEMPORANEOS). Vol. 1. Arequipa: Estab. Gráfica La Colmena, 1954. 478p. This work contains biographical sketches of 58 authors of the region of Arequipa, Perú, with a listing of their works. (No more published?)

Cabel, Jesús. BIBLIOGRAFIA DE LA POESIA PERUANA, 65/79. Lima: Amaru Editores, 1980. 143p. Bibliography is arranged alphabetically by author under the following categories: I. Libros. II. Antologías. III. Plaquetas. An índice onomástico is also included. The bibliography covers the years 1965-1979 and includes titles published in Perú and abroad.

Carrión Ordoñez, Enrique. "Biobibliografías peruanas. Nómina provisional," HUMANIDADES (Revista de la Facultad de Letras, Pontificia Universidad Católica del Peru), Núm. 2 (1968), 5-40. Indexes ten major reference sources which include biobibliographies of Peruvian authors. Entries are arranged alphabetically by author.

Castro, Emma. "Seudónimos de autores peruanos," FENIX (Biblioteca Nacional, Lima), Núm. 4 (segundo semestre de 1946), 866-893. 866 names are given in dual alphabetical listings, first by pseudonym and then by true name. Names of foreigners associated with Perú are also included. Author index is provided.

Champion, Emilio. "Bibliografía de la poesía peruana (1900-1937)," LETRAS (Lima), Núm. 8 (1937), 474-485. Selected bibliography, which is alphabetically arranged by author.

Cornejo Bouronde, Jorge. "Algunos seudónimos de escritores cuzqueños," BOLETIN BIBLIOGRAFICO (Biblioteca Central, Universidad Mayor de San Marcos, Lima), Año 13, Núm. 1/2 (junio de 1940), 1-4. Sixty-five pseudonyms of writers from Cuzco. Also given are very brief biographical facts about these writers. The listing is alphabetical by pseudonym and then lists true name of the author.

Delgado Pastor, Amadeo. "Contribución para un catálogo de seudónimos de autores peruanos," BOLETIN BIBLIOGRAFICO (Biblioteca de la Universidad de San Marcos), Año 21, Vol. 18, Nos. 3/4 (diciembre de 1948), 254-264. 430 pseudonyms are arranged by pseudonym, followed by real name. Supplements and updates Emma Castro's work. An author index is included.

Eguiguren Callingos, Rosa María. "NOTAS PARA UN DICCIONARIO DE LITERATAS PERUANAS." Tesis de la Escuela Nacional de Bibliotecarios, Lima, 1977. 189p. Alphabetically arranged biobibliographies. This bibliography also includes a list of pseudonyms and a list of sources.

Finch, Mark Steven. "AN ANNOTATED BIBLIOGRAPHY OF RECENT SOURCES ON LATIN AMERICAN THEATER: GENERAL SECTION, ARGENTINA, CHILE, MEXICO, AND PERU." Ph.D., University of Cincinnati, 1978. 372p. "The eight hundred eighty-four items of this document are, then, a supplement, extension and clarification of such sources as the PMLA annual bibliography, the Hebblethwaite bibliography, the Dauster 'recent research' article, the Woodyard-Lyday bibliography and The Handbook of Latin American Studies." The general section chapter, as well those on Argentina, Chile, Mexico and Peru, are divided into the following sections: books and reviews, articles, anthologies, bibliographies and miscellaneous items. (Dissertation Abstracts International, 39 [1979], 5502A.)

Foster, David William. PERUVIAN LITERATURE: A BIBLIOGRAPHY OF SECONDARY SOURCES. Westport, Conn.: Greenwood Press, 1981. 324p. Contents: I. Critical Works on Peruvian Literature: General References. A. Bibliographies. B. General History and Criticism. C. Collected Essays of Criticism. D. Studies on Criticism, Including Reviews and Journals. E. Peruvian Literature

ıeva de Puccinelli, Elsa. BIBLIOGRAFIA DE LA NOVELA
RUANA. Lima: Ediciones de la Biblioteca Universitaria, 1969.
. Entries are alphabetically arranged by novelist. A chronol-
concludes the work.

O RICO

eca José M. Lázaro. PUERTO RICAN LITERATURE: TRANS-
TIONS INTO ENGLISH. LITERATURA PUERTORRIQUENA:
ADUCCIONES AL INGLES. Recinto de Río Piedras: Universi-
de Puerto Rico, 1974. 38p. The bibliography's entries were
ted to the holdings of the Biblioteca José M. Lázaro. Genres
uded: short stories, essays, novels, poetry, drama, and
hologies. There are author, Spanish title and English title
ices as well as a list of newspapers indexed.

, Enrique R. AN ANNOTATED SELECTED PUERTO RICO BIB-
GRAPHY: BIBLIOGRAFIA PUERTORRIQUENA SELECTA Y ANO-
DA. New York: Urban Center of Columbia University, 1972.
p; 114p. There is both a Spanish and an English section con-
ing the same literature entries divided into obras generales,
nto, ensayo, novela, poesía, and teatro (pp. 60-84).

, David William. PUERTO RICAN LITERATURE: A BIB-
GRAPHY OF SECONDARY SOURCES. Westport, Conn.:
enwood Press, 1982. 232p. Contents: I. Bibliographies.
General Histories. III. Collected Essays. IV. Literary Criti-
ı, Reviews, and Journals. V. Literature and Other Subjects.
Relations with Foreign Literatures. VII. Women Authors.
. Special Literary Topics. IX. General Studies on Colonial
rature. X. General Studies on Nineteenth Century Litera-
. XI. General Studies on Twentieth Century Literature.
General Studies on Poetry. XIII. Colonial and Nineteenth
tury Poetry. XIV. Twentieth Century Poetry. XV. General
dies on Drama. XVI. Twentieth Century Drama. XVII. Spe-
Topics in Drama. XVIII. General Studies on Prose Fiction.
. Nineteenth Century Prose Fiction. XX. Twentieth Century
se Fiction. XXI. Special Topics in Prose Fiction. XXII. Gen-
Studies on the Essay. XXIII. Critical Works on Puerto Rican
rature: Authors (80 authors are included). Section XXIII
ıdexed in the preceding GUIDE.

y Zenón, José, and Abelardo Morales Ferrer. BIBLIOGRAFIA
RTORRIQUEÑA. Barcelona: Araluce, 1934. 453p. 500 an-
ted entries divided into three sections: (1) books written
uerto Rico since 1807; (2) books written by Puerto Ricans
h were published in Spain or other foreign country; and (3)
s written about Puerto Rico.

and Foreign Literatures. F. Special Literary Topics. G. Women Authors. H. General Studies on Colonial Literature. I. General Studies on Nineteenth Century Literature. J. General Studies on Twentieth Century Literature. K. General Studies on Poetry. L. Colonial and Nineteenth Century Poetry. M. Twentieth Century Poetry. N. Special Topics in Poetry. O. General Studies on Drama. P. Colonial Drama. Q. Nineteenth Century Drama. R. Twentieth Century Drama. S. Special Topics in Drama. T. General Studies on Prose Fiction. U. Nineteenth Century Prose Fiction. V. Twentieth Century Prose Fiction. W. Special Topics in Prose Fiction. X. Regional and Local Literature. II. Critical Works on Peruvian Literature: Authors (38 authors included; bibliographies, critical monographs, dissertations, and/or critical essays are included under the author entries). III. Index to Authors of Secondary Sources. Section II is indexed in the preceding GUIDE.

Fuentes Benavides, Rafael de la. "Autores del primer siglo de la literatura peruana," BOLETIN BIBLIOGRAFICO (Biblioteca de la Universidad de San Marcos), Año 9, Vol. 12, Nos. 3/4 (diciembre de 1939), 268-332; Año 10, Vol. 13, Nos. 1/2 (junio de 1940), 81-133. Biobibliographical studies of authors, in alphabetical order. Work stopped with the letter "G."

Leavitt, Sturgis E. A TENTATIVE BIBLIOGRAPHY OF PERUVIAN LITERATURE. Cambridge, Mass.: Harvard University Press, 1932. 37p. One listing, alphabetical by author, follows a brief list of works consulted.

Lohmann Villena, Guillermo, and Raúl Moglia. "Repertorio de las representaciones teatrales en Lima hasta el siglo XVII," REVISTA DE FILOLOGIA HISPANICA, 5 (1943), 313-343. Entries for the period 1563-1793 are arranged chronologically; a few include descriptive commentary.

Lostaunau Rubio, Gabriel. FUENTES PARA EL ESTUDIO DEL PERU (BIBLIOGRAFIA DE BIBLIOGRAFIAS). EDICION Y PROLOGO DE MIGUEL ANGEL RODRIGUEZ REA. Lima, 1980. 500p. "Literatura," pp. 288-317. Contents: I. Obras generales. II. Poesía. III. Teatro. IV. Cuento y novela. V. Literatura infantil.

Maletta, Héctor. "Cuatrocientos tesis doctorales norteamericanos sobre el Peru (1869-1976)," ESTUDIOS ANDINOS, Núm. 15 (1979), 57-134. Arrangement of entries are by year, with the following indices: "índice de universidades," "índice de autores," and "índice temático."

Mendiburu, Manuel de. DICCIONARIO HISTORICO-BIOGRAFICO DEL PERU. Lima: Solis, 1874-1890. 8 vs. 2ª edición con adiciones y notas bibliográficas por Evaristo San Cristobál. Estudio biográfico del General Mendiburu por J. de la Riva-Agüero. Lima: Gil,

1931. 11 vs. APENDICE AL DICCIONARIO HISTORICO-BIOGRAFICO ... POR EVARISTO SAN CRISTOBAL. Lima: Gil, 1935-1938. 4 vs. 3a edición (reprint of 2nd edition): Lima: Editorial Arica, 1976- (in progress). Entries are alphabetically arranged.

Monguió, Luis. POESIA POSTMODERNISTA PERUANA. México, D.F.: Fondo de Cultura Económica, 1954. "Contribución a la bibliografía de la poesía peruana (1915-1950)," pp. 207-239. Entries are arranged by author and then by year of publication for both books and pamphlets of poetry.

Mostajo, Francisco. "Contribución al catálogo de seudónimos," BOLETIN BIBLIOGRAFICO (Biblioteca de la Universidad de San Marcos), Año 9, Vol. 12, Nos. 1/2 (julio de 1939), 13-25. Emphasis on the colonial and early republican periods. Contents: I. Seudónimos de escritores arequipeños (arranged by pseudonym, followed by true name). II. Seudónimos de escritores de otros departamentos.

Mundo Lo, Sara de. INDEX TO SPANISH AMERICAN COLLECTIVE BIOGRAPHY. VOLUME 1: THE ANDEAN COUNTRIES. Boston: G. K. Hall, 1981. 466p. Contains some 1,100 annotated entries for biographical works ranging in date from the seventeenth century to the present, arranged alphabetically by author within major disciplines or fields of activity. Complete author, title, geographic, and biographee indexes supplement the main listings. Covers Bolivia, Colombia, Chile, Ecuador, Peru, and Venezuela. U.S. library locations are given.

Natella, Arthur A. "Bibliography of the Peruvian Theatre, 1946-1970," HISPANIC JOURNAL, 2, No. 2 (1981), 141-147. "The list includes works which have been presented on the Peruvian stage, published or both" [p. 141]. The bibliography is arranged alphabetically by playwright.

Ojeda, Olivia. "Iniciación de una bibliografía biográfica del Perú," FENIX (Lima), Núm. 2 (1945), 297-311.

Pastor Delgado, Amadeo. "Contribución para un catálogo de seudónimos de autores peruanos," BOLETIN BIBLIOGRAFICO (Biblioteca de la Universidad de San Marcos), Año 21, Vol. 18, Nos. 3/4 (diciembre de 1948), 254-264. Supplements and updates Emma Castro's bibliography.

Paz-Soldán, Juan Pedro. DICCIONARIO BIOGRAFICO DE PERUANOS CONTEMPORANEOS. NUEVA EDICION CORREGIDA Y AUMENTADA. Lima: Librería e Imprenta Gil, 1921. 449p. Biographical sketches with bibliographies of writings by, but not about, biographees.

Pintó Gamboa, Willy. CONTRIBUCION A LA BIBLIOGRAFIA DE LA LITERATURA PERUANA EN LA PRENSA ESPANOL versidad Nacional Mayor de San Marcos, 1965. 17 rio Bibliográfico de la Literatura Latino-Americana Contents: I. Autores peruanos que han colabora y diarios españoles. II. Autores extranjeros que sobre temas peruanos en la prensa española en re españoles. Each section is alphabetically arrange Annotated entries.

Podestá, Bruno. "Estudios latinoamericanos en Itali peruano," APUNTES (Universidad del Pacifico, L (1981), 70-91. Article includes a list of books, translations on Perú by Italians.

Rodríguez Rea, Miguel Angel. "El cuento peruano Indice bibliográfico, I, 1900-1930," LEXIS (Ponti Católica del Perú, Lima), 7, Núm. 2 (1983), 287 logically arranged entries.

_______. "Poesía peruana del siglo XX (I: 1900- HUMERO (Lima), Núm. 7 (octubre/diciembre de "Se he ordenado cronológicamente por años y, en alfabético de autores." (p. 134).

_______. "Poesía peruana del siglo XX (II: 1921 HUMERO (Lima), Núm. 8 (enero/marzo de 1981

_______. "Poesía peruana del siglo XX (III: 19 HUMERO (Lima), Núm. 9 (abril/junio de 1981),

_______. "Poesía peruana del siglo XX (IV: 19 HUMERO (Lima), Núm. 14 (julio/setiembre de

Romero de Valle, Emilia. DICCIONARIO MANUAL PERUANA Y MATERIA AFINES. Lima: Unive Mayor de San Marcos, Departamento de Public Guide to past and contemporary Peruvian autl Alphabetical arrangement by author or subjec to literary genres, periodicals, and so forth.

Tauro, Alberto. HACIA UN CATALOGO DE SEU NOS. Lima: Universidad Nacional Mayor de 66p. 861 entries are arranged alphabetically Each entry indicates the circumstances of its authors is appended.

Vidal, Luis Fernando. "LAS ANTOLOGIAS DEL PERU," REVISTA DE CRITICA LITERARIA I (Lima), Año 1, Núm. 2 (1975), 121-138. A each work is listed; arranged chronologicall

González, Nilda. BIBLIOGRAFIA DE TEATRO PUERTORRIQUENO (SIGLOS XIX Y XX). Río Piedras: Editorial Universitaria, Universidad de Puerto Rico, 1979. 223p. Contents: I. Autores, obras y comentarios críticos (S. XIX y XX). II. Obras de teatro colectivo. III. Apéndices. A. Zarzuelas y operas. B. Obras con ficha incompleta según colección Emilio J. Pasarell. C. Obras de la farandula bohemia. D. Festivales de teatro puertorriqueño del Instituto de Cultura Puertorriqueña (1958-1976). E. Manuscritos inéditos en la oficina de fomento teatral del Instituto de Cultura Puertorriqueña. F. Obras premiadas en los certamenes de teatro del Ateneo Puertorriqueño (1913-1976). G. Agrupaciones teatrales en Puerto Rico en las últimas cuatro decadas (1931-1976). H. Seudónimos. IV. Bibliografía. A. Tesis y libros sobre autores y/o teatro puertorriqueño. B. Ensayos y artículos sobre teatro y/o autores puertorriqueños. C. Estudios de carácter general sobre dramaturgos. D. Bibliografía general. V. Indice de autores. VI. Indice de obras.

Hill, Marnesba D., and Harold B. Schleifer. PUERTO RICAN AUTHORS: A BIBLIOGRAPHIC HANDBOOK. Metuchen, N.J.: Scarecrow Press, 1974. 267p. A bilingual biobibliographical dictionary of Puerto Rican authors; entries contain few biographical or critical studies.

Laguerre, Enrique A. LA POESIA MODERNISTA EN PUERTO RICO. San Juan: Editorial Coquí, Ediciones Borinquen, 1969. 217p. "Poesía puertorriqueña," pp. 205-214. Contents: I. Almanaques. II. Antologías. III. Libros de poetas. IV. Crítica sobre el modernismo puertorriqueño. A. Estudios en revistas y periódicos. B. Prólogos. V. Otras críticas. VI. Obras inéditas. VII. Revistas.

Mohr, Eugene. "Fifty Years of Puerto Rican Literature in English, 1923-1973: An Annotated Bibliography," REVISTA/REVIEW INTERAMERICANA, 3 (Fall 1973), 290-298. Works by both Puerto Ricans living in Puerto Rico and Puerto Ricans living in the United States who wrote in English are included in this selected bibliography. Sixty works of literature are discussed under the following categories: poems, novels, stories and sketches, autobiographies, para-literary editions, translations, periodicals, and bibliographies.

Pedreira, Antoino Salvador. BIBLIOGRAFIA PUERTORRIQUENA (1493-1930). Madrid: Hernando, 1932. 707p. Arrangement by subject.

Pérez Márquez, Albertina. "INDICE BIBLIOGRAFICO DE LA POESIA PUERTORRIQUENA RECOGIDA EN ANTOLOGIAS." Ph.D., Universidad Complutense de Madrid, 1962. 772p.

Quiles de la Luz, Lillian. EL CUENTO EN LA LITERATURA PUER-

TORRIQUENA. Río Piedras: Editorial Universitaria, Universidad de Puerto Rico, 1968. 293p. "Indice bibliográfico del cuento en la literatura puertorriqueña (1843-1963)," pp. 141-293. Contents: I. Indice alfabético de autores. II. Indice alfabético de títulos. III. Cuentos aislados y en colecciones. Short stories published in anthologies and in periodicals are included.

Rivera, Guillermo. A TENTATIVE BIBLIOGRAPHY OF THE BELLES-LETTRES OF PUERTO RICO. Cambridge, Mass.: Harvard University Press, 1931. 61p. Contents: I. Anthologies. II. Art. III. Bibliography. IV. Biography. V. Criticism. VI. Drama. VII. Essay. VIII. History. IX. Legend. X. Literature (general). XI. Novel. XII. Oratory. XIII. Poetry. XIV. Tale. XV. Unclassified. XVI. Writings Incorporated in Periodicals. Collections, etc. XVII. Incomplete or Doubtful Titles. XVIII. Periodicals (listings).

Rivera de Alvarez, Josefina. DICCIONARIO DE LITERATURA PUERTORRIQUENA. 2. ed. rev. y aumentada y puesta al día hasta 1967. San Juan: Instituto de Cultura Puertorriqueña, 1970-1974. 3 vs. Volume 2 (in two volumes) is an alphabetically arranged series of articles (with bibliographies) on individual authors, literary terms, movements, etc.

Rosa-Nieves, Cesáreo, and Esther M. Melón. BIOGRAFIAS PUERTORRIQUENAS: PERFIL HISTORICO DE UN PUEBLO. Sharon Conn.: Troutman Press, 1970? 487p. Emphasis is on the twentieth century.

Vivó, Paquita. THE PUERTO RICANS: AN ANNOTATED BIBLIOGRAPHY. New York: R. R. Bowker, 1973. 299p. Bibliographic citations on Puerto Rican literature, literary history, and criticism in periodicals appear on pp. 113-146 and 215-216.

SOUTH AMERICA

Yaben, Jacinto R. BIOGRAFIAS ARGENTINAS Y SUDAMERICANAS. Buenos Aires: Metrópolis, 1938-1940. 5 vs. Alphabetically arranged biobibliographies. There is a supplement in Volume 5.

URUGUAY

Bollo, Sarah. LITERATURA URUGUAYA, 1807-1975. Montevideo: Imprenta Rosgal, 1976. 351p. Brief biobibliographies of authors are included under each literary period.

Coester, Alfred. A TENTATIVE BIBLIOGRAPHY OF THE BELLES-LETTRES OF URUGUAY. Cambridge, Mass.: Harvard University Press, 1931. 22p. One alphabetical listing by author.

Englekirk, John Eugene, and Margaret M. Ramos. LA NARRATIVA URUGUAYA; ESTUDIO CRITICO-BIBLIOGRAFICO. Berkeley: University of California Press, 1967. 338p. (University of California Publications in Modern Philology, 80). Part I is an extensive essay on Uruguayan prose. Part II lists some 450 writers of the novel and short story and their works (525 novels, 7,000 short stories). Some entries include references to critical studies. Part III is the bibliographic index and author list.

Fernández Saldaña, José María. DICCIONARIO URUGUAYO DE BIOGRAFIAS, 1810-1940. Montevideo: Amerindia, 1945. 1366p. Alphabetically arranged biographical entries, but no bibliographical information is included.

Guerra, María Amelia D. de. DICCIONARIO BIOGRAFICO DE LA CIUDAD DE MALDONADO (1755-1900). Montevideo, 1974. 506p. Uruguay.

Moratorio, Arsinoe. "La mujer en la poesía del Uruguay (bibliografía 1879-1969)," REVISTA DE LA BIBLIOTECA NACIONAL (Montevideo), Núm. 4 (diciembre de 1970), 43-63. "Esta bibliografía ha sido preparada con el propósito de facilitar un panorama de la poesía de la mujer, editada en libro individual. En ella se encuentran reunidas en el país y en el exterior, reediciones y traducciones de cada autora, editadas en el país y en el exterior, ordenada por año de publicación" [p. 43]. Arranged by author.

Rela, Walter. REPORTORIO BIBLIOGRAFICO DEL TEATRO URUGUAYO (1816-1964). Montevideo: Editorial Síntesis, 1965. 35p. "Obras de creación," pp. 7-25, is an alphabetical listing of playwrights and their major works.

Scarone, Arturo. APUNTES PARA UN DICCIONARIO DE SEUDONIMOS Y DE PUBLICACIONES ANONIMAS. CONTRIBUCION AL ESTUDIO DE LA BIBLIOGRAFIA DEL URUGUAY. SEGUNDA EDICION, NOTABLEMENTE AUMENTADA Y CORREGIDA. PROLOGO DE ARIOSTO D. GONZALEZ. Montevideo: Imprenta Nacional, 1934. 351p. 732 pseudonyms and anonymous publications entries, alphabetically arranged with true name for authors given in entry. An alphabetical index to each section is included.

_______. DICCIONARIO DE SEUDONIMOS DEL URUGUAY. PROLOGO DE ARIOSTO D. GONZALEZ. SEGUNDA EDICION. Montevideo: Claudio García y Cía., 1942. 632p. Divided into three parts: "Obras, folletos, artículos periodísticos, etc. suscriptos con seudónimos," "trabajos publicados con iniciales," and "publicaciones anónimas." There are 1,684 pseudonyms. Each entry explains the pseudonym and refers to publications in which it occurs. A name index is also included.

______. URUGUAYOS CONTEMPORANEOS; NUEVO DICCIONARIO DE DATOS BIOGRAFICOS Y BIBLIOGRAFICOS. SEGUNDA EDICION. Montevideo: A. Barreiro y Ramos, 1937. 610p. Alphabetically arranged entries.

Schulkin, Augusto I. HISTORIA DE PAYSANDU: DICCIONARIO BIOGRAFICO. Buenos Aires: Editorial Van Roosen, 1958. 3 vs. A biographical dictionary for Uruguay in general, as well as the city of Paysandú, Uruguay, in particular.

Uruguay. Biblioteca del Poder Legislativo. URUGUAYOS CONTEMPORANEOS: NOTICIAS BIOGRAFICAS. Montevideo, 1965. 4 pts. in 1 vol. Biobibliographical entries. An index to biographies appears at the end of Part 4.

VENEZUELA

Arrom, José Juan. "Bibliografía dramática venezolana; apuntes bibliográficos," ANUARIO BIBLIOGRAFICO VENEZOLANO (1946), 199-209. The list of 142 titles of Venezuelan drama and dramatic literature is arranged alphabetically by author. Information includes author, title of drama, date and place of publication, as well as where the item can be found in U.S. or Venezuelan libraries. Many 19th-century titles included.

Becco, Horacio Jorge. FUENTES PARA EL ESTUDIO DE LA LITERATURA VENEZOLANA. Caracas: Ediciones Centauro, 1978. 2 vs. 1,860 items. Contents: I. Bibliografía de bibliografías. II. Repertorios biográficos. III. Historia y crítica de la literatura. IV. Teatro, ensayo y antologías. V. Antologías universales e hispanoamericanos. VI. Antologías venezolanas. VII. Antologías venezolanas editadas en el extranjero. VIII. Imprenta y periodismo venezolanos. IX. Indices de periódicos y revistas. X. Addenda. XI. Indices.

______, and Alberto Amengual. "Antologías poéticas americanas y venezolanas en el siglo XIX," in MEMORIA DEL III SIMPOSIO DE DOCENTES E INVESTIGADORES DE LA LITERATURA VENEZOLANA (Mérida, Venezuela: Universidad de los Andes, Facultad de Humanidades y Educación, Instituto de Investigaciones Literarias "Gonzalo Picón Febres," 1981), v. 1, pp. 238-249. Contents: I. Antologías poéticas americanos (siglo XIX). II. Antologías poéticas venezolanas (siglo XIX).

Cárdenas Ramírez, Julio, and Carlos Sáenz de la Calzada. DICCIO-

and Foreign Literatures. F. Special Literary Topics. G. Women Authors. H. General Studies on Colonial Literature. I. General Studies on Nineteenth Century Literature. J. General Studies on Twentieth Century Literature. K. General Studies on Poetry. L. Colonial and Nineteenth Century Poetry. M. Twentieth Century Poetry. N. Special Topics in Poetry. O. General Studies on Drama. P. Colonial Drama. Q. Nineteenth Century Drama. R. Twentieth Century Drama. S. Special Topics in Drama. T. General Studies on Prose Fiction. U. Nineteenth Century Prose Fiction. V. Twentieth Century Prose Fiction. W. Special Topics in Prose Fiction. X. Regional and Local Literature. II. Critical Works on Peruvian Literature: Authors (38 authors included; bibliographies, critical monographs, dissertations, and/or critical essays are included under the author entries). III. Index to Authors of Secondary Sources. Section II is indexed in the preceding GUIDE.

Fuentes Benavides, Rafael de la. "Autores del primer siglo de la literatura peruana," BOLETIN BIBLIOGRAFICO (Biblioteca de la Universidad de San Marcos), Año 9, Vol. 12, Nos. 3/4 (diciembre de 1939), 268-332; Año 10, Vol. 13, Nos. 1/2 (junio de 1940), 81-133. Biobibliographical studies of authors, in alphabetical order. Work stopped with the letter "G."

Leavitt, Sturgis E. A TENTATIVE BIBLIOGRAPHY OF PERUVIAN LITERATURE. Cambridge, Mass.: Harvard University Press, 1932. 37p. One listing, alphabetical by author, follows a brief list of works consulted.

Lohmann Villena, Guillermo, and Raúl Moglia. "Repertorio de las representaciones teatrales en Lima hasta el siglo XVII," REVISTA DE FILOLOGIA HISPANICA, 5 (1943), 313-343. Entries for the period 1563-1793 are arranged chronologically; a few include descriptive commentary.

Lostaunau Rubio, Gabriel. FUENTES PARA EL ESTUDIO DEL PERU (BIBLIOGRAFIA DE BIBLIOGRAFIAS). EDICION Y PROLOGO DE MIGUEL ANGEL RODRIGUEZ REA. Lima, 1980. 500p. "Literatura," pp. 288-317. Contents: I. Obras generales. II. Poesía. III. Teatro. IV. Cuento y novela. V. Literatura infantil.

Maletta, Héctor. "Cuatrocientos tesis doctorales norteamericanos sobre el Peru (1869-1976)," ESTUDIOS ANDINOS, Núm. 15 (1979), 57-134. Arrangement of entries are by year, with the following indices: "índice de universidades," "índice de autores," and "índice temático."

Mendiburu, Manuel de. DICCIONARIO HISTORICO-BIOGRAFICO DEL PERU. Lima: Solis, 1874-1890. 8 vs. 2ª edición con adiciones y notas bibliográficas por Evaristo San Cristobál. Estudio biográfico del General Mendiburu por J. de la Riva-Agüero. Lima: Gil,

1931. 11 vs. APENDICE AL DICCIONARIO HISTORICO-BIOGRAFICO ... POR EVARISTO SAN CRISTOBAL. Lima: Gil, 1935-1938. 4 vs. 3a edición (reprint of 2nd edition): Lima: Editorial Arica, 1976- (in progress). Entries are alphabetically arranged.

Monguió, Luis. POESIA POSTMODERNISTA PERUANA. México, D.F.: Fondo de Cultura Económica, 1954. "Contribución a la bibliografía de la poesía peruana (1915-1950)," pp. 207-239. Entries are arranged by author and then by year of publication for both books and pamphlets of poetry.

Mostajo, Francisco. "Contribución al catálogo de seudónimos," BOLETIN BIBLIOGRAFICO (Biblioteca de la Universidad de San Marcos), Año 9, Vol. 12, Nos. 1/2 (julio de 1939), 13-25. Emphasis on the colonial and early republican periods. Contents: I. Seudónimos de escritores arequipeños (arranged by pseudonym, followed by true name). II. Seudónimos de escritores de otros departamentos.

Mundo Lo, Sara de. INDEX TO SPANISH AMERICAN COLLECTIVE BIOGRAPHY. VOLUME 1: THE ANDEAN COUNTRIES. Boston: G. K. Hall, 1981. 466p. Contains some 1,100 annotated entries for biographical works ranging in date from the seventeenth century to the present, arranged alphabetically by author within major disciplines or fields of activity. Complete author, title, geographic, and biographee indexes supplement the main listings. Covers Bolivia, Colombia, Chile, Ecuador, Peru, and Venezuela. U.S. library locations are given.

Natella, Arthur A. "Bibliography of the Peruvian Theatre, 1946-1970," HISPANIC JOURNAL, 2, No. 2 (1981), 141-147. "The list includes works which have been presented on the Peruvian stage, published or both" [p. 141]. The bibliography is arranged alphabetically by playwright.

Ojeda, Olivia. "Iniciación de una bibliografía biográfica del Perú," FENIX (Lima), Núm. 2 (1945), 297-311.

Pastor Delgado, Amadeo. "Contribución para un catálogo de seudónimos de autores peruanos," BOLETIN BIBLIOGRAFICO (Biblioteca de la Universidad de San Marcos), Año 21, Vol. 18, Nos. 3/4 (diciembre de 1948), 254-264. Supplements and updates Emma Castro's bibliography.

Paz-Soldán, Juan Pedro. DICCIONARIO BIOGRAFICO DE PERUANOS CONTEMPORANEOS. NUEVA EDICION CORREGIDA Y AUMENTADA. Lima: Librería e Imprenta Gil, 1921. 449p. Biographical sketches with bibliographies of writings by, but not about, biographees.

Pintó Gamboa, Willy. CONTRIBUCION A LA BIBLIOGRAFIA DE LA

LITERATURA PERUANA EN LA PRENSA ESPANOLA. Lima: Universidad Nacional Mayor de San Marcos, 1965. 170p. (Repertorio Bibliográfico de la Literatura Latino-Americana, Serie B 1). Contents: I. Autores peruanos que han colaborado en revistas y diarios españoles. II. Autores extranjeros que han escrito sobre temas peruanos en la prensa española en revistas y diarios españoles. Each section is alphabetically arranged by author. Annotated entries.

Podestá, Bruno. "Estudios latinoamericanos en Italia: el caso peruano," APUNTES (Universidad del Pacifico, Lima), Núm. 11 (1981), 70-91. Article includes a list of books, articles and translations on Perú by Italians.

Rodríguez Rea, Miguel Angel. "El cuento peruano contemporáneo: Indice bibliográfico, I, 1900-1930," LEXIS (Pontificia Universidad Católica del Perú, Lima), 7, Núm. 2 (1983), 287-309. 62 chronologically arranged entries.

_______. "Poesía peruana del siglo XX (I: 1900-1920)," HUESO HUMERO (Lima), Núm. 7 (octubre/diciembre de 1980), 133-150. "Se he ordenado cronológicamente por años y, dentro de estos en alfabético de autores." (p. 134).

_______. "Poesía peruana del siglo XX (II: 1921-1930)," HUESO HUMERO (Lima), Núm. 8 (enero/marzo de 1981), 132-149.

_______. "Poesía peruana del siglo XX (III: 1931-1935)," HUESO HUMERO (Lima), Núm. 9 (abril/junio de 1981), 148-158.

_______. "Poesía peruana del siglo XX (IV: 1936-1940)," HUESO HUMERO (Lima), Núm. 14 (julio/setiembre de 1982), 186-204.

Romero de Valle, Emilia. DICCIONARIO MANUAL DE LITERATURA PERUANA Y MATERIA AFINES. Lima: Universidad Nacional Mayor de San Marcos, Departamento de Publicaciones, 1966. 356p. Guide to past and contemporary Peruvian authors and their works. Alphabetical arrangement by author or subject. Some attention to literary genres, periodicals, and so forth.

Tauro, Alberto. HACIA UN CATALOGO DE SEUDONIMOS PERUANOS. Lima: Universidad Nacional Mayor de San Marcos, 1967. 66p. 861 entries are arranged alphabetically by pseudonym. Each entry indicates the circumstances of its use. An index of authors is appended.

Vidal, Luis Fernando. "LAS ANTOLOGIAS DEL CUENTO EN EL PERU," REVISTA DE CRITICA LITERARIA LATINOAMERICANA (Lima), Año 1, Núm. 2 (1975), 121-138. Annotated contents of each work is listed; arranged chronologically 1908-1975.

Villanueva de Puccinelli, Elsa. BIBLIOGRAFIA DE LA NOVELA PERUANA. Lima: Ediciones de la Biblioteca Universitaria, 1969. 88p. Entries are alphabetically arranged by novelist. A chronology concludes the work.

PUERTO RICO

Biblioteca José M. Lázaro. PUERTO RICAN LITERATURE: TRANSLATIONS INTO ENGLISH. LITERATURA PUERTORRIQUENA: TRADUCCIONES AL INGLES. Recinto de Río Piedras: Universidad de Puerto Rico, 1974. 38p. The bibliography's entries were limited to the holdings of the Biblioteca José M. Lázaro. Genres included: short stories, essays, novels, poetry, drama, and anthologies. There are author, Spanish title and English title indices as well as a list of newspapers indexed.

Bravo, Enrique R. AN ANNOTATED SELECTED PUERTO RICO BIBLIOGRAPHY: BIBLIOGRAFIA PUERTORRIQUENA SELECTA Y ANOTADA. New York: Urban Center of Columbia University, 1972. 115p; 114p. There is both a Spanish and an English section containing the same literature entries divided into obras generales, cuento, ensayo, novela, poesía, and teatro (pp. 60-84).

Foster, David William. PUERTO RICAN LITERATURE: A BIBLIOGRAPHY OF SECONDARY SOURCES. Westport, Conn.: Greenwood Press, 1982. 232p. Contents: I. Bibliographies. II. General Histories. III. Collected Essays. IV. Literary Criticism, Reviews, and Journals. V. Literature and Other Subjects. VI. Relations with Foreign Literatures. VII. Women Authors. VIII. Special Literary Topics. IX. General Studies on Colonial Literature. X. General Studies on Nineteenth Century Literature. XI. General Studies on Twentieth Century Literature. XII. General Studies on Poetry. XIII. Colonial and Nineteenth Century Poetry. XIV. Twentieth Century Poetry. XV. General Studies on Drama. XVI. Twentieth Century Drama. XVII. Special Topics in Drama. XVIII. General Studies on Prose Fiction. XIX. Nineteenth Century Prose Fiction. XX. Twentieth Century Prose Fiction. XXI. Special Topics in Prose Fiction. XXII. General Studies on the Essay. XXIII. Critical Works on Puerto Rican Literature: Authors (80 authors are included). Section XXIII is indexed in the preceding GUIDE.

Géigel y Zenón, José, and Abelardo Morales Ferrer. BIBLIOGRAFIA PUERTORRIQUEÑA. Barcelona: Araluce, 1934. 453p. 500 annotated entries divided into three sections: (1) books written in Puerto Rico since 1807; (2) books written by Puerto Ricans which were published in Spain or other foreign country; and (3) books written about Puerto Rico.

González, Nilda. BIBLIOGRAFIA DE TEATRO PUERTORRIQUENO (SIGLOS XIX Y XX). Río Piedras: Editorial Universitaria, Universidad de Puerto Rico, 1979. 223p. Contents: I. Autores, obras y comentarios críticos (S. XIX y XX). II. Obras de teatro colectivo. III. Apéndices. A. Zarzuelas y operas. B. Obras con ficha incompleta según colección Emilio J. Pasarell. C. Obras de la farandula bohemia. D. Festivales de teatro puertorriqueño del Instituto de Cultura Puertorriqueña (1958-1976). E. Manuscritos inéditos en la oficina de fomento teatral del Instituto de Cultura Puertorriqueña. F. Obras premiadas en los certamenes de teatro del Ateneo Puertorriqueño (1913-1976). G. Agrupaciones teatrales en Puerto Rico en las últimas cuatro decadas (1931-1976). H. Seudónimos. IV. Bibliografía. A. Tesis y libros sobre autores y/o teatro puertorriqueño. B. Ensayos y artículos sobre teatro y/o autores puertorriqueños. C. Estudios de carácter general sobre dramaturgos. D. Bibliografía general. V. Indice de autores. VI. Indice de obras.

Hill, Marnesba D., and Harold B. Schleifer. PUERTO RICAN AUTHORS: A BIBLIOGRAPHIC HANDBOOK. Metuchen, N.J.: Scarecrow Press, 1974. 267p. A bilingual biobibliographical dictionary of Puerto Rican authors; entries contain few biographical or critical studies.

Laguerre, Enrique A. LA POESIA MODERNISTA EN PUERTO RICO. San Juan: Editorial Coquí, Ediciones Borinquen, 1969. 217p. "Poesía puertorriqueña," pp. 205-214. Contents: I. Almanaques. II. Antologías. III. Libros de poetas. IV. Crítica sobre el modernismo puertorriqueño. A. Estudios en revistas y periódicos. B. Prólogos. V. Otras críticas. VI. Obras inéditas. VII. Revistas.

Mohr, Eugene. "Fifty Years of Puerto Rican Literature in English, 1923-1973: An Annotated Bibliography," REVISTA/REVIEW INTERAMERICANA, 3 (Fall 1973), 290-298. Works by both Puerto Ricans living in Puerto Rico and Puerto Ricans living in the United States who wrote in English are included in this selected bibliography. Sixty works of literature are discussed under the following categories: poems, novels, stories and sketches, autobiographies, para-literary editions, translations, periodicals, and bibliographies.

Pedreira, Antoino Salvador. BIBLIOGRAFIA PUERTORRIQUENA (1493-1930). Madrid: Hernando, 1932. 707p. Arrangement by subject.

Pérez Márquez, Albertina. "INDICE BIBLIOGRAFICO DE LA POESIA PUERTORRIQUENA RECOGIDA EN ANTOLOGIAS." Ph.D., Universidad Complutense de Madrid, 1962. 772p.

Quiles de la Luz, Lillian. EL CUENTO EN LA LITERATURA PUER-

TORRIQUENA. Río Piedras: Editorial Universitaria, Universidad de Puerto Rico, 1968. 293p. "Indice bibliográfico del cuento en la literatura puertorriqueña (1843-1963)," pp. 141-293. Contents: I. Indice alfabético de autores. II. Indice alfabético de títulos. III. Cuentos aislados y en colecciones. Short stories published in anthologies and in periodicals are included.

Rivera, Guillermo. A TENTATIVE BIBLIOGRAPHY OF THE BELLES-LETTRES OF PUERTO RICO. Cambridge, Mass.: Harvard University Press, 1931. 61p. Contents: I. Anthologies. II. Art. III. Bibliography. IV. Biography. V. Criticism. VI. Drama. VII. Essay. VIII. History. IX. Legend. X. Literature (general). XI. Novel. XII. Oratory. XIII. Poetry. XIV. Tale. XV. Unclassified. XVI. Writings Incorporated in Periodicals. Collections, etc. XVII. Incomplete or Doubtful Titles. XVIII. Periodicals (listings).

Rivera de Alvarez, Josefina. DICCIONARIO DE LITERATURA PUERTORRIQUENA. 2. ed. rev. y aumentada y puesta al día hasta 1967. San Juan: Instituto de Cultura Puertorriqueña, 1970-1974. 3 vs. Volume 2 (in two volumes) is an alphabetically arranged series of articles (with bibliographies) on individual authors, literary terms, movements, etc.

Rosa-Nieves, Cesáreo, and Esther M. Melón. BIOGRAFIAS PUERTORRIQUENAS: PERFIL HISTORICO DE UN PUEBLO. Sharon Conn.: Troutman Press, 1970? 487p. Emphasis is on the twentieth century.

Vivó, Paquita. THE PUERTO RICANS: AN ANNOTATED BIBLIOGRAPHY. New York: R. R. Bowker, 1973. 299p. Bibliographic citations on Puerto Rican literature, literary history, and criticism in periodicals appear on pp. 113-146 and 215-216.

SOUTH AMERICA

Yaben, Jacinto R. BIOGRAFIAS ARGENTINAS Y SUDAMERICANAS. Buenos Aires: Metrópolis, 1938-1940. 5 vs. Alphabetically arranged biobibliographies. There is a supplement in Volume 5.

URUGUAY

Bollo, Sarah. LITERATURA URUGUAYA, 1807-1975. Montevideo: Imprenta Rosgal, 1976. 351p. Brief biobibliographies of authors are included under each literary period.

Coester, Alfred. A TENTATIVE BIBLIOGRAPHY OF THE BELLES-LETTRES OF URUGUAY. Cambridge, Mass.: Harvard University Press, 1931. 22p. One alphabetical listing by author.

Englekirk, John Eugene, and Margaret M. Ramos. LA NARRATIVA URUGUAYA; ESTUDIO CRITICO-BIBLIOGRAFICO. Berkeley: University of California Press, 1967. 338p. (University of California Publications in Modern Philology, 80). Part I is an extensive essay on Uruguayan prose. Part II lists some 450 writers of the novel and short story and their works (525 novels, 7,000 short stories). Some entries include references to critical studies. Part III is the bibliographic index and author list.

Fernández Saldaña, José María. DICCIONARIO URUGUAYO DE BIOGRAFIAS, 1810-1940. Montevideo: Amerindia, 1945. 1366p. Alphabetically arranged biographical entries, but no bibliographical information is included.

Guerra, María Amelia D. de. DICCIONARIO BIOGRAFICO DE LA CIUDAD DE MALDONADO (1755-1900). Montevideo, 1974. 506p. Uruguay.

Moratorio, Arsinoe. "La mujer en la poesía del Uruguay (bibliografía 1879-1969)," REVISTA DE LA BIBLIOTECA NACIONAL (Montevideo), Núm. 4 (diciembre de 1970), 43-63. "Esta bibliografía ha sido preparada con el propósito de facilitar un panorama de la poesía de la mujer, editada en libro individual. En ella se encuentran reunidas en el país y en el exterior, reediciones y traducciones de cada autora, editadas en el país y en el exterior, ordenada por año de publicación" [p. 43]. Arranged by author.

Rela, Walter. REPORTORIO BIBLIOGRAFICO DEL TEATRO URUGUAYO (1816-1964). Montevideo: Editorial Síntesis, 1965. 35p. "Obras de creación," pp. 7-25, is an alphabetical listing of playwrights and their major works.

Scarone, Arturo. APUNTES PARA UN DICCIONARIO DE SEUDONIMOS Y DE PUBLICACIONES ANONIMAS. CONTRIBUCION AL ESTUDIO DE LA BIBLIOGRAFIA DEL URUGUAY. SEGUNDA EDICION, NOTABLEMENTE AUMENTADA Y CORREGIDA. PROLOGO DE ARIOSTO D. GONZALEZ. Montevideo: Imprenta Nacional, 1934. 351p. 732 pseudonyms and anonymous publications entries, alphabetically arranged with true name for authors given in entry. An alphabetical index to each section is included.

______. DICCIONARIO DE SEUDONIMOS DEL URUGUAY. PROLOGO DE ARIOSTO D. GONZALEZ. SEGUNDA EDICION. Montevideo: Claudio García y Cía., 1942. 632p. Divided into three parts: "Obras, folletos, artículos periodísticos, etc. suscriptos con seudónimos," "trabajos publicados con iniciales," and "publicaciones anónimas." There are 1,684 pseudonyms. Each entry explains the pseudonym and refers to publications in which it occurs. A name index is also included.

______. URUGUAYOS CONTEMPORANEOS; NUEVO DICCIONARIO DE DATOS BIOGRAFICOS Y BIBLIOGRAFICOS. SEGUNDA EDICION. Montevideo: A. Barreiro y Ramos, 1937. 610p. Alphabetically arranged entries.

Schulkin, Augusto I. HISTORIA DE PAYSANDU: DICCIONARIO BIOGRAFICO. Buenos Aires: Editorial Van Roosen, 1958. 3 vs. A biographical dictionary for Uruguay in general, as well as the city of Paysandú, Uruguay, in particular.

Uruguay. Biblioteca del Poder Legislativo. URUGUAYOS CONTEMPORANEOS: NOTICIAS BIOGRAFICAS. Montevideo, 1965. 4 pts. in 1 vol. Biobibliographical entries. An index to biographies appears at the end of Part 4.

VENEZUELA

Arrom, José Juan. "Bibliografía dramática venezolana; apuntes bibliográficos," ANUARIO BIBLIOGRAFICO VENEZOLANO (1946), 199-209. The list of 142 titles of Venezuelan drama and dramatic literature is arranged alphabetically by author. Information includes author, title of drama, date and place of publication, as well as where the item can be found in U.S. or Venezuelan libraries. Many 19th-century titles included.

Becco, Horacio Jorge. FUENTES PARA EL ESTUDIO DE LA LITERATURA VENEZOLANA. Caracas: Ediciones Centauro, 1978. 2 vs. 1,860 items. Contents: I. Bibliografía de bibliografías. II. Repertorios biográficos. III. Historia y crítica de la literatura. IV. Teatro, ensayo y antologías. V. Antologías universales e hispanoamericanos. VI. Antologías venezolanas. VII. Antologías venezolanas editadas en el extranjero. VIII. Imprenta y periodismo venezolanos. IX. Indices de periódicos y revistas. X. Addenda. XI. Indices.

______, and Alberto Amengual. "Antologías poéticas americanas y venezolanas en el siglo XIX," in MEMORIA DEL III SIMPOSIO DE DOCENTES E INVESTIGADORES DE LA LITERATURA VENEZOLANA (Mérida, Venezuela: Universidad de los Andes, Facultad de Humanidades y Educación, Instituto de Investigaciones Literarias "Gonzalo Picón Febres," 1981), v. 1, pp. 238-249. Contents: I. Antologías poéticas americanos (siglo XIX). II. Antologías poéticas venezolanas (siglo XIX).

Cárdenas Ramírez, Julio, and Carlos Sáenz de la Calzada. DICCIO-

NARIO BIOGRAFICO DE VENEZUELA. Madrid: Garrido y Mezquita y Compañía, 1953. 1558p.

Cardozo, Lubio. BIBLIOGRAFIA DE BIBLIOGRAFIAS SOBRE LA LITERATURA VENEZOLANA EN LAS BIBLIOTECAS DE MADRID, PARIS Y LONDRES. Maracaibo: Centro de Estudios Literarios de la Universidad del Zulia; Centro de Investigaciones Literarias de la Universidad de Los Andes, 1975. 67p. An annotated bibliography of about 100 bibliographies.

_______. LA POESIA EN MERIDA DE VENEZUELA. Maracaibo: Universidad del Zulia, Facultad de Humanidades y Educación, 1971. 215p. (Monografías y ensayos, 15). Contents: I. "Apéndice (Datos biográficos sobre los poetas estudiados)," pp. 133-159. II. "Bibliografía," pp. 163-215. Section II is indexed in the preceding GUIDE.

_______, and Juan Pintó. SEUDONIMIA LITERARIA VENEZOLANA (CON UN APENDICE DE JOSE E. MACHADO, SOBRE SEUDONIMOS DE ESCRITORES Y POLITICOS VENEZOLANOS). Mérida, Venezuela: Universidad de Los Andes, Escuela de Letras, 1974. 114p. (Centro de Investigaciones Literarias, Serie bibliográfica, 6). Contents: I. Seudonimia literaria venezolana. II. Bibliografía, seudónimos: fuentes consultadas. III. Entrada por el nombre del escritor. IV. Entrada por los seudónimos. V. Apéndice: José E. Machado, "Escarceos bibliográficos: seudónimos y anónimos en la política venezolano." VI. Lista de seudónimos y anónimos en la literatura y en la política venezolanas.

Carrillo Moreno, José. APODOS, SEUDONIMOS Y SOBRENOMBRES. Caracas: Ediciones Navideñas de Saade Hermanos, 1970. 64p.

Castellanos, Rafael Ramón. "De la seudonimia literaria venezolana," in his ANALISIS CRITICO DE LITERATURA VENEZOLANA (Caracas: Imprenta Nacional, 1977), pp. 87-210. Contents: I. Del nombre al seudónimo (pp. 87-140). II. Del seudónimo al nombre (pp. 143-210).

Churion, Juan José. EL TEATRO EN CARACAS. Caracas: Tip. Vargas, 1924. 230p. Bibliography, authors and works, notable actors, pp. 199-225.

DICCIONARIO BIOGRAFICO DE VENEZUELA. Madrid: Bláss, 1953. 1,558p. Alphabetically arranged entries. In addition to who's who information, this work includes much statistical and gazeteer information.

DICCIONARIO GENERAL DE LA LITERATURA VENEZOLANA: AUTORES. Mérida: Universidad de los Andes, Facultad de Humanidades y Educación, Centro de Investigaciones Literarias, 1974. 829p. Alphabetical entries cover through 1971. "Este tomo está dedicado al estudio biográfico, bibliográfico y crítico de los escritos venezolanos; aunque también se incluye a escritos extranjeros--nacionalizados o no que hayan escrito literatura en Venezuela o sobre ella." Each author entry usually includes a selected bibliografía directa and a bibliografía sobre el escritor (mainly monographs).

Fabbiani Ruiz, José, ed. BIBLIOGRAFIA DE LA NOVELA VENEZOLANA. Caracas: Universidad Central de Venezuela, Centro de Estudios Literarios de la Facultad de Humanidades y Educación, 1963. 69p. 324 unannotated titles and 187 authors of Venezuelan novels of the nineteenth and twentieth centuries (1842-1962). Entries are alphabetical by author. A chronological appendix with authors and works, as well as an author list by century, concludes the study. A title list of novels arranged alphabetically is also included.

Grases, Pedro. "Fuentes para el estudio de la literatura venezolana," REVISTA NACIONAL DE CULTURA (Caracas), Núm. 81 (1950), 86-99. Emphasis is on three categories: (1) anthologies, (2) general studies, and (3) bibliographies.

Greymont, Sally J. "Hacia una bibliografía del teatro venezolano colonial," LATIN AMERICAN THEATRE REVIEW, 8, No. 2 (Spring 1975), 45-49. "Esta bibliografía incluye obras que se refieren al teatro precolombiano, teatro folklórico, teatro colonial y dramaturgos y dramas coloniales" [p. 45]. Includes monographs and articles, alphabetically arranged by author.

Hirshbein, Cesia Ziona. HEMEROGRAFIA VENEZOLANA, 1890-1930. Caracas: Ediciones de la Facultad de Humanidades y Educación, Instituto de Estudios Hispanoamericanos, Universidad Central de Venezuela, 1978. 574p. A bibliography of literary writings appearing in Venezuelan periodicals. Entries are grouped by genre, then arranged alphabetically by author. Writings of foreign authors are listed in separate sections.

________. BIBLIOGRAFIA DEL CUENTO VENEZOLANA: APENDICE. Caracas: Instituto de Investigaciones Literarias, Facultad de Humanidades y Educación, Universidad Central de Venezuela, 1977. A bibliography of cuentos, arranged by author or anonymous title, that were published in the journal El Cojo Ilustrado.

Larrazábal Henríquez, Osvaldo; Amaya Llevot; and Gustavo Luis Carrera. BIBLIOGRAFIA DEL CUENTO VENEZOLANO. Caracas: Universidad Central de Venezuela, Facultad de Humanidades y Educación, Instituto de Investigaciones Literarias, 1975. 315p. Bibliography includes 3,311 short stories by 332 authors. An appendix section is arranged in the following categories: I. Antologías y colecciones. II. Autores de un solo cuento. III. Cronología del cuento venezolano. IV. Nómina de autores. V. Indice alfabético de obras. VI. Cronología de antologías y colecciones. VII. Indice alfabético de cuentos.

Laverde Amaya, Isidoro. UN VIAJE A VENEZUELA. Bogotá: Imprenta "La Nación," 1889. 406p. "Lista en orden alfabético de autores dramáticos venezolanos y de sus obras," pp. 379-392.

Lollet, Carlos Miguel. BIBLIOGRAFIA DE CULTURA VENEZOLANA. Mérida, Venezuela: Universidad de Los Andes, Instituto de Investigaciones Literarias "Gonzalo Picón Febres;" Universidad Central de Venezuela, Instituto de Investigaciones Literarias, 1977. 136p. (Série bibliográfica, 11).

Lovera de Sola, Roberto J. BIBLIOGRAFIA DE LA CRITICA LITERARIA VENEZOLANA, 1847-1977. Caracas: Instituto Autónomo Biblioteca Nacional y de Servicios de Bibliotecas, 1982. 489p. Contents: I. Bibliografía de la crítica literaria y temas conexos. II. Bibliografía de la crítica teatral en Venezuela. III. Fuentes bibliográficos utilizados. IV. Indices (autores, compiladores, editores y prologuistas).

Mac-Pherson, Telasco A. DICCIONARIO HISTORICO, GEOGRAFICO, ESTADISTICO Y BIOGRAFICO DEL ESTADO MIRANDA, REPUBLICA DE VENEZUELA. Caracas: Imprenta de El Correo de Caracas, 1891. 556p.

_______. DICCIONARIO HISTORICO, GEOGRAFICO, ESTADISTICO Y BIOGRAFICO DEL ESTADO LARA. 2. ed. Caracas: Editorial Elite, 1941. 558p.

Mundo Lo, Sara de. INDEX TO SPANISH AMERICAN COLLECTIVE BIOGRAPHY. VOLUME 1: THE ANDEAN COUNTRIES. Boston: G. K. Hall, 1981. 466p. Contains some 1,100 annotated entries for biographical works ranging in date from the seventeenth century to the present, arranged alphabetically by author within major disciplines or fields of activity. Complete author, title, geographic, and biographee indexes supplement the main listings. Covers Bolivia, Colombia, Chile, Ecuador, Peru, and Venezuela. U.S. library locations are given.

Niño de Rivas, María Lya. "Escritores actuales de Venezuela: una bibliografía," ARAISCA (Anuario del Centro de Estudios Latinoamericanos "Rómulo Gallegos"), 1975, 349-382. Entries are by author. Bibliography covers mainly those authors born in the 1930's and 1940's.

LA MUJER EN LAS LETRAS VENEZOLANAS; HOMENAJE A TERESA DE LA PARRA EN EL ANO INTERNACIONAL DE LA MUJER: CATALOGO EXPOSICION HEMERO-BIBLIOGRAFICA, 5-26 DE OCTUBRE DE 1975. Caracas: Imprenta del Congreso de la República, 1976. 176p. Contents: I. "Bibliografía (libros y folletos)," pp. 27-119. (1,869 entries arranged by women authors; includes literature). II. "Hemerografía (revistas, periódicos y boletines)," pp. 121-133 (entries by Caracas and then by state).

Pintó, Juan. BIBLIOGRAFIA DE LA POESIA ZULIANA. Mérida, Venezuela: Universidad de Los Andes, Centro de Investigaciones Literarias, Escuela de Letras, 1971. 58p. (Serie bibliográfica, 3). Contents: I. Entrada por autor. II. Entrada por títulos de los libros. III. Cronología (titles are arranged by year, 1848-1969). Only books and pamphlets are listed.

Querales, Juan H. BIBLIOGRAFIA DE LA POESIA CARORENA. Carora, Venezuela: Casa de la Cultura, 1972. 23p. Contents: I. Entrada por autor. II. Entrada por títulos de los libros. III. Cronología (titles are listed by year, 1903-1971). Only books and pamphlets are included.

Ramírez y Astier, Aniceto. GALERIA DE ESCRITORES ZULIANOS: CONTRIBUCION AL ESTUDIO DE LAS LETRAS VENEZOLANAS. Maracaibo: Universidad de Zulia, 1951-1952. 2 vs. Biobibliographies for writers of the state of Zulia born in the nineteenth and twentieth centuries.

Ramos Guédez, José Marcial. BIBLIOGRAFIA AFROVENEZOLANA. Caracas: Instituto Autónomo, Biblioteca Nacional y de Servicios de Bibliotecas, 1980. 125p. (Serie bibliográfica, 2). "Literatura afrovenezolana," pp. 99-106. Citations include both works by black Venezuelans or works about blacks in Venezuelan literature.

Ramos Q., Elias A. EL CUENTO VENEZOLANO, 1950-1970. Madrid: Playor, 1979. 196p. "Bibliografía," pp. 177-187. Contents: I. Cuentos estudiados. A. Antologías. B. Libros. C. Revistas y periódicos. II. Trabajos sobre la narrativa venezolana: crítica y estudios. A. Libros. B. Artículos. C. Reseñas.

Rivas Rivas, José. ALBUM BIOGRAFICO DE GRANDES VENEZOLANOS. Caracas: Centro Editor, 1970-1971. 2 vs.

Rodríguez, Ramón Armando. DICCIONARIO BIOGRAFICO, GEOGRAFICO E HISTORICO DE VENEZUELA. Madrid: Talleres Penitenciarios de Alcalá de Henares, 1957. 887p.

Rojas, José María. BIBLIOTECA DE ESCRITORES VENEZOLANOS CONTEMPORANEOS (ORDENADOS CON NOTICIAS BIOGRAFICAS). Caracas: Rojas Hermanos Editores, 1875. 808p.

Rojas Uzcátegui, José de la Cruz, and Lubio Cardozo. BIBLIOGRAFIA DEL TEATRO VENEZOLANO. Mérida, Venezuela: Instituto de Investigaciones Literarias "Gonzalo Picón Febres," Consejo de

Publicaciones, 1980. 199p. Contents: I. Corpus bibliográfico (949 entries alphabetically arranged by author). II. Obras inéditas o no representadas de las cuales se tiene escasa información. III. Operas y zarzuelas. IV. Traducciones. V. Cronología del teatro venezolano, siglo XIX. VI. Cronología del teatro venezolano, siglo XX. VII. Indice de títulos. VIII. Bibliografía documental y crítico del teatro venezolano. Partially annotated entries.

Rubin Zamora, Lorenzo. DICCIONARIO BIOGRAFICO CULTURAL DEL ESTADO GUARICO. Caracas, n.p., 1974. 364p.

Salas, Carlos. HISTORIA DEL TEATRO EN CARACAS: MATERIAL PARA EL ESTUDIO DE CARACAS. Caracas: Secretaría General del Cuatricentenario, 1967. 383p. "Bibliografía dramática venezolana," pp. 321-383. The bibliography is arranged alphabetically by author. Only plays presented in Caracas are included. Première information is given for each play.

Sanabria, Alberto. CUMANESES ILUSTRES. Caracas: Editorial Arte, 1965. 324p.

Santiago, Pedro A. de. BIOGRAFIAS TRUJILLANAS: HOMENAJES A TRUJILLO EN EL CUARTO CENTENARIO DE SU FUNDACION, 1557-1957. Caracas: Ediciones Edime, 1956.

Sembrano Urdaneta, Oscar. CONTRIBUCION A UNA BIBLIOGRAFIA GENERAL DE LA POESIA VENEZOLANA EN EL SIGLO XX. Caracas: Ediciones de la Facultad de Humanidades y Educación, Escuela de Letras, Universidad Central de Venezuela, 1979. 367p. Contents: I. Fuentes bibliográficas y hemerográficas. II. Autores y obras (alphabetically arranged). III. Antologías y selecciones. IV. Estudios críticos. V. Apéndices: A. Nómina de autores. B. Indice de títulos. C. Cronología de la poesía venezolana. D. Antologías y selecciones: cronología. E. Premios nacionales de literatura. F. Premios municipales de poesía. Only first editions of works are listed in the "autores y obras" section.

Subero, Efraín. BIBLIOGRAFIA DE LA POESIA INFANTIL VENEZOLANO. Caracas: Banco del Libro, 1966. 118p. Contents: I. Antologías hispanoamericanas. II. Antologías venezolanas. III. Poemarios infantiles. IV. Poesía suelta. V. Folklore. VI. Indice de autores. VII. Indice de títulos.

Venezuela. Biblioteca Nacional. ESCRITORES VENEZOLANOS FALLECIDOS ENTRE 1942 Y 1947. Caracas, 1948. 72p. (Alcance al ANUARIO BIBLIOGRAFICO VENEZOLANO). Each entry has a brief biographical sketch followed by a list of published books and articles by the author and sources used to obtain the information.

Waxman, Samuel Montefiore. A BIBLIOGRAPHY OF THE BELLES-

LETTRES OF VENEZUELA. Cambridge: Harvard University Press, 1935. 145p. Contents: I. Bibliographical Sources. II. Collections of Venezuelan Authors. Venezuelan and Spanish-American Anthologies. III. Critical Works. General. Histories of Venezuelan and Spanish-American Literature. Collections of Critical and Biographical Essays on Venezuelan Writers, Artists, and Musicians. IV. Venezuelan Periodicals. V. The Belles-Lettres of Venezuela (by author).